GENERATING AND EXPLORING ALTERNATIVES IN LANGUAGE TEACHING

JOHN F. FANSELOW
Teachers College, Columbia University

Longman
New York & London

Executive Editor: Arley Gray
Senior Production Editor: Ronni Strell
Text Design: Jean Morley
Cover: Tapestry from Abomey, Benin, West Africa
Production Supervisor: Judith Stern
Compositor: The Maryland Linotype Composition Company, Inc.
Printer and Binder: R. R. Donnelley & Sons Company

BREAKING RULES

Longman Inc., 95 Church Street, White Plains, N.Y. 10601

Associated companies: Longman Group Ltd., London; Longman Cheshire Pty., Melbourne; Longman Paul Pty., Auckland; Copp Clark Pitman, Toronto; Pitman Publishing Inc., New York

Library of Congress Cataloging-in-Publication Data

Fanselow, John F.
Breaking rules.

Bibliography: p.
Includes index.
1. Language and languages—Study and teaching.
I. Title.
P51.F36 1987 418'.007 86-27678
ISBN 0-582-79733-0

87 88 89 90 9 8 7 6 5 4 3 2 1

To Dorothy for the usual rules
To Fred for the alternative rules
To both for always letting *me* learn the values of each

Contents

Acknowledgments

All the teachers I have worked with have reminded me of how much more we know in partnership than isolated. I am grateful to all who have taught me either as students or teachers, but I want to mention a few individuals in particular and the types of lessons each taught me. John Rodgers opened my eyes to the field of ESL when I was in Nigeria. Carl Graham and Marie Gadsden gave me the freedom to learn from teaching teachers they asked me to prepare. Geraldine LaRocque introduced me to educational research, including that done by Arno Bellack and his colleagues. Arno Bellack both shared his insights and introduced me to other literature in observation. Robert L. Allen shared his gusto for critical analysis and teaching. Louis Forsdale shared his insights about communication in many incidental conversations. Joseph Gleeson and David Rorick kept reminding me of the free spirit in all of us by their actions and conversations. Larry Anger showed that risk taking requires action, not just talk.

As I developed the observation system used in this book, FOCUS, my greatest insights came from questions about it raised by those I presented parts of it to and those who tried to use it extensively. In particular, these individuals were especially helpful: Ira Bogotch, Patrick Buckheister, Sandra Chen, Angelica Marta Clavero-Pamilla, Sergio Gaitan, Tilahun Gamta, Jerry Gebhard, Mary Hines, Abdullah Libdeh, Polly Merdinger, Robert Oprandy, Proskovia Rwakyada, Carol Rubin, Frances Shapiro-Skrobe, Dwight Strawn, and Rob Walbridge.

These individuals have generously given me permission to use communications they have transcribed or created: Noah Beil, Elaine Brooks, Kathryn Garlow, Tadashi Goto, Bernadine Kraf, Barbara Leroy, Michael Long, Susan Lanzano, Joy Noren, Theresa Smith, Thomas Smoyer, Themba Taole, Carol Taylor, Hillel Weintraub, Ann Wintergerest.

The following organizations and individuals have provided permission to reproduce copyrighted material: Harper & Row; Grove Press; Sky Oaks Productions; New York News, Inc.; "$20,000 Pyramid" television program 1977 Basada, Inc., All rights reserved.

The Spencer Foundation provided funds for buying videotapes that were used a great deal to analyze communications and develop FOCUS, the observation system presented in this book.

John F. Fanselow

EPISODE 1

Begin Here— A Rule Not to Break

I. YOU CALL YOURSELF A TEACHER?—INTRODUCTION

The most memorable lesson in my work in teacher preparation came during a practice teacher's class I was observing with one Mr. Ononye, a supervisor charged with showing me how to help practice teachers. Halfway through the lesson, Mr. Ononye literally leapt out of his seat and shouted these words at the practice teacher: "You call yourself a teacher? I'll show you how to teach." After a short demonstration, Mr. Ononye gave the class back to the practice teacher with these encouraging words: "Now, see if you can teach the way I want you to."

Much of what I have heard in discussions of teaching and read in books about teaching since this lesson I have interpreted through the filter this incident set up in my mind. Thus, when I read methods books or teachers' guides to textbooks or hear discussions of teaching that urge us to use meaningful material, be enthusiastic, give clear directions, or provide supportive feedback, I see these seemingly reasonable suggestions as prescriptions that imply the authors or supervisors know what good teaching is, just as Mr. Ononye acted as if he knew what good teaching was.

When I hear teachers discussing their teaching or that of others with judgments added to prescriptions such as "Your lesson was great, especially the dictation and group work, but why don't you have them write more quickly?" I hear Mr. Ononye saying "I'll show you how to teach!" Even when the prescription accompanying the judgment is communicated less directly, with the most delicate modal, such as "Great lesson . . . ah . . . but . . . I wonder whether you might want to have them write a bit faster during the dictation?" I hear Mr. Ononye, because on one level both judgments and prescribed suggestions imply we know what good teaching is.

In fact, there is little evidence strongly supporting one particular practice over another in all settings, in part because the tests that have been used to compare different practices are not always related to instruction, in part because many out-of-class variables are not controlled in comparison-of-methods studies, and in part because the practices have been described with so little precision that in some cases the differences between the practices do not exist in reality and in others the critical differences have been overlooked. [Background 1–1]

The Ononye model, or an adaptation with polite variations, methods books, teachers' notes for textbooks, and the comments we make and hear about our teaching, in addition to being prescriptive, also tend to be general. "Get them to communicate, give them less time, be clear" and judgments like "great" are general. Even a model lesson one demonstrates is general because so much is presented that it is hard to pinpoint the precise communications that are being demonstrated and thus advocated. The general words not only make it difficult to know what to do differently, but they also make it difficult to see the extent to which what we do matches the prescriptions we are given as well.

Finally, the sources of the prescriptions in books, as well as in discussions with supervisors, tend to be outsiders—experts, people in charge, or authorities. The suggested alternatives are generated from others, not by ourselves, from within. This is not to imply outsiders are necessarily bad or not liked. Many authors of methods books and articles on how to teach are popular, sought out, and acclaimed as well. Even Mr. Ononye was popular and considered very helpful in the setting we were in. [Background 1–2]

Judgments and prescriptions based on preconceived notions of good teaching given by outsiders, general in nature, and with no means to explore congruence between practices and prescriptions, obviously serve a critical function in teacher preparation and development. These practices are widespread, and almost all teachers have experienced them. It is partly because of the fact that most teachers are aware of the normal rules in teacher preparation and development that I provide a different set of practices. The practices I invite you to experience are basically the exact opposite of those most followed. Thus, I invite you not to judge, or if you do, to withhold your judgment, to substitute specific descriptions for general prescriptions, and as a result to be free to generate alternatives unrelated to your preconceived notions of good and bad teaching, to serve as your own expert rather than to depend on those in authority, and to explore congruence between what you think you do, what you want to do, and what you actually do.

Journal Entry

From time to time, you will see the words "journal entry" throughout this book. In each journal entry, I ask you to jot down in a diary, notebook, or separate log of some kind your thoughts and feelings about what you have just read in relationship to your personal experiences. Making journal entries is an important part of using this book.

The material you are about to read is basically just a way of looking at teaching from a different perspective so that you see teaching and discussions of teaching differently. I vividly remember one of the first times I realized how looking from a different perspective can make much we take for granted seem unimportant. I was 11 years old and was looking for a black washer that I had dropped on a black floor. As I was standing and looking down at the floor with intense concentration, seeing only black space and no washer, my uncle came in. He told me to lie down on the floor. I did, and in an instant, because of the different perspective, I saw the washer.

Can you recall any incident in your life that highlighted for you the importance of looking at something from a completely different perspective or point of view?

If you can, write it out in the notebook you are starting for the journal entries in this book.

It is perhaps ironic that though prescriptions mandate change and judgments about our teaching imply change, they are rarely accompanied with any means whereby we can see the extent to which we are carrying out practices others have prescribed for us. Mr. Ononye did say "Now, see if you can do it!", but he gave no help to either the teacher or me as an observer to determine congruence between what was demonstrated and what was done by the teacher after the demonstration. Nor do prescriptions such as "Be clear," "Get them more involved," "Show some enthusiasm" provide a means to see how we can see the extent to which what we do matches the prescriptions. In the case of Mr. Ononye, there is no indication of what the *it* refers to. In the case of judgments, there is normally no indication of what precisely was *great* in a "great lesson." Partly because of the general nature of both judgments and prescriptions, the communications the supervisor has in mind are often different from those the teacher has in mind. When each party is referring to a different *it*, there is little chance that each can see the same congruence between prescriptions or judgments and practices, since in many cases the practices each has in mind refer to a different moment in the lesson. In this book, I provide experiences that enable you to make it more likely that you and another person will be able to refer to the same *it*, and that the congruence between plans and actual practices can be more clearly seen.

To explore congruence between what you yourself think, plan, and actually do, I will invite you to take two steps in the following pages, over and over again. First, I'll ask you to transcribe some actual communications or find exchanges or exercises in texts or tests that you want to explore. Then I'll ask you to code them. Thus, to explore the congruence between actual practices and a general prescription such as "Get them more involved" or a global judgment such as "The students were really involved—great," I would listen to a recording of a small segment of the lesson and make a transcription that would look like this:

JAKE: This is silly work (said with annoyance)

MARIA: Come on, let's copy the sentence.

JAKE: OK, give me the first one.

MISU: (Erasing some incorrect sentences from her notebook.)

TADASHI: (Taking some stickers off his old notebook cover and putting them on his new notebook cover.)

MARIA: There were two men in the cell.

JAKE: (Writes the sentence.) This is stupid!

I'd then label some characteristics of the communications I transcribed with a metalanguage I introduce in Episode 2. In English we might describe the exchanges by saying that student 1—Jake—made negative comments about the work that was to be done in the group, and that students 3 and 4—Misu and Tadashi—did not participate in the group activity, and that student 2—Maria—was on task. In the metalanguage I introduce, I'd say that student 1—Jake—reacted with both a linguistic aural medium and a paralinguistic aural medium used to evaluate both the content being studied and the type of activity assigned. All the communications would be coded in a similar way, using terms that are part of a conceptual system. The coding—or a detailed description in English for that matter—help us see what the students were actually doing during the group activity, while the usual judgments or prescriptions do not.

Without coding, based on a set of operationally defined labels that are part of an overall concept, each of us is more likely to see and describe events through our own preconceived notions, as I see discussions of teaching through my Ononye filter. After viewing the *same* class, I have heard contradictory comments from different observers: The teacher had rapport; the teacher was condescending; there was too much silence; there was too much noise; the material was too easy; the material was too difficult; the students were involved; the students were uninterested. Such discussions are analogous to one in the Japanese movie *Rashomon*, where four people give contradictory and equivocal accounts of an event they have all witnessed. Since in *Rashomon* one of the four has supposedly killed another while another of the four, the dead man's wife, looked on, different perspectives are predictable. But in discussions of teaching, where it would seem much less intense feelings would be generated, radically different perspectives are often communicated too. Because category labels, by definition, are designed to describe, using such words in discussions of teaching can sometimes begin to move us beyond the *Rashomon* effect. This, of course, is not to deny the excitement and value of this effect. But as I said before, since most of us have a great deal of experience with this perspective, I concentrate on an alternative perspective in this book.

The coding serves an additional purpose that a specific description in normal language of what went on does not: Because all the categories are part of a limited range of options, the categories that do not appear in the coding of a particular series of communications become alternatives that can be generated in a subsequent lesson on one's own, without the advice of an expert. But there will be plenty of illustrations of this point elsewhere in the book, so I only mention the fact here. [Background 1–3]

Journal Entry

Section 1. If you have had discussions with a supervisor after a lesson you taught, write down as many things you were told about the lesson that you can remember. If you did not have any discussions, skim through some articles or books on how to teach and jot down some of the advice given.

Section 2. Now, divide the comments you remember or those you found in books and articles on teaching into two groups: those that are descriptive and those that are prescriptive and judgmental; these often contain the word *should*, or imply it.

Section 3. Finally, write down the feelings you had as you were listening to the comments or reading the advice in the books or article. Were your feelings different about the comments in the columns labeled descriptive and prescriptive?

Section 4. As I said in the first paragraph of this episode, the most powerful observation I participated in involved a supervisor who shot to his feet and shouted "You call yourself a teacher!" during an observation. At first, I was shocked. But the practice teachers got used to the rules of this supervisor, and his demonstrations were clear.

Were any of the comments you have heard in discussions of teaching or read as dramatic as those of Mr. Ononye?

The transcribing and coding I urge you to undertake in this book are, of course, based on some assumptions, which means that on one level they are based on my preconceived notions of what is important to note in looking at communications. Not only does the coding system highlight some characteristics I consider important, but it reflects an underlying premise about communications as well. The premise is that each small, precise change we make affects the entire set of arrangements we are immersed in. For example, asking students to say the name of their favorite color or film star when responding to the roll rather than saying "here" not only alters each response, thus affecting the teacher's knowledge of each student, but also alters the perceptions some will have of the teacher, requires the use of different sounds, and might alter in some way the relationships between some students. A comment after class such as "I like him too" is more likely when students state favorite film stars than when they say "here." In addition to urging small, precise changes because I believe they alter the whole arrangement between those in the setting, I urge them because as I said before, most people have experience with the global ones often urged in methods books and in the Ononye type of discussion of teaching. My premise is reflected in these words from William Blake:

> He who would do good to another must do it in Minute
> Particulars:
> General Good is the plea of the scoundrel, hypocrite & flatterer.
> For Art & Science cannot exist but in minutely organized
> Particulars. [Background 1–4]

In addition to describing my premise in lines 1, 2, 4, and 5, with the words *scoundrel, hypocrite*, and *flatterer* in line 3 Blake provides a background for the Ononye model of discussions of teaching.

II. DIFFICULT VOCABULARY—RULES

Sandals with a Suit?—The Importance of Rules

Over time, as I have seen how stable communications in classrooms and in discussions of teaching are, I have begun to describe them with the same label many others use to describe patterned communications that occur nine times out of ten: *rules*. The idea that much of what we do is controlled by rules—unconscious conventions and habits—is central to my thinking. If we tend to do the same thing nine times out of ten in a particular situation, I don't think we do it because we are particularly clever or stupid. I think the patterns that occur in our lessons and our discussions of teaching are so predictable because much of what we do is the result of following invisible rules which, although they become quite obvious as soon as we point them out, still can control us after we realize they exist.

Examples of rules we all follow in our teaching are easy to think of. Who has trained us all to say "OK now, we're going to have a test"? Though I've never seen the advice "Use *OK* and *now* to introduce a new topic or activity or a shift in activity in your teaching," I have looked in vain for classes where shifts are not usually marked by "OK now." Masters of ceremonies on television talk shows use the same markers; few of them have been trained in our profession. What methods book has prescribed such markers?

The idea that rules control much of our teaching and discussions of teaching is of course not particularly surprising, if we just reflect for a moment. After all, we follow hundreds of rules outside of teaching settings as well. You've observed people buying newspapers at newsstands. Which newspapers do we tend to take from each stack when we buy our papers? In most large cities on the continents where I have observed newspaper stands, the paper below the top one is taken, not the top one, at least by those we'd normally refer to as middle class. You know how strong the rules are that we follow with telephones. Don't you feel compelled to answer ringing telephones on empty desks, even though you are not expecting a call and there is hardly one chance in a million that the call could possibly be for you? Don't you use baby talk when you play with babies and pets, and talk differently at a funeral and a sports event? Do you wear sandals with a suit? It is hardly surprising that we follow rules in teaching and discussions of teaching, since we do in most other activities. [Background 1–5]

An Invitation—Discovering Rules

Advocating the breaking of rules, as I do in this book, might imply that I don't believe in order. I realize that rules are necessary for society in general, and classes in particular. Without rules, chaos reigns and predictions are impossible. But because the breaking of rules requires as a first step precise description of the rules we follow, by breaking rules we become more aware of them. They become more visible, and we become more conscious both of them and of alternative rules. The breaking of rules is endless because the more we know about what we habitually and alternatively do, and the consequences of both, the more likely we are to want to continue to explore.

When we see writing on classroom walls or desk tops, the rule to write on paper and blackboards that we normally take for granted literally leaps to visibility. Though we can see how strongly the pull of the front of the classroom is just by describing the fact, if we try the alternative rule of teaching from the back of the class one day, thereby breaking a habitual rule, the usual rule becomes even more visible.

Of course, if we moved around the room and broke other rules just to realize more consciously how strong the rules are, the value of such an enterprise would be limited. But each rule we break provides us with another alternative rule that is self-generated and tests the validity of our preconceived notions. If we always explain all the new vocabulary items before a reading passage, we can never see the consequences of explaining no new vocabulary items before a reading passage. If we never ask students deliberately to produce incorrect utterances, we can never compare the consequences of this practice and the more normal one of asking students deliberately to produce only correct communications. Over time, we realize that on our own, without outsiders, we are each capable of generating more variety and freer to inquire into the consequences of our teaching than we thought. [Background 1–6]

This is not to say that teaching is just the deliberate substitution of one rule for another, or the bringing to consciousness of a wide repertoire of rules in order to generate alternatives. Teaching is also sharing in the hopes, sufferings, and aspirations of those with whom we work. But I believe that to make such sharing more likely, we must feel free to do what we are capable of and to question what we do, just as the artist who created the cover of this book felt free to question some patterns of color and space and used alternative patterns. What are new trends in art, fiction, dance, advertising, and science but the questioning and the altering of normal patterns, either accidentally or deliberately? Just as alternatives in other fields are the result of the breaking of rules, so one central way alternatives in our own teaching and discussions of teaching can be generated is by breaking the normal rules of the classroom game. [Background 1–7]

As we break rules by choice and deliberate control rather than by chance, I think we can become truly self-reliant, and we can remind ourselves and others of a very central lesson of learning: never to think we have *the* answer. Like many of the lessons we learn from observing from a different perspective, this one is obvious, just as putting an important letter in full view to hide it is an obvious alternative when endeavoring to keep a letter secret. Because much of what we see as the result of breaking rules is obvious, it is all the more likely to be obscured or ignored if we look in the usual way, colored by our preconceived notions of what is right and wrong and good and bad. For example, as soon as you observe people teaching others, you notice that the person doing the teaching tends to say "OK very good" each time the learner performs some task that was set, even when the task was not necessarily performed very well. Likewise, when one person turns the doorknob the wrong way and the door does not open, an onlooker is likely to say "Turn it the other way," even though the person turning the knob might have already started to turn the knob the other way. Whether the "OK very good" and "Turn it the other way" type of comments are the result of anxiety, a belief in reinforcement, a need to maintain control, or the following of a discourse pattern is hard to determine. What is clear is that we do follow many rules like this. What is also clear, to me at least, is that change is more likely if we deliberately substitute an alternative rather than simply advise change with a general prescription such as "Give more specific feedback," or with a judgment such as "Don't continue to do such a stupid thing." [Background 1–8]

For too long, we have sought suggestions, insights, and information only from psychologists, linguists, researchers who did comparison of methods studies, advocates of particular schools of language teaching, authors of texts, or tests or other experts. Of course, these sources have been helpful and should not be discarded. But they can be supplemented by self-generated alternative suggestions, insights, and information. Initially, we may not trust our own self-generated alternatives as much as those provided by experts. But confidence comes as we remember the Socratic idea of teaching: aiding each other to remember what we each already know, helping us each see what is within each of us. Ultimately I break rules, and invite you to join me, to see more clearly what we each are capable of and how our preconceived ideas sometimes limit this capability. If we realize how much more is within us, it is more likely we will be able to aid our students in coming to the same realization. Such conscious realization, paradoxically, leads in my experience to more freedom, for as we become aware of a greater range of rules on the conscious level, we are able to use a greater range unconsciously. Said another way, as we explore our craft by describing—recording, transcribing, and coding communications—rather than by seeking prescriptions and judgments from others, rules are broken that say we teachers must seek alternatives from those in charge, rather than ourselves or our peers, and that we must work alone within our autonomous but isolated and lonely classrooms, rather than with colleagues. [Background 1–9]

Journal Entry

If you met a friend at a party and during the course of the conversation you mentioned you had just read part of the introduction to a book, and your friend said "Gee, tell me about it" (the friend perhaps would have to have had a few drinks to make such a request), what would you tell your friend about what you've read so far?

Teaching and Nonteaching Settings—Substituting Opposite Rules

We can break rules deliberately in two ways. One is to substitute rules opposite to those we follow in our teaching. For example, if we always ask students to underline words they do not understand—something that is likely to happen nine times out of ten in reading lessons of a particular type—two opposite rules are possible, at the least. One is to ask students to cross out and obscure words they do not understand, making it easier to ignore them and move on to capture the meaning from subsequent lines, as in a cloze test. Another opposite rule is to ask them to underline only the words they do understand. Some students may be astonished to realize they know more words in a passage than they don't know. Each opposite also forces us to question the commitment to the idea that individual vocabulary items are central to the reading process.

Another way to break classroom rules deliberately is to substitute in the classroom those rules we normally follow outside the classroom and other teaching settings. For example, if you look at people reading outside most classrooms and libraries, you no doubt notice that many of them read with a lot of noise or music around. You might also see many of them reading with their feet up on tables or footrests and in a lounging position, rather than sitting upright and erect. You might see some of them eating or drinking as they read and looking up from the pages occasionally. Trying these rules in classrooms or libraries would mean that the silence usually demanded during silent reading would be replaced with noise. Substituting these rules would also mean students could read in a range of positions and accompany their reading with a snack or a drink now and then. Finally, following the rules we observe in nonteaching settings for silent reading in class would mean that students would be free to look up from their books to gaze out the window, at another student, or even at the ceiling or the teacher. Such opposites call into question the preconceived notion that concentration is best obtained in total silence and reading is best done in a certain position.

Notice that whether we break classroom rules by substituting opposites from rules found in teaching or in nonteaching settings, the first step is to describe precisely and without judgment the rules we think we are following. Remember, there are no adjectives such as *clever, useful, exciting, effective*, or *rewarding* before *Breaking Rules* or before *Alternatives in Language Teaching* in the title of this book. These judgments are absent because a central purpose of the book is to see—to see differently, but ultimately just to see. By advocating the generation of alternatives to see what we are doing, including the consequences of what we are doing, I am contending, or perhaps the better word is admitting, that we do not know precisely what we are doing nor what consequences we are producing, let alone the best way to proceed to achieve particular results.

Journal Entry

Given my definition of rules, do you think I have broken any so far in this episode? If you think I have, note them and write your reactions to the broken rules. If you think I have not, note one or two I might have broken and write how you would have reacted to my breaking them.

Imagine All the Possibilities—Some Reflections on Teaching

At this point, I had better indicate that I do not consider all of us who teach to be robots programmed to follow invisible rules we neither see nor understand. We obviously exercise some control over what we do, and we vary our teaching somewhat. Some days we have students write, other days they ask each other questions. Some days we teach the entire class, and other days we work with groups or assign tasks in pairs. We might even sometimes describe part of a lesson to see what is happening, rather than to support a preconceived notion of what should be done. Indeed, we tend to rebel against sameness and routine, always searching for ways to keep out of the proverbial rut. What are criticisms of schedules, tests, texts, and lessons on one level but an expression of our boredom with things as they are?

In spite of our efforts to vary our teaching, most systematic studies, as well as many casual observations, have shown that we tend to operate within a rather narrow range most of the time. The rules of the classroom game are remarkably stable. And often what we think we are doing is different from what observers perceive us as doing. Even when we try alternatives, we are more likely to judge them in relationship to our preconceived notions of what good teaching is rather than by including the consequences of the alternatives in our descriptions and comparing them. In short, though we do exercise some control and are somewhat aware of what we do, for most of us there is a whole alternative world of possibilities to discover and try out. "So, make a wish, make a dream, imagine all the possibilities!" [Background 1–10]

III. TENNIS, ST. JAMES?—DESCRIPTION IN OTHER AREAS

Though a major reason I advocate alternate practices is because most people have a great deal of experience with common practices, some ideas about change from other areas can be related to the practices I advocate you experience. In fact, you might at first wonder whether it might seem easier to follow the usual rules in discussing teaching, ignoring actual communications, being general and judgmental so that some comments sound like clichés, limiting the alternatives we generate because of our preconceived notions of what good teaching is, and not bothering about congruence between ideas and practice. As St. James said, "Ye shall be compared to a man beholding his own countenance in a glass, for he beheld himself and went his way, and presently forgot what manner of man he was." Seeing precise details can shock! But in my experience, as we begin to observe what we see, without judgment, sometimes we experience a type of liberation. [Background 1–11]

Just as the pain we imagine we'll feel is often more severe before we get in the dentist's chair than after the drilling begins, so the fear of seeing ourselves is often decreased, if not eliminated, by observing nonjudgmentally. Though the goal of observing is to describe rather than to say how terrible or wonderful we sound or look, we usually cannot avoid seeing and hearing ourselves as a critic for a while. But as we describe more and more, fear and anxiety usually decrease. Energy is devoted to trying to describe and discover what we do, including the consequences, rather than to lamenting our looks or the sound of our voice. Since the aim of the description is only to see, not to prove or disprove our preconceived notions, comments of this type become less frequent: "I sure did a stupid thing;" "Wow, that really was great;" I handled the questions perfectly."

Using a coding system—a set of operationally defined descriptive terms—to describe communications, in place of general words that imply judgments, can provide distance from what we do to help us see differently. Gallwey—a famous tennis coach—once demonstrated on television two approaches to getting players to get the ball over the net more than three times during the opening volley. He started by shouting "Great!" after a volley was completed and "Almost" when the ball went out of bounds or hit the net. After some out-of-bounds balls, he made comments such as "Try harder—you can do it." The more he praised the players—a type of judgment—the fewer times they could get the ball over the net and back.

He then told them that rather than trying to get the ball over the net more than three times, they should just describe what was happening. He asked them to supply one word to describe the ball when the racket came in contact with it, and another word to describe the ball when it touched the ground, either inside or outside the serve lines. They chose the words *bounce* and *hit.* One player started the volley, and as he did, he, of course, said *hit* as he whacked the ball. Each player called out *bounce* as the ball touched the court on each player's side.

The players were able to keep the volley going for thirteen exchanges as they accompanied their playing with the naming of the two elements of their exchange. The coach contended, of course, that helping them to observe and describe what they were doing nonjudgmentally helped them. Rather than tightening their muscles in preparation for a judgment, or as a result of a judgment, they simply looked at what they were doing. Since they were looking at what they were doing rather than trying to decide what manner of people they were, they were free from anxiety and could let their muscles move to do the job at hand. [Background 1–12]

Whether we are on the tennis court, in a classroom, or in any other setting, much of what we do we are *not* conscious of. "Hold your feet so they give more power and sit up straight" shouts the parent teaching a child to swing in the park. If the child does not know how to determine how much power his feet are presently producing, and he is not aware of his current posture, he cannot alter his way of swinging, except by accident. "Your back is now on an angle—line it up with the chains on each side of the seat" is a command that is descriptive and so allows the child to see what he is presently doing *and* how the suggested alternative is different. It is also nonjudgmental, not implying that the child is inadequate, as the usual "Sit up straight" does.

A comment like "Get them more involved" is closer to "Sit up straight" or "Great shot!" than to "bounce-hit" or "Line up your back with the chains." I find such general, judgmental comments such as "Get them more involved" harder to translate into practice. Nor can I see how to determine the extent to which I follow the advice. So I emphasize descriptive comments that are specific, such as "Make your back even with the chains" or comments that include categories, such as "bounce-hit." As a result, we are perhaps less likely to avoid beholding ourselves, to paraphrase St. James. And perhaps we will be less likely to forget what manner of person we are as well if we continue to look and try to see ourselves over a long period of time.

IV. ONLY 2 PERCENT—FIVE VARIABLES THAT AFFECT LEARNING

Some argue that discussions of teaching, whether done with specific descriptions or with general prescriptions, with judgments or without, and whether accompanied with the citation of actual communications from classes, texts, or tests or not, are rather futile enterprises. Some argue that variables other than those we can describe affect our work the most. They contend that most of the important things which occur in a class cannot be described, only felt. Teacher and student rapport or teacher charisma would be considered such variables. Since they are so difficult to see, I call these *invisible* variables.

Others claim that prescribed texts, imposed syllabuses, and required examinations students must follow or be prepared for tie teachers' hands and prevent them from trying alternatives. These *required* variables, they argue, are even more significant influences than *invisible* variables. Still others remind us that student and teacher attitude, knowledge of first and second languages, energy levels, motivation, and previous training contribute and detract from learning a great deal: These are *foreordained* variables. Emphasizing what we actually do in classes distracts us from the great influence these *foreordained* variables have on learning. And finally there are those who remind us that administrative decisions such as the number of hours devoted to language in the timetable; the amount of money provided for paper, chalk, and materials; and the salaries provided for teachers affect learning more than anything a teacher can do in a classroom: These are *big chief* variables. Why fiddle with a few alternatives in a class when the amount of time provided for instruction is less than makes sense? [Background 1–13]

There is no doubt that the alternatives we introduce in our work make up only one variable of many that affect learning. What we do—*teacher* variables—cannot be separated from *invisible* variables, *required* variables, *foreordained* variables, and *big chief* variables. Even if *teacher* variables account for only a small percentage of the contribution to total learning that is needed, they are necessary. For the sake of argument, let's say that *invisible* variables account for 24 percent of the variance of any item a student learns. Let's assume *required* variables account for another 24 percent, *foreordained* variables account for 24 percent, and *big chief* variables account for still another 26 percent. This means that whatever we deliberately do or can alter accounts for only 2 percent of the variance that contributes to the learning of any single item.

But so what? If learning equals 100 percent, and lack of learning means anything less than 100 percent, the 2 percent we are responsible for makes the difference between learning and not learning. Whether the variables we control account for 98 percent of the variance that produces learning, and the other variables account for 2 percent, or whether it is the other way round, learning cannot take place without the variables teachers can control. Scurvy in the British Navy was eliminated by the small amounts of one vitamin in limes, one of the smallest fruits. The amount of a contribution should not be confused with its importance.

Anyway, the rules that control *invisible* variables, *required* variables, *foreordained* variables, and *big chief* variables are no more rigid than those that control *teacher* variables, the ones we are in charge of. As some of the rules that control *teacher* variables are broken, other variables might be affected. For example, while it is of course true that the daily diet of students is out of our control, this *foreordained* variable can be affected by serving snacks in class as part of a lesson. Altering *teacher* variables so that students do well on examinations, *required* variables, may affect *big chief* variables. If students do well on leaving examinations, a principal may be more willing to make more books and materials available.

Each type of variable affects the other. I hope that as you work your way through this book, the number of comments in your discussions with other teachers that mention *teacher* variables will increase. After all, these are the only ones we can control as teachers. Spending time arguing about *invisible, required, foreordained*, and *big chief* variables distracts us from *teacher* variables. But it is hard to see how conversations about these can be as effective as those about *teacher* variables, which we alone control and are responsible for.

Journal Entry

If your colleagues don't mind, record some conversations between them in the staff room and tally the comments made about *teacher* variables with a *t* and tally all other comments with an *o* for *other*. If the number of remarks about *teacher* variables is small, listen to the tape again and tally the variables that were discussed. Use an *i* for *invisible* variables, an *r* for *required* ones, an *f* for *foreordained* ones, and a *b* for *big chief* variables. Copy some of the communications in each category. After a few weeks, record and tally again and see if the pattern is consistent. Copy the remarks from the subsequent recording and see if they seem similar or different in nature from the original ones. Are they less critical or more critical, for example?

If you find none of these variables discussed—unlikely but possible—then we can establish a new category called the *couldn't be bothered* variables. In my experience, teachers are concerned and do discuss variables that affect learning. But if you find teachers not discussing *invisible, required, foreordained, big chief,* and *teacher* variables, you can put the communications you find in the category *couldn't be bothered.*

V. ABOUT YOU AND THE BOOK

Misleading Titles—Deciding Whether the Book Is for You

Though you might think the words *language teaching* in the title identify the audience, logical as such a conclusion is, they do not. The words *breaking rules, exploring, generating*, and *alternatives* are the ones that delimit the audience. If changing your teaching on your own is of little interest, and adding variety to your teaching is not a central concern, then even if you are involved with language teaching, this book is not for you. On the other hand, even if you are not involved with language teaching but are fascinated by observing, keen on generating alternatives on your own, interested in classifying communications to discover rules, have a compelling desire to explore teaching, and believe that ultimately we can depend only on ourselves to learn and develop, this book might be of interest to you. Your attitude is more critical in determining whether this book is for you than the content you teach, the age group of your students, or their capabilities and levels of achievements.

On one level, all teaching is language teaching anyway. To understand the meaning a linguist and a botanist attach to words such as *syntax* or *taxonomy* is, in fact, language learning. Discovering what *breaking rules* means to a judge, a physicist, a criminal, a linguist, a police officer, a botanist, and yourself—both now and when you finish this book—is also at one critical level language learning—realizing of course that language learning must be accompanied by the experience the language we are learning deals with.

Oh Mighty Maze, but Not without a Plan! (Alexander Pope)—Organization of the Book

If you've looked at the table of contents, you've realized that if there is a plan for how the episodes are organized, it is not clearly discernible. In fact, there is no plan, at least in the usual sense. The episodes are simply listed in alphabetical order. I could have organized them according to the classic skill sequence, putting those related to listening in the first section, those related to speaking in the second, and so on. Or I could have put those episodes related to the beginnings of lessons first, those related to the middle of the lesson next, and so on.

I rejected the usual linear organization because I do not want you to have to go through the book in linear sequence. I do not think all learning is strictly linear and sequential; I think much learning is circular or nonsequential. And I wanted to symbolize this belief by listing the episodes without any imposed order so you could start anyplace you want and move to any other place in any direction, including skipping episodes in either direction, as if you were a piece in a chess game—in the unlikely event that you ever had an ambition to be a piece in a chess game. So, except for the first two episodes, which follow the normal rule, all the other episodes can be done in any sequence. Why do there always have to be exceptions? [Background 1–14]

Start with a title that interests you, or a description of a title that makes sense. Or select a topic you are taken with listed in the index and glossary in Episode 24. Follow the topic from any episode to any other one in any sequence. Not only do you not have to go from one episode to another in linear sequence, but you need not go from front to back in any single episode. You can dip in and do sections in each on the same topic, as is possible in many reference books. Finally, as you'll see in Episode 2 and as the tables in the inside covers show, categories of the observation system used as the controlling concept for the book are cross-referenced to the episodes so you can select episodes or sections of episodes on the basis of categories that interest you.

Obviously, you can follow the normal rules of reading a book from the beginning to the end in linear sequence. But you don't have to, because each independent episode is related to all the other episodes by the conceptual framework I've based the book on. That framework is the observation system I call FOCUS, introduced in Episode 2.

VI. RULES FOR YOU—USING THIS BOOK

Rule 1. How to Use This Book

As you work through this book, with a partner or by yourself, you'll see a reduced version of the bird motif on the cover next to some of the text, like this: 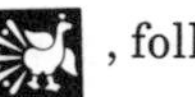 , followed by a black line along the left margin. If you are limited in time, like most professionals—with too many students and preparations, a research report due a week ago, a full-time job and a class or two to follow as you care for a family—just work your way through the material not marked with the birds: the *unrated material*. And just fly over the rated material until you have time for it later. Concentrating on the unrated material, you'll see ways to generate alternatives and begin to understand and be able to use the major categories of the observation system I introduce. [Background 1–15]

The rated materials, marked with the bird, are reserved for those with more time. If you are a teacher with released time to work with a practice teacher, a materials developer paid to compare a series of texts, a researcher investigating the consequences of different models of teaching, a supervisor charged with developing an in-service teacher development program, or a student searching for a topic for a project or thesis, these rated sections are for you.

In other words, you have before you two books in one. In the unrated material you can get an understanding of the major categories of the observation system I introduce and specific teaching ideas. You'll see alternatives to try and learn ways to generate additional alternatives on your own. In the rated sections, marked by the bird, you will get an understanding of the many details of the observation system I introduce, see additional ways to generate alternatives, see the extent to which you do what you think you do, *and* begin to look at the consequences of your work. The rated material provides ways to explore in the same way the other material provides ways to generate alternatives.

Rule 2. How *Not* to Use This Book

Both the marked and unmarked material need to be gone through in a different time frame from most other books though, because this book requires not only reading and thinking, but activity and action. Both during and after the reading of a novel, a newspaper, or a textbook, often all that is required is memory work or thinking. Both during and after the reading of *Breaking Rules*, I ask you for much more than memory and thinking. Generating and exploring alternatives requires activity—writing comments, recording, transcribing and coding communciations—and also action—substituting alternatives in communications you control.

As you might expect, a book that requires activity and action on the part of readers as well as reading and thinking has to be used differently. While a quick skim through many episodes will provide a beginning understanding of the concepts I introduce, and a number of alternatives to try, and while a great deal of transcribing and coding can be done in short courses of a few weeks or an academic term, the generation and exploration of alternatives that I am advocating is a multiyear undertaking. In each episode there are scores of alternatives. If you read one short episode per week and generate or explore even a few alternatives or categories for a few weeks after that, you are doing enough. This book is ready to be your companion for years.

Short-term quick answers is not what this book is about. This book is about gradual, long-term generation and exploration of small numbers of alternatives and categories at a time. People don't expect to master bridge or tennis by reading a book during a two-week course or school term. Nor do we feel compelled to try ten alternative bids or strokes per day or even per week as we begin to learn about bridge or tennis. So, from all the alternatives possible, from all the categories and subcategories, realize my intention is to have you select. The idea is to master a category at a time, see how it fits into the entire system, but not be concerned about mastering all the categories at once or in a short period of time. In classes, breaking too many rules too quickly by trying to alter many categories at once is more likely to block our view of teaching than to help us see it differently, one of the central aims of this book. [Background 1–16]

"I'm Going to Tell the Teacher"—An Aside about Using Books

I do hope you'll excuse my carrying on about how to use this book, as if you've never had a book in your hand before. But we are sometimes programmed so thoroughly to go through books in a certain way that I felt a gentle reminder was in order, especially since some of the uses of this book are somewhat curious anyway.

I do want to share with you an observation that illustrates the emphasis put on reading material in a certain way. I made the following observation during the silent reading portion of a reading lesson. As all the students were reading silently, one student started skipping a few pages in the section of the book that had been assigned and began to thumb through the book until he found a section he wanted to read. Just as he was about to start the new section, the student sitting next to him whispered very strongly: "You can't read that yet; you haven't finished this section yet, and you didn't answer the questions either. I'm going to tell the teacher!"

Well, I want you to know that not only would I not "tell the teacher," but also that I think a book like this is more likely to be valuable if, no matter how much time you have, you start with topics you are currently interested in and at first limit yourself to the unrated material. I trust you will have the book a long time, and in my experience, most of us have varying amounts of time during different stages in our professional lives. At some point in all our lives, there's always more time. At these junctures you can explore by working your way through the rated sections, having already engaged yourself in the generation of alternatives in the unrated sections.

On to Episode 2: "Bringing Things into FOCUS—At Least Beginning To!"

BACKGROUND NOTES

1–1. The comparisons of methods studies usually mentioned include Agard and Dunkel, Scherer and Wertheimer, Upshur (1968), Smith (1970), and the GUME Project in Sweden done by Levin and Olsson. These compared test scores of students in classes considered to be following one method or another, such as drill versus explanation. While the GUME project suggested that explanation helped, and while none of the studies supported the value of repetition, the descriptions of what teachers and students actually did were very general. The critique of the Smith study in the *Modern Language Journal* of October 1969 points out the weaknesses of these types of comparisons of methods studies.

In the field of reading, the debate has been between phonics and the whole-word approach. Again, the descriptions are global, and when tests of students taught by different teachers are compared, one never knows for sure what the teachers did, let alone what they did differently. Chall's study is the classic in this genre. Problems in research design of both comparisons of methods studies and other types of research are clearly described in a review of over 400 studies in composition published by the National Council of Teachers of English by Braddock et al.

The most readable account I have found that reviews comparisons of different treatments is in an article on stuttering by Gerald Jonas called "The reporter at large—The disorder of many theories." To put all comparisons of methods into perspective, it is important to read books that describe learning variables outside the class, such as those of the home and what the child or adult brings to the class. Jencks's report on the effect of family on achievement puts methods into a larger perspective and is a book worth reading.

1–2. Many critiques are little more than subtle negotiations for power. If the observer comes up with a suggestion and the teacher gives a reason why the suggestion cannot be followed, the observer is likely to come up with a counterargument indicating that the suggestion can be followed. One could count up the number of points each person makes and declare the one who makes the most arguments the winner. Or one can try other models of supervision. Cogan (1973) describes a number of them in his book on supervision. Gebhard does too.

The idea of listening to taped critique sessions to see what we say is a practice counselors have advocated for a long time (Blocksma, 1947). Should you find clichés in tapes you listen to, and should you want to be reminded of a philosopher's warning about clichés, read Hannah Arendt.

1–3. I used to believe that it was necessary to teach language as I was working with language teachers so those I observed and critiqued could see me in action. While some often want to see me teach so they can determine whether I can do what I say is worth trying, I see less and less value in model lessons. Just as a coach's task is to get others to break records and win games and a language teacher's job is to get others to develop language, not simply speak, read, write, and listen in front of students, so my task is to observe and critique, not to teach languages in front of others so that they can try to imitate my teaching.

Michael West wrote about this issue in a classic article in 1959. Together with Richard L. Light, I edited a series of articles dealing with issues of teacher preparation published by TESOL.

My own interest in observation using more than the usual checklists started around 1970. I made my first public presentation of my observation system at a workshop in 1973 at TESOL in Puerto Rico. I followed this with a description of the system similar to the present one in 1976 at TESOL in New York City. The description from the convention appeared in the *TESOL Quarterly* in March 1977 in an article called "Beyond *Rashomon*." I first discussed the idea of rules in a presentation at the New York State TESOL Affiliate meeting in Albany, New York, in 1976. The presentation was subsequently printed in a collection edited by Richard L. Light and Alice Osman in 1978. Carol Rubin tried out the system with materials she developed.

1–4. In *Science and human values*, where these lines are quoted, Bronowski reminds us that even in science, concepts are neither absolute nor everlasting. He argues that learning, whether in science or art, is a search for truth. His ideas are related to this book because the goal of artists and scientists is to seek unity in hidden likenesses. Socrates in his questions too was searching for truth and tried to show that the pat answers we often provide do nothing but prevent us from seeing and searching.

1–5. Many have written about the idea that we unconsciously follow rules in much of what we do. Darwin describes a bet he made and won based on his understanding of a rule. He bet a man a certain amount of money that he would be unable to spit a certain distance within a certain time. Darwin won the bet, as he knew he would, because of his understanding of the rule that saliva flow slows down under pressure. Eibl-Eibesfeldt's descriptions of rules animals follow builds on Darwin's idea that much of what all living things do is biologically determined rather than the result of habit formation, behavioral control, or planning. Substituting the word *people* for the different animals that she describes reminds us that when people flock to the front of a bus to get off in spite of signs urging that the rear door be used, unconscious flocking rules are being followed; we are not acting deliberately. Her book, incidentally, is not intended to explain why we do and do not do such mundane things as get on buses. She is ultimately writing about the need to understand the rules we unconsciously follow to discover ways to prevent war and nuclear destruction.

Though I borrowed the idea of classroom rules from Bellack, Jackson too suggests that much of what we do is unconscious. He reminds us in his description of life in classrooms that scores of split-second actions are made all day long, and there is simply no way we could deliberate about all of them.

When Bellack developed the rule metaphor to summarize his classroom observations, he was thinking of the use of language as a series of rules in a game rather than of Darwin's biological rules. But I find the rule metaphor in both senses useful because by using it, I find it easier to avoid arguments about why we do something in a particular way. Rules also remind me of games, which at least sometimes are associated with playfulness and fun. Should you be interested in reading about other words associated with rules as well as possible explanations for much of what we seem to do unconsciously, read Erving Goffman.

1–6. I deliberately use the word *consequences* rather than *results* or *effects* when I refer to what occurs after we do something. I can say with assurance that students in a class will talk to each other more in groups of four than in a group of forty when the teacher is in control and asking questions. The fact that they talk more is a consequence. Whether this consequence will produce different results on an examination or be more effective is a separate question. By distinguishing between what happens as a result of what is done—consequences—from what outcome something has—results or effects—I hope to make the study of effectiveness a separate issue rather than an excuse for not trying alternatives.

Given all the variables that probably contribute to language development, the ones that contribute to outcomes most effectively are not easy to find. Dunkin and Biddle confirm this point in their comprehensive review of decades of process product research. Their discussion of the limitations of matching specific teaching behaviors with effects needs to be read together with

Brophy and Good's review of process product research. Brophy and Good are much more confident about relationships between teacher behavior and learning. Long's 1982 review of some studies in second language teaching is in this tradition. And W. F. Mackey (1978) has developed a model for relating teaching practices to results students achieve, should you want to pursue this model of research. His title is the most explicit that I have seen in advocacy of this type of research: "Cost benefit quantification of language teaching behavior."

Judgments are often followed by the type of simple cause-effect relationships we often hear. "Calling on students with a friendly tone of voice will make them feel comfortable"; "Writing neatly on the blackboard will produce students with neat habits" are two examples of simple cause-effect relationships that I consider dangerous. If such simple relationships existed, teaching would not be complex at all. Most things we do have multiple and contrasting effects. Trying to make neat, simple cause-effect relationships about teaching and learning shows little understanding or respect for students or teachers. Jackson too points out the limitations of such one-to-one relationships.

1–7. Perhaps best known for the idea that new concepts are not developments or refinements of old ones, but rather revolutionary, is Kuhn's *The Structure of Scientific Revolutions*. Kuhn shows how Einstein replaced Newton and Newton replaced Copernicus because their explanations were found to be inadequate to describe what people experienced. Digital watches illustrate the idea as well as Kuhn's brilliant examples from the history of science. Expert watchmakers did not develop digital watches, nor were the electronic components of digital watches an outgrowth of the fine jeweled movements made by skilled craftsmen. The components of digital watches grew out of a totally different tradition. In most countries that specialize in mechanical watches, many people lost their jobs because of the revolution in watchmaking. In drama, Beckett did not build on Aristotle's ideas of drama with plot, spectacle, and so on, but wrote plays that banished these usual components from the theater. Joyce did the same thing in the novel with the publication of *Finnegan's Wake*.

Fries and others who emphasized oral models from teacher and student speech rather than oral reading in language classes were not building on the common practice of translating texts in language classrooms. They revolted against former practices. In advocating that the teacher not provide an oral model, Gattegno (1976) was not building on the work of Fries, but urging an opposite practice, believing like Fries earlier that his revolutionary practices were superior to previous ones.

Outside the classroom and the world of art, a moment's reflection brings more examples to mind. Short dresses in style one year are replaced by long ones soon after all finish buying short ones. Narrow ties are replaced by wide ones and then by a scarf or open shirts. One year's popular color is replaced by a different hue before one season has passed.

1–8. I don't have a great deal of support for this claim, though Good and Brophy have described one of the many studies done on the topic. But changing teachers, or anyone, is a complex process that does not lend itself to simple solutions. Should you be interested in treatments of the underlying idea of nonjudgmental observation as a precondition for change, I'd urge you to read those I mention in 1–12: Gallwey, Alexander, and Pirsig. And I'd invite you to study neurolinguistic programming, described by Bandler and Grinder. Also, keep in mind Christ's admonition not to judge but to love others in spite of what we may think are their flaws. Should you want more than general precepts and a rationale for nonjudgmental observation, read and do some of the suggested activities in Curwin and Fuhrmann's book about discovering your teaching self.

1–9. While rereading the *Meno* takes a lot of energy, I find Plato's statement containing Socrates' idea that all learning is but recollection exciting. "I am saying that there is no teaching, but only recollection" are the words Plato puts in the mouth of Socrates as he teaches Meno's slave geometry. To help people recollect, we need to challenge them. In the *Meno*, Socrates perplexes the student in order to put him in a stronger position, because the boy will want to overcome his misunderstandings.

1–10. The theme song of a television program called "Make a Wish," produced by Lester Cooper and with Tom Chapin as the main character, ends with the line "Imagine all the possibilities!" In the program, viewers are always invited to "Make a wish, make a dream." I invite you to do this as you work your way through the episodes in this book. If you do, perhaps the narrow range of behavior reported in most classroom observation will be broadened, and the recitation so commonly reported up until now by studies such as Hoetker and Ahlbrand's will become rare.

1–11. The quote from St. James is from Chapter 1, verse 24. But I didn't connect it to my work. I saw the quote related to teacher preparation in a book edited by Robert C. Burkhart in 1968.

1–12. The ideas behind the "bounce-hit" sequence on television are accessible in Gallwey's "inner game" books. His *The Inner game of tennis* is the one I keep looking at. Your tennis game may or may not improve, but you'll sure be exposed to a different perspective about many daily activities. I've found Pirsig useful for providing nonjudgmental perspectives too. The Alexander technique used by many actors and musicians is a variation of what Gallwey and Pirsig discuss.

1–13. While my labels for these five variables are original, and I have heard these types of comments made for years, I owe the classification of the content in discussions about teaching to Dunkin and Biddle.

1–14. In his treatment of association in *Principles of Psychology*, William James tells how looking at a clock set off a number of associations that pursued an erratic course. He argues that making seemingly unrelated associations is an ordinary process (page 375). The novelist Walker Percy presents a different argument for letting learning happen without a linear sequence. He contends that the individual gives up "sovereignty" by following the usual routes and the expected organizations and plans and sequences. So for a genuine search, each must follow an individual route, a personal sequence. Robert Coles is the source of these comments about Walker Percy (1978).

1–15. Originally, I had decided to mark more time-consuming sections with an *X*. But aside from the connotation attached to X-rated materials, X brings to mind a lot of images unrelated to reading. X for experimental is used by the military, as in the MX tank—experimental model; X also means an error to most; to represent kisses we use an X; and X also marks the spot.

The bird, suggested by my editor, Arley Gray, has none of these connotations and yet indicates whether the material is more time consuming as clearly as an X. Incidentally, before I rated the material, either with an X or bird, more people resisted coding. But once the sections for coding were made optional, not only was there nothing left to resist, but curiosity was aroused by what some considered to be forbidden. As soon as Pandora was told not to open the box, she did. As soon as the birds indicated that the material could be passed over, many decided to pass through it.

1–16. I realize some books require more time than others, having done a lot of cooking with recipes, to say nothing of having transcribed, coded, and tallied with observation guides. I have always been struck by the fact that we tend to read books about teaching as if we were reading a daily newspaper, while we spend a great deal of time on recipes, as we do on books about hobbies and games. Yet learning how to observe and teach is surely as complex as learning how to cook, stain furniture, or play bridge. If you are the type to read the same steps over and over again in recipes or other how-to materials, you'll understand the need to do the same thing in a book about observing and teaching.

EPISODE 2

Bringing Things into Focus— At Least Beginning To

I. WHAT'S IN A NAME ANYWAY?—NAME OF OBSERVATION SYSTEM: FOCUS

I have found it useful to use an observation system to generate and explore alternatives in language teaching. A system helps me discover rules, generate alternatives, and see the extent to which rules I break raise questions about my preconceived notions. I call the system I use FOCUS, an acronym for *F*oci for *O*bserving *C*ommunications *U*sed in *S*ettings. I like the acronym because the word *focus* implies change. We often hear that things are moving in and out of focus. Each time movement causes the focus to change, an alternative perspective is produced. *Focus* also implies variety. We often speak of moving from one focus to another in conversations, in our work, or in life. I also like the acronym because, like the mathematician's use of the word *focus* to refer to the place where rays of light come together, FOCUS highlights my aim of bringing together much of what we do both in teaching and nonteaching settings, all within one conceptual framework. Finally, to bring anything into focus means to look with a particular perspective. But just as a camera lens allows us to focus on distance shots or close-ups, so FOCUS is designed to help see communications in two ways. It is useful in a general way for those without a great deal of time and, at the same time, it is designed for those who have the time to describe in specific terms very small details of communications.

I like the words the acronym stands for less than the acronym itself. In fact, I find the words *Foci, Observing, Communications, Used*, and *Settings* more and more pretentious. However, they do highlight some critical features of the system that are important. For example, the first word, *Foci*, because it is plural, indicates that I describe more than one characteristic of each thing we look at. In fact, I look at five different characteristics of what we observe, or five foci. *Observing* highlights the fact that the purpose of the observation system is to look, not judge. *Communications* shows that the observation system can be used to describe more than just linguistic messages such as words—messages sent with gestures or received from music, for example. The *Used* is not the one from the car lots. My *Used* captures the active nature of communication. And the last word, *Settings*, indicates that the system is designed to be applied anywhere. That includes not just what goes on in classrooms, but also what goes on during conversations in a bar, while announcements are made at a concert hall or on a plane or when a tollbooth attendant gives directions to a driver. You'll be happy to know that I failed in my original plan to have each of the letters in the acronym stand for one of the five characteristics I distinguish with FOCUS. It's easy to get carried away!

II. MEETING A NEED NOT EVERYONE FEELS—ADVANTAGES OF A DESCRIPTIVE OBSERVATION SYSTEM

My observation instrument eliminates many of the problems inherent in the usual methods of teacher preparation, such as suggestions that either imply criticism or pay little attention to actual communications used in classes and nonteaching settings. Because the purpose of my observation system is to describe communications in order to discover rules, and *not* to improve teaching, the descriptions need not be concerned with either implicit or explicit judgments. Since describing communications to discover rules requires that the actual communications be cited, attention to what actually happened is stressed. Consequently, when using FOCUS to discuss teaching, variables often mentioned in the usual discussions of teaching, such as arguments about the principal's choice of books, or the set text or the superiority of one theory over another, are less likely because the observation system forces one to classify actual communications made in the classroom. It is hard to classify and argue about other variables at the same time.

Without an observation system, both rules and alternatives, whether suggested by others or self-generated, begin to make up an extremely large list. The list of items can become so long that it is hard to either keep track of or remember them, much less learn to use them freely without concentration. An observation system enables each rule and alternative to be seen in relation to a central conceptualization, all described with the same set of basic words.

Almost every group of words we learn has the potential for opening up an alternative world. Potential is greatly enhanced when the new words are related to one another by a unifying concept. Thus, *atom, proton,* and *neutron* make more sense when considered together with the unifying concept of the atomic theory of the universe. *Phone, allophone,* and *phoneme* make more sense when they are related to one another by the distinctive feature theory of language description. And *shrimp, herring, consomme, cream of asparagus, strawberries,* and *cheese* make one kind of sense when they are listed in different places on a menu, related to one another by the concept of the course of the meal, and another kind of sense when they are arranged in random order on a shopping list. They make still another kind of sense when related to one another by the food value they contain, expressed by words such as *calories, vitamins and minerals, fats, proteins,* and *carbohydrates.*

I think that one of the limitations in much of our discussion of the teaching act has been the fact that often the terms we use are not unified by a conceptual framework. They are closer to shopping lists than to five-course meals and closer to five-course meals than to the analytical description of food provided by *calories, vitamins and minerals, fats, proteins,* and *carbohydrates.*

Though you have probably had the chance to see observation checklists, I have included a few here because they symbolize the shopping-list model of teacher preparation. I do not include the examples to illustrate either very-well-thought-out checklists or poorly thought-out ones. I include the examples only to illustrate a different way of looking at lessons and discussing teaching.

III. SHOPPING LISTS—JUDGMENTAL OBSERVATION SYSTEMS

Example 1

Rank with a *4* if high, a *3* if average, and a *1* if low.

Attitude of Teacher

sincerity	________	enthusiasm	________
tact	________	humor	________
confidence	________	humility	________
objectivity	________	patience	________

Personal Characteristics

Appearance		Behavior	
attire	________	composure	________
grooming	________	punctuality	________
bearing	________	courtesy	________

Knowledge of Lesson Planning and Teaching

is up to date	________	defines new terms	________
has continuity	________	uses teaching aids	________
follows a sequence	________	checks learning	________
uses materials well	________	maintains interest	________
involves students	________	achieves aims	________
channels discussion	________	adapts well	________
simplifies complex concepts	________		

Example 2

Some questions to check mastery of essential teaching techniques:

1. Do I make sure all students can see and hear what I do?
2. Do I use a great range of objects and pictures to illustrate ideas?
3. Do I ask students to demonstrate meanings?
4. Do I beat around the bush or go directly to the central topic of the lesson?
5. Do I avoid unnecessary movement and distracting behavior?
6. Do I know at all times exactly what I am saying and doing, and what I will be doing next?
7. Do I do everything in an orderly, efficient, businesslike way?
8. Do I speak clearly and distinctly?
9. Do I get cues from students and use them to tell me whether they are with me or not?

10. Do I keep alert to the needs of students?

11. Do I keep a quick pace so I can keep interest high at all times?

12. Do I take care to motivate the students?

13. Do I try to see myself as my students see me?

Example 3

Rate the teacher on a scale of *1* through *5*, with a *5* being highest.

Knowledge in area of teaching	______
Ability to communicate	______
Ability to plan work without close supervision	______
Tendency to cooperate with other teachers and administrators	______
Inclination to show initiative	______
Perseveres in completing work that has been started	______
Ability to accept criticism	______
Emotional stability	______
Leadership potential	______
Loyalty to the school and its ideals	______
Trustworthy in matters pertaining to students and staff	______
Voice—enunciates well and clearly	______
Dresses appropriately	______
Personal grooming	______

Of course, observation systems can be descriptive rather than judgmental. One can simply list things teachers and students do in specific, nonjudgmental terms. Indeed, the first stage I went through in developing FOCUS was to list teacher and student activities and communications during dialogs, dictations, silent and oral reading, and pattern drills, to name a few activities I made guides to observe. Here are some excerpts from some of the guides.

Dictation Guide	Yes	No
Teacher stated a reason for giving the dictation.	___	___
Teacher stated the procedure to be followed during the dictation.	___	___
Teacher followed the procedure stated.	___	___
Teacher read the elements from the passage orally and looked at class—did not glue eyes to page.	___	___
Teacher dictated punctuation, capitalization, or spelling of difficult words—ones students could not spell.	___	___
Teacher wrote material dictated on the blackboard after students completed material.	___	___
Teacher wrote one item at a time on blackboard as students were completing each item.	___	___
Read and look up guide		
Teacher stated a reason for having students read silently, look up, and then say what they had read.	___	___
Teacher elicited a reason for having students read silently, look up, and then say what they had read.	___	___
Teacher demonstrated read and look up.	___	___

Teacher compared length of sense groups read in timed periods on one day with those from timed periods earlier in the course.	___	___
Students made vocabulary substitutions when they said what they had read silently that showed they understood what they were reading.	___	___
When students said lines, they looked at another person rather than at the ceiling, the book, or down to the floor or the desk.	___	___

After I used the guides for some time, I noticed that statements in one guide were similar to those on other guides. I then began to group the scores of separate items listed in seemingly endless progression on the guides for separate activities. Not only did the guides help me develop the categories, but they also provided some of the same distance that transcription and coding do. And, of course, descriptive guides enable us to see what we are doing and to generate alternatives the same way an observation system does, so they are still the opposite of the ones used in the usual model of teacher preparation. [Background 2–1]

Although in discussing teaching we do use words that are sometimes related to each other, such as *mechanical, meaningful,* and *communicative* to use one set, these terms are not part of the same conceptual framework as other words we use, such as *pace, drill,* and *reinforcement.* And these in turn are not related directly to *rapport, situational,* and *structure,* to name only a few of the scores of separate, largely unrelated words we usually use to discuss our work. To put it another way, though we use a great many words to discuss our work, they are not part of one central conception. Additionally, most of them tend to be ill-defined and inconsistently used. In a word, though physicists have all sorts of *-ons* to describe atoms, and linguists have *-ones* and *-emes* to describe sounds, while restaurateurs have courses to organize their food and nutritionists have percentages of fats and other basic components to describe food in still another way, we do not have the equivalent of the five-course meal, much less commonly accepted units of analysis such as *teachons* or *teachemes*! [Background 2–2]

While I'm sure that on one level you are delighted we don't have *teachemes* or *teachons*, not having considered physics or phonetics two of your favorite indoor activities, and while I suspect you prefer discussing food in terms of a five-course meal rather than the number of calories and percentages of fat the meal contains, the use of these sets of labels, each tied to a particular conceptualization, does have some advantages. For one thing, such technical words, though limited in number, can describe all the items within the framework they make up. On one level of description, for example, the words *calories, vitamins and minerals, fats, proteins,* and *carbohydrates* can be used to describe all the fantastic variety of food in the entire world. Such comprehensiveness is possible because the terms stand for categories of items rather than single items. In addition to making it possible for the sets of words to be comprehensive, the categories help show relationships between different items within the system, some of which would remain obscured without the terms. An observation system also enables each rule and alternative to be seen in relationship to a central conceptualization.

IV. DOWN TO BASICS—THE COMPONENTS OF FOCUS

Two Questions—Introduction

Since FOCUS is designed to meet so many goals—be used to code communications in both teaching and nonteaching settings, for example—it is of course multidimensional.

It contains categories to note five different characteristics of communications. The first two characteristics—the source/target and purpose of communication or move type—answer the question "What's being done?" By noting the next three characteristics of a communication—the medium, use, and content—we can answer the question "How is it being done?" [Background 2–3]

What's Being Done?—The First Two Characteristics of Communications

Who or What?—The First Characteristic: The Source/Target of the Communications

It is of course crucial to note who is saying or doing what to whom when we note the characteristics of communications. Rather than have separate words for the source and target of communications in and out of classrooms, I expand the use of *teacher* and *student* so they can be used for all settings. I use *teacher* to refer both to a person who is paid to teach and to anyone who assumes the role of a teacher by acting as if he or she is in charge or by showing and telling—like the person at the Saturday card game who feels compelled to demonstrate how his or her new watch operates, for example, or the person in line at the bank who tells everyone where the end of the line is and that each person should move quickly to the teller when his or her turn comes. Many of these teachers are not only not paid, but are not appreciated either. In fact, they are often considered an annoyance.

I use *student* to refer to those enrolled in a class, to those who must sit through the demonstration of a friend's new watch, and to those at the banks who line up and move smartly because one person has assumed the role of teacher. If there is a teacher, there has to be a group of students. I also use *student* to mean peer, or "equal." So if two friends are having a conversation on the bank line, in spite of the person who insists on keeping things moving smartly, I code both of them *students*. They are relating to each other on an equal basis.

Since the source of many communications we receive is not a person, I have another category called *other*. I use this to account for communications from noises, labels on cans, or road signs and books, to mention a few. For example, I'd code a ringing alarm clock *other*, as well as the hands on the face of a clock, if these communications structured, solicited, responded, or reacted in the settings I was observing.

If the range of sources coded *other* is small, the names can simply be written next to *other* like this: *other*, siren; *other*, approaching car. If there are a great many, they can of course be classified in some way, such as moving objects, stationary objects, and so on. In fact, the mediums, which you might recall from your previous reading as the third characteristic of communication I note with FOCUS, aid us in classifying the different types of sources and targets coded *other*.

To distinguish different sized groups of students, a *g* could be added to the *s* for student for assigned parts of entire classes and an *s* could be added for a random part of a class that is not a specified group. The *s* would suggest student*s* rather than an individual student. If you prefer to simply use a *c, g*, or say a capital *S* rather than s_c, s_g, or s_s, of course you can. As long as you use your abbreviations or symbols consistently and are faithful to the categories, any abbreviating or subscripting is fine.

To make even finer distinctions between different sources of communications, subscripts can be added to *teacher, student*, and *other*. Subscripts assigned to each individual student, s_1, s_2, s_3, can reveal which students in a class communicate most frequently, for example, or which ones communicate with which other ones.

In addition to assigning numbers to students to distinguish them from each other, numbers can be used to classify student attributes. You might be interested in comparing each individual student with each other individual student on a personal basis, as well as in comparing the frequency of participation within different groups of students. Using a particular subscript to designate sex, another to designate first language, another to designate the level of students, another to note high risk takers and low risk takers, and on and on, will enable you to see whether students in different groups communicate only to those in their groups, or whether those in some groups communicate less than those in other groups.

If you are interested in observing the sequence of the sources of communications, you could assign still another subscript. The first person who communicated would be given the subscript 1, the next person 2, and so on. It might turn out that some students are the sources very infrequently, but when they are, they tend to hold on to a sequence of communications. Others may communicate more frequently, but never follow one communication with another, neither sustaining nor building on their first communication. As you can see, once you begin to think of the great range of variables within just this one characteristic, you realize the many variables there are in the investigation of both the teaching act and communications outside teaching settings.

Only Four?—The Second Characteristic: The Move Type

After observing hundreds of classes, I came to the rather obvious conclusion, helped by reading some studies of classroom observation, that on one level only four things are being done in classrooms. Announcements are made that set the stage for or recapitulate the lessons: "Today, we're going to work on adjectives," or "Today, we worked on adjectives." Tasks are set: "Open your books and do the exercises." Tasks are performed: Books are opened, exercises are done. And comments are made about anything and everything: "Silly assignment;" "Great questions in the exercise"; "Very good."

Outside class, we do similar things, but in different proportions and sequences. We announce and set the stage for what we're about to do: "Marge, I'm off to the store now." And we recapitulate too: "I'm back—got all the stuff we needed." We ask people to perform tasks with requests, commands, or questions: "Would you please pass the salt;" "Close the window;" "What time is it?" And we perform tasks—we pass the salt, close windows, and give people the time of day. Finally, we comment on almost everything: "Wet salt"; "Tight window"; "Time sure flies."

Announcements of what we're going to do or have done I code as *structuring moves.* Setting tasks by asking questions, issuing commands, or making requests I code as *soliciting moves*, fully aware of the connotation of *soliciting* in certain contexts. Replying to solicits—in my sense, not the sense limited to the context of the street—I code *responding moves.* And all the comments we make I code *reacting moves.*

Though the four move types cover most of what we have traditionally considered important in observing in classrooms, they do not cover all possibilities. One type of communication that I find many coders asking about is the idiosyncratic communications many of us make both while teaching and in conversations. For example, some people shake change in their pockets as they teach or listen in a conversation. Others smoke, scratch their heads, or constantly touch their ears. I call these types of communications *bearing moves.* If you feel limited by the four move types, you might try coding communications without one of the four purposes of structuring, soliciting, responding, or reacting as bearing moves. At the least, by being conscious of the bearing moves you make, you might be able to substitute other moves. And it may be that bearing moves distract some students so much that the power of the other moves is diminished. When students imitate teachers in playacting, students often include many of the bearing moves a teacher communicates. So bearing moves are very obvious, at least to observers.

Given the extensive work of linguists in identifying the different purposes for which we use language, and given the work of discourse analysts in establishing so many different descriptive terms for classroom interaction, you might wonder why I did not make use of their work in selecting terms for the purposes of communication. Well, I decided to use only the four move types for the following reasons:

1. The four move types have been used extensively in studies with only the normal amount of coding disagreement; no particularly difficult coding problems have developed.

2. Perhaps this is simply a variation of reason 1, but the moves are easy to understand and talk about. Busy teachers are able to conceptualize much of their work in these terms after brief presentations; many of the other units identified by linguists overlap a great deal in some exchanges; the number of categories in many linguistic descriptions is often larger than four and a great deal of time is spent trying to fit communications into categories.

3. I have found the four move types sensible and easy to apply to communications in a range of settings, as I hope I demonstrate in this book. [Background 2–4]

If you still consider the move too small a unit of analysis for the entire description of communications, larger units can be used. A number of moves that treat the same topic can be considered as a group of moves. A group of moves on a topic in a class following one method can be compared with groups of moves on the same topic in classes following another method. Or topics in groups of moves can be compared that have been collected in teaching and nonteaching settings. Often, groups of moves in teaching settings contain many more individual moves than groups of moves in nonteaching settings, because in many conversations the topics shift a great deal. Looking at groups of moves rather than individual moves is useful for revealing some of these other rules on a higher level of analysis.

Still another way to look at a unit larger than the individual move is to look at cycles of moves and sequences of cycles. A teaching cycle is a series of moves beginning with a structuring or soliciting move that is not preceded by a structuring move. It ends with the move before a new structuring or a new soliciting move that is not preceded by a new structuring move. Twenty-one types of cycles are possible given this definition. Once the cycle is identified, the sequence of cycle types can be described, together with the source and target of the cycles and the sequences of cycles. In short, just as in a chess game we can describe individual moves, combinations of moves in the beginning game, mid-game, or end game, or an entire game, so in describing communications in and out of classes we can look at individual moves, cycles of moves, and sequences of cycles. [Background 2–5]

Four Plus Who or What—Combining Source/Target and Move Type

In Excerpt 2–1, I show how I code the source/target and move type of each communication to demonstrate how I answer the question "What's being done?" The *t*, as you'd guess, stands for *teacher* and the *s* for *student.* As you'd also guess, *str* stands for *structuring* moves, *sol* for *soliciting* moves, *res* for *responding* moves, and *rea* for *reacting* moves.

EXCERPT 2–1
In and Out of Teaching Settings*

		Communications	*Source/ Target*	*Move Type*
Setting 1: Two students are sitting in a language class before the teacher arrives. One student brought some nuts with him which he and the second student are eating. (T)				
1	Carlos:	These are great.	s/s	rea
2	Ali:	Yeah. But are they oily!	s/s	rea
3	Carlos:	They're fattening too. I'm already overweight and I really don't need them.	s/s	rea
4	Ali:	I like these as well as peanuts: I like them both.	s/s	rea
Setting 2: A flight attendant is preparing passengers for takeoff.				
5	Flight attendent:	Please fasten your seat belts in preparation for our takeoff. (Demonstrates how to fasten the seat belts.)	t/s	sol
6	Passengers:	(Fasten their seat belts.)	s/t	res
7	Flight attendant:	I want to remind each of you that there are designated areas for smokers and nonsmokers. Rows fifteen through thirty are reserved for nonsmokers and rows thirty-one through sixty are reserved for smokers. At no time are cigars allowed; nor is any type smoking of permitted at any time in the lavatories. At this time, all smoking materals should be extinguished.	t/s	str
8	Flight attendant:	I'm sorry, sir, but you'll have to put that out.	t/s	sol
9	Passenger:	(Puts out his cigarette and places it in ashtray.)	s/t	res
Setting 3: A coach and his student on a tennis court during a tennis lesson.				
10	Player:	Am I bending too much? (Said as he is bending to serve.)	s/t	sol
11	Coach:	No. Bending has nothing to do with serving.	t/s	res
12		Your serve is coming along fine.	t/s	rea
13	Player:	Damn! (Said as he sees that the ball has gone out of the serving area.)	s/s†	rea
Setting 4: Two friends at a wine and cheese party are talking about the guests.				
14	Sam:	Do you know her? (Pointing to person at other side of room.)	s/s	sol
15	Dave:	Not really.	s/s	res
16	Sam:	Do you know the girl with Susan?	s/s	sol
17	Dave:	I don't know her.	s/s	res
18		I don't think I know anyone here except you.	s/s	rea

EXCERPT 2–1 (*continued*)

		Communications	*Source/ Target*	*Move Type*
Setting 5: A language classroom. (T)				
19	Teacher:	Are these the same; he going—he's going?	t/s	sol
20	Jama:	Yes.	s/t	res
21	Teacher:	Ali?	t/s	sol
22	Ali:	No.	s/t	res
23	Teacher:	Very good.	t/s	rea
Setting 6: A small park with swings, a sandbox, benches, and a large play area with a slide. (T)				
24	Mother:	Now, I don't want you walking all over the park. We're going to stay right here next to the sandbox. And, I don't want any climbing today—you'll get hurt.	t/s	str
25	Child:	(Starts to walk away from the bench where the mother is sitting; walks toward the slide.)	s/t	str
26	Mother:	I said stay close to me!	t/s	sol
27	Child:	(Stops walking.)	s/t	res
28	Mother:	That's a good girl.	t/s	rea
Setting 7: Playing The Remembering Game on "Sesame Street," the children's television program. The characters are Cookie Monster, a muppet who loves cookies, and a Master of Ceremonies (MC) who states the rules and spins the wheel. (T)				
29	MC:	Here's your big chance, Cookie Monster.	t/s	str
30	Cookie Monster:	No can do.	s/t	rea
31	MC:	If you can remember where the other jet plane was behind the spinning wheel.	t/s	str
32	Cookie Monster:	No can eat jet plane.	s/t	rea
33	MC:	But choose one anyhow. What number do you want?	t/s	sol
34	Cookie Monster:	I think Cookie will try number three. Three.	s/t	res
35	MC:	Let's see what's behind three!	t/s	str
36	MC:	(Spins wheel.)	t/o	sol
37	Wheel:	(Reveals a picture of a jet plane.)	o/ts	res

* I have included two types of communications in the excerpts in this book. One type contains transcriptions of actual exchanges. The other type contains exchanges written either by me or by a novelist or playwright and used here to illustrate a point. I have noted all transcribed excerpts or parts of excerpts with a *T* for actual transcript, here and elsewhere. You'll notice that there is a *T* after settings 1, 5, 6, and 7 in the excerpt, for example. How accurate transcriptions are is in itself a thorny issue. [Background 2–6]

† *s to s* means that the person is reacting to himself or herself; here the student could be reacting to himself and the coach, and so it could be coded both s/s and s/t.

even how to transcribe

Practice Makes _____—Coding the Source/Target and Move Type

Though the four move types seem straightforward enough, given the ambiguity of communication, when even the source is sometimes not sure of the meaning, 100 percent agreement in coding the moves is rare. Even when two people know each other well and one says something like "I'm thirsty," the other is likely to say, "What did you mean by that?" If those involved are not sure whether such a comment is a reaction or a solicit requesting that some water be brought, how much more difficult it is for outsiders to code communications with 100 percent accuracy?

Having difficulty in classifying the move type of a communication because it does not fit neatly into one category or another can yield positive results. A comment such as "A book?" communicated after the response "A book" to the solicit "What should I take on the picnic?" can be either a reaction or a solicit. In a subsequent class or conversation, one could make a point of making comments that neatly fit only one category. Thus, in place of "A book?" one could say "I don't see the need for a book" to react, and "Why do you say you need a book?" to solicit. Sometimes, students do not know whether we are reacting to what they say or asking them to respond. One reason they cannot distinguish the purpose of a move is that we often communicate two different purposes in the same move. Having trouble with fitting communications into a category reminds us of why others may not be doing what we expect, and at the same time provides us with a way to alter our behavior: Make sure our communications fit neatly into one of the four purposes.

Practice coding is one way to keep coding consistent and to clarify move types we use in communicating in a range of settings. If you code the source/target and move type of the communications in Excerpt 2–2,* the meaning of the move types and the great amount of information revealed by the coding of just these two characteristics of communications will become clearer. Use the same abbreviations I used in the seven settings you just read in Excerpt 2–1: *t* for teacher, *s* for student, *o* for other, *str* for structuring, *sol* for soliciting, *res* for responding, *rea* for reacting. Compare your coding with mine, given in the excerpt footnote.

Though this dialog took place outside a classroom, there are elements in it that are parallel to the usual pattern in some classrooms. One person is assuming the role of teacher, asking questions and providing feedback. The other is being treated like a student. One obvious alternative that Excerpt 2–2 illustrates is that students can take the role of teacher. At a very early age, children seem to learn the classic pattern of teacher solicit, student respond, and teacher react. If language students were asked to teach a skill they knew to others in the target language, it would allow them to escape from the role that students are usually expected to play, that of people who simply respond.

If, after you do the coding, you want to check the percentage of agreement, here's one method of determining intercoder reliability. Count the total number of agreed-upon items and divide it by the total number of items coded. For example, if you code eight out of ten items the same way I did, divide eight by ten for an agreement of 80 percent. [Background 2–7]

One limitation of this procedure for checking inter- and intracoder reliability is that it assumes that each coder, or the same coder on two separate occasions, has identified the same total number of moves. In fact, often the problem of unreliability occurs because of disagreement about move boundaries rather than move types. Though

* From time to time, excerpts and tables will be a page later than their reference.

EXCERPT 2–2
Green Cakes (T)

		Communications	Source/ Target	Move Type
Setting: The living room of an apartment. Two 4-year-old boys are sitting on the floor next to a coffee table on which they have just been playing a game. After the game, the following exchange takes place.				
1	Joseph:	What you do at Janie's party?		
2	Rodney:	She had a cake.		
3	Joseph:	What kind?		
4	Rodney:	(Spreading his arms widely.) A big one.		
5	Joseph:	What kind of big one?		
6	Rodney:	A *real* big one. (Said emphatically.)		
7	Joseph:	(A bit perplexed.) What color were it?		
8	Rodney:	(Touching his lips with wandering fingertips.)		
9		What color were it?		
10		Green.		
11	Joseph:	(Waving his hand disdainfully.) Aw, you dumb. They ain't no green cakes.		

Key: 1. t to s sol; 2. s to t res; 3. t to s sol; 4. s to t res; 5. t to s sol; 6. s to t res; 7. t to s sol; 8. s_1 to s_1 rea; 9. s_1 to s_2 rea (lines 8 and 9 could also be coded as one move); 10. s to t res; 11. t to s rea.

the context, the source and the target aid in determining both boundaries and move types, practice coding, constant reliability checks and the establishment of coding ground rules, containing multiple examples of communications coded in each category, are the only ways I know to maintain consistency and accuracy in coding. [Background 2–8]

Though intercoder and intracoder agreement varies a lot and can be as high as 100 percent, an average of 80 percent is considered acceptable. Reliability checks provide support for the degree of agreement between researchers necessary to make the results acceptable, but they help ensure accuracy as well. Sometimes we code incorrectly because we get careless. Checking a dozen moves every few hundred is a useful test, during actual coding as well as during practice coding.

Rotten Cheese—Source/Target and Move Type Make Two Slots in a Substitution Table

To reply to "What's being done?" I find it helpful to think of the source/target and move type as titles in the columns of a two-slot substitution table. In place of a list of adjectives in the first column such as *rotten, fantastic*, and *big*, I put *teacher, student*, and *other*. And, in the second column, in place of a list of nouns, such as *cheese, deal, show*, and

TABLE 2–1
Two Characteristics of Communications

What's Being Done?	
SOURCE/TARGET[1]	MOVE TYPE
teacher/•	
	structure
	solicit
student (sgc)[2]/•	
	response
	react
other/•	

[1] The target in each case, indicated by a bullet, can of course be any one of the sources. One teacher can solicit another; one student can solicit the teacher or another student, and so on. To note all the combinations would take a great deal of space and defeat the idea behind the substitution table. Let it suffice to say that each source can be a target of each source.
[2] s = individual student; g = group from the class; c = entire class.

melons, I put the four move types: *structuring, soliciting, responding*, and *reacting*. As in most substitution tables, any item in the first column can combine with any item in the second column. In place of *rotten cheese, rotten deal, rotten show, rotten melon*, and so on, we can form combinations, such as *teacher to student structuring, student to teacher structuring, other to student structuring*, and on and on. Table 2–1, shows a substitution table with the two characteristics of communication I employ to reply to "What's being done?"

Journal Entry

Section 1. I'd like you to write down how long you've been holding this book without a break and how many pages you have "covered" since you took a break. I know you'll probably have to estimate the time, and perhaps even the number of pages, since I didn't tell you when you began to note either the time or the page number. But take a stab at it.

Section 2. Now, I'd like to tell you to take a break. But before I do, I'd like to ask you to write your feelings about my ordering you to take a break. If no words come to mind, draw a sketch that you think expresses your feelings, or, approximate the spelling of sounds that express your feelings.

Now, take a break no matter how many pages you have covered or how long you have been holding the book without a break. And reflect, either during the break or at another time, on how you feel about being ordered to share your personal feelings. Some teachers rarely ask students for their personal feelings; they simply are quiet and allow students to react. The reactions often contain personal feelings. I am now playing the role of a teacher who wants feelings in response to a solicit, not in reactions you make without being told.

How Is It Being Done?—The Next Three Characteristics of Communications

A Few More—The Basic Unit of Analysis

When we distinguish the move type and its source/target to answer the question "What is being done?" we at the same time establish the move as the unit of analysis. Each time a different purpose is communicated and we code a different move type, we break the communication off from the stream it's enmeshed in. It's as if we were nutritionists measuring food in ounces or cups so we could have a given quantity of butter, rice, and chocolate, for example, to compare the percentage of fats, carbohydrates, and proteins contained in each.

But while the nutritionist is eager to establish units of exact amounts for analysis, I am interested only in establishing units that have the same purpose. Whether a structuring move contains one word or one hundred words, it still counts as only one structuring move. Whether a teacher reacts with a nod, a "very good," or a long explanation of the rules of the past tense, the communication counts as only one reacting move. The way I distinguish differences between the same types of moves, and thus answer the question "How is it being done?", is to distinguish three other characteristics of each communication: the medium, the way the medium is used, and the content the mediums communicate. [Background 2–9]

A Strange Word—The Third Characteristic: The Medium

It might seem strange to describe objects, music, gestures, and other mediums in an observation system designed in the first instance for language teachers. But in fact, as you realize, mediums other than language are central to communication in language classes. The nuts in setting 1, Excerpt 2–1, are what generated the students' comments. And without the actual seatbelts and smoking and no-smoking sections, the flight attendant's structuring move in setting 2, Excerpt 2–1, would have little meaning. Most words like *these, that, one*, and *there* make sense only when we can see, hear, or feel the mediums they refer to. How could the classic "What's this?" be answered without noting mediums other than language?

I realize that the term *medium* seems a bit strange because of the connotation it has in relation to seances and other contacts with the nether world. But McLuhan's *The Medium Is the Message* both broadened the connotation of *medium* and gave added popularity to the word. And this is one reason I am using it.

I place mediums in one of three major categories. One is *linguistic*—the print in front of you and the words that you hear others say or that you say. Another is *nonlinguistic*, like a picture, an object, music, or noise. Gestures, body language, and tone of voice constitute the third major category of medium, which I call *paralinguistic*. Another medium I note is the absence of the others, or simply time. I call this category *silence*.

Our substitution table now has three columns. The three sources of communication, *teacher, student*, and *other*, now can be joined to the four move types, as well as to the four major categories of mediums: *linguistic, nonlinguistic, paralinguistic*, and *silence*. Three sources directed to three targets give us nine different combinations. These combine with the four move types to produce thirty-six possible combinations. And finally, these thirty-six combinations can be communicated in one of four major categories of mediums. That makes one hundred forty-four theoretical combinations of just the major categories of the two characteristics I employ to describe a reply to "What is being done?" and one of the three characteristics I employ to describe a reply to "How is it being done?" When you consider that these different combinations can occur in a great variety of sequences, the number of alternatives we can describe with these few categories is extremely large.

In Excerpt 2–3, I illustrate how each of the mediums in Table 2–2 can be combined with each of the move types, just as a word in one column of most substitution tables can be combined with all the words in an adjacent column. I've used the first letter from each of the categories of mediums as abbreviations: *l* for *linguistic, n* for *nonlinguistic, p* for *paralinguistic* and *s* for *silence.* And I've underlined the numbers of the lines where I have coded mediums other than linguistic ones.

On a lower level of classification, I subdivide each of the major categories, except *silence*, into three subcategories. Mediums that appeal primarily to the ear such as spoken words, noise, music, and tone of voice I call *aural/oral* mediums. Those that appeal primarily to the eye, such as printed words, phonetic transcriptions, pictures, diagrams, objects, and gestures, I call *visual mediums.* Those that appeal to more than one sense or to any of the other senses such as touching, distance, or smell I classify *other.* Braille, perfume scents, temperature, and dancing are a few mediums I would place in the category *other.* Attention to all these mediums not only reveals how many of the same move types are different, but also reveals a great number of moves that would ordinarily not be noticed because they are communicated in mediums we frequently fail to note, such as distance, pictures, and all the other ones I code.

By focusing on the mediums used in student responses, it is easy to discover that, say, speech is the only medium being used. Because FOCUS shows both what mediums are used in a particular series of communications, as well as those that are not used, alternatives are built into the system. If we discover that students use only *linguistic* mediums in column 3, it is a simple matter to point to *nonlinguistic* mediums or *paralinguistic* mediums and decide to have the students use these in place of linguistic mediums on another day. As the mediums are contrasted, we can begin to see what consequences seem to follow each alternative. Do fewer errors of meaning occur when students are told to draw or mime the meanings of vocabulary items rather than speak them, for example?

Six Words—The Fourth Characteristic: The Use

The next thing I look at to answer the question "How is it being done?" is what I call the *use*, the fourth characteristic. I find the use by asking the question, "How are the mediums used to communicate content?"

The first major distinction between different uses of mediums is easily made by noting whether the mediums are taken in or produced. In silent reading, tasting, touching, smelling and looking at pictures, mediums are simply attended to, not produced. When we engage in these receptive activities, I say we are *attending* or using mediums to *attend* to content. By putting the taking in of all mediums into the same category, I hope to highlight the fact that some of the predictions we need to make when taking in a linguistic medium such as print might be similar in some ways to the predictions we make when we look at pictures, listen to music, or read the expressions on people's faces. Obviously, seeing the word *smoke*, looking at smoke, and smelling smoke require some different mental processes. We can recognize smoke, yet not be able to read the word in a language we do not know, for example. But equally obvious is the fact that

EXCERPT 2–3
Substituting Mediums

		Communications	*Source/ Target*	*Move Type*	*Medium*
Setting 1: Working on word meaning in a math class. (T)					
1	Teacher:	Tell me what a *triangle* is.	t/c	sol	l
2	Jim:	A three-sided figure—all lines straight.	s_1/t	res	l
3	Sam:	(Draws a triangle on the blackboard.)	s_2/t	res	n
4	Lorie:	(Puts tips of both thumbs together in a line and joins both index fingers to form a triangle with her fingers.)	s_3/t	res	p
Setting 2: In a language class, lesson on adjective word order					
5	Teacher:	I didn't see what kind of a hat you wore today, Oscar. Please describe it.	t/s	sol	l
6	Oscar:	A wool beret color black.	s/t	res	l
7	Teacher:	Change the word order.	t/s	sol	l
8	Oscar:	A wool beret black color.	s/t	res	l
9	Teacher:	(Draws lines, arrows, and large X on the blackboard: _ _ _ _ X.)	t/s	sol	n
10	Oscar:	A black wool beret color.	s/t	res	l
11	Teacher:	(Holds up right-hand fingers perpendicular to the floor and with left thumb and index finger touches the top of the right thumb and first three fingers. When he gets to the small finger, he shakes it with the left thumb and index finger.)	t/s	sol	p
12	Oscar:	A black wool beret . . . color.	s/t	res	l
13	Teacher:	(Waits—does nothing so student has another chance but with no new information.)	t/s	sol	s
14	Oscar:	A black wool beret!	s/t	res	l
Setting 3: In a foyer, one person is demonstrating to another how to bow when being introduced.					
15	Larry:	Bow like this. (Demonstrates a bow with hands along side of legs.)	t/s	sol	l + p
16	Pat:	(Bows incorrectly, with hands sticking out in back.)	s/t	res	p
17	Larry:	(Takes out a pad of paper and draws a pair of hands stuck out in back and a pair beside the legs.) Draw the one that is correct.	t/s	sol	l + n
18	Pat:	(Draws the hands along side the side of the legs.)	s/t	res	n

TABLE 2–2
Three Characteristics of Communications

What Is Being Done?		*How Is It Being Done?*
SOURCE/TARGET[1]	MOVE TYPE	MEDIUM
teacher/•		linguistic
	structure	
	solicit	nonlinguistic
student (sgc)[2]/•		
	respond	paralinguistic
	react	
other/•		silence

[1] The target in each case, indicated by a bullet, can be any one of the sources.
[2] *s* = individual student; *g* = group from the class; *c* = entire class.

each activity requires taking something in. What makes the difference is which medium we in fact take in. By putting the taking in of all mediums in the same category, I want to highlight the similarities and differences between different types of attending. At the same time, it is useful to further highlight the fact that the mediums in column 3 can combine with any of the uses in column 4, just as the words in each column in a substitution table can combine with words in adjacent columns.

I put productive activities into one of five major categories. When we indicate that something is right or wrong, use category labels, and in other ways comment about language or people, I say we are using mediums to *characterize* content. The italicized words in the following sentences are examples of communications I say are characterizing content.

Bags look *alike.* (Sign at airport where bags are picked up.)

He going is *incorrect.*

Chalk is *a noun.*

Walked *has one syllable, not two.*

You did *a poor job.* (Commenting on a sentence a person wrote.)

Those directions are *stupid.*

Some items we refer to when we characterize content are examples of what I call *sets.* I say we can use mediums to set content to form another category of use. Print is used to set the words *he going, chalk,* and *walked* in the examples above. In a solicit such as "Repeat this: I'm hungry as a lion," the sentence referred to by *this* I'd classify as setting content also.

Setting content is communicating models or other items that are referred to by words such as *this, that, it,* and *one.* In some conversations, referents are never named, but they need to be identified in order to know what the conversation is about. The mediums that communicate the referents themselves are used to set the content. You've no doubt felt confused after getting into a conversation that has been going on for some time because you did not know what had been set before you came. Unless you know whether the *this* in "*This* sure didn't fit well" refers to a word, a sentence, paragraph, pipe, shoe, or whatever, you could not understand the sentence. Had the person been holding a shoe as he or she said "This sure doesn't fit," the shoe would be used to set content. The word *stuff* in these questions refers to communications that *set* content: "What stuff is this lesson about? What stuff is being discussed? What stuff do we have for homework?"

When one person uses any medium to set content, and another person repeats or copies the model, referent, or example, I say the person is using mediums to *reproduce* content. One example of reproducing is copying a series of sentences from a blackboard. Another is copying down a telephone number from an advertisement on television. When children repeat what their friends and parents say exactly as they say it, they are reproducing also.

To cite one example of the results of lack of attention to using gestures to reproduce content I will share my experience with Americans who learn Japanese. I can often tell whether a person's teacher was a man or a woman by the way the student bows. Japanese women bow with their hands crossed in front of them, while men bow with their hands at their sides. Many non-Japanese imitate not only the sets provided by their teachers' speech, but also by their gestures, even though the teacher may not ask them to imitate gestures. When I see American men bow like Japanese women, I usually find after talking with them that indeed they did have women teachers.

Mediums can also be used to make inferences and generalizations. You can say, for example, "All copulative verbs are short and they have more than two forms." That's a generalization about copulative verbs. Assuming that the generalization is not simply repeated but has required some thinking, I say that making generalizations is using mediums to *relate* content. Because finding the main idea in a paragraph and making other inferences also require some thinking, I put inferences in this category also.

Any mediums that are not clearly characterizing, relating, reproducing or setting content I say are being used to *present* content. The category *present* includes asking questions and stating information directly. "Where are you going?"; "Do you speak English?"; "Who discovered America?" are questions I'd code present. Statements that answered the questions—"Home"; "Yes, I do"; "Columbus"—I'd also code present, since they simply state information directly.

To illustrate the five ways we can use mediums to communicate content with FOCUS, I've coded the uses in an expanded version of Rodney and Joseph's rated conversation in Excerpt 2–2. I've given the unrated version in Excerpt 2–4. As you can see, except for the *d* for *reproduce,* I have used the first letter of each use for coding. [Background 2–10]

In Table 2–3, I've added the six ways mediums can be used in column 4, *Use.* As you can see, the categories are arranged in alphabetical order; they are not listed hierarchically. By simply looking at the *use,* as well as the *medium, source and target,* or *purpose,* you are provided with many alternatives. With the same categories, you can describe communications outside a teaching setting that on the surface may seem quite different but with the categories simply become a rearrangement of the same basic elements.

Different Combinations—Combining Medium and Use

Looking at the *mediums* in column 3 and the *uses* in column 4 in different moves can point out characteristics of communications we often fail to notice. It can also show relationships between communications that on the surface seem to have nothing to do with each other. In classrooms, one reaction to a student response is to repeat what the student says with a rising intonation. For example, if a student says "I am go home," a teacher is likely to say "I am go home?" with a rising intonation. The words—a linguistic medium—are used to reproduce one message. But the intonation—a paralinguistic medium—is used to present a separate message. When I order ice cream, the person behind the counter often repeats my order with rising intonation much as

EXCERPT 2–4
Examples of Uses

		Communications	*Move Type*	*Use*
Setting: The living room of an apartment. Two 4-year-old boys are sitting on the floor next to a coffee table. They have just been playing a game. After the game, the following exchange takes place.				
1	Joseph:	What you do at Janie's party?	sol	p
2	Rodney:	She had a cake.	res	p
3	Joseph:	What kind?	sol	p + s*
4	Rodney:	(Spreading his arms widely.) A big one.	res	c
5	Joseph:	What kind of big one?	sol	p + s
6	Rodney:	A *real* big one. (Said emphatically.)	res	c
7	Joseph:	(A bit perplexed.) What color were it?	sol	p + s
8	Rodney:	(Touching his lips with wandering fingertips.)	rea	p†
9		What color were it?		d + p‡
10		Green.	res	c
11	Joseph:	(Waving his hand disdainfully.) Aw, you dumb.	rea	c
12		They ain't no green cakes because flour and butter and eggs and milk ain't green and you don't put vegetables in cakes.		r

* The cake referred to is coded as a set here and in 5 and 7, since the cake is what the questions refer to.

† I code the repetition of the words reproduce and the intonation that is essentially saying "I understand" as present.

‡ The moves here and in line 12 contain two separate uses that each communicate two separate areas of content. But since the purpose of the separate uses is the same, I code the communications as only one move each.

TABLE 2–3
Four Characteristics of Communications

What Is Being Done?		*How Is It Being Done?*	
SOURCE/TARGET[1]	MOVE TYPE	MEDIUM	USE
			attend
teacher/•		linguistic	---------------
	structure		characterize
	solicit	nonlinguistic	present
student (sgc)[2]/•			
	respond	paralinguistic	relate
	react		reproduce
other/•		silence	---------------
			set

[1] The target in each case, indicated by a bullet, can be any one of the sources.
[2] s = individual student; g = group of students; c = class of students.

a teacher repeats a student response, both when it is correct and incorrect. The exchange might go like this:

CUSTOMER: Two vanilla, one chocolate.

CLERK: Two vanilla, two chocolate?

CUSTOMER: Uh-huh.

When the wrong number of cones or the wrong flavors are handed over, the customer realizes what he or she was asked about earlier. Often, no difference is heard between the words used in the ordering and in the repetition of the ordering. But when the cones come—in my system a *nonlinguistic* medium—then the difference is discovered. Well, might it be true that differences between messages are more likely to be noticed when visual mediums, rather than spoken words or rising intonation, are used? Might written words on the blackboard make it more likely that a difference will be noticed in a classroom, just as ice cream cones are more likely to be noticed outside of a class, than simply words, which appeal only to the ears? Do appeals to more than one sense or a different sense have a different impact? FOCUS enables us to describe differences specifically enough to allow us to investigate such questions.

Let me take another common communication that can be described using the *mediums* and *uses* in combination in a way that is likely to make us see what we are doing more clearly. When saying a pair of words, phrases, or any units, one normal pattern is to use rising intonation after the first sample and falling after the second. For example, it is likely that most people say "Are these the same or different—*beach* (rising intonation), *beach* (falling intonation)?" Well, to the student who listens well, they are different in intonation and the same in pronunciation and spelling. I would code the communications this way, using the asterisk on the last line to indicate that the communication is in contrast to the previous one.

Source/Target	Purpose	Medium	Use	Communications
teacher to student	solicit	linguistic aural	set	beach
		linguistic aural	set	beach
		paralinguistic aural	set	rising intonation
		paralinguistic aural*	set	falling intonation

That we use many mediums as well as words to communicate is a truism. The *mediums* and *uses* can be used to translate this truism into a precise description. To say two words or phrases with falling intonation takes deliberate effort, since it is necessary to break the normal rule we follow in presenting contrasting pairs of anything. Specific attention to the *mediums* and *uses* can both help reveal rules we follow and also provide alternatives to anyone interested in substituting different *mediums* and using them in different ways.

The mediums and uses can be used to vary the messages in any type of move communicated by any source. If students are consistently responding only with speech and if they are using speech only to *present* content, one alternative is to have them *characterize* in their response. Rather than giving answers to questions, such as "Use *plumber* in a sentence," they can be asked a series of questions that require nothing but a *yes* or *no* about a vocabulary item being taught. For example, the teacher or another student can state a fact, such as "These people work with water." Students are required to respond with either a *yes* or a *no*. Such a response requires no knowledge of grammar because one does not have to form a sentence. Responses such as "He work the water" are thus avoided, as are tangents in which such errors of grammar are treated to such a degree that the lexical information about the word in question is forgotten.

If a series of yes/no questions is asked, such as "Plumbers use planes; plumbers repair sinks; plumbers repair phones" to get at the meaning of *plumber*, students can begin to see characteristics of plumbers and at the same time get practice in making distinctions about information others state, an activity many believe is crucial to understanding. In addition, errors of form can be avoided. But aside from these arguments, the more important point is that if 90 percent of student responses have been requiring the use *present*, as in a response to "Use *plumber* in a sentence," one obvious alternative is to require more responses in the category *characterize*, as in a *no* response to "Do plumbers repair engines?" Another is to require that the response be communicated in a *nonlinguistic visual* medium rather than a *linguistic aural* medium, such as with pictures, objects, or graphs. Obviously, asking a student to draw a plumber or act the way a plumber would act with a broken pipe is not a new suggestion. What this system does that is slightly new is show how these different tasks can on one level be considered as different combinations of four *mediums* and six *uses*.

The Fifth Column Is Not Always the Most Dangerous— The Fifth Characteristic: Content

The fifth characteristic I code is the content communicated by the mediums used in different ways. I employ three major categories of content: *life, procedure*, and *study*.

If the target language is being communicated as an area of study—as information set apart and studied, tested, or practiced for its own sake, I code the content *study*. A comment such as "The burner is on too high" I would code *study* if it were said to practice the grammar represented by "too high," the lexical meaning of *burner, on*, or *high*, the pronunciation of any of the words, or any other one of the systems of language we need to learn.

To distinguish areas of study communicated in language classes and other classes, I subdivide *study* into the *study of language* and the *study of other areas*. In a chemistry class, the comment: "The burner is on too high" I would code as *study other*, since it is likely to be communicated to teach something about the use of a burner for heating different chemicals. I would code it *study other* in a cooking class too if the purpose were to communicate information about cooking as an area of *study*.

If a person said "The burner is on too high" as an indirect way of saying "It's too hot in here for me," I would code the communication *life.* I use this category to code personal feelings, such as "I'm hot," as well as personal information, such as "I was born in Chicago." I also use the category *life* to code communications that contain formulas for greetings and leave-taking or polite expressions. General knowledge, such as historical dates, prices of cars, or issues like inflation—the types of things one hears on the news or reads about in popular magazines and newspapers—I also put in the category *life*.

When mediums are used to call the roll, discipline students, give directions, or give a rationale for particular exercises. I code the content of the communications *procedure.* Collecting money for books and communicating administrative or bureaucratic information are other examples of content I'd code *procedure*. [Background 2–11]

Dickens' description of a class in Gradgrind's school in *Hard Times* illustrates both the separate categories of content and the tension between them in any teaching setting. Try coding the content of the messages in the moves in Excerpt 2–5. Use *f* for *life, p* for *procedure*, and *s* for *study*. Compare your coding with mine, which is given below the excerpt.

The same words can usually be coded in any of the three categories of content because the category is determined by the content the words communicate, rather than by the words themselves. For example, if "I'm hot" is said to share a personal feeling, I'd code it *life*. If it were said as an indirect request to have someone open a window, I'd code it the same way I'd code a direction such as "Please open the window"; as *procedure*. A response to a solicit such as "Tell me how you feel" to practice contractions and adjectives in a language class, I'd code as *study*

To distinguish between the study of language and other subjects, as I said, I subdivide *study* into two categories: *language* and *other*. I further subdivide the study of language into the many areas of language that we teach, such as grammar, lexis, mechanics, pronunciation and rhetoric, to name a few.

In describing areas of study other than language, you can set up your own subcategories by doing a content analysis of the texts, syllabuses and tests in the subject. These usually indicate what is to be taught. This type of content analysis has already been done in some subjects, and it would be practical to at least check some of these classifications before starting a new one. [Background 2–12]

Table 2–4 contains the major categories of content, as well as the other four characteristics I just described. Consequently, our substitution table at last has all five columns. The first two, containing the source, target move type, are designed to answer the question "What is being done?" and establish the basic unit of analysis. And the

EXCERPT 2–5
Facts

	Communications	*Source/ Target*	*Move Type*	*Content*
	Setting: A large, stone-walled classroom with desks in rows and a very high ceiling. Mr. Gradgring, the master teacher, is present along with another teacher. Sissy Jupe, the student being asked about horses, has been described earlier. She lives in a room with wallpaper decorated with horses. Her father raises horses, or trains them at least, and so she rides them frequently, feeds them and cleans up after them. She has had extensive experience with horses outside of the classroom!			
1	Now, what I want is facts. Facts alone are wanted in life.	t/c	str	___
2	Girl number twenty—who is that girl?	t/s_1	sol	___
3	Sissy Jupe, sir.	s_1/t	res	___
4	Sissy is not a name.	t/s_1	rea	___
5	It's father as calls me Sissy, sir.	s_1/t	rea	___
6	Then he has no business to do it.	t/s_1	rea	___
7	What is your father?	t/s_1	sol	___
8	He belongs to the horse-riding, if you please sir.	s_1/t	res	___
9	We don't want to know anything about that, here.	t/s_1	rea	___
10	Give me your definition of a horse.	t/s_1	sol	___
11	(Sissy Jupe thrown into the greatest alarm by this demand.)	s_1/t	rea	___
12	Girl number twenty unable to define a horse. Girl number twenty possessed of no facts in reference to one of the commonest of animals!	t/c	rea	___
13	Some boy's definition of a horse?	t/c	sol	___
14	Quadruped. Graminivorous. Forty teeth, namely twenty-four grinders, four eye-teeth, and twelve incisive. Sheds coat in spring; in marshy countries, sheds hoofs, too. Hoofs hard, but requiring to be shod with iron. Age known by marks in mouth.	s_1/t	res	___
15	Now, girl number twenty, you know what a horse is.	t/s_1	rea	___

Key: 1. procedure; 2. procedure; 3. procedure; 4. study; 5. life; 6. procedure; 7. life; 8. life; 9. procedure; 10. study; 11. life; 12. procedure; 13. study; 14. study; 15. procedure.

other three, the medium, use, and content columns, are designed to answer the question "How is it being done?" by revealing how moves of the same type are different.

Messages—Grouping Medium, Use, and Content

I call groupings of the three characteristics of communications that show us how it is being done *messages*. Thus, in the solicit, "Repeat Eskimo," there are two messages.

TABLE 2–4
Five Characteristics of Communications[1]

What Is Being Done?		*How Is It Being Done?*		
SOURCE/TARGET	MOVE TYPE	MEDIUM	USE	CONTENT
			attend	
teacher/•		linguistic	---------------	life
	structure		characterize	
	solicit	nonlinguistic	present	
student (sgc)[2]/•				procedure
	respond	paralinguistic	relate	
	react		reproduce	
other/•		silnce	---------------	study
			set	

[1] The target in each case, indicated by a bullet, can be any one of the sources.
[2] s = individual student; g = group of students; c = class.

In the command "Repeat," speech is used to *present* a teaching direction, content I code *procedure.* And speech is also used to *set* the model "Eskimo" that is to be *reproduced* in the response. In "Juan, repeat Eskimo," the name *Juan* is a third message. In naming the student, speech is used to *present* the name. I code names as a subcategory of *procedure.* In the reaction "That's a great tie?" said with great skepticism, the words convey one message—a positive evaluation that I'd code *characterize evaluate* +—and the tone of voice conveys the opposite message—a negative evaluation I'd code *characterize evaluate* −.

The variety in moves is a result of the fact that they contain messages made up of different combinations of mediums, uses, and areas of content. When moves consistently contain only one message, or a message with the same combination of medium, use, and content, alternatives can easily be generated by substituting a different medium, use, or area of content. Comparing messages in moves in a range of settings reveals a great many types of messages that are rare in teaching settings and frequent in other settings. Messages on television, for example, tend to contain the two mediums—music and speech—in each message while in conversations in class and most other places speech and body language are used. [Background 2–13]

Further Considerations—Medium, Use, and Content Have Subcategories

There are times, either when doing research or when discussing lessons, when two communications are obviously different in some way, yet the major categories in Table 2–4 do not reveal any differences. And these differences are beyond obvious ones such as target language or native language, and other differences noted as features of the communications with subscripts. In these cases, I use subcategories of the major categories of medium, use, and content. These subcategories are treated in subsequent episodes of the book.

As soon as the subcategories are introduced, some people begin to say that the coding system is too complex. Over a period of time, however, the subcategories can be mastered as easily as the major categories and they can help to make the major categories clearer. But even if you feel confused by the subcategories sometimes, or even by the major categories, don't feel troubled by the confusion. First of all, communication is by nature ambiguous, and so the fact that all communications do not fit neatly into the major categories or subcategories is natural. Second, all I did to develop the system was constantly to ask this question: "Are these two communications the same or different in a particular way?" It doesn't matter ultimately whether you master each subcategory. The critical thing is to classify communications that seem to be the same in some way and put them together, and separate them from those that seem different. [Background 2–14]

Can You Stand Two More Analogies?— Seeing Communications as Combinations of Basic Elements

The number of individual characteristics in Table 2–4 is small: only five. And the number of major categories of each characteristic never exceeds six, in the case of *use*. Yet the number of communications that can be described by different combinations, frequencies, and sequences of these basic elements is extremely large, since the number of possible permutations is so great.

One way to think about the elements in Table 2–4 is to consider them similar to the 103 basic chemical elements that combine to form thousands of different compounds in nature by following certain rules of combining. Or, the elements in Table 2–4 can be considered similar to the twelve-tone system used to generate classical music, jazz, and rock and roll, each according to its own rules. In the case of the elements in Table 2–4, as well as in the case of the chemical elements and the twelve-tone system, new alternatives can yet be generated simply by breaking some of the rules that now control combinations.

V. TAKING STOCK—A READER'S SUMMARY

One Joint Venture and One Monopoly—Introduction

At this point, if you aren't a bit confused, I'd be surprised. Just as a first lecture in a new subject by a professor usually ends with reactions from the students, such as "Wow, is this going to be tough." "I wasn't sure what was going on." "There were way too many new words," here too there is reason to feel at least like scratching one's head. After all, in a very few pages I have introduced around sixteen new words. In some cases, they are words you are familiar with but which have new and different meanings. But since my goal was limited to providing you with just a fuzzy picture of what the controlling framework for this book is, I have no regrets. And in working through the review, you will see that you've mastered more than you think.

Rather than restating the central characteristics and major categories myself in this review, I have designed a cloze passage so that the review can be a joint project. This will show you that you already know much of what I am saying. You have been a source and a target of communications, for example. And you have structured, solicited, responded, and reacted with a range of mediums used in different ways to communicate separate areas of content. My conceptualization and terms are, of course, a bit different, but you are already familiar with the characteristics of communications.

After you fill in the blanks, compare your entries with those a friend filled in. Then discuss them. Finally, compare your choices with the words I deleted, which are given below the summary. Count any choices you made as wrong, unless they are identical to those deleted from the original passage, allowing only for spelling errors.

The Joint Venture—Filling In Words in a Summary of Episode 2

FOCUS is an acronym for Foci for Observing Communications (1) __________ in Settings. I developed FOCUS to help me answer (2) __________ questions: "What is being done?" and "How is it being done?" (3) __________ two questions are very central.

Very often discussions of (4) __________ contain words that are ill-defined and inconsistently used and (5) __________. Furthermore, the terms are not a part of one (6) __________ conception. The terms in FOCUS are operationally defined and (7) __________ rather than judgmental. Additionally, they are part of an (8) __________ conceptualization.

To answer the question "What is being done?" I (9) __________ the source and target of communication and the purposes or move type. (10) __________ code three major sources and targets: *teacher, student, other*. (11) __________ I employ FOCUS both in teaching and nonteaching settings, (12) __________ expand the meaning of the word *teacher* to include (13) __________ who takes charge. And I expand the meaning of (14) __________ to mean peer as well as one who is (15) __________ the role of learner.

(16) __________ distinguish different individual students (17) __________ types of students and (18) __________ groupings, I add subscripts (19) __________ the categories *teacher, student* (20) __________ *other*.

I classify all (21) __________ as one of four purposes or move types. Communications that set the (22) __________ for subsequent behavior, I call structuring moves. Setting tasks (23) __________ asking questions, issuing commands or making requests, I call (24) __________ moves. Replying to solicits I code as responding moves. (25) __________ all the comments we make about other moves, I (26) __________ as reacting moves.

The (27) __________ is the unit of (28) __________ in FOCUS. Move is (29) __________ ounce or cup as (30) __________, uses and areas of (31) __________ are to fats, carbohydrates (32) __________ proteins.

Since the move is determined by deciding on (33) __________ purpose of a communication, the length of moves can (34) __________ a great deal. But length is not the primary (35) __________ to distinguish moves of the same type from each (36) __________. To distinguish moves of the same type that are (37) __________ from each other, four soliciting moves that treat an (38) __________, for example, I code the mediums used to communicate (39) __________ moves, the way the mediums are used, and the (40) __________ the mediums communicate. Describing the mediums, uses, and areas (41) __________ content helps answer the question "How is it being done?"

(42) __________ put mediums into one of four major categories. Spoken (43) __________ written words I call linguistic mediums. Noises, music, and (44) __________ I call nonlinguistic. Gestures, tone of voice, and movement (45) __________ call paralinguistic. The absence of the use of any (46) __________ these mediums, simply waiting, for example, I call silence, (47) __________ fourth category of medium.

(48) ________ for silence, each major (49) ________ of mediums has three (50) ________, determined by the sense (51) ________ appeal to. Mediums that (52) ________ to the eyes I (53) ________ visual, to the ears (54) ________, to touch and scent (55) ________. A picture is an (56) ________ of a nonlinguistic visual (57) ________, and a gesture a (58) ________ visual medium.

In determining (59) ________ way mediums are used, I first split communications between (60) ________ and productive activities. All receptive activities I call *attend.* (61) ________, tasting, and silent reading are just some examples of (62) ________ I code *attend.* Productive activities I put into one (63) ________ five major categories.

Indicating (64) ________ are right or wrong (65) ________ code *characterize.* Making inferences (66) ________ developing explanations of how (67) ________ or other phenomena work, (68) ________ they require thinking, I (69) ________ *relate.* Imitating constitutes a (70) ________ I call *reproduce.* Referents (71) ________ models I code as *sets.* (72) ________ that don't fit these (73) ________ categories I code *present.*

The (74) ________ characteristic of communication is the content that the mediums (75) ________. The three major categories of the fifth characteristic are (76) ________, *procedure*, and *study. Life* I use to code greetings, (77) ________ information and feelings, and general knowledge. *Procedure* I use (78) ________ code directions and any kind of administrative or bureaucratic (79) ________. *Study* I use to code the material we are (80) ________ or learning for its own sake.

Each combination (81) ________ one medium, one use (82) ________ one area of content, (83) ________ call a message. Each (84) ________ contains anywhere from one (85) ________ any number of messages. (86) ________ is from the variety (87) ________ messages in the moves (88) ________ much of the variety in our communications (89) ________ from.

Deleted words: 1. Used; 2. two; 3. These; 4. teaching; 5. judgmental; 6. overall; 7. descriptive; 8. overall; 9. code; 10. I; 11. Because; 12. I; 13. anyone; 14. student; 15. in; 16. To; 17. or; 18. different; 19. to; 20. and; 21. communications; 22. stage; 23. by; 24. soliciting; 25. And; 26. code; 27. move; 28. analysis; 29. to; 30. mediums; 31. content; 32. and; 33. the; 34. vary; 35. means; 36. other; 37. different; 38. error; 39. the; 40. content; 41. of; 42. I; 43. and; 44. pictures; 45. I; 46. of; 47. the; 48. Except; 49. category; 50. subcategories; 51. they; 52. appeal; 53. call; 54. aural/oral; 55. other; 56. example; 57. medium; 58. paralinguistic; 59. the; 60. receptive; 61. listening; 62. activities; 63. of; 64. items; 65. I; 66. and; 67. language; 68. because; 69. code; 70. category; 71. and; 72. Communications; 73. four; 74. fifth; 75. communicate; 76. *life*; 77. personal; 78. to; 79. information; 80. teaching; 81. of; 82. and; 83. I; 84. move; 85. to; 86. It; 87. of; 88. that; 89. comes.

The Monopoly—Answering Questions to Summarize Episode 2

Responding to questions provides another way to restate what we've read. Here are some questions that seek the same information the cloze passages did. While these questions might require more thumbing through pages than the cloze passage, such questions are the usual rule after the silent reading of passages, so I feel compelled to include them. But since I also like to break rules to make the rules we follow more visible and to prompt us to question our preconceived notions, I've made the bulk of the questions yes/no questions rather than question-word questions, requiring you to characterize in the responses. Though questions requiring choices or verification are frequent on many standardized examinations, they are rare in most classrooms, occurring less than 5 percent of the time in most classes. Socrates of course made frequent use of yes/no questions in his famous lesson on geometry in the *Meno*. But we all know what the breaking of rules led to in his case. [Background 2–15]

1. FOCUS can only be used in classroom settings. ___
2. The basic unit of analysis in FOCUS is the message. ___
3. Structuring moves must be followed by responding moves. ___
4. If a move lasts more than three seconds, you must start tallying another move. ___
5. The purpose of breaking rules is to make teaching more unpredictable. ___
6. The usual pattern of critiques of lessons is to describe what has happened using an observation instrument. ___
7. Because FOCUS provides a framework for conceptualizing the many communications we observe, it makes it more difficult to remember alternatives when using FOCUS than if we were to just list the alternatives others suggested or we generated on our own. ___
8. Soliciting and structuring are initiatory moves. ___
9. There are four categories of mediums. ___
10. Linguistic mediums are more central to coding with FOCUS than other types of mediums. ___
11. *Attend* is a category of use. ___
12. *Life* is a category of use. ___
13. How many characteristics of communications can be described with FOCUS? ___
14. FOCUS represents no preconceived notions. ___
15. These are the three major categories of content: *life, study of language,* and *study of other* areas. ___
16. I defined the use *present* in such a way that it is a kind of catchall category. ___
17. The scores of alternatives you learn to generate are *all* to be translated into action immediately and simultaneously. ___

Key: 1. no; 2. no, the move; 3. no, soliciting moves must be followed by responding moves; 4. no, moves can last any amount of time or be any length; 5. no; 6. no, not in my experience; 7. no; 8. yes; 9. yes, including silence; 10. no; 11. yes; 12. no, content; 13. 5; 14. no, it contains by preconceived notions: for example, I obviously think mediums are important since I code them; I also think it is important to look at student communications as well as teacher communications, to name two examples of my preconceived notions; all observation instruments contain the point of view of those who developed them; 15. no, life, procedure and study are the three major categories; study of language and study of other areas are two subcategories of study; 16. yes, I defined all the other uses and then said that if the communications don't fit them, code them as examples of *present.* 17. no, selection is critical. One alternative per lesson tried a number of times is reasonable. This book is meant to be a life-time companion, not a quick-fix throwaway.

Journal Entry

As you've begun to realize, the alternatives I advocate are often very small changes in the network of communications, such as substituting a diagram on the blackboard for an oral description in treating an error, as in Excerpt 2–3, line 9. FOCUS is designed to aid in very specific descriptions, after all.

I've noticed that outside the classroom small changes sometimes have large consequences. For example, millions of gallons of water can be saved per week if each person closes the faucet completely so that no dripping occurs. Small amounts of water can also cause harm, as in the case of a few drops of water repeatedly falling on a painted surface over a period of time. They can cause the surface to blister and peel and thus destroy the paint job.

One of the most striking memories many have of the 1976 American presidential campaign is of the debate between candidates Ford and Carter. A small part costing around 25 cents malfunctioned during the debate and produced a sound blackout that lasted around thirty minutes. Millions of parts were involved in the broadcast, but the one that malfunctioned had a great consequence.

Note any small changes you have observed that you think had large consequences. Comment on this idea of small changes having large consequences.

VI. SOME APPLICATIONS—YES, SOME APPLICATIONS

Last Chance to Get Out—A Few Ways to Employ FOCUS

Working through subsequent episodes will make the cloze passage totally accessible, confirm your characterizations of the rated questions you answered, and show many applications of FOCUS. To introduce you to some of the ways I apply FOCUS in other episodes, and the types of questions that can be investigated, I've included some applications and questions here.

Tallying and Questioning—Coding Live

Though Table 2–4 can be used to code five characteristics of any communication, it is not possible to describe all five characteristics simultaneously without using a tape or transcript. But it is possible to code and tally one or two characteristics live. For example, if you want to see what content students are communicating in responses and reactions, you simply need to make two columns, one headed *response* and the other *reaction*. Under each, you can tally the frequency of different areas of content by writing an *f* for *life*, a *p* for *procedure*, and an *s* for *study* each time a student responds or reacts. This tally provides a quick index of what areas of content are most frequent in reflexive student communications.

Once the rules are discovered and once we are quite sure what is going to happen in one class nine times out of ten, questions about alternatives and relationships can be asked. Are the frequencies similar across all levels taught by the same teacher? Do reading classes contain more *life*? Are the proportions different according to the level of the classes, with less *life* in beginning classes and more in advanced classes? What differences are there between classes set up with different aims that use different books and syllabuses? What happens when we change the proportions, thus breaking the rules we follow? These are just a few of the questions that the coding and tallying of content could help answer.

Generating Alternatives—Coding Transcriptions

While tallying is possible for one or two characteristics of communications, transcribing communications or listening to them on tapes may be necessary for noting all five characteristics. Once communications are transcribed and coded, the categories can be used to generate alternative communications, just as words in substitution tables can be used to generate alternative sentences. Let's say that we were interested in generating alternative messages in structuring moves, for example. One pattern we might find is this: Teacher structures with a *linguistic aural* medium used to *present* content of *procedure*. An example of this could be "Now, we're going to have a test." By definition, one aspect of structuring is to give directions, since structuring moves prepare for subsequent behavior. Knowing this, it is hard to imagine that say *life* or *study* could be substituted for *procedure*. But another alternative to substitution is addition. Stating what the test was to be about would add *study* to the content of *procedure*, as in "Now, we're going to have a test on the films we saw right before the break." We can even add *life* by adding still another statement: "Now, we're going to have a test on the films we saw right before the break. I know how much you hate tests and like films. I prefer films to tests too."

Graphically, the structuring moves with different combinations of distinct areas of content would look like this:

Now, we're going to have a test.	str	procedure
Now, we're going to have a test on the films we saw right before the break.	str	procedure + study
Now, we're going to have a test on the films we say right before the break. I know how much you hate tests and like films. I prefer films to tests too.	str	procedure + study + life

If the structuring moves that were transcribed already contained a great number of messages similar to the ones I just presented, with more than one area of content in each one, then the obvious alternative would be to subtract messages rather than add them. But whether we add, subtract, substitute, or integrate and combine categories, coding transcriptions helps us to describe what is. And it thus reveals the rules we are following and suggests alternatives we can generate so we can explore the consequences of different rules.

Changing areas of content in structuring moves, like almost all the other specific alternatives treated in this book, represents a small change that can be done with hardly any notice by students or inspectors. Partly because so many alternatives are possible, many readers may think that I'm advocating changes that are impossible because they are too different. In fact, I advocate the selection of small numbers of precise alternatives introduced gradually, not the wholesale introduction of large numbers of simultaneous alternatives.

The Electronics Industry Benefits Either Way—The Value of Transcriptions

Even if all the communications we transcribe are not coded or tallied, much less used to generate alternatives, listening to tapes of classes or viewing videotapes of them and transcribing selected communications from these recordings can be useful alone. From a tape, we often hear communications we missed while in the midst of communicating. Transcribing forces us to become an observer, since it is hard to try to catch what is being said or done, transcribe it, and at the same time judge what is being communicated. In short, forcing ourselves to *attend* to the teaching act itself and then transcribe what we see and hear can help us see ourselves, and thus begin to reveal some rules, even before we apply the categories to what we transcribe. We can focus even before applying FOCUS, if you'll excuse the play on words. [Background 2–16]

Feel Free to Leave the Class—Observing Outside Class

If transcribing communications from teaching settings, or coding, tallying, and manipulating them does not reveal enough rules or suggest variations, another tack is to collect and code communications in nonteaching settings. FOCUS is designed to be *U*sed in *S*ettings, not just classrooms. Looking at both teaching and nonteaching settings takes advantage of the fact that much of what we learn we learn because contrasts help us see what similarities obscure. For example, if we look at feedback only in classes, we will see that gestures and language are frequent and that *no* is avoided. Outside classes, at sporting events, for example, we see that noises—whistles and bells—are used, as well as gestures and speech. We will also see that indications that something is not right are not avoided. "You're out" is communicated very directly, as are other indications that the time is up or that someone is out of bounds.

Helping Get the Door Open—Conclusion

I'd like to conclude with an example of the application of FOCUS that shows how the system can aid in revealing relationships between communications in different settings that a surface description may not reveal. The example is from the area of feedback, treated in detail in Episode 12, "It goes in the other way!" If you were to drop me in a parachute almost anyplace in the world, and I observed someone trying to open a door in an unfamiliar place, and the person pulled a door that needed to be pushed to be opened, nine times out of ten another person would either say "push" or would push the door for the stranger.

What happens in a classroom when a person needs an answer, or at least does something wrong? I think we often follow a similar rule to the one we follow outside the classroom. When a student makes a mistake, what do we tend to do, nine times out of ten? Well, usually we give the answer. We sometimes indicate "no," which is less necessary in the case of a door that won't open, since the lack of movement is a kind of "no." At any rate, in FOCUS I would code the demonstration of how to open the door and the stating of an answer to treat a student error as *sets*. They are both examples communicated for others to copy.

To tell ourselves or others in a discussion to treat errors differently is unlikely to produce change. In fact, the treatment of some errors by communicating an example or the right answer—a *set* in FOCUS—seems to be a rule most of us seem to follow, both inside and outside the classroom. This rule, like many we all follow, is probably very deeply ingrained. Even some who think they have a different philosophy, and believe that giving an answer is not good, often do so because feedback, like most of teaching, is not always conscious and deliberate. By coding communications and deliberately substituting alternatives, we are more likely to become conscious of what we do and thus become better able to alter and control what we do. To prescribe change without a clear idea of what we are doing and without substituting an alternative that fills the function that the normal rule does is, in my experience, a limited strategy and fails to provide a way to compare consequences as well on to any episode!

Journal Entry

In some ways, learning FOCUS is like learning a language. Jot down what you consider to be some ways learning FOCUS is similar to and different from learning a new language.

BACKGROUND NOTES

2–1. For samples of guides based on FOCUS as well as a review of different types of descriptive guides, see Libdeh's dissertation.

2–2. Stevick used *techneme* in a 1965 article. While I don't expect *techneme* to catch on, I of course find the terms in my observation system more helpful than more global terms such as *methods* or *techniques*.

2–3. I borrowed the move and source directly from Bellack. My *content* is parallel to his *substantive and instructional* meanings, and my *uses* are parallel to his *substantive logical* and *instructional logical* meanings. While he noted some mediums, the idea of a separate characteristic devoted to mediums is my original contribution to the system. W. F. Mackey's *Language teaching analysis* did not highlight what I wanted, but it was a constant compass for me.

2–4. A summary of some of the studies using the move as a unit of analysis for classroom description can be found in a dissertation by Susan Turkel. Though Coulthard uses other terms for his units of analysis, his units are parallel to move types.

2–5. Bellack has defined a teaching cycle like this: ". . . a series of pedagogical moves that begins either with a structuring move or with a solicitation that is not preceded by a structuring move and ends with a move that precedes a new structuring or a new unstructured solicitation. Since by definition both responding and reacting moves are either actively elicited or occasioned by a previous pedagogical move, neither one can be said to begin a cycle, thus substantially limiting the number of combinations of moves" (p. 193).

2–6. I include a great many transcribed communications made from tape recordings in both teaching and nonteaching settings. As you will notice as you look at the excerpts in this episode as well as others, the transcriptions are not extremely detailed. I spell the words normally and so don't note actual pronunciation; nor do I note stress or pauses. I indicate some gestures and body language when this is necessary to illustrate a point, but otherwise omit detailed descriptions of movement. In addition, I have edited some transcriptions so that they more clearly illustrate a particular point, keeping close to what seemed the intention of the speaker and not essentially changing the communication, but not reflecting it exactly either. All perception involves some editing. We decide what parts of what is before us to see, hear, and feel as we observe. As we transcribe from a tape, we filter out information. In fact, the taping itself filters out some information, since the "feel" of a setting, such as temperature and less tangible things, is not recorded. Of course, I have tried to be faithful to the original communications, but I wanted to make it clear that my transcriptions, like all transcriptions, are *representative* of the real thing rather than the real thing. The central issues in transcription are discussed in detail in a piece by Elinor Ochs called "Transcription as Theory."

2–7. The issue of determining reliability is not as clear-cut as I presented it. Issues to consider in determining reliability are discussed by Dunkin and Biddle in their book, and by Shapiro-Skrobe and Strawn in their dissertations.

2–8. When Bellack and his colleagues coded, they worked in teams of two and discussed their choices in pairs before they checked their coding for reliability with another team (p. 35). By discussing choices and checking coding before a reliability check, many careless mistakes can be corrected and the preliminary discussions can themselves increase the reliability of the coding.

2–9. Though moves of different length are counted the same way, it is of course possible to compare the length and complexity of moves. Indeed, rather than limiting the measuring of different effects in separate classes to pre- and posttests and even regular in-class tests, the number of words in student moves can be counted. Do student responses tend to be longer when they are in small groups or in the entire class? Is there a relationship between the length of teacher moves and student moves, with longer teacher moves producing shorter or longer student moves? Do particular types of solicits produce different-sized responses?

In addition to comparing the number of words or syllables in teacher and student moves, the complexity of the moves can be compared. Simple measures such as phrases, patterns of sentences—those in the subject-verb-object pattern versus those with inversions or many clauses added—or standard measures such as T-units can be used as described by Hunt, Gaies, and Larson-Freeman.

2–10. I worked on the *use* category for many years. When I finally had the distinction clear in my mind between *characterize, present*, and *relate*, I happened to skim through Searle's *Speech Acts*. I was quite excited to find that he states it is important to distinguish between what he calls *characterizing talk, talking*, and *explaining talk*. This is not to say that my three uses reflect his ideas exactly, or that I want to use him for support. Rather, I want to share my excitement at having seen some surface similarity between the categories I had been working on for a long time and Searle's.

2–11. Bellack's *instructional* meaning is similar to *procedural* meaning, and his *substantive* meanings are similar to *study*. What I call *life* he did not treat, but the communications in this category are similar to what Dewey called *experience*. Dewey (1938) contrasted experience with education—*study* in my terms. Barnes, like Dewey, divides content into two major categories. Barnes refers to what I call *study* as *school knowledge*, and he refers to what I call *life* and what Dewey calls *experience* as *action knowledge*. My division of *study* into *language* and *other* makes it possible to see relationships between language development and other subject matter development.

2–12. If you are interested in social studies classes, Bellack is a good place to begin. Fey has classified content for mathematics classes and W. G. Anderson has done the same for physical education classes. Before you look at anything, I'd urge a look at Simon and Boyers' catalog of over 200 observation systems and Long's listing (1982).

2–13. One could easily argue that we use more than speech in conversation, since we move parts of the body as we speak. However, in making commercials, mediums are deliberately combined. When you think mediums other than speech communicate additional messages, code them, especially when you think the additional messages are quite obvious. One reason only speech is coded in most systems is that, once you consider all mediums, it is hard to know when to stop noting the separate messages in the move. I prefer the complexity of noting the range of mediums because I think looking beyond speech alone helps us see differently. Trying to reach agreement on a number of separate messages is time-consuming, but can also be revealing.

2–14. The idea of distinctive feature analysis is described in detail by Jakobson et al. To see how different people distinguish two communications that they think are different using quite a wide range of categories, I'd suggest you spend some time with Cazden's anthology (1972) containing scores of individual descriptions of similarities and differences in communications in classrooms. Long's review of designs for looking at second language classrooms (June 1982) should also be consulted to see how different people noted distinctive features of communications.

It is critical to realize that there are no definitive or best categories. It is also important to remember that any categories we develop limit our perception. FOCUS, like any category system, is simply a lens that reveals some characteristics and obscures others. Using subcategories or subscripts is one way to reveal more than the major categories. Another way is to develop or use a totally different lens. This book is about FOCUS not because FOCUS is an ideal lens, but because it is a lens I have found useful. Like all lenses, it interprets reality. Perhaps the story of three types of umpires illustrates the ways we can observe. One type of umpire describes the way he calls strikes and balls the pitcher throws in this way: "I calls 'em the way I sees 'em." Another type of umpire says, "I calls 'em the way they iz." The third type says, "They ain't nothin till I calls 'em." I am like the first type of umpire. I call them as I see them with FOCUS, not pretending to mistake my coding for reality nor thinking that I determine what is.

2–15. I don't mean to be sarcastic in recalling that Socrates had to give his life for breaking rules; in fact, though, breaking rules does often lead to some type of ostracism.

2–16. When another points out what we do, it is different from when we see what we are doing ourselves. By transcribing, we can see what others see. This is one of the lessons Alexander was trying to teach in his development of the Alexander technique.

EPISODE

3

Cigarette?

I. WARMING UP—INTRODUCTION

Nose, Eyes, and Ears—The Problem

I wish more students would be as interested in the processing of print in silent reading as in the inhaling of cigarette smoke, or as interested in listening to the target language as in listening to popular music. The activities during positive responses to the solicits "Cigarette?" and "Listen to my new record!" so often are more enthusiastic than the activities during responses to the solicits "Read this passage" or "Listen to this conversation on the tape."

Smoking, silent reading, and listening have more in common than the fact that they all require the taking in of some medium through the senses. They also cause millions of dollars to be wasted each year. Headlines highlighting problems caused by lack of skill in taking in and processing mediums with our eyes are almost as frequent as those highlighting cigarette-related diseases caused by taking in the medium of smoke through our mouths. Here are three that are representative: "Misreading of repair manuals costs Navy millions per year in ruined equipment." "Medical personnel administer wrong gas—color code misread." "Pilot mistakes county airport for municipal airport—comes within 600 feet of ground before discovering mistake."

Taking in and processing aural mediums through our ears is just as problematical as taking in and processing visual mediums. I recently saw an ad run by a large corporation that invited those reading the advertisement to send for a free brochure to improve their listening skills. The ad contends that listening errors result in the loss of vast amounts of effort and money. Even if incorrectly hearing a particular order number, date, or delivery address results in the loss of an average of only $10 per order, considering the millions of people around the world who take orders, the total amount lost must come to billions of dollars a year. The corporation that puts out this brochure prints this statement under its logo: "We understand how important it is to listen."

To show that it is just as concerned about silent reading as listening, the corporation prints this note in its listening brochure: "Thank you for your interest in listening—and for reading our advertisement closely enough to find the offer we made for this material."

Journal Entry

Look for examples that pay attention to the taking in of mediums in ads and headlines you see and hear. I found this one right after I saw the invitation to send for the brochure on listening: "At 3M, listening is more than just good philosophy. It's vital to our future. 3M HEARS YOU." List the examples that you found.

Basically, Only Two Columns—Outline of Contents of This Episode

This episode is about listening and silent reading, two subcategories of the use *attend* that we usually associate with classrooms. It is also about other subcategories of *attend* that we usually associate with out-of-class activities, such as smelling, tasting, touching, and viewing, which we rarely think of when we discuss listening and silent reading in language classes. Since one of the major distinctions between different subcategories of *attend* is based on the differences between the mediums we *attend* to, this episode is also about those mediums. For example, in listening we *attend* to aural mediums, in reading to visual mediums and in tasting to nonlinguistic visual mediums. Graphically, the components from FOCUS treated in this episode are illustrated in Table 3–1.

Since we can *attend* to mediums either on our own initiative—in structuring moves—or as the result of being told to—in responding moves—I've added the purpose of the communications to Table 3–2. Since the subcategories of *attend* tend to combine with particular subcategories of mediums—listening with the oral/aural mediums, silent reading with linguistic visual mediums—I've added the subcategories of mediums to Table 3–2 as well. These extra variables make the descriptions of the ways we *attend* more precise.

TABLE 3–1
Components from FOCUS Treated in "Cigarette?"

Medium	*Use*
l linguistic	
	a attend
	al listening
n nonlinguistic	
	ar silent reading
	as smelling
p paralinguistic	at tasting
	ah touching
	av viewing
s silence	

TABLE 3–2
More Components from FOCUS Treated in "Cigarette?"

Move Type	*Medium*	*Use*
	l linguistic	a attend
structure	la aural—spoken words, pauses, markers and fillers lv visual—printed, written or phonetically transcribed sounds, words and sentences lo other—Braille, Morse code	al listening
	n nonlinguistic	ar silent reading
	na aural—noise, music nv visual—objects, speech organs, cartoons, pictures, diagrams, maps, shape of a stop sign, musical notes, color coding of tools or wires no other—smells, temperature, lighting	as smelling
	p paralinguistic	at tasting
respond	pa aural—crying, tone of voice, volume of voice pv visual—gestures, facial expressions, posture, skin color, gazing po other—doing things with objects, movement, distance from others, touching people	ah touching
	si silence	av viewing
	Implicit communications, pauses, wait time, so-called pregnant pauses	

What We Take In and How Fast We Do It—Purposes of This Episode

The purpose of this episode is threefold. In section II, I explore the subcategories of the use *attend* inside and outside classrooms. In section III, I compare the types and combinations of mediums we *attend* to in teaching and nonteaching settings. If you think a moment, you'll realize that in nonteaching settings, we usually *attend* to multiple mediums at the same time, while in teaching settings we tend to *attend* to only one at a time. Thus, in a lounge or in our homes, we usually read while listening to music, sipping a drink, eating a snack or smoking. In a class or a library, we are expected to take in only print. Signs demanding silence and prohibiting eating and drinking make explicit the rule which demands that we *attend* to only one medium at a time in a teaching setting. In section IV, I'll urge you to increase the rate at which you communicate mediums others are to *attend* to, thus breaking the rule we usually follow which requires that we slow down our speech when speaking with nonnative speakers of a language.

Though I would hope that some alternatives generated here would lead to fewer headlines deploring poor listening and reading skills, I can't promise such results. We can find out the consequences of following different rules only after we break the ones we ordinarily follow. Exploring the rules we follow when we *attend* both in and out of teaching settings can be interesting for its own sake because of some of the striking differences that exist between teaching and nonteaching settings, however.

A Monkey Wrench—Distinguishing *Attend* from Other Uses

To illustrate the distinction between *attend* and other uses, the classic question in language teaching can be used as a starting point. If I were to ask you "What's this?" as I held up a monkey wrench, it's true that you'd have to hear the words "What's this?" and see the monkey wrench in order to respond. But the purpose of the question is to see if you can name the object, not to have you *attend* to the medium of speech in the question or the medium of the solid object itself. The response I want requires that you *attend*—if you had a blindfold on and plugs in your ears, you could not respond—but basically I'm asking you to perform by saying the words "A monkey wrench." Had I asked you to draw the wrench or write the word, you would have had to employ print and a sketch, but you would still have had to produce something, not just take something in.

To prevent the tallying of every response in which we have to hear or see mediums, and thus have no way to say when listening was being given attention and when it wasn't, I code instances of listening, and other subcategories of *attend*, when the expected response requires only that something be taken in. This does not address the problem of determining whether the person told to *attend* in some way is actually doing so, but it does make it possible to tally the proportion of responses that require that something be produced and those that require only that mediums be taken in.

I have not found a completely satisfactory way to determine whether a person asked to listen or read silently or view a picture or touch a texture stops attending, or, in fact, whether the person is attending. If a person is told to *attend* or initiates one of the subcategories of attend on his or her own, I code the fact that mediums are being taken in, in spite of the fact that I have no way to prove that they are. To compare the length of time people are attending, I simply note the amount of time in minutes that the person is given to *attend*. After all, listening to one or two notes played on a piano is obviously different from listening to an entire piece or even a long movement. Consequently, noting the amount of time a person seems to be taking something in, I think, needs to be done.

I've coded some examples of *attend* and showed how I note the duration of each example in Excerpt 3–1. I've noted other uses with an *o* in Excerpt 3–1, and I've noted instances of *attend* with an *a* for *attend*, plus the first or other letter of the subcategory: *l* for listening; *r* for silent reading; *s* for smelling, including inhaling cigarette smoke; *t* for tasting; *h* for touching; and *v* for viewing. The number after the abbreviations indicates the length in minutes and seconds allowed for the attending. I use these numbers fully realizing that a person may not be processing the mediums the senses are exposed to for the entire time noted, or even taking them in for that matter. But, at the minimum, the distinction between *attend* and *other* uses shows the frequency of each and suggests the proportion of time devoted to the uses that require processing of mediums taken in and the processing of mediums as they are produced.

Journal Entry

What are your feelings about my use of the word *attend* to refer to listening and silent reading (activities which are usually considered as receiving)? And what do you think of my putting tasting, smelling, viewing, and touching in the same category as silent reading and listening?

EXCERPT 3–1
Distinguishing between *Attend* and Other Uses

		Communications	*Source/ Target*	*Move Type*	*Use*	*Time*
Setting 1: On a tour of a building (T)						
1	Teacher:	As we walk around the building, I want you to find things that will guide you back to this room if you get lost.	t/c	sol	o	_____
2	Student$_1$:	(Looks at a large pipe painted red that carries water in case of fire.)	s_1/o	res	av	0:06
3	Student$_2$:	(Sees names of people on doors of rooms.)	s_1/o	res	ar	0:12
4	Student$_1$:	(Gets separated from group and finds his way back by following red pipe.)	s_1/o	str	o	_____
Setting 2: At the cashier's window, two friends						
5	Al:	Look at that fellow.	s_1/s_2	sol	o	_____
6	Jim:	(Looks at a person in line with a large new bag and old clothes.)	s_2/s	res	av	0:03
7	Jim:	He looks suspicious.	s_2/s_1	rea	o	_____
8	Al:	Could you describe him if a police officer asked you later?	s_1/s_2	sol	o	_____
9	Jim:	(Looks at person again.)	s_2/s	rea	av	0:06
10		Before you asked, I couldn't have.	s_2/s_1	res	o	_____
Setting 3: During an examination (T)						
11	Teacher:	Listen carefully to the lecture. If you don't hear what the speaker says on the tape, you will not be able to give the required answer.	t/c	sol	o	_____
12	Class:	(Listens to the lecture on the tape.)	c/t	res	al	15:00
Setting 4: In a restaurant (T)						
13	Waiter:	Would you like something to drink?	s/t	sol	o	_____
14	Customer:	Gin on the rocks.	t/s	res	o	_____
15	Customer:	White wine without ice.	t/s	res	o	_____
16	Waiter:	(Gives menu to the diners.)	s/t	str	o	_____
17	Customers:	(Look at the menu.)	t/o	str	ar	2:00
18	Waiter:	(Stares at ring on customer's finger, trying to read the engraving on it.)	s/o	str	av	0:20

EXCERPT 3–1 (*continued*)

		Communications	*Source/ Target*	*Move Type*	*Use*	*Time*
Setting 5: In a classroom (T)						
19	Teacher:	Read the poem thoroughly. Underline the words you don't understand.	t/c	sol	o	
20	Students:	(Look at the poem.)	c/t	res	ar	3:00
21	Student$_1$:	(Draws a line under every few words.)	s_1/o	res	o	
22	Student$_2$:	(Looks at snapshots a friend brought which are lying on the poem.)	s_2/o	str	av	1:00
23		(Begins to draw scars, eye patches and beards on the faces in the snapshots.)	s_2/o	str	o	
Setting 6: At a party						
24	Guest$_1$:	(Tastes some olives from a table of food.)	s/o	str	at	0:12
25	Host:	What da ya think?	s/s	sol	o	
26	Guest$_1$:	I like 'em better without the pits.	s/s	res	o	
27		(Puts on a record)	s/o	str	o	
28		(Listens to the record.)	s/o	str	al	0:30
29	Host:	(Here the host is taking charge and so changing roles.) Turn that damn thing off!	t/s	sol	o	
30	Guest$_1$:	(Takes the record off the stereo.)	s_1/o	res	o	
31	Guest$_2$:	(Looks at paintings and photos on walls.)	s_2/o	str	av	1:00
32	Guest$_2$:	Where did you take that picture?	s_2/s	sol	o	
33	Host:	In Tokyo.	s/s	res	o	
	Guest$_3$:	(Looks through a copy of the *New Yorker* seeing ads, cartoons, stories, notices.)	s/o	str	ar + av	2:00
35	Guest$_2$:	(Looks over shoulder of guest$_3$.)	s/o	str	ar + av	1:00
36		This month there is a special rate for new subscribers.	s/s	rea	o	

For additional experience distinguishing *attend* and *other* uses, code the uses in the *Use* column in Excerpt 3–2. Use an *o* for *other* uses and an *al* for listening, *ar* for silent reading, *as* for smelling, *at* for tasting, *ah* for touching, and *av* for viewing. Compare your coding with the samples given below the excerpt. Either ignore the column for noting the time people are engaged in the use *attend* or write in an estimate.

Mis-_____—Relationship between Errors in Different Types of Attending

I think it is important to look at ways we take in mediums other than the usual ones we think of when we teach—listening and silent reading—because in some ways it might be that we process meaning in similar ways no matter how we *attend*. We can incorrectly identify food we are tasting just as we can incorrectly identify a word we hear or a scent we smell. In one of the headlines I presented at the beginning of this episode, a pilot almost landed at the wrong airport. This was a case of misviewing landmarks, not misreading print. "Mistaken identity" is a phrase that refers to the subcategory of *attend* I call viewing. Identifying smoke from a fire and distinguishing it from that of a cigar or cigarette can mean the difference between a false alarm, a burned-out house, and a comment such as "He loves to smoke."

If students misread print, do they also "mistaste" and in other ways *attend* incorrectly? Or do those who can pick out the smallest detail in a picture miss even gross distinctions in print? Helping anyone see that some of the same processes may be involved in all the ways we *attend* might aid a few in strengthening the subcategory of *attend* they are weakest in. Of course, a simpler reason, subject to less controversy and not requiring any rationale, is the fact that to show the rules of listening and silent reading in teaching and nonteaching settings, we need to note other activities, such as viewing, smelling, tasting, and touching. This is true because people engage in these activities as they read and listen outside of classrooms, and sometimes even in classrooms and other teaching settings, such as libraries and bookstores.

EXCERPT 3–2
Experience in Distinguishing between *Attend* and Other Uses (T)

		Communications	*Source/ Target*	*Move Type*	*Use*	*Time*
1	Flight attendent$_1$:	Welcome to Flight 141 to Buffalo with continuing service to Chicago.	t_1/c	str		
2		At this time, please direct your attention to the flight attendants in your section of the aircraft.	t_1/c	sol		
3	Passengers:	(Look at the attendant.)	c/t	res		
4	Flight attendent$_1$:	In the seat pockets in front of you is a card about the safety features of this aircraft.	t_1/c	str*		
5	Flight attendent$_2$:	(Hold up the cards.)	t_2/c	str		

EXCERPT 3–2 (*continued*)

	Communications		*Source/ Target*	*Move Type*	*Use*	*Time*
6	Flight attendent$_1$:	It points out the location of the nearest exit and how to use it.	t_1/c	str		
7	Flight attendent$_2$:	(Point to exit signs.)	t_2/c	str		
8	Passengers:	(Look at the exits and listen and look at the cards.)	c/to	res		
9	Flight attendant$_1$:	Now fasten your seat belts.	t_1/c	sol		
10	Passengers:	(Fasten their seat belts.)	c/t	res		
11	Flight attendant$_1$:	And observe the No Smoking sign.	t_1/c	sol		
12	Some passengers:	(Put out their cigarettes.)	g/t	res		
13	Flight attendant$_1$:	Now take out your cards and look at the map of the exits. (The cards are in front of each passenger in a pocket on the backs of the seats.)	t_1/c	sol		

Emergency exit routes

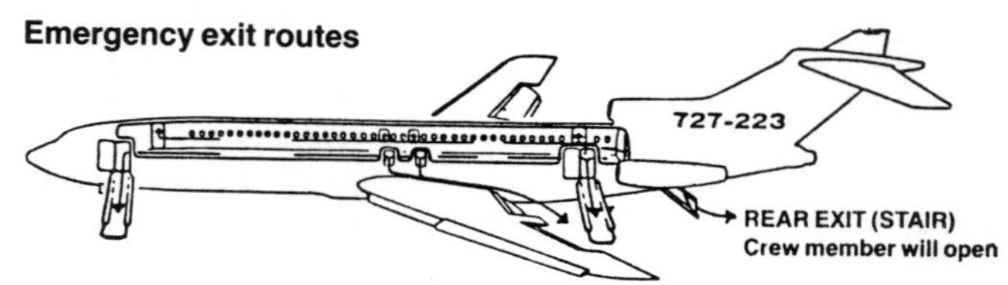

14	Passengers:	(Look at the cards.)	c/t_1 + o	res		
15	Flight attendant$_1$:	The captain has turned off the No Smoking sign.	t_1/g	str		
16	Some passengers:	(Take out cigarettes, light them and put them into their mouths.)	g/t_1	str		
17	Some passengers:	(Inhale.)	g/o	str		
18	Some other passengers:	(Browse through magazines and books as they begin to sip drinks they have been served—magazines have pictures.)	g/o	str		
19	Some other passengers:	(Listen to music on headphones they have been given, sip drinks, and look at the sky and clouds.)	g/o	str		

* Though I have coded lines 4–7 as four separate moves, you could also consider them as only two moves, one from each source, punctuated by the nonspoken communications.

Coding done by others: 1. o; 2. o; 3. av; 4. o; 5. o; 6. o; 7. o; 8. al + av; 9. o; 10. o; 11. o; 12. o; 13. o; 14. ar + av; 15. o; 16. o; 17. as + at + ah; 18. ar + at + av; 19. al + at + av.

II. TAKING IN, INSIDE AND OUTSIDE—*ATTEND* IN TEACHING AND NONTEACHING SETTINGS

A Lack of Stability on the Outside— Amount of Attending Varies Outside of Class

Inside classes, I have consistently found little time devoted to silent reading and listening. I have found the proportion of listening and silent reading and other uses much less stable outside the classroom. During conversations, the frequency of listening is usually low and people don't ordinarily say "Now, just listen!" I've heard this command at meetings, especially after a disagreement. But many meetings are like teaching settings, with one person in charge. One could argue that when a person in a conversation reacts by saying "I hear what you've been saying," the person has been listening even though he or she has not explicitly been told to. Still, in most conversations, listening is not tallied a great deal. [Background 3–1]

The amount of time spent on listening as a subcategory of *attend* while people are at concerts, at lectures for entertainment rather than instruction, and while tuned to a radio station is greater than the amount of time devoted to other uses. It is even much greater than the amount of time spent on the same use while in a language lab, because at these other settings no time is devoted to responding to questions. When people read silently on trains, buses, planes, and in parks, the amount of time spent on the subcategory of *attend*, silent reading, is greater than that spent on other uses, and greater than the time devoted to reading in most classrooms because, outside of reading lessons, we don't ordinarily read orally to people and because usually no one asks questions about what we are reading. Finally, most instances of the subcategories of *attend*, listening and silent reading, outside of teaching settings are self-initiated. The train conductor and flight attendant or bus driver do not go up and down the aisles shouting "I want you all to read your newspapers, magazines, and books now." The fact that most out-of-class attending, at least the subcategories listening and silent reading, is self-initiated means that we *attend* in structuring moves outside class and in responding moves in class.

To duplicate the out-of-class pattern in class, one alternative is to provide reading and listening materials and free time to students during parts of periods. Each time a student picks up something to read or switches on a tape or record, perhaps equipped with earphones, the student is attending in a structuring move rather than in a responding move. [Background 3–2]

Journal Entry

As you are working your way through this episode, what mediums are you attending to other than the print on the pages and spatial arrangements in the tables? In what ways are you attending in addition to silent reading? Finally, are you attending to the material in this book as a result of a solicit, in a response, or are you attending as a result of your own initiative, in a structuring move?

Definite Incongruities—We *Attend* Differently outside of Classes

Outside of teaching settings, another difference a cursory observation reveals is that people engage in subcategories of *attend* other than just listening and silent reading. People view pictures in ads or in magazines, stare at other people and buildings, taste food and drinks, smell flowers, food, animals, pollution and even other people, touch cloth they are shown, pass their hands over babies' faces, and squeeze bread, fruits, and vegetables they are about to buy or leave for a less suspicious or fussy customer.

But one of the most striking things I'm sure you've noted about the way we *attend* outside classes is that we engage in more than one subcategory of *attend* at the same time. I rarely listen only to speech. I take in people, objects, and the scents around me too. In a concert hall, I look at the instruments, the musicians, and the audience at the same time that I listen to the music.

While reading silently outside class, most people I observe have the radio on and tune in and out the music and print at various times. If they read without music, they look away from the print to objects in the room or other people as they read. Others eat, smoke, or drink as they read. In the United States, most of those who eat breakfast alone probably have the radio on as they do, and read the newspaper or the nutrition information on their cereal boxes as they either gulp down or savor their meals. The aroma of baking bread can be enjoyed along with a good record, a book, or a glass of milk.

Most train stations have arrival and departure information posted, but the information is announced as well so passengers can *attend* by listening and reading silently. Many passengers in large stations read the departure or arrival announcements and then go up to the information booth and ask for the information they just read silently so they can *attend* by listening and silent reading. In airports in most parts of the world, announcements are not made about arrivals and departures. This information is only posted. But there are check-in clerks at the gates to say things like "I see you're flying to London today" as they check tickets. So passengers have a chance to listen and read when they fly too. And just in case one does not read the posted information correctly or hear the clerk, the captain will announce the destination once passengers are on the plane. So everyone has a chance to listen again.

If listening were the only subcategory of *attend* music lovers were interested in, there would be little reason to go to a concert or watch a concert on television. But people want to *attend* by listening and viewing. The bands that are often most popular with teenagers are often those that play while lights are flashing, wear extraordinary costumes, and play flashy instruments—those that require both listening and viewing!

Teaching settings can be distinguished partly on the basis of the fact that they usually require us to *attend* in fewer ways at the same time. Have you ever tried to touch something at a museum at the same time that you are viewing it? "Don't touch the marble" says the guard in the role of the teacher. The guard's admonition is supported with Do Not Touch signs or plexiglass between the objects and you so you can *attend* in only one way. In a library, you cannot eat food and read silently at the same time; libraries are only for silent reading. Many students do more reading in lounges or coffee shops where they can *attend* in more than one way at the same time.

The language laboratory and the language classroom seem to be two of the only places in the world where we are expected to *attend* in only one way at a time. In many language labs, we sit in carrels so we can see only blank walls. And we have earphones on to try to exclude everything but the sounds electronically transmitted to our ears. Perhaps the fact that we are expected to *attend* in only one way at the same time explains the high incidence of drooping heads that need to be supported by hands holding chins and elbows braced on the desk. If I am given directions on the street, I am likely to be able to see the buildings and streets to be used as guides as they are mentioned. I can *attend* by both listening and looking at the same time at the buildings and streets mentioned. In classrooms, we often *attend* to street directions only by listening to speech or reading print; we are not able to *attend* by looking at buildings, gestures, or street signs, or smelling odors or hearing traffic noise.

Journal Entry

When you are in a strange place, either in your own country or in another country, what do you *attend* to that makes you feel uncomfortable, and what do you *attend* to that makes you feel comfortable? For example, do you seek out music familiar to you when in a strange place, or food you are accustomed to? As you *attend*, either in a familiar place or a strange place, do you tend to *attend* in more than one way at the same time, or only in one way?

If you haven't been in strange places, you might want to comment about smokers if you are a nonsmoker, and smokers or nonsmokers if you are a smoker—how to *attend* to smoke, in other words.

A Few More Alternatives—Having Students *Attend* Differently

If the rule in classrooms or language labs you are involved with allows students to *attend* in only one way at a time, try having them *attend* in more than one way at the same time, as we usually do outside classrooms. Have them view a series of slides or pictures during a listening exercise. Have the students eat or take in the scent of an herb while reading silently. Or, allow those who smoke to smoke as they read—in an area away from the nonsmokers. They can touch different textured materials as they read or listen too.

If you want to use slides, pictures, food, herbs, or textured materials that are directly related to the passages they read or listen to, you will have to spend a great deal of time searching for passages or for items to go with them. Obviously, when we are given directions, we want to view a map related to the place we're going to as we listen to the directions. And we want to hear and see the name of the same train station together. It would not be useful to hear "Morris Heights" and see a sign that had "Spuyten Duyvil" on it. Thus, the picture we view supports the words we read, and the music we listen to is directly related to both the picture and the words. We are viewing, listening to, and silently reading the same message all at the same time.

But outside of classes, not all the different things we *attend* to at the same time are related. You may want to touch marble in a museum to compare it with the formica in your kitchen, not to remember the name of the statue you are viewing. You surely do not try to find music on a car radio related to the scenery you are passing. And though we talk about what we are eating as we eat, our conversation is not limited to comments related to the food in front of us, or even to the topic of food.

The Power of Association—A Rationale for Attending Differently

While some television commercials bombard us with a single message, some present disparate material to each sense. Consequently, another alternative to try when asking students to *attend* in different ways is to select the items to smell, taste, touch, and view during silent reading or listening at random! When you remember some advertisements, you remember something that may be quite unrelated to the item being sold. Cigarette ads show pictures of waterfalls, pyramids, and tattoos; liquor ads sometimes contain scenes of far-away forests. Associations aid us in remembering not only products; but almost anything. For example, when we remember how we met a person, we often make statements like this: "I met Gloria at the dinner at Goto's where we had cinnamon ice cream."

Ask students to bring in a sample of a food from their countries or something they particularly like. Have them exchange the food and eat it as they silently read passages that do not mention eating, food, or cooking in different countries. Have different scents in class on different days during different listening lessons that make no mention of odors. Nine times out of ten, you'll begin to hear students making statements such as these: "Hot pepper—the day Mrs. Gold had a heart attack in *No Hot Water Tonight* (an ESOL reader by Jean Bodman and Michael Lanzano); "The day we read about Mr. Going-To-Do, we smelled pine-scented candles in class" (from V. F. Allen's ESOL reader *People in Livingston*). [Background 3–3]

Many reading specialists have advocated the tracing of the shapes of letters cut from sandpaper so students can profit from the tactile sense. Playing with three-dimensional blocks in the shape of letters is popular if availability of these items in toy stores is an index of popularity. And blocks with a letter on them and a picture of an object that starts with the letter are also popular—an A and a picture of an apple to view at the same time. As an alternative, have students associate different letters with different textures that have nothing directly to do with the particular letter. In other words, do not just have a rough piece of wood associated with an R for "rough," for example. On the day R is introduced, let the students pick a texture they want. Different ones may have, and indeed probably will have, completely different associations. If I say a letter or word to a group of people and ask them to write down a word that comes to mind, I get a wide range of different associations for many of them. Of course, since many words tend to be used with other words more frequently, there is a great deal of similarity in some associations. But still, there are associations very much limited to different individuals. [Background 3–4]

Though one out-of-class rule we can try in class is to have students *attend* in many ways at the same time to the same content—a rule developed to its most efficient extreme in television commercials that emphasize one message for our ears and eyes—another out-of-class rule we can try in class is to have students *attend* in more than one way to mediums that contain seemingly unrelated content, believing in the power of random association. If every listening and reading lesson takes place in the same setting, with the same four walls, the same chairs and desks in the same positions, the same students, and where uniforms are worn, the same clothes, and the same teacher, separate days blend together, overlap, and seem more and more identical. There is nothing to make one day different, separate, distinct, or memorable except the material being listened to or read itself. But often the material is all from the same book. By having students *attend* in two different ways to unrelated materials, memorable associations are perhaps more likely. Each day you have students *attend* in more than one way, say, eating and reading silently, will not only be a day for different material to be attended to, but for different associations to be made. The possibility of different associations between the material taken in by our ears and eyes and the material taken in by our hands, mouths, and noses is brought into existence. Radio and television programs have musical themes totally unrelated to the content of the programs in many cases, yet we remember the themes for years. Why not try this alternative in your classes, at least for part of a period once a week?

Even if the associations do not always make the material read and listened to more memorable, at least some of the students may incidentally learn one or two more expressions directly related to the smelling, tasting, and touching they do. And their reading and listening are likely to be as profitable as when done in isolation. But in isolation, students would not be likely to make comments such as "That smells odd—reminds me of an old suit," or "I hate hot things like that, but it sure cleans out your nose." Because some will be puzzled when they are asked to take in mediums through more than one sense at the same time, some will ask what they are doing and why they are doing it—questions unlikely during the normal routines of classroom discussion. Some will be puzzled by the presence of many objects in the class and may consider the items gifts, forcing them to ask the teacher whether they can take them home or not. Both situations provide students with a chance to use language to communicate feelings or needs.

The central point of trying out-of-class activities in class is not to make a more relaxing atmosphere or to make listening and silent reading fun. These results may or may not occur and may or may not be important. But the substitution of the rules we usually follow when we *attend* outside teaching settings inside teaching settings will allow students the chance to do in classrooms what we do outside. Over a period of time, some students may be better able to concentrate in class while reading silently or listening because they will learn to filter out extraneous information and not take in more than the printed or spoken language they want to. Some may realize concentration is easier with music on than in a very silent place, and that silence may be harder to read and listen in than while listening, eating or attending in other ways.

Journal Entry

What do you most enjoy about silent reading, listening, and taking in mediums in other ways? Do you usually *attend* in only one way at a time, or in more than one way?

III. SIT UP STRAIGHT—POSTURE AND ATMOSPHERE AS WE *ATTEND*

When I read silently or listen outside a library or classroom, I not only try to take in more than one medium at the same time, I also situate myself differently. I sit in a soft chair or even lie down on a floor or a sofa outside a teaching setting as I read or listen. My friends tend to also. And students at my institution sit in the lounge with their feet up on tables when they can, preferring the soft lounge chairs to the hard straight chairs of the library. In bookstores, as well as on trains and buses, it is not hard to find people standing as they read, often in a slouched position rather than at attention as if in a military review. In short, posture—a medium I code *paralinguistic other*—is different in teaching and nonteaching settings when we *attend*.

If students you teach always sit in hard chairs in class, invite them to sit or lie on the floor or sit in the soft chairs in a lounge with their feet up on the tables. If they never stand up when they read in class, invite them to. Of course, these opposites may have no effect on developing reading skills, but it is intriguing that so many people put their feet up and sit comfortably or stand when reading outside of classrooms. *At the minimum, introducing these out-of-class rules inside classrooms may provide a different perspective for some students, and as always using out-of-class rules in class reminds us that one task of teachers is to provide some experience with what students are expected to do outside class.*

Another group of mediums that I code as *other* are the *nonlinguistic mediums of temperature and lighting. These nonlinguistic other* mediums, like the paralinguistic mediums of posture, may have no effect on the development of reading or listening skills. Yet they are available variables. If it is always bright during listening exercises, dim the lights. Many of my friends listen to music or radio programs in the dark. During concerts, the audience sits in darkness. While I don't always like to read with dim lights, when forced to read in a darkened car, for example, my eyes adjust and I can read something if I have to. Reading in darkened places, like listening in darkened places, might enable us to concentrate on the linguistic mediums we are trying to *attend* to. Whether altering the light forces concentration or not, it is a fact that we must be able to read and listen without strong light outside most teaching settings.

Another *nonlinguistic other* medium is the temperature we experience. If it is always hot in teaching settings you are in, open the windows or leave the class and head for a shady place under some trees. If it is cold, ask students to keep their coats on and bundle up. [Background 3–5]

Since erect posture in a classroom and a reclining posture in a lounge are both coded *po* for *paralinguistic other*, and since bright lighting or dim are both coded *no* for *nonlinguistic other*, distinctions between these categories of mediums can be made by using subscripts. For example, po_s can stand for sitting up straight, po_f can stand for sitting with feet on a footrest like the ones on buses or on low tables or footstools in lounges. Dim lights can be coded no_{dl} and bright ones no_{bl}. The point is simply that we take in mediums other than the linguistic ones as we read silently and listen, and if we want to see the rules we follow more clearly, we need to observe not only how we *attend* to linguistic mediums, but also how we attend to and produce nonlinguistic and paralinguistic mediums, including those in the category I call *other.*

Journal Entry

When you read this book, do you usually sit in a straight chair at a table or in a lounge chair? Do you sit in different positions for different kinds of reading? For example, when reading a novel, do you lie down? When reading a text of some kind, especially for an examination, do you tend to sit up straight? Can you concentrate more when you try not to, as when you are in a prone position or in a lounge chair, or when you are sitting at attention on a straight-backed hard chair?

IV. SPEED LIMITS—VARYING THE RATE OF MEDIUMS WE *ATTEND* TO

Even if we are all silently reading in a similar position, have similar content before us, and are all sipping the same drink, the activity can be different for each of us because of the speed with which we take in the mediums. You may finish reading a paragraph in 30 seconds, while I may take 90 seconds. The direction "When I say 'stop,' put a line next to the word you have just read" will produce lines in many different places on the same page of text. Slowly decreasing the amount of time allowed to *attend* to the same material is an alternative implied by the fact that different people *attend* at different rates.

Of course, making someone speed up his or her reading for its own sake is not the aim of altering the amount of time allowed to read a passage silently. The aim is to show that below a certain speed, comprehension of some materials during silent reading is extremely difficult. It is also useful to be able to take in print quickly because, outside of teaching settings, we sometimes have to. For example, phone numbers and titles often flash on television screens for less than a second. And as we drive along looking for a friend's house that "you just can't miss," we often have only a few seconds to catch the words on street signs.

One way to try to get students in class to read more quickly is to ask them to look at groups of words or different signs quickly and then close their eyes. Or, hold up signs and turn them face down very quickly. And to get students to read extended print more quickly, and thus help them to read groups of words rather than word by word, we can specify that they finish a set number of lines in a prescribed period of time. There is no need to state the prescribed period beforehand. All you need to do is say "Mark your place and begin reading" at one time, and "Stop reading and mark your place" at another time. The students can count the words or syllables in between the marks and see the number of words or syllables that they read in the time allowed. Then they can be asked to start again and stop again, but with less time. As they see that their lines are being made in different places, they begin to see that they can take in more sense groups in the same amount of time. Of course, it must be realized that subsequent trips through the print make the material more familiar and account for some of the increased speed. But this fact can help readers see that a quick rate can lead to understanding as well, if not better, than a slow rate.

Just as we cannot comprehend some printed material if the time lapse between individual words is too great, and we might miss some crucial information in a contract if we race through it, so we have to learn to listen to material delivered orally at different rates of speed. One rule most of us follow when we talk to nonnative speakers of a target language, and also to native speakers who are either children or old people, both in teaching and nonteaching settings, is to slow our rate of delivery. If we want our students to be treated like children, we should speak to them only at the slower rate. But if we want them to be able to follow the native speakers that they listen to on television or the radio, at least programs not in special English, we need to expose them to a range of delivery rates.

The rule that says "slow down" to nonnative speakers, old people, and children is hard to break without tape-recording something you say and figuring out the words spoken per minute. Record yourself reading the same passage in different prescribed limits such as 30 seconds, 45 seconds, and 60 seconds. Do this with news items, dialogs in which people are buying something, lectures, and a range of items your students have to listen to. Then, play each tape in class. Even if students say they prefer slow speech, when they hear the same passage at different rates they often see how much better they can follow normal, even rapid speech. By forcing students to grasp speech at different rates of speed, some will be better prepared to follow speech outside class. They will see that slower is not always clearer or easier and that speed can help.

The comprehension of native speakers of English does not suffer until the rate reaches around 250 words per minute, which is more than 75 words per minute above average. The only way to help students see whether they listen for individual words during slow delivery and larger units of meaning during fast delivery is to provide them with passages delivered at different rates of speed. At the least, listeners exposed to a range of speech rates in class can begin to realize that listening rates must vary with the purpose just as reading rates must match the purpose of the reading. [Background 3–6]

Viewing, tasting, touching, and smelling can also be timed, though the senses may retain the image, flavor, texture, or scent long after the materials have been removed. By saying "Look at this picture quickly" and then turning it over or taking it out of another person's sight, we provide the viewer with a chance to see what can be viewed in a short period of time. On a moving bus, we must view things quickly because they disappear as the bus moves on. Watching television and movies provides no chances to *attend* again, unless we can record and replay the material. Usually, things we view move on and we have to *attend* quickly. By allowing people a long period of time to say how they felt about something they tasted, they may not as easily be able to share their first reaction. They may even become hesitant about sharing any reactions because, when they have too much time to think about the question they may start to wonder, "What does he want me to say?"

To force students to taste or view everything quickly would never give them a chance to be reflective about what they *attend* to. Thoughtful reflection about the taste of wine, the content of a painting, or a perfume we have been given as a gift is sometimes what is wanted. Here, as with the other alternatives, the point is not to increase the rate at which we want others to *attend*. The alternative is to vary the rate at which others are expected to *attend*, since this is what we must do outside teaching settings.

By varying the rate of delivery and the amount of time allowed for taking in material, everyone gets a chance to learn that both slowness and speed can be an advantage or a drawback. When first learning to balance a bicycle, a certain minimum speed is necessary to keep from failing. Once balance is achieved, it is possible to ride a bicycle at a rate below the one needed to balance the bicycle during the initial stages of learning. After riding a great deal, some can balance a bicycle while almost at a standstill.

Just as we must vary the speed of propelling a bicycle to learn this skill, so must we vary the speed of delivery and the amount of time allowed to *attend* in order to learn the consequences of breaking the rule that dictates that we always slow down when we are with nonnative speakers of a language, children, or old people. The "Are you a stu den t?" rate of delivery must be juxtaposed to the "Aryaastuent?" rate, as well as to the "Are you a student?" rate in order to compare each. Of course, the ultimate goal is more speed, but this goal must always be tempered by the fact that rate depends upon purpose. Those who can vary their rate to meet different purposes are probably the best off.

Journal Entry

When you speak to others who may not understand you, do you decrease the amount of blending you do? Do you alter the intonation pattern by tending to stress each word? When others do this to you, either in your own language or in a foreign language, how do you feel about it?

When you speak to others who may not understand you, do you alter the level of your voice? Do you lower or raise your voice, for example? If you listen to others who are speaking a language foreign to you, do they lower or raise their voices? If they do, how do you feel about it? Does the alteration ever aid comprehension? Does it make some sounds clearer than when the material is simply said over and over at the same level?

V. COOLING DOWN—CONCLUSION

How Many of What?—Tallying Subcategories of *Attend*

I use an observation guide to compare the frequency and duration of the subcategories of *attend* with other uses, to see what mediums and combinations of mediums are attended to, whether the attending is self-initiated or done in response to being told to, to note the combinations of the subcategories, and to clock the speed at which people are expected to *attend*. Observation guides permit the tallying of different variables. The resulting tallies reveal how the variables differ from class level to class level, in classes taught by teachers with different amounts of training and different preparation, in a range of teaching and nonteaching settings, and between any other contrasts you might want to investigate. [Background 3–7]

As you can see in Observation Guide 3–1, I've listed the subcategories of *attend* in the left-hand column. To distinguish instances of silent reading, listening and other subcategories that are self-initiated from those that are required by another, as well as to keep the unit of analysis constant, I've formed two columns next to the list of the subcategories. One is titled "Structuring" and one is titled "Responding." To tally the frequency of each subcategory of *attend*, all you have to do is put a check mark in the appropriate place.

OBSERVATION GUIDE 3–1
How Many of What?

Setting: ______________________________

Number of Participants: ______________ If class, type and level: ______________

Materials used: ______________________________

Time observation began: ______________ Time observation ended: ______________

Move Type / Use *Attend*	Structuring	Responding
1. listening (al)		
2. silent reading (ar)		
3. smelling (as)		
4. tasting (at)		
5. touching (ah)		
6. viewing (av)		
Use *Other*		

To discover the extent to which different subcategories of *attend* occur together, you can use the abbreviations of the subcategories rather than check marks in the tally. For example, if a person were reading silently and listening to the radio, you would put an *al* for listening next to line 2, where silent reading is tallied. If the person were eating as well, then you'd have to put an *al* and an *at* in the box on line 2. To distinguish one move from another in a sequence, you can separate each tally with a comma.

To see what mediums are attended to, you can use the abbreviations for the mediums rather than check marks or the abbreviations for the subcategories of uses in the tally. Here are the abbreviations, but it might be easier to tally while looking at Table 3–2 (page 55) because it contains examples of each of the categories as well: la = linguistic aural; lv = linguistic visual; lo = linguistic other; na = nonlinguistic aural; nv = nonlinguistic visual; no = nonlinguistic other; pa = paralinguistic aural; pv = paralinguistic visual; po = paralinguistic other; si = silence.

To note the duration of the different instances of the subcategories of *attend*, you can mark the number of seconds or minutes devoted to each instance in the columns. In other words, you can tally with numbers rather than check marks or abbreviations. Timing reading is important if you want to compare different proportions of it to other subcategories of *attend* and *other* uses. If one silent reading task takes 10 minutes to finish in a 20-minute period devoted to reading and thirty other uses are performed, it makes little sense to say that 3 percent of the activities required only that mediums be taken in and 97 percent required that they be produced when in fact the time devoted to both *attend* and *other* uses was 10 minutes, or 50 percent each. Likewise, you may observe only one listening task and one silent reading task in a class. But if the reading occupied 30 minutes and the listening occupied 3 minutes, it makes no sense to simply tally one instance of each type of attending. When tallying subcategories of *attend*, the amount of time taken for receiving the material needs to be noted, as well as the number of times a particular subcategory of *attend* occurs to provide an accurate description.

To give you an idea of what a filled-in Observation Guide looks like, I've included Observation Guide 3–1A. As you can see, I've used the abbreviations for the subcategories of *attend* in some cases, the mediums in others, and the number of seconds devoted to *attend* in others. Normally, I'd do a tally to show one thing or the other, but I wanted to illustrate what a filled-in guide looks like. As you can see, all the instances of *attend* were self-initiated. As you can also see, the people smoked and drank as they listened, and listened as they read silently. They listened for periods of time ranging from 1 to 6 minutes and read in 5-minute periods.

If you are interested in comparing the frequency with which different individuals *attend* in different ways or comparing the speed with which different individuals *attend*, you can tally with abbreviations for different individuals. The initials of the individuals can be used or numbers can be assigned to them.

In making copies of Observation Guide 3–1, it is important to fill in the line on top labeled "Setting" so that frequencies in different types of settings can be compared. How similar are the subcategories of *attend* in classes, offices, and homes? Specific information about different types and levels of classes also needs to be entered in copies of the guide. How similar are the subcategories of *attend* in classes at different levels of proficiency, composed of different age groups and designed to teach different skills?

To keep at 165 pounds, the most accurate and graphic way to check to see whether my present weight is congruent with this aim is to get on a scale. A scale and an observation guide are the same type of instrument. They each provide both a clear picture of the present state of affairs and at the same time suggest alternatives. But

OBSERVATION GUIDE 3–1A
How Many of What? (With Some Tallies)

Setting: a student lounge
Number of Participants: 14 If class, type and level: ____
Materials used: record player and magazines, cigarettes and drinks
Time observation began: 1:15 pm Time observation ended: 1:30 pm

Use *Attend* \ Move Type		Structuring	Responding
1. listening	(al)	as, at, at, as at. 120, 360, 60, 180 la + na, la + na	
2. silent reading	(ar)	al, al, al lv + nv, lv + nv 300, 300	
3. smelling	(as)		
4. tasting	(at)		
5. touching	(ah)		
6. viewing	(av)		
Use *Other*			30, 30, 60, 20 20, 20

while the scale provides only two alternatives—lose weight if the number 170 appears and gain weight if the number 160 appears, and since gaining weight is a less frequent aim than losing it, only one alternative is really offered. The observation guide for describing *attend*, however, provides numerous alternatives. First, the observation guide reminds us that we can alter the proportion of *attend* and *other* uses. And it reminds us that the subcategories of *attend* can be decreased or increased and that they can also be combined. If most of the tallies occur under the structuring column, we are reminded that we can set tasks for others in responses, rather than just letting them engage in the taking in of mediums on their own in structuring moves. Finally, we can see which mediums are attended to, at what rates, and by whom.

Journal Entry

If you are a smoker, note the times you have a cigarette. If you are not a smoker, note the times a person you know has a cigarette. Do the times coincide with times when there are no other mediums to *attend* to and when no other receptive activities are taking place? Or, do the times coincide with times when there are other mediums to *attend* to and other subcategories of *attend* are being engaged in?

Just One More Puff—A Rationale for Variety

Nine times out of ten, one consequence of breaking rules will be negative reactions from both teachers and students. Adult students may consider the taking in of mediums other than print and speech in the target language to be childish the first few times. And some young students may enjoy the taking in of mediums other than speech and print so much that they might consider it fun, not "educational." Students not used to listening to extended discourse over and over may at first rebel, especially if the material is delivered at the normal rate. They may say to themselves that if they want to listen to what they can't understand, they do so outside of class and therefore there is no reason to come to class.

It is critical to bear in mind that complaints are a normal part of any change. On the surface, such complaints may seem like a good reason to keep following the rules. But even out of class, many of the mediums we *attend* to become ritualized and we become totally unaware of what we are doing and therefore not sure of what we are failing to do. Breaking rules, because it does raise questions, helps us all look beyond preconceived notions of what the best ways to *attend* are, what the best proportions of *attend* and other uses are, what the best proportion of the different subcategories of *attend* are, what rates of delivery are best, and which combinations of mediums we need to *attend* to. And by looking at silent reading and listening in the same way we look at smoking cigarettes, which is just another subcategory of *attend* that I call *tasting*, it might become clearer why the purposes of attending are more varied than we often realize.

Just as smoking a cigarette can be a signal of the end of a meal, a sign of tension during an intense experience, or an aid in killing time, so silent reading and listening have more purposes than the usual one—to get information and help us learn. Silent reading on buses gives some an excuse not to talk, while others use a book like a cigarette to invite comments. Some are just waiting for someone to say "Oh, that book looks interesting. What's it about?" Others hope the book will serve to ward off any conversation. We can listen to a radio play or a song to relax, to escape or to puzzle out meaning, to pass time and feel a part of a larger group, as well as to seek information or improve our language. Reasons for listening, like reasons for smoking and other subcategories of *attend*, are varied, and as likely to be immediate and short term as well as long term. [Background 3–8]

As long as everything is totally predictable in any medium or subcategory of *attend*, no stretching is necessary on anybody's part. Of course, if no predictions are possible because too much new information is being taken in, frustration rather than stretching occurs. But outside class, one thing that helps us stretch rather than become frustrated is that we are forced to make predictions about the many mediums acting on all our senses. So if one prediction about a sound is frustrated, we have a scent, a taste, a scene, or some print to help us predict. And even if we are in a place where radio and television in the target language are not available, we still spend more time each day taking in mediums than producing them in most cases, so some altering of the proportions of in-class *attending* would make our out-of-class patterns more similar to our in-class patterns.

Three- and four-year-olds resist help, constantly commanding those around them to give them a chance. "I can do it alone," they shout. I hope describing the rules we follow when we read silently and listen in a range of settings and breaking the rules will decrease the frequency of headlines deploring the lack of reading skills and increase the frequency of occurrence of the statement "I can do it alone."

You Said Just One More—Other Episodes Related to This One

Though watching a person attend to a cigarette, book, concert, baseball game, sermon, or a drink provides us with some idea of how we take in mediums, we usually like to see what people produce as well. I treat the uses I have been calling *other* in some other episodes. For example, I treat oral reading and dictations in Episode 14. I explore the uses we often use with *attend* in Episode 10.

BACKGROUND NOTES

3–1. In a study of the time spent in various subjects and activities, Denham and Lieberman support my contention. Harris and Guthrie do too. Squire and Applebee in their description of English classes in American and British high schools not only describe common activities but show contrasts between the two countries. Rwakyaka describes reading lessons in Uganda in her dissertation and it is hard to know they are reading lessons except that they are called that; little silent reading is done. Shapiro-Skrobe found the same practices in elementary classes in New York City.

3–2. Within the field of language teaching, Palmer in the early 1900s advocated that more time be spent with listening. Billows echoed Palmer's plea in 1961, and Morley developed her listening text because of the need she felt to devote more attention to listening in ESL classes.

3–3. I once observed a teacher using *People in Livingston* with a group of adults living in Somalia. The adults were looking at the book with sad expressions. After class, the teacher explained that the students were not sad because they did not like the book. Rather, they were sad because they did indeed like the book, but they were due to finish the book in one more week. The students were sad because they felt they would not be able to enjoy the book anymore after they finished it. The development of characters that Virginia French Allen did so well in *People in Livingston* is done in a similar way by Bodman and Lanzano. The major difference between the two books is that *People in Livingston* treats people in a small town while *No Hot Water Tonight* treats people in a large city. They are both in the same tradition, however.

3–4. Watson's review of educational psychology and its contribution to classroom practice provides one source of support for the idea that associations can aid learning. Carrol's (1965) essay applies educational psychology to second-language learning in particular, and he too notes the value of associations.

3–5. In one of my favorite books, *Oh, What a Blow That Phantom Gave Me*, Edmund Carpenter points out that in tropical climates where people have recently achieved literacy, there are reports that people are very cold when they read, and that many people wear woolen hats when they read. He also reports that during World War II in England, two types of workers got extra rations: laborers and those who had to read all day long. Carpenter has written about many of the ideas that McLuhan has popularized. Like McLuhan, Carpenter is interested in the effects different mediums have on our perception.

3–6. An article on the variability of rate of conversation was written by Goldman-Eisler in 1954. In 1968 David Orr edited a special issue of the *Journal of Communication* devoted to compressed speech. In this issue, a number of separate investigators report similar conclusions about the effect on comprehension of increasing the rate at which speech is delivered. These articles, of course, treat the rate with native speakers of the language, not nonnative speakers. Jonas in an article on stuttering, points out the crucial role played by the rate of delivery.

3–7. Mackey developed an electronic device for tallying multiple characteristics of communications at the same time. While the purpose of tallying is a means to an end rather than an end in itself, and an electronic device might distract us from this fact, it would seem that easing the actual tallying would provide more time to analyze the data, and so moving beyond a pencil might be a great boon.

3–8. Frank Smith (1971) and Kenneth Goodman (1973) advocate that we spend more time having students read silently if we want them to read their own language. They also argue that teachers and adults should read more to children so that they have more opportunities to take in language before they are expected to read language silently. Gibson and Levin in their review of research in the teaching of reading to native speakers also urge that people be given more time to take in print. Among those who write about the teaching of listening to nonnative speakers, Gary (1981) captures the current movement in the field with the title of an article advocating listening: "Caution: Talking May Be Dangerous to Your Linguistic Health." It seems that in the 1980s we are urging that we return to 1918 and do what Palmer said we should do, spend great amounts of time taking in mediums.

EPISODE

4

Could I Ask You a Couple of Questions?

I. SURE—INTRODUCTION AND PURPOSE

"Could I ask you a couple of questions" might be associated in your mind with reporters, opinion pollsters, lawyers, detectives, doctors during examinations or bureaucrats at customs, tax or social welfare offices. But a moment's reflection reminds us that asking "a couple of questions" is as central to the teacher's role as to those of other professionals. Research in classroom interaction confirms what a moment's reflection reminds us: In all school subjects, the most frequent teacher communication is a *solicit*. Whether a class is being taught or an individual, whether the students are young or old, in a regular classroom, repair shop, hotel lobby, photography lab or dance studio, on the street or at a computer terminal or at a desk with a programmed text, solicits usually occupy from one-third to one-half of the communications. In short, as teachers, one of the rules we follow is to solicit a great deal. [Background 4–1]

Since the purpose of solicits is to get others to respond, some rules about solicits can be discovered by exploring responses. In this episode, we will do just that. In particular, in Section II, I will treat the uses *characterize, present, relate*, and *set* in responses. We will explore how we use mediums to *characterize* in responses every time we indicate that communications in solicits are the same or different, right or wrong, true or false. In addition, we will explore how we *characterize* in responses by noting the size or shape of communications, by using category names such as *adverb*, or by giving short definitions.

We will explore how we use mediums to *present* in responses by noting responses that require only that we state information directly or ask questions, either ones we know the answer to or don't. And we will explore how we *relate* in responses every time we are asked to make an inference or a generalization. Finally, we will explore how we can use mediums to *set* content by noting that in responses we can provide examples or models that are used by others to perform other uses on.

Since the same uses make up the basic components of solicits, I treat them in solicits as well in Section III. In short, the purpose of this episode is twofold: First, to treat uses in responses that are not covered in other episodes: *characterize, present, relate*, and *set*. Second, to treat these same uses in solicits. By treating uses in solicits, I will show how the difficulty of responses and mental activity required in responses can be varied even when the same category of use is expected in the response. Without knowing how to vary the uses in solicits, the six types of uses possible in responses would lack the variety that we in fact can observe in a range of settings.

In short, this episode is essentially about the uses *characterize, present, relate*, and *set* in responses and solicits. Graphically, I note these characteristics in Table 4–1. As you can see, I've included the source and target of communication and move type as well, because in order to explore how the moves are made, we need to identify the moves. But the major emphasis in this episode is on the uses in the fourth column.

If you are interested in responses that require only that mediums be taken in, go to Episode 3, where I treat *attend*. If you are interested in responses that require others to take in mediums by attending and produce mediums by guessing or making inferences, go to Episode 10, where I treat *attend* together with some subcategories of *characterize* and *relate* in reading and listening lessons.

If you are interested in copying, tracing, substitution drills, controlled composition and other responses that require that mediums be *reproduced* in the same medium they were communicated in in the solicit, go to Episode 17. And if you are interested in mediums that are *reproduced* in a different medium in the response from the one set in the solicit, as when we change the medium of print to speech in oral reading, and change the medium of speech to print in a dictation, go to Episode 14.

TABLE 4–1
Mainly the Fourth Column

Source/Target	*Move Type*	*Use**	
		characterize	*c*
teacher			
	solicit		
		present	*p*
student			
		relate	*r*
	response		
other			
		set	*s*

* *Characterize* = communicating attributes by indicating items are the same or different or right or wrong; noting size or shape of items, qualities things have or giving category labels to items; *present* = stating information directly and asking questions, either those we know the answer to or those we don't; *relate* = making inferences or generalizations; *set* = giving examples or models to perform uses on.

II. *C*, *P*, *R*, AND *S*—USES IN RESPONSES

Has a ____*Characterize*

C—Definition and Examples of Characterize

Whenever we set a task that requires someone to use speech, print, gestures or other mediums to communicate qualities of anything, I code the responses *characterize*. In a game of bridge, for example, if I ask my friend what he has in his hand, and he says he has "one heart," he is *characterizing* his hand since "one heart" stands for a combination of different cards, and does not mean literally that the player is holding only one card in the heart suit. If I asked my friend to state the cards he had, and he said, "My hand is made up of the four of hearts, the queen of hearts, the ace of spades, etc.," he would not be *characterizing* his hand, but stating directly what his hand contained, or *presenting*. [Background 4–2]

We also *characterize* in responses when we cannot remember the name of a person or the name of an object. "Herb, what was the name of the mailman who served this route for so many years?" asks the wife. And Herb responds, "You mean the one who was so friendly? Yeah, he had nice black hair, and he was always here early." When we forget the names of tools, we often tell the person asking for the name what the tools do. "Oh—can't remember the name now, but you know they can grip a screw like a vise, and you hold them in your hands; they are usually about 8 inches long." Both these extended descriptions are examples of *characterizing*.

I've provided some examples of responses I'd code *characterize* in Excerpt 4–1. All the moves are related to excerpts from *It done begin*, a pidgin version of Genesis. You'll be happy to know that by the end of the episode you'll reach the fall, when you might be in about the same mood Adam and Eve were in at that fateful time. I have indicated the communications I'd code *characterize* in responses with a *c* in the use column. Those in the negative are underlined to indicate that fact. The blank lines next to items in the Move Type column will be referred to later in the episode. At the end of the excerpt, you'll see coding done by others; ignore it all for now.

Characterizing Content Differently—Definition and Examples of Subcategories of Characterize

Binary Choices—Indicating Sameness and Correctness

As you noticed reading through Excerpt 4–1, not all the responses coded *characterize* require the same type of attributes in the responses. Those preceded by yes/no or either/or questions require only verification or negation of the information in the solicit, while those preceded by question-word questions require that attributes be communicated in the response. Yes/no and either/or questions require us to *characterize* in responses by making choices, whereas question-word questions require us to *characterize* in response by communicating attributes, or showing qualities an item has.

Those yes/no or either/or questions that require a person responding to indicate that communications are the same or different I code in a subcategory I call *differentiate*, *cd* for short. The response to "Do these rhyme? *fish—dis*" in line 58 is one example of a response I code *cd*. The classic minimal pair drill, "Are these the same or different, *lamp—lump*?" also requires a response in the subcategory *differentiate*.

EXCERPT 4–1
Using Mediums to Characterize in Responses

		Communications	*Source/ Target*	*Move Type**	*Use*
1	Teacher:	(Standing at the side of the class of students; they are turned to the side to	t/c	___ str	
2		face the teacher.) Now that we've read the first part of Genesis in pidgin from the blackboard, I'm going to ask a few questions. You can look at the board if you want, but first try without looking.			
3		(These sentences are on the blackboard in front of the room.)			
3a		It done begin			
3b		An de Lawd, He done go work hard for			
3c		make all ting dey call um Earth. For six day de Lawd He work an he make all			
3d		ting—everyting He go put for Earth. Plenty			
3e		beef, plenty cassava, plenty banana, plenty			
3f		yam, plenty guinea corn, plenty mango,			
3g		plenty groundnut—everyting. An for de			
3h		wata He put plenty fish, and for de air He			
3i		put plenty kinda bird. After six day de Lawd He done go sleep. An when He			
3j		sleep, plenty palaver start for dis place dey callum Heaven. Dis Heaven be place where			
3k		we go live after we done die, if we no been so-so bad for dis Earth.			
3l		De headman of dem angels, dey call um Gabriel. When dis palaver start for Heaven			
3m		dere be plenty humbug by bad angel, dey call um Lucifer. An Gabriel done catch			
3n		Lucifer an go beat um. An palaver stop, one time. And de Lawd tell Gabriel he be			
3o		good man too much and He go dash Gabriel one trumpet. An Lucifer go for			
3p		hellfire where he be headman now. —From John Gunther, *Inside Africa*			
4	Teacher:	Is cassava a place to live?	t/c	___ sol	
5	Student$_1$:	No.	s/t	res	c
6		It's food.			
7	Teacher:	Where is the stress in the word *palaver*?	t/c	___ sol	
8	Student$_1$:	On the second syllable.	s_1/t	res	c
9	Teacher:	How many syllables in *palaver*?	t/c	___ sol	
10	Student$_1$:	Three.	s_1/t	res	c
11	Teacher:	Which one is good?	t/c	___ sol	
12		(Holds up a picture of Lucifer and Gabriel.)			

EXCERPT 4–1 (*continued*)

		Communications	*Source/ Target*	*Move Type**	*Use*
13	Student$_2$:	(Points to Gabriel.)	s$_2$/t	res	c
14	Teacher:	Was Lucifer always bad?	t/c	______ sol	
15	Student$_2$:	No.	s$_2$/t	res	c
16		Only after he started the palaver.			
17	Teacher:	Did "de Lawd" dash Gabriel one trumpet?	t/c	______ sol	
18	Student$_1$:	Yes.	s$_1$/t	res	c
19	Teacher:	Which one is a trumpet?	t/c	______ sol	
20		(Holds up a trumpet and a bugle.)			
21	Student$_1$:	(Points to the smaller one without valves.)	s$_1$/t	res	c
22	Teacher:	Is the structure of this passage and the play we read the same?	t/c	______ sol	
23	Student$_3$:	No.	s$_3$/t	res	c
24		The play had acts and characters.			
25	Teacher:	Listen to this sentence.	t/s	______ sol	
26		*An palaver stop, one time.*			
27	Class:	(Listen to the sentence.)	c/t	res	attend listen
28	Teacher:	Now, Jericho, circle the item on the board that means the same thing:			
29		(On the board: a. The fighting stopped for good. b. There was just a pause in the fighting.)			
30	Jericho:	(Circles *a.* on the blackboard.)	s/t	res	c
31	Teacher:	Now, listen to some examples and when I say something in pidgin, say *one*. And when I say something in English, say *two*.	t/c	______ sol	
32	Teacher:	And the Lord.			
33	Student$_1$:	Two.	s$_1$/t	res	c
34	Teacher:	Which statement does this go with: *after six day*?	t/c	______ sol	
35		*de Lawd he work—de Lawd He done go sleep*			
36	Student$_1$:	The second one.	s$_1$/t	res	c
37	Teacher:	Diagram this sentence to show it has two meanings: *He go dash Gabriel one trumpet.*	t/c	______ sol	

EXCERPT 4–1 (*continued*)

		Communications	*Source/ Target*	*Move Type**	*Use*
39	Students:	(Diagram sentence to show two meanings.)	c/t	res	c
40	Teacher:	Draw an arrow to connect *He* and *ting* to the words they refer to.	t/c	_____ sol	
41		(Passage on the board is one at beginning of episode.)			
42	Student$_1$:	(Comes to the board and draws an arrow from *He* to *Lawd* in the first sentence.)	s_1/t	res	c
43	Student$_2$:	(Goes to the board and draws an arrow from *He* before *sleep* in the second paragraph to *Lawd*.)	s_2/t	res	c
44	Teacher:	Which one is a groundnut?	t/c	_____ sol	
45		(Holds up a groundnut and a cashew.)			
46	Student$_3$:	(Goes up and takes the groundnut.)	s_3/t	res	c
47	Teacher:	Which is the sound of a crunched groundnut?	t/c	_____ sol	
48		(Crunches up a groundnut and then a leaf.)			
49	Student$_3$:	The first one.	s_3/t	res	c
50		It sounds louder.			
51	Teacher:	Now, define *groundnut.*	t/c	_____ sol	
52	Student$_1$:	Small than a cashew.	s_1/t	res	c
53	Student$_2$:	Makes loud noise when you squeeze it.	s_2/t	res	c
54	Student$_3$:	Grows in the ground.	s_3/t	res	c
55	Teacher:	What part of speech is *groundnut*?	t/c	_____ sol	
56	Student$_1$:	A noun.	s_1/t	res	c
57	Teacher:	Do these rhyme? *fish—dis*	t/c	_____ sol	
58	Student$_2$:	Yes.	s_2/t	res	c
59	Teacher:	Are the initial sounds of these words pronounced the same in the variety of English you just heard?	t/c	_____ sol	
60		*thing—the*			
61	Student$_3$:	No.	s_3/t	res	c
62		They are different in English too.			
63	Teacher:	Are the yams mentioned in the passage the same or different from the yams many people in North America eat for Thanksgiving?	t/s	_____ sol	

EXCERPT 4–1 *(continued)*

		Communications	*Source/ Target*	*Move Type**	*Use*
64	Student$_1$:	Different.	s_1/t	res	c
65		They are orange—those in Africa are white.			
66	Teacher:	Now, here is a childish thing to do. Take these letters and put them in the empty slots.	t/c	______ sol	
67		(Red and white plastic letters ¼-inch high are lying on the desk together with some stencils that the plastic letters fit in.)			
68	Students:	(Fit the red letters in the stencil that reads Lucifer and the white letters in the stencil that contains the spaces for Gabriel.)	c/t	res	c

Coding done by others:

Subcategories of *characterize*: 5. ce underlined to show negative; 8. cx; 10. cx; 13. ce; 15. ce; 18. ce; 21. ce; 23. cd; 30. cd; 33. cl, two is used as a label for English; 36. ce; 39. cx_1 and cx_2—the subscripts show that two analyses of the sentence were performed; 42. cx; 43. cx; 46. ce; 49. ce; 52. ci; 53. ci; 54. ci; 56. cl; 58. cd; 61. cd; 64. cd; 68. ce.

Identification and coding of messages: 4. Is . . .? pe, cassava so, a place to live ci, a partial definition. 6. It's food cl since the student is using *food* as a category. 7. Where is the stress in the word . . .? pe, palaver, so; 9. How many syllables in . . .? pe, palaver so. 11. Which one is . . . pe, good ce, picture of Lucifer se_1, picture of Gabriel se_2*—the asterisk indicates a contrast. 14. Was . . .? pe, always ci; bad ce underlined to show *bad* is negative; Lucifer so, sentence in passage information refers to ss. 16. Only after he started the palaver ps or if you think these words indicate some type of inference, ri. 17. Did . . .? pe "de Lawd" dash Gabriel one trumpet ps, sentence in passage with information question refers to ss. 19. Which one is . . .? pe, a trumpet ps, actual trumpet se_1, actual bugle se_2*—asterisk shows a contrasting example, the same cd. 22. Is the structure of this passage we read and . . .? pe, actual passage sx_1, actual play referred to sx_2*—the asterisk indicates a contrast, the same cd. 24. The play had acts and characters ci. 25. Listen to this sentence pe, An palaver stop, one time ss. 28. Now ps, Jericho ps, circle the item on the board that means pe, the same thing cd, the fighting stopped for good ss_1, there was just a pause in the fighting ss_2*, a ps_1, b ps_2, sentences just heard ss_1—the same subscript is used to show that one set in the solicit matches another set in the solicit. 31. Now ps, listen to some examples and when I say . . . say . . . and when I say . . . say . . . pe, pidgin and one cl_1, English and two cl_2*. 32. And the Lord sp_2*—asterisked to show that it matches the label English and two, also marked with the subscript $_2$. 34. Which statement does this . . . pe, go with (meaning is correct with) ce, after six day sp_1. 35. de Lawd he work ss_2*, de Lawd He done go sleep ss_1, the sentence in the text related to the right matching, ss_1. 37. Diagram this sentence pe, to show it has two meanings ci, He go dash Gabriel one trumpet ss. 40. Draw an arrow to connect . . . and . . . to the words they refer to pe, He, ting ps, passage on the board sx. 44. Which one is a . . .? pe, groundnut ps, actual groundnut se_1, actual cashew se_2*. 47. Which is the sound of . . . pe, a crunched groundnut ps, crunching groundnut se_1, crunching leaf se_2*. 50. It sounds louder ci. 51. Now ps, define . . . pe, groundnut so. 55. What part of speech is . . .? pe, groundnut so. 57. Do these . . . pe, rhyme cd, fish so_1, fish so_2*. 59. Are the . . . of these words pronounced . . .? pe, initial sounds cx, the same cd, in the variety of English you just heard ci, thing so_1, the so_2*. 62. re if you consider the added comment an attempt to generalize or explain the *no* in the response. 63. Are the . . . mentioned in the passage . . . pe, the same cd, or different cd, yams ps_1, mentioned in the passage ci_1, yams ps_2* many people in North America eat for Thanksgiving ci_2*, passage where yams are mentioned sx_2. 65. They are orange ci_1, those in Africa are white and bigger ci_2*. 66. Now ps, here is a childish thing to do ci, take these letters and put them in the empty slots pe, red letters sl_1, white letters sl_2, stencil of Lucifer ps_1, stencil of Gabriel ps_2.

Solicit types: 4, 5; 7, 3; 9, 3; 11, 9; 14, 5; 17, 7; 19, 11; 22, 9; 25, 3; 31, 9; 34, 9; 37, 3; 40, 3; 44, 11; 47, 11; 51, 3; 55, 3; 57, 5; 59, 5; 63, 5; 66, 11.

Comprehensive coding with the givens in parentheses:

5 s res la ce I (la pe ce + la so I + la ci II)

EXCERPT 4–1 (*continued*)

6 s res la cl l (same as for 5 but this part of the response was not solicited and as a result some may consider it a reaction rather than part of the response solicited)
8 s res la cx lsp (la pe cx + la so lsp)
10 s res la cx lsp (la pe cx + la so lsp)
13 s res pv ce l (la pe ce + la ce lu + nv se_1 lu + nv se_2^* lu)
15 s res la ce l (la pe ce + la ci lu + la ce lu)
16 s res la ps lu or la ri lu (same as for 15 but this part of the response was not solicited and as a result some may consider it a reaction rather than part of the response solicited)
18 s res la ce lu (la pe ce + la ps lu + lv ss lu)
21 s res pv ce ll (la pe ce + la ps ll + nv se_1 ll + nv se_2^* ll)
23 s res la ce lj (la pe ce + lv sx_1lj + lv sx_2^*lj + la cd lj)
24 s res la ci lj (if you consider this a response rather than a reaction, the givens are the same as for line 23)
26 s res la al lu (la pe al + la ss lu)
30 s res nv cd lu (la ps pt + la ps pn + la pe cd + la cd lu + la ss_1 lu + lv ss_1 lu + lv ss_2^* lu + lv ps_1 p + lv ps_2 p)
33 s res la cl ld (la ps pt + la pe cl + la cl_1 ld + la cl_2^* ld + la sp_2^* ld)
36 s res la ce lu (la pe ce + la ce lu + la sp_1 lu + la ss_2^* lu + la ss_1 lu)
39 s res nv + lv cx lu (la pe cx + la ci lx + la ss lu) This task also requires that speech be changed to print so the student has to reproduce and change the medium: *dc* as well as *characterize examine*; it is hard to pinpoint the content here as in many of the previous responses and solicits and so again I note that the task requires unspecified study of language because more than three areas of language could be involved.
42 s res nv cx lt (la pe cx + la ps_1 lt + la ps_2 lt + lv sx lu)
43 s res nv cx lt (la pe cx + la ps_1 lt + la ps_2 lt + lv sx lu)
46 s res nv ce ll (la pe ce + la ps ll + nv se_1 ll + nv se_2^*ll)
49 s res la ce lu (la pe ce + la ps lu + na se_1 lu + na se_2^*lu)
50 s rea la ci lu (the givens are the same if you consider this a reponse rather than a reaction)
52 s_1 res la cixll (la pe p? since any number of uses could define; + la so ll + la ps pt—Now)
53 s_2 res la ci ll (same givens)
54 s_3 res la ci ll (same givens)
56 s res la cl lx or lz (la pe cl + la so lx or lz)
58 s res la cd lsg (la pe cd + la cd lsg + la so_1 lsg + la so_2^* lsg)
61 s res la cd lsg (la pe cd + la cx pe + la cd lsg + la ci ld + la so_1 lsg + la so_2^* lsg)
62 s rea la re lsg (same givens if you consider this a response and not a reaction)
64 s res la cd lwa (la pe cd + la cd lwa + la cd lwa + la ps_1 lwa + la ci_2 pe + la ps_2^*lu + la ci_2^* + lv sx_1 lu)
65 s rea la ci_1 lwa (same givens if you consider this a response and not a reaction)
65 s rea la ci_2^* lwa (same givens if you consider this a response and not a reaction)
68 s res po ce lm (la ps pt + la ci fp + la pe ce + nv sl_1 lm + nv sl_2 lm + nv ps_1 lm + nv ps_2lm)

The solicit "Was Lucifer always bad?" in line 14 requires verification in the response rather than an indication of sameness. I code such responses *ce* for *characterize evaluate* because the person posing such questions is seeking verification of a proposition. Since a response to an either/or question, such as "Which one is good?" in reference to pictures of Gabriel and Lucifer in line 11 is simply another way of finding out whether a person can verify the proposition given, using two choices rather than one in a yes/no question, I code responses to either/or questions that require verification *ce* as well. I code responses in multiple-choice tests *ce* too, since these solicits require choices.

When we indicate something is correct or incorrect in a response, I code the use *ce* too. Indicating correctness is just another way of verifying, of indicating in most cases that some aspect of the form of a communication is right or wrong rather than the meaning. Had the teacher asked students whether any individual response had been right or wrong, the responses indicating whether they had been right or wrong would be coded *ce*.

Questions such as "Do you understand?" or "Do you like cassava?" do not require verification or an indication of correctness, so I do not code responses to these solicits *characterize evaluate*. One way to distinguish solicits that are in the form of yes/no or either/or questions, but do not require verification from those that do, is to try using the verbs in the questions with *-ing*. We cannot say "Are you understanding?" or "Are you liking cassava?" Also, questions that are seeking information, such as "Do you understand?" or "Do you like cassava?" cannot at the same time be asking for verification. Responses to these information-seeking questions in the form of yes/no or either/or questions I code *present*, a category I treat right after we finish *characterize*.

Explicit Information—Indicating Size or Shape, Classifying, and Defining

Though the bulk of the examples of Excerpt 4–1 consist of yes/no or either/or questions that require responses in which binary choices are made, coded *cd* or *ce*, responses coded *characterize* are not limited to indicating that items are the same or different and correct or incorrect and true or false. The explicit information communicated about content by diagramming sentences and by indicating the size or shape of words or other communications I code *characterize examine*, *cx* for short. The word *examine* implies searching for attributes an item has. The particular attributes I code in this subcategory have to do with size or shape and are usually expressed with numbers. "On the second syllable" in line 8 in response to "Where is the stress in the word *palaver*?" is one example of *characterize* in the subcategory *examine*: *cx*.

When we indicate that a model, example, or item—*set*—has attributes that do not fit neatly into the subcategory *examine*, I put them in a subcategory I call *illustrate*, *ci* for short. The partial definitions of *groundnut* in lines 52 to 54 I code *ci* because they illustrate qualities a groundnut has without naming the food. A response to a solicit such as "What did you think of *Superman II*?" in which a person says "It had a lot of action," I code *ci* as well, since the comment clearly is stating an attribute a person feels the movie has, yet the person is not evaluating the movie and so the comment cannot be *ce*.

Another way we show attributes is to give category names to items. Indicating that *is* is an auxiliary verb, *the* an article or *a* a lower-case letter would all be examples of responses I'd code *cl* for *characterize label*. The grouping of items in categories is a central feature of all learning. [Background 4–3]

Journal Entry

Outside of classes, we are faced with many questions that force us to make decisions: the classic "Coffee, tea or milk?" on flights, the "french-fried, baked or mashed?" in restaurants, the "smoking or nonsmoking" at plane and some train check-ins, the "guilty or not guilty?" of the courtroom. In addition to these questions which force choices, we are asked for our phone numbers countless times, whether we want to rent a car or room or when we call to make a flight reservation, and our marital status when we apply for credit cards.

How do you feel about being bombarded with so many questions? Do you accept it as a matter of course? Do you think that in fact we are not bombarded with questions? Do you wonder what is done with the responses to so many questions being asked every day all over the world? Do you think the predictable questions we face each day help things move efficiently, hamper dialog between citizens, or have some other consequence?

To summarize the subcategories of *characterize*, I've called Table 4–2 Different Ways of *Characterizing*. To better understand the subcategories of *characterize*, go back to Excerpt 4–1 and add abbreviations for the subcategories of *characterize* to the responses coded *c*. Use the abbreviations in Table 4–2: *d* for *differentiate, e* for *evaluate, x* for *examine, i* for *illustrate*, and *l* for *label*. The coding of the subcategories done by others is shown below Excerpt 4–1.

As you can see, the subcategories of *characterize* are arranged in alphabetical order in Table 4–2. However, the order also reflects a sequence I think we might follow in much of what we learn. A common first step in learning anything new is distinguishing it from what we already know or from things around what we are learning. In short, a first step is often indicating whether something is the same or different from something else, or *differentiating*. A next step is often trying to verify whether the information we are exposed to is true or false, or *evaluating*.

To aid us in determining whether something is the same as something else or true, we often look at the attributes an item we are learning has: its size or shape—*examine*—or more general attributes—*illustrate*. Finally, we classify the new bit of information, putting it in the mental filing cabinet in our heads with other items it is similar to as the result of certain attributes it has. To put it another way, we often *differentiate, evaluate, examine, illustrate*, and *label* in this order in processing new information. When something does not fit in the category we put it in, we go back and look at attributes it has and then go back and compare and contrast it with other examples. [Background 4–4]

TABLE 4–2
Different Ways of *Characterizing**

characterize	*c*	Communicating attributes about communications; indicating a "has a" relationship.
differentiate	*cd*	Indicating that items are the same or different.
evaluate	*ce*	Indicating that items are correct or incorrect; verifying or negating the truth of something; *not* stating information directly.
examine	*cx*	Diagramming sentences; indicating the number of syllables, words, or larger units in words, sentences, or paragraphs; analyzing words by spelling them; dividing words or other units into smaller units; indicating anything about the size or shape of words or other communications.
illustrate	*ci*	Giving partial definitions of words and indicating attributes that do not fit neatly in any of the other subcategories.
label	*cl*	Using labels or names of categories to group items or to classify them.

* The extra space between *cd* and *ce* on the one hand and *cx, ci,* and *cl* on the other is provided to highlight the fact that *cd* and *ce* require only choices, whereas *cx, ci,* and *cl* require that attributes be communicated.

To Characterize Content Differently or Not—Exploring the Subcategories of Characterize

It Starts with f*—Advantages and Disadvantages of Characterizing*

When people I've been introduced to forget my name and ask me to say it again, I respond "It starts with *f*," rather than "Fanselow." I *cx* it in the response. I find it easier to recall things when I'm given attributes an item I'm asking about has rather than the thing itself. Of course, saying "It starts with *f*" breaks a rule, a rule that in my experience is so strong that even when I ask people to say the first letter of their name rather than their name so I can more readily remember the name, most people present their name rather than an attribute their name has, such as the letter it begins with.

Soliciting responses that require *characterize evaluate* breaks a rule too, in most classrooms anyway. Responses coded *characterize evaluate* occur less than 5 percent of the time in most classes studied. Yet in most of these same classes where yes/no and either/or questions requiring verification are almost nonexistent, we give multiple-choice tests, instruments that contain nothing but solicits which require students to *characterize evaluate* in every response. [Background 4–5]

Of course, we can think of reasons to support the rules we normally follow in classes—the rules that require us to avoid subcategories of *characterize* in responses, especially *evaluate*. A common argument against soliciting responses I code *characterize evaluate* has been that the right responses can be guessed. Personally, I consider this one of the critical reasons for expanding their frequency, should their frequency be small in classes, tests, or texts you are involved with. Guessing is just another word for expressions such as "making predictions," "floating hypotheses," and other like-worded mental operations that are the basis of development in most fields and in much learning.

Evaluating requires the type of binary choice we make every day outside classrooms. When we try to open a door by turning the doorknob to the left and find no movement, we turn it to the right. If the door still fails to open, we try pushing it; and if this fails too, we try pulling it. Most computers are designed to make binary choices. But fantastic as they are in processing millions of bits of information in very small amounts of time, they have yet to prove as versatile as our minds in making wide ranges of binary choices. At any rate, it seems that if we have a chance to provide students with an opportunity to do in class what billions of dollars are devoted to design computers to do, we should at least try the alternative. [Background 4–6]

Another objection to yes/no questions that require us to *ce* in responses is that the responses require only one word—*yes* or *no*. And in games such as twenty questions in which we are trying to eliminate thousands of possibilities to arrive at a correct answer quickly, we are likely to say only *yes* or *no*, as lines 18 and 58 of Excerpt 4–1 illustrate. In a series of written responses to yes/no questions, we are likely to circle only *yes* or *no* or write only one of the two words as well. But when we are given more than a few seconds before another solicit is made after we respond *no*, a rule we normally follow is to explain the *no* in our response. This is one reason lawyers and judges constantly have to tell witnesses to limit their responses to a simple *no*, to a one-word response. Lines 15, 23, and 61 illustrate the rule that a *characterize evaluate* represented by a *no* is likely to be followed by many words, more than the one-word responses produced by question-word questions in solicits, such as "What's this?" The teacher's

"Answer in a complete sentence" plea after the one-word responses to question-word questions stands in sharp contrast to the judge's plea for witnesses to limit their responses to yes/no questions to "Just one word."

It is hard to object to the length of responses to either/or questions that require a *ce* in the response, because when responding to either/or questions, we tend to restate one of the choices given. The length of the choices governs the length of the responses, rather than the question type. Thus, if I were to ask "When you found the money, were you walking with relatives carrying books on their backs and bags in their hands, or relatives carrying suitcases in their hands and babies on their backs?" you'd have to respond with 10 words. If I were to ask you whether you were holding "a book in your hand now or a typewriter," you'd have to answer with 2 words, the article *a* plus the noun *book* or *typewriter*. Even this two-word response will be an improvement over the responses to many question-word questions, since a response by a nonnative speaker of English to "What's this?" is more likely to be "book" than "a book." At any rate, either/or questions can be used to produce responses of variable length without the admonition to "answer in a complete sentence," since a rule we usually follow is to restate one of the choices in a response to an either/or question.

Another argument against yes/no or either/or questions is that the information required is provided in the solicit. This of course is one of the beauties of either/or or yes/no questions. They provide information! Consequently, they can teach and test simultaneously. When I say "What's this?" all the information must come from the person responding. When I say "Is this a three-legged chair or a four-legged chair?" or "Is this a three-legged chair?" the person knows the word that fits the object, whether the response itself is right or wrong. If I am in fact holding a three-legged chair and the person says "four-legged" or "no," I will say "wrong," and the person knows just as much as if "three-legged" or "yes" were the response.

Finally, some suggest that yes/no, either/or and multiple-choice questions are unable to provide students with any experience with complex mental processes. But as we will see when we explore components of solicits in the third part of this episode, the uses that we verify or negate in yes/no or choice questions are not limited. In a response, one can verify or negate a rule another has given in a solicit. We can *evaluate* a communication in the solicit in the category *relate*. Or we can verify labels provided in solicits, as in a response to "Is *am* an auxiliary verb?" In this case we would be evaluating explicit information about language that I code *characterize label*. To put it another way, we can *evaluate* explicit information and qualities an item has in solicits—components I'd code *cd, ce, ex, ci*, or *cl*; rules, generalizations, and inferences—components I'd code *r* for *relate*; as well as direct information—components I'd code *p* for *present*. When those who control the launching of rockets are asked to make their final decision about launching or not launching, they simply say "Fire" or "Abort," another way of saying yes or no. This instance of *characterize evaluate* is hardly a simple mental operation. [Background 4–7]

Out of 1,458 responses I tallied during two days of observing classes, 66 percent required uses other than *characterize*, and 33 percent required the use *characterize*. This was at a time when I was coding the responses to any yes/no questions *characterize evaluate*, including "Do you understand?" so the 33 percent is inflated. Responses to "Do you understand?" are coded *present state*. Other studies show even lower frequencies of responses in the category of use *characterize*. In one of the courtroom scenes in the movie *Witness for the Prosecution*, I found almost the exact mirror image of uses required in responses that I found in classrooms. Out of 95 responses in the courtroom scene, 78 percent required the use *characterize* and only 22 percent required other uses. [Background 4–8]

Journal Entry

As language teachers, many of us think of some subcategories of *characterize* only in terms of certain areas of content. For example, the first thing that comes to many language teachers' minds when they see *differentiate* is a minimal pair drill which requires us to combine *differentiate* with sound.

In mathematics classes, balancing equations fits *differentiate*. And in police work, matching fingerprints or marks on spent bullets fits *differentiate*. Other combinations and content and subcategories of *characterize* will also come to your mind.

Does thinking of different combinations change your view of the difficulty level of, say, a minimal pair drill? Or do you see indicating items as the same or different differently as a result of thinking of *differentiating* different areas of content from, say, the sound system?

Is a _____—*Present*

Presenting *Content—Definitions and Examples of* Present

When we ask someone to use mediums to state facts, recall information, agree, give permission, promise, assert a point of view, or ask questions with either these or other purposes, I code the responses *p* for *present.* Such information, assertions, promises, and so on in statement form I code *ps* for *present state.* When the information, assertions, and so on are in question form, I code them *pe, pq,* or *p?* for *present elicit, present query,* or *present question.*

The difference between the *pe, pq,* and *p?* subcategories is that *pe* refers to commands, requests, or questions that display language or other areas of study for their own sake or solicits others to display study for its own sake. Asking questions we know the answers to is a common communication I code *pe*. Questions that explore reality, seek to solve a problem, or seek new information I code *pq* for *present query.* When questions do not fit nicely into the subcategories *pe* or *pq*, I code them *p?*. This subcategory indicates both that the communication is a question and that as coders we question the subcategory of *present* it belongs in. Some of the questions that consistently fit the *p?* subcategory are those that are open-ended and indicate neither that a specific task is to be performed nor that a specific area of content is to be communicated. "Say something about the story" I'd code *p?*, since any type of response is possible, and *life*, *procedure*, or *study* could be communicated in the response. "Could you help me?" I'd also code *p?*, since the response could be providing help of different sorts, looking more carefully at what the person asking is doing to see what help seems needed, or even a "Yes, I'll try" or "I'm sorry, I'm busy."

Excerpt 4–2 contains examples of the subcategories of *present*. As you can see, I've coded each response with two subcategories of *present*. Only one of them fits the communication. Circle the one you think fits. Selections others have made are shown below the excerpt. The solicits and responses all refer to *It done begin*. The blank lines next to the Move Type column will be returned to later in this episode.

EXCERPT 4–2
Present

		Communications	*Source/ Target*	*Move Type*	*Use*	
1	Teacher:	Give me a verb from the passage.	t/c	____ sol		
2	Student:	*Savvy.*	s/t	res	ps	pe
3	Teacher:	Now, each of you write a sentence using *savvy.*	t/c	____ sol		
4	Student$_1$:	(Writes "I savvy the word *verb.*")	s_1/t	res	ps	pe
5	Student$_2$:	(Writes "Would you explain *savvy*?")	s_2/t	res	pe	pq
6	Teacher:	Give me a synonym for *savvy.*	t/c	____ sol		
7	Student$_1$:	*Understand.*	s_1/t	res	pe	ps
8	Teacher:	We read the story yesterday. It's still on the board. But when I ask the following questions, I'd like you to try to look at me rather than the passage. Only look if you can't remember at all.	t/c	str		
9	Teacher:	I want you to tell me the part you thought was the funniest.	t/c	____ sol		
10	Student$_1$:	The fight.	s_1/t	res	pe	ps
11	Student$_2$:	Getting the trumpet.	s_2/t	res	pe	ps
12	Teacher:	Name some foods that were mentioned in the story.	t/c	____ sol		
13	Student$_1$:	Yams.	s_1/t	res	ps	pe
14	Student$_2$:	Cassava.	s_1/t	res	ps	pe
15	Teacher:	Who was Lucifer?	t/c	____ sol		
16	Student$_3$:	The bad guy.	s_3/t	res	ps	pe
17	Teacher:	Who was Gabriel?	t/c	____ sol		
18	Student$_4$:	The good guy.	s_4/t	res	ps	pe
19	Teacher:	Say some other things about the story.	t/c	____ sol		
20	Student$_1$:	I like it.	s_1/t	res	ps	pe
21	Student$_2$:	My mom read it to me in English	s_2/t	res	ps	pe
22	Student$_3$:	Why did we read it?	s_3/t	res	pq	p?
23	Student$_4$:	I don't understand all the words.	s_4/t	res	ps	pe
24	Student$_5$:	I can't pronounce some words the way they're spelled.	s_5/t	res	ps	p?
25	Teacher:	For homework, I'd like you to write some questions about me using the language, or some of it, from the passage.	t/c	____ sol		

EXCERPT 4–2 *(continued)*

		Communications	Source/ Target	Move Type*	Use	
26	Student$_1$:	(Wrote these questions and handed them in the next day.)				
27		How old you done be?	s_1/t	res	pq	p?
28		You done be so so bad?	s_1/t	res	pe	p?
29		Your son go work hard?	s_1/t	res	pe	pq

Coding done by others:
Subcategories of *present*: 2. ps; 4. ps; 5. pq; 7. ps; 10. ps; 11. ps; 13. ps; 14. ps; 16. ps; 18. ps; 20. ps; 21. ps; 22. p?; 23. ps; 24. ps; 27. pq; 28. p?; 29. pq.
Solicit types: 1. 1; 3. 3; 6. 3; 9. 1; 12. 1; 15. 3; 17. 3; 19. 4; 25. 4.

Has a _____ or Is a _____ ?—Contrasting Characterize and Present

Remembering that a tomato is considered a fruit by the botanist reminds us that whenever we set up categories, some items will have characteristics that fit in more than one category. To put it another way, no matter how we cut the cake, there are crumbs. The problem of classifying uses is compounded by the fact that the intentions of the person soliciting need to be taken into account in coding both responses and solicits.

In addition to trying to distinguish *characterize* from *present* on the basis of definitions of each category, I try to associate *characterize* with a *has a* relationship and *present* with an *is a* relationship. About now, you are probably interested in returning to the definitions. [Background 4–9]

Maybe a few examples will help. In order to fit in the category *characterize*, communications should be able to fit into one of these slots:

X has a ________.	Water has a medium density.
X and Y have ________.	Pliers and wrenches have handles.
X is ________.	He go is wrong. He go is different from he goes.
X is a ________.	The is a function word. (Meaning has the attributes of words in this category.)

To fit in the category *present*, communications should fit into one of these slots:

X is a ________.	This (holding a pen) is a pen. (Meaning this is its name, it is this, not it has these qualities.)
________ is a/an X?	What, where, etc. is a pen?

In order to have you distinguish responses that seem to have the qualities of more than one category, and to show you another installment of *It done begin*, I've provided Excerpt 4–3. I've included a *c* and a *p* in the use column after each response. Circle the *p* if you think the use expected in the response is *present*—shows an *is a* relationship or is not a verification of information in the solicits. Circle the *c* if you think the use expected in the response is *characterize*—shows a *has a* relationship. Add the subcategories of characterize if you wish: *cd* = *differentiate, ce* = *evaluate, cx* = *examine, ci* = *illustrate, cl* = *label.* As usual, I've put the coding done by others below the excerpt. The blank lines next to items in the Move Type column will be referred to later.

EXCERPT 4–3
Characterize or Present?

		Communications	Source/ Target	Move Type	Use
1	Teacher:	For homework, I asked you to read a few more paragraphs of *It done begin.* Here are questions about the passage up to where we are.	t/c	str	
2		(Hands out a list of questions.) As you can see, the parts I've asked you to read have been written on the board next to the first parts. So, you can check if you want, but try to keep your eyes on the handout and not look up.			
3		(Section of passage on the blackboard that has been added:)			
3a		After, de Lawd done go look um dis ting dey call um Earth and He savvy			
3b		dat no man be for seat. So de Lawd			
3c		take small piece earth and He go breathe—an man day. An de Lawd			
3d		He go call dis man Hadam.			
3e		De Lawd He say: "Hadam, you see			
3f		dis garden? Dey call um Paradise. Everyting for dis garden be for you.			
3g		But dem mango tree dat be for middle garden dat no be for you. Dat			
3h		tree be white man chop, dat no be			
3i		black man chop. You no go chop um			
3j		or you get plenty pain for belly. You savvy?"			
3k		And Hadam he say: "Yessah, Lawd, I savvy." —From John Gunther, *Inside Africa*			
4	Handout:	What part of speech is the word *chop* in this phrase:	t/c	____ sol	
5		*white man chop*?			
6	One student:	(Writes "noun.")	s/t	res	c p
7	Handout:	Name the part of speech of the word *chop* here:	t/c	____ sol	

EXCERPT 4–3 (*continued*)

		Communications	*Source/ Target*	*Move Type**	*Use*
8		*You no go chop um.*			
9	One student:	(Writes "verb.")	s/t	res	c p
10	Handout:	Is *chop* a noun or a verb in this phrase:	t/c	____ sol	
11		*black man chop*?			
12	One student:	(Writes "noun.")	s/t	res	c p
13	Handout:	Are the words *chop* and *eat* synonyms?	t/c	____ sol	
14	One student:	(Writes "yes.")	s/t	res	c p
15	Handout:	What sound does the word *water* end with in this variety of English?	t/c	____ sol	
16	One student:	(Writes "*o* as in *top.*")	s/t	res	c p
17	Handout:	Is the story line the same as in other versions of Genesis that you have heard or read?	t/c	____ sol	
18	One student:	Yes.	s/t	res	c p
19	Handout:	Can you recall who the bad angel was?	t/c	____ sol	
20	One student:	Lucifer.	s/t	res	c p
21	Handout:	Name seven things "de Lawd go put for earth."	t/c	____ sol	
22	One student:	(Writes "beef," "banana," "yam" and "mango.")	s/t	res	c p
23	Handout:	What size *earth* did the Lord use to make Hadam?	t/c	sol	
24	One student:	(Writes "little.")	s/t	res	c p
25	Handout:	Write three questions about the story so far.	t/c	____ sol	
26	One student:	(Writes the following questions:) Is pidgin really used?	s/t	res	c p
27		Where can I get more examples of pidgin?			c p
28		Why did you have us read this passage?			c p
29		What does *humbug* mean?			c p
30		Why is *th* pronounced *t*?			c p
31		Do you think it's insulting?			c p

EXCERPT 4–3 (*continued*)

		Communications	*Source/ Target*	*Move Type**	*Use*
32		Is the story read in church?			c p
33	Handout:	Indicate whether these sentences are correct pidgin:	t/c	____ sol	
34		a. *The Lawd He say.*			
35		b. *You see this garden.*			
36		c. *That tree be white man eat.*			
37		d. *You done savvy?*			
38	One student:	(Writes these words next to the sentences:) a. *incorrect*	s/t	res	c p
39		b. *incorrect*			c p
40		c. *incorrect*			c p
41		d. *incorrect*			c p
42	Handout:	Divide these words into syllables and mark the syllables with primary stress.	t/c	____ sol	
43		a. *humbug*			
44		b. *savvy*			
45		c. *trumpet*			
46	One student:	(Writes the following lines and marks on the words:)	s/t	res	
47		a. *húm/bug*			c p
48		b. *sáv/vy*			c p
49		c. *tŕum/pet*			c p

Coding done by others:
c and *p* components: 6. cl; 9. cl; 12. ce since a choice is made; 14. cd; 16. ps; 18. cd; 20. ps; 22. ps; 24. ps; 26. pq; 27. pq; 28. p?; 29. pq; 30. pq; 31. pq; 32. pq; 38 to 41. *ce*; 47 to 49. cx.
Solicit types: 4. 3; 7. 3; 10. 9; 13. 5; 15. 3; 17. 5; 19. 3; 21. 1; 23. 3; 25. 4; 33. 5; 42. 3.

Is a ____ Because Has a ____— Definition and Examples of *Relate*

When we ask others to use mediums in responses to make inferences or generalizations, I code the responses *r* for *relate.* Inferences include finding main ideas, generating new patterns by combining known patterns in new ways, making analogies, completing cloze tests that require more than recall, and translating when more than literal meaning needs to be captured. All these activities I code *ri* for *relate infer*. Making generalizations, communicating rules or reasons for our actions or activities, answering why questions that require genuine explanations, speculations, and long definitions I code *re* for *relate explain*. In the vernacular, performing any task that requires "using your head" rather than simply regurgitating information is likely to be coded *relate*. *Relate* requires that we understand and can put together attributes items have and information about what items are. *Relate* thus incorporates both *characterize* and *present*.

To make it more likely that my understanding of *relate* and yours are similar, I've included some coded examples of *relate infer* and *relate explain* in Excerpt 4–4.

EXCERPT 4–4
Relate

		Communications	*Source/ Target*	*Move Type*	*Use*
1	Teacher:	Some of you were absent when I assigned the reading of the paragraphs about the creation of man, and the command from the Lord for Hadam to avoid the middle garden and the mango tree in it because it was only for the white man, "white man chop" as "de Lawd" said. Feel free to consult the paragraphs you missed. They are printed in Excerpt 4–3. But you may be able to respond to these questions from what you already know of the creation according to the account in the Bible. At any rate, before I start the questions, I want you to read what happens after the fall. If you finish this part early, you may want to go back and review the creation in Excerpt 4–1, lines 3a to 3p.	t/c	str	
2	Teacher:	Begin reading the fall, which as you can see, is on the side blackboard.	t/c	sol	
3		(Written on the side blackboard:)			
3a		Later comes the fall:			
3b		Den de Lawd done come back for Earth			
3c		and he go call Hadam. but Hadam he no be			
		for seat. He go fear the Lawd an done go			
3d		for bush, one time. Again, de Lawd call:			
3e		"Hadam." An Hadam he say with small			
		voice: "Yessah, Lawd." And de Lawd He			
3f		say, "Close me, Hadam, close me." An			
3g		Hadam he close de Lawd.			
3h		De Lawd say: "Wassa matta, Hadam, why			
3i		you go for bush?" An Hadam say: "I do get			
		cloth Lawd, so I no want dat you done see			
3j		me naked." And de Lawd he be vex too			
3k		much. He say: "What ting dis—who tell you			

EXCERPT 4–4 (*continued*)

		Communications	*Source/ Target*	*Move Type*	*Use*
		no be naked?" Den He say: "Ah ha, you			
3l		done go chop dem mango from tree for			
3m		middle garden." And Hadam say: "I no			
3n		chop um Lawd. Dem woman you done make			
3o		for me, she go put um for groundnut stew."			
3p		Den de Lawd He make plenty palaver and			
3q		He done drove Hadam and Eva from			
		Paradise.			
		—From John Gunther, *Inside Africa*			
4	Students:	(Read the passage silently; some read the creation of man as well and a few even read the creation of the earth and the battle between the angels in Excerpt 4–1.)	c/t	res	attend—read silently
5	Teacher:	Can you write or state a rule to explain the contrasting pronunciation of the initial sounds in these words: *the, them, they* and *thing*	t/c	sol	
6	Student$_1$:	When the initial sound is voiced, in English, as in *the, them* and *they, d* is used in pidgin. When the initial sound has no vibration as in *thing*, then the voiceless sound is used, the *t*.	s_1/t	res	re
7	Teacher:	What is the mango a symbol for?	t/c	sol	
8	Student$_1$	I think that the mango is bad, or at least what we should not do. Maybe doing things like eating a mango are fun and seem good, but they are not allowed.	s_1/t	res	ri
9	Teacher:	Make some comments about this doll. (Holds up a red devil doll with the word *Lucifer* printed on a sign hanging around the neck.)	t/c	sol	
10	Student$_1$:	There are live devils like that in ourselves and angels too. When we cause suffering, we become like the doll, devils.	s_1/t	res	ri
11	Teacher:	What is the attitude of the writer to the white man?	t/c	sol	
12	Student$_2$:	(Student$_1$ by now is exhausted, having responded to almost everything.)	s_2/t	res	ri
13		I think that the author respects the white man but feels separate from him.			
14	Teacher:	Write a précis of the passage now, cutting out about half of the words but keeping the ideas the same, work in pairs.	t/c	sol	
15	Students:	(Begin writing a précis in pairs.)	ss/t	res	ri*

EXCERPT 4–4 (*continued*)

		Communications	*Source/ Target*	*Move Type*	*Use*
16	Teacher:	Why are you two making noise?	t/ss	sol	
17	Students:	Because we had some questions about the passage about words we didn't understand. And then we wanted to decide who would write and you said we should work together, which makes a little noise.	ss/t	res	re

* The use *reproduce same medium—ds*—is also required here, since some parts of the passage are copied directly when writing a précis. The use *ds* is treated in Episode 17, "Two vanilla, one chocolate."

Give Me a ____—Definition and Examples of *Set*

Now that we're out of the garden, we can solicit some other text to perform uses on. To put it in FOCUS terms, we can ask that mediums be used to *set* content. When we ask others to use mediums to provide examples, models, transcribed conversations, or texts that we want them to perform other uses on, I say we are asking people to *set* content. While we tend to *set* content in initiatory moves—structuring and soliciting moves—we can *set* content in responses as well. Excerpt 4–5 contains some examples of communications I code *s* for *set* in reponses.

EXCERPT 4–5
Set

		Communications	*Source/ Target*	*Move Type*	*Use*
1	Teacher:	Now that we've finished the pidgin version of Genesis, I'd like you each to bring in something you want to read in class.	t/c	sol	
2	Students:	(Bring in magazines, books, and newspapers the next day.)	c/t	res	s
3	Teacher:	Now, that you have brought in what you want to read, write on the board the topics you want to discuss along with the things you brought to read.	t/c	sol	
4	$Student_1$:	(Having recovered from responding to all the other solicits in previous excerpts.)	s_1/t	res	
5		Energy.			s
6	$Student_2$:	Movie stars.	s_2/t	res	s
7	$Student_3$:	(Holds up his grammar book.)	s_3/t	res	s
8	$Student_4$:	(Points to computers in the magazine he brought in.)	s_4/t	res	s

I am interested in two types of information when I employ the use *set*. One has to do with the length of the *set* and the medium used to communicate it. The other has to do with the nature of what the *set* refers to. When the student *sets* movie stars in line 6, real people are being referred to. The pictures of computers *set* things. *Energy* is an abstraction whether we think of electrical energy or the energy of a student who has to do a great many things. I show how I distinguish sets on the basis of this information in Table 4–3, page 103, where I discuss *sets* in solicits.

Can't Tell—Distinguishing Uses in Responses

As you saw when you read the uses in responses in Excerpts 4–1, 4–2, 4–4, and 4–5, and in the rated Excerpt 4–3, there is overlap between the categories of use. When stating attributes of words, where should we draw the line between the uses *characterize* and *relate*? When we teach the colors, are we asking students to *characterize* in their responses or *present*? Well, given the ambiguity of communication and the lack of clear intention in much of what we do, some overlap in categories is unavoidable. Some crumbs will always appear no matter how we cut the cake. "All grammars leak," as the saying goes. [Background 4–10]

I would advise limiting to 5 to 10 minutes the time spent on trying to figure out a particular use in a response. I'd allow this much time only because the use of any particular response must be decided in relationship to those that precede and follow it. Rather than spending more time on puzzling over coding a few moves, I'd move on.

If a number of responses do not clearly fit into one of the categories, I suggest that the difficulty in coding suggests an alternative: clear-cut responses in one of the categories. Increase those solicits you and others have no difficulty coding and decrease those you do, as one alternative. As another, increase those you have difficulty coding. By seeing more of them, you may discern a pattern, or some characteristics of them, that help you code them more easily. At any rate, realize that coding the uses consistently and fitting them in the same categories time and again is difficult for all of us. And, an 80 percent rate of agreement is a much more realistic goal than 100 percent agreement. As you see more examples of uses in excerpts in other episodes, and as you code some of them, you will get a deeper understanding of the categories because you will have more examples of each in your mind.

Write at Least 100 Words—Coding Extended Responses

The bulk of the responses in excerpts that I have so far employed in this episode consist of responses of only a few words. When the task is to write a composition, longer responses are, of course, required. But no matter how long a composition is, I count it as only one response as long as it is preceded by only one solicit. The individual sentences in both compositions and extended oral responses I code in the usual categories of use. Most compositions and extended oral responses are made up messages of some combination of *characterize, present, relate*, and *set*. To illustrate how I code the uses in responses that consist of more than a few words, I've coded some samples of writing and some transcribed extended comments students made about a short story. These are given in Excerpt 4–6. I show how I note the length of responses in section IV of this episode in a rated subsection called "Beyond Uses—Additional Features of Solicits and Responses."

EXCERPT 4–6
Coding Uses in Extended Responses

		Communications	*Source/ Target*	*Move Type*	*Use*
Setting 1: In a classroom after each student read a story of his choice; individual conferences with the teacher. (T)					
1	Teacher:	Tell me what feelings you have about the story you just read.	t/s	sol	
2		(Story about a boy who stole some toothpaste.)			
3	Student:	It was long.	s/t	res	c
4		His mom got angry in the beginning.			p
5		His father was never home.			p
6		He didn't steal that much.			r
7		After he took the toothpaste, she seemed too mean because it wasn't worth hardly anything.			r
8		I felt the way he did when I took something once.			p
9		I like the boy a lot.			p
Setting 2: In a den, reading a thank-you note a father told his son to write. (T)					
10	Father:	(Had told his son to write a thank-you note.)	t/s	sol	
11	Contents of letter:	Dear John,	s/t	res	ps
12		Thank you for sending me those stamps.			ps
13		I like them very much.			ps
14		How is it in New York?			pe
15		I put some of the stamps in my book.			ps
16		P.S. We went to the circus.			ps
17		The elephant did his own act.			ps
18		He went to the bathroom on the ground.			ps
19		The funniest act was the ape act. (because)			(c)
20		The ape pulled the woman's dress and wig off.			(ps)
21		And she pulled the ape's uniform off.			re
Setting 3: A class where a teacher is watching as students write a composition on ambition. (T)					
22	Teacher:	(Had told students to write compositions on ambition.)	t/s	sol	
23	Contents of composition:	In the first place, the word *ambition* means anxiety or eagerness.	s/t	res	ps

EXCERPT 4–6 (*continued*)

	Communications	*Source/ Target*	*Move Type*	*Use*
24	The world of today is full of ambitious men and women.			re
25	Very often, people misunderstand this word and term it selfishness.			ps
26	Myself, I have a great ambition for education.			ps
27	People have different ambitions.			cd
28	The reason I have ambition of education is that I want to be one of the outstanding personalities and useful citizens of my community and without an education I shall not achieve this objective.			re
29	I have such an ambition because I know that no one in this world can make himself useful in life with folded arms.			re

Journal Entry

Usually, the task in the journal entry is clearly established. But, open-ended questions—coded *p?*—are possible in all settings. So, for a change, say whatever you want. This journal entry is wide open in task, and content. Even if you would like to write nothing after pausing to think about what you have just read, feel free.

Inside Outside—Uses Occur in Responses outside Classrooms as well as Inside

The responses I used to illustrate the *uses* tended to occur only in teaching settings, and mostly in relation to *It done begin* at that. The letter in Excerpt 4–6 thanking me for sending stamps is one of the only instances of uses that I used as examples that was not in a teaching setting. To remind you that we use mediums in different ways in our responses outside teaching settings as well as inside, as well as to provide a few more examples of some of the uses, I have prepared Excerpt 4–7. As you can see, I have coded the use in each response.

EXCERPT 4–7
Inside Outside

		Communications	*Source/ Target*	*Move Type*	*Use*
Setting 1: An elevator with people getting on and off.					
1	Person getting on:	Going up? (Said with question intonation.)	s/t	sol	
2	Person inside:	Yes.	t/s	res	ps

EXCERPT 4–7 (*continued*)

		Communications	*Source/ Target*	*Move Type*	*Use*
3	One passenger:	Is your client guilty?	s/s	sol	
4	Fellow passenger:	Absolutely.	s/s	res	ce
5	One passenger:	Will you plead guilty?	s/s	sol	
6	Fellow passenger:	Absolutely not.	s/s	res	ps
7		Isn't it for the court to decide whether he's guilty?	s/s	sol	
8	One passenger:	Unfortunately.	s/s	res	ps
9	New passenger:	(Comes in with jogging suit on, sweating.)	s/s	str	
10	Fellow passenger:	Have you been jogging?	s/s	sol	
11	New passenger:	(Nods head up and down.)	s/s	res	ps
Setting 2: A deserted house.					
12	Homeowner:	Do you want to tell me what happened? (Said to a visitor who had just arrived looking like he had been in an accident.)	s_1/s_2	sol	
13	Visitor:	Yes.	s_2/s_1	res	ps
14		If you'll give me a drink of brandy.	s_2/s_1	sol	ps
15	Homeowner:	(Gives him a glass of brandy.)	s_1/s_2	res	dc*
		You have been a policeman for four years? (Said later in the conversation.)	s_1/s_2	sol	
16	Visitor:	Yes.	s_2/s_1	res	ce
		(Takes out a knife from his boot.)	s_1/s_2	str	
17	Homeowner:	Is that for cleaning fish?	s_2/s_1	sol	
18	Visitor:	Something like that.	s_1/s_2	res	ce
19		Can you call town from here?	s_2/s_1	sol	
20	Homeowner:	I am completely isolated.	s_1/s_2	res	ps
21	Visitor:	(Moves toward homeowner with knife.)	s_2/s_1	str	
22	Homeowner:	You are the escaped convict!	s_1/s_2	rea	
23	Visitor:	(Moves closer to homeowner.) [To Be Continued.]	s_2/s_1	str	

* *dc* stands for *reproduce change medium*, a use treated in Episode 16.

So What?—A Few Asides on Setting Tasks

A common way to classify tasks students perform has been on the basis of the cognitive level of the questions asked. The usual finding in research studies that use some hierarchical framework for classifying questions is that so-called lower-level questions are asked most frequently. The emphasis on facts is usually deplored, and teachers are implored to ask questions that require more thought. The studies of questioning and the setting of tasks have tended to ignore the types of questions we ask outside classrooms, so they must of necessity avoid concluding that more higher-level questions are necessary in class to prepare students for the world outside class. [Background 4–11]

I want to emphasize that I am not urging more tasks be set that require others to *characterize* rather than *present*, or *relate* rather than *present*. I am simply urging you to see what uses occur in responses in a range of settings and to compare the consequences of the different responses. If you find no instances of *characterize* in a setting, I would urge you to solicit some. Indeed, I would urge you to do the complete opposite of whatever you are doing as far as the setting of tasks goes.

The various systems for classifying questions and the responses they solicit may be accurate for tallying one aspect of questions, but the systems have ignored two facts. First, they tend to ignore the fact that we can perform tasks in many mediums. Sequence can be shown in a table as well as in a series of spoken or written sentences. We can show meanings with mime or noise, and pictures can show main ideas as well as written words. In addition, the question hierarchies tend to be used only in classrooms. But, as I pointed out at the beginning of this episode, and as you know, judges, poll takers, and a host of others spend the bulk of their professional lives asking questions too. Imploring teachers to ask more "higher-level" questions, without knowing what types of questions we need to ask in different roles outside class, may or may not lead to consequences that are important. In fact, in much questioning—police officers interviewing witnesses, to cite one obvious example—the goal is to get the facts—*present state*. Any inferences about why a person ran a red light or robbed someone—*relate infer*—must be avoided. The classic line spoken by a detective on a popular television program called *Dragnet* was: "All I want is the facts, just the facts."

I point out some characteristics of classification schemes others have developed to remind you, first, that my system is not hierarchical and, second, that I am not urging you to increase a particular category. Of course, if you find no instance of *characterize*, for example, I would urge you to require some responses in this category. I urge a different frequency not because I think some questions are better than others, but as a means of exploring different consequences and discovering the rules we are following.

Journal Entry

Have you used any classification systems for looking at questions or responses, such as Bloom's taxonomy? In your own dealings with others, have you stopped to think about the different types of responses we require when we ask different questions? When you respond to others who ask you questions, do you think about the "level" of response required?

III. IT DEPENDS ON THE QUESTION—USES IN SOLICITS

Only Six Types?—Introduction

If we were limited in our solicits to setting only six types of tasks, representing the six categories of uses in responses, the range of possible communications we would be able to make both in teaching and nonteaching settings would be narrow indeed. But since the six categories of uses in responses also make up the components of solicits, the range of responses is much greater than six major types. When we alter the uses in solicits, we provide different kinds and amounts of information, and so the six types of tasks we require in responses are vastly expanded. To see this variety, I treat the uses in solicits in this section. [Background 4–12]

Have to Have 'Um—Obligatory Uses in Solicits

Watch Your ps *and* qs*—An Indication to Do Something*

"Could I ask you a couple of questions?" Like all solicits, this one contains an indication that a response is required. The word order of *Could, I,* and *ask*, together with the rising-falling intonation in speech and the question mark in print, signal the fact that a response is required. In a question such as "What would you like to ask?" the question-word *what,* together with the word order, the rising-falling intonation in speech, and the question mark in print signal the fact that a response is required.

The component of solicits that indicates a response is required I code as either *present elicit, present query,* or *present question.* The difference between the *pe, pq,* and *p?* component in a solicit is the same as the difference between them in a response. When the person soliciting knows the response or is soliciting in order to have another person use language for its own sake, play a role, display knowledge or a skill, practice answering questions, or express other areas of study for their own sake, I code the component *pe* for *present elicit.* When the solicit is used to genuinely seek new information, explore reality, or solve a problem, rather than to express content for its own sake, I code the component *pq* for *present query.* And when I cannot tell whether the component fits either of these two subcategories or when the solicit is open-ended and no specific task is required, I code the component *p?* for *present question.*

Of course, some of the same questions that I'd code with a *pe* component when they are asked with one intention can be coded with a *pq* component when they are asked with another intention. The intention of the source of the solicit distinguishes a genuine solicit from one initiated to test, practice, or use content as an end in itself. If I ask a person to read a sentence because I cannot see it, do not know what message it contains, and am interested only in hearing the sentence so I can get the information the words contain, then the component of the solicit that indicates a response is required I would code *pq* for *present query.* Asking a student to read a sentence orally to see whether he or she can pronounce the words means content is being displayed to test, so I would code the component of this solicit *pe* for *present elicit.* If I ask a student "How old are you?" to practice numbers, I'd code the *p* component *pe* for *present elicit.* If I ask the same question in a conversation about age, retirement, pension plans, or marriage, and do not know the answer, I would code the *p* component *pq* for *present query,* since the content is not being communicated for its own sake. Even the classic "Who discovered such and such?" can contain a *pq* component. If a child is looking at a painting of an explorer, and the title of the painting is *Discovering the Nile,* the question "Who discovered the Nile?" is a genuine request for information and not a question the child knows the answer to. Thus, I'd code the *p* component *pq* for *present query.*

Questions used for other purposes, such as asking whether you can ask a question, as in "Could I ask you if you know who discovered the Nile?", I'd code *p?*, since the first part of the solicit suggests the question may be just an opportunity to talk, with no interest in the response. "Say something about the Nile" I'd also code *p?*, since neither the task nor content expected in the response is specified.

A Set Is a Set—the Use Set *in Solicits*

In looking at the solicits in the excerpts, you cannot help but notice that they contain more than a *pe, pq,* or *p?* component. In fact, almost all solicits contain a minimum of two uses, each with a different area of content and often a different medium as well. To put it another way, almost all solicits have a minimum of two messages. The first message consists of the question, command, or request which indicates that something is to be done: the *pe, pq,* or *p?* component. The second message consists of the *what* something is to be done to. Just as in a cooking class you can't just tell someone to "chop"—you have to tell a person to chop something—chop onions or chop celery, for example—so in a language class you can't just tell someone to repeat, or define, or indicate sameness or differentness or correctness or incorrectness. You must indicate what is to be defined, repeated, or judged the same or different, or correct or incorrect. You must have the *pe, pq,* or *p?* component, together with at least one other use.

When the communication that the task in the response is to be performed on is an example, model, or text, I code the component as a *set.* In the solicit "Repeat Eskimo," the word *Eskimo* is a *set* since it is the example the *pe* component is indicating that a task is to be performed on in the response. In "Spell Lucifer," *Lucifer* is what the *pe* component refers to, and so I code it as a *set* too. *Sets* in solicits are thus defined the same way they are defined when they occur in responses. The difference is that in a solicit they cannot occur alone. They must be accompanied by a message that indicates what is to be done with the *set* in the response. Later in this section, I'll show how other uses can form the second, third, or even fourth messages in solicits. The *pe, pq,* or *p?* components can be accompanied by any uses in the solicits, not just the use *set.*

Journal Entry

Have you ever joined a conversation sometime after it has gotten started and realized that, though you understand every word said, you don't know what the people are talking about? Words such as *he* and *it* keep coming up, and you do not know what or who they refer to. Well, the items we refer to in conversations with words such as *it* and *he* are *sets.* When we have not been in at the beginning when mediums have been used to *set* content, we usually can't follow the conversations.

Have you noticed in class that sometimes some students are not following? It could be for the same reason—some lack of clarity about the sets that are being talked about.

Can you note any examples of sets you have not followed, either in class or outside, and as either a student or a teacher?

As I said when I discussed *sets* in responses, I note two types of information with the use *set.* One has to do with the length of the *set* and the medium used to convey it. The other has to do with the nature of what the *set* refers to. I note the medium and length with subcategories, and the type of referent the *set* indicates with abbreviations for features. I've listed the subcategories and features in Table 4–3.

Not Everything Is a Set*—Other Uses in Solicits*

When the *pe, pq,* or *p?* components of solicits refer to communications that are not in the category *set,* I use the categories *characterize, present* or *relate* to code them. The meanings of the terms are the same when they occur in solicits as when they occur in responses. Thus, if a person is asked whether a rule is true or false, the *pe* component in the solicit refers to a communication that fits the category *relate.* If a person is asked whether a particular word such as "snake" is a noun, the word *noun* fits the category

TABLE 4–3
One or the Other

Set *s*	Communicating models or other items that are referred to by words such as *this, that, it,* and *one.*
example *se*	*Nonlinguistic, paralinguistic,* and silent communications that we refer to as items for uses to be performed on.
less than one word *sl*	Models made up of sounds of a language or individual letters or syllables: /*p*/, *s, sa, es.*
one word *so*	Models made up of one word.
part of a sentence *sp*	Models made up of phrases, clauses, and any groups of words that do not constitute a sentence.
sentence *ss*	Models made up of complete sentences, including those in the form of questions.
extended discourse *st*	Transcriptions or actual conversations used as models for other uses to be performed on; the conversations can consist of anywhere from one exchange to any number, but they must contain an exchange to be distinct from separate sentences, *ss.*
text *sx*	Extended samples of language that are connected to each other as in a lecture, sermon, reading passage or essay.
unknown *su*	Communications that do not fit the other subcategories neatly.

Features of sets:

Those that refer to ideas or abstractions can be distinguished from others by adding a subscript, such as *a* for abstraction.

Those that refer to people could be noted with a *p* for *people.*

Those that refer to places could be noted with a *c* for *place.*

Those that refer to things could be noted with a *t* for *things.*

Those that refer to living things—animals—could be noted with an *a* for *animals* and to other living things—plants—with a *pl.*

Other subscripts can replace these or can be used to expand these for exploring relationships between what is given in a solicit and what occurs in a response. Do solicits about people produce different types of responses or longer ones? Is more time needed to respond when the solicit asks about an idea?

characterize, subcategory *label.* And, if a person is asked whether a particular object is "an apple," the word *apple* fits the category *present,* subcategory *state.* The word *snake* and the apple itself though both fit the category *set* since they are words or objects the question in the solicit indicates the task in the response is to be performed on. Both of these words *set* the content expected in the response.

One way I distinguish a *set* from a *pe* component is to see whether *one, it, them* and other words like these can be used to refer to the communication in question. In "Define groundnut," *this* can be used to refer to *groundnut.* In "Is this a groundnut?"

asked about a real nut, the *this* refers to the nut, not the word *groundnut*. Consequently, the nut is the *set*, and the word *groundnut* is a *ps* component.

Divide and C ____—Identifying Separate Messages in Moves and Coding Them

The only way the use components in solicits can make sense is to divide a few solicits into the separate messages each contains. Once the separate messages are identified, each can be seen in relationship to the others.

In a solicit like "Define groundnut," the two separate messages, *define* and *groundnut*, are easy to identify. Assuming the teacher knows what a groundnut is and wants to know whether a student does too, the word *define* is the *pe* component, and constitutes the first message. The word *groundnut* is what the *pe* component is indicating a task must be performed on. It constitutes the second message. Since it is a word that sets the content, I code it as a *set*, subcategory one word: *so*.

In a solicit like "Do these rhyme: fish—dis?" the sets *fish* and *dis* are clear. But the *pe* component is not as neat as *define* in the solicit "Define groundnut." *Do* and the question mark after *dis* signal that the communication is a solicit. But they don't make sense without *these* and *rhyme*. *These* simply reminds us that there are sets around being referred to, so we need not code it. *Rhyme* means the same as *sound the same*, though, which clearly fits the definition of *characterize differentiate*. In terms of FOCUS, this solicit has four separate messages, since mediums are used in four different ways to communicate content. Here are the four messages:

Message 1	Do these*	the *pe* component
Message 2	rhyme?	the *cd* component
Message 3	fish	one *so* component
Message 4	dis	another contrasting *so* component

* We don't code *these*, but it's a signal that sets are referred to and need to be coded.

Responses too can have more than one message. You might recall that after some students responded with a "no," they gave a reason for the response. In response to "Was Lucifer always bad?" a student said "No. Only after he started the palaver" (Excerpt 4-1, lines 15 and 16). Well, the *no* is clearly *characterize evaluate*. The second message in the response I'd code *relate explain*, since the student is attempting to give a reason for his response that requires some thinking about the passage.

To practice noting the separate messages in solicits and responses, go back to Excerpt 4–1 and identify the separate messages in these two types of moves. Since knowing the uses of the separate messages can aid in identifying both them and the boundaries, it is helpful to code the uses in each solicit and response as you identify the separate messages. I find it easiest to identify the obligatory *pe, pq*, or *p?* component in solicits first; then the sets, if they occur; and then other uses. Circling the communications that make up the *pe, pq*, or *p?* component isolates them and removes them from consideration for being coded as other uses. Drawing a line under the sets, and perhaps an arrow from the word that refers to the *set*, eliminates another message or two or three because each *set* counts as a separate message, even though all are in the same major category.

Finally, drawing two lines under the next communication that is left, three lines under the next one, and perhaps a broken line under the next leads to more and more divisions until there will be nothing else left to code. Changes in mediums and areas of content, of course, help in identifying separate messages. For example, in "Juan, define groundnut" each of the three words communicates a separate area of content. *Juan* is *procedure*, but the subcategory *name*. *Define* is *procedure*, but the subcategory *teaching direction*. And *groundnut* is the *study of language* in a language class. In a botany class or a health class studying nutrition, it could of course be the *study of other subjects*. Though circles, lines, and arrows are useful in dividing moves to identify the separate messages, in the footnote to Excerpt 4–1 there are no circles, lines, or arrows. The communications in each message are simply noted and the uses coded.

In identifying the messages and coding the uses in Excerpt 4–1, Table 4–4 might be helpful. So that you don't have to flip back and forth to two places while coding, I've included the abbreviations for *sets* just noted in Table 4–3.

The dashed line separating *set* from the other uses, both in Table 4–4 and on the inside of the back cover of the book, highlight the fact that sets are different from the other uses. When mediums are used to *set* content, I code the communication with a subcategory of *set*. So, *It done begin* is a *set*, subcategory *text* (*sx*), when the passage is *set* for us to perform other uses on. But each communication in a *set* has the potential for being another use. Consequently, each separate communication in *It done begin* can be coded as a use other than *set*. Conversely, each separate communication in an extended dialog or text can simply be coded as one of the subcategories of *set*. I coded each communication in the extended dialogs and the letter in Excerpt 4–6 as separate uses because the communications were not used to *set* content to perform other uses on. But if I asked someone to read the thank-you letter in Excerpt 4–6 silently, then I could code the entire letter as a *set*, subcategory *text*.

Up to You—Optional Components of Solicits

A number of optional components are also possible in solicits. Before you require a response, you can consciously wait a few minutes. Such waiting I code in the use category *attend*. I mention it here even though this use is not highlighted as a use I treat in this episode, because most research has shown that this optional component is in fact very infrequently observed in solicits. In one study of junior high school English classes, the amount of time that elapsed between the solicit and the response was less than 6 seconds in low-ability classes. The same lack of wait time has been found in science classes. By increasing the amount of time between the solicit and response, the length and complexity of student responses increased dramatically in some studies. The few seconds often allowed in classroom solicits is much less than the 14 seconds allowed after each solicit on the Miller Analogy Test, a standardized exam given to graduate students. And the only task in this test is to choose single words in print that seem to match each other. Many who have participated in Silent Way classes or a Quaker meeting for the first time are at first taken aback because the optional component of *attend* is so frequent in the solicits, and the length of each *attend* component is so great. But some see the rewards of waiting. [Background 4–13]

One way to add wait time to a solicit is to simply delay calling on someone to respond to a solicit for a longer number of seconds than usual. Using *attend* as an optional component of solicits in this way might also decrease the number of people who shout out answers, hoping to be the first to show the teacher they know the right answer. In written solicits, in exercises or examinations, increasing the time allowed for completing the work provides extra wait time. Since most tests are timed so that those who can work faster get higher scores, altering the amount of time provided will

TABLE 4–4
Abbreviations for Some Uses

characterize *c*	Communicating qualities of anything; a "has a" relationship.
differentiate *cd*	Indicating sameness or differentness.
evaluate *ce*	Indicating correctness or incorrectness or verifying.
examine *cx*	Indicating size or shape.
illustrate *ci*	Partial definitions and other attributes that don't fit other subcategories or *characterize.*
label *cl*	Using category names
present *p*	Communicating information directly; an "is a" relationship.
elicit *pe*	Asking questions one knows the answers to.
query *pq*	Asking questions to explore.
question *p?*	Questions that are open-ended or don't fit the other subcategories.
state *ps*	Recalling information, agreeing, promising, stating facts.
relate *r*	Making inferences and generalizations.
relate explain *re*	Making generalizations or rules.
relate infer *ri*	Making inferences, making analogies, generating new patterns.
reproduce*	
set *s*	Examples, models, or longer units used to set content other uses are performed on.
example *se*	Sets in other than linguistic mediums.
less than a word *sl*	Letters, sounds, syllables.
one word *so*	Single words.
part of a sentence *sp*	Phrases, clauses, and units smaller than sentences.
sentence *ss*	Questions, commands, statements that begin with an upper-case letter and end with a period or other end-of-sentence punctuation.
extended discourse *st*	Transcriptions or actual dialogs and other spoken language that includes some exchanges or was communicated orally in the first instance.
text *sx*	Material written in the first instance.
unknown *su*	Sets that don't fit neatly into the other subcategories.

* *Reproduce change medium* is treated in Episode 14; *reproduce same medium* is treated in Episode 17.

change the distribution of scores. On reading tests, I have seen students move from second-grade proficiency to eighth-grade proficiency by simply allowing students as much time as they need to complete the solicits in the tests. Since high scores reflect both ability to understand and ability to understand quickly, doubling the amount of time increases the scores. I treat other ways to add the optional component *attend* to solicits in Episode 14. [Background 4–14]

Another optional component of a solicit is a *characterize* that helps the person responding narrow the number of possibilities in the response. If I ask you to give me a letter from the alphabet, you have 26 choices in English, and so your chances of getting the same one I am thinking of on your first try are at most 1 in 26. If I add a comment such as "It's a vowel," you have fewer choices, so your chances are better. If I add "It's round," your chances are improved even more. All these "clues" fall in the category *characterize*. They are different from the obligatory *characterize* in questions, such as the word *adjective* in "Is cup an adjective?" or the word *correct*, as in "Is this correct?"

The category *characterize* can also be used to set criteria for responses. When a response is slow and you say "more quickly," or you say "read the passage in 3 minutes," the words *quickly* and *in 3 minutes* characterize the type of performance you want in the response. So I put them in the category *characterize*. I treat *characterize* as an optional component of solicits in Episode 5.

The admonition "Call students by name when you ask questions" reminds us of another optional component of solicits: a *ps* component with content in the category *procedure* and in the subcategory *name*. Do fewer students shout responses when an optional *ps* component, which states a particular student's name, is added to the solicit? Do fewer students raise their hands or snap their fingers for a teacher's attention when this optional component is used? The order the name is stated in can also be manipulated. When the name occurs before the question, as in "Jama, where did you go this weekend?", do fewer students think of an expected response than when the question is posed and then a student is named, as in "Where did you go this weekend, Jama?" Do fewer nervously tap their feet during class when the name precedes other components in the solicit? Although some variables may seem to be rather minor, such as how students are called on and how they volunteer, in fact such variables have a lot to do with the frequency and amount of language students process. And the whole business of turn taking is very complex. [Background 4–15]

The optional *ps* component is not limited to content of *procedure*. Formulaic expressions such as *please* or *damn* in solicits I code *life formula*. To some, a "please" added to a solicit makes a response more likely, as when a person who values politeness expressed in this way is asked "Please open the door" or "Would you mind opening the door?" To a person who considers "please" and formulaic indirectness effete, *damn* is more likely to produce a response, as in "Open the damn door!" Such formulas are optional, and trying a range of optional formulas provides a number of alternatives when soliciting that are likely to produce a range of different responses.

The optional *ps* component is not limited to formulas or to the linguistic/aural medium of speech. Expressing astonishment, anger, or other personal feelings through tone of voice or facial expressions also makes a statement, so I code these communications *ps* too. We can say "What's this?" as we hold up a snake in a matter-of-fact way. Or we can say it with curiosity, either feigned or real. We can say "Close the door" matter of factly or with observable anger, apprehension, or joy. Any time the tone of voice or body language—*paralinguistic aural* or *visual* mediums—are used to present an emotion, content I code *life personal*, I code the optional component *ps*.

Try asking questions with energy, even when you know the answer, if you normally don't. Then try asking questions in a lethargic way, if you never do. If you are usually supportive in your soliciting, try being threatening, and compare the consequences.

All these optional components constitute additional messages. Once you understand that both the obligatory components of solicits and optional components can be manipulated, you'll be able to expand the variety of questions you ask in any setting by substituting, adding, and subtracting separate messages.

Journal Entry

To many parents, the *ps* component in solicits that contains a polite formula is not optional! Many parents will not respond to children if the children do not use *please* or a similar formula in their solicits. "What do you say?" is a common question parents ask children. The expected response is to add a *please* to the original solicit.

Have you noticed parents requiring children to use *please*? Do the parents consistently use *please* in their solicits? Does the practice vary from language to language and within a language group among different individuals? In short, how firm is the rule?

Moving into 5—Uses as Content

I code uses as content when I code the content of the *pe, pq*, or *p?* component of solicits. These components of every solicit communicate a teaching direction—a request, command, or question to respond to. Each teaching direction I code as a subcategory of *procedure* I call *teaching direction*. But to code *pu* for *procedure teaching direction* as the content of each *pe, pq*, or *p?* component of solicits would provide no useful information. Consequently, I code the content of each *pe, pq*, or *p?* component of each solicit with the use that is expected in the response. Thus, if I say "Is this a groundnut?" I code the content of the *pe* component *ce* for the use *characterize evaluate*, because this is the use expected in the response. When we code the responses, we can see whether the task performed in the response is the one that was communicated in the solicit. How frequently, when the *pe* component in a solicit requires one to *present state*, for example, does *present state* appear in the response, and how frequently does another use occur? When a solicit is open-ended, coded as *p?* both in the use and the content columns, what types of uses occur in the responses? These questions of congruence can be shown by coding the content of the *pe, pq*, and *p?* components of solicits as the use expected in the response rather than as *pu* for *procedure teaching direction*.

Formulas?—Coding Solicits and Responses

Since many responses in the same category of use are different because of the uses in the previous solicits, as a convention I code the uses in solicits on the same line as the use in the responses that follow the solicits. For example, I'd code the solicit "Define groundnut" in this way if the response was "They grow in the ground": *s res ci* (*pe* + *so*). In plain English, this simply means that a student responded by *characterizing* in the subcategory *illustrate*—the *ci*—to a solicit in which a question a person knew the answer to—the *pe*—referred to a word—the subcategory of *set* I call one word: *so*. In this way, I can note the task that has been performed and the components of the solicit compactly. I enclose the messages of the solicit in parentheses to distinguish them from the use in the response. To put it another way, a person responded with such-and-such a category of use, *given* such-and-such messages in the solicit. The given is made up of the abbreviations enclosed in the parentheses.

Using the parentheses after responses makes it easy to distinguish a great number of responses in the same category from each other. For exmple, the responses to "Is apple a noun?" and "Is this [holding an apple] an apple?" are both coded *ce* for *characterize evaluate* in the responses. But the communications that are being characterized are quite different. Here is how I'd code these two responses to show that the solicits which preceded them were quite different:

Is apple a noun?	yes	*ce* (*pe* + *so* + *cl*)
Is this [holding an apple] an apple?	yes	*ce* (*pe* + *se* + *ps*)

The components *given* in the solicit highlight the fact that in one case a label is being verified and in another case the name of an object is being verified.

We can, of course, add the content and mediums of the uses to the coding, making the "formulas" a bit longer, but just as easy to see the components in. For example, identifying a suspect in a police lineup and indicating that two sounds are the same are both responses that require the use *characterize differentiate*. Yet the activities are quite distinct because the *givens* in the solicits are so different. Here is how the two tasks could be coded:

1. Which[a] of these men (six men lined up)[b] is the one[c] you think took your wallet at gunpoint?[d]
(Man in person's mind.)[e]
The second one.
s res la cd fp (*la pq cd*[a] + *nv* se_5 *fg*[b] + *nv se* fp_1[c] + *la ci fg*[d] + *si se* fp_1[e])

2. Are[a] these[b]—lamp[c], lamp[d]—the same? (The first example is said with rising intonation,[e] the second with rising falling.[f])
Different?
s res la cd l (*la pe cd*[a] + *la* se_1 *lsg*[b] + *la* se_2 *lsg*[c] + *la cd lsg*[d] + *pa se u*[e] + *pa se** *u*[f])

* Indicates the contrasting sets.

The content of the sets in the first solicit is *life*, subcategory *public, fg*, since the five people are presumably not personally known by the victim. The person who committed the crime I code *fp, life personal*, since he is known by the victim, though not as a friend, of course. The subscript 5 shows that there are five *sets* alike. The subscript 1 next to the *set* coded *nv* for *nonlinguistic visual* I note to show that the actual person is the same as the image of the person in the victim's mind, coded *silence*, but with the same subscript, 1. The description "the one you think took your wallet at gunpoint" sets limits on the attributes of the one to be selected, so I coded this component *ci* for *characterize illustrate*.

The content of the second example is *study language* in the response, since pronunciation is the topic. The fact that the intonation of the first model is different from the second I note by coding the use of a *paralinguistic medium.* I have coded the content *unspecified, u,* since the contrasting intonation is hard to fit in any other category. The normal rule, of course, is to use rising intonation in listing a series. But here we need to break a normal rule not only for the usual reasons—to help us see what we are doing more clearly and to compare the consequences of doing things differently—but also to decrease ambiguity. The detailed coding reminds us that rising intonation in one of a pair that is intended to be identical can cause a careful listener confusion.

Should you be intrigued by comprehensive coding of the givens that precede responses, you can code Excerpt 4–1 following this convention. If you have already divided up the moves into messages, it will be an easy task simply to add the mediums and areas of content and code the messages that precede each response. You can use the FOCUS table on the last page of the book for the abbreviations. Comprehensive coding of Excerpt 4–1 that others did is given in the footnote.

Just 9—One Way of Classifying Solicit Types

A popular paradigm for classifying questions that I used for many years consisted of a grid with nine boxes in it. Along the top of the grid, the three question types were listed: question-word, yes/no and either/or. Along the side of the grid were listed the words *fact, inference, experience.* Question-word questions that solicited facts in responses would be tallied in the upper left-hand corner. Question-word questions that solicited inferences in responses would be tallied in the left-hand box in the middle, and so on.

I have provided a copy of the grid in Table 4–5. I took the examples in the grid from questions teachers wrote down after I asked them to write a series of questions about the action of dropping a ball. I dropped a ball, and then asked the teachers to write questions about the action I had just performed. The numbers in each box in the grid show the frequency of each type of question. The rule that requires us to ask question-word questions which seek facts was followed most frequently by the teachers. [Background 4–16]

Not Just 9—Another Way of Classifying Solicit Types

Useful as the fact, inference, experience paradigm in Table 4–5 is, it lacks the type of specificity I am advocating in this book. The single category *facts* fails to remind us that we can ask about *grammar, lexis, pronunciation*, and any of the other subcategories of the *study of language*, to say nothing about the *study of other subjects*. The broad categorization also fails to account for procedural questions such as "What page is the assignment on?" This would be in the same box in the grid as "What does *page* mean?" since both are question-word questions based on facts. The questions in the category *experience* fail to distinguish personal information from general knowledge, and information from feelings.

The categorization of question type is also broad, and consequently fails to show how questions of each type can be radically different from each other. "Was the ball big?" is obviously different from "Is *ball* a noun?", for example. One requires only the verification of a name, and the other the verification of a category label.

On the other hand, without a system for classifying questions, the number of different types we can tally or generate seems unmanageable. Indeed, without some group-

TABLE 4–5
Nine Types of Questions with Examples

	Question-word questions	*Yes/No Questions*	*Either/Or Questions*
Fact	What did he drop? What color was it? How high did it bounce? What happened? What did you do? What did he do? 376	Did the ball bounce? Did he drop a ball? Did he drop a book? Was the ball big? Was the ball white? Was the ball heavy? Is the ball new? Was the action tiring? Is *drop* a verb? 103	Did he drop a ball or a book? Did it bounce 2 feet or 4 feet? Was the person who dropped the ball standing or sitting? Did the ball make a loud noise or a soft noise? Did the teacher drop a hard ball or a soft ball? 8
Inference	What did he drop it for? Why wasn't the sound of the thud louder? Why didn't the ball bounce higher? 63	Do balls always bounce? Was the ball heavier than a basketball? Did the teacher drop something with a lot of density? 8	Do small balls like that one bounce higher or lower than large balls with thin skins? If he had stood on a table rather than the floor when he dropped it, would it have bounced higher or lower? 0
Experience	What kind of a ball have you dropped? Where have you dropped a ball recently? When did you drop a ball recently? 58	Have you ever bounced a ball? Is your football heavy? Is your tennis ball as bouncy as this ball? Are you heavy? Do you own a ball like this? 66	Have you dropped balls or stones in water more? Is John lighter than you or heavier? Is this ball or your ball full of more bounce? 1

ing of the use component, the variety is so great as to seem overwhelming. To make the deliberate generation of alternative solicits more manageable, I have grouped the obligatory components into twelve basic combinations. Each combination represents one type of solicit. I have displayed the twelve types of solicits in Table 4–6. As you can see, the usual grouping of solicits into question-word, yes/no and either/or questions forms the basic framework on which I have grouped the twelve types of solicits. [Background 4–17]

What Table 4–6 reminds us is that all types of solicits must contain an indication to do something—a *pe, pq*, or *p?* component—and, with the exception of solicit type 4, each solicit type must also contain what the something is to be done with or on: two messages. That something the expected response is to be done with or on can be a model, object, or other type of referent—an *s* component, an attribute—a *c* component, the name of an object or some other direct presentation of information—a *ps* component, or a rule, generalization, or inference—an *r* component. In question-word questions, the *pe, pq*, or *p?* component requires that the person responding produce something not communicated in the solicit. In yes/no and either/or questions, the person responding simply has to verify or in another way comment about the information provided in the solicits themselves. In a yes/no question, this is done with a *yes* or *no*, or some variation of these words. In an either/or question, this is done by selecting one of the choices communicated in the solicit. As the footnote on either/or questions in Table 4–6 indicates, the number of choices in either/or questions must be at least two, but is unlimited. However, it is uncommon to have more than four choices, as shown in most multiple-choice tests.

Mastering the solicit types in Table 4–6 actually provides you with many more than twelve alternatives. The five subcategories of *characterize* are all indicated by *c*, and the two subcategories of *relate* are indicated by *r*. And each of the components can be communicated in any medium. *Sets* can be pictures (*nonlinguistic visual*), sounds (*nonlinguistic aural*), or any other medium, for example. And each component can contain a different area of content as well. When you consider the fact that the type of task expected in the response changes the nature of the solicit itself, the variety of solicit types is even greater. After all, a type 3 solicit can be used to elicit not only silent reading (*attend*), but also a repetition (*reproduce*), or any other use.

Journal Entry

How have you been classifying questions you have been asking or responses students or others have been making? Have you been thinking in terms of different types of exercises? In terms of cognitive levels? Or in terms of difficult or easy questions?

Should you be interested in becoming more familiar with some of the twelve solicit types listed in Table 4–6, you can code the types of solicits in Excerpts 4–1, 4–2, and 4–3 in this episode. Perhaps you've noticed that I've put a blank line before each solicit in these three excerpts. Using Table 4–6 as an aid, you can note the solicit types on these blanks, remembering that optional components of solicits are not considered in coding solicit types. The coding of solicit types done by others is given in footnotes to each of the three excerpts.

TABLE 4–6
Twelve Types of Solicits with Examples

Obligatory Components							
QUESTION-WORD QUESTIONS[1]		YES/NO QUESTIONS		EITHER/OR QUESTIONS[2]			
1. *pe*, *pq*, or *p*?	Give me	5. *pe*, *pq*, or *p*?	Is	9. *pe*, *pq*, or *p*?	Is	*or*	Which
+		+		+			
c	a noun.	*s*	*key*	s_{1-n}	key		key or keyed is
		+		+			
		c	a noun?	c_{1-n}	a noun or a verb?		a noun?
2. *pe*, *pq*, or *p*?	Comment on this:	6. *pe*, *pq*, or *p*?	Is this	10. *pe*, *pq*, or *p*?	Is this	*or*	Which of these—
+		+		+			
r	(a rule)	*r*	(a rule)	r_{1-n}	(a rule)		(rule 1) or (rule 2) is
		+		+			
		c	correct)	c_{2-n}	useful or silly?		silly?
3. *pe*, *pq*, or *p*?	Repeat:	7. *pe*, *pq*, or *p*?	Is this	11. *pe*, *pq*, or *p*?	Is this	*or*	Which is
+		+		+			
s	*key*	*s*	(holding a key)	s_{1-n}	(holding a key)		(holding a key and a coin)
		+		+			
		p	a key?	p_{2-n}	a key or a coin?		a key?
4. *pe*, *pq*, or *p*?	Say something. *or* What's up?	8. *pe*, *pq*, or *p*?	Do you have	12. *pe*, *pq*, or *p*?	Do you have		
		+		+			
		ps	a key?	ps_{2-n}	a key or a coin?		
Optional Components[3]							
a ± Wait time		*c* ± Clues or criteria for responses		*ps* ± Names, polite formulas, personal feelings such as anger, astonishment, etc. Expressed through the tone of voice, words or gestures.			

[1] *Question* is used broadly to include requests and commands—all manner of solicits.
[2] 1 − *n* means that from one to any number of components is possible; 2 − *n* means that a minimum of two of the components is obligatory but that more than two are possible.
[3] *a*, *c*, and *ps* are obligatory in some types of solicits.

IV. BRINGING THINGS TOGETHER—CONCLUSION

Did the Butler Do It?—Source and Target in Solicits and Responses

Mastery of the components of solicits and the types of tasks we can expect in responses provides us with an opportunity to provide different students with totally different tasks. The only class I know of in which different students are at the same level is any class that has only one student. And even then, it is hard to predict accurately what a person can and cannot do at a given time. Moods change, we all get distracted, and we all have different energy levels at different times. By altering the components of solicits, we can modulate the difficulty of a solicit to a particular student, thereby setting what amounts to an entirely different task, even if we still expect the same use in the response. And of course, we can alter the use expected in the response as well. If one student always shouts out the responses to solicits that require *present state* in spoken responses, that student can be asked to write responses and asked to *characterize* rather than *present*. If one student can do fifteen *characterize* tasks in 3 minutes, and other students take 3 minutes to do only five, then let it be. Different students can be given differentiated tasks based on different moods, abilities, and amounts of energy at a given time.

Over time, there is no reason students cannot learn some of the components of solicits, and they can be taught the different types of tasks that can be required in responses. Then, they can work in pairs and form many of the solicits on their own. If the usual pattern in a class is teacher to student for all solicits, two obvious opposites are student-to-teacher solicits and student-to-student solicits. The other alternatives, text to student, is also possible. But since some texts and worksheets are made by the classroom teacher, this alternative is more a change of medium, from spoken to written messages, than of source.

Journal Entry

You have probably noticed another important reason for students to ask each other questions: Their style is often different from that of the teacher. How do you feel about any differences between solicits from different sources? What types of differences have you noted?

Once upon a Time—Teaching without Solicits

The solicits in Excerpts 4–1 through 4–6 were not meant to show how questions should be asked, nor even to urge that questions be asked a lot. The solicits in the excerpts were meant only to illustrate the uses in responses and solicits. I think that the frequency of each type of response is distorted in the excerpts, since each excerpt was meant to illustrate a particular use in a response. I treated uses in solicits and responses because they occur both in teaching and nonteaching settings. But as always, there are alternatives, and teaching without solicits is one of them.

I'm sure you have seen a child playing alone, talking a great deal without the benefit of anyone asking any questions. You know that in many conversations you have, you or your partner structure and react to each other, but hardly ever solicit. On television talk shows, the task of the host is usually to keep people from interrupting each other, and to try to allow all to speak, rather than simply to ask a series of questions. One comment from either the host or a guest usually causes a whole string of reactions to be uttered. Many who write stories that begin "Once upon a time," like those who write novels, short stories, and most other works we read daily, do so on their own initiative, not as a response to another's solicit.

While it is clear that the solicit will be with us in teaching till the end of time, it is equally clear that the solicit is only one way to get people to speak. And there is some evidence that it is not the best way. So now that you have some new ways to manipulate the components of solicits and alter the types of responses you require, remember that there is always an opposite. In this case, after you have worked solicits to death, or gotten perplexed by their components, just let people in some classes talk, provide others with materials to work with, or movies, field trips, or guests to talk about. To put it another way, teach your students to say *no* to the solicit "Could I ask you a couple of questions?"—or simply don't ask the question, or any others, at least for a few minutes in the beginning and later for as much as an entire period.

If we really gave people a chance to respond honestly to "Could I ask you a couple of questions?" how many would be delighted to do so? When you ask children to sing or say a poem or say their age, or even their name, in front of relatives or guests, how many of them respond quietly? Yet when they are in their room playing or in the park with friends, how many of the same children cannot be quieted down? When children do not respond to adults, some adults say "Has the cat got your tongue?" This question is never necessary when kids react to each other as they play or work together, or even as they play or work with adults. But solicits put many people on the spot. On quiz shows, people sometimes seem to forget the simplest facts. Surely the pressure of being put on the spot contributes as much to these lapses of memory as the excitement about the possibility of winning vacations or new cars or the time limits imposed on responses. [Background 4–17]

Journal Entry

How do you feel when you are asked to do something at a party that you do a great deal among friends on your own initiative? Would you prefer to start playing the piano at a party on your own, or be asked to do so in front of all the other guests?

At the time I was writing this episode, I was relieved of some money and my wedding band at gunpoint. The power of a solicit with a gun is so great that no options are really available. But as I reflected, I realized that even without the use of a nonlinguistic visual medium such as a gun, a solicit is extremely powerful and leaves very little room for maneuvering. How put upon do you feel by solicits? How many options do you think solicits usually provide, including the option of not responding?

Reality—Questions on Solicits

In addition to pressure, other questions about solicits worth exploring include these: Do more responses requiring *relate* occur in classes where tasks are set that require students to both *characterize* and *present*? Are responses to solicits we know the answer to—those with a *pe* component—shorter or longer than those we don't know the answer to—those with a *pq* component? And when more *pq* solicits occur, are they accompanied by more student-to-teacher and student-to-student exchanges? When people are asked to *characterize* in responses, are the responses longer or shorter than when they are asked to *present*? Are responses that require a negative response longer than those that require a positive response? Does altering the amount of wait time—adding the optional component *attend* to a solicit—affect the length or complexity and error rate of student response? Do open-ended questions—*p?*—affect complexity and error rate of student responses in the same way that *attend* does in a solicit?

Obviously, the number of questions to investigate is large, and I can only list a few here to illustrate ways to manipulate uses to test the validity of what we think we should do, and what we think others should do, and what others think we should do. But the only way to discover the validity of admonitions about teaching or our own commitments to teaching one way or another is to describe what we do. Such description helps us see the rules we follow. Then, to confirm the discovery of the rules and at the same time provide a means to compare the consequences of following different rules, we can break the original rules by doing opposite things.

BACKGROUND NOTES

4–1. Of course, in classes where lectures take place the frequency of teaching moves is not necessarily much greater than the frequency of student moves. However, in the case of teacher structuring moves, the moves are much longer. Michael West was interested in the problem of teacher talk vs. student talk, and in 1956 wrote an article called "The Problem of Pupil Talking Time." Recently, Mary Hines (1982) tallied the frequency of teacher solicits and student moves in a number of ESL classes. Though West and Hines found a lot of teacher talk, in fact the teacher talk in the classes that they looked at is somewhat less than the social studies classes Bellack tallied in his research.

4–2. Frank Smith's ideas about the working of the mind parallel mine. In his 1971 *Understanding Reading* and in his 1975 *Comprehension and Learning* he talks about the use that I call *characterize*. And in the 1975 book he distinguishes the *has a* relationship from the *is a* relationship. I found this useful when I began to distinguish between my *characterize* and *present* categories.

4–3. Smith's description of cognitive functioning has been very helpful to me, and if you are interested in the way we group items, I think a very good source is Frank Smith, 1971 and 1975. Vygotsky is useful, too.

4–4. In talking about the sequence of the subcategories of *characterize*, again I would refer you to Smith, both 1971 and 1975. I have included separate background entries for all these points, even though they are related, in an attempt to emphasize the importance of Smith's books on my thinking about the categories of *use*. My subcategory terms are different from his terms but I find support for my subcategories in his ideas.

4–5. I have done a number of informal surveys in ESL classrooms and I have consistently found infrequent yes/no questions. Shapiro-Skrobe confirms all my informal tallies in her dissertation.

4–6. Wiener's books on cybernetics do not treat classroom questioning. However, in his talk about binary choices in computers I find insights into the way the mind operates and the way we can form questions to show the mind making different kinds of decisions.

4–7. The fact that launching a rocket is a complex operation hardly needs support. What does need to be said to refresh our memory is what De Bono, among others, emphasizes. That is, in all decision making we must depend on small amounts of information, for we never have all the information that we need. All decisions require much more information than we ever have available, but we have to make these decisions anyway. When we ask questions of our students, however, it is important to remind them once in a while that they have to take the chance to be wrong, since they will never have enough information to answer most complex questions perfectly. De Bono is worth reading in general for looking at things from a different point of view and for asking different kinds of questions.

4–8. In addition to looking at questions in courtrooms and other settings outside of the classroom, I have found it very illuminating to look at questions asked in medical diagnosis. Berton Rouché writes a series in *The New Yorker* entitled "Annals of Medicine." In these pieces Rouché shows the importance of yes/no questions and the importance of the use *characterize.* He also shows how we have to make some educated guesses because we usually don't always have the complete information we need. In this way, he echoes De Bono. Of course, questions that are asked to diagnose medical problems are somewhat different from both classroom questions and courtroom questions, because in medical diagnosis we are genuinely searching for a solution. In both courtroom and classroom questioning, we are often simply trying to get the students to say what we want them to say. Or we are trying to control knowledge, argues Delamont.

4–9. In my earlier references to the relationships between cognitive functions and uses, I referred to Frank Smith a great deal. Gibson and Levin also discuss cognitive funtioning in their book. While I find Frank Smith's writing more exciting, Gibson and Levin too should be consulted, not only for the *has a/is a* contrast between *characterize* and *present,* but also for some of the contrasts between other uses and subcategories of uses.

4–10. Sapir makes the statement "all grammars leak" on page 38 of *Language: An Introduction to the Study of Speech.*

4–11. Classifications of questions or other tasks is usually hierarchical. In Bloom's taxonomy, for example, there are higher- and lower-order questions. Taba also ranks question types. Squire's descriptions of questions in high school English classes in the United States and the United Kingdom also are weighted. Some questions are considered more important than others. I have arranged the categories simply in alphabetical order. *Relate* is not better than *present,* but different. I do think we need to ask a wide range of questions if we are going to make use of the different mental functions that are possible. However, in the same way, taking in mediums is not better or worse than producing mediums. Nor is the usual order—listening, speaking, reading, and writing—held to in the organization of uses. Children often spell words and write them before they read. And to assume that there is one correct order goes against the entire theme of this book. Hechinger, in a report on a project in Florida, describes children writing before they read. The project was worth an article in *The New York Times.* Most people have seen children write before they read. Yet perhaps because of their preconceived notion that reading must precede writing, they simply did not notice the difference or think about it.

4–12. Donaldson (pages 40–50) is one of the few who takes into account the words in the solicits we ask as well as in responses. Yet the alteration of even one word in a question can make all the difference in the responses. Studies tend to look at student responses, ignoring the amount and type of information contained in the solicits. People who ask questions in courts of law realize how vital the wording of questions is. They often ask judges to strike some questions from the record because of the way they are phrased. The solicits have to be taken from the record, not the responses. In looking at solicits and responses, we need to look at the messages in the solicits as well as at the expected task in the responses.

4–13. If you have gone to a Quaker meeting, you will have experienced wait time very intensely. At a Quaker meeting the participants sit and wait until one feels ready to say something. The wait times are not measured in seconds, but often in minutes. In the *Silent Way,* Gattegno too advocates long periods of waiting. The effectiveness of wait time can be extremely dramatic. Daly showed how allowing students extra time on tests meant that almost half of the students who would ordinarily be placed in remedial classes would not be so placed if they were simply allowed more time to complete their examinations. Rowe shows how the length of student responses is consistently increased when students are given more time to answer. She also shows how the complexity of the thought in responses is greater when more time is given. Hoetker and Hoetker and Ahlbrand show how consistently wait time is withheld in classroom questioning.

4–14. The Daly study referred to in note 4–13 I read many years after I compared the test scores of teachers in Africa, whose tests I marked first when they stopped at the allotted time and remarked when given unlimited time. Scores were usually at least doubled with more time. Obviously, a person who can read more quickly and get the information needed can be considered more efficient than a person who takes more time. All the reading tests in the world are predicated on the idea that you must not only read and answer questions, but you must do so in a limited amount of time. We are probably stuck with timed reading tests. However, I think it is useful to give both timed and untimed reading tests to students so that we can see how much of the so-called efficiency is due to slowness rather than to some other lack in the reading process. Basing our diagnosis and treatment of reading difficulties only on timed tests may be very deceptive. We may find that in at least half of the cases, additional time is all the students need; they do not need different kinds of treatment. And in fact the treatment we give them may make them more nervous and cause them to read more and more slowly, thus compounding the difficulty we think we are overcoming. The emphasis on speed is reflected in the educational TV program *Sesame Street*. However, fortunately *MisterRogers* serves as a useful foil to *Sesame Street*. For students who cannot follow quick delivery and who need more time, we are lucky we have Mister Rogers. However, if students have only one teacher in a class, they need to have the opportunity for that teacher to act like Mister Rogers at least part of the time and not always to act like the characters in *Sesame Street*, racing furiously forward, providing no time for reflection or the type of slower intake many of us need.

4–15. The complex issues involved in turn taking have been treated by Sachs et al. Allwright has described the importance of turn taking in language classes in a 1980 article.

4–16. As I recall, my first introduction to the nine types of questions was Gurrey, published in 1955. The article that influenced me most and made me a convert to the nine was Stevick's 1965 article entitled "'*Technemes*' and the Rhythm of Class Activity." After reading Stevick, I made many presentations about the nine types of questions and I compared the frequency of different types at various stages of training. If anything, less variety was evident as different types were advocated. Perhaps this can be explained by the fact that the teachers were in the midst of learning the new classification system and so were concentrating on one or two types of questions in any one period that I observed them in. However, I was somewhat crestfallen when I consistently found that my excitement about the nine types seemed not to be clearly evident in the teachers' use of the nine types in the classrooms I observed.

4–17. In his 1970 work, *The Study of Non-Standard English* (p. 57), William Labov emphasizes the need to avoid asking questions if we are really interested in getting people to speak.

EPISODE

5

Do You Have the Key?

I. GETTING STARTED—INTRODUCTION

Hits and Misses—The Problem

The last time I said "yes" in response to "Do you have the key?" for both my friend who asked the question and me, it meant an extra trip from our destination back to our starting point and then a second, extra trip back to our destination. In an attempt to make sure I had the key to the house we were driving to, my friend asked me whether I had the key before we left. Unfortunately, the key in my friend's mind and the key in my mind were different. He was asking about the key to the house we were going to, while my "yes" referred to the key for the place we were in when he asked the question.

I call this type of misunderstanding a *miss* and contrast it with a *hit*. Had my "yes" referred to the same key my friend was asking about, a hit would have occurred rather than a miss. I'm sure you can think of many hits and misses you have experienced both outside and inside of classrooms. In fact, one could argue that much of teaching involves altering the number of hits and misses that occur between teachers and students, whether the misses are errors in the content being taught or miscommunications, like the key exchange in which each person had a different set in mind.

Journal entry

Do you have a favorite miss similar to my key miss? If so, write it down and see as you work through the episode whether any of the alternatives here might have prevented the miss you consider your favorite.

A Clue from a Puzzle—The Use *Characterize* in Crossword Puzzle Solicits

Though the "Do you have the key?" type of question illustrates the problem of hits and misses, it is different from most classroom questions in at least two ways. First, it is a yes/no question, rare in most classrooms. Second, my friend did not know the answer to it when he asked me the question. The bulk of classroom questions we ask we know the answers to and simply want to see whether others do as well. Consequently, I did not start my search for alternatives by looking at solicits people asked to find information they did not know. Rather, I started by looking for solicits that required responses the solicitors already knew the answers to. I found such solicits in crossword puzzles. Indeed, the central purpose of a crossword puzzle is the matching of wits between the author of the puzzle and those who try to work their way through the puzzle. Given the fact that most authors and workers of puzzles never meet, and therefore can't discuss their responses, the choices in the responses have to be narrowed so that the "student" has a chance to get the response correct. But the puzzle cannot be so easy that the "student" has no challenge whatsoever. This is a problem parallel with the one we all face as teachers—making our solicits difficult enough so that the students learn something from them, and not too easy so they have no real challenge in trying to answer them. [Background 5–1]

One feature that most clearly distinguishes classroom solicits from solicits in crossword puzzles is that nine times out of ten, each solicit in a crossword puzzle contains a component I would code as the use *characterize*. Authors of crossword puzzles do a lot of *characterizing*. In fact, each solicit usually contains at least two communications I'd code *characterize*. Put another way, each solicit in a crossword puzzle contains at least two *c* components, *c* standing for *characterize*. The form of the puzzle itself, made up of boxes that indicate the length of each word that is expected in each response, constitutes one *c* component. Each clue that narrows the choices for the sets of boxes provides another *c* component. So, between the boxes which tell us how long the word is to be and the minimum of one clue per item, we have at least two *c* components in every solicit in a crossword puzzle.

Since the extra trip back to pick up the "right" key, and since I noticed that crossword puzzle solicits contain descriptive phrases or clauses about what is expected in the response that are to fit in the boxes, I rarely answer questions unless they contain *c* components. When someone asks me "Do you have the key?" or "Where is the key?" I ask another question such as "Which key?" to force my inquisitor to add a phrase or clause to describe the item in question. I request that the person soliciting add a *c* component to the solicit. After the *c* component is added, I am ready to respond. Because these solicits have a *c* component in them, I'd respond to them immediately: Do you have the key to the house in the country? Where is the key to the house in the country? Where is the key I bought last week? Do you have the key Martha lent you over the weekend? As you no doubt guessed, the *c* component in these questions consists of the identifying words. By adding a *c* component, an extra message is added to each solicit. (I treat messages in Episode 4.)

Characterizing—Episode 5 Is about the Use *Characterize* in Solicits

Because I have found the *c* components that add clues to delimit the range of responses in classroom solicits so infrequent and because I have found that adding this type of *c* component can be helpful in altering the proportion of hits and misses, I have devoted a part of this episode to the use *characterize* in solicits. I treat this component in Section II. Because I've noticed that the *c* component contains different areas of content in different settings, I treat the content of the *c* component as well in Section III. I show the relationships between the *c* component and content in Section IV, but the material in this section of the episode is rated. Finally, in Section VI describe some other char-

TABLE 5–1
Two, for an Opener

Move Type	Use	Content
	c characterize	
		p procedure
solicit	±	
		s study
	o other	

acteristics of communications that can be altered to change the proportion of hits and misses. Section VI contains a few concluding remarks.

Table 5–1 shows what this episode is about in a graphic way. The ± between the use *characterize* and the other categories of use I have noted with the word *other* simply means that in most solicits, the *c* component is optional. In the examples, you'll learn how to add or subtract the *c* component from your solicits.

II. THE BIG C—THE USE *CHARACTERIZE*

A Typical Puzzle—Identifying Instances of *Characterize*

Because the *c* component is so central to solicits in crossword puzzles, I will use a puzzle to provide examples of the *c* component. As you can see, the puzzle in Excerpt 5–1 is shaped to form a *c*, the abbreviation for the use *characterize*. The *cxs*, *cis*, and so on in the Use column are simply abbreviations for some of the subcategories of the use *characterize* treated in some of the rated sections. And the letters in the Content column are abbreviations for areas of content. Ignore the abbreviations for now and concentrate only on the fact that the clues under the down and across lists of clues, as well as the numbered boxes in the puzzle itself, are all examples of the *c* component. Ignore the dashes in the columns.

Journal Entry

How do you feel about crossword puzzles? If you like them, which types of clues do you like best? Which do you like least? If you don't like crossword puzzles, why don't you? Do you dislike the fact that the person who made up the puzzle knows the responses and you don't? Or do you simply not find them exciting for some other reason? If you do crossword puzzles, do you use a pen or a pencil? Do you like the answers close at hand so you can check a lot, or do you ignore the answers anyway?

Characterizing Differently—Subcategories of *Characterize*

As you see in Excerpt 5–1, the *characterize* component can provide information about the expected response in different ways. The boxes obviously provide information differently from the partial definitions, for example. By identifying subcategories of the *characterize* component, we can increase the number of alternatives available and make our descriptions more precise.

EXCERPT 5–1
The Big C

		Communications	*Move Type*	*Use*		*Content*	
		DOWN					
1	1.	Fill in a word with these attributes:*	sol	______		______	
2		a place where people spend a lot of time being silent		cd	ci	lp	lu
3		stress on the first syllable		cx	ci	lp	lu
4	2.	Fill in a word with these attributes:	sol	______		______	
5		used in formal papers		cd	ci	lp	lu
6		from another language		cd	ci	lp	lu
7	3.	Fill in a word with these attributes:	sol	______		______	
8		part of humans that continues after we die		ci	cx	lp	lu
9		used by the ancient Egyptians		ci	cl	lp	lu
10	4.	Fill in a word with these attributes:	sol	______		______	
11		a part of it is important for us to balance		ci	cx	lp	lu
12		rhymes with pier		cd	ci	lp	lu
13	5.	Fill in a word with these attributes:	sol	______		______	
14		black substance used for covering a roof		ci	cl	lp	lu
15		looks similar to far when written		cd	ci	lp	lu
		ACROSS					
16	1.	Fill in a word with these attributes:	sol	______		______	
17		having the same qualities		ce	ci	lp	lu
18		conjunction		cd	cl	lp	lu
19	2.	Fill in a word with this attribute:	sol	______		______	
20		a place famous for corn		ce	ci	lp	lu
21	3.	Fill in a word with these attributes:	sol	______		______	
22		very proper people		ce	ci	lp	lu
23		an abbreviation		ci	cl	lp	lu
24		both the same kind of letters		cd	ci	lp	lu
25	4.	Fill in a word with these attributes:	sol	______		______	
26		the letter is a consonant		ci	cl	lp	lu
27		it occurs in the last quarter of the English alphabet		cx	ci	lp	lu
28	5.	Fill in a word with this attribute:	sol	______		______	
29		a preposition		cx	cl	lp	lu
30	6.	Fill in a word with these attributes:	sol	______		______	
31		an abbreviation		ci	cl	lp	lu

EXCERPT 5–1 *(continued)*

		Communications	*Move Type*	*Use*		*Content*	
32		a very dangerous material		ce	ci	lp	lu
33	7.	Fill in a word with these attributes:	sol	______		______	
34		a noun		cd	cl	lp	lu
35		comes from Janus, the guardian of portals		cx	ci	lp	lu
36	8.	Fill in the letters to form the words:	sol	______		______	
37			(numbers)	ps		______	
38			(boxes)	cx	cd	lp	lu

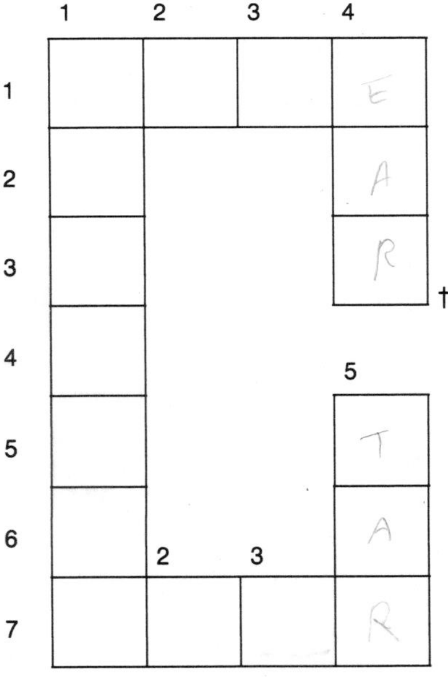

Key to crossword puzzle:

Down	*Across*
1. library	1. like
2. *i.e.*	2. Ia.—abbreviation for Iowa
3. ka	3. Br.—abbreviation for Britain
4. ear	4. r
5. tar	5. at
	6. Ra.—abbreviation for radium
	7. year

* I realize that these instructions are not usually found in the solicits in crossword puzzles. I have included the words here simply to show that the *c* component is added on to a direction to respond, a message I code with the use *pe, present elicit*, since the person asking knows the answer. And I code the content of the *pe* message *pu procedure*, subcategory *teaching direction*. This *pe* message is implicit in crossword puzzles.

† Since this book is called *Breaking Rules*, I have taken the liberty of breaking the rules of crossword puzzle construction by leaving a large gap in the middle of some words.

Coding of uses done by others: 2. ci; 3. cx; 5. ci; 6. ci; 8. ci; 9. ci; 11. ci; 12. cd; 14. ci; 15. cd; 17. ci; 18. cl; 20. ci; 22. ci; 23. cl; 24. cd; 26. cl; 27. cx; 29. cl; 31. cl; 32. ci; 34. cl; 35. ci; 38. cx.

I'd put the boxes in any crossword puzzle in the subcategory of *characterize* that I call *examine* because they indicate the length of the expected response. I put other information about the size, shape, or configuration of expected responses into this subcategory as well. Saying what a word begins with or the number of letters it contains are two types of comments I'd code as *characterize examine*. As the words in a crossword puzzle are filled in, they indicate the first or last letters of other words, and so I'd code these *cx* for *characterize examine* as well.

The partial definitions of words in the clues of the crossword puzzles—a place for corn (20), a very dangerous material (32)—to cite two examples, I put it the subcategory of *characterize* I call *illustrate, ci* for short. In addition to putting partial definitions in the subcategory *illustrate*, I code other instances of *characterize* that do not clearly fit into the other subcategories as *ci*. In short, *ci* is somewhat of a catchall subcategory.

The clues that told what the expected response rhymed with—rhymes with pier (12)—and other statements about similarities and differences, I put in a subcategory of *characterize* I call *differentiate, cd*. A classic example of this subcategory is printed on signs in baggage claim areas at airports all over the world: Bags look alike. On tours, the *cd* component is heard too: "Doesn't this remind you of Iowa—looks just like the fields there? Isn't this different from the wine we make back home?" We *characterize* in this way from an early age. One of the first things 2- and 3-year-olds say is "Isn't this like mine?" and "That one is like my dad's."

Once we see similarities and differences between things, we begin to classify them. One way we classify items is to label them. These labels were used as clues in the crossword puzzle in Excerpt 5–1: *conjunction* in 18, *preposition* in 29, *abbreviation* in 23 and 31, and *noun* in 34. Labels such as *noun* are of course school labels, but this does not mean that this subcategory is limited to school. Among children, one early category is *my things*, which is usually used in contrast to *things that aren't mine*. Another category is *fun things*. For a long time, plates and cups are in the category *fun things*, and this is one reason no doubt that children use plates and cups as they use toys, throwing them on the floor and making noise with them rather than eating from them. To the parents, the plates and cups are in a category called *functional things*. At any rate, whenever we attach names to any category or group of items, I put the communication into the subcategory of *characterize* I call *label, cl*.

Another way we group things other than using category labels is on the basis of acceptability. First, children learn that shouting and whispering are different. Then they may group shouting along with making noise, crying, and other disruptive communications. At some point, they begin to not only see similarities and differences and that things can be categorized, but that some things are acceptable and some are not. Indicating whether an expected response is to be acceptable or unacceptable, correct or incorrect, I'd classify as the subcategory of *characterize* that I call *evaluate, ce* for short. If I say to a student, "Now you have said the sentence correctly; say it with the error again," I'd code the "with the error" as *characterize evaluate*.

To firm up your mastery of the subcategories of *characterize*, go back to Excerpt 5–1 and circle the abbreviations for the subcategories of *characterize* in the Use column that are appropriate. In each entry in the Use column, I have given two *c* components. One is correct and one is incorrect. Here are the subcategories and their abbreviations: *cd—characterize differentiate, ce—characterize evaluate, cx—characterize examine, ci—characterize illustrate, cl—characterize label*. The subcategories that others have circled are given in the footnote. Extra coding practice can be done in Excerpt 5–3.

Really *Characterizing* Differently— Employing Subcategories of *Characterize*

To illustrate how conscious attention to the different kinds of *c* components of solicits can be used to change the proportion of hits and misses, I'd like you to take the role of a student. Try to respond to these four solicits by writing the correct word next to each partial definition in this vocabulary exercise.

Vocabulary Exercise

1. an undercover organization ____________________
2. word to describe apples and cherries ____________________
3. World War II entente ____________________
4. kind of school ____________________

Most people fill in very few correct words. The solicits and responses don't hit each other! Though the brief definitions in 1, 3, and 4, each an example of *characterize illustrate*, do narrow the possibilities, they still leave enough choices so it is almost impossible to write the exact word that is expected in the responses. To narrow the possibilities more in these solicits and any others, one alternative is to increase the number of *c* components. I have done this in an expanded version of the some vocabulary exercise. I have labeled the subcategories of the *c* components. Where two subcategories of the same type occur, I have distinguished them from each other by adding subscripts. See if you can make more hits with the additional *c* components for items 1 and 2 in an expanded version of the vocabulary exercise.

Vocabulary Exercise, Expanded

1. an undercover organization	characterize illustrate	ci_1
is not in the Eastern Hemisphere	characterize illustrate	ci_2
contains a letter used to grade students	characterize illustrate	ci_3
has three letters in it	characterize examine	cx_1
the first letter	characterize examine	cx_2
is a consonant	characterize label	cl
Response: ____________________		
2. word to describe apples and cherries	no characterize component	
rhymes with bed	characterize differentiate	cd_1
same as blood	characterize differentiate	cd_2
is a color	characterize label	cl
Response: ____________________		

With the third and fourth items, I have left broken lines under the original components for you to add *c* components that you think will narrow the choices and at the same time match the coding I have put next to each set of broken lines. *C* components others wrote are printed below the third and fourth questions. Since you need to know the expected responses to solicits before you add *c* components to narrow choices, I have put the responses for solicits 3 and 4 next to the original solicits. Incidentally, the answers to solicits 1 and 2 are *CIA* and *red*.

Vocabulary Exercise, Continued

3. World War II entente

a. ______________________	characterize illustrate	ci_1
b. ______________________	characterize illustrate	ci_2
c. ______________________	characterize examine	cx_1
	characterize examine and characterize differentiate	$cx_2 + cd$

expected response: Axis

4. kind of school

a. ______________________	characterize illustrate	ci
	characterize examine and characterize examine	$cx_1 + cx_2$
b. ______________________	characterize differentiate	cd
c. ______________________	characterize examine	cx_3
d. ______________________	characterize label	cl

expected response: prep school

c components others have written:

3a. A tool for chopping wood or important Christian holiday in December, etc.
3b. Has four letters or has two syllables, etc.
3c. Starts like the word *at* or ends so that it rhymes with *miss*, etc.
4a. Ends and begins or starts and finishes, etc.
4b. With the same letters.
4c. The third letter or the first letter or the second letter or the fourth letter.
4d. Is a vowel or a consonant.

I wonder whether you scored more hits in the responses after additional *c* components were added to the solicits than before they were added. More hits are usually made even though some of the additional *c* components provide no information to some readers and some of the *c* components are even distracting. This simply tends to support the idea that all of us have our own filing systems in our heads. To those who file information partly on the basis of shape, the subcategory *examine* is an aid in retrieval. To those who classify by using hundreds of category names, the subcategory *label* is an aid.

Each person who tried to state the four words you just worked on, like each person who works on crossword puzzles and makes other kinds of educated guesses, has his or her own way of retrieving information so that he or she can respond in the way expected. Adding a range of *c* components to solicits rather than relying only on one type, or using none at all, would seem to make it more likely that each person responding would have a greater chance of responding in the expected way. Even with only two *c* components rather than one, it is twice as likely that a hit will occur on the first try because the number of choices might be narrowed considerably by the addition of each *c* component.

Journal Entry

For years, I have remembered a cartoon that showed a scene between a waiter and a customer. After the customer had ordered "imported cheese," among other things, and the waiter was just about to leave, the customer turned to him and said, "And make sure it's imported because I can't tell the difference." When you order, or observe others order, how frequently do *c* components such as "imported" occur? And do they tend to increase or decrease the chances of getting the food or drinks brought the way you ordered them, rather than the way they appear on the menu? Can the quality of a restaurant be in part determined by the degree to which *c* components in orders that try to set some criteria are responded to as solicited and expected? Or are extra *c* components in solicits ordering food just a way of showing off and a nuisance?

Adjusting—Rationale for *Characterize* Components in Solicits

Not only might *c* components help some students retrieve responses by narrowing choices, as in crossword puzzles, but they might also aid in adjusting the difficulty of solicits. No matter how well we know our students, we can never know whether our solicits on particular topics will be too easy, too difficult, or just right for particular students. In my experience, the addition of *c* components after misses is the exception rather than the rule. The usual rules require one or more of these steps: Repeat the same solicit more loudly; communicate a completely different solicit; redirect the original solicit to a different student; respond yourself to the solicits students can't respond to. None of these steps provides new information. As a result, they do not give the student a chance to make use of his or her filing system or to learn new characteristics of the information he or she is being asked to retrieve. The usual rule that provides no new information might make the student think that he or she cannot respond with hits either. Rather, simply repeating a solicit louder, answering it oneself, redirecting it to another student, or trying a completely different solicit might imply to some students that they are capable only of misses. Even if none of these arguments is valid, one central reason for adding *c* components to solicits when they do not contain them is that such an alternative is an opposite.

This is not to say that the goal is 100 percent hits. If you circled all the *c* components in Excerpt 5–1 correctly, the solicits were too easy for you and you learned nothing new from them. Misses are a gauge to help us see if our solicits are pitched at appropriate levels. When they occur, we know what we need to teach. Here, I am suggesting that if you find solicits without *c* components in them, one opposite is to add them to solicits, both to adjust the difficulty level and to enable students to file information, relate it to what they have already learned, and develop ways to retrieve it. When we are asked to respond, we have quickly to pull out one of the millions of bits of information we have stored that fits the solicit. The *c* components, because they indicate features of the information we are to retrieve, can narrow the choices from say one million to just a few. We can do this because the narrowing of choices works geometrically rather than arithmetically. Indicating that something we are to guess is alive rather than dead eliminates thousands of possibilities, not just one or ten. And then indicating that what we are to guess is a person, a female, and lives in England eliminates hundreds more possibilities.

Characterizing It Leads to Bigger Things—Further Rationale for *Characterize* in Solicits

Even if the *c* components do not themselves aid learning directly, they might be important for another reason. It is a truism that language is rule-governed behavior. Many of the rules we know are unconscious, and many are never made explicit. But to the extent to which rules are generalizations, they must be based on models, samples, or items—*sets* in terms of FOCUS—and characteristics of these *sets*—the subcategories of *characterize*. A generalization can be made only by seeing differences between items and then grouping them in some way—in short by *characterizing* them.

While all learners obviously develop many rules on their own, all learners do so at different rates and probably with different degrees of efficiency. By using the *c* components in solicits, some learners may be aided in the development of the rules necessary to learning. It is hard to imagine how a person could know, either consciously or unconciously, that *-ed* endings are pronounced differently in *wanted, combed,* and *walked,* for example, without hearing many examples, or *sets*, of each type and without realizing that each ended with different sounds, requiring that a learner *differentiate* and *examine*. Then, when differences are located, the examples need to be put into different categories—*characterize label*. [Background 5–2]

A Final Note—Criteria for Coding *Characterize* Components

One final comment is needed before we leave the *c* component: not all clauses, phrases, or adjectives that occur in solicits narrow choices, and as a result, they cannot all be coded as *characterize*. To be coded as a subcategory of *characterize*, a communication must in some way distinguish between multiple possibilities. If I say to a class "Take out your green books" every day, the *green* in the solicit is simply part of the direction. A *c* component characterizes only if there are different items that are distinguished from each other in different ways during the course of a lesson. Even characterizing by evaluating with the word *correct*, as in "Give me the correct sentence," ceases to be characterizing if the word *incorrect* is never used in contrast with *correct*, as in "Give me the sentence with the error in it now." The *c* component must in some way indicate the distinctive features of the information or actions we expect in the responses.

III. OTHER THINGS CAN MATTER— CONTENT OF *CHARACTERIZE* COMPONENTS

Stress on the First; Different One—Content of *Study*

There is, of course, more to borrowing the *c* components from crossword puzzles to alter the proportion of hits and misses in responses to solicits we know the responses to. The content the *c* component communicates can affect the proportion of hits to misses as well. The solicit "Give me a word with the stress on the first syllable" (3) requires knowledge of the sound system. The solicit "Give me a word that begins with a letter in the last quarter of the alphabet" (27) requires knowledge of the spelling or mechanical system.

If I hold up two balls, one red and one green and say "Are these the same?" there is no way to know what subcategory of the study of language I am referring to. If I am working on the lexical meaning of shapes, then the correct response would be "yes." If I am working on the vowel sounds in *red* and *green*, then the correct response would be "no." When the area of the *study* of *language* is not specified, I code the content of the *c* component *lu* for the *study* of *language unspecified*.

In the present episode, rather than distinguishing the subcategories of the study of language from each other, I am just going to show how we can note whether some areas of the *study of language* are specified or not. Since stress was mentioned in one solicit (3) and *letter* in the other (27), these two *c* components obviously contain specified content—*lp* for *study* of *language specified*. But in a solicit such as "add a word to the phrase—a different one," no area of the study of language is specified. We have no idea why a different word should be added. Is it because the pronunciation of the first is wrong? Or is it because the lexical meaning does not fit? All we know is that a different word is needed. When no area of the study of language is specified, I code the content of the *c* component *lu* for *study of language unspecified.*

I've included some examples where content is specified and not specified in Excerpt 5–2. As you can see, I've included the abbreviations for both *specified* and *unspecified study of language* in the content column: *lp* and *lu*. Circle the one that is appropriate on each line. Compare your choices with those of others, which are given in the excerpt footnote.

If you find solicits that contain *c* components such as *differentiate* (*cd*) and *evaluate* (*ce*) consistently do not specify a separate subcategory of the study of language as lines 3 and 6, one alternative is to do the opposite: Specify an area of content by noting a subcategory of the study of language that pertains to the samples that you are asking about. Some may consider the solicit "Are these the same?" in reference to *corps* and *corpse* in written form curious, since they in fact appear quite different. If the teacher is thinking of the sound system while the student is thinking of the spelling system, there is bound to be a miss. Specifying the fact that the question is about the pronunciation of the two words rather than the spelling might prevent a miss. To learn some of the subcategories of the study of language, work through Episode 11.

Quickly in Three Minutes—Content of *Procedure*

Content in the category *procedure* is also communicated in *c* components, and it also can be divided into subcategories. Here are examples of the *c* component *characterize illustrate, ci*: "Read the passage carefully"; "Read the passage—it's a difficult one"; "Read the passage—the long one"; "Read the passage in 3 minutes." Each of these

EXCERPT 5–2
Specified or Not

	Communications	*Move Type*	*Use*	*Content*	
1	Are these	sol	_____	_____	
2	(*corps* and *corpse* written on blackboard)		_____	_____	
3	the same?		cd	lp	lu
4	Is the sentence	sol	_____	_____	
5	*I go the store every day*		_____	_____	
6	correct?		ce	lp	lu
7	In this sentence, *I go the store every day,*	sol	_____	_____	
8	is		_____	_____	
9	the word order correct?		ce	lp	lu
10	In these words on the board: *corps* and *corpse*	sol	_____	_____	
11	is		_____	_____	
12	the pronunciation the same?		cd	lp	lu

Coding others have done: 3. lu; 6. lu; 9. lp; 12. lp.

illustrates one of the subcategories of *procedure* that tend to combine with the *c* component.

Words and phrases such as *carefully, loudly, with a whisper, quickly, by shouting,* and others which indicate how students are to perform a task that do not refer to time or size of the expected response are in the subcategory of procedure I call *classroom behavior, language: pl.*

C components that communicate information about the difficulty or ease of a task I put in the subcategory of *procedure* I call *difficulty factor*. The father of one child I know always says things like this: "Catch this ball—it's too hard for you to do." He always includes a *c* component with content I'd code *pd* for difficulty factor. To distinguish *c* components that comment about the ease of a task from those that comment about the difficulty of a task, I add a plus sign to those that indicate a task is going to be easy.

C components that refer to time, such as *quickly* or *in 3 minutes*, I put in a subcategory of *procedure* I call *time, pe*. And those that refer to size and shape of words, sentences, sounds, or any other referents, including buildings and objects, I code in a subcategory of *procedure* I call *size and sequence, ps.*

In Excerpt 5–3, I've included some communications that contain *c* components with the four subcategories of *procedure* just presented. As you can see, there are two abbreviations in each content entry next to a *c* component. Circle the one that fits the content of the *c* component. Compare the coding you do with that done by others, given in the excerpt footnote. Ignore the dashes, as usual.

When I tell someone the task I'm setting is easy—*ci pd+*—the satisfaction of scoring a hit might be diminished. When I tell someone the task I'm setting is difficult—*ci pd−*—anxiety might be increased. When people playing a sport want to hassle each other, they often make this kind of statement: "You can give it a try, but you'll probably blow it."

If you find that the content of most *c* components is in the subcategory of procedure *teaching direction, pu*, one opposite is the subcategory *difficulty factor, pd*. If the *pd* content is always an indication that the expected response is to follow a difficult solicit, the opposite is a *c* component, which indicates that the material on which the response is based is easy. If the *pe* content always indicates that the expected response is to be fast, then the opposite is slow. If a teacher consistently says "louder" in every teaching direction, one obvious opposite is to say "very quietly."

If the subcategories of *pe* and *pd* are both varied and frequent, then information about the time the response is to be performed in can be substituted; content I code *pe* can be communicated. Or information about the size of the expected response *ps* can be given by adding phrases such as these: "a two-word answer"; "a three-sentence comment about the reading"; "a half-page summary"; "a one-word answer"; "an answer with words limited to one syllable each."

Basically, the subcategories of *procedure* and the *study of language* can be divided into two groups: those that tend to be specific and those that tend to be general. In the specific category, I would place the *study of language specified, lp*; information about size and shape, *ps*; and information about time, *pe*. In the general category, I would place the *study of language unspecified, lu*; general teaching directions, *pu*; and comments about the degree of difficulty of the expected response, *pd* + or −. The only way to see which group leads to different proportions of hits and misses to try some from each group, to alternate *c* components that are specific, such as "Listen to the end sounds," with those that are general, such as "Listen carefully."

EXCERPT 5–3
Careful, Difficult, Short, and Quickly

	Communications	*Move Type*	*Use*		*Content*	
1	Start the exam.	sol	______		______	
2	(The examination is in front of the students.)		______		______	
3	It's an easy one.		ce	ci	pu	pd+
4	Start the exam.	sol	______		______	
5	(The examination is in front of the students.)		______		______	
6	It has forty items.		ce	cx	pd	ps
7	Finish it in 10 minutes.		ce	cx	ps	pe
8	Write an essay.	sol	______		______	
9	only one page long.		cd	cx	pd	ps
10	Write an essay	sol	______		______	
11	and make it short.		cd	cx	pd	ps
12	Let's meet	sol	______		______	
13	where we met last time		cd	cx	pu	ps
14	at the same time.		cd	cx	ps	pe
15	Let's meet	sol	______		______	
16	at the entrance to the skating rink		cd	cx	pu	ps
17	at 12:30 P.M.		cd	cx	pu	pe
18	Read the passage	sol	______		______	
19	(Students have the passage in front of them.)		______		______	
20	for the important points		ce	ci	pu	pd+
21	and don't look up—		ce	ci	pu	ps
22	don't mouth the words.		ce	ci	pu	pe
23	Repeat this pattern	sol	______		______	
24	"Where are you going after class?"		______		______	
25	with a whisper.		ce	ci	pu	pl
26	Now, repeat the pattern	sol	______		______	
27	"Where are you going after class?"		______		______	
28	by shouting it.		cd	ci	pl	pe

Coding done by others:

Content: 3. pd+; 6. ps; 7. pe; 9. ps; 11. ps; 13. ps; 14. pe; 16. ps; 17. pe; 20. pd+; 21. pu—underlined to show a negative communication; 22. pu; 25. pl; 28. pl.

Uses: 3. ci; 6. cx; 7. cx; 9. cx; 11. cx; 13. cd; 14. cd; 16. cx; 17. cx; 20. ci; 21. ce because it is a prescription; 22. ce because it is a prescription (underlined because in the negative); 25. ci; 28. ci.

IV. PULLING TOGETHER—SUMMARY

Two Slots with a Few More Entries—A Table Showing Subcategories of *Characterize, Procedure,* and *Study*

Five subcategories of the use characterize and five subcategories of content of procedure, together with specified and unspecified areas of the *study of language*, might seem like a lot of debris floating around in our heads. And without a framework to fit the bits in, it is. But a central theme of this book is that, in discussing teaching, we need to attach various alternatives to a framework so that we can both see and manipulate them and also so that we can keep track of them.

Table 5–2 shows how five different ways of characterizing in solicits and the subcategories of content look within the framework of FOCUS. The ± in between the use *characterize* and *other* is a reminder that the *c* components in solicits are optional.

Seeing What We Do—Three Observation Guides

In order to investigate the relationship between hits and misses and the *c* component of solicits. I have designed Observation Guide 5–1. As you can see, I have left blank spaces at the top of the guide for you to note the type of setting the tallies are being made in. I have left extra space to describe the type and level of class if the tallies are being made in a teaching setting.

Along the top of the Observation Guide, I've listed the types of responses being investigated: hits and misses. Tallies of each type are made in the columns formed under each type. Along the left-hand margin, I've listed the two types of solicits the tally is designed for: those without a *c* component and those with a *c* component. Hits

TABLE 5–2
Two Slots with a Few More Entries

Move Type	*Use*	*Content*
		p procedure
	c characterize	*pl* classroom behavior—language
		pd difficulty factor
	cd differentiate	
	ce evaluate	*ps* size
solicit		
	cx examine	*pu* teaching direction
	ci illustrate	
		pe time
	cl label	
	±	*l* study of language
	o other	*lp* specified
		lu unspecified

that follow solicits without a *c* component, tally in the upper left-hand box. Hits that follow solicits with a *c* component, tally in the lower left-hand box. Misses that follow solicits without a *c* component, tally in the upper right-hand box. Misses that follow solicits with a *c* component, tally in the lower right-hand box. My "yes" response to "Do you have a key?" would be tallied in the upper right-hand box, since the response was a miss preceded by a solicit without a *c* component. A "no" response to "Do you have the key to the house in the country?" would be tallied in the lower left-hand box, since I did not have the key. The response would have been a hit, and it contained the *c* component "to the house in the country."

OBSERVATION GUIDE 5–1
Hits and Misses and the *c* Component

Setting: __________
If class, type (math, history, language): __________
If class, level: __________ Number of participants: __________

Solicit type \ Response type	Hits	Misses
no *c* component		
with a *c* component		

If you have tallied some solicits with Observation Guide 5–1, you'll be familiar with the type of communications that fit in each of the four boxes. Then, by using Observation Guide 5–2, you'll be able to tally the frequency of the subcategories of the *c* component. As you can see, Observation Guide 5–2 is parallel in form to Observation Guide 5–1. The major difference is that in Observation Guide 5–2, I've listed the subcategories of *characterize* next to the solicit type that contains a *c* component. Rather than tallying each *c* component anyplace in the lower boxes, you can tally them on the line next to the proper subcategory. The *c* component in the solicit "Give another word to me—*a different one*" would be tallied on the first line next to *cd*, for example, under the Hits column if the response was what was expected and under the Misses column if the response was different from expected, or incorrect.

As you tally, you may begin to find that some of the *c* components are communicated in the negative. If you find comments such as "Don't give a long answer" or "Give me the incorrect one," you can distinguish them from those without a negative word in them by underlining the tally mark of negative *c* components. If you find a lot of solicits

OBSERVATION GUIDE 5–2
Characterizing Differently

Setting: ____________________

If class, type (math, history, language): ____________________

If class, level: ____________________ Number of participants: ____________________

Solicit type \ Response type		Hits	Misses
no *c* component			
with a *c* component*	*cd*		
	ce		
	cx		
	ci		
	cl		

* *cd* = differentiate; *ce* = evaluate; *cx* = examine; *ci* = illustrate; *cl* = label.

that contain a string of *c* components, you can add a subscript to all the *c* components that belong to a particular solicit. It may be that the frequency of misses preceded by solicits with no *c* component and one *c* component are the same, but that when two or more *c* components are communicated in solicits, misses are much less frequent.

To see the relationship between different areas of content and the *c* components, you can of course tally with the abbreviations for the subcategories of content rather than with a tally mark. In addition to showing the relationship between different *c* components and different areas of content, such a tally can aid in investigating the congruence between the content in the *c* component in the solicit and the response. Had my friend said to me "Do you have the key? Answer with a two- or three-letter word," he would have provided me with a *c* component with content in the area of the study of language. This would have been incongruent with the content of my response, which was procedure. In a class, such incongruence might be as critical as outside. Are *c* components coded *procedure, teaching direction* (*pu*), such as "we did it yesterday," as helpful as a *c* component coded *ps*, such as "It starts with an *s*," when one is asked "What's this?" and is expected to name an object, such as a switch that the teacher is holding? Use the abbreviations in Table 5–2 as an aid for remembering the abbreviations for the subcategories of procedure and the study of language that are treated in this episode.

Whether you need to use subscripts and whether you need to underline some *c* components because they are in the negative, or whether you need to add other features such as the use of the first language rather than the target language or not, the guides as they are printed here are not large enough. They simply provide a format. Larger sheets of paper with more space for tallying are necessary for actual observations.

Journal Entry

When someone tells you to do something you're just learning to do, how do you react to a *c* component such as "You're handy and can do it" or "You're not handy enough to do it"? Do such comments, either positive or negative, make you feel relaxed, more reluctant to try, tense, or don't they have any effect? And when you're told to do something in obviously difficult circumstances, such as on ice, how do you react to a *c* component such as "It's slippery" along with the directions? Are you more or less likely to slip after being warned?

V. BITS AND PIECES—OTHER ALTERNATIVES

Characterizing with a Different Purpose—The *C* Component in Structuring Moves

Had my friend announced that he was about to do a check to make sure we had everything we needed for the trip to the house we were going to before he asked if I had the key, a *c* component in the solicit might not have been necessary. When the choices are not sufficiently narrowed in other ways, announcements about what is about to take place—structuring moves—can be used. When the structuring moves occur before the solicits, and when the structuring moves contain a *c* component, the need for this component in each subsequent solicit is sometimes diminished.

To demonstrate the way *c* components in structuring moves can increase the number of hits produced by subsequent solicits, I'd like you to write down some responses to solicits. In Excerpt 5–4, write down words in the empty spaces under the Communications section to the left of the moves, lines 3, 6, and 10.

EXCERPT 5–4
Soliciting minus Structuring

	Communications	*Source/ Target*	*Move Type*	*Use*
1	Tell me the word—	t/s	sol	_____
2	it grows on a stalk.			ci
3	____________________	s/t	res	_____
4	Now—	t/s	sol	_____
5	a little bird.			ci
6	____________________	s/t	res	_____
7	Last one—	t/s	sol	_____
8	blank Mae is the name of Lil' Abner's girlfriend.			ci
9	a little young flower.			ci
10	____________________	s/t	res	_____

Now, read this structuring move: "All the things I am going to ask about are *yellow*." Go back and try to respond to the solicits in Excerpt 5–4 again. The expected responses were *corn, canary,* and *daisy*. I suspect you got more hits after you read the structuring move with the *c* component. Knowing that "a little bird" in line 5 is yellow eliminates a great number of possibilities for most people.

In the structuring move "All the things I am going to ask about are *yellow*." I'd code *yellow* as a label. The reason the word *yellow* is a label here is that it is used as a name for a group of items. Any word in any language can be used as a label as long as it serves the function that the name of a category does. Let's say that I have ten screwdrivers of different sizes on a table and ten awls on the same table. If I want another person to group the two kinds of tools and I say "Put the screwdrivers here and the awls there," then the names of the tools are used as labels. I have used them to classify items on the basis of distinctive features different types of screwdrivers and awls have. Since *yellow* was used as a category label to include items such as corn, canaries, and daisies, it too is a label, and thus coded *cl* for *characterize label.*

Of course, other features of structuring moves also affect hits and misses. One is difficulty level. If the activity is described in a way that few understand it, the likelihood that misses will be decreased is small. Another aspect of structuring moves that may affect misses is the degree to which the structuring moves are related to the experiences of those who hear or see them. This topic is treated in Episode 20.

Journal Entry

One way to find out whether the solicits you write down for class use are likely to yield the responses you expect is to try them out on people outside of class who are native speakers of the language you are teaching. What people often do when they cannot respond to a question is to say something such as "You mean you want such and such." From these paraphrases, it is often possible to rephrase the solicits or generate structuring moves that will yield the responses expected. Such an enterprise would also remind you of different ways people follow solicits. Sometimes, they ask for further information, following a solicit from a teacher with a solicit from the person in the role of student.

Write a few solicits in your journal that you asked outside class, responses to them, and the solicits rephrased so that they yielded the responses you expected.

Another Source—Student Solicits

I once overheard this conversation in a drugstore:

CUSTOMER: Do you have earplugs?
CLERK: For sleeping or swimming?
CUSTOMER: For noise!
CLERK: You want sleeping.

This dialog reminded me of the fact that one of the "ultimate" alternatives many of us use to decrease misses outside the classroom is the communication of a solicit after a solicit in place of a response. The most powerful alternative to use to decrease misses might be to teach students to solicit after any solicit that they do not follow, rather than to try to respond. If the exchanges in which students follow solicits they do not understand with solicits, rather than responses, are recorded, they can be partially transcribed in class, and then investigated by teachers and students. In this way, both teachers and students can begin to see which solicits are consistently not responded to, and what characteristics these solicits lack. Sometimes students will see that the reason they had to solicit after a teacher solicit was because they were not listening. At other times, they will identify other variables. [Background 5–3]

An Invisible Component—Silence

Student solicits, like the *c* components in soliciting and structuring moves, stand out because they are usually communicated in mediums we sense easily: speech and tone of voice, to name two. There is a less visible component of solicits that can affect the proportion of hits and misses; wait time. Whenever a person soliciting in some way makes it clear that he or she is in no rush for the response, that he or she is deliberately waiting, I note the fact by coding the silence as *attend*. I code the content of *attend* with the same subcategory of *procedure* I used to code indications of time in the *c* component: *time pe*.

Since some time is allowed between all solicits and responses, one could argue that *attend* is an obligatory component of all solicits. But because some studies have shown that some types of responses tend to be longer and more complex after at least a 3-second period is allowed after the solicit, I code *attend* only if more than 3 seconds are allowed before the response is required to be made. In coding the *attend* component, since the amount of time needed to affect responses may vary, the best thing to do is note the number of tenths of a second or the number of seconds that go by between the end of the solicit and the beginning of the response. Thus, responses after short and long periods of time can be compared.

An easy way to start altering the length of the *attend* components is in the administration of timed, printed tests. By providing some reasonably comparable individuals with 5 minutes to complete twenty items and others 10 minutes for twenty items and comparing the scores, you can see the effect different durations of *attend* components have. When I've given standardized reading tests designed for native speakers to two groups of comparable nonnative speakers, one with the set time and one with unlimited time, the groups with more time consistently double their scores. Since almost all tests in all fields are a measure of the number of hits that occur in a set period of time, it is hardly startling that more time would lead to more hits. But while there is no reason to be startled by the results, we can be reminded by them that what some have called wait time, and I code *si at* pe_{1-n} units of time, affects the proportion of hits and misses. [Background 5–4]

Different Directions—Establishing Contexts, Using Other Mediums, and Naming Targets

Had my friend asked me "Do you have the key?" as I was locking the door of the place we were leaving, I might have responded with reference to the key of the place we were going to and connected with the solicit with a hit. My friend would probably not have asked me about a key he saw me using. One reason we are able to make some hits outside classrooms that we might miss in classrooms is that the context the solicits occur in and the roles we play both narrow choices. For suggestions on establishing a range of contexts and roles in classrooms, and as a result providing means to narrow choices in responses, work through Episode 13. This episode treats role-playing and the establishment of a range of contexts in classrooms.

Had my friend pointed out the window in the direction of the house we were bound for as he said "Do you have the key?" a hit would have been more likely because the gesture would have indicated which key he was asking about. The classification and use of a range of mediums are treated in detail in Episode 18. For now, the reminder that in solicits nonlinguistic mediums, such as the boxes in crossword puzzles, and paralinguistic mediums, such as pointing, can be used to help narrow choices in responses will enable you to note these other mediums while observing, and perhaps even see how solicits with these alternatives affect hits and misses.

Journal Entry

I have a friend who always refers to items with *this* or *that* and places with *here* or *there*, rather than with the names of items or descriptions of locations such as "next to the red chair." Some people he's with not only find it difficult to keep track of what objects and places are being referred to, and thus cannot pick up or go to the places he indicates, but also get angry. When people say to you "Pick that up" or "Go over there" rather than "Pick up the ice pick" or "Go to the plant by the telephone," how do you react? Are you able to make hits just as easily without names and verbal descriptions as with them? In short, what effect do paralinguistic and nonlinguistic mediums have on responses in your experience?

Had my friend been with me and another person as he asked "Do you have the key?" and not added "John," neither the context nor the extra mediums might have been enough to help ensure a hit. The third person might have answered the question rather than me. Just as some misses are the result of the ambiguity of the solicit, so some misses are the result of the ambiguity of the target. It is easy to understand why a murmur of voices might follow a solicit such as "What did that story mean to you?" And when commands such as "move away" are made in large groups, I'm sure you sometimes do not move, thinking that the command is intended for another person. Misses can occur sometimes simply because it is not clear who is expected to respond to the solicit. I treat the naming of targets in Episode 16.

VI. Really the Last—Conclusion

It seems as likely that we will never have the key to hits and misses any more than we'll ever have the key to certain diseases. A certain amount of miscommunication, like a certain amount of illness, seems inevitable. But just as the discomfort of some diseases can be eased and the prevention or cure of others can be discovered, partly as a result of systematic description of healthy and diseased cells, so the distress of some misses can be eased, and the prevention of others can be sought through nonjudgmental descriptions of the components of solicits and the systematic generation of alternate solicits. Even if the number of misses is decreased only slightly, at least as a result of the investigation, it is likely that all will conclude that most misses are caused by the rules we follow in different settings rather than the stupidity, lack of sensitivity or knowledge, or the ignorance of the participants. And even though following the rules of crossword puzzle solicits in classroom solicits and other alternatives may not always decrease the number of misses, ultimately the process of searching for the key, because the search shows how normal misses are, may be more important than finding the key.

Journal Entry

The solicits treated in this episode were mainly the type that the person asking them knew the answer to. How do you feel when you are asked such questions? Do you feel differently when you are asked totally open-ended questions? To which type of solicits are your responses longer and more complex? Which type of solicit do you feel more relaxed and less uneasy about? (The distinction between solicits we know the response to and those we do not know the response to is treated in Episode 4.)

BACKGROUND NOTES

5–1. In discussing Piaget, Donaldson talks about the importance of category names or qualifying words in questions. Payne does the same thing in his discussion of questions. He refers to questions that divide information up into categories as "bifurcated questions." Buckheister has studied the *c* component in ESL, social studies, and science classes.

5–2. Frank Smith in his *Comprehension and Learning* talks about the way we file information in our brain so we can retrieve it more efficiently. I find his discussion of cognitive processing in general particularly insightful. Gibson and Levin treat the same topic; Vygotsky does too.

5–3. Ruth Crymes was one of those who urged that students become involved in the analysis of communications that they have with each other. She described specific ways students could analyze their communications, and she presented some of the insights they discovered in a paper delivered in July 1979 at the Lackland Air Force Base English Language Center.

5–4. Rowe showed how wait time led to longer responses in science classes.

EPISODE

6

Eh? Vinegar and Water?

I. A LESSON FROM LIFE—RELATING *LIFE, PROCEDURE,* AND *STUDY*

The title of this episode comes from a conversation between two friends of mine, one a chemistry teacher and the other a homemaker. The chemistry teacher had to attend a funeral. Right before the funeral, there was a snowstorm. Going home from work to get ready for the funeral, my friend had to trudge through the snow to get to his car, and in doing this he got his black shoes wet. As you know, soon after shoes get wet, especially black ones, white lines appear all over the shoes. My friend shined his shoes three times in an attempt to cover up the white lines. But after each application of shoe polish, the lines reappeared. He had just about decided not to go the funeral when my other friend, the homemaker, stopped by. She looked at the shoes, told him to get a rag and wet it with vinegar and water. He said, "Eh? Vinegar and water?" She said, "Of course." He made the solution—just as if he were in his chemistry lab at school—wiped the shoes, and the lines disappeared.

To my chemistry teacher friend, the properties of vinegar were bits of information to be learned for their own sake, content in the category I call *study*. To our mutual friend, who it turns out had never taken a chemistry course in her life, properties of vinegar were a part of general knowledge, content in the category I call *life*, subcategory *general knowledge, fg*. She did not know that vinegar contained acetic acid, as the chemistry teacher did. She only knew that it removed white lines from shoes.

The issue of relating what we teach—*study of language* or *study of other subjects*—to what we do and are outside class—*life personal* or *life general*—is hardly a new issue. In your own experience as a student, I'm sure you've encountered some teachers who, like my friend, consider *study* to be separate from *life*. Whether the area of *study* is a subject, such as chemistry (*so*) or language (*sl*), the same issue arises. Making a comment about a chemistry class, such as "I know a lot of chemical formulas and the properties of many compounds, but I can't relate any of the knowledge to my experience," is the same as making this remark about a language class: "Those French classes are too academic; we memorize dialogs and systematically analyze the language used in them, but we never use these bits of language to share our personal experiences (*life-personal*) or talk about famous people or events (*life-general*)." [Background 6–1]

The conversation between my two friends illustrates the topic I treat in this episode: relating content I call *study* to *life general*—our knowledge of the world outside the classroom—and to *life personal*—our own personal knowledge and our feelings about the world.

To instruct the chemistry teacher, my friend solicited and so communicated a third area of content: *procedure*. Each solicit contains a direction to respond. The solicit "Get a rag and wet it with vinegar" contains an explicit direction. In a solicit such as "Where do you live?" the direction is implicit, signaled by the word *where* and the word order in speech, and in print by the question mark. I put directions in solicits in the category *procedure* because they don't contain information I code as either the category *life* or *study*. Since almost all solicits contain *procedure* together with *life* or *study*, we must discuss *procedure* along with *life* and *study*.

In Table 6–1, I've listed the three major areas of content that I treat in this episode, along with two subcategories of both *life* and *study*. As usual, I've noted the source and target and some move types as well because these are necessary to identify the units we analyze.

II. GETTING VINEGAR INTO CLASS—WAYS OF RELATING DIFFERENT AREAS OF CONTENT

It Depends—Identifying Different Areas of Content

Excerpts 6–1 and 6–2 illustrate how we have to move beyond definitions of the categories of content to identify them because we have to take into account what content people attribute to communications.

Excerpts 6–1 and 6–2 illustrate that the setting and our perception of the intentions of the speakers affect the coding of the lines. The words in Excerpts 6–1 and 6–2 in

TABLE 6–1
Major Areas of Content

Source/Target	Move Type	Content
		life *f*
	solicit sol	personal *fp*
		public/general *fg*
t/s		
	response res	procedure *p*
		study *s*
s/t		
	react rea	language *sl*
		other *so*

EXCERPT 6–1
The Cafeteria

		Communications	*Source/ Target*	*Move Type*	*Content*
1	Student$_1$:	Where do you live?	s_1/s_2	sol	p + fp
2	Student$_2$:	In Queens.	s_2/s_1	res	fp
3	Student$_1$:	My aunt lives there. I go there a lot and like it where she lives.	s_1/s_2	rea	fp
4		Do you live near the airport? Where about do you live?	s_1/s_2	sol	p + fg
5	Student$_2$:	Near the site of the World's Fair grounds.	s_2/s_1	res	fg
6	Student$_1$:	Where's that in relation to the airport?	s_1/s_2	sol	p + fg

line 2, "In Queens," I coded *fp* for *life personal* in the conversation in the cafeteria. In the classroom, I coded the same words *study language, sl*. Had the conversation taken place between a customs official and a tourist, the response could be coded *procedure*, since the intention of a customs officer is usually not to share personal feelings or information. Usually, the goal is to enforce the law, the symbol of *procedure*. A customs official is interested in where one lives or how long one has been in a country to see whether one is allowed to bring in liquor or gifts without paying duty.

That we as observers have to attribute content to communications is not something no one else does. When you say "Did he really mean that?" you are trying to decide what content was communicated. We all attribute content to communications. I once saw a class of second graders reading a small book entitled something like *Stories for Fun and Pleasure*, a title that suggests the category *life*. I saw some students smiling as they read the book silently. For them, the material might have been *life*. I saw others struggling with the meaning of individual words and sentences. Many were trying to sound out words. It is hard to code the words on the page for these youngsters as anything but *study*.

I observed one youngster skip a page in the story assigned to the class. He seemed to be attracted to a picture and a caption in an unassigned section. When the student

EXCERPT 6–2
The Classroom

		Communications	*Source/ Target*	*Move Type*	*Content*
1	Teacher:	Where do you live?	t/s	sol	p + sl
2	Student:	In Queens.	s/t	res	sl
3	Teacher:	Very good.	t/s	rea	sl

sitting next to him saw this, he said: "You can't start that till the teacher tells you. I'm going to tell the teacher." To this youngster, reading seemed to be going through motions by going over pages the teacher had assigned. To this young reader, pages seemed to contain only *procedure*.

You might argue that for students during a class, any pages or any patterns are so critical for them to learn that we should code them *life*. All learning should be coded *life*, for it all is part of their experience. But important as a target language is, when it is communicated to practice it or use it for its own sake rather than to express true information, whether personal or public, I code it *study of language*, not *life*.

How to Relate*—Ways to Relate Different Areas of Content

Are They Related—Rating Excerpts and Examples of Related Content

Just because moves contain more than one area of content does not mean that the areas are relating experience and the area of study. In this section, I have rated a number of excerpts on a scale of 1 to 5. In excerpts where I think the areas of content are related, I have given a 5 rating. In those excerpts where I do not think the areas of content are related, I have given a rating of 1. Attempts to relate content in some moves that are negated by other moves I rate close to the low end of the scale and give them a 2 or 3.

The first two excerpts, 6–3A and 6–4A, I have rated 1 even though the solicits contain two areas of content, *procedure* and *study of language—p + sl*. This is because all solicits must contain a direction to do something—*procedure*—and in most cases they contain a topic the question is about, coded either *life*, *study*, or *procedure*.

The next two excerpts, 6–3B and 6–4B, I have rated 5 because the teachers added a comment I'd code *life* to the solicits. As you look at the excerpts, you will see that the teachers indicate in their solicits that students are to share their personal feelings, as well as communicate material they were studying, in their responses. The *fp* added to the *p* and *sl* indicate this.

EXCERPT 6–3A
Homework One Way (1)

		Communications	*Source/ Target*	*Move Type*	*Content*
1	Teacher:	Copy down verbs from three advertisements you see on the bus or train or television or hear on the radio.	t/c	sol	p + sl
2	Students:	(Bring in verbs written down in notebooks.)	c/t	res	sl
3	Teacher:	(Walks around room looking at notebooks.) That's not a verb. Yes, all three are verbs. You have a range of tenses. Lots of helping verbs.	t/c	rea	sl

* The *relate* in this section is not the use *relate* in FOCUS.

According to studies that have investigated student responses to literature, students see short stories as tales to be retold, but rarely identify with the characters or relate incidents in the stories to personal experiences or experiences of their friends or relatives. Literature is *study* alone, and not related to *life*. [Background 6–2]

EXCERPT 6–4A
Comprehension One Way (1)

		Communications	*Source/ Target*	*Move Type*	*Content*
1	Teacher:	Tell what happened in this chapter of *Tom Jones*.	t/s	sol	p + sl
2	Student:	Tom drank a lot, got in a fight in order to protect servants. He almost got killed.	s/t	res	sl

EXCERPT 6–3B
Homework Another Way (5)

		Communications	*Source/ Target*	*Move Type*	*Content*
1	Teacher:	Copy down verbs from the three ads you dislike the most that you see on the bus or train or television or hear on the radio.	t/c	sol	p + sl + fp
2	Students:	(Bring in verbs written down in notebooks.)	c/t	res	sl + fp
3	Teacher:	(Walks around room looking at notebooks.) I don't like that ad either—the verb sounds out of place. I smoke Camels, but the ad is bad.	t/c	rea	sl + fp

EXCERPT 6–4B
Comprehension Another Way (5)

		Communications	*Source/ Target*	*Move Type*	*Content*
1	Teacher:	Would you like to have Tom Jones as a friend after what he did in this chapter?	t/s	sol	p + sl + fp
2	Student:	Sure—he drinks a lot, fights and is very emotional but he stands by his friends—he protected the servants here and risked his life; I like loyalty.	s/t	res	sl + fp

Whether asking students to relate personal feelings with things they read in class would lead to more self-involvement and personal associations in their comments about their reading of short stories, or about other aspects of the *study of language*, cannot be determined, of course, until the alternative is tried. But the examples in Excerpts 6–3B and 6–4B at least serve to illustrate one way to relate *study* and *life*.

This is not to say that asking personal likes and dislikes guarantees a rating of 5. Relating *study* and *life* obviously involves more than asking students for personal

EXCERPT 6–5A
Thanksgiving in the U.S. (2) (T)

		Communications	Source/ Target	Move Type	Content
1	Teacher:	Taste these cranberries—they're eaten with turkey in late November in the U.S.	t/c	sol	p + sl
2	Students:	(Taste cranberries.)	c/t	res	sl
3	Teacher:	How do they taste? (Seaching for the word bitter.)	t/c	sol	p + sl
4	Student:	Like a lemon!	s/t	res	fg
5	Teacher:	(Shakes head sideways indicating "no.")	t/s	rea	sl

EXCERPT 6–6A
Cardinal Numbers (2)

		Communications	Source/ Target	Move Type	Content
1	Teacher:	Ali, how many sisters do you have? (Holds up three fingers and is interested in seeing if students can say numbers.)	t/s_1	sol	p + sl
2	Ali:	Three?	s_1/t	res	sl
3	Teacher:	Good.	t/s_1	rea	sl
4		Yukiko, how many sisters do you have? (Holds up five fingers.)	t/s_2	sol	p + sl
5	Yukiko:	Five.	s_2/t	res	sl
6	Teacher:	Very good.	t/s_2	rea	sl
7		Now, everyone, three.	t/c	sol	p + sl
8	Students:	Three.	c/t	res	sl

feelings or information, as the teachers did in Excerpts 6–3B and 6–4B. Consider the communications in Excerpts 6–5A and 6–6A.

As you can see, I ranked these two excerpts as 2, on the low side of the continuum, because I do not think that the *study of language* and *life personal* are related, in spite of the fact that the teachers ask questions with *you* in them. If the teachers had really been interested in the personal feelings in the student responses, they would not have reacted as they did. As you see, the teacher reacts to "Like a lemon!" by indicating that the response is incorrect. This suggests that the teacher was interested in *study of language* and not *study of language* plus *life personal.* In Excerpt 6–6A, lines 3 and 6, the teacher says "Good" and "Very good" after being told the number of sisters a student has. These reactions contain no indication that the teacher is reacting to anything other than the use of cardinal numbers, content in the category *study* and the subcategory *language.*

In adapted versions of Excerpts 6–5A and 6–6A, shown below and numbered 6–5B and 6–6B, the teachers still ask about cranberries and age, but the reactions are altered in a way that has the teachers commenting on the *life personal* content of the student responses as well as stating the cardinal numbers, and noting the students' language on the board, both instances of *study language, sl.*

If you go back to the B version in Excerpt 6–3, you will notice that there too the teacher's reaction commented on both the content I code *sl* for *study of language* and *fp* for *life personal.*

EXCERPT 6–5B
Thanksgiving in the U.S. (5)

		Communications	*Source/ Target*	*Move Type*	*Content*
1	Teacher:	Taste these cranberries that Juan brought in to class today. His mother bought them to eat with turkey tomorrow. Thanksgiving Day.	t/c	sol	p + fg + sl
2	Students and teacher:	(Taste cranberries.)	c/t	res	fg + sl
3	Teacher:	How do they taste? (Interested in students' feelings and in clarifying some descriptive words used in tasting.)	t/c	sol	p + fp + sl
4	Student$_1$:	Like a lemon!	s_1/t	res	sl + fp
5	Teacher:	(Writes "Like a lemon!" on the blackboard and "Sara," the student's name, next to it.)	t/c	rea	sl + fp
6	Teacher:	Some other comments? (about Juan's cranberries)	t/c	sol	p + sl + sl
7	Student$_2$:	Sour—I don't like them!	s_2/t	res	sl + fp

EXCERPT 6–6B
Cardinal Numbers (5)

		Communications	*Source/ Target*	*Move Type*	*Content*
1	Teacher:	Ali, how many sisters do you have? (Interested in having students use cardinal numbers and finding out about their families.)	t/s_1	sol	p + fp + sl
2	Ali:	Two.	s_1/t	res	lp + sl
3	Teacher:	I do too. I have two sisters, one older and one younger.	t/s_1	rea	fp + sl
4		Yukiko, how many sisters do you have?	t/s_2	sol	p + fp + sl
5	Yukiko:	Four—all older.	s_2/t	res	fp + sl
6	Teacher:	Lots of help in doing dishes and repairing things! I couldn't afford five girls.	t/s_2	rea	fp + sl

Journal Entry

Though personal questions may get you a 5 rating, they may cause different reactions from students. At cocktail parties, many from my culture are aghast at the thought that they have to respond to personal questions. When asked "How do you feel about the president?" some do not want to respond. When others are asked how much they make or even what they do, they feel their personal life is being investigated by people they don't know. Some resent personal questions in public.

How do you feel about being asked questions that contain content I code as *life personal* in a public place, such as at a party or in a classroom? How do your students feel about these questions? Do they consider them intrusions? Do they feel like responding "None of your business!" or do they feel that such questions show personal interest?

EXCERPT 6–7A
How Say Dis? (3)

		Communications	*Source/ Target*	*Move Type*	*Content*
1	Student:	How say dis? (Pointing to the word *Hudson*.)	s_1/t	sol	p + sl
2	Teacher:	The first part rhymes with *bud* and the second part is said like *sin*—like this: Hudson.	t/s_1	res	sl
3		Class, I'd like you to use your dictionaries to find out how words are pronounced.	t/c	str	p + sl

I did not rate teacher solicits 5, even though teacher solicits contained *procedure* plus *study*, because by definition a solicit must contain both a direction to do something—*procedure*—with or about something—*life, procedure,* or *study*. I rated Excerpts 6–3A and 6–4A with a 1. However, I have given a rating of 3 to Excerpt 6–7A. The content column is coded the same as Excerpts 6–3A and 6–4A next to the solicits: *procedure* plus *study of language, p + sl*. The reason I rated Excerpt 6–7A with a 3 is that the source of the initial solicit in the excerpt is a student rather than a teacher. Generally, students solicit much less frequently than teachers, so when a student solicits—and thus relates procedure and study, life, or procedure—I think it should be judged with criteria different from those used to judge teacher solicits. [Background 6–3]

Excerpt 6–7B is a variation and expansion of Excerpt 6–7A. I have rated it 5 because not only is the same student solicit communicated, but the teacher communications relate content from different areas. Read Excerpt 6–7B, noting the content.

The student solicits about language in Excerpt 6–7B, as well as the excerpt entitled *Homework*, remind us that no matter how many hours students spend with teachers, they spend more hours without them. Except where the target language is not used outside the classroom, the best place students have to make use of the target language *is* outside the language classroom. Even where the target language is not the *lingua franca*, books and recordings are usually available. Thus, one type of ideal meshing of *life, procedure,* and *study* takes place when students learn on their own by using the target language with native speakers outside class, or at least by listening to it or reading it on their own. If for no other reason, responding to questions about learning should be encouraged because of this fact. Of course, student questions in class can never replace efforts to learn outside class because of the simple fact that the amount of time students are out of class is so much greater than the amount of time they are in class, even if they are in intensive programs.

I don't know whether you winced at the form of the language in the solicit "How say dis?" or not. If you did and you are interested in treating errors, there are many ways of doing so. I treat many of them in Episode 12.

EXCERPT 6–7B
How Say Dis? (5)

		Communications	*Source/ Target*	*Move Type*	*Content*
1	Student:	How say dis? (Pointing to the word *Hudson*.)	s_1/t	sol	p + sl
2	Teacher:	(Writes the student's question on the board.) Let's look it up in the dictionary.	t/s_1	sol	p + sl
3	Students:	(Look up the word in the dictionary.)	c/o	res	sl
4	Student:	I no understand. I hate dictionary.	s_1/t	rea	p* + fp
5	Teacher:	They are difficult. Before I understood them, I hated them too.	t/s_1	rea	p* + fp

EXCERPT 6–7B *(continued)*

		Communications *	Source/ Target	Move Type	Content
6		Look up *bud* and *medicine* and compare the marks next to them and say them.	t/s_1	sol	p + sl
7	Student:	(Performs both tasks.)	s_1/o	res	sl
8		Oh, Hudson. (Says it so it rhymes with *scene*.)	s_1/t	rea	sl
9	Teacher:	Say this—pointing to *medicine*.	t/s_1	sol	p + sl
10	Student:	Hud, Hud, son (as *scene*) Hudson (correctly).	s_1/t	rea	sl
11	Teacher:	Now look up this word. (pointing to *this* in student's question written on the board.)	t/s_1	sol	p + sl
12	Student:	(Looks up the word.)	s_1/o + t	res	sl
13	Teacher:	I'm going to keep your question on the board and I want all students to ask questions like it. They delight me. If you make a mistake in them, it is fine—we will practice saying them right.	t/c	str†	p + fp + sl

* Any indications that items are not understood I put in a subcategory of *procedure* I call *check*; communications that indicate how easy or difficult something is I put in a subcategory of *procedure* I call *difficulty factor*.

† I treat ways to relate life, procedure, and study in structuring moves in Episode 19.

Journal Entry

If you have a chance to compare communications in classrooms and in tutoring sessions, do so. And see whether there is more *life* related to *study* on the part of students when there are fewer participants and the participants have a different relationship between themselves and the teacher, as in a tutoring session, or whether the same areas of content are communicated in classes that have many participants and tutoring sessions that have few. Then, if you have used the classification of the subcategories of *life, personal*, and *general*, see whether one of these two subcategories is more likely to be related to *study*.

Congruence—Other Examples of Relating Content

There are other ways students relate different areas of content than by asking questions such as "How say dis?" Often, student responses show attempts to relate different areas of content. In Excerpt 6–8A, line 2, I think the student is relating two areas of content. If you do too, write the two areas of content you think he or she is trying to relate. Use one of these pairs of abbreviations: *p + sl, fg + sl* or *p + fg*.

An alternative version in Excerpt 6–8B shows the two areas of content the student was trying to relate. Look at the student comment in line 4.

EXCERPT 6–8A
The Right Answer

		Communications	Source/ Target	Move Type	Content
1	Teacher:	Can elephants fly? (Has an answer in mind—wants to test to see if students know elephants are heavy.)	t/c	sol	p + sl
2	$Student_1$:	Yes.	s_1/t	res	
3	Teacher:	Who knows the right answer?	t/c	sol	p + sl
4	$Student_2$:	No.	s_2/t	res	sl

EXCERPT 6–8B
The Right Answer (T)

		Communications	Source/ Target	Move Type	Content
1	Teacher:	Can elephants fly? (Is interested in learning how students perceive elephants and whether they know what one is.)	t/c	sol	p + sl + fg
2	Student:	Yes.	s_1/t	res	fg + sl
3	Teacher:	(Simply waits for student to continue.)	t/s_1	rea	p
4	Student:	I saw Dumbo on television last week—flying! (name of a flying elephant in Walt Disney films)	s_1/t	res	fg + sl

I coded the student comment in line 4 *fg + sl* because the student was relating something he had seen on television—*life general*—with the teacher's interest in the meaning of the word *elephant*—*study of language*.

This same lack of congruence between the area of content expected by the teacher and communicated by the student occurred in the first version of *Thanksgiving in the U.S.* too, Excerpt 6–6A. The teacher shook his head indicating "no" after the student responded with "Like a lemon!" to "How do they [cranberries] taste?" In both cases, the teacher was thinking of *study*, and the students were thinking of *life*, or *life* and *study*. As a result of this lack of congruence, opportunities for relating *life* and *study* were lost.

Lack of congruence does not only occur in *study* and *life*. In Excerpt 6–9, there is lack of congruence because the teacher is interested only in *procedure* and the student is communicating information I code *life personal*.

Listening and Waiting—Aids to Relate Content

One way to increase the possibility that the content of teacher and student communications will be in the same category, and therefore increase the opportunities for

EXCERPT 6–9
At the Door

		Communications	*Source/ Target*	*Move Type*	*Content*
1	Teacher:	Do you have a note from the director giving permission to come to class late?	t/s	sol	p + p
2	Student:	I feel sick.	s/t	rea	fp
3	Teacher:	I want you to show me the note.	t/s	sol	p + p
4	Student:	I'd feel better if I could sit down.	s/t	rea	fp

different areas of content to be related, is to try to avoid the "harried waiter syndrome." In restaurants, waiters ask customers questions like "Boiled or fried?" in reference to potatoes as they take orders. When a customer responds with "Rice," the harried waiter, thinking only of the two choices he gave, writes down "fried." After all, there is more of a similarity between "rice" and "fried" than between "rice" and "boiled" because of the *r* sound. The totally unexpected "rice" is like the "yes" response to "Can elephants fly?" in line 2 of Excerpt 6–8A.

In Excerpt 6–8B, the second version, the teacher might have expected "no" just as much as the first teacher. But he was willing to wait a few seconds after getting a response that was different from what he expected. Waiting gave the student time to add "I saw Dumbo on television last week—flying!" in line 4. This response shows that the student *did* know elephants were heavy, one of the goals the teacher had in asking the question in the area of study. At the same time, the response provided the student with an opportunity to relate general knowledge—*life*—to *study*, represented by vocabulary items such as *fly*, *elephants*, and *can*.

Given the time, some students may relate *life* to *study* in their responses. But for this to happen, we have to listen to the responses rather than to our expectations of the responses. Since our expectations are such a powerful factor in determining messages we receive, it is not usually possible to stop making use of our expectations by making a resolution to do so or by willing it. We have to alter the way we act.

One way to prevent our expectations from "hearing" what others say is to pause for a set period of time, say five to seven seconds, after another person says something. This amount of time gives the speaker time to expand on the comment made, and it gives you time to compare and contrast the communications produced with the communications you expected. Studies of teachers who allow students longer amounts of time before they comment on the student resonses or ask another question have consistently shown that longer periods of wait time produce communications that are longer and reflect more thought than those produced in machine-gun fashion. [Background 6–4]

Another way to stop our expectations from preventing us from "hearing" what others say is to write down what they say. As you recall, the teacher in the second version of How Say Dis? wrote the student's solicit on the blackboard right after the student said it. Writing takes a few seconds and thus automatically provides an extended period of wait time, giving the student a chance to say more. In addition, it provides the listener with a chance to stand back and look at the communication. If the words on the blackboard are different from those the student said, the student can say so. Had the teacher in *At the Door* written down "I feel sick," he could have seen that the student was communicating personal feelings, and it might have been more likely that he could have seen the incongruity between his questions in the category *procedure* and the student's response in the category *life*.

While the teacher in the first version of Thanksgiving in the U.S. indicated that "Like a lemon!" was not the expected response to "How do they [cranberries] taste?", the teacher in the second version wrote the response on the blackboard, along with the name of the student who said the sentence. Whether the writing of the student response helped the teacher make the decision to accept the response, or whether the teacher's attitude was an accepting one, we cannot know. But since writing student communications on the blackboard gives us a chance to note the area of content it is in and gives the student time to expand on the initial response, it is more likely that we will hear "rice" for "rice" than if we do not write the words on the blackboard. If the students see that we have written "fried" for "rice," they too have another opportunity to tell us that what we "heard" is different from what they said.

Another way to provide students with a chance to confirm or reject your rendition of what they say is to paraphrase or restate what they say. Though this takes less time than writing the student communication on the board, it does give the student the chance to help you know whether what you "heard" is what the student said. And this step also provides you with a little time to see whether the student communication is in the same area of content as the one you expected or in a different one. If it is in a different one, it gives the students time to expand on what they said, and allows them time to relate two areas of content, theirs and the one you expected.

See whether student communications, or communications made by your friends in conversations at parties or meetings, contain both content you asked for and content in another area when you provide them with more time to speak, either by waiting, writing their message down, or paraphrasing it. If in all your solicits you remember that responses can be in the area of *life, procedure*, or *study*, or some combination of them, rather than only in the area of your solicit, your area of expectations are broadened considerably. Remembering that a response such as "Yes" to "Can elephants fly?" can be referring not only to *study* but also to *life* might make it less likely to accept only "the right answer."

Journal Entry

One of the alternatives I just suggested was to restate what the person you are talking to says so he or she, and others as well, can comment on the accuracy and intent of the original communication. As you see people doing this, what surface manifestations do you observe that distinguish those who really care about what is being restated and those who simply restate—reproduce—as a routine?

Formulas—Coding Ways to Relate Content

In Table 6–2 I have taken the elements from Table 6–1 and arranged them in a matching-column exercise to show the alternatives suggested so far in this episode. To match the formula for each alternative, I have written a verbal description for each one. The verbal descriptions are listed on the left-hand side, and the formulas written in FOCUS are listed on the right-hand side. Next to each formula there is a blank line on which I'd like you to write the number of the verbal description that fits the coding of the formula with FOCUS. So that the matching can be done more quickly, I have arranged the alternatives in groups of four. The matching others have done is given in the footnotes.

TABLE 6–2
Coding Ways to Relate Content

VERBAL DESCRIPTIONS OF ALTERNATIVES	Code	FORMULAS FOR ALTERNATIVES *Source/ Target*	*Move Type*	*Content**
1. Teacher asks questions requiring the use of a particular item of the language or the display of knowledge of other subject matter for its own sake.	A. ___	t/s	rea	s
2. Teacher asks questions requiring the use of a particular item of the language or the display of knowledge of other subject matter and true information about the student's life or life in general.	B. ___	t/s	sol	p + s
3. Teacher comments on the form of student communications.	C. ___	t/s	sol	p + s + f
4. Teacher comments on the form of student communications and the information they contain.	D. ___	t/s	rea	s + f
5. Teacher reacts immediately after the student has communicated. If the student communication contained content in the category *study*, the teacher reaction is in the same area.	E. ___	s/t t/s	res rea	s p
6. Teacher reacts immediately after the student has communicated. If the student communication contained content in the category *study*, the teacher reaction is in a different category. The content of teacher and student communications is incongruent.	F. ___	s/t t/s	res rea	s p + s
7. Teacher, as a procedure, reacts by waiting five to seven seconds after the student has communicated before communicating information about either a particular item of language, some bit of subject matter, or the person's life.	G. ___	s/t t/s	res rea	f p + p
8. Teacher, as a procedure, reacts by waiting five to seven seconds after the student has communicated before communicating information about either a particular item of language, some bit of subject matter, or the person's life. The reaction contains content that is different from the content in the student response.	H. ___	s/t t/s	res rea	s s
9. Students ask questions of the teacher only about the subject being studied.	I. ___	s/t	sol	f + p + s
10. Students ask questions of the teacher about his or her personal life and background.	J. ___	s/s	sol	p + f

TABLE 6–2 *(continued)*

VERBAL DESCRIPTIONS OF ALTERNATIVES	Code	FORMULAS FOR ALTERNATIVES *Source/ Target*	*Move Type*	*Content**
11. Students ask each other questions about personal life and background.	K. ___	s/t	sol	s
12. Students ask questions of the teacher about anything they want.	L. ___	s/t	sol	p + f

Coding: A: 3, B: 1, C: 2, D: 4, E: 6, F: 7, G: 8, H: 5, I: 12, J: 11, K: 9, L: 10.
* The *p* before each plus sign stands for wait time in the reactions in F and G.

Basics—Planning a Lesson

Excerpt 6–10 contains some student communications I overheard after a class. Excerpt 6–11 contains examples of the language Martha and the students used during the lesson. Martha's questions and the students' answers show again that just because we ask students questions about themselves does not mean that *study* and *life* are related as a result.

As you can see as you read both excerpts, not only are the areas of content during and after class incongruent, shown by the coding of the content as well as the lines themselves, but also the patterns used by the students when they talk to each other after class are much more complex than the ones they use in class in reply to Martha's

EXCERPT 6–10
Conversations after Martha's Class (T)

		Communications	*Source/ Target*	*Move Type*	*Content*
1	$Student_1$:	I worked and I went to work with my father and I got a cut. He fixes sinks and drains.	s_1/s_2	rea*	fp
2	$Student_3$:	I haven't even had a turn!	s_3/s_4	rea	p
3	$Student_4$:	You're a big fat liar!	s_4/s_3	rea	fp
4	$Student_5$:	My sister was doing a cake in the oven and it came out real black.	s_5/s_6	rea	fp
5	$Student_7$:	There was a lot of water!	s_7/s_8	rea	fg
6	$Student_8$:	Some of the people died, I think. (Closes eyes)	s_8/s_7	rea	fg
7	$Student_9$:	Look at his stinking feet!	s_9/s_{10}	sol	p + fp

* This line could be a response too. I did not hear what came before it. If it is a reply to questions such as "What did you do?" then of course it is a response. I coded it as a reaction because it seemed to me that the students were just commenting on what each one said and did not seem to be asking each other questions.

EXCERPT 6–11
Patterns during Martha's Class

		Communications	Source/ Target	Move Type	Content
1	Teacher:	What did you do last night?	t/s	sol	p + sl
2	Student$_1$:	I studied.	s_1/t	res	sl
3	Teacher:	(Writes "Juan studied last night" on the blackboard.)	t/c	rea	sl
4		What did you do last night?	t/s_2	sol	p + sl
5	Student$_2$:	I watched television.	s_2/t	res	sl
6	Teacher:	(Writes "Maria watched television" on blackboard.)	t/c	rea	sl
7		What did you watch?	t/s_2	sol	p + sl
8	Student$_2$:	An interesting program.	s_2/t	res	sl
9	Teacher:	(Writes "She watched an interesting program" on board.)	t/c	rea	sl
10		Juan, what did you study?	t/s_1	sol	p + sl
11	Student$_1$:	English.	s_1/t	res	sl
12	Teacher:	(Writes "And he studied English" on blackboard after "Juan studied last night.")	t/s_1	rea	sl
13		You all did such interesting things.	t/c	rea	fp

questions. Attention to student communications outside class provides us with a way to discover the *life* content they talk about and the level of the *study* content they are capable of.

Read both excerpts, and after you do, I'd like you to plan a short lesson showing how you would relate the pattern Martha was trying to teach to the language and the topics the student communications after class contain. In short, relate *study of language* and *life*.

As you might imagine, the plans different teachers make vary a great deal. The first decision one teacher made to relate the conversations after Martha's class to the pattern during the class was to divide the class into groups of four, realizing that generally, outside of classrooms, we ask and answer personal questions in small groups, not in front of thirty other people. Then, the teacher told all the students in all the groups that they were to decide who in each group had done the most unexpected thing the night before, and how many had done the same thing. Then, each group was told to discover whether all the members of each group had at any time during the past week all done the same thing at the same time. The students asked each other questions such as "Well, then what did you do on Saturday? Did you do that too? When did you do that?". The teacher circulated from group to group commenting on what they had done by indicating times he had done the same thing and volunteering descriptions of other activities he had done that were unexpected, and similar or different from the students'. The teacher also treated some errors of form in the students' questions as he visited each group. Both while the teacher was with a group, and before and after the visit, students reacted to each others' questions and responses with statements parallel to some of the reactions made after Martha's class: "You're kidding." "Come on, I don't believe that."

Another teacher asked each student to write down either the most exciting thing that happened to him or her in the last few days or the most exciting event he or she had witnessed. Then, the teacher asked students to pair off, state the event each had written, and ask each other about the event. As the students talked, the teacher wrote down some of the events she considered particularly exciting. After a few minutes she said she would state some events she had heard that she considered exciting, and that students should ask her questions about the event. If she couldn't answer them, she'd have the student who wrote the event answer the questions about it. This teacher also invited students to ask the question, "Why did so and so do such and such?" This question follows the same pattern as "What did so and so do?" but usually produces longer responses since a why question invites expansion rather than short, factual responses. As students heard events that others considered exciting described, some reacted as follows: "That's not exciting"; "Exciting? That's dull"; "That doesn't make it exciting."

A third teacher divided the class into two groups. Each person in each group had to write down the name of a famous person and the thing the person did to achieve fame or notoriety. Then one student in the first group, chosen by the flip of a coin, asked a student in the other group, "What did ______ do?" (with the name of the famous person in the blank, of course). If no one in the other group knew what made the person famous, the team of the person who asked the question got one point. When someone on the other team answered the question, the right to ask questions switched to this group. No student on either team had to state the thing a person did to achieve fame that the original student had written down. Each student simply had to say something that was true, and verifiable, that had made a person famous. Many of the students repeated "What did ______ do?" with rising intonation before they answered it, as a person might say "What's this?" with rising intonation after someone touched an article he or she obviously knew the name of and asked "What's this?"

None of these "plans" is earthshaking. But, after all, most daily conversations we have out of class are matter-of-fact and routine. Each "plan" has in it, however, elements that guaranteed student-to-student communication rather than just teacher-to-student communication. And each one related the pattern "What did ______ do?" to the experience of the students.

The first two plans related the patterns to the personal experiences of the students, and the third one related it to different bits of general knowledge different ones had at their command. By dividing the students into groups or pairs, and playing a game (in the case of the third teacher), the possibility that students would communicate personal experiences was increased. The usual level of discourse in classrooms and other public places is impersonal, partly because of the number of participants involved. The smaller the group, the greater the possibility for personal remarks. One reason for silence in elevators in many countries surely is that, though the number of participants is small and the distance between them is intimate, thus calling for personal remarks, each person is usually a complete stranger to the others. Unable to follow the rules that demand intimate remarks, everyone in the elevator is silent. [Background 6–5]

As you recall, after Martha's class, a series of reactions occurred rather than a series of questions and answers. Some of these reactions were caused by disagreements: "You're a big fat liar!" (line 3). Others were caused by not following the rules: "I haven't even had a turn!" (line 2). The first two teachers, by limiting the type of experience to be recounted—unexpected and exciting—provided grounds for disagreement. The third teacher, by asking students to follow the rules of a game, provided grounds for student reactions to enforce the rules. While the usual pattern of moves in classrooms is teacher solicit, student response, followed by teacher reaction, outside the classroom these moves are combined in a much greater range of sequences. While sticking to the usual format of teacher solicit followed by student response followed by teacher reaction may enable students to follow the same sequence of moves in other classes, it does not prepare them for meeting the wide range of sequences found in other settings. The pedagogical function usual in classrooms hardly prepares one for the social function needed when talking to other individuals, for the narrative function needed when telling stories, and for all the other functions we use language for, in addition to the one that involves replying to questions a teacher asks that he or she usually knows the answer to. I list some functions in Excerpt 8–1. [Background 6–6]

Journal Entry

Describe a rule you think was being followed in a class you taught or observed right before you started this episode, and that you think was broken as a result of your experience with this episode. Describe the alternative you found in this episode that you think resulted in the breaking of the rule as well.

The Usual—Arguments about Relating *Life, Procedure,* and *Study*

Some contend that there is no need to relate the language taught in the classroom to the uses students may need to put the language to outside the classroom. In the class, the emphasis should be on the structural system and the sound system. When these are mastered, students can easily use the language to communicate whatever they want outside the class. The call "Back to the basics!" is a recurring reminder of the strength of this point of view not only in the teaching of language, but in the teaching of all subjects. "Progressive education" does not have a good connotation in all circles. [Background 6–7]

Of course, no point of view is universally accepted. There are those who argue for relating *study* to *life* with as much vigor as those who argue against doing it. Rather than leaving students' needs for out-of-class treatment, there are those who contend that we need to start language lessons with what students feel compelled to say. If the students cannot say what they need to in the target language, they are told to do it in their own language, and it is then translated into the target language. Once samples of the students' own language are available, the sound and grammatical systems can be related to them. Many in this school of thought would argue not only that student language must be related to the formal features of the language, rather than the other way around, but also that if the teacher has to choose between concern for features of the language—*study*—or the needs and feelings of the student—*life*—*study* is not the area to select. [Background 6–8]

There are always those who take positions between the extremes. By developing sequences of exercises that move from what are called practice, manipulation, or skill-getting exercises to application, realistic production, or skill-using, some argue that the mastery of patterns in classes can lead to the use of the patterns in class to communicate personal feelings or information, thus relating *study* and *life*. [Background 6–9]

Another group advocates the use of dialogs and reading materials on topics of interest to the students, and believes that, by highlighting grammatical structures and parts of the sound system in these samples of language, one can relate *study* and *life*. English for specific purposes—ESP—which is an attempt to teach a waiter only the language he will need to hear and say as he waits on tables, or a research chemist only the language he or she will have to read—study of language and study of other subjects—is a logical development of the school that tries to produce dialogs students need to use as a way of illustrating the grammatical and sound systems of the language. [Background 6–10]

Still another group believes there is little need to go outside the classroom to apply the language, and has developed a series of dialogs that illustrate the structure of English through classroom activities. To teach the *too* in "too heavy," for example, one book contains comments such as these: "Ali, can you lift your desk alone? No, it's too heavy. Farah, touch the celing. I can't; it's too high." To teach possessive pronouns, this sequence is suggested: "Touch your nose. Now, touch my nose. Touch the nose of the student next to you. Is this your nose or my nose?" Critics argue that both the language and the activities that accompany the language are so artificial that they do not reflect either *life* or *study*, much less a relationship between the two. [Background 6–11]

To counter the criticism that many class activities like moving chairs or touching noses are fake, some suggest that games and group problem-solving activities be used to relate language form and real use of language the way we employ language outside the classroom. Many of these suggestions require that the teacher not be present when the students are solving their problem. [Background 6–12]

Because role-playing combines the idea of using language students are likely to encounter, as the dialog groups advocate, with action, as the activity groups emphasize, some consider it an ideal way to relate language to the needs of the students. Drama and the teaching of language through commands that require physical responses from students are two variations of role-playing. In fact, in following a command such as "Open the oven," a student can perform the physical response required in a dramatic way and thus combine these two variations on role-playing. [Background 6–13]

In spite of the fact that role-playing, total physical response, realistic dialogs, English for specific purposes, classroom activities, and problem-solving games have been suggested as ways to relate *study, procedure,* and *life*, descriptions of some classrooms reveal that little relating of these areas goes on when the teacher is in charge of the class. Though many of these alternatives are designed to try to integrate *life, procedure,* and *study*, in my observations of classes in which these activities are engaged in, many communications contain only one area of content. Tallies of thousands of student communications in English as a second language classrooms in elementary and secondary schools, and hundreds of communications in high school French classes, have shown that *study of language* alone is communicated in almost all student responses to teacher questions. [Background 6–14]

Journal Entry

One clue to the identification of communications that relate different areas of content is the variety of mediums used to communicate the content. The students have their arms folded or hands by their sides, and they sit or stand without any movement of their bodies, unlike people using language for other purposes. In recitations, the voice is usually not modulated either. In actual language use, even on the phone, we not only change our tone of voice often, but we move our hands, eyebrows, faces, and other parts of our bodies.

From teaching you are able to observe, transcribe some taped communications in which you think different areas of content are related. Then, set the tapes aside for a few days. Return to them and select communications that are made with speech plus other mediums. See if there are many matches between the transcribed moments you thought related different areas of content and the presence of communications made by multiple mediums.

III. THE END—CONCLUSION

No I'm Not—More than Relevant and Free Conversation

You might be reacting about now with a comment like, "He's just saying make the subject relevant." I'm really not saying this. First, different people have contrasting ideas of the meaning of *relevant.* Second, areas of study are not of themselves *relevant* or *irrelevant.* One of the components of vinegar is acetic acid. My chemistry teaching friend had taught many lessons on acetic acid. He knew its chemical composition as well as its properties, and he knew that vinegar contains it. But neither in class nor out of class did he relate this information to white lines on shoes caused by getting the leather wet. Acetic acid, like a gerund, or any other topic, is not in itself relevant or irrelevant. Shakespare's "Cowards die many times before their death" can be related to our experience or treated as a line from a play with a particular stress pattern. But the line itself is neither relevant nor irrelevant.

Rather than thinking I'm advocating teaching that is relevant, you might think that I'm advocating free conversation. But there would be little point in an episode if I were simply urging that students be allowed to talk about what they want. Getting students to do this is easy. It requires no planning or training. There are almost always some students who love to talk about themselves and things that concern them. But for this type of free conversation to occur, a teacher is not needed, only a suitable setting, refreshments perhaps, and people with time. A great deal of content I call *life* is communicated before or after classes, as well as at cocktail parties, holiday dinners, play areas in parks, and in coffeehouses and tea shops. But the *life* component in these settings is not generally integrated with *study*, nor are teachers needed to cause the conversations to take place. It would seem a silly idea to hire teachers to be on hand when they talk about things that concern them, communications in the category I call *life.* And to have classes in which *life* alone is communicated would be as much a failure of relating study to *life* as would classes with *study* alone.

The alternatives suggested in this episode, as you will see, are not to have cocktail parties in class without cocktails, or tea and coffee breaks without these beverages. Nor are the alternatives substitutes for the other attempts to relate *life* and *study*, such as role-playing, dialogs, games, and classroom actions to illustrate the language. Rather, the alternatives suggested here provide specific ways for you to relate *study* and *life* in any methods or materials you use.

Not Necessarily Easy—More than Surface Behavior Is Necessary

Dividing students into groups and asking them to ask each other about unexpected or exciting things that actually happened to them are obviously only surface behaviors. While I would argue that group work, requests for exciting and unexpected things that actually happened, and personal comments are better than the absence of these types of moves, they are all only a first step. They, like all the other alternatives, are, together with the thesis of this episode, only a starting point and a series of small steps toward the goal of learning more about ourselves by learning more about our students. While I like to think students will learn more if we relate the areas of study we teach to their experiences, I cannot prove that this will happen. But I do know that understanding the concerns of students helps us recognize and admit our own concerns because both of our concerns are basically the same. We all seek to have a clearer idea of who we are, and we are all anxious about what we do and what we are not able to do. [Background 6–15]

One teacher wrote this description of her attempt to help herself see who she was by trying to relate *study* and *life* with her students:

> First words must have an intense meaning.
>
> First words must be already part of the dynamic life.
>
> First books must be made of the stuff of the child himself, whatever and wherever the child.

She followed this description for the need to have students read, speak, and write only their most intense feelings with a number of examples of student communications. Here is one of them.

> Mummy
>
> Ihaka
>
> hit
>
> cried
>
> kiss
>
> Daddy hit Ihaka.
>
> Ihaka cried.
>
> Mummy kissed Ihaka.
>
> Daddy hit Ihaka.
>
> Ihaka cried.
>
> Kiss Ihaka, Mummy. [Background 6–16]

You might think that these lines are unrelated to "Eh? Vinegar and water?" On one level, they are. Crying and kissing concern the personal part of life and white lines on shoes concern the public part. But the *personal* and *public* areas of *life* are related because they both show that our needs cannot be met by mastery of a stable, controlled body of knowledge or even a process of learning alone. Life consists not only of the logic and reason of areas of systematic study, but also of the general knowledge and emotions and feelings of life. We might use mastery of an area of study to cope with our concerns. And mastery of some aspect of a subject, or investigation of a subject for its own sake, might provide some feelings of satisfaction. But no matter how much we know in any field, our personal experiences and the things we need to know for coping outside the classroom still are our central concern. By relating *study* and *life*, we recognize this fact.

A teacher should not be expected to know how each aspect of a subject is related to his or her own or his or her students' concerns. To expect all chemistry teachers to know that acetic acid in vinegar can aid in removing the white lines that form when leather gets wet would be unreasonable. But the argument in this episode is not that teachers should know how each area of a subject can be related to experience. Rather, the argument is that part of the job of a teacher is to ask him or herself and his or her students what concerns are central, and what connections each sees between experience and knowledge, so that relationships between *study* and *life* can be discovered. Further, the argument is that needing to know how to remove white lines from shoes is the surface manifestation of the anxiety we all feel about much of life, the same way that the student's comment "I hate dictionary" (Excerpt 6–7B) is more than a literal statement about lack of affection for dictionaries.

I hope that the topic of this episode, and the few surface behaviors I have suggested as alternatives, will help you and those you work with in learning more about the self, as well as the subject being taught, no matter what set of materials or methods you use. "Tangled, muddy, painful, and perplexed" as "the world of concrete personal experiences in which [the world outside the classroom] belongs," this is the world we and our students must face. [Background 6–17]

BACKGROUND NOTES

6–1. The quotations about classroom activities in language classes reflect the central concern in education of trying to relate experience to education. In fact, that is why Dewey called his classic work *Experience and education.* Barnes in *From communication to curriculum* discusses this issue again in relationship to group work. The *curriculum* in Barnes's title refers to Dewey's *education* and my category *study*, and Barnes's word *communication* is parallel to Dewey's *experience* and my category of *content—life.*

6–2. James Squire asked students to share their reactions to short stories with him orally. He found that the bulk of their responses were restatements of the story. He found very few comments in which readers said things like "That reminds me of my brother" or "I feel just what that character felt." Purves in his discussion of responses to literature states much the same thing. Whether students don't relate their experiences to literature when they are asked to comment on stories that they read because they really don't do any relating, or because they don't think it's expected because of their experiences in classrooms, is hard to know. But the fact is that studies of responses to literature do not show much integration of the categories *study* and *life*, to use my terms.

6–3. In a study of French classes in an English-speaking country, Lobman found very few student solicits. Three of my own students found few student solicits when they studied ESL classrooms for their dissertations: Hines, Rwakyaka and Shapiro-Skrobe.

6–4. In one of the classic studies of wait time, Rowe found that students in science classes consistently talked more and made more complex responses when teachers allowed students more time to respond. In Barnes's discussion of group work, he consistently shows that students need more time to explore their thoughts. The need for teachers to have students give perfectly shaped responses is a need that can never be met. Surely one of the reasons that students stop talking in many classes when the teacher asks a question in front of the whole group is that students are unable to give the perfectly shaped responses they know are required. When students have time with each other to shape their responses and explore what they want to say as they are talking, they usually have a great deal more to say.

6–5. In *The five clocks*, Joos describes five levels of talk moving from something in print that we read, which he calls frozen, all the way to conversations between husband and wife or other people who know each other well in which only a few words need be said because so much is understood without words. From intimate to frozen, he discusses the characteristics of each clock and he also discusses the types of settings that call forth the use of each clock. If we accept Joos's classification, we can easily see why certain types of communication are not possible in a classroom simply because the setting does not allow us to communicate in some of the clocks that he describes.

6–6. Halliday discusses what he considers to be some of the major functions of language, and one of his conclusions is that the representational function, in which we simply name objects and describe, is a function used almost exclusively in the classroom. He contends that one of the reasons students might have difficulty in the classroom is that they are used to all the other functions outside of classrooms, but in classrooms they are exposed to only one function. Halliday urges that students be given more opportunities to ask questions they don't know the answers to and pretend in classrooms, since these functions are so important for language growth outside classrooms. See Episode 8, where the functions are listed in Excerpt 8–1.

6–7. When Fries developed the texts that came to be known as the Michigan Materials, he was working with students who lived among English speakers in Michigan. And as soon as the students finished their work in class with the structures that Fries emphasized, they had the opportunity to go outside class and use language to talk about whatever they wanted with the people they lived with in the community. Though Gattegno does not talk about how students are to speak outside the classroom, he also emphasizes the structural system and the sound system in the lessons he advocates. In neither of the materials these men prepared is there much allowance for students to discuss what they want to discuss. The emphasis in both cases is on the structural system and the sound system of the target language.

6–8. Curran, in *Counseling learning*, starts with communications the students feel compelled to say. The sequential development Fries and Gattegno advocate Curran ignores in eliciting initial language. Jakobovits and Gordon strike a middle road between those who advocate only the use of language for its own sake and those who urge that students say what they want to say. By setting up contexts that force certain things to be said, Jakobovits and Gordon try to integrate the experience students have and the language they need.

6–9. Paulston and Bruder present steps in their methods book to move students from practice with language to use of language for communicating what they want to say. Some texts, such as the one by Rossner et al., have sections instructing students to ask each other for personal information to get away from practice only with patterns of language for their own sake. Wilga Rivers (1972) urges that students become involved in games and small-group activities that force them to use language in a range of ways, though she urges that students be prepared for the activities by having the language they need presented to them first. The title of her aticle, "Talking off the tops of their heads," shows the importance she attaches to the use of language for expressing more than study for its own sake.

6–10. The movement in Europe that started to relate language to the needs of students, popularly referred to as English for Specific Purposes, and discussed by, among others, Van Ek, is another attempt to try to integrate students' needs, often some area of study, with the target language.

6–11. A. S. Hornby developed classroom situations to teach most of the words and sentence patterns students need. While the situations are very clever in most cases, Michel West pointed out that sentences such as *This is my nose*, while very useful for clarifying meaning, force us to say things that we in fact would never say outside of the language classroom when we had something important to say to someone. At any rate, Hornby's situations are well worth reading, as well as West's criticism of the situations he made 1955.

6–12. The best source of insight for setting up group problem-solving activities is to be found in Barnes. Though he speaks about native speakers of English, his insights are useful for any group work with any kinds of students.

6–13. Asher's directions to move to the refrigerator, open the refrigerator, take out a Coke from the refrigerator, etc., provide a very easy means of role-playing, since only actions are required of the performer in the first instance. Hines requires that students speak as well as act in her book of skits. Via, in his book about putting on plays with foreign students, also requires both action and language. But all three authors are attempting to make the language the students use and listen to be something more than simply language that expresses grammatical form and is not in any way attached to the emotions of the participants.

6–14. Lobman found very few instances of content I call *life* in student responses in high school French classes in an English-speaking area. Shapiro-Skrobe found hardly any *life* in student responses in elementary school reading classes where English was the students' second language. In ESL classes in New York City, Hines found *life* content almost unheard of in student responses.

6–15. Jersild tried to remind teachers that if they cannot share their concerns with their students, their students are unlikely to share their concerns with them.

6–16. Both quotations are from Sylvia Ashton-Warner's *Teacher*. She, of course, urged that we start with the students' feelings and move to the language rather than the other way around. Koch has put together the poems that his students wrote in New York City. He too urges that we start with the feelings students have and worry about the language secondarily.

6–17. The quote is from William James's *The present dilemma in philosophy*. I was given the quotation by Ira Bogatch as he read an early draft of this episode.

EPISODE

7

The End Is the Beginning

I. ENDS AS BEGINNINGS?—INTRODUCTION

In this episode, I summarize ways to use FOCUS to explore our work, I note some paradoxes of the exploration, and I make a few concluding remarks. Whether you are here after two episodes, seven, or any other number, don't feel you have to move on because you think summaries and conclusions occur only at the ends of books. I put this episode here rather than at the end, first because the title fits between *Eh?* and *Give* alphabetically. But another reason to put it here rather than as the last episode is because I see this book more like a merry-go-round than like a ladder or a series of steps to ascend. You can get on and off anywhere after you gain access to the fairgrounds by working through Episodes 1 and 2. Each episode after the first two is a beginning, and each is an end. And the end of any episode is really just a beginning. So, having a concluding episode far from the end of the book reminds us of the circular nature of this book.

II. IN A NUTSHELL—A SUMMARY OF WAYS TO USE FOCUS TO EXPLORE

The aim of this book is ultimately to see teaching differently. To reach this aim, I have urged you to systematically describe communications, make generalizations or rules about them, and then generate alternatives by substituting other communications and thus breaking the rules you discover. If you find that children outside classrooms who are given an oral command while looking at a toy or television program consistently ignore the oral command and pay attention only to the toy or television program, as when parents tell children to "come on" while they are looking in the window of a toy store and they don't come on, you would be led to a rule that indicated that to get attention, nonlinguistic mediums were more likely to be effective than linguistic mediums, at least with children. By avoiding orders when children were attending to nonlinguistic mediums or by distracting them with pictures that contained the orders, you could systematically test the validity of the original rule.

Just as there are opposites to try in teaching, so there are opposites in exploring teaching. One opposite of a systematic search for rules as a means to generate alternatives is the random generation of alternatives. In a game like Bingo, totally random combinations of letters and numbers are picked from a large container. We can easily generate alternatives in the same way by taking slips of paper with different combinations of characteristics from FOCUS on them and by putting them in a container in place of balls with numbers on them, as in Bingo. By pulling slips out and translating the formulas on them into communications, some exciting surprises are possible. [Background 7–1]

Another way we can generate alternatives is systematically to describe what happens only when something goes wrong and change some of the characteristics observed. Not only can we save time in looking at what goes wrong, since such incidents occur in only a small section of most lessons or incidents, but also we can see what causes them to go right. Such discoveries are harder to make "in situations of harmony because people are more likely to take them for granted and less likely to discuss them," and "by looking at what happens when speakers fail to get the message across . . . one can gain insight into the routine structures of behavior. . . ." [Background 7–2]

Moments when things go wrong I refer to as *leaden*, to contrast them with those when things don't go wrong, which I call *golden*. Here are some questions that illustrate how the exploration of leaden moments can lead to the discovery of rules and generation of alternatives. In disruptive moments in classes, are there fewer different types of tasks set than in moments that are not disruptive? Are children less likely to do what they are told, and more likely to act up, when they are told to do things in front of their friends, in front of other adults, or when no one is present? When students fail to read assignments for homework, is the material more likely to have been selected by the teacher or the students? And when students don't do homework, are they punished or provided with incentives for another chance to do homework?

One additional advantage of exploring leaden moments to seek alternatives is that description of them reminds us that they are made up of different combinations of the basic elements that constitute golden moments. By substituting different elements, we are reminded that the cause of one type of moment is not stupidity and the other type cleverness, but that both types of moments are caused by the communication of different combinations of some of the characteristics noted with FOCUS.

FOCUS is not limited to helping us generate alternatives. It can also be used to plan tests, texts, or lessons that meet student needs we have established, and to see the extent to which the plans meet the needs. For example, if one of your goals is to help students be able to obtain both literal and implied meaning from spoken short exchanges and extended conversations in out-of-class settings, the following would have to be observed in class:

Student responses that required inferences: *s res ri*.

Student responses that required listening to speech: *s res la al*.

Sets in solicits that contained more than a few words: *sol la sx* or *st*.

Sets in solicits that contain music and background noise plus speech:

sol la + na st + sx.

Sets in solicits that contain a range of content to reflect the range of topics heard in conversation and the formulas we use in short exchanges:

sol st ff + fp + fg + p + o.

In addition to using FOCUS to explore the extent to which our classroom practices parallel our goals, FOCUS can be used to explore the extent to which assumptions about learning are translated into practice. If we accept the idea that learning may occur with different degrees of efficiency and delight, it is logical to accept the idea that learning based on theories of learning would be better. Let's say, for example, that you believe in the theory that learning is more likely to stick if students are given a chance to learn what they want to learn. Well, these types of communications would be parallel with this assumption:

Student moves would have to contain content originated from students:

s str + sol + res + rea.

Students would have to have chances to share their personal feelings and opinions about the content that was used by teachers and students:

s rea fp.

[Background 7–3]

III. LOSE TO FIND—BUILT-IN PARADOXES

In another context, most of us have heard paradoxes such as these:

We have to be exposed to a lot of temptation and perhaps even lose ourselves in some excess in order to find ourselves and realize we can resist temptation.

It is in the giving that we receive.

We must die in order to live.

To be truly rich, you must give up all you have.

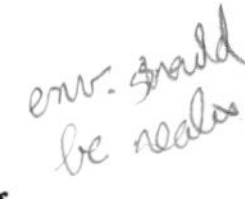

This book, like life, contains paradoxes. One of the first, if not the most glaring, is that I urge that we look *outside* the classroom to gain insight into what goes on *inside* the classroom. A central theme is to try in classes what we observe outside of classes and to realize that teaching goes on both inside and outside classrooms.

Another paradox is that by specific description I claim that you will be better able to see the general contours of what goes on both in teaching and nonteaching settings because the specific description is based on a broad conceptual framework. The idea that specific and sometimes atomic description may lead to seeing general contours and larger pictures is not as preposterous as it may at first seem, since some scientists claim to conceptualize the entire universe in an atom. [Background 7–4]

At any rate, the scores of detailed descriptions I make, the dozens more I advocate you to make, and the multitude of questions I suggest are all variations of just these few basic questions:

> In teaching and nonteaching settings, what mediums do we use, how do we use them, and what content do we communicate?
>
> How are the mediums, uses, and content communicated by peers to each other, and by those in charge to others, in both teaching and nonteaching settings?
>
> Do the mediums, uses, and content vary when we are: (1) preparing for subsequent behavior or engaged in self-initiated activity; (2) setting tasks, requesting, commanding or asking questions; (3) performing tasks, acceding to requests, following commands or answering questions; or (4) communicating in ways different from these three?
>
> What happens to the frequency and sequence of all the characteristics when one of them is altered?
>
> How do sets that are initiated by students affect other characteristics of FOCUS, and are the effects different from sets initiated by teachers? How do sets specially prepared for teaching language affect other characteristics differently from sets that come from out-of-class discourse and are not specially prepared to teach language?

The apparent lack of attention to the emotional and human side of teaching, as reflected by the questions I ask, the tallies, categories, and rules, leads to another paradox: distraction from emotion can lead to genuine expression of emotion. By concentrating on describing rather than on judging and thus trying hard to be one type of person or another, we are freed to act as we normally do. What could be less genuine than trying hard to be sincere or excited or interested? And if we judged ourselves to be lacking in sincerity and tried harder to be sincere, would this not be likely to produce the opposite effect? The predictable, flashing smiles cheerleaders are trained to exhibit hide more emotions than they exhibit.

Attempts to change in order to be judged better by either oneself or others may result in less change than attempts to change for its own sake. This paradox exists because both self-judgment and external judgment can produce tension, which in turn can prevent change. When I unlock the door to my apartment under normal conditions, it takes me only a few seconds. But when I try hard because the phone is ringing inside, and I worry about the person hanging up, or I am outside with a child who needs to go to the bathroom and I'm fearful the child won't be able to wait, it takes me at least twice as long to open the door. I try harder as the result of tension because I wonder whether I am doing well. Opening my door in different prescribed numbers of seconds just for the sake of doing it, and not to prove one way is better or that I am incompetent if I can't, would remove much of the tension since I would not be trying too hard to be judged good, but simply trying different things for their own sake.

Another paradox in many cases may be that many changes you make will result from an odd subtitle in the book or an incidental comment I make rather than from the systematic manipulation of the characteristics of communication that FOCUS highlights. In all of life, we learn a great deal incidentally. Haven't you often had a student come up and say that the critical insight he or she got from a class was something that

you had not even considered as part of your aim? I vividly remember such a case. I had just given a presentation about the classification of print, speech, pictures, and other mediums. After the presentation, a person came up to me and said that she appreciated my "opening up her mind to something totally new." I smiled, and then she added that before my presentation she had not known that it was possible to make 35mm slides of pictures. This was a side comment I had made when I showed a slide of a cover of a magazine that I had had made. After great concerts, haven't you heard someone comment about the conductor's hair or the dress worn by one of the musicians? Just as anticipated judgment can lead to fumbling from nervousness, so a book on systematic description that contains incidental comments can produce as much learning from the incidental comments as from the alternatives that grow out of systematic description.

Since you are reading about the possible value of incidental comments, you might wonder why you have been asked to code so much. Although understanding the categories of characteristics is necessary in order to code, the coding itself is only a means to an end. It is no more an end in itself than is the learning of medical terms in a health book, and this provides another paradox. We look at the proportion of white to red blood cells to see if the body is fighting an infection, not to show we know the technical terms or that we can count. In the same way, noting the number of questions teachers ask to which they know the answer—present elicit—in contrast to those they ask to which they don't know the answer—present query—is necessary in order to suggest altering the proportion to see the consequences of both, not to show that you know a *pe* from a *pq*.

The final paradox no doubt is that insights about communications in your classes and outside are just as likely to come, if not more so, at moments when you are not concentrating on the book or your teaching at all. Just as we often remember a name that is on the "tip of our tongue" by thinking of something totally different, and just as we are more likely to think of answers to exam questions after the exam when we are thinking of something else, and just as things we want to write come to us after we leave our desk and the blank paper we have been trying to fill, so are we likely to understand a use or a medium or an area of content or move type while we are not concentrating on them. Deliberate, conscious attempts to learn are effective partly because we alternate them with unplanned, unconscious moments of learning.

IV. YES, ENDS AS BEGINNINGS—CONCLUSION

While the words *breaking rules* imply change, they do not require revolution. If students want grammar lessons during class, and expect them, surely part of our responsibility is to give them. In such situations, we can break rules during a break, or after class for a few minutes rather than for an entire period. Trying an alternative for a few minutes or even a few seconds breaks a rule the same as if we try an alternative for an entire period, for a few hours or for several days. In fact, the breaking of rules for brief periods, incrementally, may lead to greater change than a revolution, which after a few unsettling periods, often settles down pretty much to things as they were before.

In fact, I've tried to break rules in this book incrementally rather than totally. I've touched on some of the same characteristics of FOCUS in many episodes in slightly different ways, not drastically different ways. I recycled the same terms in contrasting contexts, over and over, rather than treating each term comprehensively in one place at one time, and I divided episodes with journal entries so you'd have small doses rather than large ones at any one sitting. Drops of water day by day will wear the hardest stone away, as the saying goes. [Background 7–5]

Incremental breaking of rules will, I hope, lead to fewer total conversions to new trends or rejections of them. The pendulum that brings wide ties one year and narrow ties the next and bow ties the next and no ties the next seems to swing in all fields. The audiolingual method represented a great swing away from translation, which emphasized reading. The silent way represented a great swing away from the oral models so central to audiolingual teaching. Total physical response presented a great swing away from all those methods that emphasized production by eliminating the use of language in student responses for long periods, thus swinging all the way back to advice in the first part of the twentieth century to wrap students in a cocoon of language and not allow them to speak for at least a few months! [Background 7–6]

By seeing alternatives as different options, rather than better options, and by realizing each rule we follow has advantages and disadvantages for achieving certain ends, I hope that openness so characteristic of true exploration and so infrequent in advocacy can flourish, thereby limiting the number of degrees the pendulum swings in each of your classrooms.

By suggesting that systematic description on your own and with your colleagues will limit the swings of the pendulum in your teaching, I am not saying that anyone can teach a language who can speak it. Professional preparation is vital. But one of the hallmarks of a professional I hope this book helps teach is knowing what we know and what we don't know. Another hallmark of a professional I hope this book helps teach is that exploration continues indefinitely.

If we see our role as the one who knows all and can help all, we are likely to be drained very quickly. But if we see our work as constant generation and exploration, we cannot be drained quickly because we are constantly receiving. I hope the ends of many episodes in this book will be beginnings for you so that you're recharged rather than drained as you break rules. [Background 7–7]

Journal Entry

Do you miss the journal entries, extensive use of FOCUS terms, coding and tallies frequent in other episodes? Does reading this summary and conclusion put the other episodes you have worked through in a different perspective?

BACKGROUND NOTES

7–1. While you may think it is preposterous to suggest that we pull different characteristics out of a hat as if we were playing Bingo to generate different ways of teaching, in fact all methods that are advocated by people are simply different combinations of the same basic characteristics. In Episode 6, I showed how different authors who have come to be associated with different so-called methods simply advocate that different areas of content be taught. For example, Curran in *Counseling learning* urges that we start with student experiences, what I call *life*, and move to *study of language*, while Fries and Gattegno urge that we start with the grammatical system and the sound system, two subcategories of *study of language*. In the same way, Fries urged that we *present* and *reproduce* in the *use* column, while Palmer and more recently Gary urged that we *attend*, or spend a great deal of time listening.

7–2. In studying language in the classroom, Stubbs urges that we identify instances where we fail to get the message across so that we can better understand what occurs when we do get the message across. In the same way, Becker, in studying medical training, urges that we look at things that go wrong in order to better understand what goes right.

7–3. I take other learning assumptions written in general terms and translate them into suggested teacher-student behaviors in an article I wrote in response to a request to describe an approach to competency-based teacher education in 1977. Though all the activities that I describe for both teachers and students can be translated into FOCUS, I have written the activities in normal English in the article.

7–4. One of the places that I have found very small items related to larger units in the universe is in Bernstein's profile of a biology watcher in the January 2, 1978, issue of *New Yorker*. Bronowski too discusses this point.

7–5. Not only do drops of water day by day wear the hardest rock away, but very small items can sometimes have effects far out of proportion to their amount or size. In a health column that I read, Jane E. Brody talked about the importance of very small trace elements in our bodies. Without these trace elements, we cannot live. The trace elements are very difficult to detect because they occur in such minute amounts. Leonard Silk illustrated the same point in the area of economics. In order to decrease the number of gallons of fuel needed to propel a car, manufacturers began to make cars lighter. This affected the price of aluminum since aluminum was sought in place of steel. Since aluminum requires a lot of electricity to be produced, especially if the energy is oil, production costs in turn increased. To save money, aluminum companies began to use more recycled aluminum, since it requires less energy. As a result, there were fewer cans strewn in parks and on public highways because people found it more and more worthwhile to pick up and save used aluminum for selling to those who wanted to recycle it. So an increase in the price of oil helped keep many parks and highways clean.

7–6. I have been using Fries to represent the audiolingual method. I have been using Gattegno to represent the silent way. I have used Asher to represent total physical response. And whenever I speak of the importance of listening, I refer to Palmer. But as I have said elsewhere, swings in what authors advocate are simply rearrangements of some of the basic elements that I describe using FOCUS.

7–7. Fraiberg talks about the importance of self-observation in children. She says that self-observation leads to self-control. She of course uses the word *ego* to describe the observing part of the self, and she says that the more we observe, the more power we gain over the biological self. I think that her observations about the development of children apply to all of us. And I think that this ability to tolerate ambiguity as well as the ability to adapt and find solutions that in her words "bring harmony between the inner world and the outer reality" are part of the humanizing process. This ability to look at ourselves as separate entities is helped by the relationships we have with our parents.

Even if you do not accept the psychological need to continue to observe in order to explore, I think it is important to realize the value of change and the uses of different activities for their own sake. In a report on the value of placebos in *The New York Times*, Dava Sobel reminds us of how powerful placebos have been shown to be in the relief of actual pain. Mayo's study of the increase in production on the assembly lines at the Hawthorne plant in Chicago has shown that change by itself often increases interest, energy, and speed. At the Western Electric Plant at Hawthorne, Illinois, production increased when the lights were turned down or lightly dimmed. Production also increased when music was played and then increased again when music was not played. In short, any type of change that showed some interest in the welfare of the workers seemed to bring with it an increase in productivity for a time. So the value of constant exploration and change for its own sake cannot be underestimated.

EPISODE 8

Give Me the Damn Thing!

I. NOT AGAIN!—REINTRODUCING COMMUNICATIONS IN TEACHING AND NONTEACHING SETTINGS

Walking through an auto mechanic's shop to see if a friend's car was ready, I heard a voice from under a car shout "Give me the damn thing!" Though I assumed he was not addressing me, I looked around for something I could pick up anyway, feeling compelled to act because of the forcefulness of the command. Just as I was about to pick up a tool—I couldn't pick up one of the other cars, I couldn't imagine that he was asking for food, and there were tools everywhere—I saw a man running toward the car with a hammer in his hand. When I heard "about time" and the sound of hammering, I knew the "damn thing" had been delivered.

This incident highlights once again the differences between language classrooms and other settings. In fact, in the area of teaching languages for jobs and for academic courses, others have been harping on the subject too. The name for language teaching which tries to make student needs and language instruction congruent is language for specific purposes, or in the case of English, English for specific purposes, or ESP. I treat ESP in this episode, going on after this brief introduction to some tenets of ESP, and to ways to explore congruence between tenets and practices. The episode ends, reasonably enough, with concluding remarks.

II. THE GOOD OLD DAYS—TENETS OF ESP

The Usual Revolt—Specifying Needs of Students

ESP, like most movements, began as a revolt against another movement, or perhaps more accurately because of a lack of movement. Many teachers and even more students saw that after years of English, or any other language, many students were not capable of studying academic subjects in the other language that had been studied, nor were they capable of doing any jobs that required the other language. At about the same time, some administrators saw that there were more and more people in need of jobs requiring English in particular, but there was less and less time and money to teach the language needed for the job.

Before long, many people began to ask the obvious question: Why not match the language people need on a job or in a particular area of study with the language taught them? If a flight attendant only has to serve food, give safety instructions, and smile in the language of the passengers, why spend years teaching the person how to say "This is a pen" and how to read and listen to stories that begin "Once upon a time"? Consequently, teachers who taught so-called general English suddenly realized that even if a person had a thorough grounding in "This is a pen" and the subsequent points of grammar that followed, the person might not be able to say "Coffee, tea or milk?"—much less smile in the target language!

From the fact that needs were not being met grew the ESP tenet which requires that the specific needs of students be taken into account in planning teaching. The two major needs that keep cropping up are job-related and academic courses. Few people seem to want to learn how to play backgammon or chess in English, fence, play the piano, cook, build model airplanes or guillotines, play computer games or develop pictures.

One result of the fact that language needs of students and courses were supposed to be congruent was the ignoring of needs or possible interests of any students who did not have job prospects or who were not going to study academic subjects. A quick view of ESP materials reveals no cookbooks, for example. While it is no doubt economic to teach flight attendants the specific language that is likely to occur in their work, not only are such flight attendants relegated to the role of a parrot with a limited repertoire, but all other students who don't have academic or job-related needs are ignored. [Background 8–1]

Journal Entry

On one level, all English is for a specific purpose. For example, teaching "This is a pen" prepares one to say "I have two eyes" in a later lesson. We begin to see that the English is used for the specific purpose of saying words to learn meanings and patterns. On another level, even native speakers of a language cannot understand much in their own language when the language contains information they are unfamiliar with. For example, if you don't play bridge, a description of a bridge game is totally incomprehensible. Insurance forms mean little to most, and the financial sections of some newspapers are foreign to some, and the sports sections to others.

What specific areas do you find most foreign? What types of instruction do you think would help you comprehend such specific areas? As you read on, compare your instructional ideas with those advocated for ESP.

A Small Crack—Importance of Functions of Language

Fortunately for all learners without the needs that ESP materials are usually designed to meet, ESP has another tenet: Language is made up not only of grammar, but also of functions. And these functions are used to talk about many different topics or notions. This tenent means that knowing how to interact by apologizing, telling a joke, lying, or greeting a friend after not seeing him or her for ten years can be as critical as getting a verb and subject to agree. This tenet has applications for all learners because it means that a crack appears in the edifice called *grammar*. Since teachers knew for years that interacting by apologizing, joke telling, lying, and greeting friends was as important as distinguishing *he go* from *he goes*, the importance attached to functions, and the topics communicated in each, that ESP provided was encouraging. To put it another way, teachers who had for years kept secret the fact that they had students engage in games and small-group activities, even when particular patterns were not practiced during these activities, felt free to come out of the closet. If you are used to only the usual function communicated in teaching—what some have called the *representational*—or if you simply want to be reminded of the range of functions possible during different activities look at Excerpt 8–1. As you can see, I have noted that each communication could be used to teach a particular function—study of language subcategory function: *lf*. I have also noted categories of functions to show the range that is used in games and small-group activities. Letters—the Y function, the S function—could serve as well as the terms I have borrowed from Halliday. If you read Halliday's definitions of the functions, your coding may differ somewhat, since many communications have qualities of at least two functions. At any rate, I have used the terms, as I said, to illustrate range rather than to teach functions. [Background 8–2]

Remember that I have coded the content of each line *lf* only to highlight the range of functions. As I say in Episode 11, I code the subcategories of the study of language only if the preceding structuring moves explicitly indicate what areas of language are being treated, or if the reactions the teacher makes indicate a particular area is being worked on. For example, if a student says "Are we gonna use paper plates?" and the teacher says "Use the full form," I'd code the content of the statement *sound*, not *function*. If the teacher had said, "Change it to the singular," I'd code the statement *grammar*. Just because a communication is representative of a particular function does not mean that the content is *lf*.

While being able to engage in the activities in Excerpt 8–1 may not help one get a job or improve one's ability in an academic class, as you can see, engaging in a range of activities does require communicating with many different functions. The common *t str, t sol, s res, t rea* pattern of the classroom is replaced by a range of sequences whenever students have the opportunity to engage in games and small-group activities. So, don't let the inability to follow tenet 1—matching courses to student needs—stop you from following tenet 2—functions are important to language learning. Even if your students' needs are impossible to determine, you can still move beyond *t str, t sol, s res, t rea* all with content of the study of language, subcategory grammar. Divide students into groups. Then, have them get out the coloring books and crayolas, colored chalk for murals on the blackboard, wrapping paper and felt pens for putting graffiti-filled paper on the walls. Have them replace the books on the desks with jigsaw puzzles, Monopoly, cards, dice, backgammon, chess, and any other games *not* designed to teach language. Have them decorate dollhouses, and build them, make model airplanes, model windmills and landmarks. Put sand in a big low box and have them plan villages, stage famous battles with toy soldiers, lay out roads, and build sand castles. Grow plants with them; raise fish, rabbits, and white mice. And cook—but don't cook the animals you raise. And sew and have everyone clean up. Episode 6 treats this relationship between the study of language and other areas of content.

If a lot of students love grammar, the activites should be done only during breaks, of course, rather than during class. But over time, some class time can be devoted to these activities. At first, you'll have a lot of students in the role of teacher, trying to take over and teach others. They will follow the *t str, t sol, s res, t rea* pattern characteristic of the representational function. But as the sewing incident in Excerpt 8–1

EXCERPT 8–1
Functioning

	*Communications**	*Source/ Target*	*Move Type*		*Content*
Planning					
1	Are we gonna use paper plates?	s/s	sol	lf	instrumental
2	Yeah.	s/s	res	lf	instrumental
3	How much should I prepare?	s/s	sol	lf	instrumental
4	I have no idea.	s/s	res	lf	instrumental
5	It should be just a little taste.			lf	instrumental
6	Should I buy legs?	s/s	sol	lf	instrumental
7	You could also buy thighs.	s/s	str	lf	instrumental
8	You know thighs are pretty small too.	s/s	rea	lf	representational
9	And they are already cut.			lf	representational
10	Oh, yeah?	s/s	rea	lf	representational
Building					
11	It looks easy but. . . .	s/s	rea	lf	interactional
12	( )	s/o	str		
13	My God!	s/s	rea	lf	personal
14	( )				
15	I can't cut straight lines.	s/s	rea	lf	personal
16	( )				
Joking					
17	May I have the scissors?	s/s	sol	lf	instrumental
18	( )	s/o	str		
19	You're going to cut it?	s/s	sol	lf	instrumental
20	Yeah.	s/s	res	lf	instrumental
21	( )	s/o	str		
22	You're going to go into surgery?	s/s	rea	lf	interactional
23	I don't think you should.				
Sewing					
24	Well, when I saw her last week, she looked fine.	s/s	rea	lf	interactional
25	( )	s/o	str		
26	She went into the hospital yesterday.	s/s	rea	lf	representational
27	( )	s/o	str		
28	I think I'll go to visit her tonight.	s/s	rea	lf	instrumental
29	( )	s/o	str		
30	Len can make his own supper for once.	s/s	rea	lf	personal
Cooking					
31	What do you do with this?	s/s	sol	lf	heuristic
32	( )				
33	For the birds.	s/s	res	lf	heuristic
	We can keep it for the birds.				
34	Yeah, for the birdies.	s/s	rea	lf	interactional
Kibitzing					
35	Move the king's pawn.	s/s	sol	lf	regulatory
36	( )	s/o	str		
37	Shut up!	s/s	sol	lf	regulatory
38	Watch his knight.	s/s	rea	lf	regulatory
39	I said shut up!	s/s	sol	lf	regulatory
40	Check	s/s	sol	lf	regulatory
41	( )	s/o	str		

EXCERPT 8–1 (*continued*)

	*Communications**	*Source/ Target*	*Move Type*		*Content*
42	Out of check.	s/s	res	lf	regulatory
43	( )	s/o	str		
44	Music sounds nice, doesn't it?	s/s	rea	lf	interactional
45	How about a break.	s/s	str	lf	interactional
Puzzling					
46	This looks like it fits here.	s/s	rea	lf	heuristic
47	( )	s/o	str		
48	Ah, not exactly.	s/s	rea	lf	heuristic
49	Toss me that one.	s/s	sol	lf	instrumental
50	( )	s/s	res		
51	This one does.	s/s	rea	lf	heuristic
52	( )	s/o	str		

* The parentheses indicate the presence of an activity being engaged in as the words are being said.

shows, after a while, as people are engaged in an activity, not only is the activity not taught, it is not even mentioned! We begin to talk of other things than what we are doing as we feel comfortable with what we are doing. More talking about personal feelings takes place during many bridge games than during many conversations in which the participants are doing absolutely nothing except trying to have a personal conversation. When a person tries to impose the representational function as others are engaged in other activities that require other functions, that person is called a pedantic person. He is quickly squelched, an important function for all to learn, even flight attendants, though this need is rarely noted in a needs assessment for flight attendants.

If students don't know any English, one's first idea might be that they have to be taught the "basic grammar" of the language before they can begin to communicate. But even at the absolute beginning level, students can engage in games and small-group activities in the target language. The teacher can join each group for a short time, or more advanced students can. Sentences others have said during the activity can be played over and over on a tape recorder as the students are engaged in the activity and they can listen, just as we listen to music during a bridge game, for example. Then, some will repeat parts of some of the exchanges heard on the tape or heard from the teacher when the teacher was talking in the group. Others will write some language they heard. Transcriptions of the comments can be passed out with words deleted, and the students can fill in the deletions together. Making the decisions jointly about what words fit where will itself force some additional use of the target language, and is itself an activity. Exchanges advanced students or native speakers made can be taped with deletions, and students can fill in the deletions and make oral substitutions, just as they have made them in print.

The language used during games and small-group activities can also provide patterns for the regular part of the language lesson. Errors students make while engaged in group work using many functions can be treated, and communications students felt compelled to make but could not can be provided. More complex alternative versions of some things that were said during the activity can be taught too. All this careful attention to what we actually say and do in a range of activities will also remind you that not only are functions as important as grammar, but also that other subcategories of the study of language, such as context, discourse, and style, to name a few, are important. I treat all the subcategories in Episode 11.

Integration—Meshing Language and Activity

Both games and small-group activities have an even more vital lesson than the demonstration of the fact that functions are important as well as grammar. Such activities remind us of a tenet that many ESP materials should follow but often do not: Language and activity must be integrated. In Excerpt 8–1, we are ignorant of much that is going on because we have access only to the language. I left the *sets* that are referred to out, and I left descriptions of other mediums out, noting them only with parentheses and space. In the Planning section, what food is going to be prepared? Some may guess that the legs and thighs mentioned belong to chickens. But this fact is not mentioned. What is being built in the Building and Joking sections is totally unknown from the language. What is being sewed we cannot determine from the language in the Sewing section, and what is being cooked we cannot determine from the language in the Cooking section. Without the chessboard described, or before us, we have no idea how many pieces are left or where they are. All very obvious! Yet in teaching settings a great deal of time is spent naming objects and describing what we see in front of us, communicating the representational function. Teaching settings are the only places where we name and describe, and so even if we are not sure what job or academic class we need to prepare our students for, we can be sure that the emphasis on naming and describing in language classes is necessary *only* in other language classes. It is unusual in any other settings.

The need to mesh language and activity is not only ignored by many who prepare ESP materials. In 1975, I was invited to teach English to some factory workers. When I got to the factory, I was directed to the meeting room used by building managers and company officers. Shortly after I arrived a number of men came in, but because, like me, they were not wearing ties, I knew they were not the managers or company officers for whom the room was ordinarily reserved. They were followed by one tie-wearing person who had this message: "We are here to learn English so that you can get a better-paying job at this factory. This person is an English teacher who is not going to teach you general English, but English for specific purposes. He is going to teach you English you need for different jobs here at the factory, on different, more complex machines." This structuring move by the tie wearer was possible because the person who was coordinating the language teaching had primed him a bit as she convinced him to allow the program to be tried in his factory. When I asked for the tools that I could use in the class, I was told that some would be delivered. Well, around thirty minutes later, some tools were delivered. As it turned out, though, the tools that were delivered were not those used by any of the factory workers. The tools belonged to the janitor, and he used them to repair lights, stop leaks, and get doors opening more easily. These were not the tasks the workers were going to have to learn to do to get a better-paying job! To the manager, as to most people, language is language, and activity is activity. They are seen as separate. And it is assumed that one must master a great deal of grammar before one can use the language related to an activity, especially a complex activity.

Journal Entry

Having students engage in activities in groups, either as part of preparation for an academic class, or for a job, or as a way to expand the number of functions communicated in a classroom, usually raises two questions. First, people ask what can be done to make it more likely that the students will use the target language rather than their own while engaged in the activities. Second, people ask what assurances there are that any language will be learned as students engage in activities.

How would you respond to these questions, and what others do you have that you'd like to discuss with a colleague?

The Same Old Thing—Basing Teaching on Actual Communications

As it turned out, the factory manager I met on my first foray into ESP was *not* unusual because of the fact that he scheduled the language class totally separate from any activity the workers needed language to engage in. Show me an ESP class, and nine times out of ten the students won't be engaged in activities parallel to those they are learning language for. In fact, it's unlikely they'll engage in any activities. My manager's ideas are widely shared. Soon after I left the factory class totally separated from the factory, I met some teachers who were developing materials for mechanics. Though they started off by tape-recording communications between mechanics, they did not find enough names of objects in the comments, so they asked workers to name the tools. The teachers arranged these in alphabetical order, glued sketches of each tool next to the name of each tool, and went on to teach their lessons. They not only separated language from activity, but they taught what had little to do with student needs. They taught what language teachers are trained to teach: names and descriptions of objects or processes.

Even when language and activity are integrated, there is no assurance that the experience will be fruitful. I observed a group of teachers working with Chinese chefs who were learning how to cook Chinese food to work in Chinese restaurants. The master chef who was teaching cooking did not know English, so some of the language teachers translated much of what he said during class. Then, after cooking class, the teachers took some of the comments he made, added some others that named the foods and the processes, and proceeded to have students state "I am slicing the onions," as at least one of them was actually slicing onions. But when does anyone say what he is doing during an activity, except when teaching a language to another? And why do Chinese chefs have to be able to say anything about their cooking in English anyway? Even the master chef who was teaching cooking did not know any English. This lack did not prevent him from teaching Chinese cooking to Chinese-speaking trainees.

What Chinese chefs probably need to know is the English of ordering food on the telephone, the English of complaining about late deliveries or poor produce or old meat and high prices. They might have to know how to bribe a city food inspector, know the steps necessary to obtain a permit to sell drinks, and be able to check figures on invoices written in English. The teachers of the Chinese cooks failed to look beyond the cooking class to assess their students' needs, and they ignored the actual communications even there.

Unfortunately, what ESP has come to mean to many is simply the substitution of one type of lexis for another—cooking vocabulary for general vocabulary, for example. Or, ESP has come to mean a substitution of the subcategory of the study of language

I call function—*lf*—for grammar—*lx*. Or in some cases, ESP means the substitution of the study of another subject—*so*—for the study of language—*sl*. The solicit "What's the first thing you do with a piece of roast beef?" during a science class on digestion differs from the solicit "What's the idea in the first paragraph?" in a language lesson only in content. In both cases, the teacher is asking questions to which he or she knows the answer. In both cases, the language is separated from an activity. And in both cases the language differs from that used outside a classroom, such as during a discussion between two scientists or one scientist and a lab assistant.

The only way I know of to know what language is needed and what activities accompany the language is to record actual communications from the settings we are preparing students for: in short, to follow one central theme of this book. Obvious as such a step is, it is not often followed, partly no doubt because it is hard to eavesdrop, and harder still to do it with a tape recorder or a video recorder in one's hands, and partly no doubt because the rule is so strong that as language teachers we are to teach grammar, along with names of objects and descriptions.

I cannot harp enough on the need to observe in the actual settings where the language is to be used. In a vocational class, I hear a teacher saying: "Would you please give me a hammer?" and I hear the students repeating the question, at which point the hammer is presented. At the tool cage in the factory where the students are going to work, I hear a worker going up to get the tools saying "They did it again!" The person who checks out the tools reacts with "Terrible, wasn't it?" I, the outsider, have no idea who *they* is, what *it* refers to, or what was done. As time goes on, I learn that the subject was football. The home team lost again, as it turns out. After a few more reactions on the same topic, the man in the cage simply says "Want the usual?" After a "Yeah," a container was passed to the worker, who then went to his post with the tools he needed. The well-trained teacher of an ESP class who starts with "Would you please give me a ______?" might do better to watch sports on television than learn polite expressions for names of tools, if the exchanges I have heard are widespread.

The purpose of this anecdote and the one about the Chinese chefs is not to suggest that those engaged in ESP programs aren't concerned, open, or knowledgeable. I'm just reminding us of how difficult it is to break rules. Student needs are not normal starting points for instruction, nor are activities part of language teaching.

Journal Entry

The emphasis on the teaching function in classrooms to the exclusion of other functions is made clear in Ionesco's *The Lesson*. While the lines are not exact recordings of classes, they do show how involved we get in one way of communicating. Here are some lines from the play, spoken by the professor:

> *Let's try another approach.*
>
> *For purposes of subtraction, let's limit ourselves to the numbers one to five.*
>
> *Wait now, miss, you'll soon see. I'm going to make you understand. Pay attention.*
>
> *I will say the sentence to you in Spanish, then in neo-Spanish and finally in Latin.*
>
> *Pay attention, for the resemblances are great.*

To the professor, the resemblances may be great, but to the student, they are not. How do you feel about Ionesco's presentation of what he considers teaching to be?

III. YES, AGAIN—EXPLORING CONGRUENCE BETWEEN TENETS AND PRACTICES

Off Center Stage—Some Roles of a Teacher in an ESP Class

Basing instruction on student needs by requiring materials—sets—that contain actual communications, by moving beyond the area of grammar, so central in much of language instruction, and by tying language to activity, all imply a different role for the teacher of ESP. Not only must the teacher move off center stage, but the teacher often needs to move out of the language classroom, first to collect the communications needed, and second, to teach in the setting where the communications are actually to be used. Teaching factory workers in a room containing nothing but chairs, sales personnel in a room without the products they sell, or business managers who use computer terminals and printouts in a room containing only blackboards is not congruent with the tenets of ESP.

Since students will know something of the area of work or study—*pw* or *so*—the teacher will, of course, concentrate on the study of language—*sl*. Consequently, when the teacher asks about work or academic areas, the questions are likely to be ones the teacher does not know the answer to—*present query*—rather than ones the teacher does know the answer to—*present elicit.* In most classrooms, the teacher rarely asks a solicit with a *pq* component. So, over all, the role of the teacher of ESP is to be an observer in collecting materials and a learner in teaching, and often a visitor to other settings as well.

Ironically, being in classes where games and small-group activities are engaged in, or being in classes where the purpose of teaching English is tied to a job or an academic area, provides a greater opportunity for language teachers to study and teach language than being in ordinary language classes, since the range of communications provides clear evidence of the fact that language is more than grammar. We cannot advise mechanics, science students, midwives, or sales personnel to change their language and accompanying mediums unless we have studied all subcategories of the *study of language*. The usual "Is the grammar correct?" must be expanded to "Is the style appropriate for the context?" when we are standing next to a machine in a factory. The teachers who cannot accept different roles that require that different rules be followed are those who simply substitute new vocabulary items for those in the regular materials.

Just a Few—Using an Observation Guide to Determine Degree of Congruence between Practices and Tenets

As you perhaps noticed, at the beginning of this episode I did not mention the specific characteristics of FOCUS I was going to treat. You now realize I treated source and target, sequences of move type, integration of different mediums, especially the activities I code *po*, the integration of the study of language with the study of other subjects or work: *sl* + *so* or *sl* + *pw*, and the importance of all subcategories of the study of language, not just grammar and lexis, and in particular, functions. Any number of observation guides could be designed to tally these characteristics, following the two-way matrix model presented in other episodes. To see how many tenets are put into practice, I have designed a slightly different one, as you can see by looking at Observation Guide 8–1. By tallying with a *r* if the major function of most communications is to teach—the representational function—and an *o* if the other functions are observed, you can see something of the consequences of the practices each tenet implies as you

OBSERVATION GUIDE 8–1
Congruence

Practices \ Type of Class	Academic	Job preparation	Language
Grammar and lexis emphasized			
Many subcategories of *sl* treated, especially functions			
Language and activity are meshed			
A range of activities are engaged in unrelated to job or content class			
Setting is a classroom			
Setting is a classroom containing equipment or materials tied to language			
Setting is where students will actually perform a job or study another subject			
Materials are based on actual communications students will be exposed to			
Materials consist of actual communications students will be exposed to—they have not in any way been specially prepared or altered			
Materials are based on language texts with some vocabulary changed to match that used in the settings students are studying to enter			

see the practices. After all, one can say "This is a hammer" either in a factory or a classroom, and while using actual materials or those designed for a specific purpose.

IV. LIMITED DELIGHT—CONCLUDING REMARKS

While I am delighted with ESP since it encourages opposites, as exploration goes forward to see both whether tenets are translated into practice and whether in fact students learn as much language from opposite practices, I hope that in all classes the consequences of supplemental use of games and small-group activities which require a range of functions will be explored as well. As these explorations take place, I hope attention will begin to be paid to skills other than speaking. While those who write about ESP note that the channel of communication is important—meaning medium in FOCUS—and while some materials are developed mainly for reading, and while those who discuss speaking functions state that they apply equally to all skills, speaking absorbs much attention. And it does function differently. We don't interact socially with a book as we do with people. And while reading to oneself is normal, speaking to oneself is not. Writing notes to help us remember to do something is simply not something we can do in speech and so cannot be described with one of the functions used for oral communications. [Background 8–3]

Another whole avenue of exploration is necessary in the teaching of more than one language. In programs designed to nurture and develop a student's first language, and at the same time introduce the student to the *lingua franca* of the area he or she is in, ESP is hardly mentioned. But to develop one's first language or a second language, a range of functions is necessary if we are to use both languages in a range of settings. While trying to teach any language in a language class that gives no attention to the content of other school subjects and no attention to out-of-class needs is bound to fail, even in the development of the first language, more than the teaching of the language or academic areas for their own sake is necessary if we want to provide students with experience in the whole range of language functions. [Background 8–4]

Both in language and academic classes and job training, the bulk of all communications have only one function: the teaching or representational function. At the minimum, I would hope that programs designed to develop two languages would explore the use of games and small-group activities. And I would hope that they would explore the teaching of languages and other subjects so that they are tied to a range of activities as well.

Perhaps ESP practices, including the use of materials people actually encounter in a range of jobs, rather than just books designed to teach for their own sake, would be used more in programs that emphasize two languages if ESP were called something else. While LSP has been used to eliminate the implication that English is not the only language for special purposes, LSP still implies only one language. Perhaps LsSP—languages for specific purposes—would emphasize the applicability of ESP tenets and practices to language programs that develop first and second languages. Hopefully, LsSP won't be confused with the old LSMFT—Lucky Strike means fine tobacco!

In addition to the need to move ESP from special programs for job preparation, or English language institutes into schools where two languages are being developed, I think we all need to look beyond the actual language used to the underlying meaning of interaction outside of classes. Language is to communicate, goes the cliché. Well, if communication includes obfuscation and lack of communication, then language is for communication. While we emphasize functions and activities, what may be more important are beneath-the-surface meanings of language. Technical words used by mechanics to customers and doctors to patients, for example, can exert control and wield power as well as be useful in diagnosis and treatment. Or, technical information can be used to allay anxiety. Consider the nurse's comments in Excerpt 8–2.

While describing the reason for the test—the interactional function—one wonders how much of the technical information is really understood. But perhaps the understanding of the words is not important. The underlying purpose of the language may be to reassure the blood donor. *Quilk* could be substituted for *centrifuge* and *gama gamm test* for *specific gravity test*, and the underlying meaning would no doubt be the same. The language is used to do something else other than what appears, I think. To put it another way, we have to think not only of work and academic areas—*pw* and *so*—but

EXCERPT 8–2
At the Blood Bank (T)

Nurse: I'm going to take your temperature and blood pressure. And, I'm going to stick your finger to take a blood test. (After blood has been drawn, it is put into a vial of blue liquid.)

Donor: What's that for?

Nurse: The drop has to go down without coming back to the top first. I'm going to try it again and if it doesn't do it, well, then we'll have to run it on the machine which is a little more accurate. This is a little quicker; the other one is a little more accurate, but if it doesn't pass this way, we'll check it the other way. (Looks at the blood in the vial.) (Drops another drop into the vial.) It's just a specific gravity test. Has to go right down in that solution without coming back to the top first. It'll all go down eventually, but if you don't pass that, then we do it in the centrifuge. And, sometimes, lots of times, you can pass when we do it in a centrifuge where you can't pass this. But it saves time to do this first. We still give you the benefit of another chance. We don't want to turn you down unless we have to.

of life—*f*—personal feelings we and others have that we hide with language or that we try to communicate, often indirectly, through language.

Finally, we need to realize that in all teaching we must keep in mind that the building of confidence, the development of skills of getting along with others and resolving conflicts constructively, the development of inquiry, initiative, and self-learning are as central as any language we may teach, whether that language is ESP, LsSP, or general English. Just as we need to think of what we do with language beneath the surface—control people, reassure them—so we need to think of what we need to teach people beneath the surface in all our classes. We need to keep constantly in front of us the fact that success in academic classes, or on the job, or in games and activities one engages in is due not only to language ability, but to constellations of traits such as confidence, initiative, curiosity, hard work, agreeableness, stick-to-it-tive-ness, singleness of purpose, shyness, humor, and tact, to name a few. If we don't keep this fact clearly in front of us as we explore the consequences of our attempts to tie language to work and other areas of study and to activities, the results of our comparisons will be less informative. And we may never know whether when others say "Damn" if they are showing intimacy and support or anger, as in "Give me the damn thing!"

BACKGROUND NOTES

8–1. The need to look at the needs of students is described in three central works: one by Munby, one by Van Ek, and another by Wilkens. Glover et al. have developed a text called *Seaspeak*, which is a clear example of ESP.

8–2. Halliday's *Explorations in the functions of language* spells out one clear series of functions. Obviously, language could be cut up in another way to have twice as many functions or half as many as Halliday presents.

8–3. In a report for the United Nations, Sullivan provides a summary of ways people are motivated to read. He includes the desire to be accepted or commended or to please others, the need to solve problems, the drive to help others, the encouragement of one's religious practice, the need for psychological escape and political participation. Olson juxtaposes the way we use language in speech and print from a historical perspective. I find his comments particularly insightful.

8–4. Cummins has shown how important it is for subjects and language to be taught together. He reminds us that cognitive development can be limited if we only teach language for its own sake and we do not attach language to something else, such as the content areas. Ruth Crymes, in a plenary address to the New York affiliate of TESOL, talked about the contextualization of language instruction and she urged that we hitch language to subject matter for students. Urzua has done a great deal of work with elementary school children to get them to talk in a way that she considers purposeful. She does this by having them talk about something other than language itself—such as, in the early stages, shadows that they make on the wall. Using language for activity rather than for its own sake is parallel with the theme of this episode.

EPISODE

9

Gu Is Easy to Remember

I. WAYS OF LIFE—TOPIC AND ORGANIZATION OF EPISODE

In this episode, I treat the ways of life of different groups. In terms of FOCUS, this topic is a subcategory of the *study of language* I call *ways of life of different groups* (*lw*). Though I treat this topic as a subcategory of the study of language, I don't want to imply that learning a language of another group means we also learn the ways of life of another group. For example, when I was in Somalia, I found *gu*, the Somali word for rainy season, easy to remember, perhaps because I associated the gooey mud pies of childhood with gooey dirt roads in the rainy season in Somalia. But knowing individual words like *gu*, or even how to put the words together, is not the same as understanding the ways of life of different groups.

I don't want to imply that in order to teach and learn about the ways of life of other groups we need to know their language. For example, social studies teachers treat differences between different ethnic groups who speak the same language and blue- and white-collar workers from the same language background. History teachers treat patterns of thought at different points in time of groups of people who all used the same language. And ultimately all teachers need to be able to understand the ways of life of different groups. If this depended on knowledge of the languages of the groups, the task would be impossible. [Background 9–1]

I illustrate the subcategory of the *study of language* that I call *ways of life of different groups* in Section II. In Section III, I show how mediums can be used to take in or produce this area of content. In the final section, as usual, I make some concluding remarks. Since I discuss how the subcategory *lw* relates to both all the mediums and all the uses, a table highlighting these components of FOCUS would not be much different from those on the inside of the front and back covers. I have not prepared a separate one to illustrate the contents of this episode.

Journal Entry

In your attempts to see patterns within different groups, have you found any *gu* words? Has your reaction to them been mixed, like mine? Or, have you found them clearly more helpful or harmful, rather then a bit of both?

II. CUMBERSOME?—ILLUSTRATING CONTENT CODED *lw*

If you thought *ways of life of different groups* was a cumbersome name for a subcategory note that I divide this subcategory into two: *actual* and *interpretive: lwa* and *lwi*. When we *attend* by observing what a group does, for purposes of teaching or learning about the ways of life of the group, I code the content *ways of life actual: lwa*. If you are trying to discover the patterns of life of some coffee drinkers, for example, and you observe them, I'd say you are *attending* to content I'd code *lwa* because you are looking at what coffee drinkers actually do. If you made descriptive comments about your observations, I'd code them *lwa* too. These would be coded *lwa*: "Some coffee drinkers put sugar in their coffee; others milk; still others a sugar substitute; and one person put an ice cube in the hot coffee."

Should a person decide to write a soap opera or produce a documentary film about coffee drinkers, and the products were observed and discussed in order to reflect a point of view about the patterns of life of coffee drinkers, I'd code the resulting communications *lwi*. Since so few people produce soap operas or documentaries about coffee drinkers—fortunately, no doubt—I illustrate *lwi* with comments rather than such productions. I'd code these *lwi*: "Coffee drinkers don't get things done as well as non-coffee drinkers because they waste so much time drinking and talking. Then, when they finish drinking, they shake so much they can't think straight." Songs, paintings, plays, stories, and other attempts to show the patterns of a group from a particular point of view are examples of other products I'd code *lwi*, assuming they are used to teach and learn about the ways of life of different groups. Thus, just because a song is about coffee drinkers does not mean that I'd code it *lwi*. I may not even code it *study of language*. I only code the content of communications in one subcategory or another when the mediums are used to teach or learn about a particular area of content.

If you are wondering how I would code film criticism, literary criticism, music and art reviews, and other commentaries on interpretive works, since they occupy so much of the time in many classes supposedly reserved for teaching and learning about the ways of life of different groups, note that I put these in the subcategory *genre: lj*. I code these items separately because they are concerned with the characteristics of works of art and their quality, not with how different groups think, feel, and act.

Of course, some mediums can be coded either *lwa* or *lwi*, depending on the content attributed to the medium. For example, *jeans*—either the word, ads showing them, or actual ones—can be described as blue denim trousers worn by men and women in certain settings: *lwa*. Or, they can be taken as a symbol of casualness, revolt, high fashion, or almost anything else, in which case I'd code them *lwi* since they are used to interpret ways of life of different groups. In both cases, the jeans would be coded *lw* only if they were used to teach and learn about the ways of life of different groups.

By separating mediums that communicate actual and interpretive ways of life of different groups, I highlight the importance of looking both at what people do and at what either they or others think they do. By using these cumbersome labels to replace *culture*, the more usual word for the topic of this episode, I don't have to contend with all the connotations *culture* has developed, nor be limited by what others think it means.

There are so many arguments about the meaning of *culture* that any interested party can only come away from a discussion of them exhausted. And the preconceived notions of the relationships between civilization, art and literature, and culture will consume any remaining breath left after deciding on what *culture* itself means.

By using the cumbersome *ways of life of different groups*, I can move beyond ethnicity and language as markers of groups and thus code discussions of the patterns of ways of life of different age groups, occupations, sexes, economic status, color, religion, education, to say nothing about groups with varying degrees of interest in baseball, motorcycle repair, leather tanning, secret codes and etchings, to name just a few of the thousands of groups that have different patterns of operating. Many conflicts between groups or individuals occur between those who speak the same language. Many divorces take place between people who speak the same language, for example. But the ways of life of different groups each person in the marriage belongs to that are similar seem to be outweighed by the ways of life of groups they belong to that are different. Bridge groups, tennis groups, cooking class groups, age groups, car groups, eating groups, film groups, coffee-drinking groups are groups that a couple may have in common. But all this commonality in the ways of life of these groups is apparently overcome by lack of commonality in toothpaste tube rolling groups, smoking groups, and garden groups. Group identity too is no doubt partly responsible for civil wars, where, as with couples, the same language is used by both sides.

By including toothpaste tube rolling groups as an example of behavior I'd code *lw*, you may think the subcategory is so all-inclusive as to be meaningless. In fact, to be coded *lw*, a communication cannot simply be the result of a personal idiosyncrasy. Not only must the communication be common to a group, but it must also be patterned and recur in the same way over time. If either differences or commonalities between groups can be described on the basis of personality—*life*, stated bureaucratic operations—*procedure*, other subcategories of the *study of language—sl*, or on the basis of knowledge about a particular subject—*study other*, then the communications cannot be coded *lw*. To code everything *lw* would obviate the need for the subcategory.

Journal Entry

My favorite book that contains communications I'd code both *lwa* and *lwi* is Ruth Benedict's *The Chrysanthemum and the Sword*. She wrote the book without ever visiting Japan, depending mainly on Japanese living in the United States who had been brought up in Japan for information. She reminds her readers in the introduction of the importance of finding out about "the range of trivial habits in daily living"—*lwa*. She contended that they had more to do with the future of nations than "treaties signed by diplomats." This point of view I'd code *lwi*.

Do you have some favorite books about the patterns of living of different groups? Is there some actual behavior and some interpretation in it, or is there mainly only one or the other? [Background 9–2]

III. DESCRIPTION/OTHER—WAYS MEDIUMS ARE USED TO COMMUNICATE *lwa* and *lwi*

Smokers—Examples of Different Uses Coded *lwa* and *lwi*

We can take in—*attend*—and produce mediums containing either actual or interpretive ways of life of different groups. In Excerpt 9–1, I illustrate how both the actual and interpretive ways of life of two different groups—smokers and nonsmokers—can be produced as well as taken in. Had the teacher not introduced the topic of differences

EXCERPT 9–1
Smokers

		Communications	*Source/ Target*	*Move Type*	*Use*	*Content*
1	Teacher:	We're going to discuss smokers today to learn something about how they and non-smokers live.	t/c	str		
2		First, I want you to tell me what you know about these.	t/c	sol		
3		(Spreads out half a dozen packs of cigarettes, each a different brand.)				
4	Student₁:	These three are filtered cigarettes. (Picking up three packs and putting them on one side.)	s_1/t	res	cl	lwa
5		They are less dangerous than the others.	s_1/s_2 + t	rea	ci	lwa
6	Student₂:	They also have less taste.	s_2/s_1 + t	rea	ci	lwa
7	Student₃:	The tobacco in all of them is shredded.	s_3/t	res	ps	lwa
8	Student₄:	They're rolled by machine and packed by machine.	s_4/t	res	ps	lwa
9	Teacher:	Who wants to compare how they smell?	t/c	sol		
10	Students:	(Two students hold individual cigarettes from different packs up to their noses and smell them.)	$s_1 + s_2$/t	res	as	lwa
11	Teacher:	Now that we've reminded ourselves of a little information about what smokers smoke, I want you to tell me some things smokers do that annoy you, so we can see if there are any patterns in what they do.*	t/c	sol		
12	Student₁:	If there are no ashtrays, they smoke anyway.	s_1/t	res	ps	lwa
13		And, then, they put out the cigarettes on the floor and leave them there.	s_1/s_2 + t	rea	ps	lwa
14	Student₂:	Yeah, for someone else to clean up.	s_2/s_1 + t	rea	ps	lwa
15	Student₃:	They smoke in elevators even if it's not allowed.	s_3/t	res	ps	lwa
16	Student₄:	They make food taste terrible even to others when they smoke at the same table, or even in the same room, like in a restaurant.	s_4/t	res	ps	lwi
17	Teacher:	What things do you notice about smokers, as a group?	t/c	sol		
18	Student₁:	They smell—their clothes smell, their fingers smell, and the places they live in smell.	s_1/t	res	ci	lwa
19	Student₂:	Their fingers that hold the cigarettes are yellow, and some of their teeth are too.	s_2/t	res	ci	lwa
20	Student₃:	They're nervous and weak willed.	s_3/t	res	ci	lwi
21	Student₄:	Some find it difficult to stop smoking.	s_4/t	res	ps	lwa
22	Student₃:	Many gain weight when they stop because they eat more.	s_3/t	res	re	lwa

EXCERPT 9–1 (*continued*)

		Communications	*Source/ Target*	*Move Type*	*Use*	*Con-tent*
23	Student$_2$:	Many of the things smokers do they are not conscious of. The fact that sometimes a smoker will put the wrong end in his mouth and start to light the filter end is one illustration of this.	s_2/t	res	ps	lwi
24	Student$_1$:	Different smokers smoke different amounts each day.	s_1/t	res	ps	lwa
25	Teacher:	Now, I want the smokers to light up and I want the nonsmokers to too, so you can experience smoking. I want the nonsmokers to imitate the way the smokers inhale and light the cigarettes.	t/c	sol		
26	Group$_1$:	(Smokers light up.)	g_1/t	res	dc + as	lwa
27	Group$_2$:	(Non-smokers light up imitating smokers.)	g_2/t	res	ds + as	lwa

* Since what annoys people can be considered to be a personal opinion, these could be coded *lwa* + *life personal*, if the teacher were really interested in the personal opinions of the students. Here, the teacher seems to be interested only in having the students provide statements treating the ways of life of smokers.

To distinguish different kinds of interpretations—humorous, stereotyped, historical critical, for example—subscripts can be used after the abbreviation *lwi*: lwi_{hu}, lwi_s, lwi_{hi}, lwi_c, etc.

between the ways smokers and nonsmokers live, the content would not be coded *lwa* and *lwi*. Here, as in all cases, content in a particular subcategory is coded in the subcategory only when that content is attributed to the mediums used in different ways. Had the teacher said "We're going to notice function words and word order in a discussion of smokers and nonsmokers," I'd code the content *grammar form—lx*, since the content is what the teacher or others attribute to the communications.

In the Use column, *as* = attend smell, *ci* = characterize illustrate, *cl* = characterize label, *dc* = reproduce change medium, *ds* = reproduce same medium, *ps* = present state, *re* = relate explain.

Obviously, the label of any group could be substituted for the word *smokers*—taxi drivers, retired people, commercial artists, cat lovers. And a parallel word could be substituted for *cigarettes* that represented an artifact or item of importance to any group—fares and taxi regulations, retirement checks and old people's homes, drawing boards, paints and brushes, cats, litter bags and cat food. In fact, it's hard to imagine anyone not having heard conversations similar to those in Excerpt 9–1 in either a teaching or nonteaching setting. We are all engaged all the time in conversations about the ways of life of different groups such as these, to say nothing of the ways of life of different groups who also speak different languages.

Journal Entry

Feelings between smokers and nonsmokers are at about the same level of intensity as those between toilet flushers and non-toilet flushers. In areas of the world where there is plenty of water, toilets are usually flushed after each use. In areas where water is scarce, such a use of water is a symbol of great waste. When one travels to a place where there is not much water, one is accused of being wasteful. At the same time, others there seem dirty. What type of experience have you had that points up some aspect of the ways of life of different groups similar to this one?

The Same only Different—The Use *Characterize Differentiate* with Content *lwa* and *lwi*

Though the purpose of discussing smokers was to see how they compared with nonsmokers, mediums were not used to *characterize differentiate* in Excerpt 9–1. Whether the absence of this use in such discussions is universal or not needs to be determined. But if *characterize differentiate* is as rare in conversations you overhear with content *lw* as it is in Excerpt 9–1, an obvious alternative is to make it frequent, since this use is designed for making comparisons. Excerpt 9–2 shows the use *characterize differentiate* in teacher solicits and student responses as they learn and teach about the ways of life of smokers and nonsmokers. [Background 9–3]

Smokers in Excerpt 9–2 have a better chance than those in Excerpt 9–1. Though students state many facts and opinions in both—*ps*—stacking these against smokers is harder in Excerpt 9–2, because both similarities *and* differences are required. The use *cd* in solicits serves to balance the statements in responses, and the use *cd* in response does too. When we are indicating similarities and differences or stating them, it's impossible to give one-sided responses that support our preconceived notions. Telling a person to say the opposite of what he or she has just said is not likely to mean the person will immediately believe the new statement. But making it forces the juxtaposition of a current opinion or fact with a totally different one.

EXCERPT 9–2
Same or Different*

		Communications	*Source/ Target*	*Move Type*	*Use*	*Content*
1	Teacher:	Do the labels *smoker* and *nonsmoker* have the same connotation?	t/c	sol		
2	Student$_1$:	No.	s_1/t	res	cd	lwi
3		*Nonsmoker* sounds better . . . healthier.				lwi
4	Student$_2$:	*Smoker* sounds better to me . . . means an older person.	s_2/t	res		lwi
5	Teacher:	Do smokers and nonsmokers have any similar needs?	t/c	sol		
6	Student$_1$:	Yes,	s_1/t	res	cd	lwi
7		each needs satisfaction, friends, contact with others.				
8	Teacher:	Do smokers and nonsmokers meet their needs in the same way?	t/c	sol		
9	Student$_2$:	Cigarettes help smokers make contact and friends.	s_2/t	res		lwi
10	Teacher:	Give me a sentence opposite to the one Al just said.	t/c	sol		

EXCERPT 9–2 *(continued)*

		Communications	*Source/ Target*	*Move Type*	*Use*	*Con- tent*
11	Student$_1$:	Cigarettes don't help smokers make contact and friends.	s_1/t	res		lwi
12	Student$_2$:	Conversations help smokers make contact and friends.	s_2/t	res		lwi
13	Student$_3$:	Conversations help nonsmokers make contact and friends.	s_3/t	res		lwi
14	Teacher:	Make three statements about nonsmokers that parallel this statement about smokers:	t/c	sol		
15	Student$_1$:	Some smokers find it difficult to stop smoking.				lwa
16		Some nonsmokers find it difficult to stop watching TV.	s_1/t	res		lwa
17	Student$_2$:	Others find it hard to stop getting annoyed at dogs.	s_2/t	res		lwa
18	Student$_3$:	At postmen if they are late.	s_3/t	res		lwa
19	Teacher:	And about this:	t/c	sol		
20		Smokers smoke in elevators even if it is not allowed.				
21	Student$_1$:	Nonsmokers spray perfume in the air and pollute it for everyone.	s_1/t	res		lwa
22	Teacher:	Here are some pictures of smokers and nonsmokers.	t/c	sol		
23		(Lines up two groups of pictures showing people in action on the job, or engaged in sports or in social settings talking.)				
24		State some similarities between people in both groups. And, when you do, I'll tell you which is a group of smokers and which a group of nonsmokers. Oh, you can state some differences too.				
25	Student$_1$:	There are three males and three females in each group.	s_1/t	res		lwa
26	Student$_2$:	They are different ages in each group.	s_2/t	res	cd	lwa
27	Teacher:	(etc.) Do these generalizations have the same meaning:	t/c	sol		
28		Smokers are self-indulgent types.				
29		Smokers sometimes forget that those around them may not enjoy cigarette smoke.				
30	Student$_1$:	No.	s_1/t	res	cd	lwi
31		The first one means they aren't nice.				
32		But the second one means they simply may not think to ask—they may forget.				

* I treat the use cd in solicits, as well as other uses in solicits which those who respond are to differentiate, in Episode 4.

If an important goal in teaching and learning about the ways of life of different groups is seeing similarities and differences that we didn't previously see, one possible way to meet this goal is by the use *characterize differentiate*. In my experience, the use *cd* is more likely to communicate content of sound—*ls*—as in minimal-pair drills than *lw*. After increasing the use *cd* in solicits and responses, see whether students say "That seems to be the way they do it" and similar comments, rather than negative facts and opinions about the ways of life of different groups. And see whether such comparisons are followed by comments that show preconceived notions have been upset and new understandings achieved.

Suggesting that one group is simply different from another group—*cd*—and not trying to prove that one group is better than another is itself, of course, a characteristic of one type of group. Consequently, advocating that you try *cd* as an important use in teaching and learning about *lw* puts me in a bind. If I advocate constant comparisons without judgments, I am implying the superiority of one preconceived notion over the other. And, I am implying that the various ways of life of all groups are equally good or bad, an obvious fallacy. There is no logical escape from this bind. Searching for a logical escape is, of course, in itself another characteristic of some groups. In spite of these binds, I will continue to urge you try the use *cd* to see how much it forces us to find similarities *and* differences in our comparisons.

By urging you try the use *cd*, I am not suggesting all groups are the same. Nor am I implying that all groups should be the same. There is little doubt that differences between groups produce healthy tension. Students from small towns and teachers from large cities, teachers who advise description and those who advocate judgments, and other distinct groups mixed together can lead to mutual growth, increased esteem for others, and constructive resolution of conflicts, as well as deeper insight for each individual about one's place in relationship to others. But differences between groups can also lead to mutual stagnation, decreased esteem for others, and destructive resolution of conflicts, as well as fear of looking at oneself to gain self-insight about one's place in relationship to others. At any rate, without increased attention to ways to teach and learn about the ways of life of different groups, both actual and interpretive, it is hard to imagine how we can decrease the difficulties we all encounter in different groups, much less avert ultimate destruction of the human race. [Background 9–4]

Journal Entry

The American magazine *National Geographic* contains many pictures and words about the ways of life of different groups. Catalogs from stores in many countries contain pictures and words about the ways of life of different groups too. For example, Sears, an American firm, produces a one-inch-thick catalog for mail-order shopping that shows a lot about the ways of life of people. Catalogs from past years show how ways of life now and many years ago are the same and different.

In your experience, do you find that catalogs or other materials *not* developed to explicitly teach about the ways of life of groups are more informative than materials like *National Geographic*, which are designed explicitly to teach about the ways of life of different groups?

More than Objects—Using Different Mediums to Communicate Ways of Life

In my experience, mediums other than speech and print are very popular in the teaching and learning of the ways of life of different groups. The *National Geographic* magazine and Sears catalog just mentioned in the journal entry would probably be far less popular without the pictures they contain. Students with different ways of life are often asked to prepare food, wear clothing, bring artifacts, or sing and dance to music typical of the patterns of their groups. While these classic uses of these *nonlinguistic aural* and *nonlinguistic visual* mediums surely can heighten interest in the ways of life of different groups, they raise a few problems as well.

The first problem raised by the use of artifacts, food, and music is parallel to the problem of *gu* words. Eating the food of those with different ways of life, and seeing artifacts, dances, and costumes, may be equated with understanding the ways of life of the other group. The second problem is that we may treat the people wearing costumes, eating different food, and displaying different artifacts the same way we treat all *nonlinguistic visual* mediums—as objects. Finally, while different tastes and smells obviously affect us, less tangible mediums such as scowls, smiles, eyebrow arching—*paralinguistic visual*—anger or surprise shown by tone of voice—*paralinguistic aural*—distance, touching, and movement—*paralinguistic other*—and the absence of mediums—*silence*—are the ones likely to be more difficult to understand and perhaps more critical as well. [Background 9–5]

If you find yourself spending most of the time on *linguistic* and *nonlinguistic* mediums, substitute the opposites—*paralinguistic* mediums and *silence*—for some of the time. Whichever mediums you use, I'd of course advocate you compare them with responses requiring *characterize differentiate*—both same and different—and with solicits containing a *cd* component that forces responses containing information about similarities and differences, as illustrated in Excerpt 9–2.

Journal Entry

According to some reports, at the meal for the Japanese after the signing of the surrender documents ending World War II, chopsticks were provided at each place. But rather than putting both of them together at the bottom of the plate, as is the pattern among the Japanese, one chopstick was placed on each side of each plate, as knives and forks are placed. Like many examples of misunderstandings between different groups, this one involved mediums other than speech, and involved lack of knowledge of what was similar and what was different about the eating utensils of two groups.

Have you had incidents similar to this one happen to you? What feelings did you and others you were with have about the incident? Did your incident involve tangible mediums such as chopsticks, or the less tangible ones that I code *paralinguistic* or *silence*?

IV. SEEK TO UNDERSTAND RATHER THAN TO BE UNDERSTOOD—CONCLUSION

In a prayer attributed to St. Francis, we make the plea to "understand rather than to be understood." Teaching and learning about the ways of life of different groups may make some students from one place more comfortable with students from another place; it may make us feel more at ease at a place different from where we were born and raised; and we may begin to realize that some of our students' actions are the result of following patterns of a different way of life. But to me, the central purpose of comparing different ways of life is to see ourselves more clearly and to see how others perceive us. Surely one of the reasons many students in high school resist works of literature that reflect patterns of life of both theirs and other groups is that they fear self-perception at a particular age.

No matter how many times we start a journey towards understanding, on each trip it is likely that at one stage we will stereotype others, treat them as objects, and equate familiarity with costumes and food or word knowledge of other groups with understanding of the ways of life of others. This last pitfall will be especially likely if the words are like *gu* and easy to remember. All these pitfalls are probably attempts to make unfamiliar things familiar to us so that the need for predictability in a world of constant change is partially met. Yeats wrote "Things fall apart, the center cannot hold, mere anarchy is loosed upon the world." At first, exposure to the ways of life of different groups may seem to increase this anarchy. But as we seek to understand by describing similarities and by putting differences in perspective, we'll realize the anarchy loosed upon the world is not related to the ways of life of different groups, but instead is a condition all groups face. [Background 9–6]

Journal Entry

Seeking to understand is a way of life of different groups. One group that I think needs to follow this way of life is teachers. How do you feel about this idea that the teaching profession should stand for intergroup understanding and do what it can to encourage groups to seek mutual understanding?

BACKGROUND NOTES

9–1. In *Teachers for the real world*, B. O. Smith reminds the reader that all teachers need to be prepared to see differences between themselves and their students. These differences are not only of background, but of age and often of ways of studying. Smith thinks that paying attention only to one particular group, such as a mainstream group, is unfortunate because he believes there are a great many differences even among people who are supposedly from the same mainstream group. In *Memories of a dutiful daughter*, Simone de Beauvoir constantly is talking about the differences between herself and some of the other girls she grew up with, as well as the differences between herself and her parents. She laments the fact that she was subject to laws, to conventional behavior, to prejudice. As a result of this, she was always keen to support other people with an independence of spirit. The other people she was talking about in her book all spoke the same language she did; in fact, many of them shared the same religion and the same social class, but still she considered herself different in her way of life from the way of life of many of those she often associated with.

9–2. Nelson Brooks and Charles Fries spent many pages in their books discussing culture. They pointed out the fact that comparing the way people swim in different lands or the ways people play games in different lands will reveal a lot about the cultures of the different groups. Sometimes we forget that one of the central themes of much audio-lingual writing was on comparing the languages of different groups as well as the ways of life of different groups. In recent discussions of the audiolingual method, we think mainly of the emphasis on structures and the emphasis on repeating. But in addition to being interested in structure and pronunciation, Brooks and Fries, to mention two central names in that movement, were very interested in what I have called the ways of life of different groups.

For a very readable discussion of culture and the various meanings of the term presented in a broad perspective of communication in general, I'd urge Forsdale's book. For a discussion of the relationship between ways of life and economic systems, see Pfaff. See Benedict as a background to all of these.

9–3. Robert Lado (1957) illustrates the way he compared bits from different cultures. He compared the form of the communication or behavior, the meaning and what he called the distribution. For example, the contents of milk are chemically the same in both France and the United States; however, if a grownup in France is drinking milk, it does not mean the same as if an American is drinking milk in the United States. Often it means that the adult in France is ill because milk is not commonly taken by adults there unless they feel ill. The context in which milk would be consumed is also different. It is not likely that an adult French person would drink milk publicly if he or she felt ill, while it is possible for an American adult to drink milk in almost any setting. To take another example, we can compare the words *gu* in Somali and *goo* in English. The forms of the words, if we look at them or hear them, are quite similar. The meaning also is reasonably similar in that they both refer to soft, mushy, sticky material. However, *goo* is a word used usually by children in the United States, while the word *gu* is used in Somalia by anyone who wants to refer to the rainy season. It is not a word limited to children or associations with children in Somalia. I find the paradigm using form, meaning and distribution extremely useful in making any kinds of comparisons, and I urge you to read Lado's description of the paradigm. For a more detailed model of ways to view different ways of life and a much wider range of activities and readings than I am discussing, read Ann Frentzen's dissertation. In her dissertation, she describes a course she taught designed to train participants in intercultural communication.

9–4. Laiten, who was a Peace Corps volunteer in Somalia for some time, did a study of conflict resolution of a sort in Somalia. He compared the discussion techniques of Somalis when they were discussing the same issues using the Somali language and the English language. His results suggest that the Somalis were more confrontational in their discussions when they used English than when they used Somali. This shows that even though we can separate the ways of life of the people from their language, in fact they are quite deeply intertwined. The study also reminds us of the importance of the ways we resolve conflicts. One of the classics in the field of conflict resolution is that written by Morton Deutsch.

9–5. A central work on the use of mediums other than language in cross-cultural communications is of course Hall's *The Silent Language*. And La Forge wrote about mediums other than linguistic ones in *Community Language Learning in Japan*. The articles that he wrote describing these mediums, including silence, are published in a journal devoted primarily to such differences called *Cross-currents*.

9–6. In *Cynbernetics*, Wiener talks about entropy, the tendency of the world to constantly disintegrate. While this on the surface seems a pessimistic idea, it reminds us that differences between the ways of life of different people might have a very strong rationale. We might need these different regulations to hold different groups together in such a way that entropy is slowed down—since, at least according to Wiener, it can never be stopped.

EPISODE 10

Huh? . . . Oh

I. THE MEANING OF "HUH? . . . OH."—INTRODUCTION AND PURPOSE

Tell me whether the conversation in Excerpt 10–1 is more likely to occur in a waiting room at a dentist's office or in a language classroom.

EXCERPT 10–1
Huh? . . . Oh.

1	David:	(Silently reading a story in a magazine.)
2	Joe:	Excuse me, what's the theme of the story you're reading?
3	David:	Huh? ______________________________
4	Joe:	I said, what's the theme of the story you're reading?
5	David:	Oh. ______________________________
6		(Continues to read the story in the magazine.)

Nearly everyone says that the conversation could take place either in a dentist's office or in a classroom, but most opt for the dentist's office, mainly because of the fact that David ignores Joe's question and simply continues his reading. In fact, the conversation did take place in a dentist's office. Joe simply wanted to see how others would react if he asked a very typical teacher question to someone reading on his own for pleasure in a nonteaching setting. When most of us read on our own, as in a dentist's office, though we may share feelings about the material with others, or even retell it to those who have not read it, we are not usually ready to answer questions on specific areas of content determined by another person.

The conversation in Excerpt 10–1 does have something in common with conversations in teaching settings though, other than the teacher question in lines 2 and 4: the meaning of "Huh?" and "Oh." In Excerpt 10–1, write words that have the same meaning as "Huh?" in line 3 and "Oh" in line 5, on the broken lines provided. Then, see if the words you wrote next to "Huh?" can also be written after "Huh?" in line 2 of Excerpt 10–2 and after "Oh" in line 5 of Excerpt 10–2.

EXCERPT 10–2
Huh? . . . Oh. Again

1	Tour guide to tourists:	Look at the beautiful *cercis canadensis* in bloom.
2	One tourist to guide:	Huh? --
3	Tour guide to tourist:	A *cersis canadensis* in bloom.
4		*Cersis canadensis.* (Slower and louder than the first time.)
5	One tourist to guide:	Oh. --
6	Same tourist to friend:	What color is the thing in bloom I was supposed to look at? (Said in a low voice.)

The words most frequently written next to "Huh?" are "What?" or "Say it again" or "I don't understand," in both Excerpts 10–1 and 10–2. While the words written for "Oh" are somewhat more varied, ranging from "Ah, I see. I understand" to "I don't understand," most write words indicating lack of comprehension, even though in isolation, "Oh" suggests comprehension. In my experience with language learners, "Oh" and parallel comments such as "I see" and "Yes," as well as a nodding head, often are the surest signals that they are not following a word I am saying.

The "Huh?" and "Oh" of Excerpts 10–1 and 10–2 are symbols of one type of comment that occurs as we *attend* (listen, read silently, smell, taste, touch or view pictures or other visual materials— the subcategories of *attend* I treat in Episode 3). We also *characterize* by making judgments: "It was great!" We *present* by retelling what we heard or read: "The butler did it." And, we make inferences about what we *attend* to, we *relate*. What all these uses we communicate after we *attend* have in common is that they try to express what was meant by the material we read, listened to, tasted, or in any other way took in. We can never find out exactly what the materials that have been taken in by another person mean. But uses which require that we produce something are used to gauge what feelings and thoughts we have had as a result of attending, whether this has been done by silently reading a menu, tasting a wine, listening to a concert, or smelling a flower.

The purpose of this episode is to compare the uses we communicate before, during, and after we *attend* in teaching and nonteaching settings. Because uses contain different areas of content in teaching and nonteaching settings, and because the range and frequency of mediums we use in both is different, I treat the mediums and major categories of content along with the uses. But mainly, this episode is about the sequence

TABLE 10–1
Mainly Uses

Source/Target	*Move Type*	*Use*
Teacher	str	attend *a*
		characterize *c*
	sol	
Student		present *p*
	res	
		relate *r*
Other	rea	reproduce *d*

and proportion of uses and moves in teaching and nonteaching settings. In Table 10–1, I show the elements of FOCUS I concentrate on in this episode.

By describing and tallying the moves and uses that occur before, during, and after we take in mediums as we *attend* in a range of settings, rules that govern these elements can be discovered. Once discovered, the rules can be broken. Those moves and uses that occur most frequently with *attend* in classrooms can be decreased. Those that occur rarely can be increased. Those that are observed outside but not in classrooms can be introduced. And, of course, those that seem to occur together with "Huh?" followed by "Oh," meaning "I genuinely understand," can be substituted for those that produce "Huh?" followed with "Oh," meaning "I don't understand."

If we decided to have people in teaching settings alter the proportion of moves and uses only because we observed these differences between patterns in classes and nonteaching settings such as concert halls, movie theaters, stadiums, and restaurants, it might be reasonable, but not necessarily sound. After all, no one gives these audiences any directions before they *attend* in these settings, nor much feedback on the comments they make as they *attend*. But it would be hard to argue that these are practices that teachers should follow when they are teaching. If the only work the teacher had to do was arrange things for people to *attend* to—unlock the place for people to enter so the events would be available to *attend* to, and lock up afterward—there would be little need for any kind of teacher preparation, little need for books on reading, listening, or any other activities that required us to take in mediums, or any reason for providing teachers with much compensation. There is even theoretical justification for suggesting alternatives as well as the justification that they occur in nonteaching settings.

Consequently, before we explore the patterns of moves and uses in teaching and nonteaching settings, I describe a theory of the reading process. In this way, we can generate alternatives by substituting opposites to break rules and by creating patterns implied by a theory.

I describe the theory, and ask you to perform some tasks that I think it implies. Then I transcribe some communications from a reading lesson to contrast some of the patterns of moves and uses that are frequent in teaching settings with some that are infrequent in nonteaching settings. In the final section, I provide an opportunity to match incidents in which teachers and students *attend* with alternatives I suggest in this episode, based both on the theory I introduce and the rules we discover in nonteaching settings that we can try in teaching settings.

II. PRACTICAL THINGS FROM AN IDEA?— ALTERNATIVES IMPLIED BY THEORY

External–Internal—A Theory of Taking Mediums In

According to one theory of the reading process, and by extension the process involved in all categories of *attend*, to understand material we *attend* to, we must not only use the information provided by the materials themselves, but also the information we already have within us that is related to the material. The information we get from the visual, aural, tactile, or sensory messages I will call *external information*. The information we have in our heads based on our prior experience I will call *internal information*. The more we depend on the information in the material we *attend* to, the less we are able to depend on the *internal information* in our heads, and vice versa. If I give you a passage about chess to read or listen to, or tell you to observe a game of chess being played, and you have never played chess or seen a game before, you will have to labor a great deal to get any meaning from the material in front of you because you have little *internal information* to provide you with part of the meaning. But if you are a filmgoer, and I say "Read this orally: Marilyn ______" nine times out of ten, you will say "Marilyn Monroe" rather than "Marilyn blank line." If I wrote "Marlene ______," you'd say "Marlene Dietrich," and if I wrote "Wolfgang ______," you'd say "Wolfgang Mozart," though less quickly, and you'd probably follow the name with a comment such as, "He doesn't belong with movie stars; he was a composer." You can fill in the names because of *internal information* developed by seeing movies, and in the last instance listening to music as well. If you haven't seen movies with the stars I mentioned, your lack of internal information makes it very difficult to *attend* to the print and blank before you.

For another example of the interplay between *internal* and *external information*, look at the images in Excerpt 10–3.

EXCERPT 10–3
Tom's Picture

When you looked at Tom's picture in Excerpt 10–3, you no doubt "saw" four legs on both camels even though one of the legs is obscured by a boy walking beside it. You also "saw" the heads on all the sheep and cattle though some of them are obscured by the shepherds. And finally, when you viewed the faces of all three shepherds you probably "saw" eyes on their faces though the shadows make them invisible in the picture. If you *attend* to the picture again, I'm sure you'll discover other instances where you used your *internal information* to contribute to the *external information* in the picture itself. If looking at Tom's picture reminds you of a place you've been, this would be another clear instance of employing *internal information* when viewing *external information*. You'll come up with others.

What we take in from pictures and other mediums can interfere with meaning we *attend* to as well as contribute to it. If we see a person coming towards us with a gun, our *internal information*, based on previous experiences with guns, tells us that danger is on its way. To see the person with the gun flick it open, and reveal a piece of candy or a jewel to us, and then offer us these "prizes" would force us to bring the meaning of our *internal information* into line with the *external information* in front of us. [Background 10–1]

I once heard a story about a reporter's visit to a prison that further illustrates the constant interplay between *external* and *internal information*. After the warden had shown the reporter the cells, recreation areas and eating facilities, he took the reporter to the room the electric chair was in. The warden invited the reporter to sit in the electric chair so he could experience the straps and the isolation of the chair in the center of the large execution room. During the entire tour, the warden and the reporter had been accompanied by a guard, who at this time was standing off to the side of the room the electric chair was in. It was a very warm day, and just as the warden completed strapping the reporter to the chair, the guard pulled down the handle of a large switch. The reporter fainted instantly. The guard was simply turning on a fan to cool the room, but the *internal information* in the reporter's mind at that moment could connect a switch with only one event: an electrocution. His *internal information* prevented him from grasping the meaning communicated externally by the guard's action of turning on a fan. [Background 10–2]

If meaning were present only in the materials we *attend* to, the materials we *attend* to would have the same meaning to everyone. Just as the switch was perceived differently by the reporter sitting in the electric chair and the guard turning on the fan, religious books such as the Bible and the Koran are perceived differently by different groups. When holding a particular belief, people often fail to perceive an opposing point of view in materials they read. [Background 10–3]

One of the tasks of judges and lawyers is to discover the "real" meaning of laws and descriptions of events such as auto accidents, provided by drivers, passengers and witnesses. In all of perception, there is an interplay between the *external information* provided by the materials and events we *attend* to and the *internal information* in our brain, and I should add heart, based on our previous experience and current feelings. The preconceived notions about teaching that color our observations also reflect this interplay.

Some Charges—Applications of the Theory

Read Silently Plus—Performing Tasks

To demonstrate some of the applications of the theory of the reading process that suggests that what we have in our heads is as important as what is in the mediums we *attend* to, and to provide some examples of some applications of the theory, I'm going to ask you to *attend* to a passage and perform some tasks after you do, as if you were a student in a reading class. Just follow Charges 1 through 12 below, ignoring the blank lines in the use column of each charge for now. You can enjoy carrying out the charges, incidentally, if you want to.

Charge 1
Read Excerpt 10–4 silently, and as you do, with a pencil draw lines through words or larger units of meaning that you do not understand.

Source/Target	Move Type	Use	Content
s/t	res	______	p + s

EXCERPT 10–4
At the Pasar* by Hillel Weintraub

1a Once upon a ping, there was a ngeng old man named Photak.

2a He had three anak-anak, named Phare, Bare, and Pare.

3a He selalu bejalan to pasar with his anak-anak, but he selalu

4a left his bini at home so she could water the sayor-sayor.

5a He went to the pasar to sell sayor-sayor.

6a He set up his stand and began to sell his sayor-sayor right away while they were fresh.

7a An orang-kechil came by and stopped in front of Photak's stall.

8a He looked ngeng carefully at Phare.

9a Then, he saberchakap, "What a kawaii looking boy that is!"

10a Do you want to sell him?"

11a Photak didn't laly berchakap to strangers but he saberchakap,

12a "What are you, some kind of a kachang or something?"

13a Lepas itu, Photak took his anak-anak home for lunch, which by now his bini had prepared.

14a The next day, Photak went with Bare and Pare to the pasar.

15a As usual, he left his bini at home to water the sayor-sayor and prepare the meals as well.

16a He also left his youngest anak at home because he didn't want to sell him to the orang-kechil.

17a Arriving at the pasar, Photak together with his anak-anak displayed his sayor-sayor.

18a By eleven o'clock, he sold nearly all his sayor-sayor, and he was getting ready to go home.

19a Suddenly, the orang-kechil appeared and berchakap shrilly,

20a "Your kawaii anak isn't here, just the unattractive ones."

21a "You have excellent vision," saberchakap Photak. "Perhaps you can also see

22a that I don't want to talk to you."

23a With that, Photak lifted his one remaining sayor, which was by now slightly wilted,

EXCERPT 10–4 (*continued*)

24a and whacked the orang-kechil on the head.

25a After that, strangely enough, Photak, his bini and all three of his anak-anak lived

26a ngeng happily ever after.

27a The quinn of the story is: If you're looking for kawaii looking boys, the pasar is

28a no place to go.

* Some of the connections between different parts of the passage may seem a bit strained, such as the moral of the story. The passage was originally written to illustrate some words, then altered to illustrate some other points. It is reconstructed, and additionally, with the mixture of words from two languages, it is not an authentic piece of writing.

Charge 2

Read Excerpt 10–5 silently, and as you do, with a pencil write in words in the blanks that you think fit, given the meaning of the sentences. Incorrect guesses will not be penalized in any way.

Source/Target	Move Type	Use	Content
s/t	res	______	s

Though you may not think you can fill in words on the blank lines that seem to fit, you've done a similar activity many times in your life. When you've been given the name of a building, and you are looking for it through a window on a bus full of people, haven't you ever rung the bell to get off even if you only saw part of the name of the building? Let's say the name of the building was the Kingsbridge Public Library, for example. And you saw only the "Kin" and the "rary" through the window of the bus, the other letters being obscured by bodies. Would you not fill in the other letters, using your own knowledge and the size of the building and the approximate location to assist you in your guess? And after getting off the bus, you confirmed or rejected your prediction.

While on the bus, you might have done some filling in too, if you are one of those who tries to read other people's newspapers over their shoulders. After the owner of a newspaper finishes a column, and shifts his fingers slightly, thereby obscuring parts of a column you are in the midst of reading, don't you continue to read, filling in the words under his fingers with your knowledge of current events and the other information in the article itself? When he moves his fingers, you compare the meaning you filled in with the meaning you are now able to extract from the unobscured print, don't you?

But here I am, telling you to read a passage and then preventing you from doing it. I'm following the rule in a teaching setting that says the bulk of the time should be devoted to activities *before* and *after* we take mediums in, not *during* the time we take in the mediums. So, read and fill in the blanks!

Charge 3

Reread Excerpt 10–4 silently and put an *X* through those words that signal to you that the story is not a true one, but some type of fable.

Source/Target	Move Type	Use	Content
s/t	res	______	s

EXCERPT 10–5
At the ______ by Hillel Weintraub

1b Once upon a ______, there was a ______ old man named Photak.
2b He had three ______, named Phare, Bare, and Pare.
3b He ______ ______ to ______ with his ______, but he ______
4b left his ______ at home so she could water the ______.
5b He went to the ______ to sell his ______.
6b He set up his stand and began to sell his ______ right away while they were fresh.
7b An ______ came by and stopped in front of Photak's stall.
8b He looked ______ carefully at Phare.
9b Then, he ______, "What a ______ looking boy that is!"
10b Do you want to sell him?"
11b Photak didn't ______ ______ to strangers but he ______,
12b "What are you, some kind of a ______ or something?"
13b ______, Photak took his ______ home for lunch, which by now his ______ had prepared.
14b The next day, Photak went with Bare and Pare to the ______.
15b As usual, he left his ______ at home to water the ______ and prepare the meals as well.
16b He also left his youngest ______ at home because he didn't want to sell him to the ______.
17b Arriving at the ______, Photak together with his ______ displayed his ______.
18b By eleven o'clock, he sold nearly all his ______, and he was getting ready to go home.
19b Suddenly, the ______ appeared and ______ shrilly,
20b "Your ______ ______ isn't here, just the unattractive ones."
21b "You have excellent vision," ______ Photak. "Perhaps you can also see
22b that I don't want to talk to you."
23b With that, Photak lifted his one remaining ______, which was by now slightly wilted,
24b and whacked the ______ on the head.
25b After that, strangely enough, Photak, his ______ and all three of his ______ lived
26b ______ happily ever after.
27b The ______ of the story is: if you're looking for ______ looking boys, the ______ is
28b no place to go.

Charge 4
Reread Excerpt 10–4 silently and write the word "humorous" to the right of those lines you think the author intended to be funny.

Source/Target	Move Type	Use	Content
s/t	res	______	s

Charge 5
Reread Excerpt 10–4 silently and circle all the verbs, both those that are function words such as "was" and those that are content words such as "went."

Source/Target	*Move Type*	Use	*Content*
s/t	res	______	s

Charge 6
Reread Excerpt 10–4 silently and shade over all the words or phrases that refer to people, like this: Once upon a ping, there was a gneng old man named Photak.

Source/Target	*Move Type*	Use	*Content*
s/t	res	______	s

Charge 7
Reread Excerpt 10–4 silently and draw vertical lines over all the phrases or words that refer to things like this: . . . so she could water the sayor-sayor.

Source/Target	*Move Type*	Use	*Content*
s/t	res	______	s

Charge 8
Reread Excerpt 10–4 silently and draw slanted lines through all the phrases or words that refer to time like this: He selalu . . .Then, . . .

Source/Target	*Move Type*	Use	*Content*
s/t	res	______	s

Charge 9
Reread Excerpt 10–5 silently and as you do, with a pencil, write in phrases or words in the blanks that you think fit, given the meaning of the sentences. Substitute new words for any you wrote before if you think the new choices fit better. You will not be penalized in any way for incorrect guesses, so don't leave any lines blank.

Source/Target	*Move Type*	Use	*Content*
s/t	res	______	s

Charge 10
Exchange copies of Excerpt 10–5 with a friend who has also written choices in the blanks. Silently reread your friend's passage and write an *f* for *fit* above those words your friend filled in that you think fit the meaning of the sentence and passage. When you and your friend have finished marking the choices you each made with *f*s, discuss the choices not marked with an *f*.

	Source/Target	*Move Type*	Use	*Content*
A. For marking the words with an *f* for *fit*	s/s	res	______	s
B. For the discussion	s/s	res	______	s

Charge 11
If you have any unresolved meanings after you finish Charge 10, ask another friend for an opinion. But do not ask for your friend to state the correct answer. Only ask yes-no or either-or questions: "Are anak-anak female?" "Are sayor-sayor to be eaten or used for fuel?" Your friend can confirm or reject the information you state in your questions with a "yes" or "no" or by selecting one of the choices given in an either-or question. But your friend cannot suggest words.

	Source/Target	Move Type	Use	Content
A. For the yes-no or either-or questions	s/s	sol	_____	p + s
B. For the confirmation or rejection of information in the yes-no or either-or questions	s/s	res	_____	s

Charge 12
Now, have your friend read Excerpt 10–4, *At the Pasar*, to you orally. Follow along in the text as your friend reads to you, and write down any feelings you have as you hear and see the passage, or draw a picture to represent the feelings you have.*

	Source/Target	Move Type	Use	Content
A. For your friend's reading	s/s	res	_____	s
B. For the tasks you perform as your friend reads	s/s	res	_____	f + s

Journal Entry

What feelings or reactions do you have to performing the charges you just completed? If you simply performed the use *attend* and did not perform the tasks required, what was your reaction to the charges? At some point, though, do perform the tasks. Then, compare your feelings after having done them with those you had just reading them.

Attend Plus—Classifying Uses in Charges 1 through 12

Below each charge, you noticed that I coded the source of each move, the move type and, in the last column, the content: *f* for *life*, *p* for *procedure* and *s* for *study*. I left the use blank so you could code the uses. Go back to the blanks and code the uses. Write *a* for tasks that required you to *attend* by reading silently. Write *c* for *characterize*, *p* for *present*, *r* for *relate*, and *d* for *reproduce*. Write a plus sign between abbreviations when more than one category of use is required in any one response.

What Does It All Mean?—Discussing Applications

Underline/Cross Out—Two Ways of Indicating We Don't Understand

One of the purposes of asking you to cross out words as you read in Charge 1 was to remind you that the internal information in your head provides you with information

---

* *Coding of the charges done by others:* 1. *a* + *p*; 2. *a* + *p* + *r*; 3. through 8. *a* + *c*; 9. *a* + *c* + *p* + *r*—the *c* is coded because we indicate some of the words filled in are wrong; 10a. *a* + *c*; 10b. *p* + *r*; 11a. *p* + *p* + *s* or *p* + *c* + *s*; 11b. *c*; 12a. *d*; 12b. *c* + *p* + *r*.

just as much as the material you were attending to. As you know, Charge 1 is in sharp contrast to the usual direction in classes, which is to underline words that are not understood rather than to cross them out. But underlining words implies that the external information of the words or phrases themselves is the only source of information available for unlocking meaning. To the extent that underlining words or phrases isolates them, underlining implies that the external information surrounding the word in question cannot contribute to the meaning of the word that is not understood. If you stop in Excerpt 10–4 at *anak-anak* in line 2a because you do not understand the word, it is not possible to use either subsequent external information in the passage or internal information in your head to help determine what *anak-anak* are. Underlining a word or larger unit of meaning tends to focus all attention on the words that are underlined and does little to remind us that we can use the information in our heads based on our prior experience to help unlock meaning, or the other external information that follows and precedes the words and phrases we underline and thereby isolate.

By crossing out *anak-anak* in line 2a because you do not understand it in your first encounter with it, you remove attention from it rather than focus attention on it. Because the place formerly occupied by the word is now blank, you are able to focus on other words in the passage, and you are forced to seek meaning from your experience. After all, there is no way you can seek meaning from a blank. By searching for the meaning throughout the entire passage and your mind, you will at some point realize that words such as *children, sons*, or *male offspring* fit in the blank because subsequent external information in the passage tells you that the item that fits the blank was male: *boy* in line 9a and *boys* 27a. You can also learn that *anak-anak* is in a category different from both *Photak* and his *bini*—lines 1a and 4a. From your experience—internal information— you know that parents tend to live with children, especially in the type of traditional society we usually connect with fables like *At the Pasar*.

Asking someone to underline all words or larger units that aren't understood also implies that all words or phrases are important. Crossing out words and larger units that aren't understood of course implies that not all words are important. One of the most critical skills of a good reader is to be able to decide not only which words and phrases are not understood, but which ones that are not understood need to be for the purposes at hand. Many so-called poor readers are perhaps poor not because they say "I don't understand," but because they think that every time they don't understand they think they should. Knowing what we don't need to know is a vital part of understanding, and crossing out words is probably more likely to aid in developing this insight than underlining words.

Even if you think the theory of reading I am summarizing here is totally unfounded, you could still try having students cross out and obscure words rather than underlining them simply to do the opposite. Asking students to underline words they do understand is another opposite to the common rule that requires that we tell others to underline the words they don't understand. Cloze tests are made up by many teachers. By having students cross out words they do not understand, they create their own cloze passages. [Background 10–4]

Of course, whether underlining words students understand or don't understand, or crossing out words they don't understand really matters or not, you have to contrast them. If you have been asking students to *present* words and larger units they don't understand mainly by underlining those they did not understand, try asking them to *present* either by underlining those they do understand or by crossing out what they don't understand. By crossing out, they are simply substituting one type of non-linguistic medium for another: a thin line beneath a word for a large, heavy line through words. Try these alternatives in your own silent reading too.

See whether the alternatives lead to more use of both the surrounding external information on the page and the internal information in their heads and in your head. If the alternatives do, you will hear and say many more "Ohs" meaning "I see—I found it" following the initial "Huh?" expressed as words not understood are crossed out. Of course, the meaning of the "Oh," expressed as word equivalents for words crossed out are given by you or a dictionary, should not be confused with the meaning of the "Oh" expressed as meanings of words and phrases crossed out are discovered by using external and internal experience. When we say "Oh" after being given the meaning, it often means "You see—you found it" rather than "I see—I found it." The meaning of the "Oh" expressed in each case, naturally, must itself be determined by both external information—the sound of the word and the tone of voice it is communicated in—and internal information—knowledge of our students' attitudes and feelings that we have made a part of our internal memory store.

Journal Entry

When many of us study, we underline items we want to remember, or we use a light-colored felt pen to highlight the lines we want to reread in a review or go back to look at again.

Do you find you actually go back to things you underline or color? Or, does the process of underlining or coloring simply give you another chance to reread the material as you mark it or slow you down as you mark it? Do you find yourself so much in this habit that you mark books that don't belong to you?

Can't Store Anything without Organizing It— Eliminating Unlikely Possibilities by Grouping

As we separate words we know from those we don't, we also have to group them in some way because we have so many thoughts in our mind that we have to match with so many separate units of meaning in the material we *attend* to. To retrieve the information we need and to recognize it quickly enough so that we can use it, we have to classify, just as groceries are grouped in any market or store so that we can get what we need without total confusion day after day. [Background 10–5]

By saying "yes" or "no" to the questions "Is *selula* a time word?" and "Is *bejalan* a time word?" and "Is *pasar* a time word?", as required by Charge 8, you are forced to group together words that are similar to each other in some way. The attributes you use to decide which words and phrases go together may not be entirely conscious as you do the grouping, and we may each have different criteria for our groups. But if we stop to think about similarities between words that are related to time, we can think of some that many of us probably recognize and thus perhaps use. When we look at the words we know to be time words, we see that they tend to occur at the beginning of sentences, and they tend to be followed by commas: *as usual, The next day, By eleven, After that.* The words or phrases that we do not know that follow this pattern include *Once upon a ping*, and *Lepas itu*. The word *laly* is not at the beginning of a sentence, nor is it followed by a comma. But it ends in *ly* which is an attribute of some other time words such as *suddenly*. Of course, *ly* is also a part of words that do not relate to time, such as *carefully, nearly*, and *shrilly*. However, the meaning required in certain slots provides other information on which we can base our decision to classify a word with one group rather than with another. In the case of time words, we are aided by the *internal information* we possess that tells us that in a fable, we usually have to show the passage of time with time expressions rather than with detailed descriptions of intervening events, because such details might distract us from the central story line.

I am not suggesting that in the actual reading process we necessarily go through an entire reading passage over and over again classifying time words during one reading, the words that name people in another, and objects in still another, and on and on. Nor am I suggesting that the time taken to perform charges 3 through 8 is in any way comparable to the time it takes to make the kind of classifications we make as we *attend* to material. Rather, I am saying that charges 3 through 8 symbolize the process of classifying information that is probably necessary to make sense out of material we *attend* to.

In addition to symbolizing the process of grouping words and phrases we *attend* to, charges 3 through 8 may provide a way to teach people something new about categorizing items. Even though we may hear many two-year-olds indicating that new items they see or new noises they hear are similar or different to ones they have seen or heard before, different children *characterize* items at different rates. In the same way, some readers, as well as listeners, viewers and tasters, seem to be able to guess meaning very quickly, having learned on their own perhaps how to categorize both *internal* and *external information*. But some seem unable to categorize in as many different ways and seem to engage in the process only with great labor.

For years, there were two programs on radio and television in the United States that demonstrated how useful categorizing can be to discover meanings that at first seem unfathomable. One was called "Twenty Questions" and the other was called "I've Got a Secret." Though the details of the rules of each program differed slightly, essentially the aim in both was for a group of panelists to try to guess what occupations guests had or what secrets they had by asking a series of twenty or fewer yes-no or either-or questions similar in type to those in Charges 3 through 8. If the guests' secrets were not guessed by asking twenty questions or less, the guest was given a prize. Few prizes were given, however, because each yes-no or either-or question on the shows eliminated a great many possibilities, just as the questions in charges 3 through 8 can eliminate a great number of possibilities. As soon as we hear "no" to a question such as "Does your secret or your occupation involve people?" literally thousands of possibilities are eliminated. A "no" in response to "Does it involve other live things?" eliminates hundreds more. Doctors, nurses, teachers, clerks, veterinarians, waiters, police officers, to name a few, are simply not viable alternatives after negative replies to these two questions. Of course, as in all choices, some alternatives were extremely unlikely, if not impossible and no questions were needed to eliminate these. Given the setting on the shows, the "secret" could not be that the guest was an escaped convict, a person with a rare but highly communicable disease, or a secret agent.

In *At the Pasar*, as on the panels, not all alternatives are equally likely either. Given the setting, "computers" or "airplanes" are really not in the running as alternatives, for example. As soon as we eliminate the unlikely possibilities, and determine that *sayor-sayor* and *anak-anak* or any other pairs of words do not refer to the same item, we have started the process of discovering the "secret" each contains in the same way the panelists on "I've Got a Secret" and "Twenty Questions" started their process of elimination. As on these programs, each additional bit of information we get as we *attend*, whether from *external* or *internal information*, brings us closer to discovery. By moving around *At the Pasar* and seeing that *sayor-sayor* are something that need to be watered (line 4a); are sold (5a), can be fresh (6a), or wilted (23a), we eliminate all bakery goods, meats, fowl, fish, and dairy products from consideration. True, at least two possibilities still exist—vegetables or flowers. But given the setting, flowers seem a bit too much like luxury items and thus, like computers and airplanes, seem unlikely. Of course, we still cannot be sure of the exact vegetable, nor have flowers been eliminated. But if *sayor-sayor* are vegetables, we know they are not tomatoes, onions, or other round items, since one cannot "whack" someone with round items (line 24a). Our *internal information* about how some words collocate helps us make this connection.

There is a constant interplay between *internal* and *external information* as we *attend*. Though you probably never experienced an *orang-kechil* before you read *At the Pasar*, you no doubt decided that, in a pasar at least, an *orang-kechil* is a kind of person. If you did make this connection, you did not do so entirely on the basis of the *external information* provided in the passage itself. On the basis of your previous experience, you know that people talk and animals usually do not. You used this *internal information* to help you decide that the *external information* represented by the letters o-r-a-n-g-k-e-c-h-i-l means person because in both lines 9a and 20a you saw quotation marks around words that *he saberchakap*. Of course, your *internal information* might also tell you that in some fables, animals do indeed "saberchakap." But, since Photak was a man in 1a, you were able to use *external information* on the page to reject the hypothesis suggested by your experience, by your *internal information*.

Just as the guests on "I've Got a Secret" and "Twenty Questions" could *characterize* by answering only one question at a time, so as we *attend*, we can only *characterize* one item at a time. But because we can *characterize* only one item at a time does not mean that we have to *characterize* all items in a particular category before we move to another category, as Charges 3 through 8 suggest. We can determine that one word refers to time and the one next to it to a person in instantaneous succession. While searching for items that refer to things in *At the Pasar*, at the same time we can not only search for items that do not refer to things, but we can also search for items that refer to qualities—*shrilly, kawaii*—and the category "things" itself can be divided into the subcategory "places" for items such as *pasar* and *stand*, and the subcategory "not-places" for items such as *water* and *sayor-sayor*.

You might argue that giving a specific charge such as noticing time words may not help a person *attend* because the person already guessed the meaning of words such as *selalu* and *lepas itu*. One of the purposes of Charge 1 is to tell you the words readers need to *characterize*. I based Charges 3 through 8 on the words various readers crossed out in Charge 1 and were unable to fill in in Charge 2. The categories in Charges 3 through 8—time, humor, people, action—reflect items bewildering to other readers and are only examples of possibilities, not the types of categories that should be used in all exercises of this type.

Journal Entry

In the grocery store, or in a market, foods are grouped. Spices are usually all together, soaps and bleach are close together, packaged food is separate from fresh items. In other parts of our daily experience, other things are grouped, but many of the groupings, like many of the ways we group words and meaning, are unconscious. Jot down a few of the groupings you think affect you each day, but that you are not usually conscious of. Or, if you prefer, draw some of the groupings, such as a sketch of the market or store you shop in.

No Need to Be Technical—Trying a Wide Range of Groupings

To try to discover the most useful categories, researchers have given scores of deleted passages to hundreds of readers and, based on their analysis of the words filled in the blanks, have developed typologies to organize the types of meaning that seem to cause the most confusion. Investigating the words readers fail to fill in or fill in incorrectly is technically known as miscue analysis. This name highlights the fact that words, phrases, or larger units of meaning that do not fit are not to be considered errors, nor are they to be considered evil in any way. Rather, the miscues provide ways to help us see how people learn and what types of teaching they require. [Background 10–6]

Helpful as miscues are, you do not have to depend only on them to discover groupings students do not make or ones they make differently from those that are needed for the passages in front of them. Charge 11 is designed to give students the opportunity to set up categories on their own. In their formation of yes-no and either-or questions, they must do what the panelists on "Twenty Questions" and "I've Got a Secret" had to do: set up categories that will bring them closer to the "secret." If a reader asks "Are *sayor-sayor* liquid?" you find out how a student is making use of *internal information* just as vividly as if the reader fills in "water" in the blank where the word *sayor-sayor* fits. When people ask us question-word questions, such as "What does *sayor-sayor* mean?", we only know that the meaning of a particular item is unknown. But when a person asks us a yes-no or either-or question, we not only know the items that are giving some difficulty, but we can begin to understand the strategies the person uses in trying to discover meaning.

Just as the categories used to help readers use their *internal information* in understanding *external information* can be different from those in Charges 3 through 8, so the size of the units the categories refer to need not be limited to single words. The units can be as small as a letter or individual sound or as large as a thick volume. If students cannot tell whether what people are saying to them is said in an angry or neutral tone of voice, you can use a dialog as the unit. As students listen to a series of dialogs, they could indicate those that sound angry and those that do not. If students were unable to distinguish between voiced and voiceless sounds, you could present a series of sounds such as /s/, /t/, /v/, /p/, /b/ and ask those listening to indicate whether a particular sound was closer to the sound a snake makes—voiceless—or closer to the sound a bee makes—voiced.

The names of the categories need not be technical terms—*bee* serves the same purpose as *voiced*. Nor need they come from you. Not only does it make sense to *characterize* only items that bewilder students, but it also makes sense only to use labels from the students. "Sayor-sayor" words might be more memorable than "person" words or "plural" words. Since any word in any language can become the name for a group of items, the possibilities for labels are extremely great. By the age of three, most children have established and named a number of categories on their own, among them one labeled variously "mmm," "cookie," or "good-good," indicating sweet things such as candy, cookies, and ice cream, and "na na" or "no ice" indicating all other food. Just as different children use different labels, so different students probably should be allowed to use whatever labels they find helpful. Episode 5 is devoted to other ways to *characterize* items.

Just as the unit being *characterized* and the labels used to *characterize* in Charges 3 through 8 should not be taken as directions to follow in *all* classes in which students *attend*, but only examples to demonstrate a process, so the time devoted to carrying out the charges should not necessarily be followed. The time it takes different readers to *attend* and *characterize* in Charges 3 through 8 of course varies from a few seconds to a few minutes. Even if you think that the longer time seems too long, remember that when words are introduced before a reading, teachers generally spend from a few seconds to a few minutes on every word. The words introduced before the reading, or other subcategory of *attend*, are all out of context and are generally presented in a medium different from the text—speech rather than print—so students are attending by listening rather than by reading silently. Even if directions like those in Charges 3 through 8 took longer to carry out, they would still take up less time than the amount devoted to covering vocabulary items in many classes. And in Charges 3 through 8, the students are, after all, reading—the aim of a reading lesson—and at the same time, perhaps, learning some strategies of reading as well.

You Never Know—Questions about Alternatives

Whether directions similar to those in Charges 3 through 8 will produce consequences you want can only be determined by trying such alternatives. If you presently give students an equivalent or tell them to look up a word in a dictionary when they indicate they do not understand a word, in my terms you are *presenting* content rather than having students *characterize* content. If you do tend to *present* rather than have students *characterize* or ask you to *characterize* by asking you yes-no or either-or questions rather than question-word questions, the next time you are asked for the meaning of a word, break the rule you usually follow. Tell the student you will only answer yes-no or either-or questions as in Charge 11 and as guests did on "Twenty Questions" or "I've Got a Secret." Or, in the beginning, ask them questions which require that they *characterize* in their responses. "Do you think the word refers to animals?" and any other yes-no question requires either confirmation or rejection, one way to *characterize.*

To what degree these alternatives will help students develop strategies for reading on their own can only be determined by trying them with students you know well. But if the current proportion of *attend* versus other uses is say, one to ten, meaning students are expected to *characterize, present* and *reproduce* ten times more frequently than they are expected to *attend*, at least this alternative would change this proportion, since it would require that the students *attend* to the material again. At the same time, this alternative might imply to the students that they can find meaning on their own. One gauge of this would be the number of yes-no or either-or questions students asked as they read. Is the number larger than before the alternative was tried?

Questions about the other alternatives also have to be asked. As alternatives like Charges 3 through 8 are tried, do students ask for fewer word equivalents? And if they do, is it because they know you won't tell them, or because by *characterizing* as they *attend*, they have learned a strategy for discovering meaning on their own? As alternatives like Charges 1, 2, and 9 are tried, do students *attend* to the same material over and over again to try to understand it, rather than daydream after they *attend* to it once without being able to understand it? As all the alternatives are tried, do students read more quickly and yet get more out of their reading? Do they *attend* to more unassigned materials on their own than they used to and seem to enjoy them more? If the responses to these solicits are more frequently positive than negative, do students over time transfer the strategies they seem to have learned in silent reading not only to new, unassigned materials in print in the target language, but also materials in their own language? And do they make use of the strategies as they listen, view or in other ways *attend* also?

If the students say "Huh?" a lot as you try the alternatives suggested here, don't be discouraged. Indicating lack of comprehension is honest and suggests an attempt to try to comprehend. What is discouraging to me is a high frequency of "Ohs" or nodding heads or parallel comments such as "I understand, I see" which mean the opposite, which really mean "I don't understand." These "Ohs" that on the surface seem to signal comprehension but really signal lack of comprehension are often signs of resignation, of giving up, and thus are the real danger signs.

Look It Up!—Dictionaries as a Source of Meaning

The Real Thing—Dictionaries Produced by Publishers

There were no charges to use a dictionary during your reading of Excerpt 10–4, *At the Pasar*, because most of you would not have dictionaries of the language the unknown words were from. But no treatment of activities that occur during the time set aside for receptive activities could be complete without reference to what is probably *the* classic symbol of the source of meaning: the dictionary. Except in classrooms where dictionaries are unavailable, or prohibited, or students have no interest in reading, dictionaries are frequently consulted during the time set aside for silent reading.

One great advantage of the dictionary is that it gives each reader the chance to look up the words each one needs. Another is that using it requires silent reading, and thereby increases the proportion of time devoted to *attend* during the time set aside for taking in mediums. And, finally it can help readers be independent of teachers. Of course, there are disadvantages to dictionaries too. But most of these are not inherent, just the result of ignorance of their proper use. For example, it would be unfair to blame a dictionary just because it might be used by some readers to look up every other word in a passage. These readers would ask another person for the meaning if a dictionary were not available.

Asking students to look up a set ratio of words would be one alternative that would alter the practice of looking up every other word a reader came upon. "From the words you underline because you aren't sure of their meaning, select one out of every four to look up in the dictionary" would be one way to help students see that dictionaries are only one source of meaning. Another way to limit the number of words looked up would be to put different rows of students in charge of different groups of words. One row, or one pair if the class is small, would be limited to words of 1 to 3 letters, another to 4- and 5-letter words, still another to 6- to 9-letter words, and the last group or pair to words of more than 9 letters or those that began with a capital letter. Another way to divide the words would be on the basis of the letter they started with: row or pair one would take *a* through *d*, the next group *e* through *i*, and on and on to the end of the alphabet. Or, to go back to the categories in Charges 3 through 8, one group could be in charge of time words, another responsible for action words, people words, or thing words. Nouns, verbs, function words, content words, and other normal grammatical terms could also form the categories. The students could form the categories and change them as they discovered new ways to group words. As in a game in which each player has a set role and is held to the role by peer pressure, so as each group takes responsibility for a particular type of word, each group will guard its domain carefully and see to it that no group looks up words that it is not responsible for. Whether this alternative limits the number of times the dictionaries are consulted, more, or less, than the usual direction to look up fewer words, can of course only be determined if it is tried.

Being allowed to look up a set number or limited type of word may not just decrease overdependence on the dictionary. It may force readers to use the *internal information* they already bring to the page before them, and let them see that the *external information* is not hidden in individual words, but in strings of words that together have meaning. By consulting the dictionary fewer times, students will have time to reread the same passage over and over since the time devoted to reading the dictionary will be decreased dramatically. At the same time, grouping words into categories such as high priority/low priority, long/short, guessable/clueless will provide a range of specific, realizable tasks that they can perform, which may decrease the amount of anxiety they feel as they reread the passage, and believe they are not getting the total meaning from the page.

Another practice that gives dictionaries a bad name is that most users seek only lexical information when they look up a word. Oxford's *Advanced learner's dictionary*, the *Longman dictionary of contemporary English*, and the *Longman dictionary of American English* are particularly rich in nonlexical information, since they are designed for nonnative speakers of English. I've asked hundreds of students and scores of teachers who have used these dictionaries what a number of the symbols that convey nonlexical information mean. Most of them have no idea. They, like most users of dictionaries I've met, see dictionaries only as treasuries of word equivalents.

One obvious alternative to using a dictionary only for lexical information is to use it for anything but lexical information. Just as you can instruct students to limit the number or type of words they look up, so you can limit the type of information they retrieve. Of course, you can't stop the person from finding that a pillow, for example, is "a down-filled bag to rest one's head on," whatever that means, unless you black out vast lines of print in each dictionary. But you can require that a student mark down a figurative use of a word, the verb pattern it can occur in, the type of setting the word occurs in, the suffixes that can be joined to the word, the stress pattern and how it shifts when suffixes are added, to name a few.

Of course, some of the nonlexical information may be totally unrelated to the word as it is used in the passage. Much of the lexical information is unrelated to the way words are used too. But now and then, one of the apparently unrelated bits of nonlexical information will enable a student to make a connection. And at least by searching for nonlexical information, the many symbols that are used in dictionaries such as the *Longman Dictionary of American English* will be discovered. Uncovering the meaning of [C] and [U] in these dictionaries can save hours each year, if you look up words a lot. Knowing what these labels mean enables you to cut in half the amount of time it takes when looking up nouns. By learning the symbols for the verb patterns in both the Oxford and Longman dictionaries, you can find the verbs you are looking for in as much as one-third less time. Just as we all form categories to help us organize the vast amount of *internal information* we possess and the great amount of *external information* that bombards us, so compilers of dictionaries find it necessary to group items—*characterize* to use my term. The discovery of nonlexical information may show students how limited lexical information often is. It may also show students that meaning comes from grammar *and* pronounciation *and* sound-letter correspondence *and* stress *and* context *and* spelling *and* usage *and* culture, or ways of life in FOCUS terms, not just from lexis. These areas of content are treated in Episode 11.

Some teachers build up class libraries of dictionaries by buying some, requesting others as gifts, and being given others. Helpful as a uniform dictionary for class use may be, class libraries of dictionaries, if they are built up of a wide range of dictionaries, can provide very useful information to students. They can see that the information provided by bilingual dictionaries is helpful in a way different from the information provided by monolingual dictionaries. They can compare the degree to which shades of meaning can be conveyed in dictionaries compiled in a limited vocabulary intended for nonnative speakers of the language with those that are conveyed in dictionaries compiled for native speakers of the language or advanced nonnative speakers. They can feast their eyes on the wealth of information picture dictionaries provide. A class library of dictionaries helps solve the problem of dictionary addiction. If there are only a limited number of dictionaries on a shelf in class, each student cannot look up every other word during the time set aside for receptive activities. I've listed some specific dictionaries and other sources of meaning such as general merchandise catalogs in the background for this episode. Catalogs with indexes are veritable picture dictionaries and should not be overlooked when collecting dictionaries. [Background 10–7]

The Real Real Thing—Student-Produced Dictionaries

Helpful as class libraries of dictionaries may be, none of these provide the students with experience in the process of defining, classifying, and arranging words. The source of all these substitutes for individual dictionaries, as the source of an individual dictionary itself, is someone in the role of teacher. The obvious alternative source of dictionaries or word lists compiled by teachers, editors, word experts, or linguists is a group of students, each individual class. With a supply of 3-by-5 cards, or even just uniform slips of paper, students can assemble information about words they have learned. They can write word meanings in their own language as well as in the target language. They can draw sketches, or cut out and glue pictures from old magazines or catalogs to illustrate words. They can write personal experiences they have had with words or larger units of meaning. They can develop labels to categorize their words and ways to organize them for easy retrieval.

Just as experience charts, if truly from the students, should not just be small and inferior models of famous short stores, travel adventures, or poems, so student dictionaries should not be anemic copies of published dictionaries, but should reflect the originality and creativity of the students. For example, some students have divided long words from short ones with the same meaning and called the long ones "dress-up" words and the short ones "casual" words. This is not a usual category in published dictionaries. Borrowing a classification from published dictionaries, but using their own labels, students have labeled nouns that take a plural and can be counted "score" words and those we can't count "non-score" words. For head words on the first card or slip in a group, stamps from around the world have been used. Should the students decide to arrange the words alphabetically using the last letter of the word rather than the first, the decision should be applauded if the goal is to tap the creativity of the students.

Those who engage in the creative process of compiling dictionaries learn a great deal about classifying, defining, ambiguity of meaning, variation in pronunciation, and need to use mediums other than words, such as pictures and sketches, to illustrate meaning. By having students compile their own dictionaries, they will have to go through the same process and will thus learn a great many of the same things. But while professional dictionaries have to be printed and can only be revised at great expense, students can change the information on their cards or slips of paper on a daily basis. A box of cards or slips of paper strung on wire are easy to manipulate. If students sign their names and the date of their part of an entry, they can see through the year how some words have expanded as they go back and reread entries they themselves wrote earlier in the year. Assuming some students put in personal experiences related to some words, information impossible in any published dictionary, they will have a chance to relive parts of the year as they look for meanings.

Fire—Problems with Dictionaries

Whether students develop their own dictionaries, or use published dictionaries, or both, one central problem still remains that is inherent to a dictionary. Dictionaries highlight individual words, while in reading and listening, we usually get meaning from strings of words. When we do face single-word sentences such as "Fire," the surrounding words must be consulted in order to know whether something is ablaze, a bullet is going to be shot, a rocket launched, a person dismissed from a job, or a piece of pottery put in a kiln, to name a few possibilities. If something is ablaze, "Fire" doesn't tell us if we should leave, take the burning cake from the oven, bring a bucket of water, or call the fire department. Strings of words, or the setting we're in, are all necessary.

Ironically, this one inherent weakness of a dictionary might best be overcome by highlighting words. To help students learn to get meaning from many sources, I suggested allowing them to look up only a set proportion or type of words they didn't know. By instructing them to look up *every* word once in a while, some students might begin to realize how detrimental concentration on single words can be.

I've been acting as if all students love dictionaries. From your experience, you know that getting some students to look up even one word is the problem, rather than overuse. Avoidance, not addiction, is often the concern. Though a lack of curiosity about meaning can be deep-seated—frustration because the material is not making sense, anger because of having to learn a new language, a feeling that books are for weaklings—it can also be partly caused by materials that are not interesting.

Journal Entry

Have you used the dictionary at all so far while reading this episode? If you did, how many words did you look up? If you did not, does it mean you "knew" all the words you saw in the sentences in this episode?

Embellish—Extra Words as Aids to Meaning

Once upon a Time . . .—Lessons from Storytellers

If you've listened to storytellers much, either those in traditional societies charged with passing on the values of the society orally to all age groups, or those in countries where children make up the bulk of those addressed, you know that many storytellers embellish the basic stories with personal anecdotes, descriptive details and aphorisms to clarify meaning for each particular audience they are with. While reading orally to students as they follow in their own copies of the material, we can clarify meaning by embellishment in the manner of the storyteller.

To illustrate this type of embellishment, I've added some comments to the first few lines of *At the Pasar*. Though you probably know the story quite well by now, I have added some embellishments to illustrate how a storyteller might add meaning to it. I've indicated the embellishments with broken lines so it will be easy to distinguish the story itself from the embellishments.

If you can, ask a friend to read Excerpt 10–6 aloud. As your friend reads, follow

EXCERPT 10–6
***At the Pasar*—Where I Did All My Shopping in Malaysia**

1c Once upon a ping, there was a ngeng old man named Photak.

1w Churchill was ngeng eloquent when he spoke to rally the British during World War II.

1x DeGaulle was a ngeng proud mad, even in defeat.

1y If an amateur runs a mile in a little over four minutes, he is a ngeng fast runner.

2c He had three anak-anak, named Phare, Bare and Pare.

2w My father and mother had two daughters, but only one anak.

2x Because President Kennedy's father and mother had many anak-anak, President Kennedy always believed

2y that if anything happened to him, one of his brothers could take his place.

3c He selalu bejalan to pasar with his anak-anak, but he selalu

4c left his bini at home so she could water the sayor-sayor.

4w Moslems selalu fast all day long during Ramadan.

4x DeGaulle bejalan to England after the Germans invaded France during World War II.

4y Marco Polo bejalen to many countries in Asia during his short life.

4z Many men prefer to be bachelors rather than to get married and live with a bini.

along and read silently Excerpt 10–4. This will provide you with the chance to experience the embellishments as a student would, by only hearing them.

When you know a particular group you are reading to, you do not need to insert so many different embellishments. I would not read 1w, 1x, and 1y aloud in the same class. I would select one that I thought the bulk of the listeners would understand. I presented a range of comments here to illustrate the way to embellish a passage.

Of course, spoken embellishment often takes more time to state than word equivalents, either in the target language or in the vernacular. But equivalents provide no opportunity for readers to guess meanings on their own; when you give a word equivalent, you give an answer. Embellishment provides additional *external information* so that students can more likely guess the answer themselves rather than just hear the answer. There is a great deal of redundancy in any passage. The "the" in the title, for example, is not vital; like many grammatical features, it is redundant. The introductory phrase "Once upon a ping," as well as the concluding "The quinn of the story is," could be shortened or eliminated. "The quinn is" is less redundant than "The quinn of the story is," for example.

Embellishments increase the amount of redundancy in passages even more than the extra words that are used as a matter of course in all languages to increase redundancy. This means that those reluctant to guess meaning, as well as those who tend to make wild guesses rather than educated guesses, may both be aided by additional information provided in embellishments. If the embellishments contain true personal information about the teacher; or public information and general knowledge about the world that students are familiar with and talk about in their daily lives, another chance is provided for students to see relationships between language study and life itself, to see the content of *life* and *study* integrated.

If the material being read is easily understandable by a group of readers in the first place, embellishments, rather than providing added *external information* useful to the reader, might simply produce noise. In information theory, "noise" refers to any messages that interfere with communications. Static on the radio, misprints in a newspaper, or a young child's word order and pronunciation are some examples of noise in this sense of the word. But some types of noise have uses. To develop secret codes, noise of some kind is always added to try to confuse those who intercept the messages.

. . . . . . *Lessons from Cryptographers*

One way to encourage students normally reluctant to guess to do so, might be to assume the role of a cryptographer rather than a storyteller. Tell students you have hidden a message in a passage and their task is to find it by striking out those words that are extraneous. Since the extraneous words were put in by someone other than the reader, and since they were put in with the aim of deceiving the reader, and since the role of the reader is that of a person deciphering a coded message, the personal investment made in deleting might be less intense than in filling in units of meaning that have been deleted, as in Charges 2 and 9. Both filling in and deleting units of meaning can only be done by a series of hits and misses; some tries will be correct, but some must be incorrect as well. In both cases, to decide whether an item does or does not fit, you have to make a number of binary choices, both for those words that fit and those that do not. But the role the students play in deleting is different. In trying to break a code, the readers confirm or reject units of meaning others have put in with the express purpose of confusing them, so some misses are built in and inevitable. For those students who find it hard to fill in blanks, deleting extraneous words may provide a chance to engage in some of the same mental operations required by filling in deleted units of meaning, but with less risk.

To illustrate one example of a message hidden within additional letters, words and phrases, I've added some to Excerpt 10–4. The first ten lines of Excerpt 10–4 are hidden in Excerpt 10–7. Read Excerpt 10–7 silently and strike out the extraneous letters, words, and phrases that try to conceal the message. In short, try to break the code.

Since you have had so many chances to *attend* to *At the Pasar*, you probably found it easy to strike out the added letters, words, and phrases. The more one knows about the secret hidden in the coded message, the more quickly one can extract the message by striking out the extraneous items. The first time I've given readers of all ages passages with extraneous additions, I've heard many "Huhs?". The rule is that we expect what we *attend* to in silent reading, listening, tasting, and in other ways to make sense. As soon as some get into the role of codebreaker, they begin to strike out extraneous elements with the ardor of a professional proofreader and the compulsion of a codebreaker—two behaviors clearly parallel to "Oh," meaning "I understand; I got it."

The aim of breaking the rule that dictates that what we *attend* to should make sense by adding noise is not to show that material we normally *attend* to should not make sense. Rather, both asking readers to add deleted words and to strike out extraneous words are designed to show that reading, like all receptive activities, is an active process that involves an exchange between the *external information* we attend to and the *internal information* we possess. During the exchange, if we are to make sense of

EXCERPT 10–7
At the Pasar Electric

1d Once morning upone a ping, a there was up a ngeng old the man named Photak.
2d He used had three by anak-anak, vegetable named Phare, horse, Bare, and chair Pare.
3d He selalu bejalan to up pasar with his table anak-anak, but he chalk selalu
4d lefte his bini ate homei so she water could water the doctor sayor-sayor.
5d He characterize went to the pasar relate to sells sayor-sayor morning.
6d The he set ups his stand by and began count to sell his sayor-sayor right away while they were fresh.
7d A an orang-kechil brown came to by and ran stopped in front last of Photak's stall the.
8d Brown he looked selalu ngeng carefully at named Phare.
9d Attend then, he saberchakap, "Come what a kawaii looking boy brown that is going!
10d Do once upon you want to sell the moral is him?
11d Since Photak didn't laly berchakap toe strangers but he since saberchakap,
12d "Four score and seven what are you some kind of a kachang or something piano?"

what we *attend* to, we must make thousands of instantaneous binary choices: this fits/this doesn't fit; this goes with the previous three words/this goes with the rest of the sentence; this is what the passage is about/this only gives grammatical information; this is parallel to "a great old book" and is similar in meaning/this is parallel to "a great old book" but different in meaning. We have to make generalizations about our choices and make connections between widely separated units of meaning in the passage. In short, we need to *characterize* and *relate* as we *attend*.

One reason we can fill in or delete words and larger units is because languages are organized systems. The fact that they are organized systems means that the frequency of certain sequences of letters and words is much greater than the sequences of others. In English *e* is more frequent than other letters, for example. Another example from English involves the use of the words *a* and *the*. These words cannot occur after *this, there, these*, or many other words. Nor can they occur between words like *blue, big* or *silk* and words like *tie, suit* or *house*.

Another reason we can delete or add units of meaning is that languages are redundant. The fact that they are redundant means that if we miss the information communicated by one area of content, we can still understand. When you see the pattern *aftet lunch* you may even miss the *t* at the end of *aftet* because other than *after* there are no prepositions that start with *aft*. Thus, the mechanical system—the spelling—combines with the grammatical system—the fact that prepositions precede nouns in English—to provide meaning even if there is an inappropriate letter in the word. Another way to describe redundancy is to say that meaning is communicated by the mechanical system—spelling and punctuation—*and* the grammatical system—word order, suffixes that signal tense and number—*and* the lexical system—the denotative meaning of words—*and* the rhetorical system—organization of the units—*and* the contextual system—the relationship between words and the topic or setting they occur in—*and* the usage system—the connotative meaning of words—*and* the literary system—the type of material, whether a fable, poem, critical essay, set of directions, or personal letter. When we do not get meaning from the lexical system, or any other single system, we immediately try getting meaning from any one of the other systems. [Background 10–8]

Just as embellishment increases redundancy, so extraneous additions decrease it. Passages with extraneous words, letters, and phrases are abnormal. But just as biologists study diseased cells to help them understand the patterns of normal cells, so extraneous letters, words, and phrases provide an opportunity to highlight the normal. The design of a piece of cloth is sometimes more clearly discerned if there is a missing element than if we look at the design without any imperfection. Of course, native speakers of a language have a better sense of both the organization and redundancy of a language than nonnative speakers. But the organization and redundancy exist for all to make use of. And extraneous elements in passages may, like design flaws, highlight the organization and redundancy of the language rather than obscure it. [Background 10–9]

To see whether either embellishment or noise does help students realize that they can do more than they think they can with anything they *attend* to, try the alternatives. As you embellish, you'll play the role of the storyteller. As you add noise, you'll play the role of the crytographer, developing codes to try to obscure meaning and in so doing provide readers, especially those who fear being wrong, a cover, because they will be playing the roles of codebreakers, a group that can uncover meaning only by making mistakes. Secret codes are set up to baffle the readers.

Should procedural matters such as typing and duplicating of passages with noise prove too time-consuming or expensive, try not to be deferred. It's an easy matter to have a student copy passages on the blackboard and then have others copy them into their notebooks during those extra free moments that occur in even the best planned lesson. A few sheets of carbon paper will enable a part of the class to read, speak, or listen while the others make copies for themselves and another group. After a few teacher-made coded passages, students can begin to write their own to exchange with partners. After the words are struck out, the pairs can argue about their discoveries. The procedures used for developing and scoring regular deleted passages can be adapted for this type of passage. [Background 10–10]

Journal Entry

If you have not taken a break yet to *attend* to some nonlinguistic visual medium such as a cup of coffee, how do you feel after going so long without a break? If you have taken some breaks during this episode, have you reflected on what you did in the episode during the break, or have you blanked out what you were doing in the episode during the breaks? Do you ask your students these questions, especially when a great number of tasks are expected in a long period of time?

Formulas—Using FOCUS to Describe Alternatives

The alternatives that grew out of the theory of taking in mediums as an interplay between internal and external information can all be described with elements from FOCUS. All the silent reading of the *set At the Pasar* I code *a* for *attend*. The charges that required you to group items by drawing various types of lines through them are all examples of tasks I code *characterize, c*. Filling in words that I deleted required the presentation of information in some cases, a task I code *present, p*. The cases in which filling in words requires inferences, I code *relate*. The oral reading, I code *reproduce, d*. In short, the charges required that you respond with these uses: $a + c + p + r + d$.

The content of the tasks was *study of language*, except when you were asked to share feelings, as in Charge 12b. In this response, the content is *life*. In asking a question in Charge 11a, a teaching direction was necessary, since all solicits contain a teaching direction. As a result, content I code *procedure* was necessary in the solicit required by Charge 11a, as well as content *sl*.

The underlining or crossing out of words to identify words or larger units we don't understand I code *present*, since we are simply indicating the fact that we do not understand particular items. The content of these uses I code *procedure*, subcategory *check*, an area of content I use to indicate understanding or lack of understanding. To distinguish underlining from crossing out, since both are *nonlinguistic visual* mediums, I simply add a *c* to *nv* for lines that are crossed out and a *u* for *underline* for items underlined: nv_c and nv_u.

The tasks in the dictionary alternatives require that we *attend, characterize*, and *present*: $a + c + p$. Providing partial definitions and grouping words in class dictionaries requires that we *characterize*. Giving antonyms or synonyms from memory requires that we *present*. And, of course, reading the entries silently requires us to *attend*.

The embellishments I suggested, both those of the storytellers and those of the cryptographers, I code *set*, subcategory *word*: *so*, if they consist of one word and *sp* for part of a sentence if they contain a phrase, or more than a word, but less than a sentence. To contrast passages with added information from those without, I code passages without additions as *sx* for *set*, subcategory *text*. The embellishments are added, so I code passages with them like this: $sx + so + sx + sp$ or $+ ss$. To contrast embellishments that make sense from those that do not, I add the subscript *e* for extraneous words next to the embellishments I code *so, sp*, or *ss*. Thus, I'd code the text in Excerpt 10–5 $sx + sp$, or in cases where sentences were added, $sx + ss$. And I'd code *At the Pasar Electric*, 10–7, $sx + so_e$ to show that single extraneous words had been added to the text. The cloze itself, as in *At the* _____, 10–5, I'd code $sx + se$, a text and an example.

The suggestions growing out of the theory I presented, when all followed, would require responses that contained all the uses, with the smallest proportion of time devoted to the use *reproduce change medium*, oral reading. And the responses and solicits together would require all major areas of content: *life, procedure*, and *study of language*.

Journal Entry

In many places, the idea of hearing someone else read something orally is very common because it is what is done in religious ceremonies. In fact, some want to read orally in class rather than silently because they want to be able to read orally for religious purposes. Have you observed this need? Have you discussed reasons why some object to silent reading in class? It would seem likely that, to some, the idea of adding sentences to a passage while reading it orally would be quite a shocking thing to do if what is read is in any way considered sacred.

III. BEFORE, DURING, AND AFTER— ALTERNATIVES FROM NONTEACHING SETTINGS

The Usual—Introduction

I've just spent a lot of time suggesting alternatives that I think a particular model of reading implies. The usual way we generate alternatives in this book is to describe some rules followed in teaching settings and substitute others from nonteaching settings. In this section, I do just this. In the first part of the section, I describe uses I consider typical that are communicated before people see the material, or the *sets*, they are about to *attend* to. In the second part of the section, I describe uses I consider typical as we have the *sets* before us. In the third part of the section, I describe the uses communicated after the *sets* are no longer before us. But we now have alternatives implied by the model of reading that considers the interplay of internal and external information crucial to understanding mediums set for us. So we can compare patterns I consider typical in classes both with patterns in nonteaching settings and with the patterns based on a theory of reading we generated in Section II.

Journal Entry

How do you take in mediums? What do you do before you take in mediums, during the time you are taking them in, and after you have taken them in—in general terms, first? Then, more specifically. Do you make associations? If a person stops you, can you say what has been going on in your mind? Could you get any insights about the reading process, or the process of taking in any mediums, by consciously trying to describe what you do in detail, or what you think you do?

First Considerations—Before We *Attend* to Materials

Afraid—An Example of Uses in a Teaching Setting

To illustrate uses that occur in step 1 of a reading lesson, before the students see the material that is to be read, I've transcribed some communications from a reading lesson I consider typical. The major activity in step 1 usually consists of "going over" vocabulary items from the passage. In the lesson the lines are from, six words were "covered," but to illustrate the uses expected in the responses, I have displayed only two of the six words. Step 1 of the lesson, which Excerpt 10–8 is from, took about one-third of the time of the reading lesson.

In Excerpt 10–8 you'll notice that there are question marks in the boxes reserved for the target of some communications. These simply indicate that it was unclear who the target was intended to be. The abbreviations for the uses next to some lines are these: *c* = *characterize*; *p* = *present*; *r* = *relate*; *d* = *reproduce*, including oral reading.

Not all reading lessons start like the one in Excerpt 10–8, and they are not all limited to dialogs about word meanings. Some start with teachers asking students what they think the passage is about after writing the title on the blackboard. Others start with questions that lead the students to comparisons between their own experiences and those they are about to read about. But almost all reading lessons contain some questions and answers about the meaning of words in the passage before the passage is seen. The bulk of the widely used texts contain directions such as this in the reading sections: "Go over these words with your teacher before you begin reading." The patterns in step 1 of reading lessons are frequently followed in listening lessons too.

One Leads to Another—Comparing Teaching and Nonteaching Settings

One of the most striking differences between listening, reading, and other subcategories of *attend* inside and outside a classroom is that outside, each of us is usually on our own. When we go to see a concert or a ball game or a movie, nine times out of ten, we initiate the move on our own; we structure ourselves. In teaching settings, the teacher announces the activity—structures—sets the task—solicits—and comments on the per-

EXCERPT 10–8
Step 1 (T)

		Communications	*Source/ Target*	*Move Type*	*Use*
1	Teacher:	Sometimes, we walk in the street late at night, all alone. And we hear footsteps behind us.	t/c	str	
2		When you're in this situation, how do you feel?	t/c	sol	
3	Student$_1$:	Afraid.	s_1/t	res	p
4	Teacher:	You're afraid.	t/s_1	rea	d
5		You're very, very afraid; you're terrified.	t/s	rea	p
6	Student$_1$:	Terrified.	s/?	rea	d
7	Student$_1$:	Ah, I see . . .	s/?	rea	p
8	Student$_1$:	. . . a synonym for the word.	s/?	rea	c
9	Teacher:	Very afraid, More than afraid.	t/s	rea	p
10	Teacher:	You put your head on a pillow at night.	t/s	str	
11	Teacher:	Do you sleep on a pillow, Berto?	t/s_1	sol	
12	Student$_1$:	Yes.	s_1/t	res	p
13	Teacher:	It's not good. You get a double chin.	t/s_1	rea	c

formance—reacts. But when we go to a movie with a friend, neither person is in charge, so the communications are parallel to student-to-student communications. Though we might ask each other some questions, more frequently we simply react to each other's reactions. This is in contrast to a teaching setting in which a reaction is a comment on someone's performance in a response.

In Table 10–2, I show how the move types and source and target differ in many teaching and nonteaching settings. I have noted the characteristics that are different with italic type.

TABLE 10–2
Source/Target and Move Type of Communications that Occur before We *Attend*

TEACHING SETTINGS		NONTEACHING SETTINGS	
Source/Target	*Move Type*	*Source/Target*	*Move Type*
t to c	str	*s to s*	str
t to c	sol	*s to s*	sol
s to t	res	*s to s*	res
t to s	rea	*s to s*	rea
t to s	sol	*s to s*	*rea*
s to t	res	*s to s*	*rea*

The uses also differ in teaching and nonteaching settings. If we want to find out something about a record we are going to listen to, we read the record jacket silently. At a concert, we silently read the program before the music begins. Before we see a movie, we often read a review. In short, we prepare to *attend* in one way by engaging in another subcategory of *attend*, or in the same subcategory. But we often only take in mediums as preparation, we don't produce them.

In classrooms, students are asked to recall or state word meanings—*present*—before they *attend*. If people at a concert do speak before they *attend*, they generally make judgments or in other ways comment about what they are about to view. They *characterize*, rather than *present*.

If you think of an event you went to for the first time with a friend who knew a lot about the event, you will probably recall that the friend did some things before you both *attended* that I just stated do not usually occur in nonteaching settings. But if your friend, for example, asked you about the meanings of terms at a baseball game, or you asked him, you have turned a nonteaching setting into a teaching setting for each moment you *present* information. If you watch a concert or some television programs or listen to an opera on the radio, some commentators also *present*. They state facts about the music to be played or about the composer's life, the tenor's wife, the dimensions and capacity of the concert hall or the number of participants who braved the elements to hear the event in person. Commentators, like friends who teach us about baseball at games, are playing the role of teacher.

Content also differs in teaching and nonteaching settings. Here are some typical reactions I overheard before some people *attended* outside a class: "I think it's [a symphony at a concert] from his late period"; "This film's similar to Woody Allen's work"; "French food is the best"; "This is the most important game of the season"; "The paintings in this show represent pointillism better than any other show." Consider these solicits and responses: "When was the last time you saw a show here? I come every week, whether they have a special exhibit or not"; "What other films have you seen recently? I stick with the classics—*Modern Times, Duck Soup, Rules of the Game*, and even *Gone with the Wind*"; "How did you get here? I took the train and just made it"; "Where did you park? Couldn't get close—about half a mile from here." When we do *present* in solicits, responses, and reactions, the content tends to be *procedure* or *life* rather than *study*, as these quotes show.

In Table 10–3, I show some of the contrasts I have observed between uses and content in teaching and nonteaching settings. The characteristics that are different I have noted with italic type.

TABLE 10–3
Use and Content in Communications that Occur before We *Attend*

TEACHING SETTINGS		NONTEACHING SETTINGS	
Use	*Content*	*Use*	*Content*
		a	*l*
p	s	*c*	*p*
		p	s

Let 'Em Do It—Trying Alternatives from Nonteaching Settings in Teaching Settings

To have students initiate reading, listening, and other subcategories of *attend* on their own—*s str a*—all that is needed is a large range of handouts, magazines, pamphlets, comics, newspapers, cassettes, and records and other materials we take in, and the allotment of some time for the students to *attend.* Five to fifteen minutes, sometimes at the beginning of a period, sometimes in the middle and sometimes at the end, is all that is needed. If the *sets* are of interest to the students, they will continue to *attend* to them outside of class.

Students will probably react with judgments, and in other ways characterize what they *attend* to, too, if given the chance. And they will solicit and respond as peers, and communicate *life* and *procedure* and probably *study*, as well. By providing cards to write down comments as they react to what they *attend* to, you can make their reactions more personal. These note cards can later be pasted to books, magazines, cassettes, and records. They can in turn be read by other students much as we read the blurb on a book jacket, a review of a record or a book, or the information on the sleeves of records or cassette cartridges.

Whether these alternatives will produce more instances of "Oh" or not can only be determined by trying them. One definite consequence will be that the amount of time spent actually reading silently, listening or in other ways *attending* will be increased. One of the clear-cut findings I state in Episode 3 is that the amount of time spent in *attending* in classes devoted to reading is small. Another definite consequence will be that by eliminating the questions and answers about word meanings that usually occur before students *attend*, students will be forced to handle word meaning differently, maybe realizing something about the interplay between external and internal information in the process.

Journal Entry

On buses, I often read to avoid conversation. At night, many people read to children to put them to sleep. You can observe many people sitting in libraries and parks sleeping with books or magazines in their hands. What are some of the reasons you read silently at different times, in addition to the reason we often give our students, to learn?

Second Considerations—As We *Attend* to Materials

Number 3—Patterns of Uses in Teaching Settings

If you read aloud in a library, you are told to be quiet. If you read aloud on the train or bus, you will cause many people to stare at you. Few politicians around the world can orally read speeches, even to supporters, so that they are worth listening to. The texts of their speeches can be read silently in a fraction of the time. In classrooms, though, during the time set aside for reading, most of the time is spent in oral reading, not silent reading. [Background 10–11]

Oral reading is *reproducing* for the person who says sentences orally that are *set* in print. For those who are not reading orally, the spoken sentences become *sets* to *attend* to, either by listening and reading silently, if they are able to follow the printed text and spoken words at the same time, or by listening alone if their books are closed. I say "if they are able to follow" because the rate of silent reading is usually much faster than the rate of oral reading. And, in some classes, one cannot silently read ahead of the person reading orally because one has to know the place at all times, in case one is called on to read aloud. Yet, one often cannot understand what one is reading silently because one is following so slowly that the meaning is lost.

Though you are familiar with oral reading, I have included Excerpt 10–9 showing two sentences being read orally. In the lesson the excerpt is from, eleven sentences were read orally. I have included only those two that contain the words *covered* in Excerpt 10–8, *terrified* and *pillow*. The *d* in the use column stands for *reproduce*, which is how I code oral reading.

The two sentences read orally in Excerpt 10–9, lines 2 and 4, show you the context for the words *pillow* and *terrified*, "gone over" in Excerpt 10–8. If you find a lot of oral reading in classes you are involved with, and want to continue it but with some variation, take a break from this episode and work your way through Episode 14. I treat different ways of changing one medium to another in that episode, both print to speech in oral reading, and speech to print in dictations, and speech to action as in total physical response. If you are interested in comparing the ways we use mediums when we have materials before us in both teaching and nonteaching settings, continue on in this episode.

Distinctions—Contrasting Teaching and Nonteaching Settings

I think you'll find that *reproducing* at out-of-class events we attend—excuse the pun—is not as common as it is inside classes. If you try to *reproduce* at a concert by humming along with the orchestra, others will try to get you to shut up. Playing catch in the bleachers at a ball game to imitate the players, reciting lines in the balcony during a play, or copying figures on the walls of an art museum as you *attend* to the paintings will produce a firm invitation to leave. The rule in nonteaching settings designed for people to attend to mediums in is to *attend* to them, not engage in other uses.

It is true that during the time we *attend* to mediums outside of classes we also use mediums in other ways. At a concert, we *characterize* as we *attend* with comments such

EXCERPT 10–9
Step 2

		Communications	*Source/ Target*	*Move Type*	*Use*
1	Teacher:	Read the next sentence—number three. (The other sentences had been read before this.)	t/s_1	sol	
2	Student_1:	After drinking the rest of his water, he took off his shirt and rolled it into a pillow.	s_1/t	res	d
3	Teacher:	Read sentence nine now.	t/s_2	sol	
4	Student_2:	Jim watched [as the snake crawled over his legs], too terrified to do anything.	s_2/t	res	d
5	Student:	(Underlines the word *rolled*.)	s/o	rea	
6	Student:	What mean *rolled*?	s/t	sol	
7	Teacher:	Turning something over and over again.	t/s	res	

* The sentences being read are from a beginning reader.

as "This sounds wonderful." As we eat, we *characterize* too. We judge: "This tastes better than anything I've eaten in weeks." And we state attributes of the food: "It's flavored with thyme, just like my aunt used to cook it." At art exhibitions, you've overheard many judgments similar to this one as people *attend*: "I usually hate the moderns, but the colors here are so vivid." We also *characterize* during parts of performances we attend by throwing kisses, applauding, sighing, booing, or in other ways saying "You are wonderful" or "You are terrible." At a concert, we are expected to save our *characterizing* till after the performance. But in a baseball game, we can *characterize* as we *attend*, as when we shout "Great run" as we watch a home run.

Graphically, the pattern of uses that occur in teaching settings during the time set aside for taking in mediums looks like this: $p + d$. The pattern in nonteaching settings looks like this: $a + c + p$. Not only is d restricted in nonteaching settings, but the proportion of p is smaller. As I stated before, the subcategories of *attend* take up an extremely small proportion of time, often less than 10 percent in teaching settings. At a concert, a ball game, play or art exhibit, we spend almost 100 percent of the time taking in mediums by listening, viewing, and in other ways *attending*. Outside class, in a nonteaching setting, the proportion of *d—reproducing* in another medium or a different one—is rare.

A Final Distinction—Content in Teaching and Nonteaching Settings

Though we *characterize* in teaching and nonteaching settings, the content of this use, and others, is different in teaching and nonteaching settings. When students *characterize* and *present* in teaching settings, the content is often *study of language*. Out of class, the content is often *life* and *procedure*.

When I look at texts students are reading for class, I usually see a lot of the printed material covered with faint yellow lines made with a felt pen, dark lines drawn under rows of print, or individual words underlined to show they are not understood. These lines *present* content in the major category *procedure* and the subcategory *check*. The lines are saying "I understand" or "I don't understand." When I see people reading on their own, with their own book, not a book borrowed from the library, I often see them write comments like this: "You don't understand the character at all—I think she's fighting courageously"; "This passage is precious—reminds me of the time I visited my sister before she had Jennifer." I see others make sketches or doodle to show the judgments they are making as they are reading. If you see words underlined to incidate lack of comprehension, or faint yellow lines or dark lines to highlight parts to memorize for tests, invite students to share their personal feelings as they read, either in comments or sketches or doodles. Have them *characterize* and *present* with content of *life* rather than *procedure*. To ensure *life* in a class as students read silently, or in other ways *attend*, ask them to feel free to share their feelings, either in the margins of the books they are reading, or on separate cards. Suggest that they *present* and *characterize* with content of *life*, if they usually do not.

Since the *life* content of the student communications that *characterize* or *present* may be quite personal, there is no reason you should necessarily read them. You might even say that since the communications are between the student and the author, you will read them only if invited to.

It has been argued that silent reading is an antisocial activity. To the extent that burying our head in a book excludes those around us, this argument is, of course, valid. However, we exclude others only so we can interact with the author. Sharing our reactions in print or sketching symbolizes the social quality of reading. But the relationship is between the author and reader, rather than between others who might be in the room and each of us as a reader. [Background 10–12]

Journal Entry

How do you feel when you write a note to an author you are *attending* to? I enjoy it. People who borrow my books can interact both with my thoughts and feelings and those of the author, since they can *attend* to what I have put in visual mediums as well as to what the author has put in visual mediums, if they choose to read my notes or look at my doodles and sketches.

After you ask students to *characterize* and *present* with content of *life* rather than *procedure*, do you find that they seem to draw fewer lines and write more notes, draw more sketches or show surprise, elation, sadness, and other personal feelings more as they read silently, and still remember as much?

Final Considerations—After We *Attend* to Materials

Classic—Uses in Teaching Settings

Excerpt 10–10 contains some of the classic patterns of communications that occur after the time set aside for taking mediums in.

As you can see, the bulk of the responses require stating words from memory by providing names of objects or feelings that occurred in the lines in the story, or in the questions and answers before the story. There is some copying, and a direction to memorize some definitions and sentences so during the next class students can state words and sentences again. In short, students are required to *present* and *reproduce*, not *characterize* or *relate*. Except for the teacher's judgment in line 27, the teacher reacts by *presenting* and *reproducing* as well.

Parallel Classic—Responding with Uses in Teaching Settings

A parallel set of questions about *At the Pasar* would look like those in Excerpt 10–11. There are blanks under each question so you can write the responses. Do not look at the passages containing various renditions of *At the Pasar* while responding!

Were you able to answer all the questions about *At the Pasar*? If you were, did your comprehension of the story increase as a result? If you were not, did your comprehension of the story decrease as a result? One of the central concerns about questions asked about material we *attend* to is what the questions test.

Problems—Objections to Classic Patterns

100 Percent—The Meaning of Scores

Though it is hard to determine what questions test that are asked after we *attend*, they are asked quite frequently. And the implication in most classes and texts is that one should be able to respond to all the solicits correctly. Have you ever seen a statement next to the questions in a text indicating that, say, only 70 percent of the solicits had to be answered correctly? A perfect score of 100 percent seems to be the goal. "Covering" words before the material is seen and demanding word-perfect oral reading during the time set aside for us to take in mediums combine to strengthen the implication that one should be able to answer all questions correctly that a teacher or a test maker asks after we *attend*.

Scoring 100 percent on any part of a standardized reading test usually means the material is too easy for the person being tested. Such tests contain a range of passages and types of questions designed to make scores of 100 percent on each section rare. In

EXCERPT 10–10
Step 3

		Communications	*Source/ Target*	*Move Type*	*Use*
1	Teacher:	What did Jim put under his head?	t/c	sol	
2	Student:	His shirt.	s/t	res	p
3	Teacher:	Under his head.	t/c	rea	
4	Teacher:	What do you sleep on at night?	t/s	sol	
5	Student:	Bed.	s/t	res	p
6	Teacher:	A pillow.	t/s	rea	
7	Teacher:	How did Jim feel?	t/c	sol	
8	Student:	Tired.	s/t	res	p
9	Teacher:	Anybody?	t/c	sol	
10	Student:	Thirsty.	s/t	res	p
11	Teacher:	He felt the same way you do when you are very, very afraid.	t/c	str	
12	Student:	Terrified. (This is a response to the solicit in line 7.)	s/t	res	p
13	Teacher:	Terrified.	t/c	rea	
14		Everyone, terrified.	t/c	sol	
15	Students:	Terrified.	c/t	res	d
16	Teacher:	Who can use *terrified* in a sentence?	t/c	sol	
17	Student:	The boy terrified the snake.	s/t	res	p
18	Teacher:	The boy was terrified by the snake.	t/c	rea	
19		(Writes the sentence in 18 on the blackboard along with the definition from Excerpt 10–8: "very afraid."	t/c	rea	
20		Pillow?	t/c	sol	
21	Student:	I use a pillow.	s/t	res	p
22	Teacher:	(Writes the sentence in 21 on the blackboard along with the definition from Excerpt 10–8: "You put your head on a pillow at night."	t/c	rea	
23		Copy these sentences in your notebook and the definitions too.	t/c	sol	
24	Students:	(Copy the sentences and definitions in their notebooks.)	c/t	res	d
25	Teacher:	Now, you understand the words.	t/c	rea	
26		For homework, memorize the definitions and the sentences.	t/c	sol	
27		Class, you were great today.	t/c	rea	

EXCERPT 10–11
A Ngeng Easy Quiz on *At the Pasar*

		Communications	Source/ Target	Move Type	Use
1	Teacher:	Did you understand *At the Pasar*?	t/s	sol	
2	Reader:		s/t	res	p
3	Teacher:	If you wrote "yes" in line 1, I'll see if you really understood the passage by asking you a number of questions.	t/s	str	
4		First, who wrote *At the Pasar*?	t/s	sol	
5	Reader:		s/t	res	p
6	Teacher:	Name three who went to the Pasar with Photak.	t/s	sol	
7	Reader:		s/t	res	p
8	Teacher:	Who did Photak leave at home?	t/s	sol	
9	Reader:		s/t	res	p
10	Teacher:	Use *berchakap* in a sentence.	t/s	sol	
11	Reader:		s/t	res	p
12	Teacher:	Use *ping* in a sentence.	t/s	sol	
13	Reader:		s/t	res	p
14	Teacher:	Define *charge*.	t/s	sol	
15	Reader:		s/t	res	p

the unlikely event that you score 100 percent on all sections, you are immediately given a more difficult test. When deletions are made in passages in order to determine either the difficulty level of the material or the reading skill of a person reading the material, a perfect score is not expected either. Scores above 75 percent on passages with deletions suggest that the material is too easy; the amount of *external information* gained from a passage in which we can fill in more than three-quarters of the deletions is very small. If you can fill in 7 out of every 10 blanks correctly, it is time to try a more difficult passage. Filling in only 5 out of 10 is quite normal and simply means that we are learning something from the material, and that it is not too difficult. Scores of less than 50 percent usually mean the material is too difficult for us and even with aided instruction may be too frustrating. Investigations of listening suggest that in normal day-to-day activities, comprehension, measured in any number of ways to try to compensate for the imprecise meaning of the word, is closer to 50 than 100 percent. [Background 10–13]

Given the infrequent expectation that 100 percent of the questions asked in standardized tests will be answered correctly, and given the fact that when we fill in deleted words, scores of 100 percent are neither desired nor obtained, sets of questions in texts and classes that imply no errors are allowed may distort the reading process. Readers may read slowly to try to absorb every detail, may get bogged down by every word they are not sure of, and may become apprehensive about guessing, fearing that responding incorrectly to any questions will detract from a score of 100 percent. To take a risk, one must often be wrong. Guessing guarantees errors. If an expectation is developed that 100 percent scores are the ideal guessing might be discouraged, since every error of course detracts from a perfect score.

Use _____ in a Sentence—Limitations of Sentences for Showing Meanings
In addition to answering questions about the passages read, the tasks in Excerpts 10–10 and 10–11 required that words be defined and used in sentences. I don't know what your reaction to "Use *ping* in a sentence" was. Others have found the task very difficult, even though they were able to fill in a word that was suitable in the deletion task in Excerpt 10–5. The task did remind many that recognizing a word while reading it silently is very different from being able to employ a word actively in a sentence. To tell someone to use a word in a sentence is to imply that the word should be part of one's active vocabulary, rather than part of one's recognition vocabulary. The words often selected for students to use in sentences are just those words that are unlikely to be needed in any active way. Hardly anyone uses more than one word in three from the total number available. For every 100 words we use, we are able to recognize 300. Of those we can recognize that occur only once in a passage, few will be seen in subsequent materials, and it will be unnecessary ever to employ any of them actively. Even if we did encounter them again or use them, it is unlikely the subsequent context would be identical, or even similar, to the one in the original passage. Given the slim possibility that many words we are asked to use in sentences will even be seen again, let alone required in conversation or writing, the value of using words in sentences to show we know their meaning seems limited. [Background 10–14]

Not only does the practice of asking students to form sentences seem of dubious value in the learning of vocabulary and demonstration of meaning, but also it usually fails to show whether students know the meaning. Do the sentences in Excerpt 10–12

EXCERPT 10–12
Use _____ in a Sentence

1 My throat is <u>arid</u>.
2 <u>Venue</u> of football game was changed.
3 The desk be <u>coarse</u>.
4 A <u>gardener</u> garden for other people.
5 Musa's vegetables were <u>fertile</u>.
6 I <u>bestow</u> the book upon him.
7 Many things in the city <u>lofty</u>.
8 I want <u>follow</u> you Lagos in your car.
9 With small nail I <u>fasten</u> paper to board.
10 As soon I <u>know</u> my girlfriend we have child.
11 With <u>grapefruit</u> they make the wine.
12 I enjoy <u>hot</u> drinks so much because they make drunk.
13 <u>Plumber</u>, he fix the water.
14 I like that man <u>too</u> much.

indicate knowledge of word meanings of the underlined words? Each sentence is a response to the solicit, "Use ______ in a sentence."

Even if the sentences in Excerpt 10–12 did demonstrate that the speakers knew the lexical meaning of the underlined words—and when I ask observers to indicate whether they do or not, there is little firm agreement—two further problems remain. First, how congruent is the meaning in the sentences with the meaning in the passages the words are from? After reading that a desert is arid because rain seldom falls, forming the sentence "My throat is arid" seems incongruent to most observers, to cite one example. If you had formed sentences with the word *charge*, such as "Charge the battery"; "Charge it to my credit card"; "The cover charge here is too high"; "The Charge of the Light Brigade"; "I got a charge out of it"; "He used to be the chargé d'affaires"; "I was overcharged," would your ability to respond to Charges 1 through 13 be enhanced? Many words that appear in print generally occur only in print. Asking nonnative speakers of a language to speak words that are ordinarily used only in print is simply another type of incongruity added to the fact that it is usually hard to use a word in a sentence that is congruent with the context in which it is used in a reading passage. Surely many of the problems nonnative speakers of a language have with collocation stem from the burdens we place on them when we ask them to use words from passages they have read in spoken sentences.

Define ______—Limitations of Definitions

Responses requiring definitions have the same disadvantage as responses requiring words to be used in sentences. If the definitions assured observers that the words were understood, the disadvantages might be compensated for. But even many dictionary definitions fail to reveal lexical meaning. If you had never seen the animal in this definition, would the definition help? "Any of a group of edible sea crustaceans, with compound eyes, long antennae, and five pairs of legs, the first pair of which are modified into large powerful pinchers: ______ are greenish or dark gray in color when alive, but turn bright red when boiled." Unless you already had seen the animal described, it is hard to imagine how the definition could help you picture one. For one thing, no indication of size is given. Is the animal being described one foot long, or ten?

To discover that teacher definitions are not always elucidating is not too shocking when we realize that dictionary definitions, which are written by professionals hired to do the work, are often baffling. When I've deleted the words being defined from teachers' definitions and asked other teachers to then insert the words, few can fill in the correct words, even though the words are part of their recognition vocabulary, if not their active vocabulary. Try filling in the words being defined on the blank lines in Excerpt 10–13.

Of course, definitions are not made so that the words being defined must be filled in. Normally, words being defined accompany definitions. But deleting the words underscores the limitations of definitions. And the deletions remind us that if native speakers of the target language paid either to write definitions for dictionaries or to teach the language produce definitions of limited value, our expectations of definitions of nonnative speakers learning the target language must be tempered.

Responses that contain either sentences produced to demonstrate meaning or definitions both present still one more problem. Even if these types of responses suggest that the students know the denotative meaning of the words used or defined, one still has to decide what to do, if anything, about errors in pronunciation, tense, article use, word order and, when written, spelling. I've seen hundreds of notebooks around the

EXCERPT 10–13
Definitions (T)

1 Pipes are made of ______. It is a metal.

2 To ______ is to die unhappily.

3 A ______ person is intelligent and polite.

4 The ______ is a well from which the Sahara people get water.

5 ______ is something written.

6 Sailing, traveling by water is ______.

7 The cloth that charcoal is put in is a ______.

8 ______ is sending out products to different places.

9 A ______ is native to Russia, Asia and North America. It has the face of a dog, huge paws like a lion's, heavy like a cow and a buffalo.

Key: 1. lead; 2. perish; 3. refined; 4. oasis; 5. News; 6. navigation; 7. sack; 8. Distribution; 9. bear.

world containing words used in almost incomprehensible sentences and definitions which not only fail to show the lexical meaning, but also contain at least two errors in grammar, spelling, or usage per line. Nine times out of ten, in small, neat writing in the margins next to the sentences and definitions I find word equivalents in the students' own language! This student feedback is probably a stronger indictment of solicits such as "Use ______ in a sentence" or "Define ______" than any evidence or arguments I can muster.

I could suggest that you eliminate the solicits "Use ______ in a sentence" and "Define ______" from your active vocabulary. But though rules can sometimes be broken, it is difficult to eliminate the function they perform, or the need they fulfill. Alternative patterns that fulfill the need and function of these and other classic patterns are suggested in the next section.

Romantic—Alternatives

Lessons from Tests—Different Uses

If the bulk of responses require recalling and stating facts about the material—*present* in terms of FOCUS—take an alternative from multiple-choice tests: Ask the students to confirm or reject facts rather than state them—*characterize* in terms of FOCUS. Multiple-choice questions, yes-no and either-or questions require the confirmation or rejection of facts another has stated—*characterize.* They can show whatever question-word questions show. The response to the solicit "Who went to the pasar with Photak—answer in a complete sentence" tells little more than the response to this solicit: "Did Phare, Bare, and Pare go with Photak to the pasar in the opening of the story, or did Photak go with only Bare and Pare?" But responses that require students to *characterize* rather than *present* eliminate the problem of language errors that are inevitable in responses to question-word questions, especially when the solicit requires the very common complete sentence response. Errors in these types of responses make it difficult to know whether the students' problem is with the material they *attend* to or the ability to produce sentences in the target language. The response to the solicit "Who went to the pasar with Photak in the beginning of the story—answer in a complete sentence" tells little more than the response to the solicit "Did Phare, Pare, and Bare go with Photak to the pasar at the beginning of the story, or did only Phare and Pare go with him?" unless one is engaged in a study of students' language errors.

Inferences can be confirmed or rejected as easily as facts can in response to yes-no, either-or and multiple-choice questions. So if student responses require only the *characterizing* of facts, the opposite is a series of questions that require that inferences be rejected or confirmed. In place of "How did Photak treat his wife?" or "What is the tone of the story?", both requiring responses in the category *relate*, state the inferences in the question as in these examples: "The tone of the story is: (a) humorous, (b) tragic, (c) serious; Photak treated his wife with respect and as an equal, with respect but not as an equal, with disrespect but admiration, with disrespect but love; Did Photak dislike his wife?" These solicits contain communications in the category *relate* that students can *characterize* by confirming or rejecting the choices provided. More information on forming these types of solicits is presented in Episode 4.

Short and Obvious—Student as Source

If the source of all the solicits after the receptive activities is the text or the teacher, the opposite source is the student. Of course, when students form questions, we face the same problem as when they form sentences in response to "Use ______ in a sentence." But if the questions are communicated in writing rather than speech, each student can be instructed to edit his or her own before saying it, and you can edit it again before it is said. Correcting written sentences is quicker than correcting spoken sentences, and of course the corrections are individualized. Each student's unique errors are treated and only the student who made the error is given the feedback, not the entire class. More work with feedback is provided in Episode 12.

☺ *—Mediums Provide More Alternatives*

Whether students or teachers form yes-no, either-or and multiple-choice questions, all these require responses in linguistic mediums. The alternatives to linguistic mediums appealing to the eye are sketches, pictures, and objects—*nonlinguistic visual* mediums—and gestures, body language, or facial expressions—*paralinguistic visual* mediums. To elicit responses in these mediums, the solicits "Use ______ in a sentence" and "Give me a complete sentence with ______" can be replaced with these solicits: "Draw ______" or "Show how ______ feels with an expression!" or "Make the sound of a person in ______ situation."

One reader's *nonlinguistic visual* rendition of an *orang-kechil* is shown in Excerpt 10–14. The 4′ above the arrow on the right-hand side indicates that the figure is four feet tall—extremely useful information that is lacking in most sketches in dictionaries. Drawings of a rat and a bear, for example, appear the same size, with no scale used to indicate that one animal is six inches tall and one six feet tall.

When a student shows how Photak "saberchakap" to the orang-kechil, a *paralinguistic visual* medium, such as a facial expression, or a *paralinguistic aural* medium, such as the tone of voice, indicates understanding just as clearly, if not more so, than a verbal description. Asking a student to make sounds likely to be heard as Photak "whacked the orang-kechil on the head," thus requiring a *nonlinguistic aural* medium, can show understanding as well as a spoken definition. When *nonlinguistic* and *paralinguistic* mediums are used, the problem of linguistic errors interfering with communication is of course eliminated.

EXCERPT 10–14
An Orang-kechil

—After Tadashi Goto

Nonlinguistic and *paralinguistic* mediums need not be limited to fact stating and sharing of literal information. Students can *characterize* without speech or writing, by shaking or nodding their head, for example. They can also *relate*. Inferences about mood can be shown by line drawings. If a student drew this , his understanding of the mood of *At the Pasar* would be clearer than those who drew these: . As a quick glance at people's offhand sketches, serious paintings, and miming at parties shows, and as a great deal of research concludes, the expression of thoughts and emotions is not limited to linguistic mediums. [Background 10–15]

Sketches, miming, noisemaking and expressing thoughts with sounds are often considered childlike and not used as a technique with adults. Or they are considered disruptive and not used with youngsters. But most teachers feel compelled to sketch or gesture as they define and try to communicate meaning. They know the target language better than the students, and yet they are unable to communicate without recourse to *nonlinguistic* and *paralinguistic* mediums. It seems unfair to expect students to communicate without the same mediums teachers cannot do without. The problem of disruption is treated in Episode 16. The issue of childlike associations with pictures, objects, and miming is treated in Episode 13. This is an episode on role-playing. The classification and manipulation of mediums in general is treated in Episode 18.

Only One—Single versus Multiple Solicits

Whether the responses are made in *linguistic* mediums, *nonlinguistic* mediums, or *paralinguistic* mediums, and whether the source is the teacher, text, or students, the responses usually are elicited in a series of solicits. The obvious alternative to a long series of solicits is a single solicit such as "Retell what you heard, saw or read." Of course the response to a single solicit will produce the same types of linguistic errors that responses to a series of solicits will produce. But while the problem of errors is similar, the retelling of a story provides information and opportunities that responses to a series of questions do not. In retelling, students have an opportunity to explore meaning; as they speak, they make connections about the material they have attended to. While listening to the retelling, a great number of reading problems can be diagnosed. All deviations in the retelling—called miscues by those who investigate them—suggest types of work students need. If past tense suffixes are consistently left off in retelling, but are accompanied by time expressions such as *before that, earlier, in her youth*, the problem is not reading, but the ability to produce past tense markers, one of the features of English that adds redundancy to the language. In one of the miscue studies, a reader was unable to say the word *pavilion*, which occurred twenty-five times in the story. Yet in the retelling, the reader substituted the word *tent* for *pavilion*. So the meaning was obviously captured, but the problem was one of pronunciation. [Background 10–16]

How Did You Like It?—Content in Teaching and Nonteaching Settings

Though in saying we can communicate emotions as well as thoughts in pictures, or with noise and gestures, I implied that personal feelings can occur in responses and reactions related to material we *attend* to, the bulk of the communications that occur after we *attend* in teaching settings contain content exclusively related to language—*study of language*. Yet outside teaching settings, the more likely questions to be asked are those about *life* rather than *study of language*. In my experience outside classrooms, the question "How did you like it?" is more frequent than "What happened?" or "What is the theme?" I may state some facts, make inferences about the characters, of if referring to food that I *attend* to, try to guess some of the ingredients. But any information I share about the *set* I *attend* to is done to illustrate my feelings, not to prove that I understood.

The alternative to responses requiring word meaning, theme, plot—content in the category *study*—is responses requiring personal feelings and opinions—content in the category *life*. Helpful as retelling and responses to a series of questions in many mediums can be to diagnose reading difficulties and to aid student understanding, our emotions and feelings determine how often we *attend* and how much effort we expend as we *attend*. Student responses to literature have been found to consist mainly of restatements of plots. Personal involvement—"I felt just like that girl did when my father got sick once"—and personal associations—"My uncle has the same temper he has, scary"—are extremely rare. But we don't go to movies, concerts, or football games or read to be able to retell what we *attend* to or develop our vocabulary. These are emotional experiences that heighten our awareness of life. Whether increasing the number of responses and reactions with content of life will increase student involvement in the material they attend to can of course only be investigated if the alternative is tried. [Background 10–17]

Back to Internal–External—A Few Final Alternatives

Whether we ask students to *characterize* rather than *present*, to use *nonlinguistic* or *paralinguistic* mediums rather than *linguistic* ones, and whether we ask many questions or a few, by asking students to answer questions before they *attend* rather than after, we can learn which questions depend on the internal information they possess, rather than the external information in the *sets* they attend to. By allowing students to pose the questions and to see or hear the questions before they *attend*, we can probably decrease student dependence on the skill of trying to guess what the teacher "wants." And by allowing students to *attend* to *sets*, we can perhaps decrease the degree to which questions test only recall of the external information they *attend* to.

Whether you employ these alternatives or not, all responses probably require some mixture not only of internal and external information, but also of memory and skill at knowing what things teachers and test makers tend to be after. The problem with terms such as memory and skill at knowing what things teachers and test makers tend to be after is that they are lacking in precision. As a result, I have suggested only a few alternatives in the last paragraph. For now, together with these few alternatives, a reminder that responses to so-called comprehension questions about *sets* we *attend* to are complex may at least serve to help keep in mind that incorrect responses about sets we *attend* to do not necessarily mean we do not comprehend the *sets*, nor that correct responses prove that we do.

Romantic—Some Alternatives Parallel Nonteaching Settings and Theory
Some of the alternatives parallel what we do after we attend a ball game, concert, movie, or play. With those who accompany us, we make judgments: "Great movie"; "Wow, that pitching was first class." We share our personal feelings with those we went to the events with too: "I love the photography"; "I get impatient with actors who don't project." We *characterize* and *present* with content I code *life* in our reactions.

With those who did not accompany us, we *characterize* and *present* too. We restate what we saw and heard, and we judge what we attended. We communicate with *non-linguistic visual* mediums as well as speech, if we can. For example, if we get a program at an event, we use the pictures in it to make our retelling and judgments more vivid. Those who feel free to act also use many gestures and modulate their tone of voice to add drama to their retelling, thus using *paralinguistic aural* and *visual* mediums as well as the *linguistic aural* medium of speech.

When I was in Somalia, there were times when not everyone in a part of a neighborhood could see a particular movie, either because of lack of money or time. Often, groups formed and pooled their money so one member could see the movie, with the stipulation that he or she would tell the group all about it. As you can imagine, those who simply retold the plot in normal speech were not given money for any more tickets. Those who retold with drama, shared their feelings, and made judgments were the ones who got the most free tickets to movies.

Others who are paid to *characterize* and *present* in their reactions are critics. If reviews contained only the outlines of the plot or a neutral description of a ball game, as many responses do after sets are *attended* to in class, they would not be read. Since critics have to write for both those who went to an event and those who might want to go, they have to do some retelling of the story or give some description of the items or events in the program. But they also make judgments; so they *characterize* as well as *present.* Everyone has his or her favorite and most detested critic. There would be no need for more than one critic in any area if all a critic had to do was describe events by telling exactly what happened, as we often expect students to do after they have *attended* to a *set* in class.

If we consider *attending* to *sets* as an interplay between internal and external information, then the need to have students do more than use linguistic mediums to *present* the *study of language* is even more compelling. Using speech or print to only *present study of language* takes no account of what is in the heads and hearts of the students, and forces students to communicate in a medium few teachers limit themselves to.

Journal Entry

If you enjoyed any part of this episode so far a great deal, note the section and what in it, or you, made the section enjoyable.

Journal Entry

Those who develop advertisements have to look to all settings to seek alternatives. One of the problems in developing an ad is to make it grip our attention and at the same time not be too difficult. While I constantly encourage that we look outside teaching settings for alternatives, I have noticed one ad that is parallel to practices in teaching settings. In place of the usual—"The best hotel in Tokyo is the Imperial"—I saw "The best hotel in Tokyo is ———."

The customer-to-be was to fill in the blank rather than be told. Of course, the answer was given below the ad. But the interplay between external and internal information was altered by using what was really a cloze test.

See if you find some ads that illustrate the interplay between external and internal information.

IV. WELCOME WORDS—THE LAST SECTION!

Not Practicing What I Preach—Judging Alternatives

I'm really not breaking my rule of describing rather than judging. Here, I am only asking you to judge congruence, not either what happens or the consequences. I have collected some extracts that contain both descriptions of incidents related to reading and alternatives. In each extract, one of the alternatives is more congruent with the theory of taking in mediums I reviewed in this episode, or one of the alternatives is more congruent with some of the ways we *attend* to mediums in nonteaching settings. I'd like you to write a 5 on the blank lines next to those alternatives that are more congruent with patterns I reviewed in nonteaching settings or the theory of taking in mediums I reviewed. Write a 1 next to those alternatives that you think are least congruent, and write a 3 next to those items that are in between total congruence and total incongruence. I discuss my judgments under each extract.

In addition to judging the congruence between the incidents and the alternatives, I'd like you to write titles for each extract that you think capture or reflect the lesson you learned from the three alternatives in the extract, or that you think will help you remember the extract or a point you want to remember from the extract. I have provided a blank line next to each extract for you to write the titles on.

To remind you of the central points of the theory I reviewed, I have summarized the theory here:

1. The *internal information* in our heads and hearts is as important to meaning as the *external information* we *attend* to; we get *external information* not from individual words, letters, sounds, segments of pictures or single atoms of food or drink, but in strings of sounds and words and a large number of segments or atoms joined together.

2. Given the great amount of *external* and *internal information* we must process, we categorize both *external* and *internal information.*

3. There is a great amount of redundancy in all mediums we *attend* to; in languages, we get meaning not only from the shape of letters or the literal definitions of words, but also from the setting the language is used in, the grammatical features of the language, the rhetorical structure of the sentences, the pronunciation and stress system when we listen, and the punctuation and sound-letter correspondences when we read, to name a few examples.

4. We make educated guesses as we read, view, listen or in other ways attend to

mediums; as in all predicting, risks must be taken as we guess, and as in all predicting, errors are inevitable; we rarely take in 100 percent of anything we *attend* to; we can usually get the message intended even if we get scores of around 50 percent on different attempts to measure comprehension, an imprecise term that, while frequently used in discussions of receptive activities, is infrequently defined.

5. Though we probably never take in 100 percent of what we *attend* to, the activity must make some sense to us as we engage in it at the time we engage in it and cannot simply be a bewildering experience that we engage in as preparation for some future enlightenment.

6. These principles imply another: that reading, tasting, viewing and other ways of taking in mediums are active processes that are probably best developed by engaging in the activities, rather than in talking about the processes by defining words we will see or hear, describing foods and pictures we will taste or see, or asking and answering scores of questions about the material we *attend* to—all using mediums to communicate rather than to take in.

EXTRACT 10–1 ________________

A page in a textbook contains a table with 50 names on it, and 200 sets of numbers arranged in four columns. Here are three sets of directions that could accompany the table. Of course, only one of the three actually occurred in the text. But the others could be written in adapting the text. [Background 10–18]

A You are an investigator from the tax bureau. A client's lawyer has asked you to prove the allegations made by the tax bureau against his client. He has given you these six questions about the data in an attempt to refute the charges. Answer the six questions, using the material in the table. ____

B Look at the numbers and names in this table. Then, I'll ask you some questions about them. ____

C Look at the numbers in this table and circle those with more than four digits in them. ____

I rated A the most congruent. So if you put a 5 next to A, we made a similar judgment. Though the student is really not an investigator from the tax bureau, the direction gives a reason for looking at the table that is immediate, if the student can suspend his or her disbelief for a few minutes and pretend he or she is solving a problem. Because the instructions have indicated what the student has to look for, it requires the student to categorize as he or she reads. The least congruent direction is B. I looked at this table, as well as many others in other books, and many diagrams, for long periods of time. When I went to answer the questions about the tables and diagrams, I could answer only a few. While looking, I had no focus.

There is a game children play in which a number of objects are placed on a table in view of all of them for a set period of time, say 30 seconds. One child says to the others, "When I uncover these objects, look at them and remember as many of them as you can." After the time is up, the materials are covered, and each viewer writes down the names of as many objects as he or she can remember. The one who can remember the most wins. If you tell the children just to look at the objects, without the extra instruction "remember as many of them as you can," children consistently remember fewer names of objects. While looking without being told what to look for, some think of objects they would like to have, others of objects at home similar to those in front of them, and others of the shapes of the objects, to cite a few examples.

I have been given this direction many times while watching football games: "Look at that!" My ability to get meaning from this direction is limited by my experience with football. Are the alternatives Player A has lovely eyes/Player A doesn't have lovely eyes; Player B is very quick/Player A is not very quick; Players A and B have very muddy uniforms/Players A and B have torn shirts? Or should I be looking at Player X? Just because material or events are available does not mean that we know what to attend to as we *attend*.

I rated C in between A and B. It is more congruent with the principles of reading presented than simply a statement to look at the tables. And it is parallel with some of the charges you performed on *At the Pasar*. But it is somewhat less like an immediate problem to solve than the tax investigator's task, and implies that it is a means to help the reader achieve some future goal rather than an immediate end.

EXTRACT 10–2 ________________

I'm going to read another passage from Joan Morley's book on listening comprehension. The passage today is about Jules Verne and his predictions about space travel and the American Apollo moon landing. [Background 10–19]

A Listen very carefully as I read the passage to you. I'm going to read it slowly so it will be easier to follow and understand. ____

B Listen for the important facts as I read. ____

C Listen for the important facts as if you are a reporter who has to inform a group that is very familiar with Jules Verne and his work, but know nothing about the moon landing by the Americans. ____

After asking many teachers to note what they considered important facts in the passage about Jules Verne, I found a great range of choices. As we discussed the choices, we all realized that what is an important fact to someone is partly determined by one's role. For instance, if you are a historian, the dates of the moon landing are important. If you are a scientist, the speeds Verne predicted for rockets and the actual speeds required to get a ship on the moon are important. If you are a reporter working for an American propaganda office, the facts related to the American landing would be more important than the facts related to Verne's French nationality. If you are a literary critic, Verne's images and themes would be more important facts than the accuracy of his predictions.

The instruction to look for important facts forces listening and directs the listener, so it is congruent with principle 2 about developing categories, and principle 6 about developing receptive activities by engaging in them. But item C mirrors principle 5 as well, because it asks the listeners to do something at least partially real as well. So, I've rated C as 5, and B, 3.

Reading deliberately by stressing every word and slowing the speed destroys the normal organization of the stress and intonation system and distorts the pronunciation of words as well, thus decreasing the redundancy of the spoken lines, effectively negating principle 3, which holds that redundancy is an aid. Slow reading takes more time, allowing less time for reading the passage many times, and so negates principle 6—that listening aids our skill in listening—as well. Thus, A in Extract 10–2, I've rated 1 for lack of congruence.

EXTRACT 10–3 ________________

The aim in these items is to teach some new words, among them the words *foot, fits, shoe, pumpkin,* and *midnight.* All the words appear in a reading passage that the teacher wants the class to read.

A Among other things, the teacher says "This is my foot" as he points to his foot. And he asks, "Is that your foot?" He continues with other statements and questions about *shoes* and *pumpkins,* both of which he has brought to class in a bag. He also asks students to point to their own shoes, their own feet and to a clock he has set at midnight. ___

B Among other things, the teacher says "My foot is sore; I hit it on the desk during the first period." And he asks questions such as "What time do you go to bed on New Year's Eve? Do you like to stay up late? When do you usually go to bed?" He also asks a long series of questions about different kinds of pies and about traditions connected with Halloween. ___

C As I read this story, follow along in your book. "Once upon a time, there was a young lady named Cinderella . . ." (And after he finishes reading it once, he rereads the story, with animation.) ___

Since C requires students to *attend* to both print and speech, and since a story contains connected discourse arranged in a way so that predictions are much more possible than in a series of disconnected questions about separate vocabulary items, principles 4 and 6 are reflected. So it merits a 5 for high congruence. In B, the teacher tries to use the words in sentences that one might hear outside a teaching setting, so he communicates a great deal of *external information*, congruent with principle 1. But no one gets a chance to see print, negating principle 6. Thus, B I rate 3, in between high and low congruence.

Even though the teacher uses real objects in A, it is totally incongruent with the principles, meriting a 1. Even though the objects are actually there, the communications are less realistic than those about sore feet and Halloween in B. "This is my foot" and parallel comments are exclusive to language textbooks and language lessons. Michael West contrasted the three alternatives in Extract 10–3 in an essay on teaching vocabulary in these words:

> . . . The sentence "This is also a toe" is unrealistic even if the toe is actually present: it has no more teaching value than learning a word in a word-list. Whereas, . . . "I must cut my toe-nails", "There's a hole in the toe of this sock: shall I darn it for you"—these are expressions of relationship with an environment: they are real, whether the thing or action is in fact present, or not.
>
> . . . [Stories] of things which are not present in the classroom, even about fairies or ghosts or other things which have no "real" existence at all may be functionally more real than visible and tangible "realities." [Background 10–20]

EXTRACT 10–4 ________________

A class is using an issue of *National Geographic,* an American magazine noted for the color photography that accompanies its articles on topics related to geography. The magazine is being used as reading material in place of the regular textbook. Three different teachers gave these three sets of directions.

A As I read, follow along in your magazines, looking only at the words I am reading. Later, we'll look at the pictures. ____

B As I read, put a check mark on those items in the pictures that are mentioned or referred to in the text. ____

C As I read, follow along in your copies of the magazine. I will point out words that are shown in the pictures. "The climbers used pitons as they ascended the side of the mountain." Now, look at the picture on the right-hand side. Notice the long iron spikes with the eyes on the end that the climber is hammering into the rock. That is a *piton* ____

Giving someone an answer—This is a *piton*—negates principle 4, reading requires predicting, so C cannot be rated 5 for high congruence. Since in C, the pictures are made use of, increasing the amount of redundancy made available, it is congruent with principle 2, and so can be rated 3. Since A negates principle 3, I rate it 1 for low congruence. Though putting check marks on parts of pictures is not an everyday activity for anyone, it requires students to make use of two sources of *external information,* pictures and print as they listen, rather than just print, so the practice is congruent with principle 1. Marking the pictures that are referred to also is congruent with principle 3 because it provides students with an opportunity to take advantage of the increase in redundancy supplied by the pictures. Marking pictures also provides students with an opportunity to make predictions, an activity congruent with principle 4. As a result, I rate B with a 5 for high congruence.

EXTRACT 10–5 ________________

After reading a passage to the class, the teacher asks the students for the title of the passage they just heard. None of the students can state the title of the passage, though the teacher did say it before he read the passage to them.

A The teacher writes broken lines on the blackboard, with one line indicating one letter in each word, and leaves longer spaces between lines that start and end words; the teacher also writes one letter of each word in one of the blanks. ____

B The teacher repeats the request for the title, saying each word with full stress and very deliberately rather than with normal stress and intonation. ____

C After waiting more than a minute for someone to state the title, the teacher says, "Well, it was called 'Stress on the job,' a long title to remember. Now, tell me how you felt about the people in this passage."

By giving clues, one increases the amount of *external information* available, so A exemplifies principle 1. Altering the normal organization of language by distorting the oral delivery increases the noise and decreases redundancy, so B negates principle 3.

Though asking students to communicate personal feelings, *life content*, is an example of one of the alternatives suggested, providing the title prevents the students from guessing. Being prevented from taking a risk negates principle 4. As a result, I rated A, 5; B, 1; and C, 3.

EXTRACT 10–6 ______________

Some children in a nursery school are standing in front of a door with a sign on it that says "No Admittance." Earlier, the teacher had said "No one is allowed in this room; don't go in this room because the boiler is in there. It's very hot and you might burn yourself. This sign says "No Admittance' and means 'Don't go in; keep out'."

After the teacher leaves, one child points to the sign and says "Keep out." Another points to it and says "Don't go in." A third points to the sign and says "No admittance."

After observing this exchange, three separate teachers act in these three ways.

A One teacher covers up all the letters on the sign "No Admittance" except the initial *N* in "No." She makes the sound for *n* and has the students repeat it. On each subsequent day, she uncovers one letter and repeats the same process. ___

B One teacher prints a sign that says "Don't go in" and another that says "Keep out." She puts one above "No Admittance" and one below it. The teacher points to "Don't go in" as she says it. The next day, she points to the sign "Don't go in" and asks the children to indicate which sign she is pointing to. Each day, she points to a different sign as she says the words, and asks children to say the words she points to. ___

C The teacher says "This sign says 'No Admittance' and that means you should not go in; keep out, don't go in. The words say 'No admittance!'" ___

The first teacher decreases redundancy. Just as it would be harder to decide between the men's room and the women's room if the first two letters of *women* were obscured, so trying to understand single letters is usually more difficult than strings of letters. When I observe classes that start with a teacher writing an *e* on the blackboard and questions about the sound of the *e*, I am unable to say the "correct" sound, as are any students who were absent the previous day when the "correct" sound being worked on that week was revealed. Like all letters, *e* has many sounds depending on its environment. The unstressed *e* in *the*, the initial *e* in *envelope*, the second *e* in *television*—we can work out these separate pronunciations because the letters occur with others and because we have some experience with the words in our lives. When letters are in larger units, we can use our previous knowledge, our *internal information* and the *external information* provided by the shape of the word, the denotative meaning of the word, the sound–letter correspondence in all the letters, the location of the word in the sentence and the pronunciation of the word based on our knowledge of it. If we can't sound out the word, we might recognize the configuration of it, or recognize the meaning or guess the meaning that seems reasonable, given the story line and topic. If you are reading about a circus and you see the letters *trap* after "She swung from one" you are unlikely to say "trap" or "trapezoid." If *trapeze* is a word you don't know, you might say *rope* or *swing* for it and keep on reading. In fact, trying to puzzle out *trapeze* may slow you down so much that you will not be able to understand anything else in the sentence. Stopping at the *trap*, or worse yet, at the *t* would probably prevent comprehension rather than lead to it. Stopping at *n* in "No Admittance" might have the same result. Because one cannot say a letter in isolation does not necessarily mean that one cannot read, though it is true that most readers can say the alphabet. But one can learn the alphabet by reading as well as by learning it for its own sake. [Background 10–21].

The teacher in B who adds more words in pursuing a practice congruent with principle 3 because she increases the amount of redundancy, rather than reduces it, like the teacher in A. She also encourages guessing, so exemplifies principle 4. And she tries to make reading engaging rather than simply an activity to perform in preparation for some future enlightment, so she exemplifies principle 5 as well. She is not a member of the school that preaches this gospel: "If you do all these things that are so confusing and baffling day after day, someday you'll be able to make sense out of all these mysterious letters."

The teacher in C is not as incongruent as the one in A nor as congruent as the one in B. She tries to show that meaning comes from the entire sign, not individual letters, following principle 1, so she merits a 3.

EXTRACT 10–7 ______

During the time set aside for silent reading, some students mumble as they read; others look up words in their dictionaries; and some write in the margins of the material they are reading. Here are the ways three different teachers acted.

A One teacher says "No noise during reading, and put away your dictionaries. Just read—no writing either." ___

B One teacher circulates around the room asking individual students "Do you understand?" The teacher also asks students to say which words they have looked up. ___

C One teacher goes from student to student asking "What feelings do you have about this material?" and "I haven't read that—tell me about it." ___

While mumbling might indicate readers are subvocalizing, thus perhaps slowing their reading rate, and while looking up words can also decrease the reading rate, thus sometimes making comprehension more difficult, and while writing too stops the reading process momentarily, these three activities can be worthwhile. To stop them flat rather than to investigate their consequences is not a practice congruent with this episode. Thus, I rate A with 1 for low congruence.

The teacher in B I rated 3. Interest in meaning is shown. But the implication is that only the lexical meaning of individual words is important, not the meaning from sources other than denotative meaning. The question "Do you understand?" not only suggests interest in meaning, but implies some kind of perfect, overall comprehension is possible. After a "Yes," another person can always find something that one did not in fact understand. On the other hand, responding with a "No" would imply total lack of comprehension. Thus, it is almost impossible to respond to the question. As I said earlier, in my experience, a "Yes" or a nodding head or an "Oh" are three of the surest signs that the person is not understanding. The question "Do you understand?" negates the idea that comprehension is relative, stated in principle 4.

Asking for feelings and for retelling as in C, is open-ended. The person soliciting cannot have preconceived notions of the answers if he hasn't read the material. And no one can say he's right or wrong about either his feelings or the information. Additionally, the person is free to say as little or as much as he wishes. Since these alternatives were specifically suggested in this episode, of course C merits a 5 for high congruence.

EXTRACT 10–8 ______________

Students in three different classes are working on crossword puzzles. Their teachers circulate around this room to provide feedback. Each teacher provided different feedback, as these three examples show.

A One teacher, looking over one student's shoulder, says "The word that fits in 4 across and 7 down is *Eskimo*." ____

B One teacher, looking over one student's shoulder, says "I love crossword puzzles, but I usually can't fill in all the boxes. Trying to match the clues to words I know is fun though!" ____

C One teacher simply looks at each student's puzzle and continues walking around the classroom, saying nothing, but shaking his head sideways now and then as he looks at some of the puzzles. ____

Since providing an answer prevents a person from guessing, A is incongruent with principle 4. By sharing personal feelings, the teacher in B communicates *life*, one of the areas of content suggested as an alternative to *study* in this episode. As a result, B is congruent with one of the intentions of this episode. Allowing the students to continue their work on their own is also congruent, exemplifying principle 6. But the sideways shaking of his head is ambiguous. It could mean "It's wrong"—neutral information. But it could also mean "You don't know what you're doing"—a personal judgment. Therefore, C I rank 3, while B is a 5 and A is a 1.

Journal Entry

Has the use of "take in mediums" in place of "receptive activities" made you wonder? Has "use mediums to communicate" in place of "productive activities" made you wonder? I realize that when people say "receptive activities" they mean that the process is active, as active as the process we engage in for "productive activities," but I find it hard to use the terms without constant reminders that "receptive" means "productive." Do you?

Dangers—Limitations of Judging Extracts

There are dangers in judging extracts. For one thing, they may not be representative. Using extracts together with tallies helps decrease this danger. But the danger that the communications in the extracts mean something different from what we think is more difficult to overcome. The meaning of a teacher's sideways shaking head may be known to the members of the class, and still baffle an observer, or in cases where the teacher is unaware of the action, it may lack meaning even for the teacher himself. Finally, the communications that occur before and after those extracted can alter the meaning of the extracts. The teacher in Extract 10–8 might have given the word *Eskimo* to the student only because he saw the student try to get it six times, and he knew the student had a low frustration and a high anxiety level.

Just as words in isolation are harder to understand, so are extracts. This danger can be partially overcome by interpreting the meaning of the extracts in relationship to other communications, the teacher's aim, and student attitudes. All interpretations, like the judgments and the tallies they are based on, must be considered tentative. The rating we just did, though done with numbers, and therefore implying certitude, is tentative, and arguments can be made for different ratings. All coding and other forms of describing and interpretations of the evidence we find are simply attempts to find the truth, rather than the truth itself.

A New Word—Feedback

Up until now, the word *feedback* has not been mentioned in this episode. Yet the feedback provided after we take in and produce mediums probably has as much to do with the value of the activities as the activities themselves. Some have argued that appropriate feedback is the most critical aspect of teaching people to take mediums in. After expending so much effort in investigating uses that occur before, during and after we take in mediums, and breaking many rules by substituting alternative activities, it would be most unfortunate not to be able to recognize feedback appropriate to the alternatives suggested. I treat feedback in another episode: Episode 12. [Background 10–22]

One Can Make All the Difference—Conclusion

If either any of the activities you now ask your students to perform or any of the alternatives seem to consistently baffle most of them, you might stop teaching and visit the homes of some of the students who read best and worst. In the homes, you could observe what the parents, brothers, and sisters do as the students from your classes read, listen, and in other ways *attend*. I don't know of any studies about different categories of *attend* other than reading that have been done across countries. But a study of reading scores in fifteen countries concluded that a good home and a child's background are the two variables that consistently differentiate between reading scores in different countries and reading scores between different groups within the same country. Detailed descriptions of activities during the classes were not made, so the effect of different reading tasks was not able to be studied in detail. But gross distinctions between classes, such as size of group, proportion of time spent in groups rather than in the entire class, and ability grouping were not as consistently important as the student's home environment. [Background 10–23]

As a result of your visits, you may find other alternatives to try in your classroom, or you might simply decide to pair up good and poor readers and schedule a lot of home visits for them to each other's houses. In spite of the fact that reading is one of the most researched areas in education, descriptions of home practices in detail and the consequence of visits are not carefully documented. [Background 10–24]

The emphasis in this episode has been on providing opportunities for students to *attend* as an important part of developing skill in taking in mediums. Asking students to go through motions and do things they consistently consider bewildering has been discouraged. I hope that none of the alternatives will simply be substituted for activities now practiced in a way that forces the students to go through motions. If you try all the alternatives, including visits to homes of good and poor readers, I'm sure that the students will not only have a better chance of decreasing the number of "Ohs" that mean "I don't understand" as they engage in receptive activities, but also have an opportunity to learn an attitude about exploration and investigation. If you are constantly exploring and investigating with curiosity, it is likely that at least one student in each class will be excited by your attitude and may begin to have a similar attitude. And if we pass on or encourage or nurture at least one, we keep ideas we hold important alive. One can make all the difference.

Journal Entry

I asked you once before whether there was anything you found particularly enjoyable in this episode. Here's another chance.

BACKGROUND NOTES

10–1. The power of the internal information in our minds is extremely great as evidenced by this story: A viewer was watching a television talk show hosted by Stanley Siegel. As the viewer watched the show, the viewer saw a guest pull out a 22-caliber revolver. The viewer immediately called the police, and the police went to the television studio only to be told that the Stanley Siegel show was not on live, but was in fact a videotape of a show that was made much earlier. It turned out that Stanley Siegel at that time was also in his apartment watching the videotape of his show. The guest who had pulled out the gun was simply demonstrating how she had closed a Cambridge, Massachusetts, pornographic bookstore in protest against the pornographic books. Frank Smith (1971) talks about the theoretical foundation for what happened in relation to Stanley Siegel's show.

10–2. This story was told by Allen Walker Read, who was a professor in the English Department of Columbia University. He told the story in discussions we had about the power of context and perception over the language we use.

10–3. Perception is not very much changed by reading, or listening, for that matter. McKillop showed how previous perceptions failed to be changed by reading, and in fact showed that previous perceptions prevented people from seeing some of the information in the prose they are reading. Howe found that people persisted in recalling misinformation from things that they listened to or read even when they were corrected. Arnheim has argued that each individual's perception is unique. He, of course, uses visual images in his discussions rather than print, but the point he is making is the same.

10–4. For two detailed descriptions of steps in making up cloze tests and for some background on cloze with native speakers, see Haskell and Oller. For the origins of the idea, see Taylor (1953).

10–5. Frank Smith in 1971 provided a clear rationale for the need to categorize in order to help us file and retrieve information. Berton Roueché shows how we make use of our classification systems in diagnosing disease in his pieces about discovering causes of illness in "Annals of Medicine" in *The New Yorker*. Nida shows how developing categories for different words is vital in learning to listen to a new language. Vygotsky argues that children learn categories of meanings before individual words.

10–6. Kenneth Goodman, no doubt, is the best known person in the field of miscue analysis. He calls reading a psycholinguistic guessing game. The findings he and his team made are presented in an anthology edited by P. David Allen in 1976, and Goodman's description of miscue analysis is in a 1973 monograph.

10–7. A. S. Hornby's *Advanced learner's dictionary*, published by Oxford University Press, is a must. The *Longman dictionary of contemporary English*, published in 1978, and the *Longman dictionary of American English*, published in 1983, are also valuable. Many have said sarcastically that the best place to hide a secret is in the preface to a dictionary, but the value of these dictionaries in particular can be increased by learning to make use of the symbols that are explained in the prefaces. There is a veritable wealth of knowledge about the ways that languages work, as well as about the meanings of many words.

For clean representations of a great many meanings, I'd urge that you subscribe to a magazine that used to be called *Pictorial Education*, but in 1983 was changed to *Junior Education*. The publication has been delivered to schools since 1927, and the address is listed in the bibliography. Large color pictures with short, clear captions show the meanings of hundreds of words in context and do not require definitions in most cases.

If you prefer to use visual materials that have not been specifically designed to teach school subjects, as those in *Pictorial Education* have been, I'd urge you to collect catalogs. In the United States, at least, once you get on the mailing list for one or two catalogs, you'll be on the list for hundreds of catalogs. Seed catalogs contain amazing information, and I have listed the address of one seed manufacturer in Episode 15. I've also put in the address of a book called *The great book of catalogs*, which is a directory listing over 2,000 catalogs. Most of the words contained in large dictionaries will be found in these catalogs.

If the thought of using catalogs to illustrate meanings offends you, be sure and buy a copy of the *English Duden*. This is a pictorial dictionary with words arranged according to various settings; for example, one page will show a picture of a beauty parlor, and on the facing page there will be a list of words keyed to all of the items in the beauty parlor. McArthur's lexicon also is arranged by topic so you can see words related to each other on the same page, rather than in alphabetical order.

10–8. Frank Smith describes the redundancy in language in *Understanding reading*. Kahn describes the importance of redundancy in breaking secret codes. He refers to Shannon, who apparently was the person who first figured out redundancy mathematically, indicating the minimum amount of information that can be retained in a message so that it could still be made sense of. Shannon's work was extremely important in intelligence work, as well as for providing insights into our understanding of the reading process.

10–9. In a mimeographed sheet dated August 1954, John B. Carroll described a test called the Minnesota Speed of Reading Test, developed in 1936 by A. C. Eurich. In the test, the subject is supposed to read the material as rapidly as possible, indicating his or her progress by underlining nonsensical words. In 1964 Alan Davies at the University of Edinburgh wrote an English Proficiency Test Battery in which he requested those taking it to underline some irrelevant English words which hindered the meaning of the passage. Spolsky reported the use of extraneous words in listening tests in 1968.

Of course, underlining or writing extraneous words could be considered unnatural, but when we play games, we do many unnatural things. And whether they are unnatural or not, it is true sometimes that we gain insights from doing things that are different from what we normally do. If you look at children playing with each other, they often set up barriers to try to trick each other. They view these tricks or barriers as challenges to overcome. They are not discouraged by them, but rather encouraged, as long as they realize that the person they are working with is not trying to fool them, but simply trying to present them with an exciting challenge. Many like to write codes and break them for fun. Noise is a vital element in codes, as Kahn shows.

10–10. The most accessible description of the construction of a cloze test is in Oller (1979). Haskell has described the steps, too, and provided sample passages in the journal of the New York affiliate of the National Council of Teachers of English.

10–11. Chall suggests how much time is spent in various reading activities by looking at the suggestions in Teacher's Notes. Harris and Serwer describe the time spent reading in a special project they reviewed in 1966. Denham and Lieberman edited a series of studies of time on task in different subjects in California schools. Guthrie provides evidence too, as does Shapiro-Skrobe.

10–12. Rosenblatt describes, probably better than anyone else, the relationship between author and text in her classic, *Literature as exploration*. Postman argues about the antisocial quality of reading in an essay called "The politics of reading," published in 1973.

10–13. Anderson has compared a number of studies and come up with the figures I present. Bormouth reports the relationship between cloze scores and other test scores in two articles. He also discusses issues related to difficulty level (1968). Klare does too (1976).

For a sample of cloze in a textbook, you could consult Plaister. Though the book in which he uses cloze was designed for listening comprehension, the passages can also be used for reading, and either way they illustrate the use of cloze in a published textbook.

10–14. Both Diller and Marckwardt discuss the size of the vocabulary of learners of a language, and both point out the clear distinction between the words we might need to have in our active vocabulary and those we simply have to be able to recognize in print.

10–15. Arnheim, in *Visual thinking*, presents a very thorough argument for the importance of recognizing that the mind can think visually as well as linguistically. De Bono does too.

10–16. While Goodman (1973) is the person most noted for miscue analysis, Rigg has applied Goodman's ideas to nonnative speakers of English and has reported some of her work in a 1976 presentation.

10–17. In his study of responses to literature among high school students, James Squire found that the bulk of the comments adolescents made as they were reading short stories was made up of interpretations of the story, judgments of the story, or retelling of the story. The comments they made which showed that they were involved in the story, such as saying "I know just how that character felt; I felt like that once," were very infrequent. Purves, in his discussion of responses to literary work, uses some of Squire's categories in an expanded way, and Purves too urges that we encourage readers to make a range of responses to what they read and not simply retell the information contained in the material they read.

10–18. I borrowed the example in Extract 10–1 from Richard Yorkey's *Study skills for students of English as a second language*. The book contains a wealth of exercises designed for developing study skills.

10–19. This example is from Joan Morley's 1972 *Improving aural comprehension*.

10–20. This quotation is from Michael West's *Learning to read a foreign language* and other essays on language teaching which he wrote in the 1950s.

10–21. The controversy between teaching students whole words and teaching them phonics is an American phenomenon. One does not hear much about it in England or in countries outside of the United States where English is taught as a first or second language. Rudolf Flesch is a leading advocate of phonics who writes in the popular press. Jeanne Chall is the scholar most associated with the controversy and has surveyed the research on both sides of the question. Frank Smith discusses the ideas involved, rather than the studies that have shown the superiority of one approach over the other. His 1971 description is particularly exciting.

10–22. Frank Smith, in his 1971 book about reading, contends that feedback is the vital component in learning to read. The reader must feel free to ask whether the guesses made about what has been read are right or wrong. If the reader does not get the answers he or she can't progress in reading.

10–23. The international reading study I am referring to is the one that Thorndike supervised and reported in a 1973 book. Reading comprehension was compared in 15 countries.

10–24. McDermott, an anthropologist by training, has done some work in describing the types of activities children engage in in their homes that are related to reading.

EPISODE

11

I Didn't Do Well in High School English

I. MORE THAN GRAMMAR—SUBCATEGORIES OF THE *STUDY OF LANGUAGE*

When people at parties ask me what I do, I don't say I teach English anymore. When I used to say I taught English to nonnative speakers of the language, people always reacted by saying "I didn't do well in high school English." When I used to ask what they meant by their statement, most said that they didn't do well in grammar. Soon after their comment, they drifted away from me. Whether they stopped talking to me because they feared I'd begin to correct their grammar, or because they found me boring, I can never know. But I do know that they tended to equate the study of a language with the study of grammar. Given the fact that schools are named *grammar schools* and that the bulk of test items on many tests assess grammar, I can hardly blame them. But I think that the *study of language* involves more than grammar. [Background 11–1]

This episode is about additional subcategories of the *study of language* in addition to grammar. After I list these subcategories with short definitions and examples in this section, I will show how all of the subcategories can be attributed to a reading passage in Section II. In Section III, I will suggest purposes for coding the subcategories and ways to alter their proportion, as well as ways to combine them differently. I will end in Section IV by showing that many arguments about different methods are really arguments about different subcategories of the content *study of language*.

Journal Entry

While most people walk away from me at parties as soon as they hear I teach English, some stay, including other English teachers. I often ask them what they consider to be the content they teach so I can compare what they think with what students think. In addition to mentioning the names of textbooks, readers, and newspapers, and after they indicate that they teach reading, writing, listening, and speaking, the most frequently mentioned areas of content are grammar, vocabulary, and pronunciation.

What do you say to people who ask "What do you teach as a language teacher? What content are you responsible for?"

Table 11–1 with short definitions and examples to illustrate the subcategories of the *study of language*. The subcategories are meant to be illustrative of what the category *study of language* means so that it is easier to contrast it with *life, procedure* and *study other*. Should you think another list of subcategories is more appropriate for reflecting what you consider the teaching and learning of languages to require, use it.

As you can see, except for *format* (*la*) both the terms and their meanings are similar to those often used in conjunction with different types of language study. As for *format*, I use it to highlight the fact that we get meaning from how words are arranged as well as from the words themselves. To some, the major difference between a poem and prose is a matter of *format*. When children learning to read can recognize *Coca-Cola, Jello*, and *Crest* on a soft drink can, a dessert package, and a tube of toothpaste, but cannot recognize the words typed on blank cards, they are getting information from *format* too when they see the words on the products they identify. The way the letters are printed, the colors used, and the shape of the containers provide some information. Knowing that different size print as well as position or color may distinguish the paragraphs in a text from captions under pictures means we understand the subcategory of the *study of language* I call *format* too. Publishers who produce both tabloid and full-size newspapers realize the importance of *format*. They know that some people buy one newspaper rather than another partly because of different size: *la*.

TABLE 11–1
One Person's Classification of the Study of Language

lc	context	The setting communications occur in; in reading, the title or cover.
ld	dialects	In Florida, they say "Stand in line" and in New York "Stand on line."
lo	discourse	The analysis of conversations: turn taking, use of power, sequencing, use of pauses, markers and fillers
la	format	The artistic or graphic design and layout of material; speed and loudness of speech, amount of background noise
lf	functions	Use of mediums to interact, seek knowledge, pray, demand, request, etc.
lj	genres	Characteristics of poems, short stories, essays; literary criticism
lx	grammar: form	Appearances of words that signal ways languages work
lxf	function words	*The, at, through, did* and other words we can list that serve as glue
lxi	inflections	Suffixes, internal changes in words for agreement, tense signals: *ed*

TABLE 11–1 (*continued*)

lxw	word order	"Fire help" to mean get rid of workers or seek aid due to flames, depending on position each word occupies
lz	grammar: meaning	Tense, parts of speech, singular, plural, etc.
ll	lexis: literal	Naming: *That's a book.* Factual meaning: *Plants have leaves.*
ln	lexis: nonliteral	Figurative, historical, humorous, idiomatic, ironic meanings
lm	mechanics	Spelling, formation of letters, holding of a pen or pencil
lq	punctuation	Use of question marks, capital and lower-case letters, indentation
lr	register	Usage of different social groups and classes
le	rhetoric	Organization of passages, logic, sequence, details and main idea, etc.
ls	sound	Pronunciation
lsb	blending	Reductions: *he's* for *he is*; *gonna go* for *going to go*
lsg	segmental	Consonants, consonant clusters, syllabification, vowel sounds, etc.
lsl	sound/letter	Correspondence between sound and spelling; phonics
lsp	suprasegmental	Intonation, stress and rhythm, tone
lh	speech production	Your tongue should be up. The voice box vibrates. Look at my lips.
lk	style and usage	That's florid. Use that word in polite places only. Slang, etc. Shifts from formal to informal to intimate.
lt	ties: cohesion	Connections between paragraphs and sentences—noting what *it* refers to.
lv	ties: collocation	Ties between words: A desert can be arid, but not your throat.
lw	ways of life	Patterns of thinking, feeling, living, etc. of different groups.
lwa	actual	What people from different age, sex, ethnic or language groups actually do.
lwi	interpretive	Novels, soap operas, satires, magazines, plays, artistic productions and other products that contain a point of view and attempt to interpret the patterns of life of different groups.
lu	unspecified	When the area of language cannot be determined or when more than three subcategories are contained in the same communication.
		When two or three subcategories are contained in the same communication the major category *study of language* is used to code the communications: *sl.*

II. NOT INHERENT—DETERMINING THE CONTENT OF COMMUNICATIONS

Start at the Beginning—Attributing Content to Linguistic Mediums

I code the content of communications on the basis of the content attributed to them because the particular areas of content are not inherent in communications. The title of Excerpt 11–1, for example, can be used as a title of a religious reading—*fg*; a comment about a historical fact—*so*; an example of a dialect of English—*ld*; a model to practice pronunciation—*ls*; or an illustration of how a particular tense is formed in pidgin—*1x*.

In teaching settings, there are three main ways we can determine what content is being attributed to communications. We can note what is said in structuring moves. If the teacher says "I want to produce verbs," we know many of the following moves are likely to be containing *grammar*. Verbs in solicits also suggest the content that is being attributed to language. The verb *define* in "Define blunderbluss" attributes literal meaning to a word: *ll*. "Pronounce blunderbluss" attributes pronunciation to it: *ls*. *Spell* would attribute mechanics to it: *lm*. Had one person said "I blunderblussed my way in" and another said "Add a verb—*blunderbluss* is a noun," grammar meaning would be attributed to *blunderbluss* (*lz*). Feedback thus provides the third way for us to know what content is being attributed to a communication.

Because any area of content can be attributed to any communication, it reminds us that we can use a passage designed to illustrate grammar to teach and learn other content as well. And, it means that any materials not specifically prepared for studying language can be used to study language. [Background 11–2]

In Excerpt 11–1, I illustrate how each area of content can be attributed to a passage originally developed to study religion—*study other*.

EXCERPT 11–1
It Done Begin

		Communications	*Source/ Target*	*Move Type*	*Content*	
1	Teacher:	(Holds up a picture of a garden with no people, then a picture with a god-like figure standing above the garden, then two men with wings on them fighting, then two people in the garden with no clothes on.)	t/c	str	lc	context
2	Teacher:	Now, open your books to page 22 and read the title.	t/c	sol		
3	Class:	(Open books and read title.) It Done Begin (Printed in the middle of the page.)	c/t	res		
4	Teacher:	This passage is written in a dialect of English called pidgin.	t/c	str	ld	dialect
5	Student:	Teacher I.	s/t	sol		

EXCERPT 11–1 (*continued*)

		Communications	*Source/ Target*	*Move Type*	*Content*	
6	Teacher:	Remember, Jean, in a formal setting like a class, we request a chance to speak by saying "Excuse me," not "Teacher I."	t/s	rea	lo	dis-course
7		Now, note that this excerpt from the Bible is not divided into columns as passages are in many Bibles and note that there are numbers printed next to the lines so we can refer to the lines by number.	t/c	str	la	format
8	Teacher:	Now, look at the first two paragraphs and notice the numbers by each line and notice some differences between pidgin and the way you write English and speak English.	t/c	sol		
9	Class:	(Look at these paragraphs:)	c/t	res	ld + la	dialects format
	(1)	An de Lawd, He done go work hard for make all				
	(2)	ting dey call um Earth. For six day de Lawd He work				
	(3)	an he make all ting—everyting He go put for Earth.				
	(4)	Plenty beef, plenty cassava, plenty banana, plenty				
	(5)	yam, plenty guinea corn, plenty mango, plenty ground-				
	(6)	nut—everyting. An for de wata He put plenty fish,				
	(7)	an for de air He put plenty kinda bird.				
	(8)	After six day de Lawd He done go sleep. An				
	(9)	when He sleep, plenty palaver start for dis place				
	(10)	dey callum Heaven. Dis Heaven be place where we go				
	(11)	live after we done die, if we no been so-so bad for dis				
	(12)	Earth.				
10	Teacher:	Now, in the next few lines, there is some reported speech and some actual quotes. Read the lines and write down the way the language is being used in these comments—whether to regulate, to imagine, to be social, or for some other reason.	t/c	sol		
11	Class:	(Look at these paragraphs:)	c/t + x	res	lf	functions
	(13)	De headman of dem angels, dey call um Gabriel.				
	(14)	When dis palaver start for Heaven there be plenty				

EXCERPT 11–1 *(continued)*

		Communications	*Source/ Target*	*Move Type*		*Content*
		humbug by bad angel, dey call um Lucifer. An Gabriel done catch Lucifer an go beat um. An palaver stop, one time. An de Lawd tell Gabriel he be good man too much an He go dash Gabriel one trumpet. An Lucifer go for hellfire where he be headman now. After, de Lawd done go look um dis ting dey call um Earth an He savvy dat no man be for seat. So de Lawd take small piece earth and He go breathe—an man day. An de Lawd He go call dis man Adam. De Lawd He say: "Adam, you see dis garden? Dey call um Paradise. Everyting for dis garden be for you. But dem mango tree that be for middle garden dat no be for you. Dat tree be white man chop, dat no be black man chop. You no go chop um or you get plenty pain for belly. You savvy?" —From John Gunther, *Inside Africa*				
12	Teacher:	Name some.	t/c	sol		
13	Student:	"You no go chop um" is regulatory.	s/t	res	lf	functions
14	Teacher:	Tell me a few things about the passage that make it different from a short story.	t/c	sol		
15	Student:	It fits on one page—shorter than a story.	s_2/t	res	lj	genres
16		It has no developed characters—it's a tale.	s_2/t	res	lj	genres
17	Teacher:	Underline the articles in first 12 lines.	t/c	sol		
18	Students:	(most underline *de*, some, incorrectly, underline *an* as well)	c/t	res	lxf	grammar: form function word
19	Teacher:	What is the form of the third person singular in the passage?	t/c	sol		

EXCERPT 11–1 (*continued*)

		Communications	*Source/ Target*	*Move Type*	*Content*	
20	Student:	The base form—no *s* suffix.	s/t	res	lxi	grammar: form inflections
21	Teacher:	What is the position of *no*?	t/c	sol		
22	Student:	It's usually before the verb.	s/t	res	lxw	grammar: form word order
23	Teacher:	What is the tense of this: He done go work hard in line (1)?	t/c	sol		
24	Student:	Past.	s/t	res	lz	grammar: meaning
25	Teacher:	Draw a groundnut.	t/c	sol		
26	Student:	(Draws a shape like a figure eight.)	s/t	res	ll	lexis: literal
27	Teacher:	Does "white man chop" in lines (29) and (30) mean forbidden food or food made and grown by white men?	t/c	sol		
28	Student:	Forbidden fruit.	s/t	res	ln	lexis: nonliteral
29	Teacher:	Turn your passages over, and spell these words: *cassava, yam, guinea, palaver.*	t/c	sol		
30	Student:	c-a-s-s-a-v-a	s_1/t	res	lm	mechanics
31	Student:	j-a-m	s_2/t	res	lm	mechanics
32	Teacher:	Try a *y.*	t/s_2	rea	lm	mechanics
33	Teacher:	Now, look at these lines, and write the words that are capitalized other than those that start a sentence.				
34	Class:	(Looks at the following lines and writes words.) (32) An Adam he say: "Yessah Lawd, I savvy." (33) Later comes the fall: (34) Den de Lawd done come back for Earth and (35) He go call Adam. But Adam he no be for seat. (36) He go fear de Lawd an done go for bush, one	c/t	res	lq	punctuation

EXCERPT 11–1 (*continued*)

		Communications	*Source/ Target*	*Move Type*	*Content*	
		time. Again, de Lawd call: "Adam" An Adam he say with small voice: "Yessah Lawd." An de Lawd He say, "Close me, Adam, close me." An Adam he close de Lawd. De Lawd say: "Wassa matta, Adam, why you go for bush?" An Adam say: "I get no cloth Lawd, so I no want dat you done see me naked." An de Lawd He be vex too much. He say: "What ting dis—who tell you no be naked?" Den He say: "Ah ha, you done go chop dem mango from tree for middle garden." An Adam say: "I no chop um Lawd. Dem woman you done make for me, she go put um for groundnut stew." Den de Lawd He make plenty palaver an He done drove Adam and Eva from Paradise. —From John Gunther, *Inside Africa*				
35	Teacher:	Who do you think the audience would be for this dialect of English?	t/c	sol		
36	Student:	Maybe those who haven't been to school or go to schools in poor sections.	s/t	res	lr	register
37	Teacher:	In the spaces next to the lines, draw stick figures with names to show the chronological development of the passage—put days of the week or dates to show the chronology too.	t/c	sol		
38	Students:	(Draw stick figures and put numbers next to lines to show chronological organization.)	c/t	res	le	rhetoric
39	Teacher:	Say whether I'm blending these words or saying them with clear distinctions between them: *I get no cloth Lawd* *IgetnoclothLawd*	t/c	sol		
40	Student:	First one is not blended or reduced.	s/t	res	lsb	sound blending
41	Teacher:	Make the sound the article starts with in this passage.	t/c	sol		
42	Student:	/d/	s/t	res	lsg	sound segment
43	Teacher:	What letter signals that the *r* is not to be pronounced in the proper name of God?	t/c	sol		

EXCERPT 11–1 (*continued*)

		Communications	*Source/ Target*	*Move Type*	*Content*	
44	Student:	*a* and *w*	s/t	res	lsl	sound sound/ letter
45	Teacher:	Draw large boxes and small ones to show which syllables in the words I say receive heavy and weak stress. *palaver*	t/c	sol		
46	Student:	(Draws □ ▯ ▭ .)	s/t	res	lsp	sound supra-segmental
47	Teacher:	Take this sock, and holding it next to this diagram of the mouth, tongue, teeth and lips, move it to show where it should be for the initial sounds for these words: *de, palaver, Dem, trumpet*	t/s	sol		
48	Student:	(Moves sock on hand to appropriate places on diagram.)	s/t	res	lh	speech production
49	Teacher:	How would you characterize the style of this passage? Serious or humorous?	t/s	sol		
50	Student:	Humorous.	s/t	res	lk	style and usage
51	Teacher:	Draw arrows from the connecting words in sentences that are tied to other sentences. For example, in line (23), *So* connects or serves as transition for the previous sentences. Connect it to the sentence it is related to, and draw lines from other similar words.	t/c	sol		
52	Student:	(Draws a line from *So* on line (23) to *He savvy dat no man be for seat.*)	s/t	res	lt	cohesion
53	Teacher:	What is inappropriate about this sentence, given this variation of Genesis? [line (23)] *So de Lawd take small piece earth and He created man day.*	t/c	sol		
54	Student:	*Created.*	s/t	res	lv	collocation
55	Teacher:	Are the yams mentioned here the same ones you eat at Thanksgiving?	t/c	sol		
56	Student:	No. These are white and much larger.	s/t	res	lwa	ways of life actual
57	Teacher:	I think you can see from reading this passage that our ways of thinking about creation are affected by the ways we live, think and feel.	t/c	str	lwi	ways of life interpretive

EXCERPT 11–1 *(continued)*

		Communications	*Source/ Target*	*Move Type*		*Content*
58		Now, for homework, read the passage again.	t/c	sol		
59	Class:	(Read the passage for homework.)	c/t	res	lu	unspecified

The purpose of Excerpt 11–1 has been to illustrate how any subcategory of the *study of language* can be attributed to a passage, or any other *set*, not to advocate changing the subcategories of the *study of language* in every move. What content should be attributed to a *set* can be decided on the basis of present proportions, frequency, and intensity of errors in each subcategory and course purposes. But if nothing else, attributing all subcategories of the *study of language* to the same passage highlights the fact that knowing a language means more than knowing grammar. To make sense out of anything we take in, we seek information from as many aspects of language as we can. The range of content attributed to the pidgin version of Genesis also serves as an alternative to the common practice of devoting nine out of ten questions about a passage to vocabulary—*ll: lexis: literal* or *ln: lexis: nonliteral* or to meaning—*lu: study of language unspecified.*

Show the Yam—Attributing Content to *Nonlinguistic* and *Paralinguistic* Mediums

Just as the bulk of questions in many reading classes would be coded *ll, ln* or *lu*, since they concentrate on vocabulary or meaning in general that requires knowledge of, say, a few subcategories combined, so the bulk of many questions in classes where nonlinguistic visual mediums are used would be coded *ll: lexis literal*. In my experience, this is true because when we employ objects or pictures in a class, we usually ask people to name items.

But an object such as a plastic snake can be used not only to illustrate what the word *snake* refers to, it can also be used to communicate other subcategories of the *study of language*. When a student says "He has four book," one could hold up a plastic snake as a reminder to add the siblant, *s*. Snakes hiss, after all. Or, if one wants words inverted, as after a person says "You do understand?" meaning "Do you understand?" one can shape the snake like the symbol used for inverting: ~. Doing this attributes content to the snake I'd code *lxw: grammar word order*. Contrasting a snake with a plastic crab, one could illustrate paragraphs that were direct with those that were going in many directions. In this case, I would attribute the content *le, rhetoric*, to the two objects. Whether attributing content to objects other than *ll* would lead to confusion or the development of many separate associations, one cannot say until one has tried the alternative by breaking the normal rule: attributing only lexical content to *nonlinguistic visual* mediums.

The content of paralinguistic visual mediums tends to be constant too. Some teachers point over their shoulder with their thumb as if they were trying to hitch a ride to indicate past tense, thus attributing *lz, grammar meaning*, to the gesture. One could also shake one's fist after a student said "sink" for *zinc* or "pick" for *bic*—the name of a brand of ballpoint pens. The shaking fist would indicate that the initial sounds should be voiced, thus attributing the content *lsg, sound segmental*, to them. Or the fingers of the hand can stand for details in a paragraph and the thumb can stand for the main idea, and thus be coded *le* for *rhetoric*. Rather than suggesting that teachers get their fingers out of joint or be accused of being contortionists, I am simply reminding readers that the mediums in column 3 in the table on the last page of the book can be combined with many subcategories of the *study of language*, not just those they are usually combined with, so that all will remember that one of the purposes of FOCUS is to generate alternatives.

Journal Entry

In most dictionaries, diagrams are used to communicate lexical meaning. Thus, a picture of a mushroom will accompany a definition. To communicate pronunciation, phonetic spelling is used, and print is used to communicate all other areas of content.

As you compare dictionaries, see not only the extent to which sketches are limited to lexis, but also which other subcategories of the study of language are treated in different dictionaries, and which areas are ignored. Discovering the areas ignored would provide you with an opportunity to develop a dictionary which did what no other ones do.

As you browse through different dictionaries, note some of your findings here, and perhaps speculate on why some areas are always covered and others always ignored.

III. CONGRUENCE, INTEGRATION, AND ATTENTION—PURPOSES FOR CODING SUBCATEGORIES OF THE STUDY OF LANGUAGE

On the surface, determining the areas of content to teach or learn seems easy. It is just a matter of congruence between student needs, determined by errors or observed problems, and teacher lessons. If a student has difficulty with sound, treat sounds: *ls*. If a student doesn't know individual word meanings, treat lexis: *ll*. If a student continually leaves off the third-person singular inflection on verbs, teach *es* so that *he go* will become *he goes: lxi*—grammar form signaled by inflections.

Such one-to-one congruence implies that the subcategories of the *study of language* are separate and in no way interrelated. In fact, separate areas of content that make up languages probably are interrelated, perhaps explaining the frequency of *lu: study of language unspecified*. Thus, telling a student about the position of his or her teeth—*lh: speech production*—may as likely alter pronunciation as multiple rules, labels, or repetitions of the sound itself: *ls—sound*. In Excerpt 11–1, literal meaning of an individual word such as *cassava* is aided by knowing the story occurs in the tropics: *lc—context*. The literal meaning of *dash* might be guessed by knowing that after a good task is performed in many places, a reward is given: *lwa—ways of life*. The tense of verbs in pidgin is as likely to be figured out from the fact that stories tell what happened—*lj: genre*—or the *context—lc*—showing pictures with no current items in them, as from the form of the verbs: *lxf* or *lxi*. The spelling of *the* as *de* and *Lord* as *Lawd—lm*—in Excerpt 11–1 is as likely to help pronunciation as stress on the sounds of the words themselves: *ls* (though the fact that *Chicago* is closer to the pronunciation of *Shacago* reminds us of the problem of depending on mechanics—*lm*—to aid pronunciation in all cases).

To put it another way, teaching separate subcategories of the *study of language* based on congruence with student needs might have to be juxtaposed with the integration of separate areas of content. If areas of content are consistently taught separately on a one-to-one correspondence between class material and student needs, try the opposite: integrating separate areas of content.

Another reason integration might be tried is that the use of two separate subcategories can draw attention away from a problem area. When students know we're working on grammar—*lx*—as in "There aren't any books here," they often remember to produce the utterance correctly. Outside of the class, when the attention is shifted to actual books and away from form, students often falter. By using different objects in class, and thus shifting attention from *lx* to *ll*, it is possible less faltering will take place. Constant shifts between different subcategories of language being focused on and on others than distract is an alternative to try if moves tend consistently to focus on only one subcategory of content at a time. [Background 11–3]

Still another reason for trying to integrate separate areas of the subcategories of the study of language is that the boundaries between the subcategories overlap. Though theoretically we may pick up grammmatical signals from something we hear or read to understand it, we probably pick up grammatical signals plus lexical or contextual signals at the same time. We may understand *groundnut* because we are reading about the tropics—context—or because we know British English—dialect—or because we know what ingredients go into stews in parts of Africa—ways of life. In deciphering a secret code, codebreakers use many different signals that they pick up. In the same way, as we try to understand, we receive signals from many subcategories of the study of language. Which ones we pick up is not an easy task to determine. But asking questions to lead students to notice both separate subcategories and the integration between pairs of subcategories will remind them that, if they fail to follow something because they don't pick up the signals communicated by, say, grammar, they need to feel free to pick up signals from context and style, or grammar and sound, or other combinations that together make meaning clear.

IV. TRENDS—CHANGING AREAS OF CONTENT

One way to look at language teaching trends is to explore the subcategories of the *study of language* advocated by different schools. Grammar translation emphasized the meaning of grammar—*lz*—and literal and nonliteral lexis *ll* and *ln*. Audiolingual advocates substituted the form of grammar, *lx*, for meaning, *lz*. And they substituted sound and speech production—*ls* and *lh*—for *lexis ll*. Realizing that context affects meaning, some introduced situational language teaching, thus highlighting *context: lc*. English for specific purposes not only stresses the need to integrate the study of language with the study of other subjects, but considers *functions* as important, if not more so, than grammar.

Realizing that we need to teach and learn many subcategories of the *study of language* frees us from the endless wild swings of the pendulum from one subcategory to another. It also means that no matter what methods school a text was developed for, we can adapt it by attributing any areas of content we want to *sets* and other uses in a text.

Whether attention to many subcategories of the study of language rather than a selected few will decrease or increase the "I didn't do well in high school English" syndrome, perhaps at the least, future guests we party with will at least attribute their dislike of language study to a wider range of subcategories. Then, at least, the conversation can be varied with some feeling weak in functions, some in speech production, others in rhetoric, still others in ways of life and even a few left from the good old days who feel totally inadequate in grammar or style and usage. [Background 11–4]

Should you be particularly interested in either *lc: context*, or *lw: ways of life*, skip to Episode 9 or Episode 13.

Journal Entry

Next time you go out to eat, ask to keep the menu after you order so that you can attribute areas of content to it to kill the time while waiting for your order to come. Does the menu format—*la*—correspond with the atmosphere of the restaurant—*lc*? Does your knowledge of the actual ways of life of eaters of the food in the particular restaurant—*lwa*—aid you in guessing what some names of foods mean—*ll*?

What other subcategories of the study of language can you attribute to communications on the menu?

BACKGROUND NOTES

11–1. A quick look at most textbooks will show that grammar is emphasized more than most other things that are related to language study. Tests, too, tend to emphasize grammar, especially most of the standardized tests. The miscue analysis work that Goodman and his associates have done is based on a taxonomy that also emphasizes the grammatical aspects of language, though others are referred to. A survey of this taxonomy, as reported in the work edited by P. David Allen, shows a heavy emphasis on word order and word endings in looking at miscues native speakers make.

I don't think grammar is going to go away in spite of my pleas in this episode. What I would urge is that if you are interested in a very different kind of grammar, one designed with teaching in mind, a very exciting grammar is *Sector analysis*, developed by Robert L. Allen and used in a series of texts by Malkemes and Pires.

11–2. The idea that one of the criteria for materials for teaching language should be that they not be especially prepared for teaching language is one advocated by Allwright. His plea was printed in a book edited by Brumfit and Johnson, which emphasized the communicative approach to language teaching.

11–3. In his methods book, Robert Lado makes the point that it is critical to distract the student from the problem area in any kind of a drill. If the student is not drawn away from the problem area with a contrasting pattern, Lado contends that he will be unable to master the pattern under study. For example, if one was teaching a sentence such as "I speak English," one of the things the student will say is "I speak the English." Consequently, Lado would urge that the sentences "I speak the English language" and "I speak English" be taught at the same time so that the student is forced to make the correct contrast between the two forms.

11–4. One way to look at the history of language teaching is to look at shifts in the area of content that have been emphasized. Reading Kelly's *History of language teaching* with this idea in mind would give a very different view to his history; the same is true for Howatt's history.

EPISODE

12

It Goes In the Other Way

I. HOW TO SHOCK YOUR FRIENDS—INTRODUCTION

Though the referent for *It* in the title—the use *set* in FOCUS—may have been different for you than for me, I'm sure that you have been told "It goes in the other way" at least once during your life. For me, the comment—the use *characterize examine* because it provides explicit information about space—has been most frequent when I put keys in unfamiliar locks on doors. For you, maybe the *set* has been a pair of binoculars you were trying to put in a binocular case or a screw into a nut. But whatever the *set* was, no matter what the setting was, I'm sure that you heard "It goes in the other way" at the exact moment I always hear it: as soon as we discover on our own that in fact the *set* we are putting in something needs to be put in the other way.

I treat feedback in this episode. In dictionaries published twenty years ago, *feedback* was defined only in relationship to the field of electronics. Today, though the term is used in many fields, its early meaning in relation to electronics is retained. Just as electronic waves that returned to the source of transmission to confirm the accuracy of the transmission or adjust it were labeled *feedback* in the early definition, so communications that are made with the intention of confirming the accuracy of previous communications or of causing adjustments of them can be considered feedback.

This episode is unique because I do not compare teaching and nonteaching settings. I don't because I believe that whenever feedback is provided, the setting becomes a teaching setting. By definition, to teach is to provide feedback. To generate alternative ways of providing feedback, we must depend on substituting different elements from FOCUS, rather than searching for them in nonteaching settings. [Background 12–1]

After this introduction, I explore how uses other than *characterize examine* can provide feedback so that you can decrease the frequency of saying "It goes in the other way." In Section III, I show how to identify the source of the feedback and the medium it is communicated in. I also explore ways to identify what move type is communicated.

In Section IV, I explore content in feedback. And in Section V, I make a few concluding remarks and provide some excerpts for you to code.

Since I treat the major categories of all five characteristics of FOCUS and some subcategories, there is no need for a separate table to highlight the elements I am treating. The table inside the front cover shows the major categories, and the table on the last page of the book shows the subcategories that I mention.

II. IN AND OUT ARE DIFFERENT—USES IN LANGUAGE CLASSROOMS AND OTHER TEACHING SETTINGS

A frequent alternative to *characterize examine* in a language classroom after a miss—a task that is performed differently from expected, or with an error—is the use *set.* After a student fails to perform a task, the correct answer is usually given. After asking one student to ask another how old the other is, the response "How old you are?" is often followed by "How old are you?" uttered by the teacher, for example. If we were to employ this use when someone didn't put a key in right, we would simply demonstrate the way the key should go in by modeling rather than by making the comment "It goes in the other way."

In Excerpt 12–1, I illustrate how different mediums can be used differently to provide feedback. As you can see, all the examples are attempts to treat the same miss—the failure of one person to open a lock on the first try with an unfamiliar key or lock. I call the person unfamiliar with the key or lock the *guest* and the person who knows how to open the lock, whether that person is an older brother, bellhop, parent, or real estate agent, *host.*

What I have illustrated in Excerpt 12–1 is how mediums can be used to provide feedback in any of the ways FOCUS identifies in the use column. Just as you can put all types of tasks in responses into one of the six major categories of *use,* so in providing feedback in terms of *FOCUS,* you have only six major options. You can do nothing, allowing the person to simply try again—attending. Attending is not ignoring errors or even correct responses. It is simply taking in what students do and allowing them time to alter what they have done or decide that what they have done is correct, rather than leading them to expect that someone else will always make comments about what they do instead of allowing them to establish their own standards. [Background 12–2]

Should you decide to do something, either after you have *attended* or before, you can provide information about performances by *characterizing* or *relating*. Relating requires generalizations or rules. *Characterizing* requires that we indicate sameness or differences, correctness or incorrectness, size, other characteristics, or a label. Or you can give the right answer by providing a *set.* Or, you can imitate what has been done by *reproducing*. Making a statement or setting the task again are also possible, *presenting.* If you believe that knowledge of results is important, you will probably decide to *characterize* or *relate.* If you believe that praise is important, you will probably *characterize evaluate* to indicate the person did a fine job, not that the response was correct. If you believe in the value of modeling, you will provide a *set* or *reproduce.* If you believe learners must know on their own how to correct, you will *attend* and *present.* Of course, these six major options are expanded tremendously when we use subcategories of uses or when we describe the uses in terms of source and target, move type, medium, and content. [Background 12–3]

As I said earlier, in my observations in language classrooms, *set* is as frequent as

EXCERPT 12–1
Uses Outside Language Classrooms

			Source/ Target	Use
1	Guest:	(Tries to insert a key in a lock, but holds the key upside down.)	s/o & t	
2	Host:	(Does nothing—simply waits in silence.)	t/s	a
3		There's a different way to do it.	t/s	cd
4		(Shakes head sideways.)	t/s	ce
5		It goes in the other way.	t/s	cx
6		Interesting lock.	t/s	ci
7		It's a skeleton key.*	t/s	cl
8		I have trouble with that lock too.	t/s	ps
9		Try again.	t/s	pe or pq
10		When you try a new lock, always look at the key and lock first. When the smallest opening in the lock is at the bottom, the thin part of the key needs to point towards the ground or floor.	t/s	re
11		(Puts the key in upside down, imitating the guest.)	t/s	ds
12		(With another key, or the same key, demonstrates the way the key fits into the lock.)	t/s	se

* If a person knew that nine times out of ten or more skeleton keys always had the bit hanging down, this label could provide useful information.

characterize examine is when I try opening an unfamiliar lock. I find that giving the right answer is not very much affected by one's occupation. I once flew to a city in Canada called Regina. On the way there, I had to ask at least four separate airline agents this question: "Excuse me, which gate should I go to for Regina?" I pronounced the second syllable so that it rhymed with *gene*. The correct pronunciation, I learned, is for the second syllable to rhyme with *fine*. The first time I asked, I was of course unaware of how the name was expected to be pronounced. The agent said "Regina," with the *fine* pronunciation. In my subsequent questions, I kept my original pronunciation, and each agent said the name of the city correctly after my error. I can't imagine that airlines have training in error treatment for their agents! What the consistent treatment simply means is that one rule of correcting mistakes is to provide the correct answer. When I mispronounce a student's name, the student always gives me the right pronunciation rather than giving me a clue about the pronunciation, such as "the stress is on the second syllable." In scores of classes I have been in, when one student misses an answer, another student is ready to give the right answer, setting content in FOCUS.

Of course, providing a *set* such as *Regina* rather than giving some information about one's error, such as "shorter sound in the second syllable," might give the illusion of a high success rate if you can get the person to imitate or repeat the *set* immediately. But whether changing all tasks into *reproduce same medium*, subcategory *imitate*, has any long-lasting effect is open to question. Obviously, if someone simply has me imitate his or her steps, whether I am trying to open a door or say the name of a city, I can do it at the moment I am asked to. But just because I can *reproduce* a *set* does not mean that I have gained the ability to do the original task, either on my own or with other types of feedback.

The words *very good* or *OK* are as frequent after correct performances as *sets* are after incorrect performances, either complete *sets* or partial *sets*, such as one word of the expected answer that was wrong. The rule to say "very good" or "OK" after another person performs is learned very early. I have observed 4-year-olds playing school who say "very good" or "OK" after every response, whether the response is correct or not. When asked why they say these words whether a task is performed well or not, the youngsters are likely to answer that this is what their teachers do. Coding these words *characterize evaluate* in all cases implies that the words communicate more than they do. In fact, "very good" and "OK" often simply mean that the teacher is ready for another person to perform. I once observed some small children being taught for the first time by a teacher from Italy who said "One, two, three, bravo" as she had the children do some dance steps. After the class, the children asked me why the teacher had called them all "bravo" rather than by their regular names. Obviously, "bravo" was not an instance of *characterize evaluate* to these children. And *very good* and *OK* often fill the same use; they simply provide transition. I code these words *ps* for *present state* as frequently as I code them *characterize evaluate*. No matter which way you decide to code them, one central question to explore is the extent to which these types of comments serve to keep control and limit the length of student responses. There is some evidence that in fact these types of comments serve to keep students quiet and keep them from communicating, rather than serving to encourage them to communicate. [Background 12–4]

The *very good* and *OK* so frequent after correct responses are not usually juxtaposed with *very bad* or *no* after incorrect responses. After incorrect responses, a repetition of the error with rising intonation or stress on the offending element is common. When a student is asked to name an apple a teacher is holding and the student says *cherry*, the teacher is likely to look puzzled and repeat the student response as a question: "Cherry?" In a larger group of words, the teacher is likely to stress the offending element, as in "*A* apple?" I have put some typical examples in Excerpt 12–2. It is hard to capture the exact tone of voice and intonation and stress in print. But both trained teachers and ordinary citizens treat errors in the same way. They *reproduce* the response in the same medium: *ds*. Then, along with the words they *reproduce*, they use their tone of voice to indicate astonishment or other personal feelings, or a tinge of criticism or complaint. Some seem to be saying "How stupid you are" with the *paralinguistic aural* medium. This use of the *paralinguistic aural medium* to *present state* is sometimes communicated together with *characterize examine* with the stress on the offending element. The stress is used to indicate the location of the error.

Reactions like *no* or *It's wrong* are as rare after errors as *very good* and *OK* are common after both correct responses and errors. Why *ds* + *ps* or *ds* + *ps* + *cx* are used after errors rather than *ce* is worth a moment's consideration. One reason for this may be that teachers think students know that a particular stress or intonation indicates when their performances are not right. Or one might argue that saying "No"

EXCERPT 12–2
You're Kidding

		Communications	*Use*
1	Teacher:	What's this? (Holds up an apple.)	
2	Student:	Cherry.	
3	Teacher:	Cherry?!	ds_{ix}* + ps
4	Student:	A apple.	
5	Teacher:	*A* apple??!	ds_{ix}* + ps + cx

* The *ix* subscript indicates that the error is intentional.

together with "It goes in the other way" would not be necessary, since the words themselves indicate something is wrong. Another argument against using "No" might be that a negative *characterize evaluate* may be discouraging or even insulting. If *ce* is seen as a judgment of a person or a person's ability, then a *ce* may be discouraging. But *ce* can also provide information, which need not be considered a judgment. Considered as information, a "No" is as useful as "Yes." And a "No," even if it is a judgment rather than just information, as when a parent says "No!!!" as a child is taking another cookie from the jar, is hardly less insulting than the classic "*A* apple??!" [Background 12–5]

One way to cushion a negative *ce* with those not used to the use of "No" or a sideways shaking head would be to get people used to receiving information by differentiating. I overheard this conversation at a flower show:

SARA: I think it's a violet.

KAREN: Violets don't have leaves like that. *cd*

But maybe it's a different species. *cd*

I'd code Karen's two comments as *characterize differentiate*. It is unlikely that Sara still thinks the flowers are violets because of the information Karen gave. Once a person realizes that mistakes are normal and that we learn from them, *ce* can be substituted for *cd* and the consequences compared. If a person stops performing after a *ce* has been used, a substitute for "No" might be necessary. On the other hand, unless "No" is said, or indicated by shaking the head or in some other way, students will never experience it, and so when they do they may be shocked. If "No" were as common as "OK" or "Cherry??!" it is hard to imagine anyone being shocked by it. It would just seem a natural thing to say when a performance was not correct just as if you ask someone for change and the person responds "No." If nothing else, the substitution of "No" for "Very good" or "OK" or "*A* apple??!"—*ds* + *ps* + *cx*—after a performance that was not correct might decrease the development of what some have called "praise addiction." [Background 12–6]

I've illustrated some uses in Excerpt 12–3. I have selected lessons that do not involve language teaching to highlight how mediums provide feedback and to show how central feedback is to all teaching.

EXCERPT 12–3
Two Lessons (T)

		Communications	*Use*
Setting 1:		The front seat of a car during a driving lesson. The driver is learning to drive. The other person in the front seat is the driver trainer; they are not related by blood or marriage (and, indeed, if the teacher were a spouse, divorce might be the next step).	
1	Driver trainer:	Put your indicator on and turn.	
2	Driver:	(Turns corner.)	
3	Driver trainer:	That was good.	ce
4	Driver:	I go left here?	
5	Driver trainer:	Yeah.	
6		So, go over to the left lane.	
7	Driver:	(Moves to left lane.)	
8		I can go right through?	
9	Driver trainer:	No!	
10		Break your speed, break your speed. There's a car coming. My God! Turn now!	
11	Driver:	(Turns very quickly in front of oncoming car.)	
12	Driver trainer:	That wasn't too good.	ce
13	Driver:	Didn't I have the right of way?	
14	Driver trainer:	No.	
15		You can't turn like that. Whenever you're turning across the traffic, you have to yield, unless the car is far enough back that you can make the turn safely.	
16		Turn at the next stop sign.	
17	Driver:	(Turns after making a stop.)	
18	Driver trainer:	That was a little wide.	cx
19	Driver:	Um-humm.	
Setting 2:		A tennis court. A pro helping a player with her serve.	
20	Pro:	Ideally, you want to throw more to the left. (Said after a serve.)	
21		Try again.	

EXCERPT 12–3 (*continued*)

		Communications	*Use*
22	Player:	(Tosses the ball and serves it.)	
23		(Ball goes out of serving area.)	
24	Pro:	That was a little too far in front.	cx
25		Try again.	
26	Player:	(Tosses the ball and serves it again.)	
27		(Ball goes out of serving area.)	
28	Pro:	Again.	
29	Player:	(Tosses the ball and serves it.)	
30		(Ball lands in the serving area.)	
31	Pro:	Not too bad.	ce/ps
32	Player:	(Serves again.)	
33		(Ball lands in the serving area.)	
34	Pro:	That was good!	ce
35	Player:	(Serves again.)	
36		(Ball hits the net.)	
37		(Grimaces.)	ce
38	Pro:	That was too low.	cx
39		You have to serve it higher.	cx
40		(Demonstrates a serve.)	se
41	Player:	(Imitates the serve.)	
42	Pro:	That was a good serve.	ce
43	Player:	(Smiles.)	
44		(Serves again.)	
45		(Ball goes out of serving area.)	
46		Oh, too high this time.	cx
47		Darn it!	ce
48		Am I bending too much?	
49	Pro:	No.	
50		Bending has nothing to do with the serve.	

III. LOCKS HELP TOO—SOURCE AND TARGET, MEDIUM, AND MOVE TYPE OF FEEDBACK

Beyond People—Source and Target of Feedback

As teachers, we usually think of ourselves or our students as the only sources of feedback. But when I try unlocking a lock, I get feedback from the lock as well as from the person who snickers "It goes in the other way" over my shoulder. In fact, one of the reasons I think we sometimes get impatient with comments others make is that at the exact moment that the lock, or the binocular case, or the nut is indicating we need to alter what we are doing, we are provided a second source of feedback. Just as a source I code *o* for *other* gives us feedback, the source I code *t* does too!

Many a crash would take place if we all waited for a teacher to provide feedback. In the driving lesson in Excerpt 12–3, it was not just the words of the driving teacher, but also the street and sidewalk, the lines on the street, the oncoming car and the stop sign that provided feedback for the driver. When we play the piano, the noise from the wrong note we play is as much feedback as the teacher's comment "C, not B," or the teacher's rapping of our knuckles with a ruler. As we fall to the side on a bicycle, our loss of balance is as likely to cause us to shift our weight and increase our speed as "You're falling," shouted by either a teacher or a peer playing the role of a teacher.

Whether feedback from *o* or *t* aids our performances better needs to be explored, though, of course, we each have our preferences. What are yours? Do you get more or less nervous when you hear a comment about something that a source other than the teacher, one I'd code *o*, has already provided feedback about? I usually prefer to make use of feedback from *o* if I can. But we cannot just base what we do in our classrooms on our personal preferences. We need to compare the consequences of altering the source of feedback from a teacher, from a student, from a student playing the role of a teacher, and from materials.

Here are a few suggestions for manipulating the variable I call the source of feedback. From a distance, observe individual students doing puzzles, correcting their work, reading silently on their own, answering questions in a workbook with a key with the answers in it, or other activities in which materials themselves provide feedback. Count the number of times they seem to make errors and false starts, the number of times they adjust their work based on feedback from the pieces of the puzzle or the printed words in the materials. And count the number of times they give feedback to themselves with comments such as "Oh, darn" or "Got it," or with gestures such as the snapping of fingers or a smile or a grimace. Then, stand next to individual students and peer over their shoulders as they perform the same activities. Make comments parallel to "It goes in the other way" such as "That piece is too big; your questions are coming along fine; you didn't number all the answers." Act the same way your friends do when you put binoculars or screws in the wrong way. See if the number of errors, false starts, self-adjustments and self-feedback are greater or fewer when you are close than when you stood at a distance and allowed the materials—the source I code *o*—to provide the feedback. Finally, ask students to work in pairs, assigning one to the role of teacher. As the student playing the role of a teacher provides feedback, note the same consequences you did for other conditions and compare them. In short, compare the consequences when *t*, *s* and *o* are the source of the feedback, or different combinations of these sources.

Note that in making these comparisons, some students may be expecting the words "Let me do it" or "It goes in the other way" if you stay close to them as you observe them. When I tell my students in class we're going to have a video presentation, my question is: "Who has never put a videotape on a videotape recorder before?" A few people raise their hands. "Here, take it" I say. There are two ways the students can begin to put the tape on the tape deck. One way is with me next to them. With this method, it usually takes them five minutes. They get feedback from the tape deck, but also expect it from me since I'm so close. The other way is for me to go and do something else. In a minute, they have the tape on, obtaining the information from the tape deck alone, without any expectation that I'll chime in with "It goes in the other way."

The advice is given in some circles to have fellow students provide feedback, substituting say s_t for either *t* or *o*. No doubt those students who always know the right answer revel in being able to tell their peers such information as "It goes in the other way." But you have to wonder how the student receiving the feedback feels. After all, the teacher is paid to teach, and is supposed to know a lot. But if a fellow student knows a lot, those students who don't know no doubt will have a range of feelings about their lack of knowledge or skill. At any rate, if students are the source, some alternatives no doubt will appear, especially if the students are observed outside the regular classroom, where in my experience they provide feedback parallel to that of the regular teacher. In Excerpt 12–4, you can see that when a peer assumes the role of teacher, the classic teacher feedback "*A* apple??!" sounds like a compliment. Peers are hard on each other in my experience, not accepting many deviations from group norms. The type of dress worn, especially by teens, is determined by the group, not by adults, and least of all by parents and teachers. [Background 12–7]

Of course, the consequences of comparing the source of feedback will probably vary

EXCERPT 12–4
You Dumb (T)

		Communications	*Source/Target*
Setting:		The living room of an apartment. Two 4-year-old boys are sitting on the floor next to a table on which they have just been playing a game. After the game, the following exchange takes place.	
1	Joseph:	What you do at Janie's party?	t/s
2	Rodney:	(Tugging at the edge of his short pants as he speaks.) She had a big cake.	s/t
3	Joseph:	What kind?	t/s
4	Rodney:	(Spreading his arms wide.) A big one.	s/t
5	Joseph:	What kind of a big one?	t/s
6	Rodney:	(Emphatically.) A real big one!	s/t
7	Joseph:	(Looking a bit perplexed.) What color were it?	t/s
8	Rodney:	(Touching his lips with wandering fingertips.) What color were it?	s_1/s_1
9		Green.	s/t
10	Joseph:	(Waving his hand disdainfully.) Aw, you dumb. They ain't no green cakes.	t/s

from activity to activity and from student to student. A piece of a jigsaw puzzle that does not fit may provide clearer feedback than a printed word that is misread. Some students may feel the need for a teacher to be close by, making comments. Others may reject a teacher's comments but welcome those of their peers. Still others will resent a peer's comments, especially if the peer is of a different sex. Though proving that one source is always the best one is an unlikely outcome of your exploration, by looking at different sources and combinations of sources you will have to alter the sources. And you may find that the whims, habits, or prescriptions you have been basing your feedback on provided less information than the observed consequences of your exploration.

Red, Green, or Yellow—Different Mediums Can Provide Feedback

The fact that materials can be the source of feedback as well as a teacher or a student reminds us that mediums other than our own speech can communicate feedback. In one of my high school English classes, the teacher, Miss Casey, rigged up a traffic light in front of each row. As she called on one of us in a row, we'd stand up. If our response was wrong, she would press a button that turned on the red light in front of the row one of us was in. If our response was partly right and partly wrong, she would turn the yellow light on. When we were right, the green light would light, and the next student in the row would stand up. At the time, I never thought I'd use the lights as a classic example of characterizing by evaluating with a nonlinguistic visual medium. But in fact, this is what Miss Casey did: *nv ce.*

More common examples of feedback provided by a range of mediums abound. Drivers honk at each other—*nonlinguistic aural.* Crying babies are quieted by a touch—*paralinguistic other.* Red lights—*nonlinguistic visual*—blink when you misuse many copying machines. Audiences cheer after a good performance in some countries, whistle in others, clap in others, and remain silent in some. Whether one should provide feedback with a *nonlinguistic aural* medium or silence is obviously important at public performances.

The pervasive use of *nonlinguistic aural* mediums to provide feedback after dances, concerts and sports events that people consider good is equaled by the use of a nonlinguistic visual medium to provide feedback after people do things that are considered bad. The nonlinguistic visual medium I refer to is the stick or paddle. From Proverbs, these statements are known to many: "He that spareth his rod hateth his son; but he that loveth him chasteneth him betimes; foolishness is found in the heart of a child; but the rod of correction shall drive it from him; withhold not correction from the child; for if thou beatest him with the rod he shall not die" (13:24; 22:15; 23:13). Quaint as the advice may sound to some, the provision of feedback with this *nonlinguistic visual* medium is a central issue around the world. In the United States, the issue of corporal punishment in schools has been argued in the Supreme Court. By substituting another kind of *nonlinguistic visual* medium—food—for paddles, the behaviorists, in their experiments provide a different conceptualization of feedback. So we can now talk about the carrot and the stick when discussing feedback, rather than just the stick. [Background 12–8]

As usual, I am not advocating that one medium is better for providing feedback than another. But I am arguing that we should investigate the consequences of the various prescriptions we hear all the time. For example, the prescription that students should only hear words and never see them written had to have been made by those who did not systematically study the consequences of different mediums in a range of settings. Go to a ticket window at a large railroad station or airline terminal. Observe how many times most passengers repeat their destinations to the clerks. Then, go up to the same clerks with your destination written on a small card. Compare the time it takes you to get your ticket with others who depend only on spoken words—linguistic aural. Of course, the clerks will look at you strangely—providing feedback with a paralinguistic visual medium. But the linguistic visual medium will have a different consequence. In the same way, writing words on the blackboard that students say incorrectly or leave out might have different consequences from only providing the words orally—with a linguistic aural medium. And writing some of them with phonetic script—linguistic visual transcribed—is likely to have still other consequences.

When I go to a hotel where my reservation has been made by someone else, there is a sequence of communications that usually occurs, which is illustrated in Excerpt 12–5. I might also say "'That's 'F' as in 'Fred' not 'S' as in 'Sam.'" This is more effective than stressing the initial sound; I stress the *F* only to keep reminding myself of the fact that the consequences are usually not very satisfactory.

EXCERPT 12–5
Checking In (T)

		Communications	*Medium*
1	Clerk:	Can I help you?	
2	Customer:	Yes, thank you.	
3		Do you have a reservation for Fanselow?	
4	Clerk:	Sanselow?	
5		Let me check. (Checks.)	
6		I'm sorry. We have nothing listed.	
7	Customer:	*F*anselow. (With emphasis on the first sound.)	la + pa
8	Clerk:	(Checks again, still under *S*.)	
9		Sorry, not listed.	
10	Customer:	(Writes an *F* on a card.)	lv
11	Clerk:	Oh, Fanselow.	
12		(Checks under the *F*s.)	
13		Room 306.	

To start discovering the extent to which the use of different mediums produce different consequences, try these alternatives. After errors in oral work, provide the model—*set*—only in speech—*linguistic aural.* See how many tries are needed by students to produce the correct response. Then, taking a cue from observations of people in the teaching world outside a language classroom, provide the *set* only in writing—*linguistic visual.* See whether the number of tries needed by students to produce the correct response is larger or smaller than when using speech alone. Then, try doing nothing, communicating the medium of silence. Do more students chime in with the correct models to augment your feedback when you provide the answer to the erring student in speech—linguistic aural—in writing on the blackboard—linguistic visual—

or when you do nothing? If one of your desired consequences is to decrease the number of sets provided by the class to the erring student, and another desired consequence is to get the student making the error to self-correct it with the fewest number of tries, varying the mediums will alter the frequency of these consequences.

Linguistic aural mediums can also be replaced by paralinguistic mediums. If you are used to saying "Thank you, good job" after students clean up their desks properly, for example, you can switch to hugging them or shaking their hands or patting them on the shoulder. No doubt some will like paralinguistic visual mediums—a smile, a blink—some will like contact like hugging or shaking hands—paralinguistic other—and some will like spoken words—linguistic aural. But if substitutions are never made, I think the value of the communication will decrease since the medium will become predictable and perhaps so routine that it is not even noticed. [Background 12–9]

The fact that a particular medium means one thing to some and another to others needs to be remembered when substituting mediums. I remember in Somalia when I raised my eyebrows vigorously à la Groucho Marx after a student responded correctly. In my language, this gesture simply meant "Very good," and thus I intended only to *characterize evaluate* the student's response. However, the gesture in Somali meant that I was interested in an affair with the student! Alternatives may open up a whole new world.

One medium need not be substituted for another only. Mediums can be combined as well. Of course, the classic combination occurs when we stress the syllable where the error is, as when a student says "He go" and the teacher says "He go*es*," with extreme vibration of the vocal cords on the end of *goes*. In this classic communication, speech—linguistic aural—is combined with stress—paralinguistic aural—in an attempt to locate the error or imply that the person who made the error is a fool, depending on which use and area of content we determine that the mediums communicate. At any rate, the point here is simply that we can substitute, say, a nonlinguistic visual medium like a line under the inflection that was omitted. Or we can draw two lines, one for each letter. We can hold up our hand and bend down each finger one at a time to indicate each syllable that was uttered and, then, at the third finger, shake the finger rather than bend it down to indicate the location of the error. In short, we can vibrate our finger in place of our vocal cords. In fact, one central difference between teachers who have been trained to speak very little, as those prepared in the Silent Way, and those who have been trained to speak a lot, is that the oral types vibrate their vocal cords to locate errors and the silent types shake their fingers, either as the words are said or mouthed.

In teaching settings outside language classrooms, combinations of mediums are often used to provide feedback. Umpires shout "Safe" at the same time that they move their arms in a prescribed way both baseball players and fans understand. On a football field, a yellow flag is thrown in the air just before the type of violation is gestured, combining a nonlinguistic visual medium with a paralinguistic visual medium. In Excerpt 12–4, as you probably recall, Joseph accompanied his use of the word *dumb* with a hand movement: waving his hand disdainfully—*la* + *pv*.

Even when nonlinguistic aural mediums such as a horn on a car are used, paralinguistic aural mediums contribute to the communication. There are basically two kinds of car honkers. In a line of cars at a red light, the first car sometimes does not move immediately after the light turns green. The first type of driver taps the horn lightly simply to communicate to the driver in the first car that the light has changed. The second type of driver pushes the horn with great vigor over and over again, not only indicating information about the light, but also implying that the first car in the line is being driven by an idiot. "It goes in the other way," and all other oral comments, can also be communicated just with words or with accompanying emotions, expressed through the tone of voice. The extra medium of vigorous car honkers and those who feel compelled to provide oral comments with speech and a paralinguistic medium no doubt leads to a different feeling on the part of the person being honked or shouted at.

Double Duty—Determining the Move Type of Feedback

After correct moves, the move type of feedback is easy to code. For example, if you say "Very good" after a student says "an apple," the "very good" is clearly a reaction. But if a student says "a apple" and you provide the classic "*A* apple??!", you are both reacting to the response and soliciting, since you are implying that you want the student to respond again. But since the goal is to have the student respond to the original solicit correctly, I consider the feedback a reaction rather than a solicit. To show that the reaction is treating an error, I write the subscript *c* for corrective next to it. I then know that the move has qualities different from a reaction that does not imply the student is to respond again. But I consider all responses that follow corrective reactions to be responses to the initial solicit that resulted in a response with an error.

I also code feedback after structuring moves rea_c. Thus, I'd code "It goes in the other way," as well as the feedback I get from the lock itself, both as corrective reactions: rea_c. The source of the first would be *t*—the bellboy, the host, or a guard. The source of the other would be *o*—the lock itself. Corrective reactions that follow structuring moves are common in playgrounds. As a child goes into the sandbox—a structuring move—a parent corrective reaction is likely, nine times out of ten. Here's one of my favorites: "I don't allow you in the sand—*no* way!"—*t* $reaction_c$.

If a teacher reacts to an error with a clear "No" followed by a solicit such as "Now, try again," I'd code the "no" as a corrective reaction, rea_c, and the solicit as a mediating solicit, sol_m, to distinguish it from the initial solicit that was followed by the first incorrect response. If the feedback is simultaneous, provided at the same time the person is responding, as when a teacher mouths the words as another says them or signals with fingers to indicate tense, I code the reaction as both corrective and simultaneous: rea_{cs}. If you want to distinguish between immediate and delayed feedback, all you need to do is add subscripts to the moves. As usual, any features you want to add, you can.

Not all feedback consists of corrective reactions or intervening solicits, though. When the driver asked the driver trainer "Didn't I have the right of way?" in Excerpt 12–3, feedback occurred in the teacher's response. And since the turn in front of the oncoming car was completed the response was not corrective, nor was the driver's solicit. Yet because the information solicited seems to have been solicited in order to shape future action, I would consider the solicit and response feedback.

When feedback is asked for, as was the case in the driving and tennis lessons, it might be more powerful than when it is given without being asked for. And withholding feedback that is asked for might also have a more powerful negative consequence than withholding feedback that is not asked for. I once observed a girl climbing a tree while her father was walking the dog in a park. When the girl had reached the highest point in the tree, she shouted "Look at me" to her father. Rather than look, and thus provide the feedback she had requested, he said "I can't, I'm talking with the lady," referring to a woman he had just met who was also walking her dog. And the girl started to cry as a result of her father not looking at her accomplishment.

When students do ask for feedback, not only can you get a sense of what troubles them from the content of their questions, but you can also get a sampling of the language they use. If they say "How pronounce *to*?", you realize that some attention to *do* and *you* in questions is in order. "Excuse, teacher, I no understand" provides as much useful information about language that needs attention as many items on an examination. It is striking to go into many advanced classes and hear students asking basic, common questions with errors that can only raise eyebrows and cause some embarrassment when they seek feedback from some people outside of class.

If a student grimaces after he or she makes an error, as the tennis player did in Excerpt 12–3, I consider such a reaction feedback too, since the student is indicating a need to adjust the accuracy of what he or she has just done. Whether a teacher grimaces at a student after an error, or whether the student does, does not change the fact that feedback is given, only that the source is different. Likewise, a student can say "It's great" after completing a task, as well as waiting for the teacher to. One question that is worth investigating is whether a grimace about one's own error, as communicated by the tennis player, which is a sort of judgment of oneself, has a different consequence from an informative statement such as "It was low." A grimace by a tennis player made after a serve that went out of the serve area is likely to be followed by a tightening of the cheek and forearm muscles. And one wonders whether this contributes to more accuracy or less. But here, the major point is simply that a person can provide feedback to him or herself as well as to another, and that I code such feedback as a corrective reaction: s_1 to s_1 rea_c.

Not all feedback is deliberate. If students are fidgeting with their pencils and notebooks during a listening part of a lesson, or as they are reading silently, these bearing moves suggest some feelings about what they are being asked to do. Also, if a teacher is looking out the window as a student asks a question or seeks to share a problem, the lack of interest implied by the bearing move is communicating feedback. In fact, the coding of bearing moves will probably be most revealing when they are looked at as feedback.

When bearing moves suggest that all is not well, or that things seem to be going well because some students are nodding their heads a lot unconsciously during a part of a class, suggesting they are following and tuned in to what's going on, a few teacher solicits are in order. Students can be asked to translate their bearing moves made with gestures—*pv*—into responding moves made with speech—*la*. When they say what they do and don't like and why, the teacher has a chance to provide some rationale for what is being done, thus communicating content I code *procedure teaching rationale.*

Of course, we can ask for opinions about our feedback without the presence of bearing moves to remind us. After being provided with feedback such as "No" or "OK" and "*A* apple??!", students can be asked to rate each treatment. What students find helpful and like may change as more types are used and as students and teacher discuss the reasons for different types of feedback, discussions I'd code *procedure teaching rationale.* [Background 12–10]

IV. PAPER??! PRUNE??!—CONTENT IN FEEDBACK

What's Very Good or Very Bad?—Unspecified Content

Perhaps you consider it strange that I have illustrated feedback with so few examples from language classes. Well, in my observations of language classes, I have not found many examples of feedback with content I'd code differently from the way I'd code content in any other teaching setting. The ubiquitous "*A* apple??!", the right answer, and "OK very good," and their almost extinct opposites, "Very bad" or "No," are hard to determine the content of whether on a tennis court, in a car with a driver trainer or backseat driver, or in a language class. In most cases, the only category of content we can use for these classics is *unspecified: u.*

We have to use *u* because we cannot determine for sure what content is communicated. When a tennis pro says "That was good!" does it mean the serve was good—*study other*—or that the person serving is good—*life personal*—or that the person follows the pro's directions well—*procedure teaching direction?* If a language teacher follows a student response of "I extremely happy" with "Very good," it would be equally hard to pinpoint what was very good. By saying "Very good," the teacher may be indicating he or she is pleased that the student is happy. In this case, the content of the feedback would be *life personal.* Or the teacher may mean that in spite of the error in the first word the rest of the sentence is fine, thus evaluating the linguistic aspects of the sentence. In this case, the content of the feedback would be coded *study of language.* Or finally, if the student response was from a student who rarely responds, the teacher may simply want to show delight that the student answered at all and finally followed some teaching directions. In this case, the content of the feedback would be *procedure,* subcategory *teaching direction.* The teacher wanted to comment on the fact that the student responded to the task that was set, rather than remaining silent or performing a task different from the one solicited!

If the teacher had said "I'm, extremely happy," rather than "Very good," after the student had said "I extremely happy," it would be equally difficult to determine the content. Does the repetition mean the teacher too was happy, in which case the content would be coded as *life personal*? Or is the teacher meaning to provide the correct model and so indicate that a sound containing the verb is missing, in which case the content would be coded as the *study of language*? Or is there a small indication of puzzlement in the teacher's repetition, meaning "I'm not sure what you said; please try again," in which case the content would be coded as *procedure teaching direction* and *procedure check.*

Without some indication of the area of content that the feedback is commenting on, the content of uses has to be *unspecified: u.* A "No" after "I extremely happy" is lacking in specific content, as a "Very good" is. Because the source of the feedback knows the area of content the error is in, or what the "Very good" refers to, does not mean that the target of the feedback does, or that an observer does. What subcategories of the study of language do you think the teacher has in mind in Excerpt 12–6.

EXCERPT 12–6
Keeping Clean? (T)

	Communications	*Content*
1	Teacher: What did you do last night?	_____
2	Student: I watch my hair.	_____
3	Teacher: Watch?	_____
4	Student: Oh, shampoo.	_____
5	Teacher: Shampoo?	_____
6	Student: (With his hands, he massages his head as if he is washing his hair.)	_____
7	Teacher: Last night?	_____
8	Student: Yes.	_____

I feel compelled to code all the feedback *u* for unspecified, on lines 3, 5, and 7. Of course, the teacher might be interested in the *study of language*, subcategory *lexis* in line 3. To the student, it was. Yet the problem could as well be *sound*, since the student demonstrates the correct lexical meaning when he massages his head as if he is in fact washing his hair in line 6. Then, in line 7 the teacher seems to be after the subcategory *inflection*. But the student considers the content of the feedback *life personal*. He thinks that the teacher is trying to verify the personal information he thinks he has just given. "Did you really wash your hair last night and not the night before?" is what the student seems to think the teacher is wondering.

Good Job on the Shampoo, Wrong Tense, and Pronounciation—Specified Content

An alternative to unspecified content is the exact opposite: specified content. In place of "Watch?" here are some opposites: "The tense in the verb is wrong"; "The tense in *wash* is wrong"; "Add something to the verb"; "Add *ed* to wash"; (writes /sht/ on the blackboard) and says "Say it again with the past tense." Since the student might be seeking to integrate *life* and the *study of language*, when saying "I watch my hair," a comment such as "It looks great"—*life personal*—after the student response could be said before the feedback that contains some of the specific subcategories of the *study of language*. But the word "Watch?" with rising intonation has to be coded *u*, since a learner has no way of knowing whether the feedback concerns *life, procedure,* or *study of language*, let alone a particular subcategory of the *study of language* such as lexis, inflections, sound or grammar, to name a few.

In fact, "Watch?", like most feedback that contains a repetition of a student error with rising intonation or stress on the offending element, can be coded with one specific area of content rather than *u* for *unspecified* if you consider that this type of feedback contains two messages, one communicated by the intonation or stress—paralinguistic aural—and the other communicated by the words—linguistic aural. I code the words *u*. But I code the intonation *life personal* in many cases. I do this because I think the intonation is often saying "I'm shocked," a personal feeling, or "How could you do such a foolish thing?" or "You are a schnook," a personal opinion.

Obviously, the rising intonation may simply be saying "Try again," so it might be fairer to code it *procedure teaching direction*. And stress on the offending element might be saying "The error is in the third word" where there are many words, so it should be coded *procedure time/space* since, like "It goes in the other way," the comment helps to locate the error. These distinctions are signaled by subtle differences in the heights and strength of the intonation and stress.

But can we assume that nonnative speakers of English can tell what areas of content our different intensities of stress and intonation signal? Even if we could teach them to make such distinctions, why not try alternatives that show deliberate, conscious control, rather than providing the same feedback that any native speaker gives to someone who is misunderstood? Haven't you heard the exchanges in Excerpt 12–7 a hundred times? Perhaps not at a table, but surely you have heard them someplace. How are the examples of feedback in Excerpt 12–7 different from the teacher's feedback in Excerpt 12–2?

There is no question of what the nonnative speaker is asking for. But rather than saying "Sure," or "I like plums too," or "There's a lot of pepper in this already," nine times out of ten, all native speakers, whether trained as language teachers or ordinary

EXCERPT 12–7
At the Table

		Communications
1	Nonnative speaker:	I need paper. (Pointing to the pepper shaker and just finishing with the salt shaker.)
2	Native speaker:	Paper??!
	(Later in the meal.)	
3	Nonnative speaker:	Give me a prune, please. (Pointing to the dish of plums.)
4	Native speaker:	A prune??!

citizens, repeat the nonnative speaker's error with a tone of voice or stress expressing anything from puzzlement to a sense of superiority to exasperation.

In addition to indicating an area of content because it breaks a rule we all follow as native speakers, another reason for indicating the area of content is that it might mean we have deliberately diagnosed the area of content. If we have to indicate what subcategory of the study of language we want a student to alter, we have to know the subcategory responsible for an error. When teachers correct compositions, "Very goods" are rare, and there are hardly any rewritten sentences with the error underlined in the copied sentence. Rather, teachers tend to indicate specific errors in compositions with symbols—*characterize label*—that contain specified content: *K* for awkward style, *agr* for agreement, etc. While many of the symbols are for the subcategories of grammar, mechanics, and word order, rhetoric and style are sometimes mentioned. At any rate, the practice highlights the fact that with print, we specify content more than we do when we provide feedback to spoken communications. Perhaps this is because we have more time to decide on a specific area of content. If this is part of the reason, writing student oral communications on a card or the blackboard, or having students do so, can provide the data in the same medium we have in compositions. Even a quick glance at the *lv* form of the student communication provides the extra part of a second for either you or the student who made the error, or other students, to diagnose the error and then either edit it or provide feedback in the area of content where the error occurred. Even if we don't write down the entire utterance, trying to transcribe might force more careful listening. [Background 12–11]

Grades too—*characterize evaluate* with a subscript *g* for grade or *characterize label* if the grade puts you in a category of students such as basics, flunkies, eggheads or college-bound—tend to have content specified more in compositions than in oral work. Some put two grades on a paper, one for the strength of the information—*life*—and one for the quality of language—*study of language*. A 60/80 would mean the language was less impressive than the ideas, for example.

On report cards, an A in classroom decorum—*procedure classroom social behavior*—might contrast with a C in arithmetic—*study other*—and a D in composition—*study of language*. But unless the D in composition or a B in reading is broken down to show what a student can and cannot do, the same questions can be raised about grades that I raised about feedback. Does a B in reading mean the student performs tasks expected—*procedure teaching direction*—relates readings to experience—*life* and *the study of language*—or reads well in subject classes—*study other*? And if the B in reading refers to study of language, does it imply all subcategories are mastered to the same degree? An unlikely condition! If the rule in providing grades is not to specify content—*u*—the alternative rule is of course to specify it.

No matter which rule about content grades follow, grades on compositions and for courses remind us that in oral feedback we have another alternative. *Very good* can be replaced by 95, *so so* by 50 and "A apple??!" by 25. It's curious that grades are almost universal in written work, but are the exception rather than the rule in oral work, whether in responses to questions about reading or listening or in conversations.

As you begin to break the rule that says to provide feedback with unspecified content by providing feedback that indicates a specific subcategory of language, you can break still another rule. You can do the unheard of by providing feedback that contains specific subcategories of the study of language for both what is right and wrong in a communication. In Excerpt 12–8, I juxtapose the usual rule of repeating the student error with rising intonation and stress on the offending element with one of the rarest alternatives—good ______, bad ______ or right ______, wrong ______ .

EXCERPT 12–8
Two Ways

	Communications	*Use*	*Content*
	One way:		
1	Teacher: 2 plus 3, please.		
2	Student: Faibu. (Student is a native speaker of Japanese.)		
3	Teacher: Fai*bu*?		u
4	Student: *Hai.*		
5	Teacher: Who knows the right answer?		
	Another way:		
6	Teacher: 2 plus 3, please.		
7	Student: Faibu.		
8	Teacher: Good addition.	ce	so
9	Bad pronunciation.	ce	ls-sound
10	Pronounce it as one syllable.	cx	

Here's another example. After a student says "My throat is very arid, and I'd like a glass of water," the teacher says "Nice grammar; the fourth word doesn't fit; the collocation is wrong." One can also say "I'm thirsty too" or give the student a glass of water before the treatment of the error. After "Since then, we have never ment," one could say "Fine clause; pronounce the last word again to rhyme with bet," keeping in mind that lexis is probably not the problem, but sound is. Though in the beginning some students will be confused by the labels, by the juxtaposition of so much information, and by being given a glass of water, over a period of time students will learn the labels and begin to see the many areas of language that they know and can develop. For ideas on some of the areas of content language study involves, see Episode 11.

Specifying content in feedback also requires that we establish criteria. If students are exchanging lines in dialogs, unless we want them to do more than remember the lines, there is little we can be specific about. But if one thinks that the relationship between tone of voice and meaning of words is important, then one could say in the structuring move before the students started that they are expected to act tired if they say "Oh, am I tired," and to be astonished if they say "Oh, what a surprise!" If I take a tape recording of dialogs in five countries with different language backgrounds, they will sound more similar to each other than we might think because each will be a recitation, and the rhythm and intonation in recitation is similar around the world. Choral repetition in five countries will be the same too—singsong. One can do little more than say "Very good" if one has no criteria other than that students remember the words. But if meaning and expression are to be matched, after a student says "I lost my wallet" with glee, one can say "Right words, but the expression is off; you need to sound disappointed or frustrated, not happy." For students to know which is which, they need to hear and say both; they need to hear and say the right words with the wrong expression, and the right words with the right expression. In fact, students sometimes are more troubled by the lack of congruence between the lines and experience than teachers. Consider Excerpt 12–9.

EXCERPT 12–9
Friendly

		Communications	*Content*
1	Teacher:	Now, what we're going to do every time you hear an error is raise your hand.	
2	Student_1:	What's error?	
3	Teacher:	A mistake	
4	Student_3:	(Begins to recite dialog.)	
5	Student_2:	That's wrong! He's supposed to be friendly with the girls because men are always friendly with girls.	life
6	Teacher:	No.	
7		I want you to signal only grammatical mistakes.	lx-grammar

The content of feedback can be clear in some cases without specifying the area of content, as Excerpt 12–10 illustrates. The act of spelling out the word makes it reasonably clear that the *study of language*, subcategory *mechanics*, is the content of the feedback.

Whether the content of feedback is specified or not, or clear or not, the question of what an error is still needs to be addressed. Deciding what will be acceptable and what will be considered an error is the basis for determining criteria. After observing a great deal, I have concluded that it is not fair to call only mistakes that an observer notes errors. What teachers treat as errors must be considered incorrect too, though a different subscript might identify them. After all, students who leave a class in which teachers treated something as an error probably consider the items treated as wrong. I recall observing a series of classes in which the same tie was used. In one class, the only acceptable response to "What's it made of?" was *cotton*. In another, only *wool* was

EXCERPT 12–10
At a Bar (T)

		Communications	Content
1	Waiter:	Would you like a cocktail?	
2	First customer:	I'd like a Pimms' Cup.	
3	Waiter:	A Pimms' Cup?	
4	First customer:	Pimms' Cup--p-i-m-s. It's a base for a mixed drink.	
5	Waiter:	(Goes to the bar to check.)	
6	Second customer:	It's p-i-m-m-s. There are two *m*'s.	lm-mechanics
7	First customer:	I think he got the idea though.	

accepted, and in still another only *polyester* was accepted. *Cotton* in the *polyester* and *wool* classes was identified as an error. When transcribing and coding communications, I think continuous discussion is necessary to determine what errors are, because observers and teachers, to say nothing of the students, all have different ideas. To say that a famous personality who speaks with an accent, for example, is constantly making errors is not very meaningful. And at one stage of development, one might accept a behavior and not accept it at another, as when we allow 5-year-olds to fall asleep during a conversation but expect adults not to.

By employing the subcategories of the *study of language* in so many examples that specify content, and by mentioning language errors, I do not mean to ignore *life* or *procedure*. The truth of what people say, write, draw or in any other way communicate needs to be noted. And tasks that are solicited and other procedures too can be done either correctly or incorrectly. Remember that "It goes in the other way" is feedback about *procedure*. So *life* and *procedure* can be specified in feedback as well as study. And when they are not, the *u* for unspecified has to be used. If anything, the content *life* is more important to specify, as this example illustrates. In response to the solicit "Say something important that has happened to you recently," one student said "My mother had a baby." "Very good" followed this response. On the surface, what could the content of the reaction be but *life*? But the next student said "My mother died last week," and "Very good" followed this response too. Surely the teacher did not want to say this personal information was good information. After I observe many examples of feedback I consider unspecified, I begin to code words like "very good" as *procedure*, subcategory *transition*, because I think they are simply signaling that the teacher wants to move on. They are no different from a pause, a marker such as "Oh" or a filler such as "hmm."

When the *very good* is said with the intonation we use when addressing children, pets and the senile, I code the words *u* or *procedure*, subcategory *transition*, and the para-linguistic aural medium of the tone of voice *life personal*. I think the tone of voice is saying "you are a schnook," as I said before. And such a comment is a personal opinion. One advantage of my high school English teacher's traffic lights was that they conveyed only *study*, not *life*. A red light simply meant incorrect, not that the person responding was stupid. And the green light did not mean you were bright, only that you were right.

By emphasizing the content of *ce* and negative *ce*, I do not mean to suggest that the other uses cannot specify content. They can. In fact, if you want to express personal feelings, believing that traffic lights are cold and impersonal, you can do so by using speech to *present state*. I'd code "I don't like what you said" as *life personal*, just as I'd code the intonation in "*A* apple??!" *life personal*. "I like the idea in your sentence; I don't like the grammar"—*ps* and *ps*—I'd code *life personal* as well. Those who counsel make a strong distinction between saying we like or dislike a person or thing, and judging that thing. If you find that you express personal feelings more with the use *ce*, substitute *ps*. In some areas of counseling, the distinction between negative *ce* and *ps*—"You're bad" and "I don't like you"—and positive *ce* and *ps*—"You're good" and "I like you"—are critical. People who say "I like you; you're cute" to children on the street *ps* and *ce*. Christ's "You're sinners, I love you" is perhaps the classic negative *ce* followed by a positive *ps*. [Background 12–12]

The content of some other uses, such as *characterize label*, is almost always specified. If you say "noun," the content of the *cl* is *grammar*. If you say "voiced sound," the content is *sound*. At least the content is grammar and sound to you, who know the terms. Whether the content of such labels is understood by students is a question to explore. One alternative that might make the content of labels clear to students would be to have them provide the labels. I heard some students use the label *sail* for contractions because they thought the vowel was just "sailed over." For the full form, they used "fist," since they considered the full form tight. For count nouns, I have heard the label *pause* since the article before count nouns forces one to stop to insert an /ə/ or a /ðə/. Mass nouns were labeled *nonpause* words. Both teacher and student labels can be used in explanations which, by definition, are explicit and therefore specify the content communicated. If you find most instances of *re* are in one subcategory of the study of language, the alternative is not only another subcategory of the study of language, but a subcategory of life or procedure. Some classes are given a lot of feedback in the form of rules about classroom social behavior—*pi*—and never a word about why certain tasks are set. Substituting teaching rationale—*pr*—in explanations for *pi* might decrease the need for rules about how students should behave, since they will know why they are being asked to do what they are doing.

The student and teacher labels used in the uses *cl* and *re* can be used to specify the area of content in *characterize differentiate* as well. In place of "Those two are different," one can say "Those two sail words are different." In place of "Those two are the same," one can say "Those two pause words are the same." Procedure too can be specified in the use *cd*. Instead of "That's different from what I wanted," one can say "Your repetition is different from answering the question," communicating *procedure teaching direction*—*pu*—in the use *cd*.

V. EXPUNGING, THROWING THEM BACK, SPECIFYING, OR EXPLORING—CONCLUSION

If students are used to very good, OK, *A* apple??!, or the presentation of a right answer after a response, the piling up of specific areas of content and the juxtaposition of a *good* and a *wrong* in the same corrective reaction may be distracting. There is a long list of authors who would not suggest specific feedback of this type. F. L. Billows represents them well:

> He [the teacher] can follow the correction of them [mistakes] by enough examples of the correct form to expunge the memory of the incorrect form from the minds of his pupils. . . . There is no need to point out the mistake, it is just rolled flat by the correct form repeated over and over again. [Background 12–13]

Of course, one doesn't have to go far to find the exact opposite advice, as this quotation from Gattegno shows:

> I do not correct learners; I only throw them back onto themselves to elaborate further their criteria and to use them more strongly. Against the demand, common among teachers for immediate correctness through so-called imitation, I take upon myself the burden of controlling myself so as not to interfere, but to give time, . . . [The teacher] neither approves nor disapproves but throws them [the students] back upon their own tools of judgment. . . . [Background 12–14]

Since FOCUS is an instrument designed to describe rather than judge or model, my prejudices are as clear as those of Billows and Gattegno. But in the unlikely event that I'd see a teacher use *only* specified content in feedback and provide no correct answers, I'd urge that teacher to try correct answers and to provide time for the students to work out their own corrections.

I can urge different and even contradictory types of feedback because I contend that our central task is to explore, not to conclude. Just as many who say "I got an A in English; he gave me an F in math" are not aware of the juxtaposition of *got* and *gave me*, so in providing split-second feedback we cannot be constantly aware of what we do, let alone realize the consequences our feedback is having. Many studies suggest that in our feedback we are vague and inconsistent, that the content of our corrective reactions is incongruent with the content of the error, and that we use a narrow range of feedback. But are prescriptions based on such findings likely to produce teachers who would provide feedback that would be different from these findings? I would think such prescriptions would be no more powerful than simply getting teachers to substitute one alternative for what they do. Unless we continue to explore, all that will happen is that a new narrow range will replace the old, and a new problem will replace one reported in earlier studies. [Background 12–15]

In exploring, try not to get too sidetracked by discussion of probable causes for your actions. Of course, it is conceivable that *OK* and *Very good* are symptoms of teacher anxiety, of the teacher's need to keep the class moving, of the need to keep in control. Important as these reasons may be, waiting to break rules by substituting alternatives while the reasons are waiting to be resolved is not likely to do anything but increase the intensity of some of the emotions. Start putting it in the other way rather than talking about it!

Journal Entry

As you may have noticed, there have been no journal entries in this episode till now. I thought that in an episode on feedback, as an alternative, I'd just put one here at the end rather than intersperse them throughout.

Now, at last, you have a chance to comment and give some feedback. Did you mind waiting? Do you usually fill in the entries in other episodes as you go along, or do you just read them? What reactions do you have to feedback in this episode?

EXCERPT 12–11
Macramé (T)

		Communications	*Source/ Target*	*Move Type*	*Medium*	*Use*	*Content**
1	Carol:	We're going to work around this way like this.					
2		(Demonstrates)					
3	Ann:	(Imitates Carol)					
4	Carol:	You went around twice.	t/s	rea_c	la	ce cx	pu pe
5		Take it apart.					
6	Ann:	(Undoes her work and tries again)					
7	Carol:	Exactly, exactly!	t/s	rea	la + pa	ce ps	so u
8	Ann:	This is fun!	s/t	rea	la + pa	ce ps	so u
9	Carol:	Now look at this.					
10		(Holds up finished one)	t/s	rea_c	nv	ps s	so u
11	Ann:	(Looks at it)					
12		Oh, I have to make mine tighter.	s/t	rea_c	la	ci ce	pu so
13		(Tightens the thread)					
14		Now, it looks just like yours.	s/t	rea	la	cd ce	so u
15	Carol:	Here's thinner thread to tie up the middle (Hands over the thread)					
16	Ann:	(Ties the middle up with the thin thread)					
17		Looks fantastic!	s/t	rea	la + pa	ce ps	so u

* *pe* stands for *procedure time/span*; *ps* stands for *procedure teaching direction*; *so* stands for *study other*; and *u* stands for *unspecified content*.

Answers: 4. *cx pe*; 7. *ce u*; 8. *ps so*; 10. *s so*; 12. *ci pu*; 14. *cd so*; 17. *ce so*. In fact, the content is hard to determine in most of the feedback; some that is coded *so* could as well be *u* and when the tone of voice is used to exclaim perhaps personal feelings are being expressed and life is being communicated as well.

To help you gain some more facility with the characteristics of communication I note with FOCUS, I've provided Excerpt 12–11 and Excerpt 12–12. *Macramé* is a continuous lesson. *Exchanges* is a series of different treatments of the same error. Simply circle one of the choices in the use and content column and compare your choices with those others have made, given in the footnotes.

Journal Entry

One of my favorite anecdotes is one Maria Montessori tells in *The discovery of the child* about a babysitter and her charge. When the babysitter announced that it was time to go meet the child's parents, the child was filling a small bucket with

EXCERPT 12–12
Exchanges*

		Communications	*Source/ Target*	*Move Type*	*Medium*	*Use*	*Content*
1	Teacher$_1$:	Where did the boy go at 8:30 a.m. with his lunch bag and books?					
2	Student:	School.					
3	Teacher$_1$:	You need a glue word.	t/s	rea$_c$	la	ce cl	l u
4	Teacher$_2$:	Something is missing.	t/s	rea$_c$	la	ce ps	l u
5	Teacher$_3$:	(Writes /t/ on the blackboard.)	t/s	rea$_c$	lv	ce s	l u
6	Teacher$_4$:	School?	t/s	rea$_c$	la pa	ce ds ce ps	l u fp l
7	Teacher$_5$:	(Shakes head sideways.)	t/s	rea$_c$	pv	<u>ce</u> ps	l u
8	Teacher$_6$:	Very good.	t/s	rea$_c$	la	ce ps	l u
9	Teacher$_7$:	Right word.	t/s	rea$_c$	la	ce ps	l u
10		Grammar is wrong.	t/s	rea$_c$	la	<u>ce</u> <u>ps</u>	l u
11	Teacher$_8$:	(Waits for the student to try again.)	t/s	rea$_c$	si	a s	l u
12	Teacher$_9$:	(Holds up two fingers, shakes first one.) (Each finger stands for one slot.)	t/s	rea$_c$	pv	cx ps	l u

* Though the exchanges here take place during oral work in class, these and all other examples of feedback can be used when students are not present, as, for example, when going over homework. In fact, feedback on homework is more critical to many students because they invest a great deal of time in their out-of-class work, and they expect the teacher to reciprocate. If the feedback on their homework is less instructive or thorough than in-class feedback, some are very disappointed.

Coding done by others: 3. *cl l*; 4. *ps u*; 5. s l; 6. *ds u*; *ce* or *ps fp*; 7. <u>*ce*</u> *u*; 8. *ps u*; 9. *ce l*; 10. <u>*ce*</u> *l*; 11. *a u*; 12. *cx l*.

gravel. After the babysitter announced that they had to leave, the child started to cry. Thinking that the crying was due to the fact that the bucket was not yet filled, the nurse started to help the child fill the bucket. As soon as she did, the child cried even louder and more intensely.

Montessori makes the observation that the child cried because she was interrupted in her task of filling the bucket, first by the announcement that it was time to go home and then by the babysitter's help. The child was interested in filling the bucket on her own, claims Montessori. And the process of filling the bucket was the critical point, not the filled bucket. She urges us to "let them fill their own buckets" whenever we are working with children.

What is your reaction to this advice, which is essentially about the source and target of feedback on one level?

Before this bird-rated coding, there was only one other journal entry, since I had wanted you to be able to experience an episode without having to provide feedback. Now, I've broken the rule that you'd only have one journal entry in this episode. How do you feel about it? [Background 12–16]

BACKGROUND NOTES

12–1. Whether feedback should be given or not seems perhaps on the surface not to be an issue, but in fact some questions have been raised about the value of feedback. Dulay, Burt, and Krashen specifically state "correction of grammatical errors does not help students avoid them." Since they specifically mention grammatical errors, it is unclear whether they are against feedback in general or just the correction of grammatical errors. The need for feedback as a central aspect of all teaching is argued by Carroll (1971) and Smith (1971). A comprehensive review of research on feedback and human behavior was written by Annett. In this review, he states the major findings in research done from a psychological point of view.

12–2. Gattegno says that the student must develop inner criteria so that he or she knows what is right and what is wrong. For the student to develop inner criteria, one of the things the teacher must do is step back and get out of the student's way. Those who write about miscue analysis also feel that it is important for students to have a sense of their own errors and correct their own errors. This view is contained in a book of readings edited by P. David Allen.

12–3. Those interested in information processing theory as described by Wiener probably believe in knowledge of results. Those that believe in other theories of learning may provide other types of feedback. Behaviorists obviously believe in rewards, for example.

12–4. Mary Rowe believes that the usual comments serve only to keep the teacher in control and in fact should not be regarded as feedback. Donaldson also makes this point in her book about children's minds. A report in the *New York Times* of a study of a feedback makes the same conclusion. In the summary, written by Blakeslee, this statement is made, "Teachers praise youngsters despite poor academic performance primarily to keep classrooms in control."

12–5. Strawn and I (1977) have described the actual feedback behavior in some ESL classes. Zahorik (1968) has described feedback provided by elementary school teachers in regular classes. Andrew Cohen provides a summary of the different directions error correction was going up until the middle of the seventies.

To see how limited we have been through the years in the type of feedback we have been providing, I would urge you consult Van Riper, who wrote about feedback for those with speech impediments or speech defects. The original edition was published in 1939 and the sixth edition in 1978.

12–6. Richard Curwin, who I met at the National Technical Institute for the Deaf in Rochester, New York, gave me a mimeographed copy of a paper he had written with the title "Praise addiction." His book on teacher preparation, written with Fuhrmann, contains the same idea, but the idea was first presented to me in the mimeographed paper.

12–7. After studying the attitudes of some gangs in New York City, William Labov (1969) concluded that the major reasons that many children in New York City did not learn to read in school was that the peer pressure outside the school was very great for them not to learn how to read. It was impossible to become a leader in a gang if you were able to read. I think when you look at the clothing that teenagers wear, you realize that the styles are set by the wearers themselves, not by adults or other authorities in the community.

12–8. Jeanne I. Maeroff entitled a feature article on discipline in the *New York Times* in 1977: "Spanking rule found an aid in discipline." The article goes on to report authorities hailing the Supreme Court's decision that paddling can be an aid in establishing the teacher's authority. In some states, teachers must still ask the parents for permission to paddle the students. Representatives from the teachers' union said that teachers simply want options in order to maintain a healthy atmosphere. One continues to see articles about paddling, even about the size of the paddle, in reports in newspapers from time to time. On June 15, 1978, I saw a UPI special from St. Louis which described a new thin rattan paddle for punishing students. The rattan was said to be flexible, not rigid.

12–9. Schachter described a hand signal for providing feedback in a *TESOL Quarterly* article, and, of course, in the Silent Way, Gattegno has urged teachers to provide feedback by shaking the finger that represents a word in a sequence that is incorrect; but I am not simply advocating the gestures be used in place of other mediums. I am suggesting that we constantly alter the type of feedback we provide. If we begin using a gesture, for example, such as a thumb pointing back over our shoulder to represent the past tense in place of saying past tense, the pointing thumb will begin to have a predictable meaning just as the words *past tense* begin to have a predictable meaning.

12–10. Cathcart and Olson asked students and teachers for the type of feedback they prefer. In addition to finding that students wished to be corrected when they made errors orally, they found out that the students liked to be provided with the correct model, and they liked to have the error compared with the model. They did not like teachers to say "Mmm" or simply to answer their statement with a question such as "What?" Zahorik asked elementary school students for their preferences for error correction too. The students liked to be told when they were correct, but they also liked to be told when they were wrong. "That's wrong" apparently did not bother the students.

12–11. In addition to providing time to think about a treatment for an error, transcribing also allows us to decide whether in fact an error has been made, and whether the error is worth bothering with. One of the things that becomes noticeable after a while is that false starts are often self-corrected by students. And transcribing serves the function of providing the student with more time to form the response that is expected, so the transcribing of errors has a dual function.

12–12. If you pick up any book on counseling, you will find the constant emphasis to accept, not to evaluate. A good example of a text containing this type of information is by Brammer and Shostrom.

12–13. This quotation, as I have shown in the text, is from Frederick Lionel Billows' *The techniques of language teaching*, page 33.

12–14. As I have indicated, the contrasting quotation is from Caleb Gattegno's *The common sense of teaching foreign languages.*

12–15. Zahorik discusses relationships between feedback and content development in a 1970 article in the *Journal of Educational Research.*

12–16. Montessori.

EPISODE

13

John, Are You Sitting?

I. NOT REALLY—BACKGROUND AND PURPOSE OF EPISODE

The number of times I have seen lessons that contain the question "Are you sitting?" during observations of classes is astonishing. At both beginning and intermediate levels, lessons on *to be* plus the *ing* form seem to be one of the favorite choices to show visitors. Perhaps one reason for the popularity of this verb form is the fact that in many texts and teacher's notes, it is accompanied by actions that illustrate its meaning. "Am I writing?" asks the teacher as he or she writes on the blackboard. "Who is walking?" asks the teacher after telling Juan to walk around the room. And to visitors, the teacher can ask "Are you sitting?", or in my case, "John, are you sitting?"

I must admit that I have often been tempted to respond "Not really, I'm planting tomatoes" or a similarly odd response, so that the response is more in tune with the seeming oddness of the solicit. Though the solicit "John, are you sitting?" may sound odd, I think it illustrates a basic urge we all have: to tie language to contexts we are in and roles we play. The purpose of this episode is to explore ways to translate this urge into action. [Background 13–1]

In Section II, I first suggest ways to match language and contexts, and language and roles. Then I show ways we can match roles and contexts in other skills, especially listening. And in Section III, I discuss some reasons for the alternatives I suggest.

In terms of FOCUS, I concentrate on the uses *characterize* and *present* as they communicate a subcategory of *procedure* I call *roles*: *po*, and a subcategory of the *study of language* I call *context: lc*. These elements of FOCUS are highlighted in graphic form in Table 13–1.

TABLE 13–1
Presenting and Characterizing Two Areas of Content

Use	Content
	procedure *p*
characterize *c*	roles *po*
	study of language *l*
present *p*	context *lc*

II. HARK! I HEAR THE CANNON ROAR!— CONTEXTS AND ROLES AS AIDS TO MEANING

Beyond Memorization—Matching Language with Contexts

Courthouses and Hen Houses—Some Contexts for "John, Are You Sitting?"

A first step in matching language to a context is simply to ask in what situation or setting outside of a classroom a particular sample of language is used. In the case of "John, are you sitting?" two come to mind. One might use the pattern in a discussion of court cases, asking whether a judge was holding court or not, as in "Is the judge sitting?" Or, we could ask whether hens were warming their eggs, as in "Are the hens sitting?" But even here, "Are the hens setting?" is perhaps more likely.

If the first contexts you come up with that match the language seem farfetched, sometimes some words can be added to the pattern to fit a less farfetched context. In a game requiring people to stand, sit, kneel, bow and perform other actions on command, "Are you still sitting?" would be possible to confirm that a person missed the command and was therefore out of the game. The word *still* added to "John, are you sitting?" would be possible also if someone had expected me to leave or thought I had been sitting too long. Then, stress on *still* would be required, along with a plaintive tone: "John, are you *still* sitting?" Even here, a location word such as *there* would be needed, together with *still*, as in "John, are you *still* sitting *there*?" In fact, location words suggest at least one other context for the question. While searching for something another has lost, a question like this is possible: "John, are you sitting on my ring?" (or wallet, or book or anything else that cannot be seen).

Noting versus Describing—Presenting or *Characterizing Context: p lc* or *c lc*

In the teaching of dialogs, in fact, settings often are noted. For example, the patterns "How much?" and "How many?" often are put in dialogs in a store or a market. And "What are you doing?" is often put in a setting in which people are performing actions, as we saw with "John, are you sitting?" But simply stating the setting—*ps*—does not necessarily establish any criteria for the communication of the patterns. Stating the setting only serves to provide a suggestion for ways the patterns are used outside the classroom, and perhaps provides an association to aid in remembering the pattern. By *characterizing* the setting as well as stating it, students are provided with criteria that can be used to judge their performance. By having students *characterize* samples in different settings, they can see relationships between language and settings that otherwise would be ignored.

To find contexts to match patterns you are teaching, simply stop and think of a nonteaching setting in which the language is likely to occur. Or, alternatively, record short exchanges in many settings, and you will have a ready-made connection between contexts and patterns.

The pattern "Did I tell you ______?" and "No, ______ didn't" and "Yes, ______ did" occurs in many settings, often to exchange recent news. Places we exchange recent news include where we work and shop and public transportation settings. If you wanted to teach a series of exchanges using these patterns, one option would be to place the conversation on a bus. But unless additional information about the bus was mentioned, we would only be presenting the context, not characterizing it. By adding facts that would in some way alter the way the patterns would be said, we would be *characterizing*. Thus, if we said that the bus was hot, crowded, had no seats and was behind schedule, and therefore moving quickly, we would distinguish the bus in some way. If a conversation were said under these conditions, it would be different from one said on an empty bus that was going very slowly. On a crowded bus, we would be more likely to be standing closer to each other, we would probably speak softly so others could not overhear, and we would have to concentrate on listening if the other people and the speed of the bus made noise.

Once the dialog was played on a tape or said by the teacher to reflect the conditions that the context dictated, individual lines could be said and students could be asked to indicate whether the lines were appropriate to the context. Thus, a line could be shouted, and a student could say "Not this bus," thus *characterizing* the sample given. In a few minutes, students could hear the lines many times, said both in a way congruent with the setting that was *characterized*, and in other ways. Their only task would be to say "This bus" or "Not this bus." The reasons for this task and other variations of it are described in Episode 5. Here, I only want to say that by providing students with the opportunity to characterize lines before they are asked to say them, they have a chance to hear them many times and associate them with certain specified conditions so that they know that any line can be said in different ways to signal different meanings.

If differences between the ways the lines are said in crowded buses and empty buses are quickly discovered, different contexts can be *characterized*. If the topic of the questions and responses using the patterns with "Did" was the birth of a baby, it would be stated differently at an office party where everyone might also be close together. More giggling would be likely there, for example. By emphasizing the way the lines are said, rather than saying the lines for their own sake, memorization is given less priority. [Background 13–2]

Journal Entry

After a class in which students supposedly memorized a number of patterns in dialog form, I asked the students to volunteer to present the dialog after class for me to tape. When I asked for volunteers after class, they said: "We can't say the lines—we forget them as soon as the class is over!"

In your observations, have you noticed that many patterns recited in class are not tied to any other settings?

I Need My Hat—Communicating Context (lc) with Other Mediums

A sketch of a bus on the blackboard would present the context the same as "This takes place on a bus." Sketching in many people on the bus and drawing lines along the side of the bus to suggest speed would *characterize* the context. A picture of hens or judges could establish a hen house or courthouse for "Are you sitting?" as clearly as words. Moving students or furniture around would be necessary if you wanted to have the linguistic and other mediums congruent. If all students sat in their seats as they said the lines supposedly spoken by people standing on a crowded bus, the spoken context would be neutralized.

Even the most basic prop, a blindfold, can be very useful in setting a context. By using blindfolds, and thus establishing a context of a guessing game, many question words can be taught less artificially. Give objects to students to place around the room, blindfold one, and both the question "Where is the ______ ?" and the response "On the teacher's desk?" become parallel to questions and answers in a nonteaching setting in which hiding games are played. Having the blindfolded students go to the desk to check the veracity of the response and pick up the item would show understanding. "What color is the ______ ?" or "What color is that?", "Are you holding a ______ ?" or "What shape is the ______ ?" are just a few of the other questions that can be put into the context of a game, if blindfolds are used. Should blindfolds be too hot, participants can simply close their eyes when playing the guessing game.

Sketches or other mediums can also be used to set the sequence of the dialog or suggest the meanings of individual lines. On the blackboard, a series of sketches can be listed next to a series of lines. Each picture aids the recall of the meaning of a line. By using pictures rather than the words themselves, or nothing, the idea that the meaning is what is central to remember is emphasized. If students say some lines differently, but keep the meaning appropriate for the context, they have met the goal. Just a sketch can serve as an association for the entire dialog, so sketches next to individual lines can serve to develop associations for individual lines.

Play a Part—Matching Language with Roles

Pert, Evasive, or Direct—Presenting and Characterizing Roles in Speech

A reporter, the judge's husband, a criminal, and a lawyer might all ask "Is the judge sitting?" differently. If you had $100 in a wallet, you'd ask "John, are you sitting on my wallet?" with more anxiety than if the wallet was empty. What we say is determined by the role we are assigned, as well as the context. If a person saying lines is not assigned a role, even if the context is stated or characterized, the only role he or she can play in a classroom is that of a student trying to memorize lines. The role requires matter-of-fact responses in which neither the emotions nor the words themselves are altered.

But just as a crowded bus might make us speak more softly than an empty bus, so excitement might make us speak differently than boredom. To know one is saying what a character named "Pert" has said may create an association for a line. But, like knowing we are on a bus, such naming does not supply any criteria for the way we say the lines. Just as if contexts are established just by naming them, an alternative is to *characterize* them. So if roles or characters are just named, an alternative is to *characterize* them. After indicating the name of a person—Pert—we can say the person is in an excited mood, does not like to share everything even with close friends, is nervous generally, and tries to evade direct answers. In fact, we can say anything, as long as we then point out when lines that are said are inappropriate for the role we have characterized.

Once we characterize the roles, we can say the lines in ways that fit the roles and do not, and the students can be asked to state either that the lines fit or not, or they can be asked to state individual characteristics that are reflected in the lines or not. If I were to say "Did your sister have her baby?" and Pert responded "Yes, she did," the words would be inappropriate if she were one to evade direct answers. The class would then shout "Too direct." Once the students have heard the lines a few times, produced in different ways, they can be asked to say lines given certain parts of the role. "Say the question as if you were excited" is one type of direction.

Party Time—Communicating Roles (po) with Other Mediums

One of the times I have consistently seen native speakers of languages act differently from the way they normally do is at parties where the partygoers wear costumes. I am not speaking about elaborate costumes. At some parties I've seen people act in ways that are different from the way they normally act after they don a party hat or a mask that covers only the area around their eyes. Obviously, the context—a party—is partly responsible. But I have seen some people who wear glasses only occasionally seem to put them on when they want to change their role, even when they are not at a party. I have seen small children unable to perform a particular action because they don't have a particular part of their "costume" with them. I've seen children refuse to play baseball without their baseball cap. I've seen children who forgot their dancing shoes refuse to dance at a dancing lesson, even though the dancing could be done barefoot. If, in fact, even minimal costumes seem to free us to act in a particular way, an obvious alternative to stating roles and characterizing them is to hand out symbols of the roles—*nonlinguistic visual* mediums. Dark glasses can be given to a student who is to act very private and not share information. A bright hat can be put on a student who is to be excited, and a dull gray jacket can be worn by a student who is supposed to be bored.

Props can be used as well. Giving a student a cigarette to hold or a cane or a screwdriver as roles are played may have the same consequence as having a student wear dark glasses. In the case of these props, if a pencil could be used in place of the objects themselves, students would have to add even more meaning to their lines, perhaps using more body language. Many props need not be real. Objects can play different roles as well as people!

Just as movement is necessary to distinguish different contexts, so movement is necessary if students are to say lines with roles they have been assigned. If students are only allowed to sit in their normal seats, or are forced to come up to the front of the classroom in pairs, the obvious alternatives are to have them present their lines in a corner of the room or in the back of the room, so they can act their roles with less deliberate display.

Journal Entry

One of my favorite jokes about acting concerns the part a person was supposed to play that required saying only one line: "Hark, I hear the cannon roar." The director of the play saw just the man he wanted to play the part on a street corner. The man had had no experience in acting, but the director thought that since only one line had to be said, the person could play the part. Day after day, the person chosen said the line over and over to himself, and he said it in front of the mirror. Unfortunately, the only thing the director told him was that he would say the line just as the curtains opened and the cannon was fired. The person had no idea of the context of the play and did not know what role he was playing.

On opening night, the new actor went on stage right behind the curtain. The director asked him what he was going to say. He replied "Hark, I hear the cannon roar." A few seconds later, the curtain went up, a loud thundering sound was heard that was supposed to be the cannon and the actor, startled, shouted: "What the hell was that noise?"

Have you had any similar experiences where there was so much emphasis on the lines themselves and so little attention to the meaning of the lines, or the purpose for saying them, that you forgot them and said something less appropriate given the setting and role you were supposed to be in?

Where and Who?—Contexts and Roles for Reading, Writing, and Listening

Roles and contexts are not limited to producing oral patterns. The fact that students are told to read for different purposes shows the importance of roles and setting in reading. Finding a definition in a dictionary while taking a test, writing a paper at home, or relaxing in the library are three different tasks because of the different roles and settings. Looking for a phone number in an emergency and checking a friend's number in one's own address book while drunk look different to an observer. Simply listing the roles we read in in different settings will produce some ideas for *presenting* and *characterizing po* and *lc* during reading lessons.

In writing, each of us may assume a narrow range of roles, and we may write in only a few settings. But if we look at people in different professions, we can discover a wider range of roles required. People have to write final reports of projects that others have funded to convince them of the value of the project. Nine times out of ten, there are deadlines for such reports and admonitions against exceeding a certain specified length. Editors have to cut down articles others have written to fit predetermined spaces, and they too have deadlines. In place of asking a student to cut an essay, one could ask a student to play the role of an editor faced with space for only 100 words needed by the printer in exactly 15 minutes. Rather than simply asking students to write what they did over the weekend, or why they came to a particular school or country, they can be asked to write on such topics as people who like to exaggerate both good and bad things. On other days, the same topic can be used and students can be asked to write as if they are constrained by their background from writing anything personal. Instead of asking the students to write alone, in a quiet place, they can be asked to write with a tape going that contains people pounding away on typewriters and ringing phones, so they can feel how many journalists write in their settings. As with finding alternatives for roles and settings in speaking, one only has to observe where people write outside classrooms and what roles they assume as they write in order to seek more alternatives. [Background 13–3]

Perhaps in listening, the need seems less clear than in reading or writing for different settings and roles. But different roles and settings require different kinds of listening too. As a keeper of minutes at a meeting, we need to keep track of more facts than as a participant. Facts in the same lecture that are important to a journalist may be different from those important to a student who will be examined on the content of the lecture. If students were told to listen for important facts in a story or television program as if they were a spy, a journalist, or other specified person, it is likely that they would note different bits of information than if they were simply told to listen for the important facts. They would probably listen differently if they were told they had no chance to listen again, and if they were told they had to listen to the sound at the lowest possible level in order not to be discovered by police who were nearby looking for them.

Given different roles and settings, what would be important facts to different individuals listening to a broadcast about space travel? Let's say the broadcast included these facts: speed of the vehicle, thrust of the rockets, date of the event, personal facts about the flight crews' families, menu for the crew, types of exercises the crew would engage in on the flight, education and training of the crew. Well, to a scientist, speed and thrust would probably be significant. To an ordinary citizen, personal information about the crews' families and the menu would probably be important facts. To potential flight crew members, education and training of the crew and the types of exercises would be listened for. A spy would be interested in everything, perhaps. But after the information was sent to headquarters, different people there would be interested in different facts; all would not be interested in everything or consider everything important. [Background 13–4]

Those who play Simon Says for listening comprehension feel the need for roles and settings a bit more than those who concentrate on answering questions about passages used for listening. Though the context of Simon Says is constant—play time—and the role is that of either an attentive listener who moves only when the command is accompanied by "Simon says," or an inattentive listener who moves even without the command, the game is an attempt to establish a context and rules during a listening lesson.

The idea behind Simon Says can be expanded and used with listening books that contain series of commands. I have reproduced one series in Excerpt 13–1. As you can see, I've preceded the solicits with space to write a structuring move in which roles and a context can be *characterized* and *presented*. Write a context and some roles the communications could be used in. [Background 13–5]

Others have suggested these contexts and roles: (1) burglars in a hideout rehearsing for a very carefully timed bank theft; the burglars are drunk at the time; (2) a friend of a recently blinded person getting the blind person ready to be independent; the blind person is very nervous and the friend is overprotective, acting as if the blind person is completely helpless; (3) two terrorists, one unfamiliar with the area, the other giving instructions via a radio transmitter across the street from the bank; the new agent is very nervous, and the one who knows the area is full of confidence. By *characterizing* the roles—drunk, overprotective, nervous—as well as presenting them—burglars, recently blinded person—we provide criteria for performance. Just as in saying lines, we can say lines in different ways and have students *characterize* the lines, so in translating speech to movement, we can move nervously or confidently and students can simply *characterize* our movement as a first step before they are asked to move themselves. If we *characterize* the setting—indicating the bank is crowded, getting ready for closing, hot with open windows, watched by three guards with guns—we provide extra information that affects the movements. In this way, even more criteria for performance are provided.

You Are Interested in Deciphering Secret Codes in Books on Teaching While Relaxing at Home—Matching Communications and Categories

In Excerpt 13–2 I've provided some examples of structuring moves that *characterize* and *present roles—po—*and *contexts—lc*. In the Use column, write a *p* for *present* next to lines that name content, and a *c* for *characterize* next to lines that more than name content. In the Content column, write *po* if roles are mentioned and *lc* if the setting is. Coding by others is given in the footnote.

EXCERPT 13–1
Learning through Action*

	Communications	*Source/ Target*	*Move Type*	*Use*	*Content*
1	______________________	t/c	str	p	po
2	______________________			c	po
3	______________________			p	lc
4	______________________ ______________________ ______________________			c	lc
5	Go to the bank.	t/s	sol		
6	(Gets up and walks to the side of the room.)	s/t	res		
7	Open the door and go in.	t/s	sol		
8	(Mimes opening a door and walking through the doorway.)	s/t	res		
9	(After each of the following solicits, students	t/s	sol_{1-n}		
10	change the medium of speech into movement.) Walk to the window. Wait in line. Move up. Move up again. Go to the window. Give a check to the teller. (or note) Say, "Please cash this check for me." (or "give me money") Pick up your money. Walk to the door. Open the door and walk to your car.	s/t	res_{1-n}		

* From James J. Asher, *Learning Another Language through Actions: The Complete Teacher's Guidebook*, Los Gatos, California: Sky Oaks Productions, 1977.

EXCERPT 13–2
Deciphering

	Communications	*Move Type*	*Use*	*Content*
1	This row be John and this row be Sara.	str		
2	This dialog takes place at school.	str		
3	Take the part of the dentist.	str		
4	The patient is nervous and would like to read while waiting to see the doctor.	str		

EXCERPT 13–2 (*continued*)
Deciphering

	Communications	*Move Type*	*Use*	*Content*
5	He is in a very, very hot waiting room, but he is sitting down while some others are standing. There are 12 chairs and 15 people. There is a magazine on a table across from him.	str		
6	You are an insurance salesman.	str		
7	Read the policy silently and circle the advantages of the policy, but not the costs or the stipulations. You are not a scrupulous person.	str		
8	The meeting place is a bar, poorly lit, but your customer has a pen flashlight with him. He has a copy of the policy too.	str		
9	(Draws a circle two feet in diameter on the floor. Hands a yardstick to one student to serve as an umbrella.)	str		
10	You are strangers, but you start to talk. It rains, and you stay under the umbrella together, within this circle, one acts shy and the other open.	str		

Note: Coding done by others: 1. *p po*; 2. *p lc*; 3. *p po*; 4. *c po*; 5. *p* and *c lc*; 6. *p po*; 7. *c po*; 8. *p* and *c lc*; 9. *p lc*; 10. *c lc* and *c po*.

III. NOT TO BE REAL—REASONS FOR THE ALTERNATIVES

Pretending to be nervous or excited is not more real that stating a line matter-of-factly. Nor is listening to a tape recording as if one were a spy being observed more real than simply listening as a student learning a language. But the purpose of *characterizing* and *presenting* roles and contexts is not primarily to be real.

One of the purposes of the alternatives suggested in this episode is to provide examples of language that reveal relationships between different areas of the *study of language*. As roles change, sounds are changed because one role may require the same lines to be blended, and another role may require the full form. As the context shifts, style often has to be altered. The register and dialect of the same words too is affected by shifts in the mood of speakers, their task, or the setting. Delivering the same lines in different ways provides examples of shifts of many of the subcategories of the *study of language*, content I treat in Episode 11.

Contexts and roles provide information that can help make meaning clear too. Once we know the setting is a forest, we know the word *hare* is not the *hair* at a barber shop. Hearing *jam* said in a kitchen at a meal brings forth a meaning different from *jam* in traffic, though the image of being stuck may be similar. An *X* on a street preceded by *no* and followed by *ing* helps us fill in *cross*, while on a greeting card the same *X* suggests Christmas, or on a scoring card at a bowling alley, a strike. Contexts and roles can mean the difference between wild guesses and educated guesses in our search for meaning, and can decrease the need for definitions and explanations of words.

Should you believe in the value of roles and contexts to show relationships between the different subcategories of the study of language and see the value of narrowing the range of possible meanings, but fear you are tampering with character development, stop worrying. Providing lines in different roles is not likely to cause character changes. Shy students are likely to remain shy even if they are asked to pretend in a class for a few minutes that in fact they are not shy. Even in plays we ultimately are acting as ourselves. If we miss a line in a play, we don't say afterward "Oh, Caesar forgot the line." We say "I forgot the line." One of the reasons different people play Caesar, or any other character, differently, is that each person is basically giving his or her own interpretation of the character. It is unlikely that students who are called enthusiastic, plaintive, or loud before they identify roles and say lines with different roles will be called anything else after they do these tasks. Since I have pretended I was a hen or a judge when asked "John, are you sitting?" I have not felt that I have acted any differently at times when I do not assume these roles. [Background 13–6]

Journal Entry

Forget FOCUS for a minute, and comment on these alternatives. Collect recordings of dialogs from students and friends. Write them out minus a description of the setting or the characters or what is being talked about. Then, have students in pairs guess different contexts and characteristics of the people talking to each other.

Then, either with dialogs students have worked with or fresh ones, have them write alternate meanings for each line. Even such a seemingly simple question as "What time is it?" can mean very different things in different settings. In a class, followed by "Very good" it means display knowledge to me by showing me you can tell time. If a police officer asks a young teenager "What time is it?" a possible response is "I didn't steal it." If we want to leave a dinner party, "What time is it?" is likely to mean "Oh, it's time to go." Seeing the relationships between contexts or settings, roles of those in the exchanges, and the meanings are more critical than learning set pieces, especially those constructed for a textbook to illustrate some point. If one wants dialog material, it is hard to improve on real exchanges, though dialogs from Shaw in plays and Hemingway in novels are quite exciting, as are those of other modern writers.

BACKGROUND NOTES

13–1. Using the materials produced by Gabriel, Hines, Maley and Duff, and Via, any teacher can provide some experiences for the class and for him or herself that will provide contexts and roles. The fact that publishers are putting out these types of materials means there is a demand.

13–2. Bloom argues that, for native speakers, the major task of language development in the school years may be to learn to use a linguistic code independent of a context. If this is true for native speakers, how much more necessary must contexts be for nonnative speakers of a language! Dewey (1933) too notes the vital role of context in all learning (page 99). Moffett urged the use of a context for the teaching of English to native speakers. And both Jakobovits and Wardhaugh put the word *context* in the titles of their books about second language teaching.

13–3. Raimes, in her book on composition, suggests at one point that the student rewrite a passage about enzymes "as if he was a historian of science in the year 2500." In another direction, the student is asked to pretend he or she is a witch and has to prepare a monstrous witch's brew to serve to his or her enemies. Of course, real roles can be used for writing and other skills too. We do often have to write notes indicating we are not going to come to an event we have been invited to in such a way that we do not tell the real reason and still not offend the host. And we do have to write notes complaining about service and requesting refunds or additional service.

13–4. The idea of the space trip is from a passage in Morley's materials. Though she does not assign roles when asking questions about the passages or when she assigns passages to be listened to, her materials, like others, can be adapted by simply assigning roles and establishing contexts.

13–5. Hornby has developed a series of contexts to teach scores of structural words and sentence patterns. Each context is set in a classroom, and by establishing a situation that requires the use of a particular pattern, he goes a long way towards establishing the meaning of the construction. For example, to teach *too heavy* he instructs the teacher to ask a student to move the teacher's desk. Of course the desk is too heavy. Then the teacher says, "The desk is too heavy—Ali can't move it." The teacher then reaches for the ceiling, but alas, "It is too high—I can't reach it." And so on. While no different roles are assigned and few different contexts established, the situations are a first step toward establishing meanings. One can ask some students to pretend they are weak and others strong, and establish a small group of movers who have been hired to rearrange the furniture in an old house. But with the situation thought out, such roles and contexts can be developed more easily since part of the work is done.

Asher's directions, too, lack roles and contexts. Why would anyone go up to an icebox and remove different items in response to a command to do so? Well, that is why I am asking you to establish contexts.

Carolyn Graham establishes contexts in her jazz chants by the use of sound effects—a real advantage for classes that are not at a level to understand verbal descriptions of contexts.

13–6. Perhaps the classic example of the fact that we are ourselves both in the roles we are assigned and in real life is that of the language professor John A. Rassias. He was written up in a series of articles to try to show how important his use of drama was in teaching foreign languages at Dartmouth. In a piece by Wolkomir in *The Smithsonian*, pictures were shown of Rassias lying on the floor in class, first hugging a student, and finally standing in a corner with his shirt sleeve ripped off as a result of an extremely energetic move in the class. To those who have met John Rassias outside class, such descriptions and pictures are no news; they are all in character, so to speak. This person is simply quite a dramatic type.

Open Your Books to Page 22

I. DO YOU WANT TO KEEP IT OPEN?—WHAT THIS EPISODE IS ABOUT

A Ritual—Introduction

One of the most frequent directions I have heard in classrooms around the world is "Open your books to page 22," or its equivalent in other languages. The page number varies a great deal of course—I used "22" because after Joseph Heller's *Catch 22*, the number "22" frequently comes to my mind. But the task that follows the command does not vary much at all, in language classes at least. The most frequent task I have observed following the command "Open your books" is oral reading, either chorally, or individually around the room.

Oral reading is so frequently done by students and it is done with so little variety that it reminds me of a ritual. I often wonder whether in fact many teachers and students see oral reading as just that, a ritual which, if carefully observed, will make them literate, just as the repetition of some words in some other rituals is believed to have effects on our physical or spiritual well-being.

All about Changing Mediums—Purpose of This Episode

One purpose of this episode is to introduce an alternative method of oral reading frequently used outside of classrooms that makes use of the high motivation and regard teachers and students have for oral reading, and at the same time has other advantages over the usual type of oral reading done in classrooms. Another purpose of this episode is to relate oral reading to other activities. As widespread as oral reading is, it is usually not related to other activities, but considered an activity that stands on its own. I will relate it to other activities in this episode by considering it as simply one example of a whole series of tasks that require that one medium be changed into another. Looked at this way, oral reading is an example of changing print to speech, just as a dictation can be considered an example of changing speech to print, and performing actions to show comprehension of commands can be considered an example of changing speech to action, and drawing figures can be considered changing speech to diagrams. Still another purpose is to show how the steps in the alternative method of reading I introduce can be used in all activities that require students to change one medium to another.

Six More Sections—Outline of This Episode

To achieve thise purposes, I have divided this episode into seven sections:

> In Section II, I introduce the alternative way of reading orally that I think makes use of the high motivation and regard teachers and students have for oral reading, and at the same time has other advantages.
>
> In Section III, I show how the steps I urge for oral reading can be applied to dictations.
>
> I provide some theoretical support for the steps I advocate for oral reading and dictations in Section IV.
>
> In Section V, I show how the changing of the mediums of print to speech in oral reading and print to speech in a dictation are simply two ways of changing one medium to another, and so relate oral reading and dictations to a whole range of activities.
>
> In Section VI, I show a few ways to alter the level of difficulty of mediums we ask others to change.
>
> In Section VII, I suggest a few questions to help explore the consequences of the alternatives I advocate you try in this episode.

To relieve you of any anxiety you might have about working your way through so many sections in one episode, I will say now that Sections IV through VII are rated, as are some parts of Sections II and III. And I have provided a journal entry between Sections III and IV to remind you to take a break.

All the sections are united by the use *reproduce—d*—and the subcategory *change medium—dc*—because in FOCUS I code oral reading, dictations, and all other changing from one medium to another *reproduce change medium*. The alternative way I urge you to have students read orally and perform parallel tasks requires that they wait for a little while before taking in one medium and changing it into another. I code this waiting as *attend*, and so I treat this use—*a*—together with *dc*.

Since changing mediums requires mediums, I mention the categories of them too. And I refer to *characterize examine—cx*—when I discuss counting words, and *characterize evaluate—ce*—when I urge responses that require only verification of labels used in solicits. I mention a few other uses a few times too. But the major uses I treat I've noted in Table 14–1, together with the categories of mediums.

II. OUTSIDE AND INSIDE—TWO WAYS OF READING ORALLY

Eye Contact—Oral Reading outside the Classroom

Just as oral reading in a classroom is not often looked at in relationship to other classroom activities, it is not often looked at in relationship to oral reading outside the

TABLE 14–1
Changing Mediums

Medium		*Use*	
speech	la		
print	lv	attend	a
Braille	lo		
noise/music	na	reproduce	d
pictures	nv		
odors	no	change medium	dc
tone of voice	pa		
gestures	pv		
movement	po		
silence/waiting	si		

classroom. And though only an extremely small percentage of people are ever required to read orally outside the classroom, among the small number there are some who follow a different pattern, as you well know if you have ever seen actors do oral readings. They look at their books to get the lines, but they say them to the audience rather than to the book, which is the usual place stared at during oral reading in the classroom. In many dramatic readings by actors or poets, the readers rivet their eyes on various people in the audience as they say the lines in the books they are reading.

Apparently eye contact is considered important by the few who read orally outside of classrooms. Many politicians and some newscasters who cannot read like actors, by glancing at the material and then saying what they have read, go to great lengths to make it appear that they in fact can read and keep eye contact, the way actors do during dramatic readings. In an effort to appear to be keeping eye contact, some politicians and newscasters have the material they have to read printed in large letters on a roll of large paper or transparent plastic. This roll is mounted on a device next to the television camera, or beneath it. To the television viewer, it appears that the person is saying the lines from memory, or as a result of a few quick glances the speakers make to the papers in front of them to strengthen the illusion that they are reading the material from the desk, rather than from the material moving between the reels. But in fact the lines are being read the same way they are read in classrooms, with eyes glued to the material.

Even before television, devices had been used to make it appear that public figures were speaking to audiences rather than reading lines out loud to pieces of paper on the top of a podium or desk. I once saw a newsreel of President Herbert Hoover speaking to a rally. For an instant, the camera photographing the event moved from the president's face to the right of the podium. Next to the podium was a tall music stand with pages of the speech attached to it at eye level. Next to the music stand, an aide was removing pages one by one as the president finished saying them. To the movie audience, and to many looking at the presentation of the speech from a distance, it appeared that the president was in fact delivering a speech. But to those who were close, and of course to the aide who was removing pages from the stand, it was clear that the president was looking at print rather than people, though he wanted to give the impression that he was able to look at people as he gave his speech. Of course, listening to such performances carefully usually reveals the fact that some type of prompter is being used because speeches delivered in this way are marked with pauses and breaks at totally inappropriate places, caused by the fact that the readers are reading word by word, rather than in groups of words that make sense together.

A few observations of actors learning their lines could save a great many of those who address people a great deal of trouble, including students who read orally in classrooms. In learning lines, as well as in delivering lines, they have not learned, many actors precede the delivery of their lines with two steps. First, they silently read a group of words on a line that makes sense—a sense group. Then they look up, away from the material, and to a person in the audience. And finally, after these two steps, they say the sense group they have read silently, and in some way their mind has acted upon it in the brief time before they actually say the sense group. By adding these two steps, actors not only are able to keep eye contact, and usually decrease the amount of time taken to learn material as well, but also prevent themselves from reading word by word, which is how many students read when they read orally around the room, either individually or chorally.

Read-and-Look-Up—Outside-the-Classroom Reading inside a Classroom

The Most Valuable Method—A Claim and a Rationale

Michael West, who called the type of oral reading some actors do *read-and-look-up*, was so enthusiastic about the idea that he made this claim: "Of all methods of learning a language, *Read-and-Look-Up* is, in our opinion, the most valuable. It is possible to master a language by this method alone, carrying a book in the pocket. You read a little [silently] and then look up and say it to someone. Gradually you are able to take in larger and larger units, at first only a line, later two or three lines . . . as you become more and more proficient, you paraphrase more and more, until eventually you are gathering the ideas from the book and expressing them in your own [words]." [Background 14–1]

Though it is hard to find anyone else as enthusiastic as West is about the need to read in sense groups, others have noted the crucial importance of avoiding word-by-word reading. Here are two other pleas for reading in sense groups: (1) "In native-language reading fluent readers look ahead to the right word group and relate it to what preceded before reading it aloud. . . . It is more difficult to do this with a foreign language text unless the material of which it is composed is very familiar. Students, therefore, need much practice in reading in 'meaningful mouthfuls,' never producing orally a new segment until they have identified the word grouping to which it belongs." (2) "To distribute his pauses intelligently, it is first of all necessary that a speaker understand the full meaning of what he is saying. . . . The foreign student's most frequent error with regard to pauses is a failure to organize his sentences into thought groups which can be recognized as such. His pauses are too timid, or bear no relation to meaning. . . . Within thought groups, words and syllables are not pronounced as separate units. . . ." [Background 14–2]

EXCERPT 14–1
It Done Begin

An de Lawd, He done go work hard for make all ting dey call um Earth. For six day de Lawd He work an he done make all ting—everyting He go put for Earth. Plenty beef, plenty cassava, plenty banana, plenty yam, plenty guinea corn, plenty mango, plenty groundnut—everyting. And for de wata He put plenty fish, an for de air He put plenty kinda bird.

—From John Gunther, *Inside Africa*

Experience Is the Best Teacher—Read-and-Look-Up!

To experience read-and-look-up, read the lines in Excerpt 14–1 to a friend, or if one is not available, to yourself, looking in a mirror. The lines are written in a dialect of English you are probably not familiar with in order to make the experience more like that a nonnative speaker of a language has with the language he or she is studying. Remember, the aim is to read in sense groups and to say each sense group to a face without looking back down to the page. You should not look up from the page until you are able to say however many words you have chunked to the face in front of you. There is no need to read letter perfect or word perfect. In fact, as West has said, expressing the meaning from the passage in your own words is the clearest evidence that you are understanding what you are reading.

Tape-record your reading. Then replay it, and when you pause at the end of a sense group, draw a slash mark like this / at the places in Excerpt 14–1 where you pause. Each pause signals the boundary of a sense group. Replay the tape again and write down above the words in the passage anything that you said differently from the original passage. Cross out words you omitted. When you have marked Excerpt 14–1 with the sense groups you found, the substitutions and omissions you made, and any other differences between the passage and your reading of it, you can compare the marked passage with my marked rendering in Excerpt 14–2.

Here is the way I said the pidgin version of Genesis you just read and recorded.

EXCERPT 14–2
Reading, Looking Up, and Speaking

An de Lawd,/He done go work hard/for make all ting dey call um Earth./For six day/de Lawd He work/an he done make all ting/—everyting He go put/for Earth./Plenty beef,/plenty cassava,/plenty banana,/plenty yam,/plenty guinea corn,/plenty mango,/plenty groundnut/—everyting./And for de wata/He put plenty fish,/an for de air/He put plenty kinda bird./

—From John Gunther, *Inside Africa*

Faithfulness—Comparing Your Experience and Mine

You might have been more faithful to the pronunciation, grammar, and vocabulary of the original version than I was, and so your version may sound more like the original passage. If your sense group boundaries vary a great deal from mine though, try recording your reading again. This is not to say that your sense groups need be the same size as mine, only that you chunked the groups of words in a similar way. For example, it is possible to read the entire first line as one sense group. It is also possible to pause after *An, make, ting,* and *um.* But pausing after *de, go, work, for, all,* or *call,* I think, does not capture the meaning well.

Though your version might have been more faithful to the original than mine as far as the pronunciation, grammar, and vocabulary went, if you omitted some words that did not make sense to you, such as *cassava, guinea corn,* and *groundnut,* this is not unusual. Indeed, omissions can show understanding just as substitutions can. Reading a word that means nothing to you usually decreases the meaning of a sense group. And so, leaving out meaningless words in the final oral rendition of a sense group is really just the mirror process of making substitutions, a process Michael West has said we should applaud.

Journal Entry

I was in Somalia at a time before Somali was widely printed in materials and books, and few students, especially in the lower grades could change the print into speech. I could say the words since they were printed in a Roman alphabet, but knew the meaning of few of them. Students who listened to me told me in English what I had read in Somali. Because I could say the words and they could not, at first, they were convinced that I knew the meaning of what I was saying. But it was not hard to expose my ignorance. How often, though, we forget that changing print to speech is possible in almost any language once we know the alphabet. I remember asking students in many countries who read lines in books used at religious services in a language they did not know; they rarely knew the meaning, but it seemed not to matter. Many people who sing in choirs sing songs in many languages with little meaning, just changing print to speech. Recall some of your experiences with this phenomenon and note your reactions to it.

Word by Word—Oral Reading inside a Classroom

The lines in Excerpt 14–3 show what might have happened to me had I read my lines in a class where the aim of oral reading was word-perfect or letter-perfect reading, rather than saying "meaningful mouthfuls" to another person. To put it another way, if the goal of reading Genesis had been to communicate content in the subcategory of *study of language pronunciation, sound-letter correspondence,* rather than to communicate content in many areas all at once, including *grammar, lexis, pronunciation,* and *ties,* to name a few, the oral reading would look like that in Excerpt 14–3.

As you can see, the students *reproduced* in the same medium by repeating what the teacher had said—*ds*—as much as they *reproduced* in a different medium by changing print to speech—*dc.* And the students also simply recalled and stated facts from memory: *ps.*

One and Many—Steps for Oral Reading and Read-and-Look-Up

For students to read orally, all that is necessary is that the teacher, or a student in the role of the teacher, tell a student to read. Whether the students stand to read or sit in their seats depends more on traditions in the place the students are than on

EXCERPT 14–3
Oral Reading inside a Classroom

		Communications	*Source/ Target*	*Move Type*	*Use**
1	Teacher:	Begin reading the passage.	t/s	sol	
2	Student:	And the lord (Said, like the following words, with eyes on the text.)	s/t	res	dc
3	Teacher:	*da* again.	t/s	sol	
4	Student:	And da lord	s/t	res	ds + ps
5	Teacher:	No *r—lawd.*	t/s	sol	
6	Student:	Lawd.	s/t	res	ds
7		Sorry.	s/t	rea	
8		He worked	s/t	res	dc
9	Teacher:	*Done go work*—read what's on the page.	t/s	sol	
10	Student:	done go work	s/t	res	ds
11	Student:	very	s/t	res	ps
12	Teacher:	There's no *very—hard.*	t/s	sol	
13	Student:	hard to	s/t	res	ds
14	Teacher:	for make	t/s	sol	
15	Student:	for make	s/t	res	ds
16	Student:	ever . . .	s/t	res	ps
17	Teacher:	all ting	t/s	sol	
18	Student:	Oh.	s/t	rea	
19		all ting day	s/t	res	ds + ps
20	Teacher:	Yes, not *they*	t/s	rea	
21		Now, Yoko take the next line.	t/s	sol	

* *dc* = *reproduce change medium*; the responses are in a medium different from the set in the solicit; *ds* = *reproduce same medium*; the responses here are all simply imitations, a subcategory of reproduce same medium; *ps* = *present state*, recalling information.

procedure. Whether the person in the role of teacher stops the students after each slip, substitution, omission or mispronunciation, and whether the teacher provides a model, a label, or an explanation or simply gives the reader another chance, or whether after acceptable readings the teacher says "good" or in some other way indicates approval, are all matters of feedback, which is a separate topic. Feedback is treated in Episode 12.

For students to read-and-look-up, the first step is to demonstrate the activity. One way to do this is to ask a student to state the commands "Read silently, look up, speak" to you. After each command, you perform the action demanded. Another way is to pretend you are two people. Stand in front of the class facing sideways and say: "Read silently." Then walk forward a few steps, turn around, put on a hat or pair of glasses, and read a sense group in some material you are holding silently. Then walk back to your original place and say "look up," taking off your costume of a hat or a pair of glasses. Walk forward a few steps, turn around, put on the hat or pair of glasses again, and look up. Return to your original station, remove your costume, and say "speak." Walk forward, turn around, and with hat or glasses on say the lines you have read silently, had your mind act on while you were looking up, and moved around.

If the demonstration does not completely exhaust you, you can indicate the sense groups in the material the students are to read. For material written on the blackboard or on handouts prepared beforehand, the sense groups can be marked with slash marks / or arrows ↗ ahead of time. If the material is in the student's books, it can be dictated: "An de Lawd *slash* He done go *slash* work hard *slash* for make all ting *slash* dey call um Earth *slash*," or "An de Lawd *arrow* He done go *arrow* work hard *arrow* for make all ting *arrow* dey call um Earth *arrow*," or "Mark a pause after *Lawd*, *go*, *hard*, *ting*, *Earth*," for example.

The purpose of indicating sense groups is not just procedural. Of course, if each student has marked the same sense groups, unison choral reading is more easily done and individual students can more easily follow each other in saying sense groups in sequence without overlap. But the indication of sense groups with slashes can aid in a substantive way as well. First, they can help students learn boundaries of sense groups. Second, slash marks can serve to show students that they can take in larger units of meaning. Just as the students can be told to mark sense groups with their pencils, so they can be told to erase marks they have made. After the first reading of a passage, students can be told to erase every other slash mark or arrow. Many students will then see clearly that they can chunk larger units of meaning than they thought they could.

After the sense groups are marked, students are told to read a sense group silently, then to look up at another student or the teacher, and finally to say the sense group, in the same manner as they just saw demonstrated. These steps need not be indicated only with words such as "Read silently, look up, speak" or "Read to yourself, look at your partner, say as many words as you've read that make sense." A system of sounds can be used, such as one tap for silent reading, two taps for looking up, and three taps for signaling that the words are to be said. [Background 14–3]

Though to introduce read-and-look up it is useful to go through the steps I just described, once a person understands the idea, a teacher is not needed. Any individual can mark his or her own sense groups, read them silently, look up, and say them, assuming the person understands the material. In fact, the sense groups need not be marked with a pencil either; the end of the last word in a sense group or the space between sense groups serves as well as slashes or arrows once the idea is understood. A partner is not needed either, or at least is not a necessary requirement. One can do the reading alone, though of course it is less social, since one is not saying the sense groups to another person. This can partially be compensated for by using a mirror and pretending that one is speaking to someone else rather than oneself, though this is obviously not very social. The mirror can serve as a reminder to look up. One advantage of doing read-and-look-up in pairs rather than alone is that in pairs, readers can argue about the divisions that were made and in the process learn the types of groups of words that do and do not make sense.

Some students believe that one aim of read-and-look-up is to show everyone how quickly they can read, so they say the words very quickly. While it is useful to vary the time between the commands "read silently," "look up" and "speak" so that students realize that when pushed they can chunk a unit of meaning more and more quickly, there is no need to say the units of meaning quickly. Indeed, at all times the aim is to pause in a leisurely way and say what has been read at a normal rate of delivery rather than at a frenetic one. When a teacher waits an extra few seconds between saying "look up" and "speak," the students are more likely to say the sense groups with normal stress, rhythm, and intonation and without racing.

If mispronunciation occurs in words the students may have to use, the pronunciation problem can be noted and treated in another part of the lesson. If slips occur that obscure the meaning, students can be asked to read the section of the line again silently, then look up and finally say it orally. The same thing can be done if omissions occur that obscure meaning or substitutions. But substitutions that show comprehension do not require that the students reread the lines. Substitutions that show comprehension provide evidence that students are reading in sense groups rather than word by word. In short, the usual "errors" that occur during oral reading which usually cause teachers to stop students are to be handled mainly by asking students to silently reread the material before them. All the teacher need say is "Read silently again, look up again, speak again." Even when students say groups of words that are not sense groups, these are the only directions usually needed.

There are times when, even after being given another chance, students still falter a great deal while doing read-and-look-up. This can be the result of any number of causes. First, the material may be too difficult for the students. If students cannot chunk a passage into sense groups, in fact, the inability is usually an indication that the material is too difficult. Repeated oral renditions of the passage by the teacher, using read-and-look-up, can make a passage more familiar, and therefore less difficult. Another reason some material cannot be chunked well is that it might be too complex for oral reading. Much of what is written is meant only to be read silently. During silent reading, we often go back over the same lines many times, perhaps refer to notes at the bottom of the page or a sketch on another page to fill in meaning. While sense groups are still the basic unit in silent reading, looking up and saying some sense groups is a task that can be counterproductive with some prose written to be read silently. Actual dialogs between people and many narrative passages lend themselves particularly well to read-and-look-up, but technical prose meant to be read silently does not.

Once the students begin to master the steps in read-and-look-up, some of them begin to go through the steps in a mechanical way. Their sense groups stay the same, average length. When they look up, they look at the ceiling, the windows, or other desks, or even look back down to the page, rather than at a person. When they say the sense groups they have read silently, they do so with primary stress on each word, or identical intonation contours on every group of words, in spite of various meanings each sense group contains. Additionally, when the students are not told to read-and-look-up, they don't. For example, if a student is asked to read the directions for an exercise to the class before a class does the exercise, the student simply says the words into the page, one by one.

When such a lack of transfer is evident, or when students do not lengthen the sense groups they say during subsequent readings or over a period of time, and do not match their tone of voice, intonation, and stress to the meaning, the cause might be a lack of understanding of the rationale for the enterprise. Being told that substitutions are permissible, even encouraged, after long periods of instruction and feedback that demanded letter-perfect and word-perfect reading can be mystifying. Marking a book—even with a pencil—after instructions not to write in books, and saying words to another person rather than to a book can seem odd after keeping one's eyes on material for a long time. Even the concept of sense groups can be threatening after reliance on single words.

One way to decrease the mechanical nature of read-and-look-up is to indicate or solicit the rationale for it. Walking across the front of the classroom with short steps, perhaps putting the heel of one foot right in front of the toe of the other, can demonstrate word-by-word reading. A regular walk across the front of the classroom can symbolize reading in sense groups. Reading a story alternately with eyes on the class and on the page, in sense groups and word by word, and then asking students to indicate which they prefer, can clarify the rationale for some. And for others, having them figure out the average number of words in sense groups they chunk at different times during the course can help make the rationale clear, since the number will increase over time if they are really using them.

The clearest rationale, though, results when a student suddenly realizes that the understanding of a passage is clearer when it is read in chunks rather than word by word. And this can occur even if a student may not be able to say what he or she's read very strongly, and if he or she may not be able to look at another student without some blinking. In making the rationale for read-and-look-up clear, it is important to indicate that read-and-look-up is a means to an end rather than an end in itself. The end includes these goals; prevent calling words without attaching meaning to them; prevent word-by-word reading; develop the ability to read in sense groups; increase students' silent reading efficiency by being able to chunk larger and larger units of meaning in a passage; diagnose and evaluate students' production of sounds; memorize or master some parts of passages that contain things students are likely to be called upon to say; give students practice in saying sense groups to others and thus help build confidence in speaking the target language; concentrate readers' attention on the material before them; learn to identify sense groups.

Highlighting Differences—Describing Oral Reading and Read-and-Look-Up in FOCUS

One way to describe the reading shown in Excerpts 14–2 and 14–3 is with the ordinary terms used in discussions of reading. We could say that in Excerpt 14–2 I used the read-and-look-up technique and in Excerpt 14–3 I read orally, and the teacher was interested in letter-perfect and word-perfect reading. To be more specific, the fact could be added that in both excerpts I made substitutions. The fact that I repeated models the teacher provided in Excerpt 14–3 could be mentioned as well. And the observation that I read silently before saying the words in Excerpt 14–2 could be noted also.

Another way to describe the communications in Excerpts 14–2 and 14–3 is to use FOCUS. By using FOCUS categories, I can show relationships between activities that in ordinary descriptions seem to be totally unrelated to each other, such as oral reading and dictations, or even oral reading and read-and-look-up. In Table 14–2, I've used FOCUS to highlight some of the distinctions between the reading and looking up I did in Excerpt 14–2 and the oral reading of students in Excerpt 14–3.

TABLE 14–2
Two Ways of Reading

Excerpt 14–2 **Reading, Looking Up, and Speaking**			**Excerpt 14–3** **Oral Reading inside a Classroom**		
ENGLISH DESCRIPTIONS	FOCUS DESCRIPTIONS		ENGLISH DESCRIPTIONS	FOCUS DESCRIPTIONS	
	*Medium**	*Use†*		*Medium**	*Use†*
Silently reading the material	lv	ar			
Chunking each sense group with a pause	si	cx			
Looking up and letting the mind act on the sense group just read	si	a			
Saying words orally on page	lv → la	dc	Saying words orally on page	lv → la	dc
Making substitutions for words on the page from memory	la	ps	Repeating words teacher or other students give as models	la	ds

* *si* = silence; *la* = linguistic aural, speaking; *lv* = linguistic visual, writing or print; *lv→ la* = changing one medium to another; the first one is changed into the second.

† *ar* = *attend,* read silently; *cx* = *characterize examine; a* = *attend,* waiting; *dc* = *reproduce* by changing one medium into another; *ds* = *reproduce* in the same medium as when we repeat a model another has given; *ps* = *present state,* recalling information from memory or stating facts.

III. SPEECH TO PRINT—TAKING NOTES AND WRITING DICTATIONS

"An de Lawd"—Changing Speech to Print in a Classroom in Three Ways

I've transcribed three dictations of "An de Lawd" being given. The uses in the first two, those in Excerpt 14–4 and 14–5, parallel the uses in most oral reading in classes. The uses in the third, the one in Excerpt 14–6, parallel the uses in read-and-look-up. The major distinction between different dictations and different types of oral reading to me is that in oral reading we change print to speech, while in dictations and note taking we change speech into print.

In Excerpt 14–4, consider the student responses as mirror images of the student responses in Excerpt 14–3. In both cases, single words are being translated from one medium to another, rather than, say, letter by letter, or sense group by sense group, or sentence by sentence.

In Excerpt 14–5, the changing of mediums is done sentence by sentence. But as you'll see as you look at the communications and the coding, the student tasks are not limited to changing mediums.

EXCERPT 14–4
An—de—Lawd

		Communications	*Source/ Target*	*Move Type*	*Medium*	*Use*
1	Teacher:	Write what I say. Listen carefully so I don't have to keep repeating the words. And keep your eyes on your own papers. Get ready. Here's the first one.	t/c	str		
2		An—de—Lawd (Dashes indicate there is a three second pause between the words.)	t/c	sol		
3	Some students:	(As soon as teacher begins dictating, begin to write.) An de	ss/t	res	la → lv	dc
4	Student$_1$:	Again?	s_1/t	sol		
5	Teacher:	An—de—(Reading from text.)	t/c	res	lv → la	dc
6	Some students:	(Continue writing.) An de	ss/t	res	la → lv	dc
7	Teacher:	He—done—go—work	t/c	sol		
8	Some students:	(As teacher begins dictating, begin to write.) He done go	ss/t	res	la → lv	dc
9	Student$_2$:	Capital *I—o* or *a*?	s_2/t	sol		
10	Teacher:	Pay attention. Listen.	t/s_2	rea		
11		hard—for—make—all—ting—dey—call	t/c	sol		
12	Students:	(Write as many words as they can as they try to listen to the words as well.)	ss/t	res	la → lv + la	dc + al
13	Student$_3$:	What comes after *for*?	s_3/t	sol		
14	Teacher:	make—all—ting—dey—call—um—Earth. (Reading orally from what he just wrote.)	t/s_3	res	lv → la	dc

The first two dictations, in Excerpts 14–4 and 14–5, like the oral reading required in Excerpt 14–3, allow no time during the dictation for the mind to act on the material. While it is true that asking students to prepare a passage for homework, as the teacher did in Excerpt 14–5, provides each student with an opportunity to *attend* to the material over and over again, preparing for *attending* to speech—*la*—and *attending* to print—*lv*—are obviously different from having time to *attend* to speech during the actual dictation. During the dictation itself, no time was provided for processing the material that was said.

In Excerpt 14–6, page 318, the teacher employs the same steps West suggested for getting students to read-and-look-up. The only difference is that in the dictation in Excerpt 14–6, the students are changing speech to print rather than print to speech, as in read-and-look-up.

EXCERPT 14–5
An . . . Earth

		Communications	Source/ Target	Move Type	Medium	Use
1	Teacher:	You've read "It Done Begin" for homework so you should know it. I'm going to read it completely three times. The first time, just listen. The second time, write it sentence by sentence. The third and final time, as I read it through, correct your sentences so you can hand in a perfect paper.	t/c	str		
2		Now, listen. (Reads through the passage orally, eyes on paper, pausing at the ends of sentences.)	t/c	sol		
3	Students:	(Listen to the oral reading of the sentences in the passage.)	ss/t	res	la	al
4	Teacher:	Now, write this: An de Lawd, He done go work hard for make all ting dey call um Earth.	t/c	sol		
5	Students:	(Write as much as they can, starting to write as teacher begins speaking.)	ss/t	res	la → lv	dc
6	$Student_1$:	Please repeat . . .	s_1/t	sol		
7	Teacher:	I'll read it a third time for you to check.	t/c	res		
8		Here's the next one: For six day de Lawd He work an He done make all ting—everyting He go put for Earth.	t/c	sol		
9	Students:	(Write as much as they can, starting to write as teacher begins speaking.)	ss/t	res	la → lv	dc
10	Teacher:	(After finishing the second presentation.) Now, here's the last reading.	t/c	sol		
11	Some students:	(As teacher says sentences, write words or parts of words they missed before.)	ss/t	res	la → lv	dc
12	Other students:	(As teacher says sentences, look at the papers of their neighbors and copy items they missed and are not sure of.)	ss/t	res	lv	ds

EXCERPT 14–6
Listening, Looking Down, and Writing

		Communications	Source/ Target	Move Type	Medium	Use
1	Teacher:	We're going to have a dictation now.	t/c	str		
2		Copy the title from the blackboard and the numbers 1–5 on the left-hand margin, as you see them here. (Indicates blackboard.)	t/c	sol		
3	Students:	(Copy the title and numbers 1–5 in their notebooks.)	ss/t	res	lv + nv*	ds
4	Teacher:	When I say the lines, look at me. When I finish, and say "pencils" pick up your pencils and look at your notebooks, ready to write. When I say "write," write as much of the line that I've said that makes sense you can remember.	t/c	str		
5		One. An de Lawd, He done go work hard for make all ting dey call um Earth.	t/c	sol		
6	Students:	(Listen with their eyes on the teacher.)	ss/t	res	la	al
7	Teacher:	(Finishes.) Pencils!	t/c	sol		
8	Students:	(Pick up their pencils and look at their notebooks and wait.)	ss/t	res	si	a
9	Teacher:	Write!	t/c	sol		
10		(Walks around room looking at notebooks.)	t/c	str		
11	Student$_1$:	(Writes *An de Lord, He done go work hard.*)	s_1/t	res	la → lv	dc†
12	Student$_2$:	(Writes *An de lawd, he done go work hard for make all ting dey call um earth.*)	s_2/t	res	la → lv	dc
13	Teacher:	Juan, say what you've written to the class.	t/s_2	sol		
14	Juan:	An de Lawd, He done go work hard for make all ting dey call um Earth. (Reads and looks up and says the words in a group.)	s_2/s + t	res	lv si lv → la	ar a dc

EXCERPT 14–6
(*continued*)

		Communications	Source/ Target	Move Type	Medium	Use
15	Other students:	(Listen and look at Juan.)	s/s_2	res	la	al
16	Teacher:	Pencils!	t/c	sol		
17	Students:	(Pick up pencils and prepare to continue writing.)	ss/t	res	si	a
18	Teacher:	Write!	t/c	sol		
19	Students:	(Write as much as they can from the entire sentence., taking from 15 to 35 seconds to write a line.)	ss/t	res	la → lv	dc
20	Teacher:	(Tells Juan to change three letters to capitals.)	t/s_2	sol		
21	Juan:	(Changes *l, h, e* to *L, H*, and *E*.)	s_2/t	res	lv	ps‡
22	Teacher:	(Asks Juan to write his sentence on the blackboard after changing letters.)	t/s_2	sol		
23	Juan:	(Writes his sentence on the board.)	$s_2/s + t$	res	lv	ds
24	Teacher:	(Points to third word—*Lord*—on paper and to board.)	t/s_1	sol		
25	Student$_1$:	(Changes *or* to *aw* in *Lord*.)**	s_1/t	res	lv	ds

* The *nv* is used to code the numbers.
† To distinguish full lines from partial, a subscript can be used.
‡ I code this *ps* for *present state* because the student is simply recalling something and writing it down from memory.
** Students and teacher continue the same steps until all the lines have been written correctly by all the students.

Journal Entry

When you studied foreign languages, or in dictations you have observed, do you remember titles such as "Dictation" or "Sentences with the *-ing* form" or "The break in" and other narrative type titles better? When you observe, which titles do the students seem to enjoy more—those that are strictly procedural like "Dictation" or those that describe the area of study like "Sentences with the *-ing* form" or those related to the action contained in the material dictated?

Lessons from Grocery Lists—Changing Speech to Print in and out of Classrooms

Some of the same steps employed in Excerpt 14–6 are used outside classrooms. Watching people make grocery lists that their parent or spouse dictates, for example, usually reveals that items are not written until they have been said completely. Also, though the words used to name the groceries are usually few in number, shorter than many sentences, they are said as a unit or group rather than one by one with long pauses in between. For example, "a large loaf of whole wheat bread" is more likely to be said as "a large loaf" pause "of whole wheat bread" than as "a" pause "large" pause "loaf" pause "of" pause "whole" pause "wheat" pause "bread." Grouping of words often takes place when phone numbers are given or words spelled too. A grouping such as "seven nine four" pause "three two" pause "three two" is more likely to be written without requests for repetition than a telephone number given without grouping such as this: "seven" pause "nine" pause "four" pause "three" pause "two" pause "three" pause "two." You may have heard the schoolchild riddle in which the word *baseball* is spelled letter by letter with a few-second pause between each letter. After the word is spelled, one is asked what the word is. Few can say, since the pauses between each letter put such a strain on our usual way of processing information that it is almost impossible to keep the first letter in mind long enough to connect it with the second one, let alone all the other letters.

For longer utterances, such as business letters or reports that are dictated, the usual sense groups have to be used. Pausing at random is no help. If one cannot take shorthand, or take simultaneous transcriptions on a machine such as court stenographers use, one must usually record the material. When the recording is played, or the transcription looked at before typing, one has to break up the words into groups that make sense. Then, one has to stop the machine, or look away from the stenographic marks, look at the typewriter, and type what has been heard or seen that makes sense. The stopping of the recorder or the pausing and looking away from the stenographic marks fulfill the same function as the pause or slash mark in read-and-look-up does, and the grasping of a sense group in the writing of a dictation does.

In an office, the dictionary serves the same purpose as the student's written model on the blackboard in Excerpt 14–6, and as the student's sentence in his notebook does in the last line of Excerpt 14–5. Each serves as a touchstone with which the material that has been written can be compared. When the student in Excerpt 14–5 looked at his neighbor's notebook so he could copy the right spelling, he was doing the same thing many of us do when we aren't sure of our internal information: we check with some source of external information. Many teachers spend a great deal of effort trying to encourage students to use dictionaries to check spelling, and yet when the same students perform a parallel activity such as checking a neighbor's paper, they are asked to keep their eyes to themselves.

An alternative to telling students to stop checking sources outside themselves would be to tell them some steps to follow in copying that may lead to more retention. They could be told that whenever they copy, either from a dictionary or another person's paper, they should look at the word or larger unit to be copied, then look away and pause before finally writing the material, rather than just copying it letter by letter while looking at it. These steps may give the mind a chance to process the letters, perhaps group them in some way, and as a result increase the likelihood that some mental processes can come into play. When some people follow these steps, either in copying or in taking down telephone numbers or items for a grocery list, they remember them longer than if they just write letter by letter or number by number, with long pauses in between, even if they lose the note they wrote the material on. Haven't you written material heard in some type of group or copied some and then remembered the material even though you lost the note?

Journal Entry

If you haven't taken a break yet, take one now.

Journal Entry

Do dictations seem dictatorial to you? Their origin is of course the same, meaning to speak, but their denotative meanings have diverged. Do they connote similar feelings to you?

Two Languages for Everyone—Comparing Varieties of Oral Reading and Dictations in English and FOCUS

In order to highlight the fact that oral reading and dictation can be looked at as mirror images of each other, and at the same time provide additional help in making clear the meaning of FOCUS elements, I've developed Table 14–3. On the blank line at the end of each description in English, write in the letter of the description in FOCUS that fits. The matching done by others is given in the footnote.

TABLE 14–3
Oral Reading and Dictation in English and FOCUS

DESCRIPTIONS IN ENGLISH		DESCRIPTIONS IN FOCUS		
		Source/ Target	*Medium*	*Use**
1. A person running for election as a member of a school board reads a speech to a group of parents and never once removes his eyes from the speech in front of him. ___	a.	s/t	la → lv	dc
2. Students write down the sentences their teacher dictates word by word. ___	b.	t/o + c	lv → la	dc
3. An actor looks down at a poem, grasps a sense group, looks at the audience and lets his mind act on the sense group, and finally says the sense group to the audience, making a substitution in one place. A member of the audience who knows the poem says the line loudly after the actor finishes the line. ___	c.	c/t	la	al
		c/o	si	cx*
			si	a
			la → lv	dc
4. A caller writes down a telephone number recited to him by the telephone operator, but before he writes it down, he repeats groups of the number to the telephone operator. ___	d.	s/t	la	al
			si	cx*
			la	ds
		s/o	la → lv	dc
5. Students write sentences their teacher dictates, but never start writing until they have heard the entire sentence, and then chunk only a part of the sentence that they can process before actually writing. ___	e.	t/o	lv	ar
			si	cx*
			si	a
		t/c	lv → la	dc
		s/t	la	ps

* The *cx* can be used to incidate that the person is dividing the passage into sense groups; usually, this use is communicated so we can observe it. But as a convention, I sometimes try to contrast those who break *sets* into sense groups from those who don't by coding *characterize examine* communicated by *silence*—in short, done in the head.

Matching done by others. (1) *b*; (2) *a*; (3) *e*; (4) *d*; (5) *c*.

IV. AFTER A BREAK—CHANGING ALL MEDIUMS

Eighty-one—Coding the Changing of Many Mediums

If you followed my directions in the last journal entry and took a break between the end of Section III and the beginning of this section, you changed print into movement: *lv* → *po*. And you were reminded that we are not limited to changing only linguistic aural and visual mediums in oral reading and dictations. As diverse as the variations of oral reading and dictations are in Excerpts 14–3 to 14–6, they are alike in one way: They require the changing of only *linguistic aural* and *visual* mediums.

In Table 14–4 I've listed the mediums I code with FOCUS in two rows in the medium column to show how theoretically any type of medium can be changed into any other type of medium. The *eighty-one* refers to the number of changes possible without subgroupings of any of the subcategories of mediums, so in fact even more than eighty-one changes are theoretically possible.

To make some of the theoretically possible changes of mediums illustrated in Table 14–4 concrete, I've described a number of medium changes in Excerpt 14–7. As you can see, I've left the medium column blank so you can fill in the mediums that are being changed in the activities I describe. Use the abbreviations from the mediums in Table 14–4 as an aid in your coding. If you find it easier to use a *to* in place of an arrow between the mediums that are being changed, do so. The arrow I used in the other excerpts is just a convention; *to* can serve as well. Compare your coding with the coding done by others, given in the footnote.

TABLE 14–4
Eighty-one

*Medium**	
la	si
lv	po
lo	pv
na	pa
nv	no
no	nv
pa	na
pv	lo
po	lv
si	la

* *la* = *linguistic aural*: spoken words; *lv* = *linguistic visual*: written or transcribed words; *lo* = *linguistic other*: Braille, and other letters we can feel but not see or hear; *na* = *nonlinguistic aural*: music and noise; *nv* = *nonlinguistic visual*: pictures, objects, maps, diagrams and lines; *no* = *nonlinguistic other*: odors, temperatures and what we sense; *pa* = *paralinguistic aural*: tone of voice; *pv* = *paralinguistic visual*: gestures; *po* = *paralinguistic other*: doing things with objects; movement, touching; *si* = *silence*: waiting, or the absence of other mediums.

EXCERPT 14–7
Coding the Changing of Many Mediums

	Descriptions of Communications	*Source/ Target*	*Medium*	*Use*
1	A teacher asks a group to write words to match these pictures:	t/g_1	______	dc
2	The teacher writes the words *restaurant, women's toilet, men's toilet, coffee shop* and *telephone* on cards and asks another group to draw signs for each word to post at an airport. The groups will compare results.	t/g_2	______	dc
3	Simon Says is being played. The teacher says "Simon says raise your right hand" and most of the students do.	t/s	______	dc
4	The teacher says "Raise your left hand" and a few students do; they are asked to stand to the side of the class and no longer participate. [Background 14–4]	t/s	______	dc
5	Sketches of cassava, banana, yam, guinea corn, mango and groundnut have been drawn on a handout. Students are asked to color the sketches with the appropriate colors.	t/s	______	dc
6	Teacher points to a red square on a chart and a student says a sound. The teacher points to a blue square and another student says a different sound. [Background 14–5]	t/s	______	dc
7	Each student is given a card with the phonetic symbol for a vowel on it. Each student shapes his or her mouth the way one has to in order to say the vowel on the card in isolation.	s/s	______	dc
8	All the other students look at the mouth of the student forming the sound, and the first one who thinks he or she knows which vowel is being formed, either from the lip position or jaw position—each of which is usually somewhat exaggerated—calls out the sound.	s/s	______	dc
9	The teacher plays a tape with short segments of music on it and students are asked to identify the moods they feel during each segment by drawing a face on which the eyes and mouth are shaped differently to reflect different moods.	t/s	______	dc
10	Teacher plays tape of a foghorn blowing, water splashing and surging against what seems to be a hard surface, loud crunching sounds, static on a radio, and a siren, in this sequence. He then asks the students to write words to represent the sounds in the same sequence so a person would know what happened. [Background 14–6]	t/s	______	dc
11	After reading a description of population trends, students are asked to make a graph showing the trends, using symbols for the groups represented in the graph rather than words.	t/s	______	dc
12	One student "uhms" the stress pattern in a sentence, and another student draws large and small boxes to represent the dis-	s/s	______	dc

EXCERPT 14–7
(*continued*)

	Descriptions of Communications	*Source/ Target*	*Medium*	*Use*
	tinction between stressed and unstressed syllables. The sentence *It's mine* would sound like uhm UHM and be drawn like this: ▭ □, to cite a simple example. [Background 14–7]			
13	A student is asked to give another student a tool from a pile of tools. The particular tool that is to be picked up and given is indicated by the teacher who makes the noise the tool makes. So after "bang bang" the student picks up a hammer, after "zzzz" the student picks up a saw.	t/s	_____	dc
14	A person stands in front of another person lecturing and signs the lecture for those in the audience who are deaf.	t/s	_____	dc
15	I have given you each a picture of a person in a particular mood. One at a time, I want you to make your face and body reflect the mood of the person in your picture to the student I assign as your partner. When you each finish, your partner will look at the picture and say whether you accurately reflected the mood in it.	s/s	_____	dc
16	Change each of the word problems I have written on the blackboard into mathematical formulas.	t/s	_____	dc
17	Act as if it is late at night, and everyone in your house is sleeping—all is quiet. Now, news of an accident has just been announced and a hush falls over an audience. Now, you are in an empty store, and there is no noise. [Background 14–8]	t/s	_____	dc
18	Draw a triangle, each side one inch long. Now, draw a box one inch square in the upper-right-hand corner of your paper so the sides of the box are one inch from the top and side of the paper.	t/s	_____	dc
19	Students connect points on cards to form different shapes. Here is one example: 1 2 7. 8. 9.3 .4 6. .5	t/s	_____	dc
20	One person throws two dice. Another person holds up six fingers to indicate to those who cannot see the dice that a "six" has been thrown.	s/s	_____	dc

Coding done by others: 1. *nv* to *lv*; 2. *lv* to *nv*; 3. *la* to *pv*; 4. *la* to *pv*, which is an error and *la* to *si* which is what the direction requires since omitting Simon says means one is to do nothing but wait and should not move; 5. *nv* to *nv*; 6. *nv* to *la*; 7. *lv* to *nv*—though the mouth can be used as body language, here it is used as an object and is no different from a sketch or model of the mouth; 8. *nv* to *la*; 9. *na* to *nv*; 10. *na* to *lv*; 11. *lv* to *nv*; 12. *pa* to *nv*; 13. *na* to *nv*—the action of giving the tool is not what communicates, but the tool itself that is selected; 14. *la* to *lo*; 15. *nv* to *pv*; 16. *lv* to *nv*; 17. *la* to *si* and perhaps *la* to *po* since some movement is involved too; 18. *la* to *nv*; 19. *nv* to *nv*—numbers in this form are not linguistic—one, two, etc., are; 1, 2, etc., are nonlinguistic because they are rendered differently in different languages, e.g., *uno, dos, ichi, ni*; but the dots and numbers are different types of nonlinguistic visual mediums, and therefore changing one to the other still is an example of reproducing in a different medium; 20. *nv* to *pv*.

Journal Entry

In the construction of tall buildings, a derrick is often used to lift steel beams or equipment to the upper stories. The person operating the derrick cannot see where the material to be lifted is, and must be told whether to move the material to the right or left, or up or down by a person who either stands on the material as it is raised, or is in a position to see it. An electric bell system is used to signal the derrick operator rather than a walkie-talkie because the bells are more reliable. "Nothing gets lost in the translation" is what those who work with derricks say. With a walkie-talkie, *noise* can interfere with the message. But using one ring of the bell to mean left, two to mean right, three to stop, four to mean up, five to mean down removes all ambiguity. For the correct action to be performed, *non-linguistic aural* mediums are preferred to *linguistic aural* mediums.

In your experience, what are some other times when *linguistic* mediums are avoided for changing mediums into actions?

V. PROVE IT TO ME—THEORETICAL SUPPORT FOR DOING IT WITH *a + dc*

We Forgot the Lines—Short-Term and Long-Term Memory

If the theory of remembering that divides memory into short- and long-term memory is valid, any oral reading that we do without pausing is unlikely to aid in retaining anything for more than a few seconds. As a group of students said at the end of a class I observed when I asked them if I could please tape-record them saying a dialog they had just read orally about fifteen times, "Oh, we forget the lines we read as soon as we stop reading them and the class is over." I could not record the dialog they had been reading orally word perfectly for the entire period because, for one thing, the students were simply employing their short-term memory—the memory we use to pay attention to something for the moment. Items that enter short-term memory as separate bits of information, such as the individual letters or words we say in the type of oral reading shown in Excerpt 14–3, have no meaning, and as a result are forgotten as soon as our attention is directed to something else. [Background 14–9]

In read-and-look-up, the act of looking up, away from the print, either forces us to read "meaningful mouthfuls" rather than individual words or forces us to flirt with the page, glancing down for another peek as soon as the few words we can put into our short-term memory are said. This is why it is so critical for readers not to look back to the page after once looking up. Keeping our eyes on the print prevents us from engaging anything but short-term memory. But if we look up and pause before we say what we have read, there is a chance that some of the material will be processed in our long-term memory.

Though Michael West did not refer to the theory of short- and long-term memory when he wrote about read-and-look-up, he knew the crucial role the time of the pause for looking up played in memory. By looking away from the material to a person, he pointed out that "the connection is not from book to mouth, but from book to brain, and then from brain to mouth," and that this "interval of memory constitutes half the learning process." [Background 14–10]

To store one bit of information in long-term memory takes more than a few seconds. And so, if the bit is one word, and we have to immediately say another word, without more than a few seconds' pause, the first word fails to move from our short-term memory into our long-term memory before we say the second word. But if we read for the meaning, and if, after each series of words that makes sense, we pause for a few seconds so our mind can in some way act on them, before we say them or look at another series of words, it is likely that the pauses between the series of words will enable the series—"meaningful mouthfuls"—to move into long-term memory. Once in long-term memory, items are considered learned, and if the right conditions exist, the items can be retrieved. It takes about the same amount of time for a word to move from short-term memory to long-term memory as it does for a group of words that constitute a sense group to move from short-term to long-term memory, if the group makes up one bit of information, that is, if they contain meaning. [Background 14–11]

One way to find out whether someone is making use of only short-term memory, or in fact moving meaning from short-term to long-term memory is to see whether the person flirts with the page or not. Glancing down to check the words usually means that the reader is reading individual words, retaining them only long enough to say them, and thus not moving them from short-term memory to long-term memory. Another way to see whether long-term memory is being used is to see whether the person is reading letter and word perfectly or not. If the reader is, then long-term memory is probably not being employed, and the person is reading words rather than meaning. The substitutions I made in my rendition of the pidgin version of Genesis in Excerpt 14-2 would have been impossible if I had been using only short-term memory because short-term memory allows us to communicate only what is before us.

More than Mediums—Internal and External Information

The substitutions I made in Excerpt 14–2 illustrate another aspect of taking in mediums and producing mediums: the interplay between what is in our heads—internal information—and the print, noise, voices or other mediums we take in or produce—external information. Read-and-look-up is based on the premise that the page in front of us supplies only part of the meaning, and that our own experience enables us to supply the other part. The substitutions I made in Excerpt 14–2 as I read Genesis show that meaning came from external and internal information, not just from the external information supplied by the letters and words on the page. If I had gotten all the meaning only from the external information on the page, I could not have said "He worked very hard" for "He done go work hard," or "in the water" for "for de wata." As we shall see, this interplay between external and internal information, like short-term and long-term memory, affects all the changes we make from one medium to another, not just the changing of print to speech in oral reading. [Background 14–12]

It's Not Wrong—Miscue Analysis

The changes I made in my oral reading of the pidgin version of Genesis in Excerpt 14–2 were not a random series of accidents. Like the changes students make when reading their own langauge, or a langauge they are studying, my substitutions and omissions can, if studied, reveal something of the reading process and also indicate areas particular students or groups of students need instruction in. For example, if a group of readers said the word *read* in the present tense, even when past-tense indicators such as *yesterday* or *last week* preceded the verbs, some instruction in the ties between time words and tense could be given. But since the present tense pronunciation might be used simply because the past-tense version is not known, indicating that *read* is pronounced to rhyme with *bed* when it follows time words is also called for. The point is simply that while substitutions and omissions can show comprehension, they can show confusion and lack of understanding as well. When they do, they can be treated as miscues, not errors, and serve as a basis for deciding some areas that students need instruction in. Without some miscues, it is unlikely that students are being provided with mediums and content that provide something for them to learn from. We know what we need to learn from the miscues we produce. [Background 14–13]

VI. TOO EASY OR TOO DIFFICULT?— MODULATING THE LEVEL OF DIFFICULTY

Give Me, Give Me—Introduction

After coding the mediums changed in Excerpt 14–7, some react by saying "the examples are either too easy or too difficult for students I am involved with." The task of changing mediums, like all tasks, needs to be adjusted so it is neither too difficult nor too easy. If each person does the task perfectly, it is obviously too easy. If few can do the task without a miscue, it is obviously too difficult. To assure that each individual must expend more effort to perform a task and at the same time give the student at least a 70 percent chance of performing the task correctly, the difficulty of the task can be adjusted in a number of ways. [Background 14–14]

Give Me Time—Altering the Time Provided

Since the first step in changing a medium is to take in a medium, the first step that can affect the difficulty level is the amount of time given to *attend* to the medium before the task to change it is solicited. While one could argue that we must take in a medium as a step in the performance of any task, I have taken the position that we should only note the taking in of a medium as a separate step if the step is deliberate, as it is in read-and-look-up and a dictation in which students are not allowed to write until a deliberate interval of time elapses.

If students are not deliberately allowed a period of time to *attend* before *changing mediums*, and errors occur, the alternative is deliberately to allow, say, three seconds to *attend* to the medium, then three seconds to *attend* in silence so the mind can process the medium. If students are changing mediums without any miscues after being allowed three seconds to take in the medium and another three to process the mediums, one alternative is to decrease the time allowed for students to *attend*, both to the observable medium and to the medium I code as *silence*. In read-and-look-up, the time can be increased or decreased for *attending* to the material by saying "look up" sooner or later than the time that produces large or small numbers of miscues. In a dictation, the time can be varied by saying "write" sooner or later. In "Simon Says" and other spoken commands that require speech to be changed into action, the time allowed for compliance can be shortened or lengthened.

The time allowed for changing mediums can be varied also. In many classes I've observed, eight-word sentences in dictations take fifteen seconds or so at the beginning of a term and sixty at the end. When students are not required to do more, they sometimes do less. If we do not constantly expect more in a deliberate way, many students will do less unconsciously simply because more effort is taken to take in mediums provided quickly than those provided slowly. Within a group of more than two, the amount of time different people take to finish the sentences in a dictation varies just as widely. One rule seems to be that the time allowed for changing a medium, at least in the case of dictations, is used!

Except for students with physical limitations, such as broken fingers or sprained wrists or arms or broken pens, students can usually change speech to writing in less and less time, with fewer miscues over a period of time. One alternative to try after miscues is more time for changing the mediums. Another alternative is to provide less time. If a class writes an eight-word sentence in thirty seconds one day, require them to write it in fifteen seconds the next day, and allow sixty seconds on another day.

One way systematically to vary the time allowed for students to *attend* and *reproduce change mediums* is to introduce the material electronically or mechanically. By using a tape recorder, record player, or slide projector, you are freed from concentrating on what you are doing and what you want the students to do, so you can circulate and provide help on an individual basis as the medium is being communicated. Knowing that the machine moves relentlessly on makes concentration easier for some. The material can be presented identically over and over in this way, as well, and if any disputes arise, the material can be presented again for evidence.

The idea of varying the amount of time provided for *attending* and *reproducing* in a different medium is not to make students fail, only to make the material they *attend* to and *reproduce* in a different medium equal to their ability, and if they don't produce miscues, it is below their ability.

Journal Entry

When most of us do pushups or other exercises, there comes a point when we seem to be unable to do any more than we have just done. But, after a short break, we can resume the exercises and do at least a few more, in most cases. In trying to adjust the difficulty level, how do your students react to small breaks? Are they able to do things that just a moment before they seemed incapable of doing? How do you react to small breaks? Do they give you the needed recovery time to do what just a moment before seemed impossible?

If you now feel the way you do when you have reached your limit in pushups, take a break and see how the next sections seem after the break.

Give Me Less—Changing the Amount of Information Provided

The amount of information in the materials *attended* to and *reproduced* can be varied just as the time can. Decreasing the amount of material presented is one obvious way to alter the amount of information. If eight-word sentences produce a miscue, four-word sentences can be tried. If unfamiliar words are misunderstood, their number can be decreased. If pictures with background and objects produce five misunderstandings in ten responses, pictures without background can be tried. If six objects in a picture produce misinformation from each student, pictures with one or two objects can be tried. If students continually miss lines in a song they've been asked to transcribe, a recording of a song without accompanying music can be tried.

Even if the amount of information itself is not decreased in size, the available information provided can be increased by requiring the students to perform only part of the task. The other part can be performed by the teacher or a student who has mastered the material. For example, words likely to be misspelled can be written on the blackboard during a dictation so they can be copied by those who cannot spell them. Marks of punctuation can be written on the board or dictated along with the words. Or, the papers students write on can have parts of the sentences being dictated printed on them. In a drawing task, students could be asked to complete a sketch rather than start from scratch.

If, on the other hand, the students change the mediums of the material with ease, steps need to be taken to partially obscure the message. To be technical, *noise* can be added to the message. If an eight-word sentence is changed perfectly, a sixteen-word sentence may be long enough to obscure part of the information available from one glance at the sentence. Static, background sounds like coughing, shuffling feet, and the moving of chairs can provide *noise* during dictations and other changes of mediums as well. After all, most people can understand at least part of most messages under ideal conditions, but the times when we usually most need to capture messages occur in less than ideal conditions. The critical time to understand a child is when the child is speaking and crying at the same time. If we are told to move a bicycle or a car, for example, it is likely that the command will be given in a noisy place rather than in a quiet place. In short, we are likely to have to *attend* to *linguistic aural* mediums and *nonlinguistic aural* mediums at the same time—*la* + *na*—and extract the linguistic message and change it, possibly losing some of it in the process. [Background 14–15]

Another kind of *noise* that can occur in a dictation is *paralinguistic aural*: the distorted rhythm and stress and intonation of sentences that are dictated at a rate of delivery slower than normal. Because an extremely slow delivery distorts the normal rhythm, stress and intonation of a sentence, it is more difficult to write such a sentence than one given at a normal rate. A slow delivery is thus another kind of *noise*. To discover the normal rate, record the person dictating during a dictation and when speaking outside the classroom, and compare the number of syllables spoken per second. To see which speed is easiest and hardest to make sense of, the rate used on one day in a dictation can be doubled for another day and halved on another day and the number of errors compared. [Background 14–16]

To increase *noise* in the presentation of pictures or gestures, the distance between the students and the teacher can be increased, or in the case of pictures, small ones can be used rather than large ones. The parallel alternative for aural mediums is to decrease and increase the volume of delivery: whisper and shout or play a recording at very low volume and then normal and finally at extra loud. In a large room, walking around the room as one speaks gives different students a different volume of delivery because the distance between speakers and targets varies.

Students can be asked to cover one eye, or the gestures can be done at the side of the room rather than at the front so students are able to see less than normal. In a dictation, obscuring the mouth and face by standing in back of students removes the small amount of information provided by these mediums. Words can also be deleted from passages to be dictated or read so students will have to produce them. The deletion of words as well as the addition of extraneous words to obscure and clarify meaning are treated in detail in Episode 10.

Of course, another alternative is to replace the material used with easier or more difficult material. But this is more easily said than done, once the activity is underway. And no matter how well material is selected, knowing how well or poorly students can change the mediums it is communicating is hard to predict. Furthermore, simply changing the material itself—introducing a different passage, set of commands or noises, pictures, or actions—implies that the external information provided by the material itself is the central variable. One of the aims of adding and deleting noise from the mediums and thus modulating the amount of information the mediums communicate is to help all the participants realize that to *attend* to mediums and to change them, different proportions of external and internal information are needed. At first, when *noise* is introduced, some students are baffled. But as messages are whispered, shouted, shown out of focus, interfered with by coughs, students learn to make more and more use of their internal information.

Though miscues need to be used as signals to vary the amount of information provided, the goal of varying the amount of information is not to cause miscues, but simply to raise the ante, increase each participant's stake in changing the medium. Student miscues, once they show how well the material is matched to the students, and signal the need to modulate the level of difficulty, can be eliminated. If students use copy books, or keep any kind of permanent record of their work, the final work in their books should probably be perfect.

Give Me Categories or Choices— *Characterizing* before *Changing Mediums*

Should altering the time provided for changing mediums not decrease the miscues, and should the alteration of the amount of information provided not decrease them either, students can be asked to *characterize* the *sets* that are provided, rather than change the mediums the *sets* are communicated in. Since incorrect chunking in oral reading prevents a person from reading orally properly, there is little point in requiring a person to change print to speech if it is clear that the sense groups are not chunked in the right way.

If students consistently *change mediums* correctly less than 70 percent of the time, one alternative is to precede the task of *changing mediums* with the task of *charac-*

EXCERPT 14–8
Dash-ing

		Communications	*Source/ Target*	*Move Type*	*Use*
1	Teacher:	In your dictations, you often substitute *are* and *did*. Today, before the dictation, I'm going to say the sentences, and I want you to draw a dash on the lines of sentences I say with a form of *do* and write an *ing* on the lines of sentences I say with a form of *are*. For example, What did he put on?—a dash What was he putting on?—an *ing*	t/s	str	
2	Teacher:	Number 1. What did he sing?	t/s	sol	
3	Most students:	(Write a dash.)	s/t	res	ce
4	Some students:	(Write an *ing*.)	s/t	res	ce
5	Teacher:	A dash is the right answer.	t/s	rea	
6		Number 2. They're leaving the room.	t/s	sol	
7	Most students:	(Write an *ing*.)	s/t	res	
8	Teacher:	For 2 *ing* is the right answer . . .	t/s	rea	
9		Now, I'll say each sentence and if it's correct, write a *c*, and if it's incorrect write an *x*.	t/s	str	
10		Number 11. What did he singing?	t/s	sol	
11	Most students:	(Write an *x*.)	s/t	res	ce
12	A few students:	(Write a *c*.)	s/t	res	ce
13	Teacher:	Number 11 is wrong. *What did he sing?* is right.	t/s	rea	
14		Number 12. They're leave the room.	t/s	sol	

terizing. Chunking in read-and-look-up and dictations is only one way to *characterize*. This way of *characterizing* I call *characterize examine, cx*. In this subcategory I include any indication of the size or shape of words, letters, sentences, or paragraphs. Another way of *characterizing* content is to indicate an item is right or wrong, a subcategory I call *evaluate, ce*. We can evaluate by making choices in responding to either-or questions or multiple-choice questions too.

Excerpts 14–8 to 14–10, pages 330 to 332, contain examples of *characterize evaluate*. In these excerpts, the teacher uses labels: *do* and *ing* in Excerpt 14–8; *full form, contraction, stilted*, and *blended* in Excerpt 14–9; and *sense group* in Excerpt 14–10. The students have to choose one of the labels that fits the examples—sets—given. In other excerpts, students simply have to indicate whether something is right or wrong. In making choices from labels provided by the teacher in the solicit and in indicating the correctness or incorrectness of items given, the students are *charcterizing* by *evaluating*. The *ce* next to the responses indicates this fact.

EXCERPT 14–9
What?

		Communications	*Source/ Target*	*Move Type*	*Use*
1	Teacher:	I'll say a sentence. You write *full form* or *contraction*.	t/s	str	
2		Number 1. I did not take them.	t/s	sol	
3	Some students:	(Write *contraction*.)	s/t	res	ce
4	Most students:	(Write *full form*.)	s/t	res	ce
5	Teacher:	Number 2. I could've taken them.	t/s	sol	
6	Most students:	(Write *full form*.)	s/t	res	ce
7	Some students:	(Write *contraction*.)	s/t	res	ce
8	Teacher:	Number 1 was the full form and 2 a contraction.	t/s	rea	
9		(After fifteen more examples.) Now, I'll say the same sentences again, and you write *blended* or *stilted* on each line, next to the words *full form* or *contraction*. For example, "Where'd ya buy 'em?" is blended. "Where'd you buy them?" is stilted.	t/s	str	
10		Number 1. I-did-not-take-them. (Stressing each word equally.)	t/s	sol	
11	Most students:	(Write *stilted*.)	s/t	res	ce
12	A few students:	(Write *blended*.)	s/t	res	ce
13	Teacher:	That was stilted—"I didn't take 'em" is blended.	t/s	rea	
14		Number 2. I coulda takn 'em.	t/s	sol	
15	All students:	(Write *blended*.)	s/t	res	ce
16	Teacher:	That, as you all realized, was blended.	t/s	rea	

EXCERPT 14–10
Nonsense

		Communications	*Source/ Target*	*Move Type*	*Use*
1	Teacher:	When I pause, write down *yes* or *no*—*yes* if I pause at the end of a sense group and *no* if I pause within a sense group. Follow along in your copy of the passage.	t/s	str	
2		An de	t/s	sol	
3	Some students:	(Write *yes.*)	s/t	res	ce
4	Most students:	(Write *no.*)	s/t	res	ce
5	Teacher:	That was not a sense group.	t/s	rea	
6		And de Lawd	t/s	sol	
7	All students:	(Write *yes.*)	s/t	res	ce
8	Teacher:	That was a sense group.	t/s	rea	

Your first reaction to the coding of the tasks requiring students to write *stilted* or *incorrect* or other words might be that writing the words is another example of changing speech to print. But while students have to write words that have only been said when they characterize in Excerpts 14–8 through 14–10, the task they are performing is indicating whether an item fits in a category that has been presented or not, or whether an item is correct or incorrect. I code *reproduce change medium—dc*—only when the task is primarily to change a medium, not when the task requires another mental operation, such as indicating whether an item is correct or not or making choices that another person offers, as when a student writes *full form* or *contraction.*

You might also have thought that it would have been more logical to code the writing of labels *characterize label* rather than *characterize evaluate*, as when students wrote *stilted* or *blended.* But the label is given by the teacher in the solicit, and all the students have to indicate is whether a particular label belongs with one item or another. They are making a choice, and I code making choices *characterize evaluate*, since a choice is an indication that one thing is correct or true and another is not.

Give Me the Material Again—Making the Material Familiar

Asking students to *characterize* before they change the medium not only shows the teacher whether it is likely that the students will be able to change the mediums without a high percentage of misses—if students *characterize* an item incorrectly, it is less likely that the student can change the medium correctly—but also provides the students with extra opportunities to become familiar with the material. Because the *characterize* tasks take only a few seconds each to perform, at the most, the students can be provided with multiple presentations of the material in literally only a few minutes. Yet in the three minutes devoted to many three-second *characterizing* tasks, students have a chance to *attend* to the material many times. By directing the students to *attend* to a different aspect during each presentation, the students get a chance to perceive different features of the communications during each presentation.

Faced with evidence that the material presented is too difficult, the alternative of presenting material over and over is often selected. In fact, one rule seems to be that when a message is not understood, it should be communicated again and again until it is understood. The rule also requires the person communicating to say something such as "Look again, carefully," or "Look again more closely." But if the message is not understood, it means that the amount of *noise* exceeds the amount of information. Faced with a great deal of *noise* and a small amount of information, it is often hard to know what to look at or listen for. These rules seem to apply both in teaching and nonteaching settings.

The *characterize* tasks in Excerpts 14–8 through 14–10 provide one way to narrow what the students are to *attend* to. Other ways to narrow choices are treated in Episode 5. However choices are narrowed, the aim is the same: to provide a focus for looking, listening, or in any other way sensing the material so that the number of possible choices is reduced, making the amount of noise smaller, the amount of information larger, and the chance to use the information in our heads greater.

Give Me the Right Stuff—Taking Content into Account

As you read Excerpts 14–8 through 14–10 and coded the mediums in Excerpt 14–7, you could not help but notice that the content in the communications varied as much as the mediums that were changed and the type of choices students made when they *characterized*. In Excerpt 14–7, drawing symbols for words—line 2—requires lexical knowledge.

The fact that we can change mediums with different subcategories of the *study of language* not only provides variety, but is also helpful because it allows us to determine the real difficulty a student is having in some aspect of the language. When a student identifies a man as a woman in a picture of people wearing long, dresslike garments, this does not necessarily mean the student does not know the lexical item for male and female gender. It is also possible that the difficulty is in the area of the subcategory of *study of language* I call *ways of life*. If we think of language only as grammar, pronunciation, and literal vocabulary, which many texts and tests do, we are not only limited in variety, but we are also likely to err when we try to identify the misunderstanding a student has. [Background 14–17]

In the same way, when a student spells *going* as *go* in a dictation, a first thought might be that the student is having trouble with spelling—the *mechanical* system of the *study of language*. But if the *-ing* suffix is consistently omitted, the problem may well be with the *grammatical* system, reflecting a lack of mastery of forms of the verb. Inability to distinguish *could have* and *could a* obviously involves the *sound* system. But information can also be provided to help detect the distinction by the *sound production, style,* and *contextual* systems. Looking at another's mouth as the blended and unblended forms are produced reveals much less lip and chin movement when blended forms are produced. And realizing that a comment made between close friends at a bar—*contextual* system—and that they are talking informally—*style* system—can aid as well. Talk at a bar between close friends who are talking informally requires blending. Knowing these facts increases the amount of internal information that is available and enables us to realize blending occurs even if we cannot hear it clearly.

We get meaning from a combination of many different areas of language, not just the *lexical*, *grammatical*, and *sound* systems that many books emphasize. Should you find that these three receive the bulk of attention in observations you make either in classes you observe, or in texts or tests used, the alternative is to introduce changes of medium that require other areas of language as well. The subcategories of the *study of language* are treated in Episode 11. The *contextual* system, which affects all the other subcategories so much, is treated in Episode 13.

The study of other areas can also be communicated when we change mediums. What is a chemical experiment done with experiment as we read a lab manual but the changing of print into action? And baking a cake by following a printed recipe also shows how we can change mediums and communicate the study of other areas.

VII. TOO WIDE A RANGE—COMPARING CONSEQUENCES AND CONCLUSION

First reactions to the use of the subcategories of the study of language are often positive. The reactions to the tasks that require students to characterize include these: "Labels are confusing"; "Letting students see and hear errors is dangerous"; "When students have only two choices, they simply guess the right answer." Some also indicate that making choices is one part of the information processing theory of learning. [Background 14–18]

First reactions to the variety of mediums changed in Excerpt 14–7 include comments like these: "I don't want dice in my classroom" reacting to line 20, "I don't teach the deaf" reacting to line 14, "Drawing is fine for children but not adults" reacting to lines 2, 5, 8, 9, and "Kids get out of control after games, actions and making noises" reacting to lines 3, 4, 10, and 13. The drawings remind a few of the fact that *nonlinguistic visual* mediums are processed in a different part of the brain from *linguistic* mediums too. [Background 14–19]

While it is true that some adults may at first resist communicating in *nonlinguistic* and *paralinguistic* mediums, actions and games can be noisy, dice connote mischief to some, *characterize* tasks can confuse and choices can be guessed, all of these communications occur outside classrooms. Outside classrooms, people of all ages are more likely to be called upon to change *nonlinguistic* and *paralinguistic* mediums than to read orally or write a dictation. And if we cannot guess when we observe outside the classroom, we are unable to make sense out of much that goes on.

Even if we did not have to change a wide range of mediums outside class and make guesses based on choices presented, these activities might be helpful in class because they provide a greater likelihood that different students can be successful, assuming we accept the premise that different people learn differently. By providing a range of tasks that require different mental operations, different styles of learning are more likely to be catered to. Student communication in *nonlinguistic* and *paralinguistic* mediums may enable some to be successful who have few successes with only *linguistic* mediums. Teachers may see that some students know material they thought they did not because of their problems with linguistic mediums. Some students, by having their attention drawn away from the linguistic aspect of what they are trying to learn, may be more relaxed and thus freer to absorb the target language as a result of communicating in *paralinguistic* and *nonlinguistic* mediums part of the time. Finally, if the truism "variety is the spice of life" or the research that has shown that variety tends to increase learning is valid, changing many mediums rather than a few, and *characterizing*, *attending*, and *changing mediums* rather than just *changing mediums* provide more variety. [Background 14–20]

As natural as both positive and negative reactions are, and as persuasive or unconvincing as arguments for and against different practices may be, they are different from actual consequences. The aims of this episode, like all the others, is to show ways to describe present practices so that the rules that control us can be discovered and, by trying alternatives, broken. The aim is not to argue for the superiority of one type of communication over another.

These questions indicate some consequences that can be compared: Do fewer errors occur when students *attend* and *characterize* before they *change mediums*, or when they *change mediums* immediately? Do students volunteer more when the mediums they change and the areas of content they communicate are varied or similar? Do teachers get a chance to see more meanings students know when they change only *linguistic* mediums or when they change *linguistic*, *nonlinguistic*, and *paralinguistic* mediums as well? Do teachers feel they can demand more accuracy when students change mediums, and get more accurate responses, when the teachers combine *characterize* and *attend* tasks with tasks that require the *changing of mediums*? Do *characterize* tasks that initially baffle some students lead to both the clarification of distinctions between categories and the *changing of mediums* with fewer miscues? When students read orally or silently or write dictations, do they chunk without being told more after read-and-look-up or normal oral reading? Over a period of time, do students who read-and-look-up make more meaningful substitutions when they read than students who just read orally as they look at their books? Responses to these solicits will produce more valid support for following the rules you find rather than breaking them than the types of initial, natural reactions we often have to anything new.

Even if there is little oral reading and only rarely a dictation in classes you are involved with, the questions about consequences can be investigated because the alternatives to little oral reading and a rare dictation are a lot of oral reading and frequent dictation. Whether these activities, and any other changes of mediums, are related to the content of other parts of the lessons, whether the material changed is authentic or made up to teach particular points, are separate issues. Whatever you decide about them will not alter the activities described in this episode. They can be used with any material and at any level in any kind of class.

Should you yourself want to experience the rest of *It done begin* by reading it orally and thus changing print to speech (*lv* to *la*); by drawing pictures of Gabriel and the devil and thus changing print to pictures (*lv* to *nv*); by making the sound a trumpet makes and thus changing print to sound (*lv* to *na*); by making facial expressions to show how Adam and Eve felt after the fall and thus changing print to gestures (*lv* to *pv*)—in short, if you want to try some of the activities described in this episode with the rest of the pidgin episode of Genesis—do! All you have to do to experience the rest of *It done begin* is "Open your books to page 75 or 253." I use *It done begin* to illustrate the subcategories of the *study of language* in Episode 11, and to illustrate some of the uses in responses in Episode 4.

BACKGROUND NOTES

14–1. I have already introduced Michael West by name in the paragraph I quote him in. The title of the book I took the quote from is *Teaching English in difficult circumstances*, surely one of the best titles for a book ever conceived. Though there is no proof that Read-and-Look-Up works as well as West claims, West would not have written lessons that he himself had not tried in classes of 40 to 60 students in poorly equipped classrooms.

14–2. In his manual called *American pronunciation*, Prator talks about sense groups; and Wilga Rivers talks about sense groups in her 1968 book, *Teaching foreign language skills*.

14–3. These suggestions are taken directly from West's lesson plans in *Teaching English in difficult circumstances*.

14–4. Asher's book on learning another language through actions is a variation of some of the usual games teachers play with their students in which they ask the students to translate spoken commands into actions.

14–5. I code Gattegno's use of colored boxes to represent sounds nonlinguistic visual rather than linguistic visual because the color, shape, or location of the box is what indicates what the sound is. There is no linguistic symbol used in the beginning to indicate the sound. In fact, much of the Silent Way requires the translation of either boxes into sounds, or rods into different structures. There is a heavy emphasis on the use of nonlinguistic visual mediums by the teacher. One way to look at differences in methods is simply to see the extent to which different mediums are translated differently.

14–6. Maley and Duff have put together a great number of examples of ways that sounds can be translated into speech in a book called *Sounds intriguing*.

14–7. In *Living English speech*, W. S. Allen uses boxes as well as musical notes to represent different supersegmental phonemes such as stress and rhythm.

14–8. Michael West talks about pindrop silence in his *Teaching English in difficult circumstances*. He tells his readers that when he is in the classroom and he wants silence, he puts his two fingers up in the air as if he has just dropped a pin. By the time the pin drops to the ground, he wants the class to be silent enough so that he can hear it drop (as if he in fact had really dropped the pin). Maria Montessori also talks about the importance of translating noise into silence in her work, and she reminds the reader that there are many different kinds of silences: silence so that a baby can sleep, silence so that we can read, and the silence of the night as we are home alone. One of her central points, of course, was that children in particular are capable of much more than we think they are, and one way they can demonstrate this even if they don't know a great deal of language is to show how they can be silent in different ways.

14–9. Frank Smith presents a very clear description of the difference between short- and long-term memory in *Understanding reading*.

14–10. West's tips in *Teaching English in difficult circumstances* coincide with theories of reading popular twenty years after he wrote his book.

14–11. As usual, Frank Smith is illuminating on the subject of bits of information. Gibson and Levin also talk about this concept in their book on the psychology of reading.

14–12. I have used Frank Smith and Gibson and Levin to support my ideas about short- and long-term memory and internal and external information, but I cannot use them to support my larger claim that all the things they write about in reference to reading affect all the changes we make from one medium to another. That is a personal claim, and I do not want to implicate any of these other authors.

14–13. Though Goodman is most known for miscue analysis both as reported in his own writing and in works such as those edited by P. David Allen, Edward L. Thorndike in 1917 wrote a monograph in which he showed how studying mistakes in paragraph reading can help us discover difficulty students are having so that we will know what we need to teach them. Thorndike was interested in how readers misreasoned as they read. He was less interested in very specific miscues such as the leaving off of suffixes or the substitution of words than Goodman is. However, he was interested in studying mistakes to help us see what we need to learn, and I think it's important to read his study together with the more recent studies by Goodman and his associates on miscue analysis. Shaughnessy's insights about errors in writing too are important.

14–14. The 70 percent I use is quite arbitrary. I have visited many classrooms where students are not expected to get more than 50 percent of any series of tasks correct. And I have also seen classes where students are expected to get everything correct. I would just urge that a number of different criteria be set rather than only one. The fact that different criteria are set in different places shows there is no set number that is preferable to another in all cases.

14–15. The word *noise* in its technical sense refers to any interference, and not just background noise during a conversation, for example. I have found Kahn's definition of noise in a technical sense most appealing. He defines noise technically in a book on secret codes, and he shows how a person making up a secret code incorporates as much noise as possible into the code so that the enemy has a more difficult time breaking it.

14–16. Orr et al., in a 1968 special issue of *Journal of Communication* present a number of figures about syllables per minute and words per minute in both regular delivery and in what they call compressed speech. They present 175 words per minute as normal. In a survey of different speakers on television and radio, using simply a stopwatch to time a tape-recorded version of what I had listened to, I came up with some of these rates: Disc jockey announcements were delivered at 350 words per minute; Walter Cronkite, who was a famous American broadcaster for many years, delivered the news at 263 words per minute, according to my calculation; the weather report on the radio was delivered at 343 words per minute. Some of the students I was working with at the time in a teacher preparation program, all native speakers of English, varied from 118 to 276 words per minute.

14–17. I have been emphasizing the category *study of language* as I have been talking about translating mediums. Students can, of course, also share their personal feelings or general knowledge in drawings. A book called *Drawing out*, written by Bassano and Christeson in 1982, provides many exercises in which students are asked to share personal feelings and general information—content I call *life*—through sketches, rather than just the category *study of language.*

14–18. Smith, in *Comprehension and learning*, would be one person who probably would support the use of labels by students so that they can classify the information they receive and make it easier for retrieval. Wiener might also support the idea because of his belief in information processing as a model for the working of the mind.

14–19. Caleb Gattegno, in his book *Towards a visual culture*, suggests that the images we take in are processed in a different part of the brain from other mediums. Sagan also discusses this fact, and Laubach, in his discussions of literacy, tells of cases where people he was working with in developing literacy misunderstood pictures sometimes even when they had no difficulty with print. The fact that they could understand print but not pictures suggests they were processing these two mediums in different places in their minds.

14–20. Naiman et al., in their study of the good language learner, found that students consistently liked classes in which there was a great deal of variety. Moskowitz, in her study of outstanding foreign language teachers, also found that students consistently liked variety. Politzer's research supports variety too. Mayo, in his classic study of production at a Western Electric plant in Hawthorne, Illinois, found that workers consistently increased the amount of work they did when changes were made in their work environment. Of course, the changes suggested to many of the workers that the managers were interested in their welfare, so this might be part of the reason why production increased. But production might also have increased because of the fact that variety in the environment made them even unconsciously simply want to do more.

EPISODE

15

Red, as I Recall

As you can already see, this episode is simply a list of items cited in the other episodes, especially in the Background Notes at the end of each episode. The boldface numbers after each entry indicate which episode and background notes the items are cited in. In most book entries those numbers are followed by the call number assigned to the item by at least one library. Even if the number varies somewhat from the one assigned at the library you use, you will in most cases be very close to the item if you are looking at the books on the shelf yourself.

While call numbers, authors' names, and titles are obviously more useful in teaching settings such as libraries, I have found descriptions of covers more useful when trying to remind others of a particular book at a party or in other nonteaching settings. So I have included short descriptions of some book covers along with the other information. One reason I think I have heard "Red, as I recall" so much, is that so many covers are red!

The blank lines and spaces between a number of the entries are provided for you to enter items you have found useful and think should be cited along with those I have cited, or in some cases in place of items I have cited. Given the almost infinite number of publications, any list is quite limited. Your entries in the blank spaces provide one kind of journal entry for this episode. Another kind of journal entry can be made by writing annotations next to my entries and yours. And since you have the option to cross out entries, you have still another way of making a journal entry.

In this episode, I've used the bird symbol to indicate the entries I spent the most time with. I've kept the birds away from the entries I skimmed or used as references. Francis Bacon's "some books are to be tasted, others to be swallowed and some few to be chewed and digested" distinguishes my types of books in a judgmental way. The birds are not judgmental; they signal the amounts of time I spent with the various references, not the amount of time one *should* spend. Since I spent more time with the rated books, they have tended to influence me more.

Bibliography

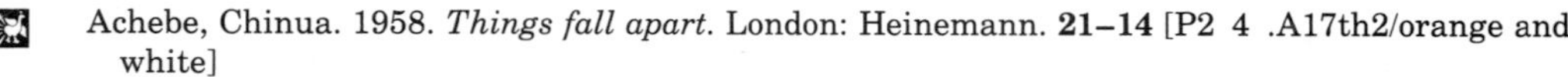

Achebe, Chinua. 1958. *Things fall apart.* London: Heinemann. **21–14** [P2 4 .A17th2/orange and white]

Agard, Frederick Browing, and Harold B. Dunkel. 1948. *An investigation of second language teaching.* Boston: Ginn.**1–1, 17–1, 22–2** [407 Ag15]

Alexander, Frederick Matthias. 1969. *The resurrection of the body: The writing of F. Matthias Alexander.* New York: University Books.**1–8, 1–12, 2–16, 23** [BF 161.A37]

Allen, P. David. 1976. *Findings of research in miscue analysis: Classroom implications.* Urbana, Ill.: National Council of Teachers of English.**10–6, 11–1, 12–2, 14–13, 21–10** [LB1050.33 .F56/ handwritten red symbols around part of the title, all on a white background]

Allen, Robert Livingston. 1972. *English grammars and English grammar.* New York: Scribner. **11–1, 17–5, 17–9** [425 A]

Allen, Robert Livingston, et al. 1975. *Working sentences.* New York: Harper & Row. **11–1, 17–5, 17–9** [fPE 1375 .A4/black]

Allen, Virginia French. 1953. *People in Livingston: A reader for adults learning English.* New York: Crowell. **3–3** [PE 1128 .A47/light green background and sketches and figures in brown of Livingston]

Allen, William Stannard. 1967. *Living English speech: Stress and intonation practice for foreign students.* London: Longman. **14–7** [PE 1128 .A448/yellow and black and shape of notches or crenels around edge]

Allwright, Richard L. 1979. Language learning through communication. In C. J. Brumfit and K. Johnson (Eds.), *The communicative approach to language teaching.* London: Oxford University Press. **11–2, 17–3** [P 53 .B79]

Allwright, Richard L. 1980. Turns, topics and tasks: Patterns of participation in language learning and teaching. In Dianne Larsen-Freeman (Ed.), *Discourse analysis in second language research.* Rowley, Mass.: Newbury House. Pp. 165–187. **4–15** [P53 .L37]

Anderson, Jonathan. 1976. *Psycholinguistic experiments in foreign language testing.* Queensland, Australia: University of Queensland Press. **10–13**

Anderson, William G. 1980. *Analysis of teaching physical education.* St. Louis: Mosby. **2–12** [GV 362 .A5]

Annett, John. 1969. *Feedback and human behaviour: The effects of knowledge of results, incentives and reinforcement on learning and performance.* Baltimore, Md.: Penguin Books. **12–1** [BF 319 .5 .F4A5/seven circles of light red dots on a white background]

Arendt, Hannah. 1977. Reflections—Thinking. *The New Yorker,* November 21. **1–2**

Arlen, Michael J. 1977. The air—Hosts and guests. *The New Yorker,* January 3. **19–3**

Arnheim, Rudolf. 1969. *Visual thinking.* Berkeley: University of California Press. **10–3, 10–15, 18–11, 23** [N 70 A693]

Asher, James J. 1977. *Learning another language through actions.* Los Gatos, Calif.: Sky Oaks Productions. **6–13, 7–6, 13–5, 14–4** [PB 36 .A8]

Ashton-Warner, Sylvia. 1963. *Teacher.* New York: Simon and Schuster. **6–16, 16–5, 18–2** [371.9793 A]

Ausebel, David Paul. 1968. *Educational psychology: A cognitive view.* New York: Holt, Rinehart and Winston. **20–2** [370.15 A]

Bandler, Richard, and John Grinder. 1979. *Frogs into princes: Neuro linguistic programming.* Moab, Utah: Real People Press. **1–8** [RC480.5 .B313/a frog and a prince with green background]

Barnes, Douglas. 1976. *From communication to curriculum.* Harmondsworth, Eng.: Penguin. **2–11, 6–1, 6–4, 6–12** [LB 1084 .B365/color photo of students in a classroom—5 standing aside the teacher's desk and 7 apparently working individually at tables]

Bassano, Sharon, and Mary Ann Christison. 1982. *Drawing out.* San Francisco, Calif.: The Alemany Press. **14–17**/two sketches with crayons on cover—a disco and a stove with person next to it and lasagna in oven]

Becker, Howard Saul, et al. 1961. *Boys in white: Student culture in medical school.* Chicago: The University of Chicago Press. **7–2** [R 737 .B4]

Bellack, Arno, et al. 1966. *The language of the classroom.* New York: Teachers College Press. **1–5, 2–3, 2–5, 2–8, 2–12, 4–1, 20–1, 23** [LB 1620 .B379/a green chalkboard with the title handwritten on it]

Benedict, Ruth. 1946. *The chrysanthemum and the sword: Patterns of Japanese culture.* Boston: Houghton Mifflin. **9–2** [952.1 B43]

Bernstein, Jeremy. 1978, Profiles: Biology watcher. *The New Yorker,* January 2. **7–4**

Bernstein, Rosella. 1976. English at your fingertips. In John F. Fanselow and Ruth H. Crymes (Eds.), *On TESOL '76.* Washington, D.C.: TESOL. **17–11** [PE 1128 .A205/blue and white batik resembling X-ray of ribs]

Billows, Frederick Lionel. 1961. *The techniques of language teaching.* London: Longmans. **3–2, 12–13, 20–3** [PB 35 .B53/red]

Blakeslee, Sandra. 1975. Study rebuffs a view of minority learning. *The New York Times,* October 14. **12–4**

Blatchford, Charles. 1970. Experimental steps to ascertain reliability of diagnostic tests in English as a second language. Dissertation, Teachers College, Columbia University, New York. **21–3**

Blocksma, D., and E. Porter. 1947. A short term training program in client-centered counseling. *Journal of Consulting Psychology,* 11, 55–60. **1–2**

Bloom, Benjamin. 1964. *Taxonomy of educational objectives I: The cognitive domain.* New York: David McKay. **4–11** [370.1 B615]

Bloom, Lois, 1974. Talking, understanding and thinking. In Lyle L. Lloyd and Richard L. Schiefelbusch (Eds.), *Language perspectives—Acquisition, retardation, and intervention.* Baltimore: University Park Press. **13–2, 17–13** [RJ 496 .S7L354]

Bodman, Jean, and Michael Lanzano. 1975. *No hot water tonight.* New York: Collier-Macmillan. **3–3** [PE 1128 .B63/light blue street scene—white back cover]

Bormuth, J. R. 1967. Comparable cloze and multiple-choice comprehension test scores. *Journal of Reading,* 10, 291–99. **10–13**

Bormuth, John R. 1968. *Readability in 1968: A research bulletin.* Champaign, Ill.: The National Council of Teachers of English for the National Conference on Research in English. **10–13** [PN 204 .N3/orange with readability printed in white 23 times in two columns]

Braddock, Richard Reed, et al. 1963. *Research in written composition.* Champaign, Ill.: The National Council of Teachers of English. **1–1** [PE 1066 .B7/yellow]

Brammer, Lawrence M., and Everett L. Shostrom. 1982. *Therapeutic psychology: Fundamentals of counseling and psychotherapy.* 4th ed. Englewood Cliffs, NJ: Prentice-Hall. **12–12** [RC480.5 B7/white, blue, and red letters—textbook looking]

Brody, Jane E. 1979. Personal Health. *The New York Times,* January 10. **7–5**

Bronowski, Jacob. 1956. *Science and human values.* New York: Harper & Row. **1–4, 7–4, 23** [503 B78/black with white stars and graph lines and a blue marigold; paperback edition]

Brooks, Nelson. 1960. *Language and language learning: Theory and practice.* New York: Harcourt, Brace and World. **9–2** [407 B79/light blue]

Brophy E. Jere, and Thomas L. Good. 1974. *Teacher student relations.* New York: Holt, Rinehart and Winston. **1–6** [LB 1033 .B67]

Buckheister, Patrick E. 1984. Exploring narrowing characteristics in classroom demands, requests and questions. Dissertation, Teachers College, Columbia University, New York. **5–1**

Buckheister, Patrick E., and John F. Fanselow. 1984. Do you have the key? In Jean Handscombe, Richard A. Orem, and Barry P. Taylor (Eds.), *On TESOL '83*. Washington, D.C.: TESOL. **5–1** [PE 1128 .A2C6843/white with blue print]

Burkhart, Robert C., Ed. 1968. *The assessment revolution: New viewpoints for teacher education.* Buffalo: Teacher Learning Center, Buffalo State University College. **1–11** [2838 .B87]

Carpenter, Edmund. 1974. *Oh, what a blow that phantom gave me.* New York: Bantam. **3–5, 18–1, 23** [301.151 C/color picture of a man in New Guinea holding a portable radio next to his ear]

Carroll, John B. 1965. The contributions of psychological theory and educational research to the teaching of foreign languages. *Modern Language Journal*, 49, 273–81. **3–4**

Carroll, John B. 1971. Current issues in psycholinguistics and second language teaching. *TESOL Quarterly*, 5, 101–14. **12–1**

Catalogs:

Edmunds Scientific, 101 E. Gloucester Pike, Barrington, NJ. 08007. **10–7, 18–5**

Great Book of Catalogs, 3rd ed. Pinkerton Marketing, Inc., 136 Oak Terrace, Box 8P, Lake Bluff, Ill. 60044. **10–7, 18–5**

George W. Park Seed Company, PO Box 31, Greenwood, S.C. 29647. **10–7, 18–5**

Cathcart, Ruth L., and Judy E. Winn Bell Olson. 1976. Teachers' and students' preferences for correction of classroom conversation errors. In John F. Fanselow and Ruth H. Crymes (Eds.), *On TESOL '76*. Washington, D.C.: TESOL. **12–10** [PE 1128 .A205/blue and white batik resembling X-ray of ribs]

Cazden, Courtney, et al. 1972. *Functions of language in the classroom.* New York: Teachers College Press. **2–14, 23** [P 41 .C38]

Chall, Jeanne. 1967. *Learning to read: The great debate.* New York: McGraw-Hill. **1–1, 10–11, 10–21** [LB 1573 .C438/dark rose]

Chastain, Kenneth. 1976. *Developing second language skills: Theory to practice*, 2nd ed. Chicago: Rand McNally. **17–8** [407 C/black, white and red and a star, and *the, año, ça*, etc. to show different scripts and languages]

Clark, John L. D. 1978. *Direct testing of speaking proficiency: Theory and application.* Princeton, N.J.: Educational Testing Service. **21–12** [fPB 71 .5 .D57]

Cogan, Morris L. 1973. *Clinical supervision.* Boston: Houghton Mifflin. **1–2** [LB 2805 .C584/dark green with title in metallic blue letters]

Cohen, Andrew D. 1975. Error correction and the training of language teachers. *Modern Language Journal*, 59, 414–422. **12–5**

Cohen, Andrew D. 1980. *Testing language ability in the classroom.* Rowley, Mass.: Newbury House. **21–8** [428.0076 C/green]

Coles, Robert. 1978. Profiles—The search I and II: Walker Percy. *The New Yorker.* October 2 and 9. **1–14**

Coulthard, Richard M. 1977. *An introduction to discourse analysis.* London: Longman. **2–4** [410 C]

Critique of the Pennsylvania project. 1969. *Modern Language Journal*, 53, 386–428. **1–1, 17–1, 22–2**

Crymes, Ruth H. 1978. The contextualization of language instruction. 8th annual convention, New York State ESOL/BEA, Lake Placid, New York, October 21. **8–4**

Crymes, Ruth H. 1979. The second language teacher as discourse analyst. Lackland Air Force Base English Language Center, July 11. **5–3**

Cummins, J. 1979. Linguistic interdependency and the educational development of bilingual children. *Review of Educational Research*, 49, 222–251. **8–4**

Curran, Charles. 1972. *Counseling-Learning—A whole person model for education.* New York: Grune and Stratton. **6–8, 7–1** [LB 1027 .C93]

Curwin, Richard. No date. Praise addiction. Mimeographed. National Technical Institute for the Deaf, Rochester, New York. **12–6**

Curwin, Richard L., and Barbara S. Fuhrmann. 1975. *Discovering your teaching self: Humanistic approaches to effective teaching.* Englewood Cliffs, N.J.: Prentice-Hall. **1–8** [LB 1025 .2 .C87/ light yellow]

Daly, Joseph. 1968. The effect of time limits on a university placement test. *Journal of Educational Research*, 62, 103–104. **4–13, 4–14**

Darwin, Charles R. 1913. *The expression of the emotions in man and animals.* New York: Appleton. **1–5** [QP 401 D25]

Davies, Alan. 1964. English proficiency test battery short version, form A. University of Edinburgh, Scotland. **10–9**

de Beauvoir, Simone. 1958. *Memoirs of a dutiful daughter.* New York: Harper Colophon Books. **9–1, 17–14** [PQ 2603 .E362Z5231/photo of the author smiling on a yellowish tan cover]

de Bono, Edward. 1976. *Teaching thinking.* London: Temple Smith. **4–7, 4–8, 10–15, 18–11, 23** [black with gold letters]

Delamont, Sara. 1976. *Interaction in the classroom: Contemporary sociology of the school.* London: Methuen. **4–8, 21–19, 22–3, 23** [371.102 S/red and colored photo of four people in an art class]

Denham, Carolyn, and Ann Lieberman, Eds. 1980. *Time to learn.* United States Department of Education, National Institute of Education. California Commission for Teacher Preparation and Licensing. **3–1, 10–11, 18–10** [LB 2838 .T55/light blue border around photographs of classes and a clock at 9:55 in the middle]

Deutsch, Morton. 1973. *The resolution of conflict: Constructive and destructive processes.* New Haven, Conn.: Yale University Press. **9–4** [301.63 D]

Dewey, John. 1933. *How we think: A restatement of the relation of reflective thinking to the educative process.* Boston: D. C. Heath. **13–2** [153.42 D]

Dewey, John. 1970. (orig. 1938). *Experience and education.* New York: Collier Books. **2–11, 6–1, 23** [LB 875 .D3943]

Diederick, Paul Bernard. 1971. Pitfalls in the measurement of gains in achievement. In William C. Morse and G. Max Wingo (Eds.), *Classroom psychology: Reading in educational psychology.* 2nd ed. Glenview, Ill.: Scott Foresman. **21–17** [fLB 1051 M725]

Diller, Karl Conrad. 1978. *The language teaching controversy.* Rowley, Mass.: Newbury House Publishers. **10–14, 18–10** [P53 .D5/different shades of blue waves with white tops]

Donaldson, Margaret. 1978. *Children's minds.* Glasgow: Fontana/Collins. **4–12, 5–1, 12–4, 22–4** [LB 1115 .D59/photo of child's face from nose up, dark brown hair]

Dulay, Heidi, Marina Burt, and Stephen Krashen. 1982. *Language two.* New York: Oxford University Press. **12–1** [P 53 .D84]

Duncan, Starkey. 1969. Nonverbal communication. *Psychological Bulletin*, 72, 118–37. **18–3**

Dunkin, Michael J., and Bruce J. Biddle. 1974. *The study of teaching.* New York: Holt, Rinehart and Winston. **1–6, 1–13, 2–7** [LB 1025 .2 .D86/orange to brown]

Dykstra, Gerald, and Richard and Antonette Port. 1966. *Ananse tales: A course in controlled composition*. New York: Teachers College Press. **17–10** [PE 1413 .D9/red spider web and grey spider on white background]

Eibl-Eibesfeldt, Irenäus. 1974. *Love and hate—The natural history of behavior patterns*. New York: Schocken Books. **1–5, 23** [BF 575 .A3Eeel3/animal mouth in center and human face on each side smiling—very light orange cover]

The English Duden: A pictorial dictionary. 1960. London: George G. Harrap. [PE 1629 .E5] and *The Oxford Duden pictorial English dictionaries*. 1981. New York: Oxford University Press. [PE 1625] **10–7**

Eurich, A. C. 1936. *Minnesota speed of reading test for college students*. St. Paul: University of Minnesota Press. **10–9**

Fanselow, John F. 1977. Beyond *Rashomon*—conceptualizing and describing the teaching act. *TESOL Quarterly*, 11, 17–39. **1–3**

Fanselow, John F. 1977. The treatment of error in oral work. *Foreign Language Annals,* 10, 583–593. **12–5**

Fanselow, John F. 1977. An approach to competency-based teacher education in second language teaching. In John F. Fanselow and Richard L. Light (Eds.), *Bilingual, ESOL and foreign language teacher preparation: Models, practices, issues*. Washington, D.C.: TESOL. **7–3** [428.007 B]

Fanselow, John F. 1978. Breaking the rules of teaching through self-analysis. In Richard L. Light and Alice Osman (Eds.), *Collected papers 1973–76*. New York: NYS ESOL BEA. **1–3**

Fanselow, John F. 1980. It's too damn tight. *TESOL Quarterly*, 14, 141–156. **18–6**

Fanselow, John F., and Richard L. Light (Eds.), 1977. *Bilingual, ESOL and foreign language teacher preparation: Models, practices, issues*. Washington, D.C.: TESOL. **1–3** [PE 1128.A2B48/ two black stick figures on ivory textured cloth]

Fey, James T. 1970. *Patterns of verbal communication in mathematics classes*. New York: Teachers College Press. **2–12, 20–1** [QA 11 .F48]

Fish, Marion C., and Elizabeth E. Loehfelm. 1975. Verbal approval: A neglected educational resource. *Teachers College Record*. 76, 493–98. **16–3, 16–9**

Flesch, Rudolf Franz. 1981 *Why Johnny still can't read: A new look at the scandal of our schools*. New York: Harper and Row. **10–21** [372.4145 F]

Forsdale, Louis. 1981. *Perspectives on communication*. Reading, Mass.: Addison-Wesley. **9–2, 18–1** [P 90 .F657/green border and photographs on cover]

Fraiberg, Selma M. 1959. *The magic years*. New York: Scribner. **7–7** [137.735 F84/photo of child on swing—red titles]

French, Frederick George. 1960. *English in tables: A set of blue prints for sentence builders*. London: Oxford University Press. **17–4, 17–6** [PE 1128 .A2F7/green]

Frentzen, Ann. 1982. A model for training in intercultural communication for ESOL teachers and other professionals. Dissertation, Teachers College, Columbia University, New York. **9–3**

Fries, Charles Carpenter. 1945. *Teaching and learning English as a foreign language*. Ann Arbor, University of Michigan Press. **1–7, 6–7, 7–1, 7–6, 9–2, 17–4** [fPE 1128 .A2F72/blue]

Gabriel, Gary. 1981. *Prose and passion*. New York: Regents. **13–1**

Gaies, Stephen J. 1980. T-unit analysis in second language research: Applications, problems, and limitations. *TESOL Quarterly*, 14, 53–60. **2–9**

Gallwey, Timothy, W. 1974. *The inner game of tennis*. New York: Random House. **1–8, 1–12, 21–9, 23** [GV 1002 .9 .P75G34/yellow with black spine]

Gamta, Tilahun. 1976. Selected behaviors in four English as a second language classrooms. Dissertation, Teachers College, Columbia University, New York. **20–1**

Gardner, Howard. 1980. *Artful scribbles: The significance of children's drawings*. New York: Basic Books. **18–2** [155.413 G]

Gargan, Edward A. 1981. Unprocessed parking tickets plague agency. *The New York Times*, September 13. **17–10**

Gary, Judy Olmsted. 1981. Caution: Talking may be dangerous to your linguistic health. *International Review of Applied Linguistics in Language Teaching*, 19, 1–14. **3–8, 7–1**

Gattegno, Caleb. 1969. *Towards a visual culture: Educating through television*. New York: Outerbridge and Dienstfrey. **14–19** [LB 1044 .7 .G34]

Gattegno, Caleb. 1976. *The common sense of teaching foreign languages*. New York: Educational Solutions. **1–7, 4–13, 6–7, 7–1, 7–6, 12–2, 12–9, 12–14, 14–5** [P 51 .G334/blue]

Gebhard, Jerry G. 1984. Models of supervision: Choices. *TESOL Quarterly*, 18, 501–514. **1–2**

Gibson, Eleanor J., and Harry Levin. 1975. *The psychology of reading*. Cambridge, Mass.: MIT Press. **3–8, 4–9, 5–2, 14–11, 14–12** [BF 456 .R2G46/brown]

Gleason, Henry Allan. 1965. *Linguistics and English grammar*. New York: Holt, Rinehart and Winston. **17–9** [425G/gray]

Glover, A., et al. *Seaspeak*. Elmsford, N.Y.: Pergamon Press. **8–1**

Gnagey, William J. 1955. *Controlling classroom misbehavior*. Washington, D.C.: Association of Classroom Teachers of National Education Association. **16–2, 16–6, 16–8, 16–9**

Goffman, Erving. 1959. *The presentation of self in everyday life*. Garden City, N.Y.: Doubleday. **1–5** [HM 291 .G6]

Goffman, Erving. 1981. *Forms of talk*. Philadelphia: University of Pennsylvania Press. **1–5** [P 95 .G58]

Goldman-Eisler, Frieda. 1954. On the variability of the speed of talking and on its relation to the length of utterances in conversations. *British Journal of Psychology*, 45, 94–107. **3–6**

Good, T. L., and J. E. Brophy. 1974. Changing teacher and student behavior: An empirical investigation. *Journal of Educational Psychology*, 66, 390–405. **1–8**

Goodman, Kenneth S. 1967. Reading: A psycholinguistic guessing game. *Journal of The Reading Specialist,* 6, 126–135. **10–6, 14–13**

Goodman, Kenneth S. 1973. *Miscue analysis: applications to reading instruction.* Urbana, Ill.: ERIC Clearinghouse on reading and communication skills. **3–8, 10–6, 10–16, 11–1** [LB 1050 .33 M57]

Gould, Stephen Jay. 1981. *The mismeasure of man.* New York: Norton. **21–6, 21–18** [BF431 .G68/ red spine and half of front and gray photo of skull on book jacket]

Graham, Carolyn. 1978. *Jazz chants: Rhythms of American English for students of English as a second language.* New York: Oxford University Press. **13–5** [fPE 1128 .A2G68]

Greenhalgh, Carol, and Donna Townsend. 1981. Evaluating students' writing holistically—An alternative approach. *Language Arts,* 58, 811–822. **21–12**

Grommon, Alfred H. 1976. *Reviews of selected published tests in English.* Urbana: Ill.: National Council of Teachers of English. **21–6** [PE 68 .U5N2/light tan with white numbers and letters representing a test answer sheet of the type scored by computers]

Gunther, John. 1955. *Inside Africa.* New York: Harper and Row. **4, 11, 14** [960.01 C95/black]

Currey, Percival. 1955. *Teaching English as a foreign language.* London: Longman. **4–16** [819.08 G96]

Guthrie, John T. Ed. 1981. *Comprehension and teaching—Research reviews.* Newark, Del.: International Reading Association, pp. 203–226, 255–276. **3–1, 10–11** [LB1051 .45 .C65/child's face on cover in sepia shades like an old photograph]

Hahn, Emily. 1978. Getting through to the others I and II. *The New Yorker,* April 17 and 24. **18–4**

Hall, Edward T. 1959. *The silent language.* New York: Fawcett. **9–5, 18–1, 23** [HM 258 .H3]

Halliday, Michael Alexander Kirkwood. 1973. *Explorations in the functions of language.* London: E. Arnold. **6–6, 8–2** [P 49 .H34]

Harris, Albert J., and Blanche L. Serwer. 1966. The CRAFT project: Instructional time in reading research. *Reading Research Quarterly.* 2, 27–56. **3–1, 10–11**

Harris, Sydney J. 1964. Strictly personal: School exams fail to pass test. *Chicago Daily News.* **21–9**

Haskell, John F. 1975. Putting cloze into the classroom. *The English Record,* 26, 83–90. **10–4, 10–10**

Heaton, John Brian. 1975. *Writing English language tests: A practical guide for teachers of English as a second or foreign language.* London: Longman. **21–1, 21–8** [PE 1128 .A2H395/green and greenish tan checkers]

Hechinger, Fred M. 1982. Learning switch: Writing to read. *The New York Times,* August 25. **4–11**

Herbert, John, and Carol Attridge. 1975. A guide for developers and users of observation systems and manuals. *American Educational Research Journal,* 12, 1–20. **22–3**

Hines, Mary Elizabeth. 1973. *Skits in English as a second language.* New York: Regents. **6–13, 13–1** [fPE 1128 .A2H54/dark green]

Hines, Mary Elizabeth. 1982. The relationship between teacher behavior and student language in fourteen adult English as a second language lessons. Dissertation, Teachers College, Columbia University, New York. **4–1, 6–3, 6–14, 20–1**

Hoetker, James. 1968. Teacher questioning behavior in nine junior high school English classes. *Research in the teaching of English,* 2, 99–106. **4–13, 21–19**

Hoetker, James, and William P. Ahlbrand. 1969. The persistence of the recitation. *American Educational Research Journal*, 6, 145–167, **1–10, 4–13**

Hornby, Albert Sydney. 1961. *The teaching of structural words and sentence patterns*, I–IV. London: Oxford University Press. **6–11, 13–5, 17–4** [PE 1128 .A2H58/green, red, salmon, gray—one color per volume]

Hornby, Albert Sydney, et al. 1963. *The advanced learner's dictionary of current English*. London: Oxford University Press. **10–7** [PE 1628 .L4/blue, dark]

Howatt, A. P. R. 1984. *A history of English language teaching*. New York: Oxford University Press. **11–4** [dark green]

Howe, Michael J. A. 1970. Repeated presentation and recall of meaningful prose. *Journal of Educational Psychology*, 61, 214–219. **10–3**

Hunt, Kellog. 1970. *Syntactic maturity in school children and adults*. Chicago: The University of Chicago Press. **2–9** [LB 1103 .S6]

Ianni, Francis, and Elizabeth Reuss-Ianni. 1979. School crime and the social order of the school. IRCD Bulletin, Institute for Urban and Minority Education, Teachers College, Columbia University, 14, 1. **16–1**

Iglauer, Edith. 1979. Profiles: Seven stones—Arthur Erickson architect. *The New Yorker*, June 4. **18–2**

International review of education—Special number: The classroom behavior of teachers. 1972. 18, 427–588. **22–3**

Jackson, Philip W. 1968. *Life in classrooms*. New York: Holt, Rinehart and Winston. **1–5, 1–6, 22–3** [LB 1032 .J3/green]

Jakobovits, Leon A., and Barbara Gordon. 1974. *The context of foreign language teaching*. Rowley, Mass.: Newbury House. **6–8, 13–2** [P 51 .J3/yellow and white]

Jakobson, Roman, et al. 1961. *Preliminaries to speech analysis: The distinctive features and their correlates*. Cambridge, Mass.: The MIT Press. **2–14** [414 J]

James, William. 1952. *Principles of psychology*. Chicago: Encyclopaedia Britannica Great Books of the Western World. **1–14** [028.3 G79 v. 53]

Jencks, Christopher, et al. 1973. *Inequality: A reassessment of the effect of family and schooling in America*. New York: Harper Colophon Books **1–1** [370.193 J/black apple with two yellow windows on it on white background with *inequality* in red and author's name in red]

Jersild, Arthur Thomas. 1955. *When teachers face themselves*. New York: Bureau of publications, Teachers College, Columbia University. **6–15** [LB 1731 .J45]

Johnson, Marguerite. 1935. The effect of behavior of variations in the amount of play equipment. *Child development*. 6, 56–68. **18–6**

Jonas, Gerald. 1976. The reporter at large—The disorder of many theories. *The New Yorker*. November 13. **1–1, 3–6**

Joos, Martin. 1967. *The five clocks*. New York: Harcourt Brace and World. **6–5** [808.042 J]

Junior Education, formerly *Pictorial Education*. Scholastic Publications, 141–143 Drury Lane, London WC2B 5TG. **10–7, 18–5**

Kahn, David. 1967. *The codebreakers—The story of secret writing*. New York: Macmillan. **10–8, 10–9, 14–15** [358.24 K and 652.8 K12, depending on how one reads the code/black]

Keating, Raymond J. 1963. *A study of the effectiveness of language laboratories*. New York: Teachers College, Columbia University. **18–9** [PB 36 .K4]

Keller, Eric, and Sylvia Taba Warner. 1979. *Gambits 3: Responders, closers and inventory*. Hull, Quebec, Canada: Public Service Commission of Canada, Language Training Branch. **19–1** [PE 1131 .K45/checkerboard cover—blue and white]

Kelly, Louis G. 1969. *Twenty-five centuries of language teaching*. Rowley, Mass.: Newbury House. **11–4** [407 K]

Klare, George R. 1976. A second look at the validity of readability formulas. *Journal of Reading Behavior*. 8, 129–152. **10–13**

Koch, Kenneth, and students of PS 61 in New York City. 1970. *Wishes, lies and dreams: Teaching children to write poetry*. New York: Chelsea House Publishers. **6–16** [811.008 K]

Kounin, Jacob Sebastian. 1970. *Discipline and group management in classrooms*. New York: Holt, Rinehart and Winston. **16–4, 16–6, 16–7, 20–2** [LB 3013 .K6/green, orange print and silhouette of classes in tan and orange on cover]

Kucera, Henry, and Nelson W. Francis. 1967. *Computational analysis of present-day American English*. Providence: Brown University Press. **19–1** [fPE 2839 .K8]

Kuhn, Thomas S. 1970. *The structure of scientific revolutions*. Chicago: The University of Chicago Press. **1–7, 23** [Q 175 .K95/pinkish red]

Labov, William, and Clarence Robins. 1969. A note on the relation of reading failure to peer-group status in urban ghettos. *Teachers College Record*, 70, 395–405. **12–7**

Labov, William. 1970. The logic of non-standard English in language and poverty. In Frederick Williams (Ed.), *Language and poverty*. Chicago: Markham Publishers. **18–8**

Labov, William. 1970. *The study of nonstandard English*. Champaign, Ill.: National Council of Teachers of English. **4–17** [427.973 L/orange and yellow waves]

Lado, Robert. 1957. *Linguistics across cultures*. Ann Arbor: University of Michigan Press. **9–3** [407 L12/orangish]

Lado, Robert. 1964. *Language teaching: A scientific approach*. New York: McGraw-Hill. **11–3, 17–7** [407 L/purple]

LaForge, Paul. 1978. Cultural silence in the interpersonal dynamics of community language learning. *Cross Currents*, V, 51–66, 37–56. **9–5**

Laitin, David. 1977. *Politics, language and thought—The Somali experience*. Chicago: The University of Chicago Press. **9–4** [JQ 3585 A38L34]

Lamendella, John T. 1979. The neurofunctional basis of pattern practice. *TESOL Quarterly*, 13, 5–20. **17–14**

Larson, Darlene. 1980. It works. *TESOL Newsletter*. **22–1**

Larson-Freeman, Dianne. 1978. An ESL index of development. *TESOL Quarterly*, 12, 439–448. **2–9**

Laubach, Frank C., and Robert S. Laubach. 1960. *Toward world literacy: The each one teach one way*. Syracuse: Syracuse University Press. **14–19** [379.23 L/tan]

Laye, Camara. 1969. (orig. 1954). *The dark child*. New York: Farrar, Straus and Giroux. **18–8** [B Laye]

Levin, Lennart, and Margareta Olsson. 1971. *Learning grammar: An experiment in applied psycholinguistics*. Gothenburg School of Education, University of Gothenburg. **1–1, 17–9**

Lewin, Kurt. 1935. *A dynamic theory of personality: Selected papers*. New York: McGraw-Hill. **17–14** [BF 698 .L4]

Lewis, E. Glyn, and Carolyn E. Massad. 1975. *The teaching of English as a foreign language in ten countries. International studies in evaluation IV*. New York: Wiley. **21–16** [PE 1128 .A2L4]

Libdeh, Abdalla A. 1984. Developing and using observation guides to describe teaching performance in ESOL classrooms. Dissertation, Teachers College, Columbia University, New York City. **2–1**

Lobman, Frances. 1979. Patterns of verbal communication in selected high school third-year foreign language classrooms. Dissertation, Teachers College, Columbia University, New York. **6–3, 6–14**

Long, Michael. 1980. Inside the "black box": Methodological issues in classroom research on language learning. *Language learning*, 30, 1–42. **2–12, 2–14, 22–3**

Long, Michael. 1982. Does second language instruction make a difference: A review of research. TESOL Convention, Honolulu. **1–6**

Longman dictionary of contemporary English. 1978. Paul Procter (Ed.). London: Longman Group. **10–7** [ref PE 2835 .LG/black, Longman ship logo in gold]

Longman dictionary of American English: A dictionary for learners of English. 1983. White Plains, N.Y.: Longman. **10–7**/yellow and red stripes]

Lozanov, Georgi. 1978. (orig. 1971). *Suggestology and outlines of suggestopedy*. New York: Gordon and Breach. **16–10** [BF 1156 .S8L6813]

Lurie, Alison. 1981. *The language of clothes*. New York: Random House. **18–7** [GT 525 .L87]

Mackey, William F. 1965. *Language teaching analysis*. Bloomington: Indiana University Press. **2–3** [P 51 .M3/gray]

Mackey, William F. 1976. Polychronometry in lesson analysis. *System: A Journal for Educational Technology and Language Learning Systems*, 4, 48–68. **3–7**

Mackey, William F. 1978. Cost benefit quantification of language teaching behavior. *Die Neueren Sprachen*, Heft 1, February. Verlag Moritz Diesterweg, Frankfurt am Main. **1–6**

Madsen, Charles, H. Jr., and Clifford K. Madsen. 1974. *Teaching/Disipline: A positive approach for educational development*. Boston: Allyn and Bacon. **16–3, 16–9** [LB 3011 .M25/purple]

Maeroff, Gene I. 1977. Spanking rule found an aid to discipline. *The New York Times*, April 25. **12–8**

Maley, Alan, and Alan Duff. 1978. *Drama techniques in language learning*. Cambridge, Eng.: Cambridge University Press. **13–1** [LB 1578 .M34/brown and red]

Maley, Alan, and Alan Duff. 1979. *Sounds intriguing*. Cambridge, Eng.: Cambridge University Press. **14–6** [PE 1128 .A2M332/dark green]

Malkemes, Fred, and Deborah Singer Pires. 1983. *Looking at English, Books* 1–3 Englewood Cliffs, N.J.: Prentice-Hall. **11–1, 17–9**

Marckwardt, Albert H. 1978. *The place of literature in the teaching of English as a second or foreign language*. Honolulu: The University Press of Hawaii. **10–14** [PE1128 .A2 M34/black]

Mayo, Elton. 1933. *The human problems of an industrial civilization*. New York: Macmillan. **7–7, 14–20, 20–4** [338.4 M45]

McArthur, Tom. 1981. *Longman lexicon of contemporary English*. Harlow, Essex, Eng.: Longman. **10–7** [AG 5 .M32/reddish brown and Longman ship logo in white]

McDermott, R. P., et al. 1982. When school goes home: Issues for a discussion of homework. New York: Elbenwood Center for the study of the family as educator, Teachers College, Columbia University. **10–24**

McKillop, Anne Selley. 1952. *The relationship between the reader's attitude and certain types of reading responses*. New York: Bureau of Publications, Teachers College, Columbia University. **10–3**

McLuhan, Marshall. 1964. *Understanding media*. New York: McGraw-Hill. **18–2, 23** [P 90 .M26/purple eye, red figure, computer card all on black in the shape of a television screen—on a white background]

McLuhan, Marshall. 1967. *The medium is the message*. New York: McGraw-Hill. **18–2, 23** [P 90 .M258]

Moffett, James. 1967. *Drama: What is happening—The use of dramatic activities in the teaching of English*. Champaign, Ill.: National Council of Teachers of English. **13–2** [PE 1066 .M55]

Montessori, Maria. 1967. *The discovery of the child*. New York: Ballantine. **12–16, 14–8** [LB 775 .M7/photo of child's face with tongue out, trying to place some round and square pegs on a table]

Moody, Kate. 1980. The research on TV: A disturbing picture. *The New York Times*, April 20. **18–10**

Morley, Joan. 1972. *Improving aural comprehension*. Ann Arbor: University of Michigan Press. **3–2, 10–19, 13–4** [fBF 323 .L5M63/two shades of light blue]

Moskowitz, Gertrude. 1976. The classroom interaction of outstanding foreign language teachers. *Foreign language annals*, 9, 135–157. **14–20**

Munby, John. 1978. *Communicative syllabus design*. Cambridge, Eng.: Cambridge University Press. **8–1** [PB 36 .M85/lilac book jacket]

Myers, Isabel Briggs. 1976. *Myers-Briggs type indicator*. 2nd ed. Center for applications of psychological type, 1441 N.W. 6th St., Suite B 400, Gainesville, Fla. 32601. **21–15**

Naiman, Neil. 1974. The use of elicited imitation in second language acquisition research. *Working papers in bilingualism*, 1–37. **21–4**

Naiman, Neil, et al. 1975. *The good language learner*. Toronto: Modern Language Centre, Department of Curriculum, The Ontario Institute for Studies in Education. **14–20, 22–4** [fPB 36 .G66]

Nida, Eugene A. 1957. *Learning a foreign language: A handbook prepared especially for missionaries*. Ann Arbor, Mich.: Friendship Press. **10–5** [P 51 .N5/red]

Ochs, Elinor. 1979. *Transcription as theory in developmental pragmatics*. In Elinor Ochs and Bambi B. Schieffelin (Eds.). *Developmental pragmatics*. New York: Academic Press, Inc. **2–6** [P 99 .4 .P72D47]

Oller, John W. 1979. *Language tests at school: A pragmatic approach*. London: Longman. **10–4, 10–10, 21–8** [LB 1575 .8 .044/tan and green curious design]

Olson, David R. 1976. Towards a theory of instructional means. *Educational Psychologist*, 12, 14–35. **8–3, 18–2, 21–2**

Olson, David R. 1977. From utterance to text: The bias of language in speech and writing. *Harvard Educational Review*, 47, 257–281. **8–3**

Orr, David B. 1968. Special issue on compressed speech. *Journal of Communication*, 18, 3. **3–6, 14–16**

Palmer, Harold Edward. 1968. (orig. 1918). *The scientific study and teaching of languages*. London: Oxford University Press. **3–2, 7–1, 7–6** [PB 35 .P2/white]

Papert, Seymour. 1980. *Mindstorms: Children, computers, and powerful ideas*. New York: Basic Books. **17–11, 18–9** [QA 20 C65P36/orange with main title in red]

Paulston, Christina Bratt, and Mary Bruder. 1976. *Teaching English as a second language: Techniques and procedures*. Cambridge, Mass.: Winthrop. **6–9, 17–8** [PE 1128 .A2P34/purple]

Payne, Stanley Le Baron. 1951. *The art of asking questions*. Princeton, N.J.: Princeton University Press. **5–1** [LB 1027 .P385]

Pfaff, William. Reflections: Economic development. *The New Yorker*, December 25. **9–2**

Pirsig, Robert M. 1975. *Zen and the art of motorcycle maintenance*. New York: Bantam. **1–8, 1–12, 23** [GT 275 .P648A33/pink]

Plaister, Ted. 1976. *Developing listening comprehension for ESL students.* Englewood Cliffs, N.J.: Prentice-Hall. **10–13** [PE 1128 .P55]

Plato. 1952. *The dialogues of Plato.* Chicago: Encyclopaedia Britannica Great Books of the Western World. **1–4, 1–9, 2–15, 23** [two tone brown with gold bands on the spine]

Polirstok, S. R., and R. Douglas Greer. 1977. Remediation of mutually aversive interactions between a problem student and four teachers by training the student in reinforcement techniques. *Journal of Applied Behavior Analysis*, 10, 707–716. **16–9**

Politzer, Robert Louis, and Louis Weiss. 1969. *The successful foreign language teacher.* Philadelphia: Center for Curriculum Development. **14–20** [LB 1576 .CU]

Postman, Neil. 1973. The politics of reading. In Rosemary Winkeljohann (Ed.). *The politics of reading: Point-counterpoint.* Urbana, Ill.: National Council of Teachers of English and the International Reading Association. **10–12, 21–13** [white]

Postman, Neil. 1981. Disappearing childhood. *Childhood education.* 58, 66–68. **17–11**

Prator, Clifford Holmes. 1951. *Manual of American English pronunciation for adult foreign students.* New York: Holt, Rinehart and Winston. **14–2** [PE 1137 .P8/green]

Purves, Alan C., and Victoria Rippere. 1968. *Elements of writing about a literary work: A study of response to literature.* Champaign, Ill.: National Council of Teachers of English. **6–2, 10–17** [PN 81 .P8/lavender]

Quirk, Charles Randolph, and Sidney Greenbaum. 1973. *A concise grammar of contemporary English.* New York: Harcourt Brace Jovanovich. **17–9** [PE 1112 .Q5/red]

Raimes, Ann. 1978. *Focus on composition.* New York: Oxford University Press. **13–3** [PE 1408 .R15/concentric circles as if in a lens going out from the 0 in composition, black and white and as the old riddle goes, "read all over"]

Rigg, Pat. 1976. Reading in ESL. In John F. Fanselow and Ruth H. Crymes (Eds.). *On TESOL '76.* Washington, D.C.: TESOL. **10–16** [PE 1128 A205/blue and white batik resembling X-ray of ribs or fish bones]

Rivers, Wilga M. 1964. *The psychologist and the foreign language teacher.* Chicago: The University of Chicago Press. **17–1** [PB 36 .R58/brownish]

Rivers, Wilga M. 1968. *Teaching foreign language skills.* Chicago: The University of Chicago Press. **14–2** [PB 35 .R43]

Rivers, Wilga M. 1972. Talking off the top of their heads. *TESOL Quarterly*, 6, 71–81. **6–9**

Rosenblatt, Louise Michelle. 1968. *Literature as exploration.* New York: Noble and Noble. **10–12** [PN 59 .R6/blue]

Rossner, Richard, et al. 1979. *Contemporary American English*, Books 1–6. Dallas: Melton Peninsula Publishing, and London: Macmillan. **6–9, 18–3**

Roueché, Berton. 1982. Annals of medicine—Prognosis in Omaha. *The New Yorker*, January 25. **4–8, 10–5**

Rowe, Mary Budd. 1969. Science, silence and sanctions. *Science and Children*, 6, 11–13. **4–13, 5–4, 6–4, 12–4**

Rubin, Carol Beth. 1977. Prototype development of self-instructional materials for categorizing communications. Dissertation, Teachers College, Columbia University, New York City. **1–3**

Rwakyaka, Proscovia. 1976. Teacher student interaction in ESL classes in Uganda. Dissertation, Teachers College, Columbia University, New York City. **3–1, 6–3, 17–2, 20–1**

Ryan, Charlotte. 1979. *The testing maze—An evaluation of standardized testing in America*. 700 North Rush Street, Chicago, Ill. 60611: The National PTA. **21–6** [a maze on rose background and silhouette of child taking a test in middle]

Sachs, H., et al. 1974. A simplest systematics for the organization of turn-taking for conversation. *Language*, 50, 696–735. **4–15**

Sagan, Carl. 1977. *The dragons of Eden—Speculations on the evolution of human intelligence*. New York: Ballantine. **14–19, 18–4, 19–2, 23** [BF 431 .S2/title in gold foil letters on white]

Sakamoto, T., and K. Makita. 1973. Japan. In John A. Downing (Ed.). *Comparative reading: Cross national studies of behavior and processes in reading and writing*. New York: Macmillan. **18–3** [LB 1050 .D67]

Sapir, Edward. 1949. (orig. 1921). *Language—An introduction to the study of speech*. New York: Harcourt Brace and World. **4–10, 18–3** [P 105 .S2]

Schachter, Jacquelyn. 1981. The hand signal system. *TESOL Quarterly*, 15, 125–138. **12–9**

Scherer, George A. C., and M. Wertheimer. 1964. *A psycholinguistic experiment in foreign language teaching*. New York: McGraw-Hill. **1–1, 22–2** [PF 3066 .S3]

Schuman, Francine M., and John H. Schuman. 1977. Diary of a language learner: An introspective study of second language learning. In H. Douglas Brown, Carlos Yorio and Ruth H. Crymes (Eds.), *On TESOL '77*. Washington, D.C.: TESOL. **21–11**

Scout Handbook (8th ed.). 1972. New Brunswick, N.J.: Boy Scouts of America. **18–5** [369.43 B]

Searle, John. 1969. *Speech acts—On essay in the philosophy of language*. London: Cambridge University Press. **2–10, 23** [B 840 .S4/white, two brown stripes, blurred picture of an ear and something else]

Shah, Idries. 1970. *Tales of the Dervishes*. New York: Dutton. **23** [white with pentagon design in red]

Shapiro-Skrobe, Frances. 1982. Interaction in elementary school ESL reading lessons before and after teacher workshops. Dissertation, Teachers College, Columbia University, New York City. **2–7, 3–1, 4–5, 6–3, 6–14, 10–11, 17–2**

Shaughnessy, Mina P. 1977. *Errors and expectations*. New York: Oxford University Press. **14–13, 21–10** [PE 1404 .S5/red]

Silk, Leonard. 1979. Lighter cars add problems. *The New York Times*, January 17. **7–5**

Simon, Anita, and E. Gill Boyer. 1970. *Mirrors for behavior*. Philadelphia: Research for Better Schools, Inc. **2–12** [fLB 1131 .5 .S56/silver—to remind one of mirrors]

Smith, Bunnie Othanel. 1969. *Teachers for the real world.* Washington, D.C.: American Association of Colleges for Teacher Education. **9–1** [LC 4091 .S6/red with a photo on the cover]

Smith, Frank. 1971. *Understanding reading: A psycholinguistic analysis of reading and learning to read.* New York: Holt, Rinehart and Winston. **3–8, 4–2, 4–3, 4–4, 10–1, 10–5, 10–8, 10–21, 10–22, 12–1, 14–9, 14–11, 14–12, 23** [LB 1050 S574/three boxes one inside the other in shades of blue on a white cover]

Smith, Frank. 1975. *Comprehension and learning.* New York: Holt, Rinehart and Winston. **4–2, 4–3, 4–4, 5–2, 14–18** [LB1051 S6218/pinkish circles and a silhouette of a head]

Smith, Phillip D. 1970. *A comparison of the cognitive and audiolingual approaches to foreign language instruction.* Philadelphia: Center for Curriculum Development. **1–1, 17–1, 22–2** [PB 38 .U6S6]

Sobel, Dava. 1980. Placebo studies are not just "all in your mind." *The New York Times*, January 6. **7–7**

Spolsky, Bernard. 1968. Preliminary studies in the development of techniques for testing overall second language proficiency. *Language Learning*, Special Issue, Number 3. **10–9**

Spolsky, Bernard (Ed.). 1972. *The language education of minority children: selected readings.* Rowley, Mass.: Newbury House. **21–15** [LC 3731 .S67]

Spolsky, Bernard. 1979. *Some major tests.* Arlington, Va.: Center for Applied Linguistics. **21–6** [fP 53 .S65]

Squire, James R. 1964. *The responses of adolescents while reading four short stories.* Champaign, Ill.: The National Council of Teachers of English. **6–2, 10–17** [BF 456 .R2S669]

Squire, James R., and Roger K. Applebee. 1968. *High school English instruction today—The national study of high school English programs.* New York: Appleton Century Crofts. **3–1, 4–11** [LB 1631 .S67]

Squire, James R., and Roger K. Applebee. 1969. *Teaching English in the United Kingdom—A comparative study.* Champaign, Ill.: National Council of Teachers of English. **3–1, 4–11** [LB 1631 .S673]

Stevick, Earl W. 1965. "Technemes" and the rhythm of class activity. In Harold B. Allen (Ed.), *Teaching English as a second language: A book of readings.* New York: McGraw-Hill. **2–2, 4–16** [PE 1128 .A2A38]

Stevick, Earl W. 1982. *Teaching and learning languages.* Cambridge, Eng.: Cambridge University Press. **17–8** [P51 .S854/black but red book jacket]

Strawn, Dwight J. 1976. Teacher feedback to students in selected English as a second language classrooms. Dissertation, Teachers College, Columbia University, New York City. **2–7, 12–5**

Stubbs, Michael. 1976. *Language, schools and classrooms.* London: Methuen. **7–2** [LB 1576 .S87/red]

Sullivan, George. 1976. *A reason to read: A report on an international symposium on the promotion of the reading habit.* New York: Academy for Educational Development. **8–3** [brown cover with a black box in the center of the cover with the title in it]

Taba, Hilda. 1966. *Teaching strategies and cognitive functioning in elementary school children.* San Francisco: San Francisco State College. **4–11** [fLB 1062 .T32]

Taylor, Robert, Ed. 1980. *The computer in the school: Tutor, tool, tutee.* New York: Teachers College Press. **17–11, 18–9** [LB 1028.5 C547/orange, yellow, purple and red teethlike designs]

Taylor, Wilson L. 1953. Cloze procedure: A new tool for measuring readability. *Journalism Quarterly,* 30, 415–433. **10–4**

Thomas, Abby. 1976. Learning in social situations. In John F. Fanselow and Ruth H. Crymes (Eds.), *On TESOL '76*. Washington, D.C.: TESOL. **22–4** [PE 1128 A205/blue and white batik resembling X-ray of ribs or fish bones]

Thorndike, Edward L. 1917. Reading as reasoning: A study of mistakes in paragraph reading. *Journal of Educational Psychology*, 8, 323–332. **14–13**

Thorndike, Robert L. 1973. *Reading comprehension education in fifteen countries: International studies in evaluation III*. New York: Wiley. **10–23** [LB 1050 .T46]

Thorndike, Robert L., and Elizabeth Hagen. 1977. *Measurement and evaluation in psychology and education*, 4th ed. New York: Wiley. **21–5** [LB 1131 .T59]

Turkel, Susan Beth. 1977. Patterns of verbal communication in the mathematics center of open classrooms at the elementary school level. Dissertation, Teachers College, Columbia University, New York City. **2–4**

Upshur, John A. 1968. Four experiments on the relation between foreign language teaching and learning. *Language Learning*, 18, 111–124. **1–1, 17–1, 22–2**

Urzúa, Carole. 1981. *Talking purposefully*. Silver Springs, Md.: Institute of Modern Language. **8–4**

Van Ek, J. A. 1977. *The threshold level for modern language learning in schools*. London: Longman. **6–10, 8–1** [PE 1128 .A2E38/blue]

Van Riper, Charles. 1978. (orig. 1939). *Speech correction: Principles and methods*. Englewood Cliffs, N.J.: Prentice-Hall. **12–5** [RC 423 .V35]

Via, Richard A. 1976. *English in three acts*. Honolulu: East West Center and The University Press of Hawaii. **6–13, 13–1** [PE 1128 .V43]

Vygotsky, Lev Semenovich. 1962. *Thought and language*. Cambridge: Mass.: The MIT Press. **4–3, 5–2, 10–5, 19–4** [P105 .V913/black, ochre and white letters]

Wardhaugh, Ronald. 1976. *The contexts of language*. Rowley, Mass.: Newbury House. **13–2** [P106 .W314/2 green stripes—Light and dark—And green letters for title on white background]

Watson, Goodwin. 1961. *What psychology can we trust?* New York: Teachers College Press. **3–4** [tan]

West, Michael. 1955. *Learning to read a foreign language and other essays on language teaching*. London: Longmans **6–11, 10–20** [407 W524]

West, Michael. 1956. The problem of pupil talking-time. *English Language Teaching*, 10, 71–73. **4–1**

West, Michael. 1959. Practice-teaching in the training of language teachers. *English Language Teaching*, 13, 149–154. **1–3**

West, Michael. 1960. *Teaching English in difficult circumstances*. London: Longman. **14–1, 14–3, 14–8, 14–10, 16–5** [819.08 W52/brown]

Wiener, Norbert. 1948. *Cybernetics and the machine*. New York: Wiley. **4–6, 9–6, 12–3, 14–18, 23** [Q 310 .W5]

Wiener, Norbert. 1967. (orig. 1950). *The human use of human beings, cybernetics and society*. New York: Avon. **4–6, 23** [Q 310 .W49/silhouette of head with compartments in it, some with geometric shapes, others with a bird, two hands, a ball, and a circuit]

Wilkins, David Arthur. 1976. *Notional syllabus*. London: Oxford University Press. **8–1, 17–3** [P 53 .W46/green]

Winn-Bell Olsen, Judy. 1977. *Communication starters*. San Francisco: The Alemany Press. **19–1** [yellow]

Witkin, H. A. 1973. *The role of cognitive style in academic performance and in teacher-student relations*. Princeton, N.J.: Educational Testing Service. **21–15**

Wolf, Thomas. 1977. Reading reconsidered. *Harvard Educational Review*, 47, 411–429. **18–11**

Wolkomir, Richard. 1980. A manic professor tries to close up the language gap: John A. Rassias. *The Smithsonian*, 11, 80–86. **13–6**

Yorkey, Richard. 1970. *Study skills for students of English as a second language*. New York: McGraw-Hill. **10–18** [fPE 1128 .Y6/green and red]

Zahorik, John A. 1968. Classroom feedback behavior of teachers. *Journal of Educational Research*, 62, 147–150. **12–5**

Zahorik, John A. 1970. Pupils' perception of teachers' verbal feedback. *Elementary School Journal*, 71, 105–114. **12–10**

Zahorik, John A. 1970. Teacher verbal feedback and content development. *Journal of Educational Research*, 63, 410–423. **12–15**

EPISODE

16

Shut Up So I Can Hear What You're Saying

I. LOOK HERE SO YOU CAN SEE WHAT'S UP—INTRODUCTION AND TOPIC OF EPISODE

As you no doubt guessed from the title, in this episode I treat what most people refer to as discipline or classroom management. Since I concentrate on subcategories of *procedure* to discuss this topic, I concentrate on these subcategories in this episode. In Table 16–1, I list the subcategories I treat. These subcategories, like others, both enable more specific description and help to illustrate the meaning of the main category. As you can see, I have no subcategories for assault, drug dealing, or gang fighting. Though these could be covered under *other*, I don't treat them in this episode or in this book. [Background 16–1]

I heard a teacher say "Shut up so I can hear what you're saying" during a particularly noisy class. The quote is both a classic example of a common means employed to control classroom social behavior—issuing a slightly angry order—and a symbol of the dilemma we face as teachers, particularly language teachers: the need for a great deal of expression and quiet so we can hear and see what is expressed.

Since an angry order is so common both in classes and outside class teaching settings—witness the father in a restaurant shouting for his 5-year-old to stop tapping his fork and to sit up straight or else be slapped—I assume you have not only discovered this rule, but mastered it. Additionally, there is some evidence that though angry orders may quiet a disruption, they may also develop associations of fear with the setting they occur in. Consequently, we'll explore other alternatives we can try in managing classes. [Background 16–2]

)ther		
	p	Administrative or bureaucratic information
	pa	Class routine, record keeping, taking roll
	pc	Checking understanding: Do you understand? I don't follow; It's not clear; not performing a task
classroom language behavior	pl	Comments about language activity: Say it louder; I can't see the board; Can you hear this?
classroom social behavior	pi	Expected actions in teaching settings: You are making too much noise; No smoking here; Don't throw paper.
name	pn	Ali . . . Maria . . . Teacher . . . *Owls*, it's your turn.
teaching directions	pu	Indicating uses are to be performed: Repeat; define this word; do the exercises.
time	pe	Waiting for an answer, a train or question; comments about time: Finish quickly; You have three minutes
other	pp	Communications that don't neatly fit in the other subcategories of *procedure* listed here or those listed on the table at the end of the book

II. YOU CAN MANAGE—RELATING SUBCATEGORIES OF PROCEDURE TO CLASSROOM MANAGEMENT

Up to You—Determining Appropriateness of *Classroom Social Behavior*

Agreement in the coding of a communication in one of the subcategories of Table 16–1 does not, of course, assume agreement in the acceptability of a communication coded *classroom social behavior*. Just because two people agree that two students whispering the assignment to each other should be coded *pi* for *classroom social behavior* does not mean that the two agree on the appropriateness of the communication. One teacher may judge it inappropriate and thus add an *x* to the abbreviation, just as we use an *x* to note language errors. And one may judge it appropriate and thus not add an *x*. Once communications are consistently identified as classroom social behavior, each teacher has to determine whether they are appropriate or not. Since student and teacher age, expectations of students, school practices, principals' policies, and the *ways of life* of all are involved, there is no way I can declare what should be acceptable behavior in a classroom and what should not be. In fact, one of the first steps in the treatment of inappropriate classroom social behavior is to identify it, and then make it clear to the students what is and is not acceptable. The alternatives I suggest in the next sections will be useful only to the extent that you have established criteria for acceptable and unacceptable behavior. [Background 16–3]

Even though appropriateness varies, distinguishing *classroom social behavior* from other subcategories of *procedure* does not. By coding the communications in Excerpt 16–1, it is more likely that my meaning of *classroom social behavior* and some of the

EXCERPT 16–1
Red Tape

		Communications	Source/ Target	Move Type	Content	
1	Teacher:	What's your name?	t/s_1	sol	pu + pa	pu + pc
2	Student$_1$:	Melissa.	s_1/t	res	pa	pn
3	Teacher:	Melissa,	t/s_1	sol	pa	pn
4		please give me the money for the notebook.			pu + pa	pu + pl
5	Student$_1$:	I don't understand.	s_1/t	rea	<u>pa</u>	pc
6	Teacher:	I'll say it louder.	t/s_1	str	pa	pl
7		Pay me the money for the notebook I gave you.	t/s_1	sol	pu + pa	pu + pl
8	Student$_1$:	(Sits and stares at the teacher.)	s_1/t	rea	pa	pe
9	Teacher:	(Takes out money from his pocket.)	t/s_1	str	pa	pu
10	Student$_1$:	Now, I understand.	s_1/t	rea	pa	pc
11	Teacher:	I hear a noise I shouldn't be hearing.	t/s	rea	pl	pi
12	Student$_1$:	(Drops the change on the floor.)	s_1/o	res	pa	pi
13	Student$_2$:	(Laughs.)	s_2/s	rea	pa	pi
14	Teacher:	Stop laughing.	t/s_2	sol	pu + pa	pu + pi
15	Student$_2$:	(Tries to stop laughing.)	s_2/t	res	<u>pa</u>	<u>pi</u>
16	Teacher:	There is no reason to laugh.	t/s	str	<u>pa</u>	<u>pi</u>
17		Everyone sit up straight and be quiet now.	t/s	sol	pu + pa	pu + pi
18	Student$_3$:	(Mumbles.)	s_3/t	res	pa	pi
19	Student$_4$:	(Drops a coin.)	s_4/t	res	pa	pi
20	Other students:	(Keep quiet and sit up straight.)	g/t	res	pa	pi

Coding done by others: 1. pu + pa—each solicit contains a teaching direction; 2. pa; 3. pn; 4. pu + pa; 5. <u>pc</u>—the underscoring simply indicates that the communication is in the negative; 6. pl; 7. pu + pa; 8. pe; 9. pa; 10. pc; 11. pi; 12. pa—assuming the action is not intentionally made to disturb; 13. pi; 14. pu + pi; 15. <u>pi</u>; 16. <u>pi</u>; 17. pu + pi; 18. pi; 19. pi; 20. pi—an X could be put next to 18 and 19 if you consider these inappropriate.

other subcategories of *procedure* and yours will be similar. Using the illustrations of the subcategories in Table 16–1 or the table at the end of the book, circle the subcategory that fits each communication. Coding done by others is given in the footnote.

Keeping Things Going—Preventing Inappropriate *Classroom Social Behavior*

Though each teacher has to decide when to designate something coded *pi* as inappropriate, once a communication is noted with the subscript x, examining other communications that preceded the inappropriate one may provide a hint for some alternatives. For example, if the instances of pi_x are preceded by a number of incorrectly performed administrative tasks—a lot of pa_x—one way to try to reduce future inappropriate classroom behavior would be to communicate administrative information differently. If routines are not followed, producing a lot of pa_x, either requests can be made that they be followed, or the routines themselves can be changed.

Waiting for students to perform administrative tasks also sometimes is related to inappropriate *classroom social behavior*. If a lot of pi_x abbreviations are noted, that are preceded by a lot of moves with content I code *time, pe*, in them, one alternative is to eliminate the moves that communicate only *time:pe*. Waiting for others to do nothing or forcing others to wait just for the sake of waiting often produces a lot of communications I'd code pi_x, such as whispering, jingling of keys, tapping of fingers, subdued laughing and other noises to break the silence that is communicating *time* alone. Long pauses together with routines that are not clear or are not followed decrease the smooth movement of classes and have been shown to increase inappropriate *classroom social behavior* as a result. [Background 16–4]

Beyond Beethoven—Treating Inappropriate *Classroom Social Behavior*

Means for trying to get students to be quiet as classic as "Shut up so I can hear what you're saying" have been reported in books about teaching. One teacher reports humming the first two measures of Beethoven's Fifth Symphony to obtain silence. Another reports holding up thumb and forefinger above the head as if holding a pin. The students knew that this meant "pin drop silence," having been told earlier by the teacher that when he pretends he is about to drop a pin, he wants everyone to be quiet so that the sound the pin makes when it hits the floor could be heard. But while such treatments may have worked for these individuals, some research, as well as your own experience no doubt, shows that just because one teacher gets silence by, say, flicking the lights on and off does not mean all teachers can get silence this way. There seem to be other variables that affect the consequences of different treatments. [Background 16–5]

One variable that seems to be important in keeping communications coded pi_x to a minimum is keeping a class occupied. You have observed this rule being followed. What do children do while waiting in line with nothing to do? What do people sitting at a doctor's office before an appointment do? What do children or teens do in an empty room with nothing to do? In most cases, they communicate *classroom social behavior* onlookers would code with an x, even though they all had different ideas about what behavior is inappropriate because when given nothing to do, the things many do are not very pleasant to behold.

If classes you are involved with have many structuring moves, solicits and reactions that contain *classroom social behavior*, as when a teacher says "Now, I'm not going to start until everyone is quiet"; "Sit up straight and fold your hands"; "That's not nice to do," one alternative is to substitute *teaching directions* for *classroom social behavior* in these moves: *pu* for *pi*. Children waiting in line with a pencil and paper draw monsters, copy words, or play pencil and paper games rather than pull on people's coats, throw pebbles, run and make noise. At a doctor's office with toys, children engage in tasks and don't keep tapping their feet, pulling leaves off plants or asking the receptionist for water. Throw a ball in an empty room and people perform tasks with it rather than sit and think of ways to make noise and disturb people. So, if students are asked to perform tasks—to *attend, characterize, present, relate, reproduce,* and *set* content in the categories *life* or *study*—it is less likely that they will be able to communicate *procedure* at the same time. [Background 16–6]

Journal Entry

I have seen teachers wait for up to fifteen minutes before they hand out something for students to read, because they have started a class by announcing to the class that the papers would not be handed out until absolute silence obtained. I have seen other teachers say nothing about silence hand out papers for students to read. As they started to hand out the papers, there was a lot of noise. As soon as students got their papers, they started to look at them and read them. By the time all the papers had been handed out—about three minutes in most classes—there was absolute silence in the classes.

Have you seen instances where tasks requiring *study* have brought a class to attention faster than tasks requiring *procedure* alone, especially the subcategory of *procedure* I call *classroom social behavior*?

Obviously, substituting *pu* for *pi* is not the answer to inappropriate *classroom social behavior*. Out of a class of fifty or even ten, nine times out of ten, at least one will communicate inappropriate *classroom social behavior* rather than perform the tasks. So, another rule seems to be, even if the bulk of a group is communicating *pu* or moves with other content initiated by moves containing *pu*, some will communicate pi_x as well. If this is true, then our task must be to look and listen—*attend*—to both communications produced by teaching directions—*pu*—and those that contain pi_x. And as we see instances of pi_x, especially as we see those that occur in back of us or in a place where a student thinks we don't know what's going on, we need to indicate that we see or hear them. Indicating to students that we know what is going on even when they are trying hard to hide from us what they are doing that they should not be doing can in fact be helpful in limiting the inappropriate behavior. [Background 16–7]

While holding up your thumb and forefinger as if about to drop a pin or humming the first bars of Beethoven's fifth are worth trying, other alternatives are available for treating communications coded pi_x. One is to name those engaged in the inappropriate behavior. Use the subcategory *name*—*pn*—by saying "John, stop that" rather than "Stop that." What thief has ever stopped running when the command "Stop thief" has been shouted? Whether a criminal like Dillinger would have more likely given up if "Stop, Mr. Dillinger" had been shouted in place of "Stop, thief and murderer," we'll never know. But for a class, the alternative can still be tried, and then the consequences can be observed. So, if a person is not named in communications that treat inappropriate social behavior, try naming the person involved.

Of course, some people when named say "I ain't doin' nothin'." So, along with specifying the person engaged in the inappropriate activity, one can specify the inappropriate communication itself. "John, stop writing your name on the desk with that knife" can be substituted for "John, stop doing that." To distinguish specified *classroom social behavior* from *unspecified*, I add the subscript *s*. As the subscript *s* for specified after *pi* increases, if the subscript *x* for inappropriate goes down, one consequence of specificity will be evident. [Background 16–8]

Though "Shut up so I can hear what you're saying" I'd code with an *s* since the behavior is indicated, the anger suggested in the order may override the specificity. Therefore, though an increase in *s*'s may decrease the *x*'s, if it does not, it will not necessarily mean specificity is not an important variable. It may mean only that other variables are operating as well. In "Shut up so I can hear what you're saying," for example, not only is *classroom social behavior* communicated—*pi*—but also personal feelings, content I'd code *fp* for *life personal*.

Journal Entry

Have you ever been struck by the fact that much *classroom social behavior* is communicated in the negative? "Don't squeeze the Charmin" is a classic ad for toilet paper, and even here the rule that we need a negative in a command about managing classroom behavior is evident. "Don't smoke here," "don't litter," "don't make noise." The list is endless. What would happen if we said instead, "Enjoy clean streets without dog dirt," "relish the quiet and listen to the birds and insects"?

How do you feel about a *no* in moves that try to manage what you do? And, is the feeling different from communications without *no*'s?

You're Coming Along Fine—Treating Appropriate *Classroom Social Behavior*

You don't need to have students make moves you'd code pi_x for inappropriate *classroom social behavior* to manipulate subcategories of *procedure*. If you had a class that always acted appropriately and tried hard, you could see whether making the type of comments in Excerpt 16–2 would prevent inappropriate classroom behavior. Research suggests that the commonly held belief that nurturing actions you want to take place and ignoring those you don't is as important, if not more so, than treating ones you don't want to take place. Whether the communications that you and I consider nurturing are important, though, is a central problem. If students continue to misbehave after their acceptable behavior is followed by comments you consider nurturing, one of the reasons may be that the students do not consider them nurturing. [Background 16–9]

In the reactions in Excerpt 16–2, the teacher is communicating classroom social behavior. But the content is being used to *characterize evaluate* the students' actions in a positive way, not to criticize them or prescribe a particular type of behavior.

EXCERPT 16–2
You're Coming Along Fine

		Communications	*Source/ Target*	*Move Type*	*Use*	*Content*
1	Student:	(Picks up paper that was lying on the floor.)				
2	Teacher:	Fine thing to do.	t/s	rea	ce	pi
3	Student:	(Erases the blackboard at the end of class.)				
4	Teacher:	I appreciate your doing that.	t/s	rea	ce	pi
5	Student:	(Keeps quiet while teacher is having a meeting with a parent after class.)				
6	Teacher:	Keeping quiet was great.	t/s	rea	ce	pi

Whether characterizing desired classroom social behavior will encourage such behavior and decrease the frequency of inappropriate behavior can only be determined by trying the alternative.

III. JUST A FEW MINUTES—NAMES AND CLASSROOM MANAGEMENT

What's in a Name?—Names as Symbols of Identity and the Generation of Alternatives

The subcategory of *procedure name* can not only specify the individuals who are not acting appropriately, but more positively can help teachers know their classes. And it can be combined with other elements to generate a large number of alternatives. Since relationships are partly symbolized by the way we use each others' names, varying this subcategory of content may also affect the subcategories of *procedure* I code *classroom social behavior.*

Of course, given the fact that naming people in a class occupies just a few minutes—two minutes to call the roll and a few seconds more any time a student is named in moves during the class—it is reasonable to ask why I treat the subcategory at all, much less in some detail. Well, in addition to providing an illustration of how to generate alternatives that require combining other content and other characteristics, I have overheard people make very opinionated comments about the way they're called during attendance and other class activities. I have included some of the comments I have heard, which you've probably heard too, in Excerpt 16–3.

EXCERPT 16–3
What's in a Name?

1 He ran a tight ship—from attendance on—all business.

2 He always called us by name and title, both during attendance and when he called on us, always respectful.

3 I could tell he never liked me by the way he said my name when he called the roll.

4 He never said my name correctly, but he wanted us to pronounce everything just one way.

5 My English teacher gave me an English name and never used my own name; he had no respect for my heritage.

6 I couldn't write my name before. But since the others taught me how to sign in, I can. I don't feel humiliated anymore.

7 Signing in is degrading—as if they don't trust us.

8 Mr. Aki—he's the manager—not only knows my name and uses it, he knows my kids' names and my husband's name too.

9 He never cared if I as a person was there or not. He just wanted good attendance so he'd look good.

10 He never misses a day. He expects us to be there too—so thorough about keeping track of us; he must care about us.

11 I'll never know why he never taught me an English name so I could use either it or my own name in my own language.

Whether the people who make comments like those in Excerpt 16–3 would be less likely to make the comments if the roll were taken in a range of ways, and whether this range would in any way affect *classroom social behavior*, we can only know if we try some alternatives. But at the minimum, since different people expressed conflicting opinions about the same behavior, alternatives will increase the number of individuals we treat the way they expect to be treated.

Before introducing alternatives, though, I want to remind you that if a person is named during the taking of attendance, I code the solicit *pn* to note the name. But since the teacher is asking about an administrative matter, I put the student response in the subcategory *administration: pa*. If a student responds by saying "here" or "Sir," or "Madame," or "Teacher" with a challenge or support for authority shown in the tone of voice, I code it *pa* for the content of the words. But since the tone of voice adds a second message that does more than indicate that a person is not absent, I put the tone of voice in the subcategory *classroom social behavior*. If you considered a challenge to authority in the tone of voice of a student inappropriate, you would code the message pi_x.

If students are required to stand as they respond to the roll, another opportunity for inappropriate *classroom behavior* presents itself. One can say "Sir" as one is in the process of getting up briskly, and one can stand up straight as one completes the word. Or, one can say "Sir," or another title, or "here," in a bent-over position, with one's hands on the desk to support oneself, without looking at the teacher and with one's eyes down toward the desk. Even a salute in the military to indicate one is not absent can be strictly a matter of administration—*pa*—or it can communicate disrespect—pi_x—together with *pa*.

Journal Entry

In calling the roll, as when we meet others outside class, names are optional. What feelings do you have when people you consider important call you by your name when they greet you outside of the setting where you work with each other? Are the feelings different when they greet you or talk to you without even mentioning your name?

Some clerks who see you a lot will no doubt ask you your name if they can't learn it by looking at checks you cash, credit cards you use, or a bill with your name on it. And after they learn your name, they use it. Others never use names of customers. In the same way, some customers try to find out the names of people who wait on them, and others never do. Many phone operators and airline and railroad personnel in some countries state their names before they ask if they can help us. And, as soon as they get our names, they address us with them. If fact, once I gave my credit card number to a person I asked about an error in my statement and almost before I finished giving the number, he said: "Well, John, I think we can work this out." Even though I knew he had gotten the name from a printout as a result of typing in my number, I was still impressed that he said my name so quickly.

Do you seek out other's names when you shop and meet the same people over and over? Does it matter to you if those who wait on you in some way use your name or not?

Beyond Administration—Combining Routine and Names (*pa* and *pn*) with Other Areas of Content

Naming people and asking them to say "Here" or "Sir" can be efficient. But the calling of the roll can be used to provide the person in charge with more information about the people in the group—*life*—and can teach some new information to the students as well—*study*. Since calling roll is so similar in all teaching settings—movies about prisoners and soldiers, for example, often have scenes in which a guard or a master sergeant calls out names and the individuals respond in a routine way—*pa*—or with some disrespect—pi_x—we need to look in nonteaching settings for some ideas on alternatives.

One out-of-class activity related to the calling of the roll is the "tell me about yourself" section of an interview. Before the main questions are asked, an interviewer usually asks a number of questions about the person being interviewed that require responses in the category of content I call *life*. The "tell me about yourself" interview is also used sometimes before or after people engage in some type of contest or game. After an athlete breaks a record, for example, the athlete is brought to a microphone and asked questions so that "people can get to know the athlete as a person." In Excerpt 16–4, I've listed some of the questions I've heard in interviews of this type. As you can see, I've left a blank with broken lines after each solicit. You should respond to the solicits on the broken lines only if you have the time—the responses are rated tasks.

I've coded the content of the responses *fp* for *life personal*. If such questions were asked both to get personal information and to determine who was in class on a given day, I would code the student responses *life personal* and *procedure administration: fp + pa*.

Of course, in a classroom, each solicit would have to contain the name of the person you called on: Yoko, what do you do in your spare time? In this way, a response would tell you both that Yoko was present, or absent, and if present, what in fact she did in her spare time. Such responses would take longer than a "Sir!" But over a period of time, they would provide both teacher and students with information about all participants that might make the individuals know each other better. And they might

EXCERPT 16–4
Tell Me about Yourself

Communications	*Source/ Target*	*Move Type*	*Content**
What do you do in your spare time?	t/s	sol	
--	s/t	res	fp
What is your favorite food?	t/s	sol	
--	s/t	res	fp
What was the most recent movie you saw?	t/s	sol	
--	s/t	res	fp
How do you like to spend your vacations?	t/s	sol	
--	s/t	res	fp
Where were you born?	t/s	sol	
--	s/t	res	fp

* If responding to the question showed that a person was present at the same time, each response would be coded *fp + pa*. Responses are rated.

then begin to see themselves as more than a group of people who were just in the same class together.

To save time, you might ask personal questions just once in a while, and just ask a few students during any one taking of the roll. By entering the information in the responses on three-by-five cards or on the register, it would be possible to get a lot of information to use in relation to class activities. If a large number of students respond in a particular way, the responses provide topics for subsequent classes. When a large number of students have seen the same movie or like the same food, this information can be related to the areas of study being taught.

In Excerpt 16–5, I've included some other questions I have heard interviewers ask people. As you can see, they concern the meaning of the person's name, content I would code *study of language*, subcategory *lexis ll*. When you have the time, feel free to respond to the solicits by filling in the broken lines. The responses are rated tasks.

In order for these questions to fulfill their administrative function, they would have to contain the names of the people you were calling on. But as students gave the meanings of their names, etymology would be introduced as part of lexical meaning. And if as you asked the names, you asked about their pronunciation and found you were mispronouncing them, you could begin to use some student names as touchstones for pronunciation of many sounds. In addition, students would hear many types of questions that people outside classes are likely to ask, especially if the people they meet have watched interviews or listened to them on the radio.

Asking students what they like and don't like and what their names mean in front of a class might be considered very private by some students. One alternative is to have students write down what they feel and the personal information you are seeking. The cards could be collected or left on the teacher's desk. Another way to decrease the pressure students might feel about sharing personal feelings and information would be for all participants to assume a role, just as participants in plays and dramatic presentations do. I've listed some suggestions that could be used to get students to develop roles for themselves in Excerpt 16–6.

The suggestions in Excerpt 16–6 do not require that complete descriptions of each characteristic be given each day. This would be extremely time-consuming. Rather, the idea is to spend five or more days on each characteristic. One series of periods would

EXCERPT 16–5
Yes, What's in a Name?

Communications	*Source/ Target*	*Move Type*	*Content**
What would you like me to call you?	t/s	sol	
--	s/t	res	fp
What does your first name mean?	t/s	sol	
--	s/t	res	fp + ll
What is the meaning of your surname?	t/s	sol	
--	s/t	res	fp + ll

* If the responses showed that a person was present, they would be coded *fp* + *pa* or *l*. Responses are rated.

EXCERPT 16–6
Developing Characters

	Communications	*Source Target*	*Move Type*
1	On each day, when I call your assumed name, tell me one aspect of your appearance.	t/s	str
2	Every day, tell me one character trait you'd like to have under your assumed name.	t/s	str
3	Describe the kind of clothes the person you are developing likes to wear.	t/s	str
4	Let us know the types of drinks the person you are impersonating likes.	t/s	str
5	Tell us some facts about the background of the person you are developing a character for.	t/s	str
6	We'd like to hear about the heroes your character has.	t/s	str

be devoted to favorite foods, and another group of lessons would be devoted to the communication of a word each day that described a series of character traits. In large classes, only a few students would state characteristics each day; others would respond to the roll in the usual way, or be marked present on the chart.

Journal Entry

In some classes, teachers ask students why they were absent in front of the entire class. Do you prefer to tell others why you were absent, or late, in front of a group or privately?

If you or some students do prefer to share reasons privately, this option is open. People can write notes explaining private reasons for not being present too. But another way students can explain why they are not there is to explain their absence in terms of the person they are developing as a character. If they were developing a person who had many outside duties, then the absence could be the result of other tasks to be done. Of course, you would not get the "real" reason. But in front of a class of students, we often do not get the "real" reason anyway.

As the characters develop, attributes of characters can be stated rather than names, and the person who is developing the role of a rich, hard-to-get-along-with, 35-year-old author of mysteries would respond to this description rather than his or her own name during the calling of the roll. By having each student develop a distinct character on an incremental basis, it will give students a chance to grow into roles if a great deal of role-playing is done in the class. (Role-playing is treated in Episode 13.) Even if role-playing is not done in class, students may begin to play the role of the characters they establish over a period of time. [Background 16–10]

Journal Entry

I once heard American linguist and lexicographer Allen Walker Read, who was a professor at Columbia University in New York City, read a story he had written while studying in England. The story treated his feelings about answering the roll during his first university class in England. Professor Read normally spoke American English, since he was American. As the roll was being called during the first class, each British student answered "here" without the pronunciation of the *r*.

Should he imitate the other students or pronounce *here* the way he normally did? Would the others think he couldn't imitate them if he used his own idiolect? Or would they consider him lacking in pride in his own idiolect if he imitated them? Or might they think him uppity if he kept his own pronunciation of *here*?

Have you ever wondered how to act in such a setting? The instant taken to respond can have consequences far greater than the percentage of time and effort taken to respond. Would you have said *here* in British English as the other students did, if you were not English? Or, would you have used your own idiolect? Would you have wished that you could have played the part of another character rather than have to be yourself?

Another out-of-class activity related to calling the roll that provides a way to integrate *procedure* and *life* is the opinion poll. Though the questions in polls are usually about public issues or public candidates, what is sought is an individual's personal opinion of a public figure or problem. To keep the confidential nature of an opinion poll intact, two alternatives are available. One is to have students put their heads down on their desks with their eyes closed as the teacher asks each student if he or she is for, against or undecided on a particular issue or candidate. Raising the right hand could indicate for, the left hand against and the head, with the eyes still closed, undecided. When the students' names were called, they would then raise either their right or left hands or their heads to indicate their opinions. Since the aim of a poll is the tally rather than the identity of each person voting, there is no reason for each student to see how each other student feels. The teacher can note the results of the poll on the blackboard after the attendance is taken. But by taking the roll with a poll rather than just by calling names to elicit a series of "Sirs," the teacher and students not only know who and how many are absent, but also know how many in a class feel a particular way about public issues or candidates. School policy, classroom procedures, types of tests to be administered and other issues more closely related to each student could also be polled in this way.

Another alternate way of not forcing students to reveal their own personal opinions about issues—some might resent having to state in front of others in the group their views on abortion, welfare, or even political candidates in the country they are from or the country they are in—would be to have the students given the opinion of the character they were pretending they were. This would give students a chance to work out the personalities of the people they were pretending to be, and would give other students and the teacher a chance to tell the person that their voting on a particular issue was inconsistent with their personality! It would add a dimension of realism to the world of imagination being used for development of roles.

A Kind of Summary—Matching English Descriptions of Alternatives and Coding Done with FOCUS

I have prepared a table for you to match FOCUS descriptions of alternative ways of employing some of the subcategories of *procedure, life personal* (*fp*), *life public* (*fg*), and *study* (*s*) and the mediums with English descriptions. Check the abbreviations for the mediums in the table at the end of the book if you need to, and use the subcategories of procedure from this episode. As you will see when you start matching, neither all the coding nor English descriptions for the alternatives have been mentioned in this episode. The new ones highlight the fact that one of the primary aims of each episode is to provide you with a means to generate alternatives on your own from the elements of FOCUS. The FOCUS descriptions and the English equivalents are grouped in fours in Table 16–2. Matching done by others is given in the footnote to the table.

TABLE 16–2
Some Alternatives

			FOCUS DESCRI			
ENGLISH DESCRIPTIONS			*Source/ Target*	*Move Type*	*Medium*	*Content*
1. Student smiles and beams at teacher as he indicates that he is present by saying "here."	______	a	s/t	res	pv	pa + s
2. Student indicates presence by standing bent over, looking down at desk rather than at the teacher.	______	b	s/t	res	la + pv	pa + fp +*
3. Student models the pronunciation of his name as he responds to the roll so the teacher can hear how it is said.	______	c	s/t	res	pv	pa + pi –*
4. Student responds to roll with a facial expression showing an emotion that the teacher requested each student to demonstrate.	______	d	s/t	res	la	pa + s
5. Student responds to roll by stating how many brothers she has.	______	a	s/t	res	lv	pa + s
6. Student writes what mood he's in on a card which the teacher collects and records in attendance register.	______	b	s/t	res	la	pa + fp
7. Student responds to roll by giving the name of the captain of the soccer team that just won the World Cup.	______	c	s/t	res	la	pa + fg
8. Student writes the spelling of a word the teacher asked him to spell when he called his name; teacher collects card to indicate presence.	______	d	s/t	res	lv	pa + fp
9. Student calls the roll by calling fellow students by name.	______	a	s/s	sol	la	ps + pa + pn
10. Student takes attendance by looking at each student and asking the student's opinion about smoking in public places.	______	b	s/s	sol	nv	ps + pa

TABLE 16–2 (*continued*)

ENGLISH DESCRIPTIONS			FOCUS DESCRIPTIONS *Source/ Target*	*Move Type*	*Medium*	*Content*
11. Student asks fellow students to pass sketches of themselves to front of the room to indicate they are present.	_____	c	s/s	sol	la + nv	ps + pa
12. Student calls roll by pointing to students' numbers written on the blackboard; each student has an assigned number.	_____	d	s/s	sol	pv + la	ps + pa + fp + fg
13. Teacher calls roll briskly, in a matter-of-fact way.	_____	a	t/s	sol	la + pv	ps + pa + pn + fp +*
14. Teacher calls each student's name and as he does, he looks at student, smiles, or nods pleasantly.	_____	b	t/s	sol	la	ps + pa + pn
15. Teacher calls each student's name with tone of voice that suggests he's doing something he hates to do.	_____	c	t/s	sol	la pa	ps + pa + pn lsp –*
16. Teacher calls roll in an adult class with the stress and intonation pattern parents used with 3-year-olds—stresses each syllable, uses a high pitch and rising-rising intonation rather than rising-falling intonation.	_____	d	t/s	sol	la pa	ps + pa + pn fp –*

* The plus sign indicates a positive emotion; the minus sign unacceptable classroom behavior. A *ps* at the beginning of an item indicates that the use *present state* is expected in the responses.

Matching done by others: 1. b; 2. c; 3. d; 4. a; 5. b; 6. d; 7. c; 8. a; 9. a; 10. d; 11. c; 12. b; 13. b; 14. a; 15. d; 16. c.

IV. PUT YOUR NAME ON THE DOTTED LINE—SOME CODING AND REFLECTING

Same or Different?—Developing New Subcategories of *Procedure* on Your Own

If you find yourself coding a lot of communications *pp* for *other* because they don't fit the subcategories of *procedure* I treated in this episode or those I treated elsewhere, then you might find you can be more specific in your description if you attach your own labels to some of those communications you code *pp*. In establishing a subcategory, the major task is simply determining whether each communication is the same or different from each other one you compare it with.

I've listed some communications in Excerpt 16–7 that fit established subcategories, and I've listed a few that could form a new subcategory or two. Leave the content line blank next to lines you think fit one of the established subcategories. Write in an *n* for *new* if you think a new subcategory is needed to describe the communication specifically. I have put coding done by others in the footnote.

Rather than *n* for *new*, lines 9 to 11 could be *administration*, but if teachers being observed say a lot of things similar to these lines, a more specific description would be possible by establishing a new subcategory. If teachers being observed consistently gave advice about what students might wear in class to prevent illness, unless they could be considered to be teaching health and thus it could be coded *o* for *study other*, such talk could also form a new subcategory. By using subcategories in FOCUS as a contrast for establishing new ones, FOCUS allows the generation of alternatives in a different way. Rather than substituting an infrequent, established subcategory for a frequent one, new subcategories can be substituted for established ones.

EXCERPT 16–7
Same or Different?

		Communications	Source/ Target	Move Type	Content
1	Teacher:	Martha, Lisa, Juan, Yumiko and Ab,	t/g	sol	______
2		now that you have the tests,			______
3		please check to see that you have 2 pages each.			______
4	Students:	(Check their papers.)	g/t	res	______
5	Teacher:	You may begin now.	t/g	sol	______
6		It's 9:05 and you have till 9:45 to do it.	t/g	str	______
7	Students:	(Write in their test booklets.)	g/o + t	res	______
8	Teacher:	Most of the questions are easy.	t/g	str	______
9		That is, if you have reviewed the chapters I have assigned you.			______
10		Do as much as you can.			______
11		Don't dwell on any one question too long.			______
12		When you're finished, hand the papers in.			______
13		And, you may leave the class quietly.			______

Coding done by others: 1. *pn*; 2. *pa*; 3. *pu* + *pa*, since a task is set here; 4. *pa*; 5. *pu* + *pa* + *s*, since the test is on some area of study, and not on administration or procedure; 6. *pe*; 7. *s*; 8. *pd*—difficulty factor, treated in Episode 5; 9. *n*; 10. *n*; 11. n; 12. *pa*; 13. *pi*.

From Within—Conclusion

Given the wide diversity of values of those we teach, the consequences of some of the alternatives suggested in this episode may vary from place to place. In a school where the principal advocates paddling, substituting teaching direction—*pu*—for information about how we want students to act—*pi*—may have different consequences than in a school where paddling is prohibited. In any school, a teacher's ideas about appropriateness of *classroom social behavior* and treatment cannot be entirely separated from the ideas and standards of the students either, since student values can affect behavior as much as the principal's. We often forget that all students, even those we might consider rowdy, have views on appropriate *classroom social behavior* and its treatment.

In fact, the more we can observe each student dealing with him or herself and with each other student, the more we can learn ways to be less centrally involved in communicating classroom social behavior or treating inappropriate instances of it. Ultimately, each person has to take personal responsibility from within for managing his or her own behavior if we are to have either classes or societies where we can all live in harmony. Having a soldier with a gun on every street corner and in every store, and police officers in every class, is not as powerful as the control that comes from within each individual.

Whether careful observation of student communications containing classroom social behavior over a period of time will yield information about the development of control from within or not, such specific observation is bound to be more revealing than discussion of the issue in global terms. Just as some of the alternatives for teachers I reviewed in this episode have been informed by specific, detailed descriptions of teachers and students in actual classrooms rather than by discussion of such clichés as *rapport, firmness*, and *respect*, so I hope that by specific description of students, you'll be able to discover ways in which the general term "control from within" is practiced. Such a discovery will not only decrease the need for saying "Shut up so I can hear what you're saying," but also the need to discuss the issue of classroom management at all—perhaps an unrealistic dream, but parts of some dreams come true.

Now, if you'll just sign on the dotted line: . . . .—*pa*—I'll be able to name you when we meet—*pn*—to share your discoveries about *pi*. And we won't have to worry about anyone overhearing our conversation because, with these terms, no one will know what we are talking about.

BACKGROUND NOTES

16–1. By not treating drugs, violence in classrooms, and other crimes, I do not mean to suggest the problems are not important, or even grave. The issues of drugs and crime in schools merit concern. Others devote their efforts in this direction though, and I urge that they be consulted. In addition to police and social agencies concerned with crime, a useful list of sources and a short review of research in the area that would serve as an introduction is "School crime and the social order of the school" by F. and E. Ianni, 1979.

16–2. A review of research in classroom management that presents research findings to support this view that I found useful is Gnagey's 1955 monograph. In Gnagey's words, "In cases of repeated severe punishment, children may learn to react with fear to the teacher, the classroom, the test, and the subject," page 25.

16–3. Madsen and Madsen, and Fish and Loehfelm all urge teachers to withhold approval for unacceptable behavior and in some way reward behavior that is acceptable. But in order to do this, the teacher must explicitly indicate what is expected.

16–4. Kounin has written one of the classic studies of classroom behavior. He and his teams spent weeks observing tapes of classes. He found that what he called "slowdowns" consistently caused some noise and deviant behavior.

16–5. West (1960) urged pin-drop silence, and Sylvia Ashton-Warner hummed the opening lines of a Beethoven symphony.

16–6. Kounin found that variety in seatwork and challenges in the tasks students were expected to perform were consistently correlated with a low incidence of misbehavior. Gnagey reports that teachers control better or have fewer things to control when the classes are interesting.

16–7. Kounin calls this being aware of what is going on "withitness." He calls being able to follow more than one thing at a time "overlapping." "Withitness" is the more important of the two variables for decreasing deviance.

16–8. "Clarity produces results" is the title Gnagey gives to the section in his monograph on teacher behaviors aimed at indicating who is doing what is unacceptable and stating what the unacceptable behavior is. If we do not name the person involved, clarity is decreased a great deal.

16–9. The nurturing of acceptable behaviors is urged by Gnagey, and Madsen and Madsen. They are both behaviorist-oriented in their point of view, and they refer to many studies that have been done that support their points of view. They wrote their suggestions twenty years apart and yet, in that time period, more research was accumulated that supports their points of view. Fish and Loehflem also urge approval.

Polirstok and Greer also are behaviorists. But they thought it might be easier to train students to act differently toward teachers, rather than to train teachers to act differently toward students. A problem student was trained outside class to react to a teacher's reprimand with a "thank you" or pleasant comment. The problem student was given lessons in role-playing outside the class. When the teacher said "Wrong" or "Not so good," the student was trained to say something pleasant. The student was also trained to say things like "Fine lesson," or "Interesting point" during the lessons. The observers found that the student was treated very differently over a period of time by four teachers. They all decreased the number of disapproving comments made to the problem student. The researchers concluded that it might be cheaper and more efficient to train students outside class in ways to act and ways to respond to disapproval than to train the teachers involved. If nothing else, the study is an example of what this book is about—trying opposites.

16–10. Lozanov developed his own suggestology for increasing the efficiency of language learning. But his suggestions about assuming rules, as well as his suggestions for a variety of tasks, relaxed atmosphere, and high expectations of students, are all suggestions that are also made by those who have done research in classroom management.

EPISODE

17

Two Vanilla, One Chocolate

I. ENTERING THE FRAY—TOPIC AND ORGANIZATION OF THE EPISODE

The ease with which a waiter taking dessert orders restates "Two vanilla, one chocolate" after I request two dishes of vanilla ice cream and one dish of chocolate in no way reflects the difficulty we all encounter when we try to redo what another has demonstrated or modeled as we are learning something. Artists-to-be trying to imitate the masters, and dancers-to-be trying to leap as high as the dance master, and potential Olympic shot-putters trying to put the shot as far as gold medalists do, and attempts to imitate a sound, let alone a phrase, in a language foreign to us remind us that trying to redo in the same medium what another has done—what I call *reproduce same medium*—is not necessarily an easy task.

And the nonchalance with which sweet-toothed customers hear restatements like "Two vanilla, one chocolate" is diametrically opposed to the intensity with which language teachers discuss the value of such restatements for developing language skill, and to the importance attached to restatements by many methodologists. Battles about communications which I code as *reproduce same medium*, or *drill* in the vernacular, have raged both in language teaching and in other areas of teaching for a long time. [Background 17–1]

I enter the fray in the episode by treating the use *reproduce same medium—ds*, for short. But in order to keep tempers calm as long as possible, I delay any statements that suggest a fray until Section IV. In Section II, I provide examples to illustrate the use *reproduce same medium: ds*. In Section III, I describe some ways to develop and employ material to be reproduced, eager to make a Xerox machine salesperson happy. Even in Section IV, I merely state some possible benefits and rejoinders to criticism of what many, those fond of dentists perhaps, call *drill*, and what I, a former botany enthusiast, call more awkwardly *reproduce same medium*. But in my experience, even mentioning the topic of redoing what another has done in the same medium means one has entered the fray, so strongly do some people feel about the topic.

If you prefer *reproducing* in a different medium, as when we *reproduce* print in the form of speech in oral reading, or when we *reproduce* speech in the form of print in dictations, or when we *reproduce* speech in the form of movement or gestures as in complete physical response, go to Episode 14, where I treat the other subcategory of *reproduce: reproduce change medium, dc.*

Journal Entry

Though at first distinguishing ways we give our orders to people who serve us meals may seem much ado about nothing, think of how many people have their meals ruined when dining out by receiving mixed-up orders. Realize too that very strict rules have been developed about giving orders. On trains in the United States, for example, all orders *must* be written by the customer on the order slips. The waiters only take written orders to the kitchens. In some restaurants, all orders are oral, and the waiters don't even write down the orders after they are given by the customer; nor do they repeat them.

What reaction do you have when the wrong order is brought to you? Do you find any difference between frequency of correct orders and the mediums the orders are given in, or changed into, or the frequency of restatements of the orders?

II. AVOIDING *DRILL*—DEFINING *REPRODUCE SAME MEDIUM: ds*

Pretty Sweet—Subcategories of *Reproduce Same Medium: ds*

I employ subcategories of *reproduce same medium* in the same way I employ other subcategories in FOCUS, to illustrate the meaning of the larger category, to enable us to describe communications more specifically, and to provide alternatives. Since all subcategories share something in common, each being related so to speak to the major category, potential overlap between subcategories is built in. Consequently, discovering overlap as you code should not drive you crazy. It goes with the territory.

Essentially, I use *ds* to code mediums used to repeat exactly in the same medium what was just communicated, or to repeat previous mediums with some variation, such as in a larger or smaller form, or with some substitution in the repetition. The variations can be indicated specifically by the person requesting the reproduction, as when a person is told: "Rewrite *He was happy* in the plural." Or the variations can be indicated generally, as when a person is asked to paraphrase what another has just said, or to edit a paragraph. Finally, the variations, as well as the exact repetitions, can simply be communicated without any indication to vary anything made by any source outside the person communicating.

In Excerpt 17–1, I have coded some examples of communications in the subcategories of *reproduce same medium* I employ. As you'll see, the meanings I attach to the terms are parallel with those generally attached to them. The subcategories can be altered to match ways people use mediums to *reproduce* in settings you are in.

The *p* in the content column stands for *procedure*, and the *sl* stands for the *study of language*. I have not used subcategories of content so you can concentrate on *reproduce*, and to remind you that determining what single subcategory of the *study of language* is being reproduced is not an easy task. The *sl* stands for the category *study of language* and also indicates that two or three subcategories of the *study of language*

EXCERPT 17–1
Pretty Sweet

		Communications	*Source/ Target*	*Move Type*	*Use*	*Content*
Setting 1: At a restaurant.						
1	Customer:	I'd like two dishes of vanilla ice cream and one dish of chocolate ice cream.	t/s	sol		
2	Waiter:	Two vanilla, one chocolate.	s/t	rea	ds reduce	p
3	Customer:	And two glasses of chocolate milk and one glass of white milk.	t/s	sol		
4	Waiter:	And two glasses of chocolate milk and one glass of white milk.	s/t	rea	ds repeat	p
5	Customer:	And, please bring it quickly. We have to leave to meet some friends.	t/s	(part of previous sol)		
6	Waiter:	You want me bring right away.	s/t	rea	ds paraphrase	p
7	Customer:	I want you to bring it right away.	t/s	rea	ds edit	sl + p*
8	Waiter:	Two dishes of vanilla and one dish of chocolate—right away.	t/s	sol		
9	Server:	Two vanilla, one chocolate.	s/t	rea	ds reduce	p
10		(Dishes up ice cream and hands to waiter.)	s/t	res		
11	Waiter:	(Serves ice cream and milk to customer.)	s/t	res	dc reproduce change medium	
Setting 2: In a classroom.						
12	Teacher:	Make these two sentences into one: *I want two dishes of vanilla ice cream. I want one dish of chocolate ice cream.*	t/c	sol		
13	Student:	I want two dishes of vanilla ice cream and one dish of chocolate.	s/t	res	ds combine	sl
14	Teacher:	You want two dishes of vanilla ice cream and one dish of chocolate.	t/s	rea	ds substitute	sl

EXCERPT 17–1 (*continued*)

		Communications	*Source/ Target*	*Move Type*	*Use*	*Content*
15		Now, ask the question with the pattern starting with *do*.	t/s	sol		
16	Student:	Do you want two dishes of vanilla ice cream and one dish of chocolate?	s/t	res	ds transform	sl
17	Teacher:	With *customer.*	t/s	sol		
18	Student:	Does the customer want two dishes of vanilla ice cream and one dish of chocolate?	s/t	res	ds substitute and change	sl
19	Teacher:	Does the customer really want two dishes of vanilla ice cream and one dish of chocolate ice cream?	t/s	rea	ds expand	sl

* I have coded *p* plus *study of language* because I think the customer is providing a sample of correct language in order to correct the errors in the waiter's speech.

are being communicated, but that the specific ones are hard to agree on. In reproducing "Two vanilla, one chocolate," for example, you could be interested in grammar, showing that no plural inflections are needed. Or you could be working on sound, the pronunciation of particular sounds or stress. Or the lexis of the words *vanilla* and *chocolate* might be the focus of attention.

The neat distinction between subcategories in Excerpt 17–1 should not make you think that all instances of *ds* fit neatly into only one subcategory. When a student changes a teacher model like *I'm holding a red felt pen* to *He's holding a red pen* after the teacher says "Try again," the sentence no longer contains an error. Since an error was eliminated, *ds edit* seems appropriate. But the student changed *I'm* to *He's—ds substitute change*—and dropped *felt—ds reduce.* As I said when I introduced the subcategories, overlap occurs. Employ the subcategories to look more specifically at communications that are reproduced in the same medium. And, as always, if you find no instances of some subcategories and many of others, simply substitute infrequent ones for frequent ones.

Where there is always overlap, solicit some responses that allow only one subcategory. For example, you could have students pretend to be legal secretaries who needed to rewrite a will because the beneficiaries were changed from the person's sisters to his daughters. This would certainly require *ds substitute change.*

Humming and Drawing Too—*Reproducing Different Mediums*

I employ the same subcategories no matter which mediums are used to *reproduce* content in the *same medium*. Thus, I'd code a piano student trying to repeat a pianist's chords as *ds repeat.* Noting the medium *na* would distinguish it from an aural/oral repetition, which I'd code *la*.

Going through the series of steps required in some controlled compositions I'd distinguish from the aural/oral examples in Excerpt 17–1 by noting the medium. Thus, when a person is asked to copy a story, change all female characters to male, add *in 2001* to sentences, and match the verbs with the new time, I'd say the students were using print—*lv*—to *ds imitate, ds substitute, ds expand*, and *ds substitute change*. Doing a series of steps to the left in a dance class after seeing the steps demonstrated to the right, I'd code *ds transform* and distinguish the steps from other communications by noting the medium as *po* for movement.

It may seem curious for me to suggest that we use mediums other than speech and print to *reproduce mediums: ds*. Reproducing strange sounds—*nonlinguistic aural*—however, might make some people feel more at ease when asked to *reproduce* sounds of the target language, as strange as grunts from pigs and chirps from birds sound to those who are just hearing them for the first time. If students never *reproduce* gestures, facial expressions, and body language in the target language, they might say the right thing when they are introduced, but shake hands, smile, or bow inappropriately. Copying triangles, boxes, or outlines of leaves and other figures might aid both the mechanics of holding a pencil and prepare some for copying and forming the shapes in letters. Reproducing another's humming, a *nonlinguistic aural* medium, might make the rhythm of the words of a new language clearer than constant reproduction of the words themselves, which are *linguistic aural* mediums alone.

Mediums are also important to distinguish moves that contain only the use *reproduce* from those that contain more than one use. "Two vanilla, one chocolate?!" with a tone of voice suggesting puzzlement, as when a waiter would say them after a customer sitting alone had ordered three dishes of ice cream, is a move with two messages. The tone of voice—*paralinguistic aural*—is used either to *characterize* the customer, implying he or she is crazy, or to *present* the message "Do you mean this?" The words are used only to *reproduce* the customer's words, and so the *linguistic aural* medium does not change the meaning of the move; the *paralinguistic aural* medium does.

When children mimic adults, or adults mimic children, the mediums again are a critical factor. If one person says "I want you to go," and the other mimics it by saying "I want you to go" in a nah, nah, nah tone of voice, I again code the words *reproduce same medium* and the tone of voice *characterize*. The tone of voice used differently from the words indicates that the move contains two messages, one in which the medium *pa* is used to communicate content one way, and one in which the medium *la* is used to communicate content another way. I treat moves that contain one message that *reproduces* and one that does something else when I discuss feedback in Episode 12.

Distinguishing among the Popular Hits—Coding Mediums Used to *Present, Reproduce Change Medium,* and *Reproduce Same Medium: p, dc, ds*

Since the most frequent student uses in classrooms tend to be *present, reproduce change medium* and *reproduce same medium*, distinguishing these three uses is important for accurate description. One place all three are communicated is at a children's dance recital. A few begin to dance on cue, remembering their steps and movements; they are *presenting*. Some, with spoken comments like "move to stage left and wave arms" remember what to do; they are *reproducing* by *changing the medium* of speech to movement. The bulk of the chidren aren't sure what to do with an audience of three hundred people in front of them, rather than the one teacher they have been used to during

EXCERPT 17–2
Popular Hits

		Communications	*Source/ Target*	*Move Type*	*Use*
1	Teacher:	Pretend you're eating ice cream.	t/s	sol	
2	Student:	(Mimes eating an ice cream cone.)	s/t	res	p dc
3	Teacher:	What kind of ice cream do you like best?	t/s	sol	
4	Student:	Chocolate mint.	s/t	res	p dc
5	Teacher:	What did I draw on the blackboard? (Draws an ice cream scooper on the board.)	t/s	sol	
6	Student:	An ice cream scooper.	s/t	res	p dc
7	Teacher:	Now, each of you draw it.	t/s	sol	
8	Students:	(Draw scoopers.)	s/t	res	dc ds
9	Teacher:	Now, write these words under it: *an ice cream scooper.* (said, not written.)	t/s	sol	
10	Students:	(Write the words *an ice cream scooper.*)	s/t	res	dc ds
11	Teacher:	Now, draw three cones with scoops on them.	t/s	sol	
12	Students:	(Draw cones with scoops on them.)	s/t	res	dc ds

Coding done by others: 2. dc; 4. p; 6. dc; 8. ds; 10. dc; 12. dc.

dance lessons, so they look to their right and left and imitate various fellow dancers; they are *reproducing in the same medium.*

To provide you with an opportunity to distinguish these three uses, I've included Excerpt 17–2. In each line in the use column, circle the appropriate use. *P* stands for *present*: communicating information directly; *dc* stands for *reproduce change medium*: reproducing print in speech, as in oral reading, or speech in print, as in a dictation; *ds* stands for *reproduce same medium*: redoing what another has just done in one medium in the same medium, either identically or with slight variations. Coding done by others is given in the footnote. [Background 17–2]

III. TABLES AND STEPS—DEVELOPING AND EMPLOYING MATERIALS TO BE REPRODUCED

What Would You Like?—Preparing Material for Reproduction

Since any communication can be *reproduced*, finding material to *reproduce* is easy. However, to provide opportunities for students to do more than *reproduce imitate*, we have to find communications that are not just single ones, such as "How do you do?", which is normally said only to any one person once, the first time we meet someone, and cannot be manipulated at all. For example, we can't say "How does Fritz do?" or "How does a horse do?"

In selecting communications for students to *reproduce*, I follow these steps. I start by listening to tapes of students engaged in group activities during class, in conversations before class and during breaks, or engaged in teacher-to-student moves in class. As I listen to students engaged in activities such as building model airplanes or discussing a cloze passage, I discover some communications the students feel compelled to make but cannot. If they say "That there, this here" with no verbs as they are directing each other to fasten or glue or pass parts around, I know some verbs are needed. As students talk in any of these settings, I also hear communications that contain errors which need treatment. And if the students use their own language during breaks, I ask about the topics so I know some language that needs to be introduced in class to discuss what interests them. If students are discussing a baseball game in the vernacular, I realize that communications such as these need to be introduced: "He made a hit, a home run, a first-base hit, a double, a triple."

If the students are taking an examination that consistently contains particular items, I select patterns from the examination for them to *reproduce*. If there is a prescribed text, I select communications from it, though I don't necessarily follow the same sequence as the book. I used to be religious about following sequences, but when I began to realize that the reason many books follow the same sequence is simply because the authors and publishers borrow them from each other, I felt freer. Proof that patterns in the beginning lessons in books are in fact easier than those later on is not easy to find. Even if as time goes on, some so-called natural sequence is discovered, student needs and interests may continue to be more crucial variables in learning than the sequences based on linguistic considerations alone. [Background 17–3]

In some cases, student needs may not be able to be determined from tapes of what they feel compelled to say, from their errors, from examinations, or from prescribed texts. When students are studying a language for a job or as preparation to study a specific area of study other than language, such as horticulture, beekeeping or glassblowing, material must of necessity come from the setting they are preparing to enter. In this case, taping the people who the student will be communicating with is vital. And the communications that these future colleagues or teachers make must form the basis for the course. I treat other aspects of this topic, language for specific purposes, in Episode 8.

Between student immediate and future needs, texts and tests, there will be no dearth of communications available to *reproduce*. But communications from these sources will tend to be immediately usable, ordinary, and common. They might, as a result, be limiting. What if you love moths and insects, karate or embroidery? Or what if only one student is interested in electronics? Should these singular interests and some of the communications that are necessary for the interests be ignored? Are we paid only to meet obvious needs of large numbers of students? Or are we paid as well to expand horizons, spark interest, and create new needs? If 100 percent of the communications students *reproduce* come from needs, introduce totally unnecessary communications as an alternative! A bit of absurdity may creep in, a bit of humor may, a bit of your own interest or an intense interest of only one student. But can't you remember some curious communications better than the everyday, common ones from a language class or other classes?

Once the students and I determine the pattern to *reproduce*, I try to find a context it naturally occurs in and roles people assume when they use the patterns. Since I treat establishing contexts and assigning roles in Episode 13, I will go right on to the next step here: developing a substitution table.

A substitution table is simply a display in columns of the pattern to be reproduced. As you have noticed, I arrange the elements of FOCUS in substitution tables. Table

TABLE 17–1
Tabular Array

1	2	3	4	5	6	7	8	9	10
	I	'd	like	two	dish	es	of	vanilla	ice cream

17–1 shows the first step in making a substitution table with the solicit "I'd like two dishes of vanilla ice cream." [Background 17–4]

Once I have arranged the elements in columns, as you might expect, I add words that can be substituted in each of the columns. A thesaurus is one aid in finding words to fit each column; a class of fifty students is another. I mention a large class simply to highlight the fact that the more heads making suggestions, the greater will be the range of appropriate items. By appropriate, I mean able to fit the slots and collocate with other columns, *not* ones usually found in school texts or used mainly in teaching settings.

As you will see in Table 17–2, there are at lest three kinds of words we can substitute: normal, abnormal, and nonsensical. I've grouped each type so you can get a clearer sense of my meaning of these words. Using three types of words may allow some students to alter the way they communicate because they will use some words they've never experienced before in their reproduction. If a person has been saying *He run* for a few years, it is more likely that the third-person singular inflection will be reproduced if it is embedded in a word unfamiliar to the person, such as *slings, jingles,*

TABLE 17–2
Substitutions

1	2	3	4	5	6	7	8	9	10
A An	I He She They We The child	'd	like	two three four (to any number)	dish bowl cup spoon plate	es s	of	vanilla chocolate banana strawberry peach	ice cream cookies pudding yogurt soda
	glutton dieter gourmet epicure connoisseur		relish	one hundred (to any number)	liter scoop order gallon quart tin can bottle			almond pistachio marshmallow	popsicles pastries eclairs flavoring
	boing cling zong		boing klin zil		boing karp slik			boing qualch	boing quish

or *whips*. Nonsense words enable the form of the communication to receive total attention. In "He boinged the boing because it was a very boing day," you don't have to worry about lexical items in the slots for the content words. [Background 17–5]

I would not start a lesson with all the words in Table 17–2, but I would hope that I could end a lesson with most of them. Items such as the *A* and *An* in the first column and the two forms of the plural in column 7 are necessary at some point though, because they provide something for students' minds to do as they *reproduce*. Selecting no article, an *a*, or an *an* makes it difficult simply to rattle off a word from each column.

The collocation between the content words in columns 6, 9, and 10 provides another diversion that prevents simple regurgitation of a word from each column. Bottles of pistachio soda, cans of marshmallow pastries, or gallons of banana, or any other kind of pastries, aren't possible. Some argue that all items in each column must collocate with all items in each other column. The types of impossible combination I illustrate in Table 17–2 are considered confusing. I address all such prescriptions and admonitions in the same way: to see more clearly what we do and the consequences of what we do, we must do the opposite. If tables always contain only possible combinations, the alternative, tables with some impossible combinations, needs to be tried. [Background 17–6]

In addition to diversions within the pattern, at some point the pattern needs to be contrasted with one it is likely to be confused with. If you've based a table on student errors, the contrast between the errors and the forms with which the errors are confused is easy to discover. If you've based a table on other considerations, as soon as a few students *reproduce* the communications, you'll know the areas that need to be contrasted. One pattern I'd contrast with "I'd like two dishes of vanilla ice cream" is "I like vanilla ice cream." I'd also contrast the solicits "What would you like?" and "What do you like?" since these two questions produce the two patterns I'd contrast.

Another way to divert students as they *reproduce* from the pattern at hand is to communicate with more than one medium. While repeating songs accompanied by music, for example, the words—a *linguistic aural* medium—are reproduced, but the music—a *nonlinguistic aural* medium—is not.

Whether different mediums are used to divert students or contrasts based on errors, or contrasts based on patterns that are likely to be confused with the pattern you start with, the diversions or contrasts need not be introduced during the first steps of reproduction. Error rate and speed of reproduction can aid in determining the time to raise the ante. If students are reproducing without any errors or at a speed beyond the normal—just spewing out words ritualistically with no sense of meaning—it is probably time for a diversion or a contrast. No matter when you do divert, or introduce a contrast, or whatever means you employ, though, I just want to stress here again a central tenet of the pioneers of substitution tables and pattern practice: the necessity of diverting students and providing them with patterns that contrast with those being introduced. [Background 17–7]

I have been stating these steps as if I have joined the prescription club. Though I have been very direct in stating the steps, I have not swerved from my advocacy of description. In my experience, many of the steps I have just stated are not followed. If you do follow them—always diverting students and providing contrasting patterns—then, of course, your task will be different: to have students *reproduce* sets with no diversions or contrasts. But if you have been following a great many texts and follow the rules I have observed most frequently, your task will be to use diversions and contrasts.

Journal Entry

Not only waiters *reproduce* outside of class, of course. And the purpose of reproducing is not always tied to procedural matters like ordering food. In one Marx Brothers film, Groucho plays the part of a recently appointed college president. At a meeting shortly after he takes over, a professor asked him this question: "I'm sure the students would appreciate a brief outline of your plans for the future." After Groucho said "What?" the professor again said, "I'm sure the students would appreciate a brief outline of your plans for the future." To which Groucho retorted: "You just said that. That's the trouble around here. Talk, talk, talk!"

How do you see people *reproducing* in the same medium in nonteaching settings? If you hear *reproduce* along with humor, are the examples funnier than the Groucho Marx example, or even less so?

All of 'Em—*Reproduce* with Other Uses

The sequences and variations with which we can use substitution tables border on the infinite. They have been written about extensively, and rather than *reproduce* what others have said, I hope to suggest some alternatives, and more important, remind you of how you can generate almost endless variations and sequences on your own. [Background 17–8]

First, realize that though I treat *reproduce same medium* separately, the use need not be used separately and in isolation from other uses. If it normally is, I would employ it along with all the other uses in the same lesson, starting, for the sake of simplicity, with the first use in the use column, *attend*, and then moving right down the column in alphabetical order. Thus, the first step would simply be to have students look at a table or listen to the words in the table being said. Since the possible combinations of words in even a short table like Table 17–2 is in the thousands, there is no need, of course, to say every combination for students to listen to. This activity alone could fill the period!

After the students look at the table or listen to different combinations from it for a few minutes, they can be asked to *characterize* what they have *attended* to. Comments like these would be likely about "I'd like two dishes of vanilla ice cream" and the substitutions in these slots: "Most containers need only an *s*"; "*Dieter* is different from the other words"; "'*d* is not pronounced the same all the time with all the subjects"; "*Of* is a preposition." Asking students simply to note differences or similarities, or to note what they think is distinct about the words in columns or the combinations, is all that is needed to produce responses with the use *characterize* in them.

When given a chance to *present*, by asking students to ask about the table, these are some likely communications: "Why is the '*d* there?"; "What does *pistachio* mean?"; "What was *marshmallow* first made from—sounds like a plant?" Asking students to make statements after *attending* to the table and *characterizing* it will produce either recalled parts or personal statements. The recalled parts might be words from just a few columns—strawberry yogurt, chocolate pastries—or words from many columns—A glutton'd relish one hundred, a dieter'd like one dish. Some may even *present* the entire sequence from memory: "I'd like four gallons of peach yogurt." Statements about the table might be personal preferences: "I like pastries." Or they might be personal information; "I never saw pistachio ice cream."

After students *present* and *characterize*, doing each for a few minutes, some may want to *relate explain*, which incorporates these two other uses. Whether the generalizations students make are completely accurate or not, they meet some students' perceived needs. Since those who devote their life to making generalizations about how language works often err or disagree in their work, it's hardly reasonable to expect nonnative speakers of a language to be perfect as they *relate*. [Background 17–9]

To expand the number of substitutions available, if the hundred-plus combinations are not for some reason sufficient, students can produce additional *sets* as they become familiar with the columns. Those *sets* they suggest in the development of the table may be harder to produce than some after they have spent more time with the table. Once a few written *sets* or spoken *sets* are added, *sets* in other mediums can be added too. Pictures of fruit or real fruit could expand the entries in column 9. Actual containers could be added to column 6 and noise—words that sound like *slurp*—could be added to column 4 containing *like* and *relish*.

Adding noises—*nonlinguistic aural*—and real containers or pictures of other fruits or flavors—*nonlinguistic visual*—would, of course, mean that the task for the students might be changed to *reproduce change medium* as well as *reproduce same medium*. But for one thing, such an added task means we have in fact employed all the uses as part of a lesson involving *reproduce same medium*. And for another thing, *reproducing* in a different medium can be used to divert a student from the form that is providing difficulty. If a student has to change a picture of a fruit into a word—*dc*—it is hard to think of the contrast between *a* and *an* at the same time, or the need to form *'d* one way with some subjects and another way with other subjects.

Within the use *reproduce same medium*, once the students *reproduce imitate* and *reproduce substitute*, they can be asked to employ the other subcategories by changing the communications to the negative, turning questions into statements, statements into questions, changing the statements into the emphatic form—"I said I *would* like . . ."—adding prepositional phrases or clauses after nouns and adjectives or before, substituting an *and* for the period and indicating two items they'd like, or not like, and on and on. By simply noting the subcategories that were employed and those that were not, other tasks could be set that would require other subcategories.

If communications were selected to be *reproduced* from student errors, some additional steps can be employed. For one thing, the central contrast when treating communications based on errors is between the correct and incorrect form. When students say "I speak English language" or "I speak the English" in place of "I speak the English language" or "I speak English," the part of the lesson devoted to characterize can require students to *characterize evaluate*. The incorrect *sets* can be intentionally stated or written, and the students' task is to say "correct" or "incorrect." While students are sometimes asked whether a student communication is right or wrong immediately after it is made, the alternative I am suggesting is different in at least two ways. First, the error is communicated intentionally. Second, students are asked to *characterize evaluate* each *set* communicated, both right and wrong ones. Usually, students are asked whether something is right or wrong only when it is wrong.

Later, another section of the lesson can be devoted to *present*, and in place of asking students for personal statements or questions, they can be asked to present both the correct and incorrect responses on command, as the students in Excerpt 17–3 are doing.

I realize that intentional use of error is not universally advocated. Indeed, the rule seems to be to avoid the intentional error. This, of course, is one reason I advocate that it be tried; to see what we do and the consequences, we must break the rules we follow and try the opposite. If nothing else, employing *characterize evaluate* in a solicit to force students to *present* incorrect responses and asking students to *characterize evaluate* intentional errors will slowly be seen as the same use of mediums as the correction of

EXCERPT 17–3
No The, The

		Communications	*Source/ Target*	*Move Type*	*Use*
1	Teacher:	(Holding up a Somali flag.) Language, incorrect.	t/s	sol	
2	Student:	I speak Somali language.	s/t	res	p*
3	Teacher:	(Holding up a French flag.) Language, correct.	t/s	sol	
4	Student:	I speak the French language.	s/t	res	p
5	Teacher:	(Holding up a Somali flag.) What do you speak? Incorrect.	t/s	sol	
6	Student:	I speak the Somali.	s/t	res	p
7	Teacher:	Correct.	t/s	sol	
8	Student:	I speak Somali.	s/t	res	p

* Changing the flag, nv, to speech, la, also requires the use *reproduce change medium*, dc.

their compositions, which requires first that they indicate what is wrong and then that they *present* the correct form: *reproduce edit* the incorrect form.

Using *characterize evaluate* in solicits also highlights a way of adding variety to responses. In place of asking students simply to reproduce sets the same way they were communicated in the solicit, they can be asked to reproduce them as if they wanted a large crowd to hear them at one time, and as if they were telling a secret at another time. Or they could be asked to act shy as they say them at one time, angry at another, and like a gourmet or dieter another time. Whenever we establish criteria like these, we are *characterizing* in the solicit. I treat the use of the *c* component in solicits in Episode 5.

A New Era—Features of *Linguistic Visual* Mediums We *Reproduce*

Reproducing tables in print long ago led to the advocacy of controlled composition, where a number of related sentences in a story are copied and then recopied one at a time, with variations covering the subcategories of *reproduce same medium.* Using a typewriter, word processor, or computer keyboard and terminal screen for reproducing the *linguistic visual* medium is less widely advocated. Yet for most students, a job that requires mechanical or electronic reproduction is more likely than one that requires the hand reproduction developed to such an art form by monks during the Middle Ages, but which ended with the printing press in the West. [Background 17–10]

Electronic and mechanical reproduction make use of the *linguistic visual* medium, but because the characters are either on keys or formed electronically on a cathode ray tube screen, and not formed by hand with pencils or pens, I add a subscript to note these features. When assigning students out-of-class work, requesting they *reproduce* with typewriters, word processors, or computer keyboards will not only provide a clear alternative, but will also enable some to master the keyboard, help others to have experiences close to those required in some jobs, and show others a way to devote out-of-close time to language development in a different way. Here, as in the substitution of most opposites, a slight alteration has the potential for consequences out of all proportion to the size of the alternative itself. [Background 17–11]

The subscripts *m* for mechanical or electric typewriters and *e* for electronic devices such as word processors or computers are not the only ones useful for distinguishing different mediums in the same category that we *reproduce* from one another. If one student copies a map from the blackboard and another traces a map from an atlas, they are both *reproducing* a *nonlinguistic visual* medium. But tracing and copying are different. If I sing a refrain after I hear it rather than along with a song leader, I am using words—*linguistic aural*—both times. But each time the mediums are different. To distinguish mediums that we *reproduce* simultaneously from those that we *reproduce* immediately after another communicates them, I add the subscript *s*. Thus, if a teacher says a pattern or mouths it along with a student rather than before the student says it, I add the subscript *s* next to the medium of both teacher and student: *t* la_s set, *s* la_s reproduce repeat.

Journal Entry

I used to have students work their way through controlled composition texts religiously. In most of those I used, the first task was to copy the passage exactly—*reproduce repeat*. The students and I became very frustrated because time and again, even the best students made at least one error when they tried to copy the passage exactly. As an alternative, I once asked students to start with step 3 rather than step 1. Step 3 was something like recopying the passage and at the same time changing all the male characters into female characters. To my astonishment, I found that students were able to *reproduce substitute change* with fewer errors and in less time than they had been able to *reproduce repeat*. Then, recently, I saw an article in the newspaper about people who write traffic tickets. One of the tasks in writing a ticket—or citation in British English—is to copy the license number from the license plate on the car to the form. It turns out that an astonishingly large number of fines are never collected because the number of errors made when license numbers are copied is extremely great.

When one stops to think about copying, suddenly one realizes how tedious it is and how little the task engages the mind. In your experience with *reproduce repeat*, in contrast to other subcategories that require more than copying or imitation, have you noticed any differences in error rate or speed with which the tasks are performed?

Beyond Sets—*Reproducing* Other Uses

While I code the bulk of communications students *reproduce* as *set*, since, like the tables, they are words, sentences or parts of either used as models, or examples which need to be *reproduced* in another medium, any use can theoretically be *reproduced*. If one person *characterizes* as in "*Glutton* is a noun," and another repeats the communication, the use *characterize label* is being *reproduced*. If a person repeats a rule over and over again, as when we used to write a hundred times "I must obey the teacher because if there is no line of authority and control in a class, we won't learn how to act, and chaos will reign both in class and in the world," then we are *reproducing* the use *relate explain*. When we rephrase a motion at a meeting, if the motion requests information, we are *reproducing* mediums another has *presented*. This is the same case as when a waiter repeats "Two vanilla, one chocolate." The use *present* is being *reproduced*.

In comprehensive coding, I distinguish the uses that are being reproduced from one another by coding them. I code the uses being reproduced in parentheses on the same line as *reproduce.* Thus, if a person *reproduces* a label in a response, the coding would look like this: *res ds* (*cl*). If a person reproduced a statement in a reaction, as a waiter might when restating an order, I'd code the reaction like this: *rea ds* (*ps*). The information in the parentheses I call a *given.* And though here I am only coding the use that precedes the move I'm coding, the medium and content can be coded as a given as well. Should you want more examples of this type of coding, go to Episode 4.

Journal Entry

While you are thinking about the uses from preceding moves that are reproduced, perhaps you also thought of the mediums that occur in moves that precede *reproduce.* The classic "I am touching my nose" was not considered an acceptable model in some places where I have observed unless it was accompanied with the touching of one's nose. When students *reproduced*, they were to touch their nose and repeat the model, imitating the gesture and the language in the preceding move. Have you noticed whether the mediums that precede *reproduce* are all expected to be *reproduced*, or are only the linguistic mediums to be reproduced? How do you feel about asking others to both say and do what you have done, as in "I am touching my nose?"

Can't Always Tell—Content and the Use *Reproduce*

As you might recall, back in Excerpt 17–1, when waiters and students were *reproducing* "Two vanilla, one chocolate," I noted that at a restaurant the content was *procedure* and in the classroom *study of language.* I further noted that determining one specific subcategory of the *study of language* was often difficult because, when observing any reproduction, two to three subcategories are usually involved. For example, to *reproduce* "I'd like two cups of almond pudding" involves grammar, lexis, pronunciation, and collocation, at the minimum. In an arithmetic class for native speakers of a language, all these subcategories of language would be taken for granted, and I'd code the content of "Two vanilla, one chocolate" and all the other numbers *study other*: arithmetic, unless the teacher said some other content was being communicated. If students were told to copy numbers to see how they were spelled, for example, I'd code the content *study of language*, subcategory mechanics, even though the reproduction was being done in an arithmetic class.

Specifying the subcategory of content that is being communicated is one of the ways to have students *reproduce* content that observers can code in a subcategory because specifying content attributes content to the uses being reproduced. If I'm told to look at a table starting with *I'd like* and ending with *ice cream* to find all the unstressed vowel sounds, all instances of schwa, then the content attributed to the *sets* could easily be coded in the subcategory of the *study of language* I call *sound.* If I'm told to write three sentences with content words that don't fit each other, I know the subcategory of the *study of language* being attributed to the sets is *ties*, or *collocation.* If you want to review the subcategories of the *study of language* that you can attribute to uses that are going to be reproduced, go to Episode 11.

If no specific content is attributed to communications in moves that precede *reproduce*, the errors that are treated provide clues to the content being *reproduced.* If a teacher says "great" after a student reproduces, even when there are many language errors in the response, maybe the teacher is only attributing *procedure, teaching directions* to the uses, happy that the student reproduced rather than presented, for example. We have all had students say "fourteen" when we have asked them to repeat "How old are you?" and so performing the task expected—a matter of procedure—could be an area of content attributed to uses.

If a teacher were to ignore the omission of *of* in "two dishes of marshmallow ice cream" and correct the pronounciation of marshmallow, I'd code *sound* as the content, not *grammar: function words*. But if no content is attributed to uses that are reproduced, and errors are not treated in specific areas of content, then we can do nothing but code the content of the *reproduction* as *sl* for *study of language* if two or three subcategories are involved and *lu* for *study of language unspecified* if more than three subcategories are involved.

IV. LEAVING THE FRAY—SUMMARY AND CONCLUSION

Before I state some rejoinders to criticism of drill, or *reproducing* in the *same medium* in FOCUS, I summarize some ways I have shown how we can *reproduce* in the *same medium*. In this way, I will delay entering and leaving the fray a few more minutes. For the summary, I have prepared Table 17–3.

The summary I just gave you, like most summaries, is *not* an example of the use *reproduce same medium* because the communications I printed were not based on others

TABLE 17–3
A Summary: Reproduce Same Medium

ds	=	redoing what another has just done in one medium in the same medium or redoing what was done earlier, say in print, but is still available to take in as we engage in redoing it
combine	=	putting two elements together: go + ing to going; I'm happy. I'm old. to I'm happy and old.
edit	=	changing a use to correct it but not completely recasting the original, and not being told what to correct or how to correct.
expand	=	lengthening any communications: I'm happy to I'm very happy.
paraphrase	=	rephrasing what another has communicated to show understanding
reduce	=	shortening a communication: She's getting mad as a hatter to She's mad as a hatter or She's getting mad.
repeat	=	redoing what another has just done with the idea of staying as close as possible to the original communication
substitute	=	replacing one or more elements in parts of communications: a p to b as in pig to big; a snake for a worm in I saw a worm.
substitute and change	=	replacing one or more elements in a part of a communication that forces a change in another part: replacing I with dieter in "_____'d like" forces a change in the pronunciation of 'd
transform	=	changing the order or sequence of a communication: Once upon a time, he was happy to He was happy, once upon a time; mid to dim, but to tub

that had just immediately been communicated or that were staring you in the face on the same page. The summary in the table contains *characterize label*—the names of the subcategories—*characterize illustrate*—the short definitions of the subcategories—and *sets*—the examples. If you were to copy the table by hand, you'd be using print to *reproduce same medium*. If you get a copy of the table from a copying machine, I would not code your work *reproduce same medium*. Without subscripts, I can't easily code what copying machines do.

The inevitable is now upon us, but knowing that entering the fray is followed by leaving the fray, here goes. "Repeating is artificial" say some. Well, say I, remember that we repeat in nonteaching settings all the time, so what does artificial mean? I copy down order numbers from catalogs when I order things through the mail. I copy down telephone numbers all the time too, preferring copying to taking dictation. I find myself restating numbers others give me orally over and over, hoping that if I keep rehearsing them in my mind, they will stay in my short-term memory long enough to get to a pencil, pen, or a pile of sand where I can trace out the numbers. I observe children all the time playing hopscotch. When a newcomer arrives, after a few minutes of watching, attempts to hop take place. Even though immediate perfection is not attained, the newcomers get an idea of what is possible, and trying to *reproduce in the same medium* may help some see where they are in relationship to where they can be, want to be or should be.

All the reproducing we might observe outside a language classroom, one might answer, does not change the fact that repeating "I'd like two dishes of vanilla ice cream" when one is a diabetic and sugar would put the person in a coma is artificial. Nor does the fact that we *reproduce* outside language classrooms change the fact that telling a person to change a statement to a question is artificial. But the fact that these tasks are artificial does not mean that we cannot learn distinctive features of the language from performing them. By juxtaposing patterns that are slightly different, some learners see and hear how parts of the language go together. Contrasting *sets* serve for some to reveal what others need rules—*relate explain*—or labels—*characterize label*—to see. And, always trying to reproduce what others have communicated reveals to us what is possible and what we can hope to do one day. [Background 17–12]

"Anybody can repeat" say some. Well, anybody can repeat some things, but we obviously cannot repeat everything others do or say. In fact, repetition can be used to diagnose what people can't do or don't know since, in order to repeat many things, we have to combine what we already know and can do with the new information that the communications contain and we are trying to *reproduce*. Care needs to be taken in using repetition to find out what people can and cannot do, though, because people can sometimes not repeat utterances they have themselves previously produced. In one classic study, a child's language was recorded and transcribed one day and given as a *set* to be reproduced the next day. The child was not able to repeat what he had previously produced—back to the artificial! [Background 17–13]

"Repetition can be a waste of time." It sure can, especially if the time devoted to it is large, or the belief is strongly held that repetition leads to fluency. As we follow a leader doing calisthenics, we all know that we can repeat something twenty times after a break or a change in activity that we could not repeat even one more time during the time we were repeating. Twenty additional push-ups can be done only a few minutes after the twenty-first could not be done, for example. If only a few minutes are spent reproducing, only a little time might be wasted. Contrasting a little time and a lot of time will also reveal a lot about the strength of the belief that repetition leads to fluency.

If the implicit information contrasting *sets* can provide is enough, and you feel even a few minutes is too much to spend reproducing if it is a waste of time, and is more likely to lead to truancy than fluency, perhaps the group spirit and precision work of a class of fifty *reproducing* will provide a bit of a rationale. Group cheering at sports events directed by cheerleaders may not really help in the game, but the *reproducing* is exciting to many, and so can the use *reproduce same medium* be when done in groups. [Background 17–14]

This fray could be endless! Since I promised to both enter and leave the fray quickly, let me *present* once again my catechism: Substitute description and exploration for prescription and argument. If you are involved with classes where only *reproduce repeat* is used, substitute *reproduce substitute*. If students *reproduce* only parallel *sets*, try contrasting *sets*. In short, *attend* to what is being done by viewing or listening to tapes, *reproduce change medium* by transcribing tapes, *characterize label* by coding some characteristics of the transcripts, and then *reproduce* by substituting alternatives—it's a never-ending cycle, almost as exciting as entering and leaving a fray or ordering ice cream.

Journal Entry

The jargon of FOCUS is minimal when you compare it with the number of special words developed for discussions of drills. One of my favorite bits of drill language is *backward buildup*. The term refers to the repetition of a model from the back to the front. The first step in repeating "I'd like two dishes of vanilla ice cream" would be to repeat *cream*, the second step *ice cream*, the third, *vanilla ice cream*, and on and on until the entire *set* had been *reproduced*.

One rationale for this type of repetition is that we remember best what we have just heard. Another is that keeping the rhythm and intonation constant is better done this way. Finally, backward buildup distracts one from the meaning of a model. One can concentrate just on the sounds and form.

What is your favorite bit of language from the language of drills?

BACKGROUND NOTES

17–1. Agard and Dunkel, Smith and Upshur all compared classes where drill was supposedly emphasized with classes where it was not emphasized. The *Critique of the Pennsylvania project* (1969) points out the types of problems these types of studies did not overcome. Wilga Rivers probably has been the central figure in raising questions of a psychological nature about the value of drill. Her 1964 study called attention to serious theoretical flaws in many of the tenets that had been used to support drill as described in the audiolingual method.

17–2. Rwakyaka coded tapes of high school English classes in Uganda and Shapiro-Skrobe coded tapes of elementary school ESL classes in the United States. The most frequent uses in both of these studies were *present, reproduce change medium*, and *reproduce same medium*.

17–3. The fact that Allwright suggested that a central criterion for materials for ESL classes should be that they not be specially prepared for ESL students, and the fact that Wilkins has urged that materials be sequenced according to the purpose of the language—to argue, to request information, etc.—mean that the idea of a linguistic sequence is not an accepted principle. Proof of the difficulty level of different sequences is difficult to find in spite of the fact that sequencing has been an issue for scores of years around the world. One reason for this dearth of research must be that sequencing is not as important as some contend, or that it is not possible to determine difficulty or interest or teachability on the basis of linguistic sequencing alone.

17–4. Albert Sydney Hornby and Frederick George French are the two central figures from England who developed substitution tables; Charles Carpenter Fries is the central figure from the United States. In French's *English in tables: A set of blueprints for sentence builders*, he tells users how many separate sentences can be generated from each table. Hundreds of separate sentences can, in fact, be generated by most of his tables.

17–5. "Boinguage" was Robert L. Allen's name for the use of *boing* in all its variations.

17–6. As on most topics, there is divided opinion on this one. French, for one, urges that all combinations be possible in any table.

17–7. Lado is the knight in shining armor who has always advocated the vital importance of contrast in all pattern drills.

17–8. Paulston and Bruder's book and Chastain's book both give step-by-step directions for a wide range of drills. Though Earl Stevick is often associated with people who do not use drills in the usual sense, such as Gattegno and Curran, it was, in fact, Stevick who described steps for conducting drills in his 1982 book. Armed with these three books, one can drill one's way through anything.

17–9. For what I consider to be the most coherent grammar for teaching, I'd urge you to read about Robert L. Allen's sector analysis. Some explanations and examples of this grammar can be found in Malkemes' text, as well as in a book by Allen et al. For a very fine comprehensive review of schools of grammar, Gleason is hard to beat. To study fine points of grammar for nonnative speakers, delve into Quirk and Greenbaum. And to support your urge to explain grammar, read the results of a study of learning grammar described by Levin and Olsson in the famous GUME project done in Sweden.

17–10. One of the early controlled composition books is the one by Dykstra and Port. If you use this book or others like it and students copy with errors, do not think it unusual. According to an article about parking tickets by Gargan in the *New York Times*, one-third of the 9.6 million parking tickets issued in New York City each year cannot be processed. The most common problem is that the license plate numbers on the ticket have not been copied correctly. In 1981 these errors in reproducing in the same medium cost the city $50 million in lost fines.

17–11. Postman reminds us that the main reason for schools starting up in the 15th and 16th centuries was because of the need to teach reading and writing. Many contend that the need to learn to use electronic means to write is as central as the revolution caused by the printing press. Taylor presents some of the most important authors in the United States who hold this view in his anthology about computers. Papert reminds us of his strong convictions on the issue in his book describing his development of his computer language. Should you not be electronically inclined, but like typing, read R. Bernstein for a report of the use of typewriters in ESL classes.

17–12. In a discussion of substitution tables, Ruth Crymes reminded me of the fact that substitution tables as well as drills that require students to manipulate the elements of sentences provide implicit information about how the languge is put together. Whether a student can describe or make a generalization or not as a result of the implicit information may not matter. The fact is, multiple contrasting examples manipulated by changing statements into questions or singulars into plurals, etc., provide implicit information about how the target language works.

17–13. Lois Bloom recorded a child's conversation one day, and on a subsequent day she asked him to repeat the sentences he had said the day before. He could not repeat them. Obviously, the context was totally different. But the point is that the boy's spontaneous speech exceeded in length what he was able to say when repeating his own language.

17–14. Drills are an eternal topic of debate. Simone de Beauvoir had intense feelings about many things. Of "tiresome exercises," she says: "I was frustrated and filled with guilt: I got through such impositions as quickly as possible, bashing them out on the rocks of my impatience" (*Memoirs* *of a dutiful daughter*, page 69). Lamendella reminds us that, from the point of view of those who describe the workings of the brain, there is absolutely no support for pattern practice—a nice contention to start a debate with. Lewin too feels that repeating has little value. He speaks from the point of view of personality theory. When repetition leads to satiation, the quality consistently goes down. He cites an example of the student required to write "I will not talk" fifty times. Most write the "I" first fifty times, then the "will's," etc. The variations in copying the sentence suggest the activity is less and less positive as the person continues to copy.

"U" Can't Miss It

I. NOT BY SPEECH ALONE—RATIONALE FOR EPISODE AND INTRODUCTION

As you might guess from the way I've written the "U" in the title of this episode—*U* as a symbol, *nv*, rather than a word, *lv*—I treat mediums in this episode. I choose the title because it can be communicated in both a *linguistic* and *nonlinguistic visual* medium and because it illustrates the vital link between our bodies and our speech. Gestures are not ancillary to speech nor speech ancillary to gestures; these two mediums, like all mediums we communicate with, are intertwined as part of a network of mediums we are constantly immersed in.

As the tollbooth attendant concludes his directions to the lost driver with the unduly confident words "You can't miss it!"—which usually means that in fact the driver will miss it—he has his finger pointed in the direction we are heading. But who other than a person coding mediums with FOCUS is looking? Surely not the driver. The driver is not looking at the pointing finger because, for one thing, he has to look at the road. But for another thing, the finger is above the driver's head, separated from the tollbooth attendant by the roof of the car. In fact, all the pointing and gesticulating the tollbooth attendant did while he was giving his directions were also hidden from the driver or the passengers in the car. All a driver can see is an attendant's stomach and hands as money is passed. Yet tollbooth attendants around the world move their hands and point fingers as they give directions. When you stop to think about it, though, haven't you caught yourself enumerating points on your fingers as you are talking on the phone to a person who cannot see you? Haven't you seen people put on eyeglasses after they answer the phone, arrange their hair, and make sure they are dressed, even though the other person cannot see who he or she is talking to? While people from different places use their bodies differently, they all use them as they speak. Notice that people partially paralyzed by strokes usually have impaired speech *and* movement:

la and *pv*. When the vocal cords move without the body, as in a repetition of something we don't understand in a language class, I would argue that the disengagement of the body prevents linguistic development, although I have no proof whatsoever for this contention!

Teachers who thought I was interested in mediums other than speech and print used to try to please me by teaching lessons on gestures. But teaching gestures implies that they are separate from speech and ancillary to it, some kind of an appendage. Many teachers also consider objects or pictures to be visual aids. But outside of a language classroom, many mediums bombard us all the time. Who is to say that some are central and some ancillary? A driveway with a sign saying *Drive Slow*—have you ever seen *Drive Slowly* on a sign in spite of the efforts of generations of English teachers?—is likely to have bumps built into it—a *nonlinguistic visual* medium—to ensure that drivers do in fact slow down. While one may ignore the *linguistic visual* medium, ignoring the *nonlinguistic visual* medium will produce a broken axle. Various colored paints on curbs—*nv*—usually accompany the *linguistic visual* medium in No Parking signs. When we buy food, the food itself—*nv*—is observed along with the *linguistic visual* labels on it or the *linguistic aural* comments of the butcher, greengrocer, or clerk. Many trucks are equipped with a bell that rings when the trucks back up so we can hear the truck—*nonlinguistic aural*—before it runs us over if we fail to see it—*nv*. The printed words—*lv*—*Keep out—danger* are less likely to deter people than a *nonlinguistic visual* medium such as a fence topped with barbed wire. On almost every bus I've been in around the world, I've seen signs that contain the equivalent of this *linguistic visual* message: Please use the rear exit. The only buses where this request is complied with are those with a turnstile next to the driver that turns only one way, allowing passengers into the bus but not back out. The *nonlinguistic visual* medium, the turnstile, accomplishes what the *linguistic visual* sign cannot.

The anthropologist Carpenter argues that Mendel's ideas about heredity based on his experiments with peas were ignored for many years because they originally were presented in print alone—*lv*—without any visual illustrations or diagrams—*nv*. To inform people of a fire in a building, bells are used rather than words. Can you imagine a voice saying "Excuse me, the building is on fire" over a loudspeaker system? People sometimes start to hit each other with their fists after they have decided that the words they have been "hitting" each other with have failed. A great deal of the tension we feel in other cultures is caused by having to take in different facial expressions, gestures, use of space and time, new and different odors, not by having to take in only the different sounds, words, and letters in another language. [Background 18–1]

How did we come to call mediums other than speech and print *audiovisual aids*? Do movie directors call their films *audiovisual aids*? Does a cooking teacher refer to the foods being cooked as *visual aids*? Do recording stars refer to the records and cassettes they produce as *audio aids*? Do you refer to your stereo and radio as *audio aids* when you have friends in? It's hard to imagine anyone at a dinner party asking the guests whether they would like to listen to some music on one's *audio aid* or view some *visual aids* in the form of paintings or collections of rare china or chess pieces. To me, eyeglasses are visual aids and hearing aids are audio aids.

While McLuhan's aphorism "The medium is the message" may be something of an overstatement, if you have experienced any of the examples I've just given, you must believe that different mediums do convey different kinds and amounts of information, and that they are all central to communication, at least in nonteaching settings. It is hard to deny, for example, that looking at a picture of an avocado, holding up a real avocado, looking at the phonetic spelling of *avocado*, and hearing someone shout *avocado* all must spark the image of a pear-shaped food in our minds differently. One purpose of this episode is to encourage thinking about mediums as simply different ways to convey information, rather than thinking about mediums other than speech and print as simply audiovisual aids. I am trying to accomplish this purpose in this introductory harangue, known in some circles as a rationale. Another purpose is to provide many examples of the categories of mediums I code with FOCUS. I provide the examples in the next section, where I also give you a chance to do some coding of mediums, if you have the time. By pointing out ways mediums interact outside teaching settings in Section III, I hope to make some of the alternatives I suggest in Section IV seem normal rather than radical. [Background 18–2]

Journal Entry

Another way of looking at what we do in a regular way time after time is to think of being "locked in" rather than being controlled by rules. In terms of FOCUS, locks are *nonlinguistic visual* mediums. Though usually not described in classroom observations, they serve as symbols. While it is true that cabinets are cabinets, a locked cabinet is different from one that is not locked, and probably both communicate a different message to students. Locked and unlocked drawers probably do too. Carrying a lot of keys probably sends some type of message. How do you feel about the signals sent by locked cabinets in classes and by teachers who carry a lot of keys and are constantly opening and closing things? By looking at a lot of mediums, do you think your views of mediums will be unlocked? Or do you think your views are already unlocked?

II. BEYOND AUDIOVISUAL AIDS—CLASSIFYING AND CODING MEDIUMS

A Bit of Jargon—One Person's Classification of Mediums

As you must have sensed, I consider the term *audiovisual aids* misguided. However, I realize that even though the terms I use to describe mediums may be more comprehensive, they are not felicitous and are unlikely to gain much currency, much less replace *audiovisual aids*. Obviously, *audiovisual aid* sounds less pretentious than *nonlinguistic visual* or *nonlinguistic aural*. And speaking or talking is more acceptable to most ears than *linguistic aural*. And while *linguistic other* is a logical third category of linguistic mediums, after naming print and writing *linguistic visual*, the common terms *Braille* or *sandpaper letters* are clearly more widely known.

In spite of the jargonistic nature of my categories, they do highlight the fact that mediums other than speech and print, or talking and writing, aren't just audiovisual aids. The terms also give distance to discussions of teaching. Asking a teacher to substitue a *nonlinguistic visual* medium for a *linguistic aural* one may lead to less defensiveness than saying "You talk too much—use more visual aids!" In fact, the *aural*, *visual*, and *other* subcategories of mediums make the substitution of alternatives easy because mediums that appeal to the ear are clearly opposite to those that appeal to the eye or other senses. The categories also make clearer than the ordinary linguistic/nonlinguistic dichotomy the fact that objects are different from gestures, and noise and music are different from tone of voice.

TABLE 18–1
One Person's Classification of Mediums*

Linguistic	aural	la	1. Elements of words: letters, phonemes, syllables. 2. Individual words: names of objects, commands, comments, examples 3. Vocalizations: *OK*, *hum*, *uh*, and other pauses, markers, and fillers 4. Words in groups: phrases, sentences, paragraphs, dialogs
	visual	lv	1. Printing or lettering of aural mediums 1–4 above, plus punctuation: typewriter keys, signs, books, computer terminals 2. Transcribing phonetically of aural mediums 1–4 above 3. Writing of aural mediums 1–4 above, plus punctuation: cursive or script 4. Ideograms
	other	lo	1. Linguistic mediums that appeal to other senses: drawing a letter on a hand with a finger, letters made of sandpaper 2. Symbolic systems: Braille, signing, Morse code
Nonlinguistic	aural	na	1. Noise from animals: barking, meowing, roaring, squeaking 2. Noise from things: clapping, footsteps, ringing bell, rustling leaves, screeching wheels, tickertape 3. Noise from people: belch, cough, humming, whistling 4. Organized "noise": chanting, music
	visual	nv	1. Real: clothing, darkness, food, furniture, light, live things, objects, people, shadows, speech organs, things with moving parts or electric power 2. Representational: cartoons, pictures, silent movies, sketches, snapshots, television without the sound, puppets 3. Schematic: blank spaces, diagrams, erasing, globe, layout, map, underscoring 4. Symbolic: color on gas cylinders, cracked glass to show "fragile," shape of a stop sign, a rod to represent piece of meat, musical notes, logos from corporations, symbols such as % or $; numbers: XI, 11
	other	no	Smells, temperature and other items that appeal beyond the ear and eye
Paralinguistic	aural	pa	Crying, laughing, tone of voice, volume of voice, whimpering
	visual	pv	Facial expressions, gazing, gestures, movement of the body, posture, skin color, tilt of the head, other actions
	other	po	Doing things with objects, space—distance from others, touching people, movement, dance
Silence		si	1. Implicit communications—students know they are to repeat when a model is given 2. Wait time—doing nothing but waiting before or after others have communicated; observing silently 3. What is in our heads—what we bring to the other mediums from experience 4. Time devoted to an activity

* Some features: size, electronic, mechanical, distorted, natural, authentic, etc.

In Table 18–1, I've listed some examples of the subcategories of the four major categories: *linguistic, nonlinguistic, paralinguistic*, and *silence*. Though the examples illustrate the distinctions, read these definitions to see why I classify the mediums the way I do. Communications expressed with sounds, or words of a language produced with the vocal cords and tongue, or written representations of such communications I consider *linguistic*. Communications that are made with instruments or parts of the body used as instruments, and things made from tools or produced artistically, mecha[illegible] or naturally, such as pictures, objects, and music, I consider *nonlinguistic* sin[illegible] from language. Communications expressed by the body, inc[illegible] ords of a language, but are made with the vocal cords an[illegible] one of voice, movement, or touch, I consider *paralingu*[illegible] d with language, they are intertwined with language. W[illegible] unicating with other mediums, I note the fact with the ca[illegible] 18–3]

[illegible] that within each subcategory I've listed some mediums th[illegible] from each other—food and speech organs are both *non-li*[illegible] Whenever you find two mediums that you consider dis-t[illegible], you can distinguish them by using the numbers in the [illegible] 2 for words, 4 for groups of words in *linguistic aural*, for [illegible] her characteristics such as the content, or you can use [illegible] e medium itself next to the category. For example, if food [illegible] ved, you could code them like this:

	Medium	Content
[illegible] ition of his tongue [illegible] teeth to illustrate the	nv—tongue and teeth	study of language—speech production
[illegible] of tongue to illustrate [illegible] a delicacy by some.) [illegible] popular in New York	nv—tongue of animal	study of language—ways of life

[illegible] rd in a book from one on a computer terminal, I'd add the [illegible]. To distinguish a voice produced from a tape recorder from a [illegible] me subscript. As always, you can use your own subscripts to [illegible] iums you want to distinguish. If you see a paragraph projected [illegible] erhead projector in one class, and you want to distinguish it from [illegible] en on a blackboard in another class, add a subscript and the distinction will be highlighted.

Remember as you look at the examples of mediums in Table 18–1 that mediums can be used in any move types, and there is no limit to the number of different mediums that occur in any single move. Each medium that is used differently or communicates a different area of content within the same move I call a *message*. Remember too that mediums can be either taken in or produced. In either case, I code the medium in front of the use. For example, if a person is listening to music on his or her own, I'd code it this way: *str na attend*. If a person were playing music, I'd code it this way: *str na present*.

Journal Entry

Chalk is not only something that you find in all kinds of classrooms. It is also a medium that fits a lot of categories. The items produced with it can be words—*linguistic visual*—or sketches—*nonlinguistic visual*. And, when we squeak it, we can place it in *nonlinguistic aural*.

Squeaking chalk is very piercing and disturbs many people a great deal. One alternative to squeaking chalk is the sound of breaking chalk into two pieces. If a regular piece of chalk is broken in half before it is used, a snap is substituted for a squeak. Breaking the chalk also might give one a sense of confidence and present an image of a teacher who knows what he or she is doing and is really in charge.

Have you seen many teachers break chalk? How do you feel as a student in classes when the chalk squeaks? Have you ever told anyone to stop squeaking chalk?

Do you think such a minor noise deserves a journal entry, or have I blown this point out of all proportion?

Give Me an *l*, Give Me a *v*, Give Me a *p*, Give Me an *o*!—Coding Mediums

Using the abbreviations in Table 18–1, code the mediums in Excerpt 18–1. As usual, compare your coding with that done by others, given in the footnote. If you want to add subscripts and note features of different mediums, do so. I have noted a few, but others can be noted. The practice is designed to make you more facile with the categories and to take note of the mediums we often fail to observe.

EXCERPT 18–1
Coding Mediums

		Communications	*Mediums*
1	Clerk:	(Wearing a T-shirt with these words:	
2		*Our pleasure to serve you.*)	____
3		(Has a snarl on his face.)	____
4	Father:	(Humming to his baby.)	____
5		(Patting baby on the back.)	____
6		(Walking around room with baby.)	____
7	Teacher:	Tell me the time.	____
8		(Holds up a digital clock.)	____
9		(Holds up a clock with a face on it and numbers.)	____ + ____
10	Teacher:	Pronounce this word.	____
11		(Writes *photographer* on the board.)	____
12		(Draws these under word: .)	____

EXCERPT 18–1 (*continued*)

		Communications	*Mediums*
13	In an ad:	Diamond Shamrock	______
14			______
15	Teacher:	(Whistles after a student error.)	______
16	Student:	(Touching and looking at a contour map.)	______ + ______
17	Class:	(Makes a lot of noise.)	______
18	Teacher:	(Stops talking as the noise from class increases.)	______
19	Student:	(Yawns.)	______
20	$Label_1$:	Diapers for newborns	______
21		6–12 lbs.	______
22		(Green strip on package.)	______
23	$Label_2$:	Diapers for babies	______
24		12–18 lbs.	______
25		(Blue strip on package.)	______
26	Tag on package:	(Background in red.)	______
27		(The word FRAGILE is printed on the top.)	______
28			______
29	Post card:	(Tuberculin Tine Test® is printed on top.)	______ + ______
30		Instructions: Feel the skin where the test was given.	______
31		Mark an X in the circle of the box below in which the raised bumps feel most like those on the skin. (In each of the boxes, bumps are embossed so they can be felt.)	______ + ______

EXCERPT 18–1 (*continued*)

		Communications	*Mediums*
32		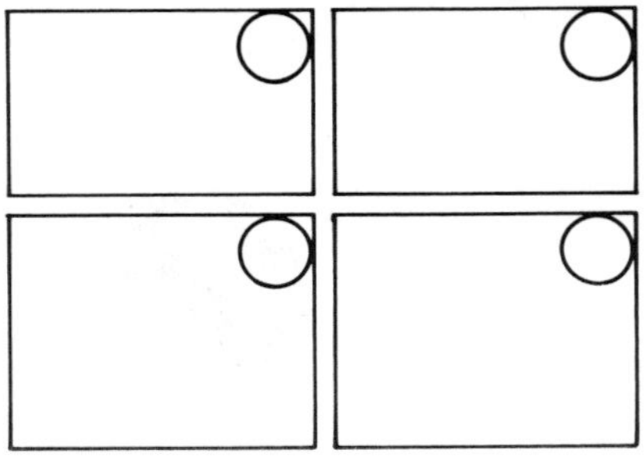	______
33	Page of music:	(Notes are color coded.)	______
34		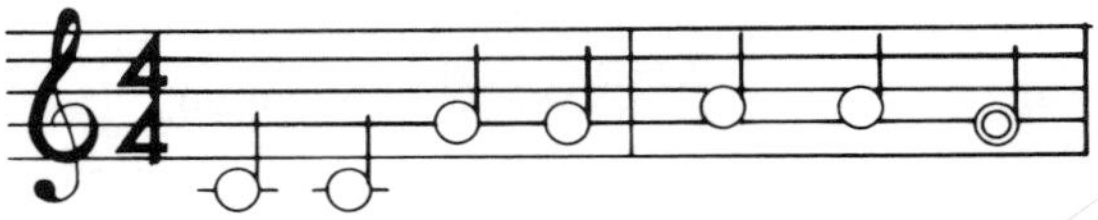	
35		1 1 5 5 6 6 5	
36		Twin - kle, twin - kle, lit - tle star,	
37			
38	Sign at store:	Please leave exact written instructions. We are *not* responsible for oral instructions.	______ + ______
39	Teacher:	(Cups hand over ear.)	______
40	Class:	(Bang on desks three times, harder the first time.)	______
41		(Say *mag ni fy*.)	______
42	Salesman:	(Holds up a vacuum cleaner to show customer.)	______
43	Tired person:	(Slouches in seat.)	______
44	Teacher:	Pay attention!	______ + ______
45		(Snaps fingers as the words are said.)	______
46	Student:	(Traces "s" on the hand of another student.)	______
47	Priest:	(Burns incense at ceremony.)	______
48	Sign:		______
49			______ + ______
50	Speech pathologist:	(Mouths sounds for a deaf student.)	______
51	Teacher:	(Mimes putting on a tie.)	______
52	Child:	(Turns red from anger.)	______

EXCERPT 18–1 (*continued*)

		Communications	*Mediums*
53	Teacher:	(Puts his arms around shoulder of child.)	___
54	Teacher:	(Holds up a picture for class to look at.)	___

Coding done by others: 2. lv; 3. pv; 4. na; 4. na; 5. po; 6. po; 7. la; 8. nv; 9. nv_3 + nv_4—numbers are symbols; face is schematic; 10. la; 11. lv; 12. nv; 13. lv; 14. nv; 15. na; 16. no + nv; 17. na; 18. si; 19. pv; 20. lv; 21. nv_4; 22. nv_4, both symbolic; 23. lv; 24. nv_4; 25. nv_4—an asterisk can be added to the medium to indicate that there is a contrast, as with the two colors and the different sizes noted by the pounds; 26. nv_4; 27. lv; 28. nv; 29. lv + nv_4 to note the registered trademark symbol; 30. lv; 31. lv + nv for the X; 32. no—like the contours on a contour map in 16, these bumps are machine-made and so nonlinguistic: no, since they are not seen or heard but felt; 33. nv; 34. —the treble clef, nv; 35. 4/4 nv; 36. the numbers over the words, nv; 37. the words, lv; 38. lv + nv, the underlined word—if it is in italics, it is coded as lv but with a subscript to show that it is different from the print in the other words; 39. pv; 40. na; 41. la, and pa if the stress is more than normally required; 42. nv; 43. pv; 44. la + pa—the tone of voice; 45. na; 46. lo; 47. no; 48. lv; 49. nv_2 + nv_4 because the red line has come to mean "don't do" or "no"; 50. nv—speech organs; 51. pv; 52. pv; 53. po; 54. nv—not nv + pv since the medium we are to look at is the picture; coding the gesture of holding it up would add no information; if the teacher points to part of the picture, this would be coded pv, since new information is added by pointing.

III. TOGETHERNESS—NETWORKS OF MEDIUMS OUTSIDE CLASSROOMS

Outside of teaching settings, one thing networks of mediums do is narrow choices. When a car stops beside me in the street as I'm walking near a highway in New York City, there is no chance that the oral solicit will require information about Oregon. The spoken words—*la*—together with the buildings, the streets—*nv*—together with street signs—*lv*—all together provide information. As a result, before the driver, or passenger, rolls down the car window, let alone finishes the solicit, literally thousands of possible topics have been eliminated and the probable information required has been greatly narrowed.

I'm sure you have experienced the value of the network of mediums, including gestures, noises, and objects, in narrowing choices when trying to respond to children's questions. I find it very difficult to do what children ask me to do, or more accurately order me to do, without taking in different mediums together. I cannot give a child butter in response to "Give me some ba" unless we are in the kitchen and the butter is on the table. The butter—the *nonlinguistic visual* medium—must accompany the word "ba." This is especially true after I have just been in the bedroom with the child and had given her a doll in response to "Bring me the ba." Just as I have to take in the doll itself and the butter along with words, so children learning outside classrooms must constantly consider mediums together. Otherwise, when told to open the cabinet, for example, they could not know what to do or with what if the cabinet was not there and there was nothing to get from it. This, of course, assumes that the words themselves are unknown to the child.

One limitation of telephone conversations, or any conversations that take place away from the persons, places, things, or actions referred to, is that the network of mediums is broken. Perhaps this is why we continue to use gestures as we speak on the phone even when they cannot be seen. We are trying to keep the network complete. But when the person says "it's a nice day," and you are on the other end, it is hard to know what that means without feeling the temperature. And orders on the phone can get confusing. If a person says "Give me six dozen" while standing next to the person taking the order, and a pile of shirts, or sheets or anything else, the network of mediums is complete. On the telephone, and in some classrooms, the usual network of mediums is not available in many cases.

Looking at mediums as part of a network not only narrows choices, but helps us perhaps more easily value each separate medium on its own merits rather than as a part of some hierarchy. When one student wants to express meaning by drawing and another by mime, we are delighted rather than disappointed that speech was not used. I have rarely seen a teacher provide the meaning of a word without speech used with gestures and often a sketch as well. To demand that students use only speech denies that speech is part of a network of many mediums.

By failing to recognize the fact that mediums are part of a network, research into animal communication was slowed. For many years, researchers tried to teach chimpanzees to speak languages. No matter how many different ways the words were presented, the vocabulary the chimpanzees could communicate was very limited. In the seventies, sign languages were taught to chimpanzees, substituting *linguistic other* for *linguistic aural.* In some cases, they were able to communicate 200 words, rather than the 10 to 20 they could communicate with speech. [Background 18–4]

Most important, by considering mediums as part of a network, we see their interrelationshps more clearly. Read the remarks about gloves, a screwdriver, a pair of pliers, and a hammer in Excerpt 18–2.

As you have just seen, we are not sure what the referents are from the excerpt itself. Other than *gloves* and *wires*, names are not used. Without the few words I gave in the introduction and the incomplete comments I put in parentheses, it would be hard to make any sense from the exchanges. Separating speech from the network often means we cannot know what is happening.

Journal Entry

Much we do is, of course, a matter of habit. For example, in some countries, ballots are folded after they are marked. I have often written notes on ballots in elections that I have conducted at small meetings. One I frequently write is "No need to fold." In spite of the fact that after I collect the ballots many recall reading the words, almost everyone folds the ballots.

Have you experienced cases similar to this in which either by force of habit or other reasons mediums did not communicate, perhaps because they were seen as added to the normal network of mediums and therefore out of place?

EXCERPT 18–2
Damn

1	Sam:	Where're my gloves? Who the hell took 'em? I need 'em right away.
2	Joe:	Loosen it. You can't let it down till it's looser.
3	Rick:	I can't. It's too damn tight.
4		Twist the wires together to hold it steady. Not so fast. You'll break 'em.
5	Sam:	Damn! (After the wires break.)
6	Rick:	Why the hell didn't you listen? Hit it now.
7	Sam:	Ow! Damn, damn, damn. (After hitting finger rather than object.)

IV. SEPARATENESS—NETWORKS OF MEDIUMS INSIDE CLASSROOMS

Being Grandiose—Designing Classrooms to Provide Different Networks of Mediums

One reason objects and recordings are considered audiovisual aids, no doubt, is that in most language classrooms the network of mediums is limited to the desks, the numbers on a calendar, a flag perhaps, a clock, and the doors and windows. In specialized classrooms such as science labs, nursery schools, or sewing rooms, mediums like cages, plants, blocks, cloth, sewing machines, scissors, test tubes, sinks, and paint, to name a few, make the network of mediums more varied. One alternative way to expand the number of mediums in the network is to redesign language classrooms. I have done just this in a dream, which I have translated into a *nonlinguistic visual* and *linquistic visual* medium in Excerpt 18–3, on page 408.

As you can see, the class in Excerpt 18–3 is not made up of only a single area, but many pie-shaped divisions, each with different networks of mediums that require still different networks of mediums to be taken in and produced when people are present. If a student spent all his or her time in any one wedge, or in the garden outside, he or she would have a chance to experience only a limited network of mediums. For example, if a student spent all the time in the bar and coffee shop, he or she would have no chance to experience the network of mediums in a classroom. The reason the title of the excerpt contains the word *classroom* rather than the word *classrooms* is that no single network of mediums contains all the possibilities. To make an ideal language classroom, a range of networks of mediums is needed, not just one or two. To complete the circle, all the segments are necessary, and the garden outside fills in any spaces left between the wedges.

I realize that the plan in Excerpt 18–3 is nothing more than the dream I had with the vision in it. In the real world, though, we can still expand the networks of mediums. If you can't have language class in specialized classrooms even on a rotating basis, areas in regular classrooms can be substituted for the wedges in the circle. Items students bring in can be substituted for items that would need to be purchased by official bodies. Insects and flowers and leaves can be collected and dried to be mounted on paper or in discarded cans or jars that have also been collected. Old cans can also be cleaned and flattened and then shaped into geometric shapes, designs, or silhouettes. Used jars and bottles can be cleaned and used to store liquids and mix them; they are as efficient as beakers or test tubes. Packing crates can be used to store items as well as to make cabinets. Student designs can brighten packing crates or other furniture, should the students desire such decoration. Around the world, one can observe student names carved in desks and sketches on desks. The skill used to make these can be used to decorate alternative surfaces. Posters or pictures are available from discarded calendars. Many students have games and musical instruments at home and would bring them to class if asked. In fact, some students always have decks of cards in their pockets or dice, but take them out only during breaks or after classes are over. Plastic cigars, party hats and masks, miniature figures like those on charm bracelets, and other novelties can be collected from students at the rate of a few per month. By the end of a term there will be enough to fill a cabinet. Tools professional craftsmen discard are often good enough for amateurs, as long as they are in good repair, kept sharp, and oiled. Ways to improvise and use basic tools and other materials are described in scout manuals and magazines for the person interested in tinkering so that the ideal classroom in Excerpt 18–3 can become the classroom in Excerpt 18–4. [Background 18–5]

EXCERPT 18–3
An Ideal Language Classroom

DRAWING OF COMMUNICATIONS	CODING OF COMMUNICATIONS			
	Source/ Target	*Move Type*	*Medium**	*Use*
	other	str	nv_{1-n}	set

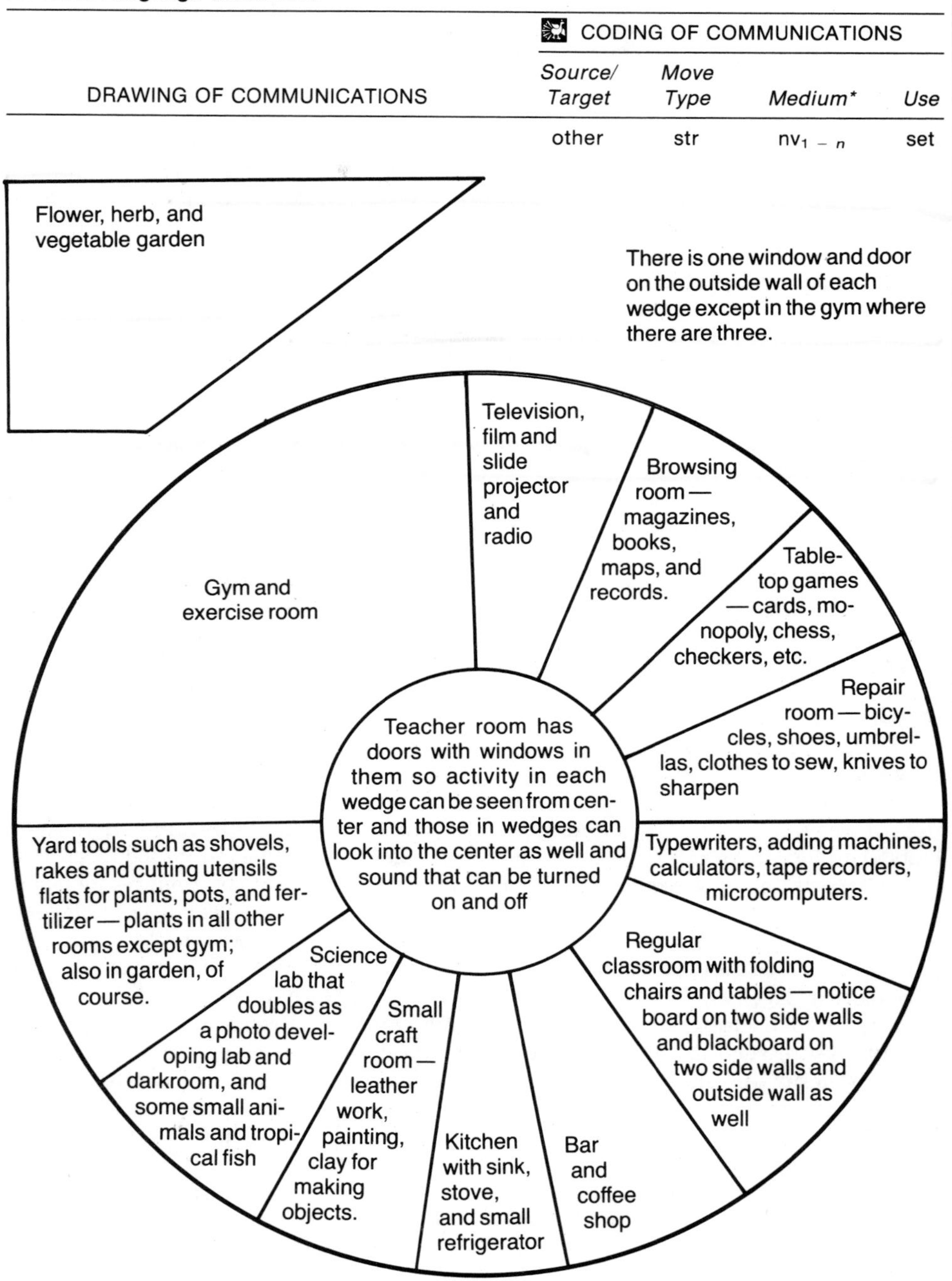

* The 1 – *n* means 1 through any number; a number can be substituted for *n* equal to the separate, different nonlinguistic visual mediums that are observable in addition to the few that are normal in all classrooms: desks, seats, blackboards, and notice boards.

EXCERPT 18–4
A Realistic Ideal Language Classroom

DRAWING OF COMMUNICATIONS*	CODING OF COMMUNICATIONS			
	Source/ Target	*Move Type*	*Medium†*	*Use*
	t/s/o	str	nv_{1-n}	set

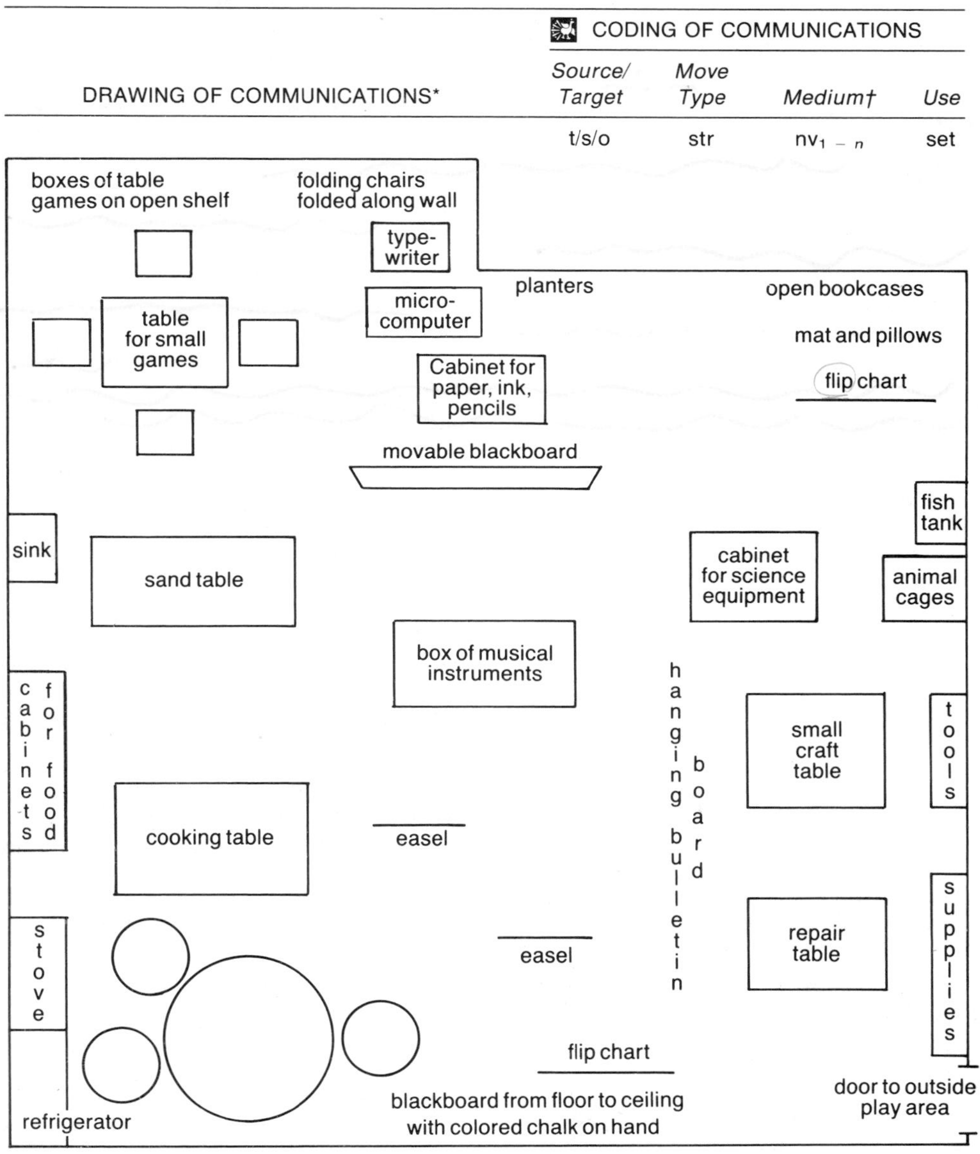

* The tables are all folding tables, the large boxes and cabinets not attached to the walls are all on wheels and easily movable so a large area can be easily cleared either for exercises or movement or to set up the folding chairs to form a regular class or any other type of grouping. A sand table is simply a table with boards six inches high attached to the edge of the table to keep the sand from falling on the floor. Children can use the sand to shape castles and to do the other usual things done in sandboxes; adults and teens can demonstrate movements in battles, show geographical features, plan parks or neighborhoods, to cite a few examples.

† The $1-n$ means 1 through any number; a number can be substituted for *n* equal to the separate, different nonlinguistic visual mediums that are observable in addition to the few that are normal in all classrooms: desks, seats, blackboards, and notice boards.

Aside from the expense for some supplies to equip the type of classroom I am suggesting in Excerpt 18–4, especially in places where buying books, paper, and pens is sometimes a problem, some of the group activities the different networks of mediums require might lead students to communicate in their first language rather than in the target language. One alternative that makes some students use the target language more is the mixing of students from different language levels. The advanced students in classes with beginners often like to use the target language, since they can play the role of language teacher. Another alternative is to have students communicate only with mediums other than speech: *la.* If students write notes in the target language rather than their own language, it makes it easier for the teacher to see which language the students are using. Another altnerative is to play tapes of their own language very loud so they are totally enmeshed in it. Because the target language blends less with the taped sounds of their own language, it is sometimes employed more. If the communications required by the different networks of mediums are very different from ones in their own language, they also sometimes use the target language, since they do not know some of the language needed to talk about the new activity. Even if they use the target language only part of the time when the networks of mediums are expanded, there is no doubt that when they use it, they will use it very differently from the way they use it in classrooms where the network of mediums is limited to desks, a clock, windows and doors, numbers on a calendar and a flag. [Background 18–6]

Journal Entry

I have urged that students be invited to bring in objects, draw murals, and in other ways be the source of the mediums to expand the usual network in a language classroom. One of my lifetime ambitions is to see a campus or park in which the users are invited to plan the walks rather than the architects.

On campuses around the world and in many public parks, people establish walkways and paths by walking over the grass, and they ignore the concrete, sand, or brick walks and paths that exist. If the paths or walkways were put down *after* users had made it clear with their paths where they were going to walk, would parks and campuses no longer have paths made by users and walks made by architects? Though this might seem far removed from the network of mediums, it reminds us of the importance of the source of a medium as a vital variable.

Being Austere—Designing Teaching to Produce Different Networks of Mediums

Most Things Can Be Anything—Improvising

A parent is sometimes startled when a child says "Look at my new cane," because all the parent sees is a broken radio aerial. To children and many actors, improvised props are even better than the real thing because they excite the imagination. If you have absolutely no access to specialized classrooms and for some reason you can't bring or keep any mediums other than chalk into a language classroom, the network of mediums can be expanded by pretending. A broken radio aerial found in a garbage can can serve not only as a cane, but as a baton, fencing foil, dagger, pointer, tongue depressor, large pencil, telescope, periscope, riding crop, thermometer for an elephant, or lightning rod, to name a few, and even as a radio or television antenna! One piece of chalk used to sketch on the blackboard can conjure up almost any scene in the world. To provide background noise for sketches, or any other activity, student hands, breathing apparatus, and feet can produce many types of noises. Tapping fingers can be made to sound like gentle rain on a roof, clapped hands like thunder, panting like runners finishing a race, a woman in labor, or dogs on a hot afternoon. Students can shriek like people or animals and can make the sounds of many animals, though the animals may not be fooled. These *nonlinguistic visual* and *aural* mediums are free, and though they require no rearrangements of rooms, they will result in a change in the network of mediums.

Right on Our Backs—Clothing as a Medium

If improvisation seems too strained, the universal essential, clothes, provides an opportunity for changing the network of mediums. By wearing different clothes at different times, we change the network of mediums just as much as if we carry a puppy into class or some other *nonlinguistic visual* medium. Inviting individual students to wear some part of a national costume from time to time will also change the network of mediums.

Many students are much more concerned about what they wear than about what they say or do. Clothes can be seen whether a person talks or not and whether one does anything or not. Just sitting in a room with certain clothes on communicates a message to those around. How closely does each teacher conform to the dress of the other teachers or the students? Does the teacher wear clothes from an earlier era or ones that are current? Are the clothes well kept, or wrinkled and with buttons missing? Students talk about these things anyway. By deliberately altering one's costume, substituting one *nonlinguistic visual* medium for another, the network is changed.

As dress becomes a topic, heated discussions may ensue. Some people can't stand red clothes or anyone who wears them. Some men never carry an umbrella because it is unmanly, or so they think. At a going away part for a missionary who had spent around forty years in a country, one of the most frequent comments heard was "His cassock was always clean." The place where the missionary lived was very dusty in the dry season and very muddy in the rainy season. But his white cassock was always sparkling clean and pressed, and this fact about his life was considered vital. So if you always dress neatly with your hair well groomed, go in one day with unkempt hair and wrinkled clothes. Ask students to do the same thing now and then. In addition to producing a great many incidental reactions, this alteration of the usual network of mediums will produce a number of solicits. "Is anything wrong?" and "What happened to you?" are some of the likely ones. [Background 18–7]

Keep Moving—Deliberately Using po *to Alter the Network of Mediums*

If *nonlinguistic visual* mediums, whether improvised or worn, become tiring, movement—*paralinguistic other*—can be substituted. In this way, even without introducing anything new into the classroom, such as the *nonlinguistic visual* mediums just discussed or illustrated in Excerpts 18–3 and 18–4, the network of mediums can be changed. If the lines of communication radiate from the teacher to the students and from individual students back to the teacher in classes you are involved with, the furniture can be moved, when not bolted down, or students can be asked to sit sideways or backwards when the furniture is bolted down.

If the network of mediums is not changed by altering positions, different patterns of communication are almost impossible. The usual patterns are so strong that when one student asks another a question, the student responding often looks toward the teacher in front of the room rather than at the other student in another part of the room. Comments such as "Don't look at me (the teacher), you are speaking to him," or "Don't answer her with the back of your head" are sometimes used to try to overcome the usual pattern. Changing the network of mediums by changing positions—substituting *po* for *linguistic aural* comments—provides one alternative.

Journal Entry

I've found that moving chairs around before an audience comes to a presentation I am going to make is a waste of time if I leave the room after I make the changes but before the participants come. If I put the chairs in a circle and leave, they are likely to be in rows, theater style, when I return. If I turn the chairs in the last rows around to discourage people from sitting there, always hoping against hope that some will come and sit in the front, people turn the chairs around and sit in them, leaving those in front, which would not have to be moved, vacant.

If we have a break, each participant returns to the exact seat occupied before the break. At a concert, even when seats are not reserved, once we sit in one, we lay permanent claim to it, it seems.

Why do you think we "claim" the same space and so often want the chairs to be lined up at public presentations? Have you had other types of experiences from your observations of seating?

If student desks are bolted down or students refuse to sit sideways or backwards in their seats, don't despair. There is always another alternative. Instead of having the students move, the teacher can. In my experience, though, teachers, like others in charge of events, such as masters of ceremonies, actors, singers, priests, ministers, rabbis, mullahs, judges, and political leaders at news conferences, stay put in front of the room. I used to be shocked when I saw teachers in countries where teachers' desks were placed on seven-inch platforms in the front of classrooms. Aside from the fear I always had that a teacher would fall off, I thought the platforms separated the teachers from the students. But when I have drawn chalk lines on the floor in the front of classrooms without platforms, I find that teachers hardly ever move outside the lines. With or without platforms, we don't move. It's as if anyone in charge of an event has a ten-foot cord attached to the back that is plugged into an outlet much like a television set on wheels. Moving beyond the length of the cord removes the source of energy and the television goes blank!

If the teaching you are involved with reveals little teacher movement, a clear alternative is to use the *paralinguistic other* medium of movement. But in the execution of this alternative, frenetic movement, as if one were an expectant father, is not the goal. Quick movement in a small area for its own sake does change the network of mediums; it focuses even more attention on the teacher. "Our teacher moved like quicksilver" recalled the West African novelist Camara Laye about one of his first teachers. The movement captivated the class and pulled all eyes toward the teacher. While this alternative surely needs to be tried, deliberate, slow movement around the room does too. [Background 18–8]

By walking up and down the aisles during silent reading or a dictation, an opportunity is provided for giving individual reactions to each student on a private basis. If the teacher stays in the back of the class, the students have a chance to look at each other when they speak rather than at the teacher, center stage in the front.

Journal Entry

Observe the power of seating in classes on a casual basis. See the extent to which the pattern of teacher in front and students facing the front obtains. As I was writing this episode, I observed a teacher reading a book to three eight-year-old children at a table. The teacher was sitting on the side of the table facing the front of the room, and the three students were sitting on the side of the table facing the back of the room. The teacher held the book so that the students could see it. But in holding it this way, the teacher had to turn it toward her each time she wanted to read a sentence. I was observing the class with another teacher. The other teacher heard me suggest after the class that the teacher try sitting on the same side of the table the children were on so that she would not have to strain her neck, trying to read the story and show the book to the children at the same time. Later in the day, the teacher I had been observing with taught a class. She read a story to three children as part of her lesson. They were seated on one side of the table and she was seated on the other. When I entered the class, she looked at me, suddenly remembered the discussion we had had about the lesson we observed together, and went around and sat on the same side of the table as the children so they could all look at the pages at the same time. She smiled after she changed seats. She had thought it was so obvious that sitting on the same side as the students was the "normal" thing to do, and she could not understand why the other teacher stayed on the opposite side of the table during the observation and discussion.

Remember when you jot down ways you have observed the power of seating that I am not suggesting that sitting on one side of the table is better than sitting on the other side. I am only saying that room arrangements are part of the network of mediums. But moving from one place to another does show what rules we are following.

Keep Cool, Keep Smelling—Deliberately Using no *to Alter the Network of Mediums*

An even more austere alternative requiring the least change involves the *nonlinguistic other* medium, temperature. Obviously, in an extremely hot and humid region such as New York City during the summer, there is little that can be done to alter this medium if no fans or air conditioners are available. One just has to sweat. Yet I'm sure you yourself have often been astonished at the frequency with which teachers are oblivious to room temperature in places where all that is necessary to cool or warm a room is to open or close the windows and door, or draw or raise the shades or blinds, or adjust the shutters. Yet the *nonlinguistic other* medium of temperature can have a great impact on the network of communication, at least as much as language laboratories do, and at much less cost. [Background 18–9]

Scents are another medium in the subcategory *nonlinguistic other*, and by using them to establish one atmosphere or another, you can alter the network of mediums. The smell of food, the sea, spring flowers and tropical blooms, bus or truck exhaust, dead animals, perfume, after-shave lotion, or medicine can set the stage for the generation of different patterns of communication. In many nonteaching settings, one of the first things we comment on when we enter a place is any striking scent, because this medium is taken in without any effort on our part. To see a teacher's new suit, a student has to look; to smell new after-shave, one has no choice.

The "Bloody Tyrant"—Time, a Part of the Subcategory Silence

By emphasizing the mediums we see and feel, I do not mean to obscure the invisible medium Shakespeare called the "bloody tyrant." Time, which I consider one type of *silence*, also affects the network of mediums. Before a teacher is hired, perhaps even before most teachers now teaching were born, the number of hours allotted for the teaching of whatever target language we teach was established. Within many schools and programs, this medium is altered as little as the position of most permanently attached student desks. Year in and year out, as new texts are bought, new methods urged, new courses developed, neophyte teachers trained, and the next generation of students taught, the number and length of periods provided for language study remain constant.

One way to compare the "bloody tyrant" in different classes is to compute the proportion of time spent in class in different programs. Another way is to compute the proportion of time per year devoted to class instruction in the target language out of all the time available. If a class meets for five 40-minute periods per week for 36 weeks, the total time spent in instruction is of course 5 × 40 divided by 60 minutes per hour × 36 weeks for a total of 120 hours, in round numbers. This comes to around 2 percent of the waking time in a year: 16 hours per day × 365 days per year equals 5,840 hours, which when divided by 120 hours yields .02054, or 2 percent.

Knowing either the total amount of time devoted to the target language in class or the proportion of waking time per year devoted to it can be misleading if one tally is computed in an immersion program and one is not. In an immersion program of three weeks with classes scheduled eight hours per day, the total time per year would be 120 hours, the same as a 36-week program of five 40-minute periods per week. Differences in the intensity of courses can be shown by following the amount or proportion of time with a slash mark and the number of days of instruction. Using this convention, the 36-week course would look like this: 120/180 or 2%/180, and the 3-week intensive course would look like this: 120/15 or 2%/15.

Of course, immersion is impossible with the usual timetables. But when you realize that during a two-day immersion you can provide three times more instruction—16 hours at 8 hours a day for 2 days—than during a month of 40-minute periods—13 hours at 40 minutes a day for 20 days, and when you realize that in an 8-hour-a-day, 5-day-a-week immersion during a month break in the regular calendar, you can provide more hours than during 40 weeks of five 40-minute periods per week, you realize that one alternative is to ignore the timetable and provide instruction during times when the timetable or regular schedule is not in force, such as during vacations. [Background 18–10]

If the time is varied, and thus silence alters the network of mediums, any comparisons need to observe the other mediums as well. Otherwise, any different consequences will not be instructive. Sitting in a class for eight hours using only speech—*la*—may not be any different from sitting there for eight minutes. Spending the bulk of the eight hours in silence—*si*—would no doubt limit as well the consequences of an intensive program.

Normal or Radical—Conclusion

Time, seating arrangements, movement, dress, pictures, objects, temperature, and smells—that they exist is obvious. That altering them can affect the pattern of communication too is obvious. What I think is less obvious is that these mediums are not extra or aids, but part of a network of mediums. In any setting, combinations of silence, linguistic, nonlinguistic, and paralinguistic mediums are part of a network. By changing one part of the network, the normal balance in any setting is changed. For example, in an elevator, distance—*po*—and lack of talking—*si*—are usually observed. But if you enter an elevator with a large package, jogging clothes, or a costume—*nv*—the network of mediums is changed. People talk, asking "What's in the package?" "Going jogging?" "Great mask!" One consequence of adding *nv* to the network of communication is for *la* to be produced.

To me, a jogging suit, a mask, or a large package in an elevator are normal, as is the different pattern of communication that is one consequence of the change in the network of mediums. What is radical to me is considering the changing of the network of mediums in a class something exceptional or special. That is why I prefer to describe mediums as part of a network, rather than as elements in some hierarchy in which any mediums other than those that exist when the builders leave a classroom are considered special and given a label such as *audiovisual aids*. We can think with pictures—*nv*; music—*na*—expresses feelings as clearly as speech—*la*; temperature and smells—*no*—affect our lives as well as the newspaper—*lv*. None is more special than the other. All are needed and reflect mental activity. And as Excerpt 18–5 shows, even with a careful transcribing of speech, without the other mediums in the network noted, "U" can miss it. What are the people talking about in Excerpt 18–5? What could you accuse the two of stealing? [Background 18–11]

EXCERPT 18–5
Sneaky Sound of a Shady Deal

Setting: A hearing room in a state office building. Investigators are listening to a tape that the State Investigation Commission said proved that a representative of a firm under investigation was guilty of a shady deal because of what the person said to a state informant. A transcription of the tape appears below.

1	Informant:	Hello. Eddie. This is . . . (the informant)
2	Eddie:	. . . (Repeating the name of the informant.)
3		From who?
4	Informant:	From Nice 'n Easy. Remember?
5	Eddie:	Yeah, where the hell have you been?
6	Informant:	I've been able to get a driver who has a guy on a platform who's stealing it, so I've got five pieces for you.
7	Eddie:	Five cases?
8	Informant:	Yeah.
9	Eddie:	An' what numbers?
10	Informant:	(States available colors.)
11	Eddie:	How much does it come out to?
12	Informant:	Oh, 45 a carton.
13	Eddie:	How many in a case? Three?
14	Informant:	Three dozen, yeah.
15	Eddie:	There's no markings on them or nothing is there?
16	Informant:	Nothing.
17	Eddie:	O.K.
18	Informant:	If anything is on them, I'll have them removed.

BACKGROUND NOTES

18–1. Hall's *The silent language* has been one of the works that has brought the importance of gestures, etc., to people's attention. Forsdale discusses these silent mediums from a broad view in relation to communication. And Carpenter criticizes films and pictures which suggest that because people smile in different places, we are all just one happy family and that differences in movement and other silent mediums are not important. He considers them vitally important and too often ignored or dismissed.

18–2. David Olson has devoted many articles to the crucial differences between speech and print and the powerful effects these differences have. McLuhan has reminded millions of the different effects different mediums have in his widely read *Understanding media* and *The medium is the message*. Ashton-Warner discusses not only differences between the first words of students she taught in the country and first words of city children; she also says: "Tongan children's first drawings are of trees. Samoan five-year-olds draw churches and Chinese draw flowers. In New Zealand a boy's first drawing is anything that is mobile; trucks, trains and planes, if he lives in a populated area, and if he doesn't, it's horses. New Zealand girls, however, draw houses, first wherever they live" (*Teacher*, page 28). In discussing the architect Arthur Erickson, Iglauer says that Erickson saw the images of what he built and thought in images, not words. Gardner studies children's drawings, and from the comments in his book we realize how significant each medium is and how different each is.

18–3. Duncan provides a comprehensive classification of nonverbal communication. Sapir divided up mediums in different categories when he was describing language. And Sakamoto and Makita, in discussing reading in Japanese, point out the fact that Japanese readers must take in two major different types of mediums: characters and symbols for syllables and individual vowels. Rossner et al. have produced a series of ESL texts that provide a wide range of mediums, should you want to practice classifying mediums.

18–4. Sagan, in his book about intelligence, reports on chimpanzee research. Hahn discusses chimpanzee talk and other animal communication in relation to thinking in a monograph in the *New Yorker*, "Getting Through to the Others."

18–5. Scout handbooks are usually available in bookstores. Many libraries have them if bookstores don't. Ordering the catalog of catalogs I list in the references episode (Episode 15) will enable you to order catalogs that sell games, scientific equipment for tinkering around, and tools and handicrafts. *Junior Education* contains pictures of many items that will generate ideas for making models from cardboard, colored paper, and paint.

18–6. Johnson, in an early study (1935), showed the effect of varying the amount of play equipment in play areas for children. And in a 1980 article, I juxtapose how we normally refer to objects—by *it, them*, etc.—when we use them outside a teaching setting and how we name them in a teaching setting.

18–7. Lurie has written an entire book on the language of clothes.

18–8. Labov (1970) tells how by having an interviewer lie on the floor and talk with kids, he was able to increase the amount they said. The interviewer also ate potato chips with those he was interviewing. He used a nonlinguistic medium—the chips—and a paralinguistic other medium—being on the same level with the kids rather than looking down at them—to alter the amount of linguistic aural production. Laye's account of his education is useful for more than this point about movement.

18–9. I have seen thousands spent on language laboratories around the world. Usually, no money is provided by the government that presents a school with the gift for maintenance of the equipment. Nor is money provided for staff or even tapes in many cases. Students are walking all around school compounds and in hallways carrying radios and often cassette tape recorders. Radio programs in the target language and production of tapes for students to check out and use on their own machines or those of friends can not only provide a savings in investment, but will prevent students from having to sit in a silent room at a booth staring into a blank wall or booth partition. Why language labs became such a prestige item for schools to get from foreign governments and why governments felt so compelled to provide them is a mystery to me, especially given Keating's finding that the labs seemed not to affect learning.

Now that the microcomputer age has arrived, I suppose this device will start to be provided. The fact that microcomputers have so many different uses, though, and the fact that there is evidence that they make use of different parts of the brain than most instruction does mean that should microcomputers be given, their impact will no doubt be greater than that of language labs. Papert and Taylor's anthology of authors writing about computing should be read for its powerful arguments for getting students involved with microcomputers.

18–10. Diller states the number of hours needed to gain proficiency in different languages as calculated by the Foreign Service Institute in the United States. He also speaks of the issue of time in class as a variable in learning. Denham and Lieberman have co-edited a series of findings about "time on task" in the learning of regular school subjects in California. Newspapers in 1982 started to run articles comparing the number of days students in the United States, Europe, and Japan spend in school and the number of hours they spend in school per day. Many started to think that increasing the number of days and hours per day might be one of the most powerful ways to increase learning. Some, of course, remind us daily that time is money. Increasing the school year and the number of hours of instruction per day increases the number of days teachers have to be paid.

At the same time that discussions about time on task in schools were heating up, we were reminded of the time children in the United States were spending in front of the television. Moody reports that many children spend twenty-six hours per week watching television in the United States, which is as much time as they spend on task in many schools, and which is more time on task than in many other schools. So time is vital both in schools and in the home.

18–11. Arnheim argues strongly for the need to develop visual thinking as well as the thinking we usually associate with words and language. Wolf, in discussing reading, reminds us that reading maps and other mediums is an important as reading print and probably involves different mental processes. DeBono says flatly,: "Thinking does not have to take place in words. Nor are concepts limited by the availability of words to describe them. Thinking can take place in images and feelings which are quite definite but too amorphous to be expressed in words. . . . A coherent and fluent essay may show language skill but does not thereby show thinking skill. We should look beyond language skill and seek to develop thinking skill as well." (pages 35 and 36).

And even without reading about the issue, a quick glance at works by Michelangelo and a few minutes of listening to Beethoven or Mozart reminds us that genuis can be exhibited in mediums other than print or speech.

EPISODE

19

Very Much

I. GETTING VERY MUCH STARTED—INTRODUCTION

Basic Vocabulary—Topic and Rationale of Episode

The usual way we think about a basic vocabulary is in terms of, say, two hundred words. This episode is about an alternative basic vocabulary—one of only nine words: *please, thank you, you're welcome, excuse me, I'm sorry*, content I code *life* in the subcategory *formula, ff.* After I introduce this topic in Section I with a rationale and some ways to use formulas, in Section II, I suggest some tasks students can perform to learn some rules we follow in using formulas. I also point out some other basic vocabulary: greetings and expressions of leave-taking, and conversation formulas. Then, in Section III, I end the episode with some reflections, as is my pattern.

This area of content is considered critical by many. The five expressions I just listed have an impact far in excess of almost any other group of nine words in English. In English-speaking places, I have seen parents refuse to do anything their children asked them to do if the children did not accompany their requests with the word *please*. I have seen parents actually take back candy from a child who did not say *thank you* after being given candy. I know people who stop sending birthday cards to friends who do not either call and thank them for the cards or send a thank-you note after they receive the card. And to belch, drop a piece of food, bump into someone, get up from the table, or leave the room without saying *I'm sorry* or *Excuse me* are actions that can lead to condemnation and criticism at the minimum and to blows at the maximum. [Background 19–1]

Many nonnative speakers of English I have come in contact with have apparently, and probably luckily, not experienced teachers with attitudes like the parents who take back candy from children who do not say "Thank you." When I hold a door open for a person studying English or light a cigarette for him or her, my action is as frequently followed by silence on the part of the other person as a "Thank you." And when I say "Thank you" in many places where English is not the native language of the people

I'm with, it's been followed with "Very much" as frequently as "You're welcome" and "Don't mention" almost as much as "Don't mention it."

If students you are in contact with, after months or even years of studying English, or any other language, say "Very much" or its equivalent as a reaction to "Thank you," or if you are interested in polite expressions either for their own sake or as a means to teach students how to discover some of the rules that control communications, please continue here. This episode is very much for you.

Journal Entry

At award ceremonies, the people receiving awards usually thank a number of people who have helped them in their work. At meetings a large number of people helped organize, the person in charge often says "I'd like to thank so and so." If you are one of those being thanked, does the remark please you? If you are just an observer, how do you feel about the long litany of polite expressions? If you have worked with someone, and you are not publicly thanked while others are, how do you feel?

Touchstones and Jumping-Off Points— Ways Formulas Can Contribute to Language Learning

Important as I think it is to make sure students learn to say polite expressions in the target language correctly, both inside and outside the language classroom, I do not think the expressions should be taught only for that reason. In addition to teaching polite expressions so that students will use them and thus not be considered rude, impolite, or even ungrateful by some native speakers of the language, bits from the expressions can be used as reference points, as sort of touchstones, for helping students master other aspects of the target language.

Because polite expressions constitute a basic vocabulary that students at any level can master the general use and pronunciation of in a few periods, the expressions can be used as key words to teach some letters of the alphabet and as touchstones to refer to when errors in other aspects of the language are made. Among students who tend to say "I going" rather than "I'm going," for example, the expression *I'm sorry* can be printed on a flash card and referred to whenever the error occurs in other sentences. The *you're* in "You're welcome" can be used as a touchstone for contractions with *you*. And to cite one more example out of many, the initial sound in "Thank you" can be used when the initial unvoiced *th* is mispronounced in any words.

Though formulas are stored in a different part of the brain from other aspects of language, and so mastery of the production of *I'm* in a formula may not transfer directly to the use of *I'm* in other sentences, reminding the students that they have mastered a bit of language in one expression may in some way affect their confidence in their ability to produce the form correctly in another sentence. [Background 19–2]

Formulas can also be used as takeoff points to teach features of the language related to the use of formulas. The modals are used together with formulas, and so formulas can provide a jumping off point for modals. From "Please open your books" it is a short road to "Would you please open your books?" or "Could you please get ready for the break now?" Contrasts between verb forms that accompany different modals would quickly come to the attention of the students as they heard questions like "Would you mind opening the door?" "Could you please open the door?" and "Would you mind opening the door, please?"

II. MOSTLY FOR STUDENTS—TASKS FOR STUDENTS TO PERFORM TO LEARN FORMULAS

Formulas Can Do More Than Get Candy—Introduction

Polite expressions can serve an even more central need than either the practical one of getting more candy from those who feel that the only way to show politeness is to use polite formulas, and the linguistic one of using formulas as touchstones for teaching other aspects of language. The polite expressions that I code as formulas—*ff*—can be used as the basis for student investigations of rules that control polite expressions.

Quite frequently, nonnative speakers of a language are interested only in the rules of tense, agreement, and word order, aspects of language associated with traditional grammar. By observing the frequency of polite expressions and the relationship between frequency, setting, and participants, some students, even at the beginning levels, can learn that there are rules—systematic patterns—that control all aspects of communication, not just items like subject-verb agreement and other aspects of what is traditionally referred to as grammar. Some will begin to see that there is a grammar of polite expressions as well as a grammar of word order, agreement, and word endings.

What Is and What Isn't—Identifying Formulas

In any investigation, the first thing to do is to list what we are looking for. If at the same time we can note where the items are likely to be found and who uses them, it is useful, because such information can narrow the search. In the exploration of polite expressions, words that seem to occur only as appendages to other questions, statements, or actions are the first items to identify. By asking students to cross out words that are not basic to the questions, statements or actions in a dialog, like the one in Excerpt 19–1, students can begin to identify which words and phrases are formulas of polite expressions and which are not.

The characters in Excerpt 19–1 are a customer and a clerk waiting on him. Since a customer is usually waited on, I called the customer "teacher" and the clerk "student." Sometimes a clerk takes a superior position, and in these cases he or she would be labeled "teacher." And sometimes clerk and customer treat each other like peers, in which case each would be labeled "student." The setting is a jewelry store.

Though Excerpt 19–1 alone would not provide enough information for students to decide which words and phrases were formulas and which were not, many dialogs similar to Excerpt 19–1 would provide enough information. As students collect dialogs from stories, movies, or radio or television programs, they can begin to notice that certain words appear over and over. In fact, the greater the range of dialogs, the easier it is to pick out the formulas, since they alone remain constant from setting to setting. If students do not live in an area where the target language is used and have no access to dialogs in books or in the media, they can be asked to write down polite expressions used as a matter of course during the class. An alternative that would probably produce more accurate information would be to have individual students write down each use of a polite expression and the communications that accompany it. [Background 19–3]

Journal Entry

Is your choice of store affected by the use of polite expressions on the part of those who wait on you? In Geneva, clerks say "Thank you" as you leave a shop, even if you just were browsing. In New York City, many clerks do not say "Thank you" if you purchase hundreds of dollars worth of goods. Do you feel better with Swiss customs, or those in many stores in large American cities like New York?

EXCERPT 19–1
Polite Expressions

		Communications	*Source/ Target*	*Move Type*	*Content*
1	Clerk:	Would you like a cigarette?	s/t	sol	
2	Customer:	No, thank you.	t/s	res	ff
3	Clerk:	A cup of coffee?	s/t	sol	
4	Customer:	Yes, please.	t/s	res	ff
5	Clerk:	(Gives customer coffee.)	s/t	str	
6	Customer:	Thank you.	t/s	rea	ff
7	Clerk:	You're welcome.	s/t	rea	ff
8		What can I do for you?	s/t	str	
9	Customer:	Would you please show me that diamond?	t/s	sol	ff
10		(Points to diamond in showcase.)			
11	Clerk:	(Takes diamond out of showcase and shows it.)	s/t	res	
12	Customer:	Thank you.	t/s	rea	ff
13	Clerk:	You're welcome.	s/t	rea	ff
14	Customer:	And that one, please?	t/s	sol	ff
15		(Indicating another diamond.)			
16	Clerk:	(Takes out the other diamond and drops it.)	s/t	res	
17		I'm sorry. Please excuse me.	s/t	rea	ff

* In lines 9 and 14, *please* is underlined to indicate that it is the part of the solicit that is coded *ff* for *life formula*.

By noting formulas on their own, students will not only get to know the words and phrases of the formulas, but also begin to see what calls them forth: when we ask another to do something, when another person does something for us, when we do something to another person, or they do something to us. By noting the *please* in "Please open your books" in class, students will find it easier to hear and note *please* in other settings. If they are thanked in class for performing an action they have been asked to do, they will better know where to look for *thank you* outside of class.

Formulas exist in notes and cards as well as in conversation: *la* and *lv*. If transcribing is hard for some students, they could be asked to collect notes and note cards that contain formulas. They could get some from stationery stores. Others, you and other teachers might duplicate for them. One note of the type I am talking about is given in Excerpt 19–2.

EXCERPT 19–2
Dear Friend's Father (T)

Thank you very much for your present. That was very nice of you. I think I will buy something useful with it. Thanks again.

Love,
Yumiko

As students hear more and more formulas in more and more settings, between more and more people, some will begin to see that formulas can mean the exact opposite of what the literal meaning suggests. The *please* in "Would you *please* leave the room?" is used to make the order stronger, and the speaker is unlikely to have politeness in mind. In a comment like "I said thank you!" the speaker is just as likely to be annoyed as to be gracious. By underlining formulas in a wide range of communications, students will be able to begin to gauge the meaning of the formulas based on the contexts of the comments they occur in. [Background 19–4]

Journal Entry

When I hand out pieces of paper in class, even tests, students often say "Thank you." But when I have students hand things out, the frequency of student reactions is smaller. When you are given something when you are in a group, do you say "Thank you" or the equivalent in some other language? When you hand things out, do you expect others to thank you, even when what you are giving out is from someone else and you are just a sort of messenger?

Fine Thanking You—Still Further Steps

The "Fine thanking you" in the title of this part of the episode is a student response to "How are you?" that I've heard hundreds of students chant at the beginning of classes all over the world. While the *-ing* of *thanking* may be what strikes you about the response, what always struck me as much as the *-ing* was the ritualistic manner with which it was said, and the fact that the greeting never changed even if everyone was in the worst mood possible!

If I had had my eyes closed in all the classes in all the great variety of many different countries where I heard the response, I would not have been able to tell where I was, so similar was the manner in which the response was uttered. The class would chant "Good morning teacher" after the teacher had said "Good morning class." Then, in response to "How are you today?", usually said with primary stress on each of the five syllables in the question, the class chanted back "Fine, thanking you" with primary stress on each of the four syllables. When I met many of the students after class and asked them how they were, they tended to reply "Fine thanking you" with the same primary stress on each of the four syllables in the same way they had responded to the teacher in class. If a student had his arm in a sling, seemed tired, or even sick, the response was still "Fine, thanking you."

In spite of this divergence, or perhaps because of it, I find the exploration of the rules of greeting and leave-taking critical. And since substituting alternatives during the few seconds at the beginning or end of class can so easily reflect the great variety of greetings and leave-taking, it seems appropriate to exchange, say, twenty different greetings three times each on each one of sixty days, rather than to exchange the same greeting each day for sixty days. To cite a simple but real problem, the greetings not only were ritualistic, but totally lacking in variety. Pity the poor students who study a language only in the morning. They never get a chance to say "Good afternoon" or "Good evening." I once was greeted by a guest who had been taught by a teacher who never opened an evening class with a greeting, but always ended it with the taking of his leave. When my guest entered my apartment for what I had thought was to be an evening, he startled me with these lines: "Thank you for inviting me; good night." He stayed the evening, and learned "Good evening" as well.

Journal Entry

An editorial titled "You'd be dead" emphasized to me the importance of knowing what to do and not to do when we meet others for the first time in a range of settings and circumstances. The editorial described advice a victim of a robbery received from the police. The man whose house was robbed told the police he wished he had had a gun in his hand when he discovered the thief. The policeman said, "If you had, you'd be dead."

The victim said he was a good shot, but the policeman said that had nothing to do with who would win the shooting match. The policeman went on to explain that decent people say something when they see another person in their home before they shoot because they think there might be a mistake or a kid might be in the house for a prank. The thief gives no such warning greeting. The instant taken for the greeting by a homeowner gives a thief just enough time to shoot. And the voice of the homeowner also indicates exactly where he is, making it even easier for the thief to do the killing.

Have you experienced any instances where knowledge of rules of greetings in a particular setting and under certain circumstances was such a grave matter?

Terrible—Greetings and Leave-Taking

I would suggest that as students master polite expressions and study the rules that govern them, some might be interested in exploring a range of greetings and expressions of leave-taking as well. Not only can *terrible, worn out, I have a headache,* and other responses be substituted for "Fine thanking you," but "How ya doin'" and other greetings can be substituted for the opening move. Several holiday greetings can be introduced as well—Merry Christmas, Happy Birthday, Happy St. Patrick's Day, Happy St. Valentine's Day, Happy Hanukkah. There is a surprising range.

Greetings can be used as touchstones just as polite expressions can. The *thank* in "Thank you" could serve as a key word to illustrate the initial voiceless *th* sound. Even the incorrect "Fine thanking you" could be used, as a reminder that we use the present participle in continuous sentences rather than the base form, as in "He's making that strange noise again." Over a period of time, some students might see that the *-ing* in the *thanking* in "Fine thanking you" is not needed, but that it is needed in continuous sentences.

Key words from holiday greetings—cut from greeting cards, thus substituting *lv* for *la*—can serve as touchstones as well. Rather than hanging specially made alphabet cards on the walls, Valentine cards can supply a *V*, St. Patrick's Day cards an *S, P,* and *D*. St. Patrick's Day can also serve to illustrate an apostrophe. Other greeting cards can be used as touchstones for rules of grammar too: word order, *very merry, the very best, greatest birthday ever*; modals: *I hope you have . . . May you have. . . .* Whether you use the expressions as touchstones or examples for pronunciation, mechanics, grammar, lexis, or any other of the subcategories of the *study of language* I treat in Episode 11, realize that the few minutes devoted to exchanging greetings and taking leave can teach more than the expressions themselves.

Teaching a range of greetings can be critical. First impressions are crucial, and no matter how fluent students of another language may be, the opening and closing impressions are often the ones that are remembered most. Some teachers say "How can she be in this class, she can't even say 'Hello' properly?" I know people who judge school districts, corporations, and most other organizations on the basis of the type of greeting they get, either on the phone or on a visit to the offices. Many government officials around the world are notorious for their impersonal attitude, reflected in part by the fact that many of them "don't even bother to say hello."

On buses in many large cities in the United States, greetings between drivers and entering passengers are so infrequent that bus authorities give a "Bus Driver of the Month" award to those drivers who greet their passengers. Of course, criteria other than the use of greetings are used for granting the award. Drivers must be punctual, not have accidents, and drive well. But greeting passengers contributes a great deal, since it is such a rare thing. Passengers are so delighted by greetings that they write letters to the bus authorities recommending "their" driver for the award.

The way we interact in public is in part symbolized by the way we greet and take leave of each other. Nomads in many places greet strangers by saying "Peace," and probably hope the stranger shares the same feeling. Those who don't say "peace" or its equivalent seem to be excluding themselves from the group. Perhaps the importance of these expressions as links between people explains why you hear so many parents urging their children to say "Bye-bye" or its equivalent as the children take leave of others, and to say "Hello to the nice man" after a child is greeted by a total stranger.

In *Julius Caesar*, Shakespeare has Brutus explain how much a greeting can tell us about another person.

BRUTUS: [How did Cassius receive you?]

LUCILIUS: With courtesy and with respect enough;
But not with such familiar instances,
Nor with such free and friendly conference,
As he hath used of old.

BRUTUS: Thou hast described
A hot friend cooling: ever note Lucilius,
When love begins to sicken and decay.
It useth an enforced ceremony.
There are no tricks in plain and simple faith;
But hollow men, like horses hot at hand,
Make gallant show and promise of their mettle . . .
(Act IV, Scene 2)

This exchange not only shows how much greetings reveal, but suggests that as students explore the rules that govern spoken greetings and those in cards, they will begin to see the importance of gestures and facial expressions—*pv*—and may even realize the meaning of the *paralinguistic aural* chanting that year after year accompanies "Fine thanking you" in so many classes.

Journal Entry

The greetings in letters and the way we end letters can of course leave lasting impressions too. For example, some people always put "Enjoy, enjoy" at the end of their letters, no matter how good or bad the news in the letter is. When you end a letter, do you vary the expression you use at the end depending on who you are writing to, the mood you are in, or for some other reason?

And when you receive a letter from a very close friend signed "Sincerely yours," does it seem appropriate, or do you wonder why a more personal formula wasn't used? Or don't you notice these expressions in letters, greeting cards, or day-to-day discourse? Or do you just notice such expressions when used by nonnative speakers of a language? When I used to receive letters from nonnative speakers signed "I remain your humble and obedient servant," I used to think it odd. But then I realized that some people only have access to greetings and closings in conversations and letters from novels of other centuries. They pick up expressions this way and think they are appropriate.

OK—The Same Further Steps

Entering and leaving conversations, pausing, using *OK, Huh?*, and all the other transitional sounds I code as *procedure transition* to juxtapose these communications with formulas. Like greetings and formulas, these items are few in number, but exceed their frequency with their importance. If you have learned another language, you realize how crucial these are. If you observe native-speaking children of the same language, you realize that one of the problems between adults and children is simply that the children have not yet mastered all the ways of taking a turn, getting into and out of a conversation, and pausing and marking their comments with the right amount of hemming and hawing.

III. THE OIL CRISIS—PERSONAL REFLECTIONS ON THE MEANING OF FORMULAS

Just as more systematic observation will reveal more formulas, so combined with tallying and generalizing, polite expressions, greetings, and conversation markers will be shown to be rule-governed, like all aspects of what we do. Such exploration will remind us that one of the rules of rule-governed behavior is that there are times when the rules are deliberately broken. Rules are hard to break, however, when they are completely mysterious. And one of the themes of this book is to discover rules of teaching so that we can make them a little less mysterious. To deliberately remain silent after a close friend has experienced a tragedy rather than to say "I'm sorry" or to simply touch the person are two alternatives that are possible only if a person has learned more than a set of formulas. To know that silence is more appropriate than saying "Thank you" after a taxi driver returns a tip he considered too small demands more than a set of formulas. These and other exceptions demand some understanding of the rules that control the formulas with different people in different settings.

As revealing as systematic identification, tallying, and generalizing may be, involvement in these activities may obscure the ritualistic nature of polite expressions, greetings, and conversation markers. Ritual connotes religion or academic or military convocations to many. But the use of the "very much," "Fine thanking you," and "OK" of this episode is ritual too. And beyond the words, tone of voice, gestures, or print, and even the rules that control them, is the underlying purpose they fulfill: to ease exchanges between individuals. Ritual, like oil, decreases friction and smoothes abrasive elements. And just as oil can cool down the heat produced by friction, so ritual can too. Too much oil, like too much ritual, can make things slippery as well as cool and smooth, but I prefer this alternative anyway, very much, fine thanking you, OK?

Journal Entry

I observed this exchange between an ESL student at work and a native speaker of English who gave out equipment the ESL student needed for his work. Student: How are you today? Person handing out tools: (silence) Then, I saw this exchange between another worker and the person handing out tools: Worker: They did it again! Person handing out tools: They're shit! The *they* it turns out was a football team. So greetings vary with settings and interests of the participants. In different settings I have found many usual greetings are not appropriate. I have also found that the usual greetings or polite expressions that I might consider important if I were handing out the tools or mail are not necessarily the oil that is needed. Sometimes bringing a cup of coffee to the person now and then is helpful. Other times, calling the person by his or her nickname is important, even if the name is not one that is flattering, such as "boondoggler" or "bum." A question about a soccer game may be more appreciated than a "Please" or "Thank you" or "Good morning."

What types of oil have you found helpful in interacting with those you meet on a regular basis to get things from?

BACKGROUND NOTES

19–1. Basic vocabulary is usually made up of words to name objects we come in contact with and actions we perform. Thrown in are function words—*the, a, an.* Word lists tend to be based on running text and not conversations. And frequency does not necessarily suggest importance. Even word counts done with computer assistance, such as the one by Kučera and Francis, cannot reflect the importance of some items to a particular context.

One book that contains ways to open conversations is Winn-Bell Olson's. Another is one by Keller and Warner.

19–2. Many people I have met can greet others in their own language but cannot do much more in the second language. Sagan discusses the role of different parts of the brain in memory and in the processing of different mediums and different parts of language. Perhaps you have visited someone who had had a stroke and can remember greetings but not other expressions or information.

19–3. Michael Arlen reflects on the fact that television has changed the greeting patterns of many people in the United States because it has made people who live far apart familiar with each other. Rituals in small communities that are used as greetings also serve the purpose of separating outsiders. But with television there are few outsiders, since so many can come into everyone's home. Ironically, though, he believes television has changed the greeting patterns for the better because he feels less involved greetings make people more accessible. He believes that on television talk shows people are becoming more and more formal and are just play-acting at being hospitable. "Why are the hosts on television so afraid?" he asks.

19–4. In *Thought and language*, Vygotsky presents Dostoevski's description of a conversation between six drunks which consisted of one unprintable word. The conversation was possible because the way the word was said by each of the drunks gave it a totally different meaning. At another place in the book, Vygotsky tells of the director Stanislavsky requiring actors to give the same greeting with forty different meanings at auditions.

EPISODE

20

We'll Be Landing in Three Minutes

I. LETTING PEOPLE KNOW WHAT'S HAPPENING—DOING JUST THAT TO YOU

One, Two, Three—Purpose, Introduction, and Organization

In this episode, I treat structuring moves. In this section of the episode I introduce a classic example of structuring and the need for this type of move. In Section II, I suggest ways to alter the classic way we structure in terms of the source of the move and the content. In Section III, I provide an opportunity for you to see the alternatives in FOCUS and English. In Section IV, I provide an opportunity for you to verify or negate the contentions I make in Section II. And in Section V, I remind you of some of the consequences of different structuring moves that we can investigate.

In Table 20–1, I note the elements from FOCUS I treat in this episode.

TABLE 20–1
Source and Content of Structuring Moves

Source/Target	*Move Type*	*Content*
t		life f
		formula ff
		personal fp
		public fg
	str	procedure p
		administration pa
		classroom behavior social pi
s		teaching direction pu
		teaching rationale pr
		study s
		language l
		other o

We'll Be Landing . . . —A Classic Example of Structuring

In almost all airplanes I have been on, announcements of destinations are made. Yet, everyone on the plane knows the destination because it is posted at the check-in gate. And each passenger's ticket, which also has the destination written on it, is seen by at least one attendant at the check-in counter before boarding. Not only are destinations announced on planes, but other information is also announced. Excerpt 20–1 contains some typical examples of the way pilots let passengers know what's happending in their structuring moves.

As passengers, we can feel the airplane gain speed before it takes off, so we know we are about to take off, even without the announcement. Most flights last at least one hour, so one wonders why a three-minute time span should be so critical that it is mentioned in the last line. True, I and most other passengers cannot tell whether we are taking off from the south, east, north, or west runway without being told. But after I am told which runway we are taking off from, I still don't really know which runway is which. I have no map of the runways or any idea which direction is which, unless the sun is clearly setting in the west or rising in the east at the time. Nor do I know if there is something particularly good about the south runway. Has it been recently repaved? Is it less crowded than the other runway? Is it shorter or longer?

Likewise, I do not find the information on altitude or speed too informative in the second line, though it is reassuring to know that we are flying at our "assigned altitude" rather than at an altitude the pilot just has a particular affection for. But unless I am given some information about 32,000 feet in relation, say, to Mount Everest or the Empire State Building or a two-story building, I find it hard to imagine what 32,000 feet is anyway. And when we fly at "532 miles per hour," is that using all the power of the engines? Is it slower than planned or faster? How much speed does the wind add or subtract?

Reassurance—Need for Structuring

Since announcements on planes usually fail to increase my knowledge about runways, altitude, or speed, they must have some other purpose. Pilots, like others responsible for groups, probably make announcements about what they are doing and about to do partly to reassure those they are responsible for. Most of us like to know what's happening, what's going to happen, and what has happened, whether we are on a plane or in any other settings where we are not in control. Self-initiated communications that set the stage for subsequent behavior, describe recently completed activities, or provide information—what I'm calling structuring moves—seem expected.

EXCERPT 20–1
A Classic Example of Structuring (T)

1	Pilot:	We'll be taking off for New York in two minutes . . . on the south runway. (After some time has passed.)
2		We are now cruising at our assigned altitude of 32,000 feet at 532 miles per hour. (After more time has passed.)
3		We'll be landing in three minutes at New York's Kennedy International Airport. (Said a moment after the sound of the landing gear dropping into place is heard by passengers.)

Structuring moves seem to be expected not only in planes and other public places, but also in conversations between individuals. Consider these structuring moves made by husbands and wives: "Now, I'm going to get the apartment cleaned up for the party"; "Now, I'm going to take a nap"; "After I finish this, I'm going to mow the lawn"; "I'm going to get the mail while I'm out"; "I've just finished shaving"; "The attic is cleaned up now," and on and on. We all communicate structuring moves.

Journal Entry

Do you hear structuring moves of disc jockeys such as "You're about to hear John Denver," or "You've just heard the Beatles and Ob-la-di ob-la-da," and those of newscasters who say "Still to come, threat of a strike, more corruption found in banking probe"? Or do you tune them out and just listen to the music or the entire news stories? Or do you tune in and out selectively? If so, what are the characteristics of the structuring moves that you tune in and the structuring moves you tune out?

II. ONE THROUGH EIGHT—BREAKING EIGHT RULES OF STRUCTURING

Who's in Charge?—Source of the Structuring Move

In my experience in teaching settings—whether on a plane listening to the captain, at a prize fight trying to follow the announcer, or in a classroom being told about an impending lesson—the person in the role of the teacher makes all the structuring moves. Studies of classroom interaction have consistently shown that it is practically unheard of for students to make structuring moves in classrooms. [Background 20–1]

Yet even if only a few students ultimately become classroom teachers, all students are called upon to assume the role of a teacher outside classrooms all the time. To play a new game with a friend, share a recipe, or show another how to transplant a plant, structuring moves are necessary. Even if a person is unusual and rarely teaches anything, the need to know how to communicate structuring moves is important. As we saw, wives and husbands announce what they are about to do or have done, and other types of partners do the same thing. We do not assume the rule of a teacher when we say "I'm going to mow the lawn" or "I've just finished shaving." But if we don't make such statements, some may consider us uncommunicative, and others may consider us rude. Some structuring moves seem to be expected both in teaching and nonteaching settings.

To break the cardinal rule of classroom teaching which says that almost all structuring moves must be communicated by the teacher hired to be in charge, you could begin to have students structure! A story is told of a small high school in Iowa, a farm state in the middle of the United States known for its fine education system. It seems that the graduating class from one small high school always received more of one of the most prestigious scholarships in physics per capita than any high school in the country. Puzzled, a reporter went to investigate so he could share with others the teacher's methods. Every lesson the reporter saw was taught by a student! At the end of each lesson, the teacher gave some reason why he could not teach the next day, and each time a different student would assume the responsibility. To teach, the students had to structure.

Journal Entry

Have you ever had the chance in a class you were a student in to structure? In short, as a student, have you ever had the opportunity to play the role of teacher? If you have, how did you feel about the experience?

Guess What Class This Is—Integrating *Procedure* and *Study*

Given the purpose of structuring moves, to set the stage for subsequent activity or to comment about present or previous activity, some procedural information is built in. In fact, as you saw in the pilot's comments in Excerpt 20–1, a structuring move can consist entirely of content I code as *procedure*.

If you find structuring moves that contain only *procedure*, try adding some information about the area of study being taught. Rather than "Pay attention," try "Pay attention to the verbs in the sentence"—*p* + *l* or "Pay attention to the dark lines on the map"—*p* + *o*. By mentioning an area of study in a procedural comment, we integrate *procedure* and *study*. The easiest way to determine whether a structuring move contains only *procedure* or *procedure* plus *study* is to see whether you can guess the type of class it is from by hearing the lines. A comment such as "You have five minutes to finish" or "Pay attention" could occur in any type of class. You cannot tell what is being taught from the comments. In fact, one criterion to use in determing whether a communication is in the category *procedure* or not is to see whether it is subject-specific or not. If it is not, it is probably a procedural comment only.

In Excerpt 20–2, I have noted the content of different lines in a structuring move from Ionesco's *The Lesson*. Though the move contains separate messages with content of *procedure* and *study*, the separate messages themselves do not contain integrated content, except in line 6.

Integrating *study* with *procedure* can in some cases prevent students from responding in ways different from those the teacher has in mind. In Excerpt 20–3, you can see that the teacher is interested in practicing the pattern "Yes, I do," while the student

EXCERPT 20–2
The Lesson

	Communications	*Source/ Target*	*Move Type*	*Content*
1	Let's try another approach.	t/s	str	p
2	For purposes of subtraction let's limit outselves to the numbers one and five.			o
3	Wait now, miss, you'll soon see.			p
4	I'm going to make you understand.			p
5	Pay attention.			p
6	I will say the sentence to you in Spanish, then in neo-Spanish and finally Latin.			p + l
7	Pay attention, for the resemblances are great.			p
8	For the resemblances are great.			p

EXCERPT 20–3
Trousers (T)

		Communications	*Source/ Target*	*Move Type*	*Content*
1	Teacher:	I'm going to ask some questions now.	t/s	str	p
2		Alright, Carlos, do you wear trousers?	t/s_1	sol	p + l
3	Carlos:	Alway . . . All my life.	s_1/t	res	fp
4	Other students:	(Laugh.)	$s/t + s_1$	rea	fp
5	Teacher:	Always you've worn.	t/s_1	rea	
6	Carlos:	I have . . . Eh wear, wear . . .	s_1/t	rea	l
7	Teacher:	Do you wear trousers?	t/s_1	sol	p + l
8	Carlos:	I wear.	s_1/t	res	l
9	Student:	Yes, I, I do.	s_2/t	res	l
10	Teacher:	Yes, you do.	t/s_2	rea	l

thinks the teacher is interested in personal information: *fp*. You will note that there is no statement that can be coded *l* for study of language in the structuring move in line 1.

Had the teacher said something which indicated that the intention of subsequent solicits was *study* and not *life*, Carlos might not have responded differently from the way the teacher expected him to respond. Here is an announcement that might have indicated what was coming, and that does integrate *procedure* and *study*: "We're going to practice responses to questions like 'Do you wear trousers?' Use 'Yes, I do' or 'No, I don't' in your answers. I'm not interested in the true facts about your way of dressing, but the language in the patterns we're practicing." Whether a structuring move like this with integrated coontent would have prevented the laughter is hard to say. Perhaps Carlos was in a tug-of-war with the teacher, trying to show that he exerted some control in the class, and he would have responded with content *fp* even if the structuring move had made it clear what content was expected. Trying structuring moves that contain only *procedure* and those that contain *study* and *procedure*, and then comparing the subsequent responses, would indicate the consequences of both types of structuring moves.

Walter—Integrating *Procedure* and *Life Personal*

In Excerpt 20–4, the teacher intersperses personal comments as he makes a structuring move mainly devoted to *procedure*.

I don't know what your reaction to Excerpt 20–4 is. Personally, I like to see content in the category *life personal* integrated with *procedure* in structuring moves. Procedure, almost by definition, tends to be impersonal. Adding a comment that is personal to an announcement can decrease the feeling of distance often produced by structuring moves that contain nothing but *procedure*.

I remember the effect a personal comment had in the midst of procedural comments

EXCERPT 20–4
Walter (T)

		Communications	*Source/ Target*	*Move Type*	*Content*
1	Teacher:	I'm going to try to read the way Walter Cronkite reads.	t/s	str	p
2		I watch the six o'clock news on Channel 5 and then I switch to Walter Cronkite on Channel 2 at seven o'clock.			fp
3		(Writes the name on the blackboard.)			fp
4		I've been watching him for years.			fp
5		If you notice, when he reads the news, he reads as though he's talking to you.			fp + p
6		That's why I call him Walter, because he's talking to me—as if he's talking to me.			fp + p
7		So what he does is he reads, he looks up at the camera and it appears as if he is looking at you.			p
8		This is the way I'd like us to practice reading.			p
9		I'm going to try to do it now.			p
10		I'm going to pretend that I'm a newscaster.			p

in a class that was expecting to have an important test returned. Read Excerpt 20–5, both with and without the personal comment in line 4, so you can see how you would have felt if you had been a student in the class.

Much as a teacher might like to increase the frequency of communications in structuring moves in the category *life personal*, there are some reasons why personal comments are often not made. When stating administrative information, for example, the person in charge has to give the same information to everyone to assure fairness to each participant. If each individual or group is not given the identical procedural information, it might be considered unfair. Even adding a comment such as "Good luck" to the instructions to one group and not to another during a contest might be thought to give some an advantage over others. And a more personal comment such as "Before I start to answer this type of question, I usually feel nervous—you might too—but as soon as I begin, I calm down" might be considered even more unfair, say, in a testing interview.

Personal remarks can lead to confusion as well as to charges of lack of fairness. If each pilot said what came to mind on every flight, some standard operating procedures might not be followed. And passengers and flight crews both would probably wonder if the captain was in charge or knew what to do. Pleasant as we may consider a phar-

EXCERPT 20–5
Getting Personal

		Communications	*Source/ Target*	*Move Type*	*Content*
1	Teacher:	I was going to go over your tests with you.	t/c	str	p
2		But I didn't grade them over the weekend as I had promised, so I can't hand them back today.			p
3		We'll start the new unit instead.			p
4		If my wife and daughter had not gotten sick late Friday night, I would have gotten the tests back. I had to take them to the emergency room Friday night and take care of them all weekend.			fp

macist who admits not liking the taste of medicine, we want to feel that the information about the amount to take is more than the pharmacist's personal opinion. So, procedure without any personal remarks can sometimes be reassuring.

The size of a group also works against the communication of personal information and feelings. While a comment such as "That's my house over there" can be added to "We'll be landing in three minutes," such a comment presupposes some familiarity between the pilot and the passengers. If a pilot that you and a hundred other passengers never saw in your life announced "That's my house over there," the comment would sound absurd because personal information is usually not publicly shared with large groups of total strangers. This constraint, as well as the need to be fair and to reassure in communicating *procedure*, supports the contention that structuring moves without content I code as *fp* tend to be impersonal.

Just because a teacher uses *I* in a structuring move does not mean that the move contains content in the category *fp*. Note that only one line out of eight in Excerpt 20–6, line 3, contains personal information—*fp*. This is not to say that the teacher is not trying to relate the topic to the students' experience. When he says he believes students have heard about Malcolm X—line 2—he is communicating content in the category *life public*: *fg*. If personal comments are hard to make for some, comments relating the topic to public knowledge or general information that many know is another way to integrate *life* with *procedure*, simply using a different subcategory.

Unless one really wants to share personal information or feelings with students, and unless one expects students to do likewise, comments of a personal nature could begin to sound empty, especially if they are added just to alter the proportion of different areas of content. It can be argued that adding statements of a personal nature in a deliberate way alters the proportion of *life personal* in the same way that genuine empathy might increase this area of content. And, in fact, I agree with this argument. But the more predictable such insertions become, the more they will cease to be communications in the category *life personal*, and the closer they will come to being formulas, *ff*. A formula is part of the major category *life*, but is less personal and more ritualistic than a personal remark. I treat formulas in Episode 19.

EXCERPT 20–6
Malcolm X (T)

		Communications	*Source/ Target*	*Move Type*	*Content*
1	Teacher:	I have a story about Malcolm X.	t/s	str	p + s
2		I believe you have all heard about him and maybe read about him.			fg
3		I first read this book when I was in college. I saw how little I knew about the country when I first read the book.			fp
4		What I want us to do is read and look up just as you have been doing with the other teachers.			p
5		First, I'll read the whole story while you follow.			p
6		Where I pause or stop, I want you to put a slash.			p
7		Now, I'll read.			p

Stop, Please—*Procedure* and Formulas

Because formulas are ritualistic does not mean that they have no place in communications. If you observe structuring moves that contain no formulas, compare your feelings about them with your feelings about those that contain formulas. "No smoking, please" is more agreeable to some than "No smoking." Many prefer "Sorry, we're closed" on an office door to "Closed." Announcements in class can be made without or with formulas. If you note that structuring moves contain no formulas, try adding some. In place of "I'd like everyone to get into groups now after I tell you what I want you to do," we could say "I'd like everyone to please get into groups now after I tell you what I want you to do." Trying *p + ff* could be a first step before trying *p + fp*.

Journal Entry

Do you feel shocked when you hear a formula in a series of directions you are trying to follow? Do you prefer that people in charge of procedural matters not mix their personal feelings and personal information? Do you prefer that business and personal affairs be kept separate? How do others you work with feel about these questions?

Differences Are Great, Too—Subcategories of *Procedure*

I have been discussing *procedure* as if all comments about getting things done were the same. In fact, as you no doubt sensed as you read the transcripts, the *p* for *procedure* is given next to a very diverse series of communications. To highlight this diversity, I have subdivided *proceduure* into many subcategories. I treat just four of them here: *administration*: *pa*, *classroom behavior*: *social*: *pi*, *teaching direction*: *pu*, and *teaching rationale*: *pr*.

The pilot's "We'll be landing in three minutes" I code as *pa*. Directions that concern details, such as payments, the filling out of forms, and other statements that do not fit

EXCERPT 20–7
In the Park/At a Crime Scene

		Communications	*Source/ Target*	*Move Type*	*Content*
1	Mother/ child:	After you play in the sandbox for fifteen minutes, we'll go.	t/s	str	pa
2		When we get home, you'll take a nap.			pa
3	Police officer/ suspect:	First, I'm going to read you your rights.	t/s	str	pa
4		Then, I'm going to interrogate you.			pa

the other subcategories, I code as *pa*. The exchanges in Excerpt 20–7 contain other examples of lines I'd code as *pa*.

Where Ionesco had the professor say "Pay attention" (in Excerpt 20–2), we have a good example of content I code *pi* for the subcategory *classroom behavior: social*. In addition to administrative regulations we all have to follow and announce, we have to make the rules we are supposed to follow in classrooms that keep things under control clear. The rather delicate term *classroom management* is often used to refer to the job of keeping a class quiet. Some lines in Excerpt 20–8 are coded *pi* for *classroom behavior: social*, a term almost as delicate as *classroom management*.

EXCERPT 20–8
Enjoy, Enjoy!

		Communications	*Source/ Target*	*Move Type*	*Content*
1	Librarian/ class:	Now, yesterday we found books in the card catalog by looking up the authors.	t/c	str	
2		Today, we will find them by looking up the titles from the list your English teacher gave you.			
3		(Holds up a list for all to see.)			
4		As you work, I don't want any talking.			pi
5		If you talk, I'll send you back to your English teacher.			pi
6		When you pull the chairs out, do it gently so they don't make noise.			pi
7		If you tear cards in the card catalog, make noise, make up books or tear out pages, I'll send you to the principal's office.			pi
8		OK?			
9		Now, let's enjoy the library.			

EXCERPT 20–9
The $20,000 Pyramid*

		Communications	Source/ Target	Move Type	Content
1	Master of ceremonies/ contestants:	Now, contestants, as you know, this is a word game.	t/c	str	pa
2		You are divided up into pairs.			pa
3		One of you will be shown a word on a screen.			pu
4		You have to give your partner clues to help you partner guess the word.			pu
5		If you give an unacceptable clue, the bird (cuckoo sounds) will signal like that.			pa
6		You will have 30 seconds to try to guess seven words.			

* Adapted from the TV show "The $20,000 Pyramid."

Of course, it is possible to structure in a classroom without either administrative comments or remarks about classroom social behavior. But what cannot be avoided in teaching settings are teaching directions, the next subcategory of *procedure, teaching directions: pu.* The *u* stands for *use* and reminds us that directions in this subcategory are those related to ways we use mediums. I illustrate this subcategory in Excerpts 20–9 and 20–10.

EXCERPT 20–10
This Is the New One (T)

		Communications	Source/ Target	Move Type	Content
1	Pharmacist/ customer:	This is the new one.	t/s	str	pa
2		(Holding up a full bottle just filled with cough syrup.)			
3		This is the old one.			pa
4		(Holding up empty bottle customer had brought to show the name of the drug and the prescription number.)			
5		The dose is a teaspoon every four hours.			pu
6		Mix it with juice if the taste is too bitter.			pu
7		I don't like the taste myself, but I like the smell.			fp

EXCERPT 20–11
Directions from a Text

		Communications	Source/ Target	Move Type	Content
1	Text/ student:	In the following passage, some words are missing.	x/s	str	
2		These words are not necessary to understand the passage.			pr
3		You can probably read the story faster and understand the story more without the words.			pr

Should a teacher try to explain the reasons for following one set of teaching directions rather than another, I indicate the fact by coding such communications *pr* for the subcategory *procedure teaching rationale.* The lines coded *pr* in Excerpts 20–11 and 20–12 illustrate the subcategory *pr* because they try to give reasons for a particular way of teaching.

Though Dickens may have intended to remind his readers that Gradgrind's emphasis on facts was unfortunate, and he might have intended Gradgrind's rationale to be considered weak by his readers, the statements are still clear examples of content I code *pr* for *procedure*, subcategory *teaching rationale.* The excerpt also contains an example of *procedure* integrated with *life personal*, in line 5.

Obviously, there is no ideal proportion of communications containing different subcategories of *procedure.* But if one subcategory is used exclusively, other subcategories can be substituted for it. If most of the time is spent in some classes on making remarks about book money, tuition, seating arrangements, and scheduling, one obvious alter-

EXCERPT 20–12
Hard Times

		Communications	Source/ Target	Move Type	Content
1	Gradgrind/ class:	Facts, mark that, children.	t/c	str	s
2		Facts alone are wanted in life.			pr
3		Count nothing else.			pr
4		The minds of reasoning animals, and that is what you are and what I am, and that is a fact, can be properly formed only by fact.			pr
5		That is the principle on which I bring up my own children.			pr + fp
6		And in this school you will be brought up on it too.			pa
7		Stick to facts, sir, that is your charge here.			pu

native is to talk more about the uses students are expected to include in their responses and other moves. If the bulk of procedural comment is about the classroom behavior of students, giving reasons for the activities students are expected to engage in is an alternative that needs to be tried. Though setting norms for classroom social behavior—*pi*—may be necessary, when accompanied with reasons for class activities that students understand, quieter classes might be the result. I treat classroom social behavior in Episode 16. [Background 20–2]

Journal Entry

One of the places *procedure* cannot be integrated with *life* is in textbooks. When a language is taught as a foreign language, as French is in the United States and English is in Japan, the structuring moves that contain *procedure* which tell students how to do the exercises are often in the students' first language rather than in the target language.

As a student of a language, did you have directions in texts written in your own language rather than the target language? If you did, how did you feel about the practice? If you did not, how did you manage to follow? Given the fact that many terms and patterns in directions are repeated a lot, and that some exercises can be followed because of the format itself, do you think that communicating *procedure* in a person's first language rather than the target language ignores a target of opportunity for learning the language of *procedure*?

Forget the Teacher or the Content—The Setting as a Source of Structuring

Though I have not yet mentioned the fact that much structuring is done by the settings we're in, rather than what the people in the settings indicate we should do, I'm sure you remember times when you observed that the setting determined what people did. In a bookstore, playground, shopping center, or carpentry shop, and most other settings, the materials in the settings themselves set the stage, just as the props do in any play. People browse through books because they are on the shelves, not because of recorded announcement saying that they should browse. People keep their distance from electric saws in a carpentry shop because of the noise. You surely have observed that many people fasten their seat belts before an announcement; the presence of the seat belts suggests that they should be buckled. In a park, you see some children playing on the swings, some in the sandbox, and others on the slides, all without oral structuring moves. The participants themselves may announce "I'm going to play in the sandbox now," or "I've had enough of the swing and I'm going to climb now." But the materials themselves set the stage for the activities. In a class with cassettes and cassette recorders available, books and magazines present, and a coffee maker and a number of table games ready for use, the participants will engage in some activities without any spoken structuring moves by the teacher, and without any printed structuring moves, because the materials themselves structure. Structuring moves communicated by non-linguistic mediums, such as the location of chairs, books, food, or toys, are treated in Episode 18.

Journal Entry

Are you conscious of the fact that you often announce what you are about to do or have just done to the person you are with? Or don't you make such announcements? As a result of becoming aware of your structuring—if you do—are you structuring less both inside and outside of classes? If you have not been accustomed to structure either inside or outside of class, are you structuring more now?

One Long One or Many Short Ones—Breaking Structuring Moves Up

Because the pilot is usually busy as the plane is landing, the announcement "We'll be landing in three minutes" is short. When the flight attendants describe the use of the seat belts, life vests, and oxygen masks, the structuring move is made up of a long series of statements, so the move is long. (A structuring move made by flight attendants is given in Episode 13.)

In classes too, some structuring moves are long, and others are short. If you find yourself or others you work with providing all the information you think is needed in a long structuring move at the beginning of class, one alternative is to divide up the move into as many separate parts as you have to give, and intersperse them during the lesson. If an opening structuring move takes three to five minutes, break it up into three or five one-minute separate moves, and communicate each one at the time during the lesson when students have to do what you are announcing.

An Announcement at the End?—Structuring at the End of Events

Since structuring moves are defined as communications that set the stage for subsequent behavior, it is hard to imagine them being communicated at the end of an event. If directions or announcements are necessary for an event to get underway, of course they must be made. One way to see just how necessary structuring moves are at the beginning of an event is to eliminate them. Then, to see what participants' perceptions of what went on is, they can be given an opportunity to announce what has happened. Such announcements at the end of an event are not unusual outside of a class, though they usually accompany announcements that have been made at the beginning. "We have just heard the Third Symphony" is common on radio programs as a program ends. Some structuring moves might be better understood when made after the events they are mentioning, since the participants have additional knowledge they have just gained from participating. If structuring moves occur only at the beginning and some parts of them are not understood, there is only one opportunity to match experience with language. By structuring at both ends of an event, an extra opportunity for connecting language and experience is provided. And by structuring only at the end, an opportunity is provided for seeing the extent to which the information in the structuring moves is helping people know what they are doing.

III. LET'S HAVE A TEST—CODING DESCRIPTIONS OF DIFFERENT ALTERNATIVES

"Let's have a test" is an example of a structuring move as classic as "We'll be landing in three minutes." Both contain only *procedure*. In Excerpt 20–13, I've provided an opportunity for you to code the content of a number of structuring moves in which *procedure* is integrated with other areas of content, and some in which you can code the subcategories of *procedure* I treated in this episode. Use these abbreviations to note content:

life: *ff* formula; *fp* personal; *fg* public

procedure: *pa* administration; *pi* classroom behavior: social; *pu* teaching direction; *pr* teaching rationale

study: *l* language; *o* other areas of study

As you can see in Excerpt 20–13, I've added a column called Features. In this column, you can distinguish structuring moves that precede and follow events. Write the subscript *r* on the blank line in the Features column if the structuring move comes after an event in order to review the event.

Though the source and target are easy to code, I am asking you to code them too, since one of the alternative ways to structure is to provide opportunities for students to structure to different targets. Use these abbreviations for source and target: *t* for teacher, *s* for individual student, *c* for an entire class, and *g* for part of a class or other group. Coding done by others is given in the excerpt footnote.

EXCERPT 20–13
Summary Descriptions of Structuring Moves for Coding

	Descriptions of Communications	*Source/ Target*	*Move Type*	*Content*	*Features*
1	Students make summary statements in their notebooks about patterns taught at the end of the class and then exchange their books.	___ to ___	str	___	___
2	Teacher introduces a geography lesson with a personal comment.	___ to ___	str	___	___
3	The teacher says "I like the topic of today's class" almost every time he introduces the language topic to be taught.	___ to ___	str	___	___
4	The teacher posts a sign saying "No smoking in the classroom" at the beginning of a workshop.	___ to ___	str	___	___
5	A teacher starts a lesson on commands by writing the words *draw, shade, darken, extend, shorten* in a column on the blackboard and then says "Tonight, we're going to draw a person dancing. As you draw, I'll come around and tell you ways to change your drawings, using some of these words." (Pointing to the list on the board.)	___ to ___	str	___	___
6	A teacher ends an introduction to a dictation with this statement: "The reason we're going to have a dictation with the radio on is that I want you to have experience hearing a person speak with background noise. After all, this is usually the way we have to listen outside of a classroom.	___ to ___	str	___	___
7	After class, one student tells some students who were absent what topics	___ to ___	str	___	___

EXCERPT 20–13 (*continued*)

	Descriptions of Communications	*Source/ Target*	*Move Type*	*Content*	*Features*
	were covered in the science experiment.				
8	At the end of class, the teacher outlines the way he expects students to behave on a class trip that is to be taken later in the day.	____ to ____	str	____	____
9	Now that you have done this exercise, you see that an *-ed* after a voiced sound is pronounced /d/ and after a voiceless sound is pronounced /t/.	____ to ____	str	____	____
10	A disc jockey ends his program with an announcement that the records just played are in the top ten although they have only been out for two weeks.	____ to ____	str	____	____
11	At the beginning of a news broadcast, after greeting the audience, the announcer states the headlines of the stories to be covered.	____ to ____	str	____	____
12	A wife outlines her activities for the day to her husband who is taking care of the children so he knows when to contact her should the children want to talk to her.	____ to ____	str	____	____

Coding done by others: 1. s to s, l, r; 2. t to c, fp + o; 3. t to c, ff + l or o; 4. t to c, pi; 5. t to c, pa + l + o; 6. t to c, pr; 7. s to g, o, r; 8. t to c, pi; 9. t to c, l, r; 10. t to g—g rather than c because not everyone listens to the program—fg, r; 11. t to g, ff + fg; 12. s to s, pa.

IV. SEVEN IN ONE—AN OBSERVATION GUIDE FOR TALLYING ELEMENTS IN EPISODE 20

The alternatives I have proposed cannot fairly be called alternatives until it is clear what content is now being communicated and what the source and target of communications are. Altering the proportion of different subcategories of *procedure*, or integrating different areas of content, or breaking up structuring moves into shorter ones are suggestions that presume a particular pattern.

In order to see in fact what present practices are, I have designed Observation Guide 20–1. By tallying with the abbreviations for subcategories of procedure, life, and study rather than tally marks, you can see the degree to which different subcategories of *procedure* are used, and what subcategories of content they are integrated with.

As you can see, I have noted the source and target along the top of the guide. Along the left-hand side I have noted both the subcategories of *procedure* and whether the structuring moves occur only at the beginning of an event, intermittently during an event—*i*—or as a review or wrapup at the end of an event—*r*. In tallying, use the usual abbreviations: *ff*, *fp*, *fg*, *l*, or *o*.

OBSERVATION GUIDE 20–1
Content, Source, and Target in Structuring Moves

Setting: ____________________
Number of participants: ____________ Characteristics of participants: ____________

If a teaching setting, type of class: ____________ Level of class: ____________
Subject: ____________________

Source and target / Subcategories of procedure	t/c	t/g	t/s	s/c	s/g	s/s
pa						
pi						
pu						
pr						
p other						
pa i						
pi i						
pu i						

OBSERVATION GUIDE 20–1 (*continued*)

Subcategories of procedure \ Source and target	t/c	t/g	t/s	s/c	s/g	s/s
pr i						
p other i						
pa r						
pi r						
pu r						
pr r						
p other r						

If you find that the subcategories of *procedure* I treat in this episode are never communicated, with all of the tallies in the *p other* box, the obvious alternative is to use the subcategories. If neither *study* nor *life* are ever found together with any subcategories of *procedure*, they can be added. If all the tallies are under the *t/c* box, by giving different directions to different groups in a class or to different individual students, some tallies will be able to be made in the *t/g* and *t/s* boxes. And at some point, if students teach, some tallies will be able to be made in the *s/c*, *s/g*, and *s/s* boxes. Using different structuring moves for different targets implies a recognition that different people in the same class have different needs and abilities and so might just profit from different and distinct structuring moves which contain different combination and types of content. Finally, if no tallies are made in the boxes next to the intermittent and review structuring moves, structuring moves could be broken up and provided before each separate activity in an event, rather than all at the beginning. Or the moves could be communicated at the end of an event rather than at the beginning. If you find some structuring moves occur both at the beginning and end of an event, the abbreviations for content could be circled to highlight them.

Observation Guide 20–1, like all observation guides, provides a framework for investigating frequencies and a summary of a series of alternatives. Guides are not meant to serve as precise instruments that cannot be altered to meet the needs of a particular setting or to highlight some of the elements from FOCUS that you discover are critical. For example, if you found that mediums played a particularly large part in a series of structuring moves that you were observing, you could tally with the abbreviations for the mediums, or substitute the medium abbreviations for the source and target abbreviations along the top of the guide. If you find that the use of the vernacular is more frequent than intermittent or reviewing structuring moves, you could add a *v* for vernacular in place of the *i* for intermittent or the *r* for review.

Whatever you finally decide to tally and whatever alternatives you try as a result, keep in mind that the goal of trying alternatives is to gain more control over what is done. Mastery of a number of alternatives enables the generation of some new alternatives, much as many pianists who have mastered the variables of the keyboard and the tone system are enabled by such mastery to improvise variations in the music they play. Though the keyboard variations might have started as deliberate steps, they soon become a part of a player's repertoire, if both player and audience enjoy them. In the same way, if students and a teacher consistently feel better when *life personal* is integrated with *procedure* in structuring moves in a deliberate way, it is likely that communications with two areas of content will become part of that teacher's repertoire.

V. DON'T WAIT—TRYING ALTERNATIVES WITHOUT "EVIDENCE" THAT THEY ARE BETTER

Ideally, you may want to introduce different alternatives only after thoroughly and systematically trying them and comparing the consequences. But such work is extremely time-consuming. I hope even some small positive consequences will occur to provide enough "evidence" to make you feel confident about continuing to try alternatives. For example, if you share personal feelings and information with students, thus integrating *life personal* and other areas of content in your structuring moves, at least one student will no doubt have a different feeling about you—and you, I am sure, will feel differently too. A pilot who does not know the passengers cannot add "That's my house over there" to his procedural statement "We'll be landing in three minutes" because of the distance between the passengers and the pilot. But one way to decrease distance between people is to communicate personal feelings and information about oneself.

Though "evidence" that integrating life, either private or public, with procedure may take a long time to become obvious, perhaps the knowledge that the comments coded *life* will probably serve as associations to help students remember some procedures or areas of study may encourage you to act. Walter Cronkite and Malcolm X and other people, places, or things you mention may not, of course, be known by students. But even without "evidence" you will be able to see that the use of such words provides a perfect opportunity for making the meaning of the items mentioned clear. And students can begin to see more and more that language, like all subjects, is more than just study. Students can begin to see that language, in particular, is a means to communicate life itself, "slices of experience." [Background 20–3]

If you have individual students teach other individual students or small groups games, crafts, skills, or a school subject other than the target language in the target language, or even a bit of the target language, I'm sure there will be at least *one* student who will get an entirely different view of learning languages as a result. Again, this represents only a small desired consequence, and for the one student who gets a new insight about language learning there might be another who gets confused. But both of these represent changes. And if you limit the amount of time in class for students to teach each other to around five to seven minutes every few days, I'm sure at least one pair will continue teaching and learning the skills, crafts, and games started in class outside of class.

Of course, I don't want to discourage exploring consequences more systematically so that "evidence" is found. But if you are planning to avoid generating and trying alternatives because you don't have time to explore the consequences thoroughly, don't. Let the small changes that are almost sure to result provide enough support for exploration. It is unlikely that there is any more "evidence" to support present practices than alternatives.

Once started, you can move into more systematic exploration of the consequences of the alternatives you try. For example, after integrating *life personal* and *study*, either of language or other subjects, ask students to write down, say, two to five statements you made during the week at the beginning and at the end of classes. If they write more communications you'd code *fp* than *l* or *o*, it suggests that communications which contain personal information and experiences are remembered longer.

If you had students structure by teaching other skills, ask how many students continued to teach and learn the skills outside class, and ask the students who taught to write down some of the sentences they communicated. See whether they are longer, more complex, and contain fewer errors than those they produce in response to questions you ask them in class.

Finally, remember to observe the students as the alternatives are tried. Do students look at you more attentively when you integrate content in structuring moves? Or do they gaze at the blackboard or fumble with their books as if they have heard it all before, acting like many plane passengers do during routine announcements?

If we were to wait for totally convincing evidence to support trying alternatives others suggested and generating our own alternatives, we would never try anything. I hope you will be encouraged to continue trying and generating alternatives even on the basis of seemingly slight positive changes that occur. For one thing, the alternatives will help you understand the rules that control much of our behavior better. For another thing, even if the observed consequences are very slight, remember there is evidence that the process of changing itself has been shown to produce growth and increased involvement, if not learning. [Background 20–4]

Of course, if you don't feel good about the suggestions here right now, don't try them. They'll be here for a long time, and you can always come back. If you think you'd feel better about trying them if a rationale was provided, read the background notes for this episode. If you wonder about the need for structuring moves, then the alternative to explore is the lack of structuring moves.

When I'm on a bus or train and am not sure when my stop is coming up, I listen intently for the announcement of the stops, and I get angry when the stops are not called out, when the driver or conductor takes it for granted that all the passengers know what stops are coming up next, or when the announcements are not even considered part of the driver's or conductor's job. But when I know the route and the place I'm getting off well, I like to look out the window, stare at passengers, or read. I don't even hear the structuring moves that contain the announcements of the stops. Or, if they are so loud that I can't help hearing them, they disturb me.

While "Next stop Broadway" or "We'll be landing in three minutes" may reassure us, when structuring moves are *not* communicated by the person in charge, I notice that people usually talk to each other more than when announcements are made. "What's the next stop?"; "How far are we from New York?"; "Do you think we'll be landing soon?"; "Boy, I don't see why they can't even make the effort to tell the passengers where we are" are some of the questions and remarks I've heard when the bus drivers and pilots do not structure.

Though much research indicates that getting others ready for learning increases learning, it is not only a fact that lack of structuring can lead to more peer-to-peer communication, but it is also possible that contrasting the presence and absence of structuring moves may produce more benefits that structuring all the time or structuring none of the time.

Having come full circle, I will now, as Falstaff said, "end my catechism."

Journal Entry

Having landed, and thus ended this episode, how do you feel about content in announcements by pilots? Or about lack of structuring moves by bus drivers or conductors? Do you feel the way I do, or differently?

BACKGROUND NOTES

20–1. Bellack found few student structuring moves in social studies classes—less than 2 percent. Fey found the same in mathematics classes. Gamta, Hines, and Rwakyaka also found very infrequent student structuring moves in the ESL classes they coded using the move as the unit of analysis.

20–2. David Ausubel has devoted a great deal of attention to "advance organizers"—introductions to the topics that are to be taught. Kounin has shown that setting rules for class management in structuring moves is related to less deviant behavior in classes.

20–3. The quote from Billows captures the spirit of his entire book on language teaching. It is filled with his feeling about what language is for, and the spirit he has can be exciting.

20–4. Mayo's classic study of workers and the increase in production when changes were made has come to be called the Hawthorne effect, after the name of the Western Electric plant at which he did the research.

EPISODE

21

What Mean *Work*?

I. BETTER TEST SCORES USUALLY—PURPOSE AND ORGANIZATION OF EPISODE

I heard "What mean *work*?" at a workshop on English teaching for nonnative English-speaking teachers. It was asked after the person conducting the workshop had claimed some suggestions he had just made for use in language classes would "work." After the teacher asked what *work* meant, the presenter went on to say that students who were in classes where his suggestions were followed would show gains in test scores greater than those who did not have the benefit of the treatment he was advocating.

I am writing this episode to suggest some alternative meanings and implications of the word *work* in response to the question "What mean *work*?" I present my response in three sections. In Section II, I present my interpretation of some results of tests other than scores, and I indicate some of the obvious incongruities between communications in tests and in nonteaching settings. In Section III, I show again how the idea that doing the opposite is an easy way to generate alternatives. Using this idea, student self-evaluations and student-made tests are two obvious alternatives to teacher-made and -evaluated tests. Another alternative from this idea is the substitution of observation of people for testing of people. In Section IV, I argue that any indication that something has worked has to be greeted coolly, whether we make the claim on the basis of results of the usual tests or on the basis of results of unusual tests or observation.

Though I compare and generate alternatives using FOCUS as a framework, I don't treat the characteristics of FOCUS. What I do do is present my personal prejudices toward many of the uses we put tests results to. So the content of this episode is, on most pages, what we would have to code *life*, subcategory *personal, fp*. I hope you will greet the content coded *fp* as critically as I urge you to greet the results of most tests and other measures.

II. INTERPRETATIONS AND INCONGRUITIES— WHAT TESTS DO BESIDES TEST; DIFFERENCES BETWEEN TESTS AND WHAT WE DO IN NONTEACHING SETTINGS

Interpretations—What Tests Do Besides Test

Good Scores Mean Good People—Things We Take for Granted about Tests

Tests—whether they measure driving, typing, swimming, botany, cooking or language—have a number of things in common: They are usually given only periodically; they focus the attention of those being tested on the skill or knowledge being tested (one's attention during a driving test is on the road, not on the scenery); they are often timed; and an attempt is made to present the results in the form of numbers of labels—an 80 or a B are more likely than long descriptions or sketches. This form of reporting the results gives them an aura of absoluteness, truth, accuracy, and finality like that of an accountant's ledger.

Tests are usually based on the assumption that they accurately sample total knowledge or ability. The typing rate for three minutes is considered representative of the possible rate during an entire day. A fifteen-minute drive is considered representative of a fifteen-hour drive. And a fifteen-minute oral interview is considered representative of the language one would use during ordinary discourse for weeks on end.

Results often are used to predict related behaviors as well. Accurate typing, for example, is sometimes taken as an index of neatness and efficiency. Attention to road signs, slow acceleration, and giving another driver the right of way are seen as indications of a safety-minded driver, as well as one who simply knows the traffic laws. A pleasant, relaxed attitude during an oral interview may not only contribute to the judgment that one's language is good, but also may suggest that one is a good person to be with.

Journal Entry

Can you remember the first test you were given in school? And your reactions to it and your score on it? Can you remember the first test you were given outside school and your reactions to it and your score on it? What things do you think you do extremely well that you have never been tested on? Do you think the fact that you have not been tested on these things decreases the excellence of your performance? In short, what is your reaction to things you can and cannot do well, and how does testing affect your reaction?

Count Backward from 1,000 in Nines—Tests as Shapers of Curriculum

No matter how many millions of dollars it costs to develop tests, and no matter how deeply you realize that they are only a means to sample a curriculum (the material being taught), those whose future will be determined by them will see them as the entire curriculum. Observe classes anywhere in the world that are evaluated on the basis of a test, and you will find that the content taught and types of questions being asked parallel the tests that are given. If you want students to read poetry in class, give a test on poetry that will determine their future. If you want students to be able to count backward from 1,000 in nines, design a test that requires this. If you want all students to learn the names of twenty trees, don't plan a new curriculum or buy a new text. All you have to do is ask all those taking the exit examination to include questions requiring the identification of twenty trees on the test.

This is not to say that because a student is tested, he or she will really learn, nor that he or she will necessarily remember what has been studied for the test. It is only to say that one rule of teaching is that, when tests are used to determine the future of students, the test, not the curriculum, the text, teachers, principals, determines what is to be taught. Try teaching conversation to classes who take written grammar tests to get into college, thus breaking a rule of teaching, and you will be stoned, either literally or figuratively. Talk to teachers about alternatives in their classes where tests are given that determine either the teachers' or students' future, and you will hear the comment, "We have to prepare the students for the tests; we can't change what we do." Observe classes that will be subjected to external examinations mandated by courts or educational authorities, and you will find a proportion of every semester devoted exclusively to preparation of the students to take the mandated tests. [Background 21–1]

On Your Own—Tests as Shapers of Values

During one's first test, a natural thing is to do what we do whenever we have a problem we can't figure out on our own outside a classroom or testing setting: we ask someone for help. If we are lost on a street or in a building, we ask for directions. If we start sinking while swimming, we shout for help. If we can't find a book or magazine in a library, we ask for assistance. If our car is stuck or our bicycle has a flat, we search for tools, if not people, to give us a hand. Many teachers encourage students of all ages to work together so each can learn and teach peers—except on tests! Then help is called cheating! Timed, individual tests may teach that individual effort is better than group effort at the same time as they determine the content and skills that are important for students to learn.

Of course, in addition to having the potential for shaping values such as individual versus group effort and competition, to name only two, tests also transmit the idea that measurement and quantification are powerful ways to determine the worth of individuals. After all, test scores are used to limit access to some kinds of instruction, institutions, and jobs, as well as to compare groups, in order to try to discover what "works."

Incongruities—Differences between Tests and What We Do in Nonteaching Settings

"Cat Got Your Tongue?"—Source of the Communication

Outside classrooms, most students communicate with their peers as well as with those who are older or in a superior role or position. Though they communicate with both strangers and friends, most tend to communicate more with friends than strangers, except with strangers they will never see again, such as people they sit next to on long bus or train rides.

In almost all tests, purchased or made, the teacher or unknown test maker in the role of a teacher is the source of the test items. In the case of published tests, the source of the items not only often lives in an entirely different environment from the students taking the test, but also might speak and write in a different dialect of the target language, have a different value system, and maybe a different way of thinking as well. Even when people from the same local area of a school are used for oral interviews or administration of tests, they are likely to be strangers to those taking the tests, and in some cases different in age from the students, if not in color, shape, size, and dress.

While all students who take a particular test may be equally distant from those who develop or administer a particular test or interview, if everyday experience can be used as a guide, the type of person asking a question and the role relationship between the two is bound to affect the answers. Not only do we tend to say less to a police officer than to a neighbor, but when we are asked questions by strangers, we are as likely to appear startled or puzzled as to respond. Though this occurs at all ages, it is particularly visible between children and adults. Surely you have seen children clam up when strangers ask their names. When the stranger reacts to the child's silence with "Cat got your tongue?" or "Shy, huh?" the original silence is not immediately changed into a string of utterances.

Journal Entry

One of the most frequent opening questions on oral tests is "What's your name?" This is often asked immediately after the tester has asked the person being tested, by name, to enter the testing area with a comment such as "Mr. Abe, please come in." In normal discourse, we usually say "What's your name?" only after we state ours. When we don't, we are often in the role of inquisitor. A police officer, for example, might ask a person suspected of some wrongdoing his or her name. What is your reaction when others ask your name without first giving their own? Have you observed the reactions of people in testing situations when they are asked their names? If so, what have their reactions been?

Don't Be Nosy—Move Types in Tests and Nonteaching Settings

The differences between the types of moves required in tests and outside classrooms are just as great as the differences between the sources of the communications. One rule of all tests is that the person taking the test is allowed to respond only to solicits—questions, commands, or requests the test or interviewer communicates. But outside teaching settings, each participant is required not only to respond, but to structure: set the stage for what is about to occur; solicit; make requests, ask questions or give commands; and react—make reflexive communications about what others have said or done that are not requested. People who do nothing but ask questions outside classes are often considered nosy, and are even viewed suspiciously by some. Suspicion can lead to devious responses and avoidance instead of extended, direct responses.

Logical but Limited—Mediums Required in Tests

Another rule of language tests is that they allow students to take in or produce only *linguistic* mediums—speech or writing. Sometimes solicits in tests contain *nonlinguistic visual* mediums—pictures or maps, for example. And students are allowed to use a *nonlinguistic visual* medium such as a circle to indicate the right choice in a response. But by and large, *linguistic* mediums form the core of the test or interview.

As logical as testing language with language is, the exclusive attention to *linguistic* mediums does not take place outside teaching settings. Except on a test, we show understanding of a joke or react to absurdity with laughter or a sardonic smile just as often as with words, if not more so. We are judged by the way we shake another's hand or bow during an introduction as well as by our pronunciation outside a testing setting. When we want to make ourselves clear, we often use our hands to mime the way a tool works or an animal moves as well as using words. Often, we omit words. Yet, it is rare to find an oral interview that considers *paralinguistic* mediums—gestures, eye contact, pauses, giggles—let alone rates their appropriateness or uses them as an index of knowledge or understanding. And in what language test can a student show an attribute of a word in means other than *linguistic*? While it is true that stating an attribute of a bird such as "has feathers" or "flies" or "whistles" is different from actually whistling like a bird, moving one's arms up and down like a bird, or drawing a beak or claws, using these mediums does show more about the person than silence. At the same time, they represent a normal way of communicating, except on most language tests.

Asking a dancer and choreographer to discuss themes in dance, a weaver to explain texture and color in cloth, a sprinter to describe movement and speed, and a musician to share feelings about improvisations is, on one level, absurd. These people all communicate some aspects of their lives through *nonlinguistic* and *paralinguistic* mediums. Limiting people in tests to *linguistic* mediums not only fails to provide us with information about what they know and can do, but implies that the only important mediums are *linguistic* ones. Our brain processes many mediums, and by testing only one, the talent and potential tapped may be severely limited. [Background 21–2]

Lack of Congruence—Ways Mediums Are Used

The variety of ways we take in or produce mediums is much more varied in everyday life than on most tests, just as the mediums themselves are more varied, as you realize if you've stopped to think about it for a moment or you've worked your way through episodes in this book on taking in and producing mediums—Episodes 3, 4, 10, and 14.

Though the way we take in and produce mediums in class is usually not as varied as the way we take in and produce mediums outside classes, there is an even greater lack of congruence between most tests and most in-class communications. One of the rules of classroom questions is that either-or and yes-no questions are to be avoided. They are the least frequently asked questions in most classrooms. Yet every multiple-choice test is nothing but a series of either-or questions! The only difference, other than the fact that questions on the test are written and those in class are spoken, is that the either-or questions on tests usually have three or four "ors" rather than one, though some research suggests that fewer are just as good. [Background 21–3]

Another lack of congruence between the way mediums are used in language classes and the way they are expected to be used on language tests concerns copying and repetition. In many language classrooms, one of the most frequent ways speech is used is to repeat what another has said. Yet on most language tests this task is not required, even though there is some evidence that the task is in fact an accurate gauge of certain abilities. [Background 21–4]

What Mean* Work*? or What* Mean *Work?—Content of Communications

The question "What mean *work*?" illustrates still another characteristic of communication that can be used to illustrate differences between communications on tests and interviews and outside teaching and testing settings. Except on most language tests and in some language classes, "What mean *work*?" would call forth more than lexical information. The content requested in the question goes way beyond the study of language alone. But on a test, or during parts of lessons when errors are treated, even the lexical information one might want to provide to give some meaning to *work* will probably be ignored, not to mention the other areas of content the word is related to. On a test, "What mean *work*?" is likely to serve as nothing more than an example of the omission of the function word *does*. It could then be followed by a direction to indicate whether it is right or wrong, or a direction such as "circle the letter next to the correct question." And in this case, the directions could be followed by questions such as these:

"What does mean *work*?" "What does *work* mean?" "What do *work* mean?" Questions are used as examples of grammar, lexis, and spelling in written tests, and pronunciation in oral tests, as often as they are used to request the communication of content that involves one's work or one's life—content in the category *life*. And they are used to contrast *life* with grammar and lexis—content in the category *study of language*.

The fact that the same words in the same order could be a comment about a job, if made by a person after observing, say, a person scaling a skyscraper to seal a gas leak on a windy day, would probably not be considered on a test. And if a person taking the test read "What mean *work*?" as "What mean work!", rather than being applauded for being able to show knowledge of different functions of language or the relationship between context and language use, that person would probably be penalized.

As I show in Episode 11, and as you know from getting meaning from messages every day, we get meaning from areas other than just grammar and lexis, and pronunciation and spelling. We also bring meaning to language from our personal experiences and from areas of study we pursue. As rich as our personal knowledge might be, and as learned as we may be in areas of study such as chemistry, weaving, or chess, and as much as we may be able to take in or produce communications in these areas of content in the target language, tests will not necessarily tap this knowledge.

Even if language tests attempt to tap experience and areas of study other than language, the problem of understanding the directions in the tests—content I call *procedure*—may prevent one from completing the test or responding correctly. Outside a testing setting, if we don't understand directions, we usually have the chance to ask for clarification. And if we begin to proceed the wrong way anyway, we are told to stop and are allowed to try again and again until we can follow the directions. But since the directions in a test are themselves often in the language being tested, or if in the person's own language, in a style different from ordinary discourse, the directions too are part of the test. They can cause misunderstanding that leads to the incorrect completion of individual items or whole sections. [Background 21–5]

Can't Beat Tables—Summary of Differences

To highlight the five characteristics of communication I just used to describe differences between communications required by students during tests and in nonteaching settings, I have developed Table 21–1. On the left, I've noted the characteristics of communications in most language tests and oral interview tests; on the right, I've noted the characteristics of communications in nonteaching settings.

If the subcategories of the characteristics were shown, as well as the major categories, the difference in range would be even broader than shown in the table. For example, the *c* in the Use column stands for *characterize*. It contains five subcategories: *cd* indicating items are the same or different; *ce* responding to yes-no or either-or questions or rating the correctness or truth of items; *cx* indicating the shape and size of items; *ci* communicating attributes of items; *l* attaching labels to items or categorizing items. On many tests, the only subcategory of *characterize* required is *ce*, making choices in multiple-choice items, which is simply a variation of responding to either-or questions.

The variety in content usually tested is just as narrow as the range of uses tested. Most language tests tend to concentrate on grammar, lexis, and pronunciation, or the mechanics of spelling and punctuation. But the meaning of communications in all settings depends on many aspects of language besides these few, as Episode 11 shows, and as you know from your own experience not only in communicating, but in trying

TABLE 21–1
Summary of Differences between Communications in Tests and Interviews and Nonteaching Settings*

TESTS AND INTERVIEWS					NONTEACHING SETTINGS				
Source/ Target	*Move Type*	*Medium*	*Use*	*Content*	*Source/ Target*	*Move Type*	*Medium*	*Use*	*Content*
t/s	res	la† + lv	a + c	sl	t/s + s/s + s/t	str + sol + res + rea	la + lv + na + nv + pa + pv	a + c + p + r + d + s	f + p + l + o

* *la* = linguistic aural: spoken words; *lv* = linguistic visual: written words; *na* = nonlinguistic aural: noise or music; *nv* = nonlinguistic visual: pictures or objects or lines; *pa* = paralinguistic aural: tone of voice, laughing, pauses and fillers—*huh*; *pv* = paralinguistic visual: body language and gestures.

a = attend: taking in mediums in activities such as silent reading, listening; *c* = characterize: communicating attributes of items; *p* = present: communicating information directly; *r* = relate: generalizations or inferences; *d* = reproduce: repeating or copying or changing mediums; *s* = set: models, examples, materials.

f = life: personal information and feelings or general knowledge; *p* = procedure: directions, regulations, and administrative information; *l* = study of language; *o* = study of other areas.

† In many tests, students neither have to write nor speak; they simply have to fill in blanks with lines or draw circles around their choices, thus communicating in a nonlinguistic medium. But the nonlinguistic medium makes sense only in relation to the spoken or written words they are used to indicate, so I do not note the medium separately.

to decide whether a particular item on an examination is testing grammar, lexis, or something else.

III. UPSIDE DOWN AND INSIDE OUT— TWO ALTERNATIVES TO USUAL TESTS

Doing the Opposite—Substituting Characteristics You Don't Find for Ones You Do Find

By having students produce test items, or even set up interviews for testing each other, we can replace the teacher or test developer as the source of the moves in tests. Though the publishers of printed tests and commercial oral interview schedules continue to include claims about the value of their instruments in the booklets they send with the tests, the number of published instruments continues to increase, implying that those on the market have flaws which the new ones are designed to overcome. How much better these published materials will be at helping test students is a question worth investigating. [Background 21–6]

To compare standards, students may want to take some commercial tests. But they can also compare standards by noting differences and similarities between test scores and self-ratings. Each student can be asked to rate his or her own language proficiency, as well as to make up test items for peers. Of course, a student score can be compared to a teacher score, or scores of other native speakers of the language of varying ages and backgrounds, thus enabling students to be the source and target of most combinations of source and target in column 1 of the FOCUS framework. [Background 21–7]

Because students have to give directions, form questions, and provide feedback in developing tests, the use of all move types is guaranteed when students themselves make tests, administer them, and score them. You can't make a test by communicating only responses! There are plenty of specific, practical, and easy-to-follow directions for constructing paper-and-pencil tests and oral interview schedules in a number of places. [Background 21–8]

Though the larger testing corporations spend millions of dollars to develop their instruments, student-constructed tests are not the least bit expensive. Printing and distribution costs are nil. And the money corporations spend to hire test writers and buy computer time is unnecessary. The students can do item analyses and make other computations by hand or with pocket calculators.

Student-made tests will not assure that mediums, uses, and areas of content communicated in nonteaching settings will be tested. If students follow the rules they have been exposed to, they are likely to test only grammar, lexis, and pronunciation. And they will probably require only linguistic mediums in the responses. But at least in making up the tests they will have to communicate *procedure*. And as they argue about distractors in multiple-choice tests, some will discover that other areas of content affect meaning in addition to the big three usually tested. At any rate, no law says that to be congruent with nonteaching setting communications, a test has to follow the preconceptions about communication contained in FOCUS. In making up tests, though, so many of the usual rules will be turned upside down and inside out that some wider range of mediums, uses, and areas of content are likely to be tested.

Doing the Opposite—Substituting Observation for Testing

The opposite of testing, whether done with commercial tests or interviews or those made by teachers or students, is one of the themes of this book: observing. The question the non-native-English-speaking teacher asked about the claims made at the workshop where I got the question "What mean *work*?" symbolizes the alternative. How many test items would need to be written to discover that in asking a question about the meaning of a concept, a particular teacher had mastered the pronunciation, stylistic, and functional aspects of a bit of language, to name a few areas of language content the teacher had mastered, but had not mastered the use of one function word in a particular question?

During the five to twenty minutes needed to develop one multiple-choice item—without pretesting it—five to twenty student communications can be written on note cards. If the communications are made during a break by students to each other, or are made as students are engaged in the actual solution of a real problem, such as the putting together of a jigsaw puzzle, or in a conversation of their own, the communications are likely to be more similar to those they ordinarily make than responses to questions in tests. They may be less inhibited as well, and as a result a more valid picture of capability may result.

You no doubt have seen a student who rarely responds to a teacher in class talking away with a friend during a joint project. And during breaks, after class, and in other settings, some who speak only laboriously in class and communicate only silence during tests cannot be stopped from talking. Some children who won't say their names when asked by an adult will blurt them out to peers and even add the names of their brothers and sisters and other friends. Sometimes, they are as exuberant with peers as they are reticent with those in the role of teacher in a superior position.

If you and those you work with already employ observation as an alternative to testing, you realize that getting samples of student communications both during language class, in classes in other areas of study, and in nonteaching settings is not as difficult as it might at first appear. What those who observe usually do is to take the money used to buy tests and pay monitors and scorers and use it to buy tape recorders, and then to pay people to transcribe tapes or observe and write down live exchanges in a range of settings.

One advantage of noting communications live as they occur is that mediums other than those you can hear on a tape can more easily be noted. Mediums other than those heard on a tape can be noted even when only a tape recording is available because the words often refer to other mediums. "It smells"; "It's very long," and comments like that make sense only in relationship to the mediums they refer to. But noting what people refer to, materials they read and write, is easier during live observation than from recordings.

Casual observations by teachers and students of each other before and after language classes, especially if they are made in a playground or lounge, can provide samples as representative as tests, assuming that the students are in a place where the target language is used. When combined with visits to other classes, including art, physical education, and music, such observations will show what students communicate in either the target language or their own language, and also what they communicate in other mediums. Perhaps observing students use a range of mediums outside the language class will provide some impetus for using more mediums in the language class.

As students record and transcribe or take notes of communications in language classes, other classes, and nonteaching settings, they not only provide teachers with an index of the types of communications mastered, but also themselves see what they have mastered and what they have not mastered. And as we use observation and notation of student communications in a range of settings to aid us in the discovery of evidence of what works, we may see more clearly what students can and cannot do. In addition, we may decrease the power of tests to shape curriculum and teach values as well. And of course we decrease the problem of the lack of congruence between characteristics of communications in tests and in other communications, both in teaching and in nonteaching settings.

A Similarity and an Opposite in Opposites—Sampling and Relaxing

I used the word *decrease* very deliberately in discussing congruence because I realize that what we observe people do may be incongruent with what people need to do on a job or in some setting we do not see them in. In fact, observations are limited in the degree to which they are congruent with a person's need in a way similar to the way tests are limited. An observation of language in use is a sample, just as any test is a sample of the entire range of language a person possesses. But we have to keep two things in mind: First, just as a small vial of blood usually shows the composition of the many pints of blood in our bodies, so a six-minute test or observation may result in an accurate index of a person's entire language behavior; second, just as a doctor usually can get an accurate measure of one organ by looking at another, as when a jaundiced eye is used as a symptom of liver disease, so a test or observation that samples a conversation about cars may provide an index of a person's ability to converse in general. And a look at how a person reads silently and in other ways attends may provide some index of abilities to speak and write.

Though similar because both are only samples, tests and observations are opposite when it comes to pressure. Observations can probably provide samples produced under less pressure than tests can. While it is common knowledge that pressure, tension, fear, and time constraints force our bodies to produce chemicals to spur us on and provide added energy we need during a crisis, it is also common knowledge that during a competition many athletes pull muscles that they do not pull during practice, many hunters shoot other hunters they mistake for animals when they get excited, and a large number of us, when nervous, drop keys or larger objects, or some of the words we use to communicate.

Some of those who make a living interviewing people realize the effects of pressure and try to substitute relaxation for it. I remember reading one columnist's method of interviewing. This particular columnist would invite the person he wanted to interview out to lunch. During the meal, the interviewer pretty much let the conversation flow naturally, answering questions as well as asking them, and reacting and listening to the reactions of his lunch guest. As the lunch was about to end, the guest invariably asked when the interview was going to start and where it was going to be held. To these queries, the columnist replied: "It's over!" He believed that true samples of behavior can be better taken in a relaxed atmosphere than one in which a person is under some kind of pressure. [Background 21–9]

Journal Entry

In observing oral interview tests, I have noted that nine times out of ten the people being tested keep their hands at their sides or held together in their laps. The body is usually held very erect, much as it is during a classroom recitation. When pictures are used, the person often looks at the pictures while talking rather than at the person doing the testing. What have you noticed about the body language of people during test interviews? What does the body language suggest about the test?

Number Count—Evaluating Opposites

Whether students, teachers, or commercial test makers make the tests, numbers still count. In discrete item tests, the number right and wrong needs to be noted. In interviews or essays given to evaluate specific areas of content, scores for grammar, organization, interest, spelling, or whatever have to be assigned. If a cloze passage and dictations are used as tests, counting errors cannot be avoided.

If observations are substituted for tests, numbers still count. To evaluate communications observed, the number of errors made can be counted just the same way incorrect answers on tests are counted. To show the proportion of correct to incorrect communications, the number of incorrect ones can be written above the number of correct ones, as when scoring a test. If there are five incorrect communications out of fifty, the ratio is one over ten or 1/10, for example.

The problem with such counting is it suggests that each incorrect communication contains only one error. The real frequency of errors can be distorted. Another way to note error frequencies is to note those linguistic communications with one error or more than one error out of a total number of communications.

The frequency of incorrect linguistic communications can be more informative if the type of each error is noted. A forty-sentence composition with twenty spelling errors, one incorrect verb form, and one missed preposition reveals a very different profile from a forty-sentence composition with twenty verb-form errors, one spelling error, and one central organizational problem. Yet the frequency of errors in both cases is 22/40. [Background 21–10]

In addition to noting the frequency and type of errors, it is possible to note whether the information in the communications is true and whether the information in them is communicated or not. Since the teacher's "What mean *work*?" has elicited a response, we can say that it communicated. Had the teacher said "What does *work* mean?" and not elicited a response, it would be fair to conclude that, though the question was correct in form, it failed in its purpose.

I have designed Observation Guide 21–1 to make it easier to tally the frequency and type of language errors in relationship to the truth and effectiveness of the content communicated. As you can see, by dividing the columns under true and untrue into four, under the headings *str, sol, res,* and *rea*, I have made it possible to show the relationships among these four purposes of communications and error rate. Finally, by providing three lines for tallying each person's communications, one for communications of one to three words, one for those four to seven words in length, and one for those of more than eight words, the guide enables you to see relationships among purpose, frequency of error, and complexity. To show the type of error, you can tally with the abbreviations for the subcategories of *study of language* described in detail in Episode 11. Should you want to show the number of errors in each communication, you could tally with numbers rather than abbreviations for the subcategories of *study of language*, a 3 indicating three errors in a communication, for example.

As with all guides, you will need more space than that provided on the guide itself. I simply want to show one way communications can be tallied and utlimately compared. Noting the number of errors and correct communications for the same individuals in a class and in another setting, and noting the length of the communications in both settings, plus the proportion of different move types, will show which kinds of settings reveal information that more closely resembles the needs of individuals.

Though Observation Guide 21–1 is designed in part to show what is wrong with communications, it is important to remember that evaluation requires an indication of what a person can do as well as what a person cannot do. The columns in the guide for tallying communications that are true and communicate information as well and the use of a plus mark or other sign for noting correct communications are two things that can be done to show what students can do along with what they cannot do.

Other measures are possible as well. The number of long words—three or more syllables—that are used can be counted and a ratio formed between long words and the total number of words spoken or written. The number of clauses can be counted, as can the number of different tenses and patterns. In fact, the type of readability formula used to determine complexity can be used with observed communications just as they can be used with reading material. If people self-correct when they speak or are able to edit their written work so the number of errors is decreased, this too is an indication of competence in the language.

While test results and tallies lend themselves to the manipulation of numerical information—the finding of averages, means, and ratios and the computing of statis-

OBSERVATION GUIDE 21–1
Tallying Correct and Incorrect Communications

Setting: ______
If class, level and type: ______ Number of participants: ______
Relationships between participants: ______
Type of activities going on: ______

Effect and purpose of communications / Source and length of communications		Information was true; information was communicated				Information was untrue; information was communicated			
		str	sol	res	rea	str	sol	res	rea
individual$_1$	1–3								
	4–7								
	8–n								
individual$_2$	1–3								
	4–7								
	8–n								
individual$_3$	1–3								
	4–7								
	8–n								
individual$_4$	1–3								
	4–7								
	8–n								
individual$_n$	1–3								
	4–7								
	8–n								

tical comparisons—they should not overshadow the importance of prose descriptions of student communications. A case study of prose containing examples of correct and incorrect communications made in different settings and examples of test items missed provides data as valuable as many sets of numbers. One advantage of writing communications on note cards while observing is that the information can be used to provide data for case studies. Students can help in noting communications on note cards, and they will be able to begin their own language diaries as a result. These would, of course, provide very useful information for teacher-, or student-produced case studies. [Background 21–11]

In addition to comparing test results and tallies with case studies, another alternative is to compare them with global judgments that you or others make. Often the first step in evaluating oral interviews is to make a global evaluation. Some editors who select material for publication often start their ratings this way. Then, after they have judged the overall quality, they go through the material again, seeking those elements that seem to support their overall evaluation. By separating all the note cards containing student communications that you consider great and terrible, and then seeing the features of the communications on the cards in each group, you will probably be better able to make the criteria for your global evaluations explicit. The communications on the cards rated *great* will help you see how much students can do, and those on the cards rated *terrible* can show what students need to work at. [Background 21–12]

Journal Entry

I once saw a newspaper cartoon by Bob Thaves which showed two architects in Renaissan[illegible]ress. They were both standing at an angle. One is shown reading a letter to [illegible] these words: "Those crazy people in Pisa claim there's somethi[illegible] we designed for them!" How often have you felt that tes[illegible] world the way another person wanted you to? [illegible] think that tests simply force them [illegible]?

Do [illegible] through observ[illegible] she wishes, and [illegible]

IV. G[illegible]INE

Stro[illegible]

As w[illegible], or tests, making eith[illegible]aning of the word *work* [illegible]kes it clearer that what we choos[illegible]lues. When we see two students hug each o[illegible]zle and say "We do good job" in place of "We did a goo[illegible] in the comment and ignore the intensity and joy of the embrace, [illegible]he completion of the jigsaw puzzle, we are saying a communication in one [illegible]s more valuable than another. Of course, if we note the hug and the puzzle and ignore the comments, we do the same thing.

Some of the values we have can be seen by looking at what we test in comparison with what students do or what issues are of concern to them. One issue in many cities around the world, for example, is racial and class conflict. By giving math tests and reading tests to students affected by these issues and not in any way attempting to describe the personal values of students, their sense of justice, self-worth, ability to accept differences or attitudes toward other groups, it is possible to conclude that we value skill in two subjects rather than personal qualities. If we compare the amount of time many students around the world watch television or listen to radios or tapes with the amount of time they read, and see that we test a skill they use less and ignore skills they use more, we realize that much of what we choose to test is a reflection of the values we hold rather than the needs of those being tested. [Background 21–13]

That our values affect, if not control, what we evaluate is not in any way abnormal. Every group evaluates would-be entrants to the group on the basis of the values of the group. Revolutions are on one level attempts to evaluate individuals on the basis of different values. In *Things Fall Apart*, a novel about changing values in a part of Nigeria, the opening scenes show the hero, Okonkwo, winning a wrestling match, being hailed for his strength and shrewdness, and lamenting the weakness of his father, who was known as a flute player rather than a champion or warrior. The middle scenes show people who learn to speak, write, and read English beginning to assume the power that Okonkwo and his peers had traditionally held partly on the basis of their strength, shrewdness, and courage. The closing scenes report Okonkwo's suicide and the establishment of schools in which ability to read, write, and speak English was valued over physical prowess and courage, symbolized by Okonkwo. [Background 21–14]

Because it is natural that values affect, if not control, what we evaluate that doesn't mean we should stop evaluating. Though there is no way to be value-free, there are ways to compensate for the fact that our evaluations are value-laden. One way is not to equate incorrect or correct communications with good or bad, but simply consider both correct and incorrect communications as bits of information. The words we usually use in reporting results of evaluations suggest we attach a positive value to communications without error and a negative value to those with errors. Nine times out of ten, we state the positive results first. Then we say "but" and add the negative results. That we note errors in speech because we value correct speech should in no way mean that those who do not speak correctly are in any way inferior to those who speak correctly, according to our standards. Nor does it mean that those who speak correctly are superior as people, any more than Okonkwo was better than his father because he was physically strong and his father was not.

Journal Entry

The idea that the quality of one performance is related to the quality of another is widespread and not at all limited to evaluation in school tests or observations. A comment like "I always order lasagna first in an Italian restaurant—if it tastes good, it means everything else will be good" reflects both a value and the belief that one good dish is related to many other facets of restaurant quality.

What are some of the litmus tests you use to judge quality that reflect your values? On what evidence do you base your comments? And on what basis do you relate the quality of one thing to the quality of another?

Ignoring the Obvious—Influence of Personality and Learning Style on Evaluation

As we test and observe, we have to realize that many of the things both we and our students do in life—caring for siblings, reacting to our environment, dancing, eating, playing, working with tools, engaging in sports activities, traveling with peers and parents, to name a few—we not only fail to evaluate, but hardly even take into account in making our evaluations. Each of the activities we engage in every day reflects our personality as well as our language skill.

On one level, evaluating language is more clear-cut than evaluating other skills and areas of knowledge. So information we share might seem to have the potential for great accuracy. If a person chooses "Good morning" on a test as a choice after "greeting used before noon," rather than "Good evening," you know the person can recognize two separate greetings and associate one with the meaning. Noting that a nonnative speaker asked "What mean *work*?" shows us the person can ask a question in English. We also know that in one setting, the teacher said the question differently from the way most native speakers of English would have.

But our advantage in being able to test and observe the language people use can be a disadvantage too, for it can easily obscure other variables. If a person does not ask a question, it may be because he or she is not confused rather than that he or she does not know how to ask a question. It may be that he or she asks questions only of peers, or when in the role of a person in charge. He or she may discover information through observation, or the reactions of others, rather than through questions. To limit the meaning of *work* only to a description of the frequency and types of communications made on tests or in a range of settings suggests that learning is related only to teaching rather than to teaching plus other variables, such as the students' personality characteristics and methods of processing information.

This is not to say that our task as language teachers is to try to develop ways to describe personalities and the way people's minds work. Nor is it to say that our task is to teach people we consider shy to be aggressive and those who need to visualize things not to. It is only to point out that the word *work* cannot be completely defined either on the basis of results of tests designed to measure the areas of study we teach, or on the basis of results of descriptions of characteristics of communications in a range of settings. Personality factors too affect what works. While as teachers we are neither trained to alter personalities nor to describe them, some instruments are available that can, if nothing else, point out different dimensions of personality. By using an instrument designed to provide descriptive information about attitudes and feelings, another meaning of the word *work* is revealed. By comparing scores of different groups distinguished from each other by personality measures, you may discover that students who are comfortable with ambiguity do well without rules, and those who need closure do not, for example. Many large studies that have tried to determine what works have failed to include the dimension of personality in the definition of *work*. The scores of students who had one type of class are compared with the scores of students who had another type of class without any attention to type of personality or learning style, which might affect the scores of students in all classes. [Background 21–15]

Even if comparisons of the scores of groups of students classified on the basis of personality measures and observation do not reveal startling differences as the result of distinct treatments, at least we are reminded again of the obvious fact that to find the meaning of *work*, we cannot depend on any one measure or type of measure given only once or twice. As in the determination of the worth of a medical treatment, a new farming method, or the effect of an afternoon nap on one's teaching, multiple means designed to describe the areas taught and the feelings of the subjects, plus observations of multiple characteristics of communications in a range of settings are a fairer definition of *work* than a hunch or a score on one measure or one observation at only one time. As obvious as this conclusion is, the rule in many countries of the world is to depend on the administration of one examination to determine the future of students. [Background 21–16]

Journal Entry

Though moving from class to class and achieving a particular level is a common goal, some people seem to go on and on and yet not make the grade they obviously have the ability to. One interpretation of this lack of achievement is that some people fear success. By completing a class and achieving a goal, an individual is faced with the task of setting a new goal and starting all over again. Have you ever put off completion of something or done less well than you probably could have because you feared success? Have any students you have worked with acted as if they too seemed afraid to succeed?

Another type of person always does well, but never does well enough to be satisfied. A 99.9 on a test for such a person is a defeat. Perfection seems to be sought after in a way that makes satisfaction almost impossible. Have you experienced such a person? How did the person cope with the realistic demands of daily life? Did this striving for 100 percent on everything diminish over time or increase?

Doing the Right Thing—Ethics of Testing and Observing

After tests are scored, there is always the question of who is entitled to see the results. If you enter public races, the times are public. How well you do in a spelling bee open to the public or what answers you give on a quiz show on television cannot be hidden. These are activities that we take part in of our own free will, knowing full well that anyone can see the results of what we do. But even if we get permission from students or their parents to test them and describe communications they make in order to try to discover what works, it does not mean that the students are agreeing to public disclosure. And in the case of examinations given for placement and eligibility, students or parents are not only not asked for permission before they are tested or their communications described, but they are often mandated to take tests as a condition of instruction. Without tests, admission and exit are often both impossible. Even if scores are not given to anyone, when a student is placed in one class rather than another, required to take a class again or not even admitted, the results of the scores are just as public as times in a public race. The only alternative that will guarantee that scores will not be shared or made public is to stop all testing of the type used to support the caste system that education is based on in most institutions around the world—an unlikely event. The reason alternatives which suggest that the only thing that has to be done to protect the privacy of students' test results is to keep them confidential are inadequate is that even if the scores themselves are kept confidential, the actions based on them can be observed. And even if peers or parents never see scores, they are frequently passed from one "authority" to another as students move from one educational institution to another.

In the case of observations, we face two questions. We have to determine who should see the data observed, and we have to determine whether the collection of the communications themselves is right. Writing communications on note cards or transcribing tapes of conversations is an invasion of privacy. That our concern is with the areas of the *study of language* communicated cannot prevent us from hearing the personal information communicated. But before sharing communications, privacy can be protected by the deletion of personal names, references to people, things that indicate the souce of communications or that would embarrass any individuals, and the identity of the speakers. By having students transcribe their own communications, and having them delete the items that identify people or places they are talking about, privacy can be protected even more.

The same care that is needed to preserve the privacy of individuals is needed in reporting the results of what we do, either to colleagues or to those we have tested or observed. Even such a seemingly simple thing as reporting differences between means of test scores or tallies observed made at two or more points of instruction is ultimately an ethical question, because reporting the differences implies that the differences are the result of intervention. Yet there is evidence that scores increase a certain amount over time just as a result of the passage of time itself. To report that those who started with low scores raised them a great deal more than those who started with high scores implies that the intervention was even more powerful. But again, there is evidence that it is normal for low scores to increase a great deal more than high scores. And as even casual attention to athletic records indicates, many more athletes move from average to above-average times than from above-average to record times. [Background 21–17]

In the matter of reporting more sophisticated measures than individual scores or group means, such as measures designed to show the statistical significance between means or the statistical relationships between different types of scores, the same ethical issue exists. It is almost impossible to find results of research in which such statistical terms are explained in specific, nontechnical terms or in which the rationale for the use of one statistical measure rather than another is presented. The term *statistical significance* is a particular problem because the words themselves connote a kind of proof. Yet when the difference between means is statistically significant, it means only that the difference between the means in a particular case is unlikely to have been caused by chance. Practical significance—whether the differences observed are worth the effort expended in the treatment being investigated and whether the differences observed are important and mean anything in practical terms—is much more critical yet is hardly ever even mentioned, much less discussed. To find that mean scores of students with five hundred hours of instruction are different enough to show statistical significance from mean scores of students with one hundred hours of instruction does not mean that five hundred hours is better than one hundred hours and that even if the extra instruction costs five times more, it should be given. These are matters requiring judgments about practical significance, a different matter from statistical significance. [Background 21–18]

Even if in our role as teacher we have little need to report anything more than what we have seen an individual student do, and we are able to avoid averages and more complex statistical measures in sharing results with students, one of the rules seems to require that inferences about the meaning of scores or tallies be given. The questions "What does it mean?" or "What do these figures show?" are often heard after any scores or tallies are given, whether at the doctor's office, tax bureau, executive suite, or in a conference with a parent or student. To break this rule, one alternative is to say that the results have no meaning beyond what they have on the surface. If a student said "Fine, thank you" in response to "How do you do?" a statement such as "seems to have trouble with introductions" moves beyond the data in the same way that saying "movies are better than ever because profits are higher" moves beyond data about profits. High profits may or may not be related to the quality of movies, just as one unrelated greeting may or may not be related to introductions. High profits are high profits, and saying "Fine" in place of "How do you do?" is saying "Fine" in place of "How do you do?"—period. Tests and observations can help us see what we need to teach. But it is important to realize at all times that the value of those we teach is neither diminished by what they don't know and can't do, nor increased by what they know and can do! Speaking correctly, like playing baseball well, need not be equated with being good, successful people. As soon as playing first flute or knowing a word begins to mean a person is a leader, a person qualified to discuss marriage and the economy and offer sound advice on many topics, we are in trouble. Part of the ethics of testing and observation is avoiding the making of inferences about the results.

Another part of the ethics of testing and observation is to keep constantly in mind that the sense of precision implied by scores on admission, placement, final, and eligibility examinations is greater than the accuracy the scores actually possess. This fact must make us fight any unethical requirements such as ones that mandate decisions to be made on the basis of one measure taken at only one time. Such a requirement fails to take into account the fact that people are complex and that numbers fail to reflect this complexity.

A final danger we must strive to overcome is treating people differently as a result of scores they have made on tests. This does not mean that we should not provide different types of work for different people, but it does mean that, in providing different tasks and feedback, we must not classify people into categories of "can learn" or "can't learn." There is evidence that in fact we do treat students very differently as a result of test scores they have made, expecting a great deal less from those who score low. By having others score tests and report results, we can perhaps avoid classifying people. [Background 21–19]

A Funny Sketch—Tapping Potential

No matter how long our test is nor how long we observe, no matter how much proof can be offered that a short interview or a short test is as representative of what a person can do as long interviews or tests, we still tap only one area of the brain. The tests that attempt to discover mental operations tap another area, but they are rarely used. Even when both types are used, unless personality measures are used as well, the psyche is ignored. With complete batteries of test instruments, other variables, such as persistence in spite of hardship, moral code in the face of temptation, interest level in the face of peer pressure, patience in adversity, and "boiling point" under stress, to name a few, are still unaccounted for. While in each decision we make about the fate of others on the basis of tests or observations we may not explicitly state that these and other traits do not count, determining people's fate without attention to these is just as clear as an explicit statement, and perhaps even more powerful in its impact. The areas we test, like the areas in a budget that receive the largest allotments, are those that begin to take on importance.

Looking at only one measure can be as catastrophic as looking only at the bottom line in the financial report of a business. If we look only at the quarterly or yearly profits and ignore the effects of plant closings on communities, destruction of the environment, degradation of workers and managers, to name a few effects that can result from only looking at profits, we invite disaster. And we invite disaster in the same way if we look at the results of only one test score to determine a person's future. No one score can reflect the complexity of an individual, any more than a number in an accountant's ledger can reflect the complexity of a business enterprise.

In both learning and business, and indeed anything we do, we need our hearts and bodies as well as our heads, and we need all parts of our heads. No one measure can describe all these facets. Consider the sketch in Figure 21–1. Note the small dot on the person's head. I have used the dot to symbolize what one test or observation might

Figure 21–1 A Funny Sketch

be able to get at. If we believe that a person's personality affects learning—represented by the heart in the illustration; and if we believe the way a person processes information affects learning—the part of the head I have shaded in; and if we believe the information a person has stored in his or her head affects learning—the part of the head I have left blank; and if we believe that the way a person uses his or her body affects learning, as when we learn how to hit a nail by handling a hammer or when we speak and make facial expressions at the same time, then the requirement that one measure should be used to determine a great deal seems absurd.

Journal Entry

A teacher presentation at a conference or even a regular lesson observed by a supervisor or other outsider is comparable in some ways to a one-shot test that determines one's future. As in an exit examination of placement test, one chance is given to show how well we can do something. Before such presentations or observations, one is often asked, "Are you nervous?" And after such presentations or observations, one is often asked, "How did it go?"

Do you think your performances in these situations are the same as everyday performances? How do you feel before they take place, while they are taking place, and when they are over? When others ask questions about them, is it hard to be completely honest?

Because our means for describing what we know, understand, and can do are limited to certain areas and are not perfect does not mean that we need to stop trying to find ways to describe what *works*, or should stop placing students, grading them, or determining whether they should move on or not. Every discovery of what students cannot do is an indication of potential that has not yet been tapped. And every indication that students are able to do each task we set is an indication that our expectations of them are too low. One advantage of observing students in a range of settings is that as students communicate in different ways—discussing an issue with gusto in their own language or dialect, painting a door frame without getting a drop on the adjoining wall, driving nails with precision, caring for a pet with great sensitivity—we are reminded of their potential. We can also see the standards they have established in areas not often covered by tests. By seeing how many things they do and the high standards they try to meet, our expectations are raised.

One invidious thing about some examinations is the low requirements they have. Examinations that attempt to test "minimum competence" are examples. Low requirements suggest low expectations; high requirements suggest high expectations. Requiring a lot is another way of saying we expect people are able to do well and we respect their potential.

One of the tragedies of our time is that we do so often associate excellence only with unusual accomplishments. Excellence can be achieved in any task. To have a gas station attendant not fill the tank so gas spills out as one drives away is excellence at one level, in my value system. To keep doors oiled so the hinges don't squeak is another. So is to cultivate a garden and keep it free of weeds. So is a prompt, accurate, friendly reply to an inquiry at a store or office. And a note that expresses sincere thanks in correct form written in the target language can represent excellence too if it is written by a beginning student. From an advanced student, such a note would be normal and expected. A fine essay would be necessary to show excellence at an advanced level. Though I dislike seeing graffiti, some are much more skillfully drawn than others. Those who draw graffiti obviously have their standards of excellence in each graffito.

Because I believe excellence is possible in everyday things we do, no matter how small, as well as in grand achievements usually associated with excellence, such as Olympic medals and Nobel prizes, I consider it unfortunate that the usual rule is to recognize excellence only on a grand scale and in one or two dimensions of a person's life. Of course, language skill is critical for all areas of study, so it would seem logical to demand excellent command of the language used in a place where one is going to study. But it is possible that at least some who are excellent in hundreds of other things they do, and whose language potential has not been tapped, will be denied space because others who are less excellent in hundreds of little ways, but whose language potential has been tapped, seem more suitable.

Journal Entry

One alternative to selecting students on the basis of scores on language tests, especially when only one place exists for every hundred candidates, is to select on the basis of chance. Mean scores on language tests, or any other tests, may be lower, but if we could measure a host of other personal qualities, areas of knowledge, and skills, we would probably find that in some areas group means were higher and that in most groups there are similar numbers of instances of excellence.

What do you think of this suggestion? How do you think it would affect learning? Would it mean that institutions which traditionally accept only the "cream" would have to work harder to produce results with the people who came to them? Would it mean that the kind of mixing of different groups that various court mandates tried to achieve in the United States would occur as a matter of course? Would standards ultimately be lowered, or would groups excluded in the past achieve as much as others had?

Consequences—Conclusion

By urging that we remember we can all be excellent in many different ways, I am not arguing against the gatekeeping function of tests. Some people *are* better piano players. All groups set standards for entry. Not all kids can meet the standards set by a gang of thieves or a team of basketball players, any more than all kids can be equally fluent in reading, writing, speaking, or listening to a language. I am not arguing against the gatekeeping function of tests or observations as much as trying to bring to the surface these simple but often ignored facts:

1. All measures are approximate.

2. Transferring information from results of one measure to judgments about other abilities or talents is invidious.
3. Tests or observations we make reflect the values we hold, and anything we fail to test or observe becomes by implication unimportant and lacking in value.
4. All attempts to keep up standards tend to develop castes and keep divisions between people as well as show what some can do better than others.
5. Single measures used to determine the superiority of one method or practice over another are invalid if we believe that most practices have multiple effects.

A classic example of the problem with using one measure to determine the best thing to do is provided by the joke in which a doctor says that the operation was a success, but the patient died. Using one test score to determine what works and ignoring student attitudes toward using the target language or subject being taught, or feelings students have about continuing to learn on their own, or amount of time students use the material learned, and other consequences, fails to prove anything. Every move has multiple consequences, and tests are limited in helping us compare them all. Claims of the superiority of one method usually are made on a single measure or only a few measures. By mentioning consequences throughout this book, I have tried to reflect the complexity of comparing the value of different moves we make.

As language teachers, we are paid to develop language and to focus attention on language with measures we may make. But if we only pay attention to excellence in the performance of tasks requiring the target language or dialect, and ignore talents in the student's own language or dialect, or talents not clearly related to language, we will fail to realize that a communication such as "What mean *work*?" does a great deal more than reveal the absence of a function word and a different word order in one person's speech!

BACKGROUND NOTES

21–1. Heaton calls the fact that people spend all their time preparing for tests the "backlash effect." In New York City, many schools spend at least one day per week for the entire school year going over test items. In Nigeria and Somalia, during the last few months before the examinations all class time was devoted to test practice. When we remember that the idea of a test is to sample what people have been doing, it seems that emphasis on preparation for tests defeats the entire purpose of sampling.

21–2. Olson argues that even when we test people with objects we want them to manipulate or comment on, our claims for results are distorted by our view of the world as determined by print.

21–3. In Table 4–5, p. 95, I show that in one tally of questions I asked teachers to make up, there are more than twice as many question-word questions as yes-no questions. In fact, in tallies in classes I find even fewer yes-no questions. The idea that more distractors in multiple-choice tests make a better test has been questioned by Blatchford, who found that two choices—in effect a variation on a yes-no question, or more accurately an either-or question—produced results not too different from items with more choices.

21–4. Elicited imitation has been used in second language research by, among others, Naiman, in 1974.

21–5. Thorndike and Hagen have warned about directions and other problems with tests in their comprehensive book on measurement and evaluation. Also keep in mind that to some, rules for taking tests and directions on a test are symbols of bureaucracy, and they are resented no doubt because of this symbolic meaning.

21–6. The national PTA in the United States has put out a booklet for parents by Ryan that presents an evaluation of standardized testing in the United States. Grommon has reviewed selected published tests in English for native speakers, and Spolsky has done the same thing for some major ESL tests (1979). Stephen Jay Gould has presented a critical review of the whole tradition of standardized testing. His book has the additional theme that our preconceived notions prevent us from seeing objectively even when we use methods considered to be objective.

21–7. One can ask students to rate on a five-point scale their ability to read, listen, speak, and write in a particular language. This format is printed on many job application forms for teachers of ESL and on some applications for admission to teacher preparation programs. One can make much more specific questions and ask people to rate on a five-point scale their ability to order a meal, bargain in a market, discuss an overcharge in rent, write a complaint to a store, listen to a song on the radio, read directions on a food package, and so on.

21–8. Cohen and Heaton present step-by-step directions for making multiple-choice tests and other regular test-type items. Oller presents steps for making a cloze test.

21–9. I cut out an article in which Sydney J. Harris wrote about the problems of pressure in 1964. His column was called "Strictly Personal," and the title of the one I saved was "School exams fail to pass test." He also spoke against standardized measures given once, upon which so much depends. Gallwey, of course, would agree that pressure distorts ability to perform and probably would urge that tests be used to help describe rather than judge. Now they are used almost exclusively for judging—doing well means one is good, and doing poorly means one is bad.

21–10. Those who do miscue analysis, as described in the book P. D. Allen edited, are concerned with defining errors. Mina Shaughnessy was concerned with this issue in her book on writing as well. The errors marked in many compositions are mechanical ones—spelling, function words, and incorrect word endings, for example. Transition, rhetoric, word choice, and other matters that are less clear-cut are often not considered errors. So many tallies of errors are distorted, since the types of errors noted are limited.

21–11. Schuman and Schuman have reported on a diary of a language learner.

21–12. John L. D. Clark describes the use of holistic rating for oral skills; Greenhalgh and Townsend describe holistic rating for evaluating writing.

21–13. Postman (1973) points out what he considers to be a distorted view of what constitutes skills needed by most people because of our emphasis on reading as a central part of all testing.

21–14. Aside from illustrating the point that different groups have different ways of measuring achievement, Achebe's book is useful to use with nonnative speakers because the language is clear and the themes are mature and complex without being confusing.

21–15. Spolsky points out limitations of tests used with minority children. Witkin believes that tests do not take into account different cognitive styles. And Myers and Myers have developed one of many types of tests designed to describe personality characteristics. But their test, like many, is not usually used for comparing groups. Standardized achievement tests or measures of what is in the head seem more critical than what is in the heart or other parts of the body.

21–16. In business, people like to look at the bottom line. We have begun to look at people the same way we look at money—as one figure. In the United States we have GREs, SATs, and other one-time measures. In most other countries, students take national examinations in one sitting and their futures are determined by the results. In comparing foreign language teaching in ten countries, Lewis and Massad did not use a wide range of measures over a period of time. We are into bottom lines in everything we do.

21–17. Diederick points out how deceptive gains are when reported by groups, because the lower groups always seem to gain more.

21–18. For the issue of statistical significance and other matters related to the numbers we use to classify people, Gould is required reading.

21–19. Delamont, in her observations of classrooms, presents instances where students are treated differently as a result of test results; Hoetker does too.

EPISODE 22

/what/would/you/like/to/see/

The words *what would you like to see* are usually used to form a question during teacher workshops I've been at. The most popular reponses include these three:

> I'd like to see lesson plans that work.
>
> I'd like to see proof that one method is better than another.
>
> I'd like to see constructive criticism—judgments—of my teaching so I know how I'm doing.

It is almost unheard of to hear teachers say they would like to see ways to record and transcribe parts of their own teaching or see ways to generate alternatives from such transcripts by coding selected communications or explore alternatives they generate on their own.

Journal Entry

Perhaps at workshops you've been at, you've heard teachers say: "I'd like to see more jobs, better benefits and lighter loads." I have heard these responses too. In this book, as you can see, I separate these professional issues from concerns with actual teaching. How do you mesh these issues with the concerns of actual teaching? Are you actively pursuing these issues in professional organizations?

Lesson plans that work would be exciting to see. Yet though through the years publishers have supported scores of teams to produce texts and accompanying teacher's notes, lesson plans that work seem as elusive as ever. Scores of articles describing lessons have been printed in professional journals and newsletters as well, but these too have apparently not met the need. And even if a plan does seem to work, we rarely know what in it worked or what *worked* means. So expecting to see plans that work may be unrealistic. Even if we tried to teach another's plan to our students, since both the students and the teachers involved are different, the plan would probably be executed differently. After all, when different actors take the same parts in the same plays, each producing exactly the same lines, the plays can be hits or flops, depending on the execution of the lines. If such differences are possible when the lines are identical, how much more are differences likely when different teachers follow the same plan, which is so much less complete than scripts? [Background 22–1]

Proof that one method is better than another would perhaps be even more exciting than seeing lesson plans that work, rivaling a cure for the common cold! Yet most comparisons of methods studies have so far produced only ambiguous results. When the reports have been written, in addition to describing what methods were to be compared—different amounts of time devoted to different skills, for example—they have consistently indicated that just because one teacher or group supposedly had students speak more does not mean that they did. Nor does it mean that some teachers from both groups did not give a lot of homework or sing in class or discuss recent television programs. Even these few examples remind us how ambiguous and useless the word *methods* is, both in comparisons of methods studies and in day-to-day discussions of what teachers do. [Background 22–2]

Whether seeing more comments that tell teachers how they are doing would be more exciting than lesson plans that work, or proof of the superiority of one method over another, is hard to determine. But it is not hard to determine that teachers usually prefer a judgment to a description. While many supervisors and teacher trainers make judgments all the time, teachers often still want to see more judgments, or judgments that are more constructive.

Though it is almost unheard of to hear teachers say they would like to see ways to record, transcribe, code, and discuss their own teaching, teachers do make tapes. At professional conferences, workshops, and special presentations, they often record what people do. But here, as in the search for lessons that work, proof of the worth of a method, or constructive criticism, the search seems to be for a single product. Trying to see such products can never result in anything but an illusion, however, since teaching is not cut and dried. Only by engaging in the generation and exploration of alternatives will we be able to see. And then we will see only that we must continue to look. Fortunately, engaging in a process, though seemingly more fatiguing, provides renewed energy. After all, as we record and transcribe, more comes back to us than goes out, as when we face a mirror and cannot prevent the reflected image from coming back to us.

Turn your recorder on yourself, away from the experts! Separate *to see* from *what* and *would* and *you* and *like*. And in response to "What would you like?" shout "To see!" While I have found the observation system FOCUS helpful as I engage in the process of exploring teaching, I could not have started the exploration without recording and transcribing. If there is any first step that needs to be taken, it is this. By now you have learned this indirectly, as you have worked through the episodes and read the many samples of transcriptions I have included in the excerpts. But if I have failed to make this message clear so far, I am saying again: record, transcribe, and discuss communications from your classes and other settings. Just as to learn a language your students have to do homework outside class, and just as they must engage in the process of exploring the target language on their own and with their peers, so too in order to see teaching, we must engage in out-of-class activity. Ironically, it is less likely that we will see what we would like if we continue to request lesson plans that work, proof that one method is better than another, and knowledge of how we're doing from others, than if we engage in the recording, transcribing, and discussion of what we do—because in products there is less to see than in processes.

In fact, teachers know that the process of making a plan is more important than the plan. Researchers know that actual investigations of methods reveal more than the findings. And teachers know that judgments they seek indicating how they are doing are often not believed, whether they are good or bad. We probably ask for plans that work, methods that are good, and judgments of how we are doing because we feel the need for security and support in an ambiguous world. Outside teaching settings, ads constantly try to teach us that products can help us cope with any problems or deficiencies. So it is only natural to seek them in our teaching. But as tantalizing as products are, they are not up to the tasks we set for them. They cannot make us secure. Freed from this illusion, security perhaps is more likely to come from other means, such as engaging in the process of exploring what we do.

Because our need for security may be central, even recordings, transcripts, and codings as ends in themselves may be viewed as products rather than as means to other ends. That is why discussions of recordings, transcriptions, and coding are so vital. In discussing them, with or without an observation instrument, we see similarities and differences. We can compare what we did with what we had planned to do and with what we thought we did. Discussion will raise questions that will require us to listen to the tapes again. In relistening, we can see that we misheard some students, failed to transcribe some comments that we and they made, note some times when silence made people anxious and other times when it provided them ease to speak, and realize that much went on we were totally unaware of not only during the class, but also during initial sessions with the tapes. When viewing and listening to videotapes, the discussions have even more information to process, of course, since we have so many more mediums to pay attention to. [Background 22–3]

In exploring actual communications, we become teaching learners in the same way our students must become language learners if they are to be able to use the target language. A text to a student is a product, just as a plan is to a teacher. As a starting point to engage in the process of exploration, they can be helpful. But as ends in themselves, they will do nothing but stop us from seeing. As many who travel are quick to point out, a journey to a place is more revealing than the destination. The pleasure of getting someplace is often more intense than arriving. [Background 22–4]

At the next workshop, break a rule. When asked what you'd like to see, respond *myself*, preceded by *to see*. Then say you'd like to see yourself by learning ways to record, transcribe, and discuss lessons specifically and nonjudgmentally in a way that would lead to the self-generation of alternatives. Say you have no interest in lessons that work, methods that have been proved successful, and clear-cut judgments of what you do. Say these products are elusive, at the least. As you break the rule, you will also be realizing that genuine confidence can come only from within. And you may refresh others in the group as well. Aren't you refreshed by my breaking a rule in this episode? I didn't mention one single category of FOCUS. And you survived.

Journal Entry

Though recording others usually goes without a hitch, self-recording usually does not, in my experience. When I ask beginning teachers to record their lesson, at least six tries are usually necessary. This is after the practicing teacher finally brings the recorder to class, a step that can take up to five weeks.

At any rate, once the recorder is in hand, the hitches begin. First, the cord is not long enough to reach the outlet. Or the batteries are dead or weak. Or the batteries are not in the recorder. Then the recording button is pushed, only to find that no tape had been inserted. Then the tape is inserted and the play button is pushed, but the recording button is not pushed. Then the batteries are new, the record button is pushed, and a new tape is in the machine, but the teacher is too far from the mike. Can these all be accidents? Or are they unconscious attempts to avoid starting the process of seeing?

In your experience with recording your own lessons or in your experiences with others recording themselves, have you encountered similar delays?

BACKGROUND NOTES

22–1. Among the most widely read lesson plans were probably those written for Darlene Larson's column in the *TESOL Newsletter* entitled "It Works." Materials published as texts with teacher's notes constitute another widely used type of plan. In fact, "It Works" and texts with teacher's notes provide scores of useful recipes for lessons. Used with an observation system that reveals the basic elements in each plan, I think such plans are strengthened. But they are very useful alone, especially in the first stages of teaching.

22–2. Perhaps the critique of the Pennsylvania study most clearly points out the limitations of comparison of methods studies as they have been conducted. Reading the studies by Agard, Scherer and Wertheimer, Smith, and Upshur reveals the limitations as well.

22–3. The observation system I use to see teaching differently represents only one perspective on observation. Delamont presents one that looks at classes from a sociological point of view without a basic unit of analysis like the move. Jackson also looks at classes from a wider point of view. Reviews of some of the issues in observations were discussed in a special issue of the *International Review of Education* (1972/4). Herbert and Altridge discuss ways to develop observation guides in all subject areas, and Long (1982) reviews the instruments that have been developed for second language classrooms.

As I said in Background 2–14, FOCUS, like all lenses, interprets reality. Any lens reveals one perspective and at the same time obscures other perspectives.

22–4. Naiman et al. discuss some of the tasks language learners engage in on their own, and present learners' views of classes. Thomas also discusses language learning from the learner's point of view. Whether one is learning languages or teaching, what propels us forward no doubt is what Donaldson calls "a fundamental human urge to make sense of the world and bring it under deliberate control" (page 111). While she is discussing children's minds in her book, her comments can refer to humans of all ages. And she argues—quoting Jung—that school is a way to strengthen the integration of consciousness. This book too has had as an aim the development of consciousness and the deliberate mastery of what we do that goes with consciousness (page 123).

EPISODE

23

Where Is This Guy Coming From?

What one professes or proposes is normally built on some theoretical or methodological base. This is true in medicine, economics, and most other fields, as well as in the study of teaching and the preparation of teachers. Germ theory undergirds and informs much of medical practice, just as the ideas of Marx, Smith, and Keynes are used to try to explain economic issues.

If my own work grew out of one central school of thought, part of a discipline or a particular way of doing things, I could easily supply an answer to the friend who told me he was asked by a reader to state the theory or method I based my work on. Well, asking where one's base is—where one is coming from in the vernacular—is, of course, a legitimate question. But in fact I don't have one clear, central base for my work.

Because I deal primarily with the observation of actual communication and recordings and transcriptions of communications, and because I stress observation, I could say I'm a phenomenologist. This term might be incongruous as a response to "Where is this guy coming from?" but it would be accurate. Once I move beyond saying what I am with a general yet technical term, I have to use many more references. The idea of rules and moves comes directly from Bellack's study of classrooms. He says his work was informed by Wittgenstein's ideas about language functions. The pervasiveness and strength of rules I have found support for in the field of the biology of behavior through the writing of Irenaus Eibl-Eibesfeldt. The idea of using opposites and breaking rules grows out of my understanding of the theory of scientific revolutions as described by Kuhn, and from DeBono's writings about lateral and vertical thinking, and from Shah's stories.

A stress on description and categorization is often associated with science. But I find ideas on information processing described by people like N. Weiner and F. Smith central to my thinking about description and categorization. The use of categorization for teacher preparation fits the anthropologist Hall's concept of technical learning. Because labels can help us get distance from what we do and so help us see ourselves, categorizing is also supported indirectly by those such as Alexander, Gallwey, and Pirsig, who write about the need to get distance by observing and describing.

The idea that we can't really teach another person what we know, but that we have to provide ways for the other person to engage in processes to learn, is supported by Plato. The idea that one of our tasks as teachers is to help people see, thus revealing what we don't know, is also presented by Plato through Socrates. Once Socrates makes Meno's slave realize that what he thought he knew he did not really know, the slave has a problem and can thus begin to learn. But I'm not a philosopher and don't pretend to claim my views on this point are based on Platonic conceptions, only that I hold them.

In addition to coming from a lot of places in my general ideas about studying teaching and preparing teachers, I come from more than one place when it comes to the characteristics in FOCUS. The anthropologist Carpenter, the communication seer McLuhan, the astronomer and popularizer of science Sagan, and the scholar Arnheim all consider the impact of different mediums. Their work informs my attention to mediums. Searle's ideas on speech acts can be tied to uses. But no central theory jumps to mind to buttress uses. Dewey's ideas of relating education and experience inform my categories of content. It almost seems embarrassing to relate the source, target, and setting to a theory of any sort, since the impact of these factors on what we do is so obvious. But in fact setting, source, and target have been ignored in many discussions of teaching, and attention to these factors is partly a result of work by educators such as Cazden and Delamont.

Observing communications in both teaching and nonteaching settings is a requirement for any language teacher, since language students need to use what is taught in class outside of class. But reading Dewey on the need to relate education and experience makes me more excited about the task: "Education in order to accomplish its ends both for the individual learner and for society must be based upon experience—which is always the actual life-experience of some individual" (*Experience and Education*, 1970 edition, page 89). How can we fail to observe both in nonteaching and teaching settings if we believe what Dewey has urged?

To put it another way, I don't come from just one place. I'm coming from a lot of places, and not yet at the point where I'm interested in being firmly rooted in one theory or methodology. I'm still coming! The background notes provide details about the work of people I mention, as well as about the work of many others that inform language teaching.

As you read the background notes at the end of each episode, you'll see that where I'm not coming from are the two fields often considered central to language teaching: psychology and linguistics. Crucial as the concerns of these disciplines are, I think we would do well to draw on a wider spectrum of fields, given the complexity of our task. I think our work is illuminated differently by exploring people on a lot of different wavelengths coming from different places in the spectrum. This makes it harder to see where someone is coming from, but makes it easier to see that he or she is in fact coming. The habit of truth is not limited to single fields, as Bronowski, among others, reminds us.

EPISODE

24

Yak? Not in This Book; Try *Soliciting*

As you will see, there are two types of entries in this episode, because this episode is both an index and a glossary. Words used generally in their ordinary sense have only page numbers as ordinary entries in any index do. Words from FOCUS, the metalanguage used in this book to describe communications, as well as some other words I attach particular meanings to, are followed by brief definitions as well as numbers that refer to episodes or pages. These definitions, like most definitions, make sense only if you have experienced the words in other contexts—in this case, done some coding as well as read the words in a range of contexts in the episodes.

attend. A category of use to code moves in which we simply take in mediums, as when we read silently, look at pictures, touch textures, smell scents, or listen to music or lectures. By classifying the taking in of all mediums in the same category, the similarities between these activities can be highlighted as well as the differences. Noting these different activities in the same category also highlights the relationship between the use and medium—another characteristic noted. On one level, silent reading is different from listening because of the fact that in one case we take in print—a linguistic visual medium—and in the other case we take in speech—a linguistic aural medium. 3, 10 Wait time is also coded *attend.* 4, 6, 14

bearing move. A catchall category of move for communications that do not fit neatly into one of the four major move types: structuring, soliciting, responding, reacting. Bearing moves include idiosyncratic communications many of us make, such as shaking change in our pocket as we talk, touching our ear as we listen, and other moves that cannot fit the four major types. Bearing moves are even less conscious than the four moves concentrated on in this book. Ethnomethodologists devote a great deal of time to describing these moves. In teaching, a teacher may avoid a particular student's eyes all the time. Without frame by frame or millisecond by millisecond analysis of video tapes the lack of eye contact will be missed. While the importance of bearing moves cannot be denied, a theme of this book is that altering the frequency and sequence of other moves alters the bearing moves we make as well. But discovering the bearing moves is a much more time-consuming process and trying to change them deliberately is probably more difficult than changing the other types of moves. 2

characterize. A category of use; using mediums to comment on something else, such as indicating that items are the same or different, right or wrong, good and bad, large or small, or giving category names to groups of items. There are five subcategories of characterize: differentiate—cd; evaluate—*ce*; examine—*cx*; illustrate—*ci*; label—*cl*. 2, 4, 5, 9, 10, 12, 13

classroom management, 16

cloze, 10, p. 209

code breaking, 10, p. 220; 13, p. 301

collocation, 11, p. 262; 12, p. 284; 17, p. 390

comparison of methods, 1, p. 2; 22

consequences, 1, p. 6; 10, p. 214; 21

content. One of the five characteristics of communications noted with FOCUS. The content the mediums communicate refers to the topic being communicated. Three main categories of content are employed: *life, procedure,* and *study*. Study is divided into *study of language* and *study of other subjects*, such as history or dance.

The same communication can express content in any of the three major categories because words and other communications have meaning only as a result of what we attribute to them. Thus, a wave of the hand could mean "Hello" and thus be coded *life*; a wave could mean "Be quiet" and thus communicate *procedure*. When studying language, a wave could be a sample of a gesture to be learned and thus coded *study*, subcategory *language*. In a karate class, the same wave would be coded *study*, subcategory *other*. 2, p. 39; 6; 10, p. 229; 11; 12, p. 280; 17, p. 390; 20

context, 13

contrasts, 17, p. 385

criteria, 12, p. 285; 13, p. 294; 21

culture, 9

dictation, 14

dictionaries, 10, p. 215; 11, p. 263

differentiate. One of the five subcategories of the use *characterize*; when mediums are used to indicate that items are the same or different, they are coded *cd* for *characterize differentiate*, as in these examples: tin and bin *rhyme*; "a" and the "e" in italics are pronounced the *same*; bags *look alike*. 4, p. 77; 9; 12, p. 271

discipline, 16

drill, 17

either-or questions, 4, pp. 86, 111

elicit. One of the four subcategories of the use *present*; *present elicit* (*pe*) refers to commands, requests, or questions which ask that language or other areas of study be displayed for their own sake; *pe* also is used to code solicits we know the answer to; *query, question,* and *state* are the other subcategories of *present*. 4, p. 101

English for specific purposes, 8

errors, 12, 17, 21

ethics of observing, 21, p. 464

evaluate. One of the five subcategories of the use *characterize*; when mediums are used to indicate items are correct or incorrect and good or bad or when one prescribes what should be done, the communications are coded *ce* for *characterize evaluate*, as in these examples: that's *wrong*; that's *stupid*; you *should not* smoke here; it's *great*; is this correct? *yes.*

To indicate the distinction between positive and negative evaluations, the *ce* is underscored in negative cases.

To distinguish between a *yes* or *no* which simply indicates information about a performance or about information and does not attribute any positive or negative value to the evaluation from comments such as "That's stupid," the content of *life* is employed. Thus, "It's wrong" is simply coded *ce* with content of *study*, since the comment is supplying information about something that is wrong. But if the tone of voice in a comment such as "It's wrong" suggests that being wrong is stupid, then the content *life* plus *study* is coded. The suggestion of stupidity is a personal opinion which attributes a negative value to the error. 4, 5, 12

examine. One of the five subcategories of the use *characterize*; when mediums are used to indicate size or shape, as when diagramming sentences, breaking sentences, words or syllables into smaller units, or indicating what letters words begin or end with, or spelling for purposes of word analysis, the communications are coded *cx* for *characterize examine*. 4, 5, 12

explain. One of the two subcategories of the use *relate*; when mediums are used to make generalizations, communicate rules or reasons for our actions or activities, respond to *why* questions with genuine explanation, speculations, or long generalizations, they are coded *re* for *relate explain*. The other subcategory of relate is infer. 4

external information, 10, pp. 202, 238; 14, p. 326

features. Whenever two different communications are coded exactly the same and one wants to show the difference, subscripts can be used to show differences. When the combinations of categories and subcategories fail to highlight differences that seem to exist between two communications, subscripts can represent features the five characteristics of FOCUS do not reveal. For example, if one student says "Come here" and another says "Ven aqui," they both solicit, they both use speech to *present question*, and both moves contain the same subcategory of *procedure*. To show that one is in one language and the other is in another, a *v* for vernacular can be put next to the coding of whichever communication is, in fact, in the student's first language. 17, p. 388; 18, p. 401

Here is a list of some features and the subscripts used with them in this book. Just as categories can be modified, so, of course, can features. These can be altered, and new ones added; these are simply illustrations of possibilities and a reminder that with FOCUS, more than the categories can be noted.

Features	*Examples*	*Subscripts*
Contrasts	Are these the same? go goes*	*
Errors	He goes the store.	x
Intentional errors	Is he a noun?	ix
Communications in the negative	Don't do that.	_____ (underline)
Communications in a nontarget language	*Si* if in an English class. *Yes* if in a Spanish class.	v
Homework or tasks assigned outside class	Read the text for Friday.	h
Repeating the same move again	Stand up. Stand up.	sol_{ds}
Repeating the same move with a slight change—double but different length—numbers from 1 through *n* to represent syllables, letters, or words or time	Very good. Very good. (louder)	rea_{dd}
	He is here now. He is here now for sure.	4 if words 6 if words
	or + for long and − for short	

Features	*Examples*	*Subscripts*
High inference descriptions—first three letters in word used to describe	Very good. (seems sarcastic) Very good. (seems mean)	sar mea
Two moves made at the same time		s for simultaneous
When treating errors, often there are many solicits; I note the initial one with an *i*, the ones that give extra information with an *m* for modulated, and those that correct the errors I note with a *c* for corrective	Define groundnut. Grows on a screw. Is a groundnut food? I think so. Where does it grow? Under the ground.	sol_i res sol_c res sol_m res
Electronic, as when reading from a TV screen	(words appear on a TV screen attached to a computer)	lv_e

feedback, 10, 12

FOCUS. An acronym for foci for observing communications used in settings, the name of the observation instrument treated in this book. The system is designed around two questions: What's being done? How is it being done? Five characteristics of communications are noted to treat these two questions. The source/target and move type are used to answer the first question. The medium, use, and content are the three characteristics used to answer the second question. Depending on one's purpose, one can use from three categories to over one hundred.

The categories of each characteristic serve both to define the characteristic and provide alternatives. Thus, the categories of *source* and *target* are teacher, student, and other. If feedback is usually provided by the teacher, the obvious alternatives are the two other categories of source: student and other.

Just as the numbers 1 through 9 and 0 are used in various combinations to generate distinct telephone numbers for millions of people, so by combining the categories and subcategories in FOCUS one can describe differences and similarities between communications that are in some way different. 2

formulas. In normal English, greetings, polite expressions; in FOCUS, a subcategory of *life—ff*; *life* is one of the three major categories of the fifth characteristic noted with FOCUS, the content. Messages in these items could all be coded formula if not being treated as objects of study: birthday cards, invitations, thank you notes, holiday greetings, sayings printed on T shirts, bumper stickers and plaques, cups, plates, or spoons containing proverbs, or other fixed forms of words or conventional sayings. 6, 19, 20

functions of language, 8, p. 174

genre, 11

givens. Reflexive moves such as responses can themselves be identical, but the messages in the preceding moves can influence the response; for example, one can say "yes" to "Is 'he go' correct" or "Is 'he go' the same as 'he goes'?" In addition to distinguishing the responses in FOCUS, it is possible to distinguish the solicits by noting the messages they contain on the same line where one codes the responses themselves. 4, p. 108

golden moments, 7

grammar. In normal English, a range of things from rules to "proper" usage; in FOCUS, a subcategory of the study of language, a central area of the fifth characteristic noted with FOCUS, content. 8, 11

greetings, 19

hits. Expected responses; if one asked a student his age and the student repeated the question rather than stating his age, a miss would have been communicated; had he given the age, a hit would have been communicated. 5

illustrate. One of the five subcategories of *characterize*, itself a category of use in FOCUS; when mediums are used to give partial definitions or indicate attributes that do not fit clearly into the other subcategories of characterize, they are coded *ci* for *characterize illustrate*; A horse has *four legs*; Say something about this raincoat—it's *for the water*. 4, 5, 12

infer. One of the two subcategories of the use *relate*; the other one is *explain*. When mediums are used to make inferences, such as when finding a main idea, making an analogy, completing a cloze test, generating a new pattern by combining known patterns in new ways, or capturing more than literal meaning, the communications are coded *ri* for *relate infer*. 2; 10, p. 222

internal information, 10, pp. 202, 238; 14, p. 326

judgmental. Attributing positive or negative values to what we observe, as when we say "That was a great lesson." When we say "You should talk less," we are implying a negative value to talking a lot. In this book, the aim has been to try to avoid attributing good or bad to what we do or see. This is not to say one must avoid liking what one does. But as soon as one says "I like it and therefore it is good," one has moved into judging. In this book, the aim has been to try to describe. In place of saying a teacher talks too much, one can say "The teacher communicated 40 solicit moves and the students 3, so for the next lesson, if the goal is questions from students, reverse the proportion." More student soliciting is not considered good, nor is less teacher talk good or bad.

This is not to say that we observe with nothing in mind. By deciding to look at a characteristic such as mediums, a decision was made that mediums were important. But finding a certain type, frequency, or sequence of mediums does not provide support for a good or a bad lesson. Finding mediums provides some data about what is happening and may lead to seeing what is being done in a different light and can show congruence between aims and practices.

The aim of describing on one level is to learn how to behave like an umpire who simply says where a ball is, rather than like the fans who boo a pitcher on the opposing team when he throws a strike and cheer when he throws a ball. 1, 7, 9, 22

label. One of the five subcategories of *characterize*, itself one of the categories of use; when mediums are used to give category names to items, as in these examples, one codes *cl* for *characterize label*: Is *z* a *voiced sound*? Horse is a *noun*. An electrician and a person who works at a factory are both *blue-collar workers*. Why don't you ask *open-ended questions*? And how many *solicits* were there? Any word in any language can be used as a label; the distinguishing feature of a label is that it is used to name groups of items rather than individual items. 4, 5, 12, 14

language. One of the subcategories of study, itself one of the three major categories of content; examples of the nineteen or so subcategories of the study of language—context, dialects, etc.—are listed in Episode 11; the subcategories are listed in the content column in the table in the inside back cover as well. Most of the subcategories retain the meanings given in dictionaries. 11

leaden moments, 7

lesson plans, 6, p. 155; 22

life. One of the three main categories of content, the fifth characteristic of communication coded with FOCUS. The other categories of content are *procedure* and *study*, either of language or other subjects. Greetings are coded *life*, subcategory *formula, ff*. Information about the world is coded *life*, subcategory *general knowledge, fg*. And personal feelings or information are coded life, subcategory *personal, fp*. 2, 6, 20

linguistic. One of the major categories of medium, divided into mediums that appeal to the ear, such as speech, the eyes, such as print, and other senses such as touch, Braille. 2, p. 32; 12; 14; 18

linguistic aural. One of the subcategories of medium, the third characteristic of communication noted in FOCUS; spoken words, sounds, sentences, and larger units of language are coded *la* for *linguistic aural*. 2, 14, 18

linguistic other. One of the subcategories of medium, the third characteristic of communication noted in FOCUS; language that we take in or produce in a channel that appeals to senses other than our ears or eyes, such as sandpaper letters we distinguish from each other by touch. 14, 18 *linguistic visual.* One of the subcategories of medium, the third characteristic of communication noted in FOCUS; printed, written, or transcribed sounds, words, sentences, or larger units; ideograms, characters, and punctuation marks—language that appeals to our eyes rather than ears or other senses. 12, 14, 18

listening, 3, 10, 14

long-term memory, 10; 14, p. 325

medium. The channel of communication used; the medium is the third characteristic of communication noted with FOCUS. 2, 18

message. A grouping of medium, use, and area of content. In the solicit "Repeat Eskimo" there are two messages because there are two uses with two different areas of content. In the solicit "Juan, repeat Eskimo," there are three messages because there are three different uses and three areas of content. Each medium that is used differently or communicates a different area of content within the same move is coded as a separate message.

Variety in moves is a result of the fact that they contain different combinations of medium, use, and content and therefore can contain many separate and different messages. 2, p. 41; 4, p. 104; 17, p. 381; 18

method. A word used with labels such as audiolingual, silent way, or grammar translation that is meant to distinguish different groups of teaching practices. The term can lead to discussions of teaching that lack specificity, and the words attached to *method*, such as audiolingual, have connotations that often stimulate arguments about the advantages of one method over another; in fact, the term *method* is too global to permit many useful comparisons. 1, 22

miscues, 10, p. 213; 14, p. 326

misses, 5

move. The basic unit of analysis of FOCUS; together with source and target, the move tells us what's being done—structuring, soliciting, responding, or reacting after Bellack et al.; In FOCUS, a fifth move type, a bearing move, is used to code communications that don't fit one of the four basic move types. 2, p. 25; 4

noise, 10, p. 222; 14, p. 328

nonjudgmental. Abstaining from attributing good or bad to what we see or do; "He's a great teacher" is judgmental; "I like that teacher" is nonjudgmental; "That teacher varies the areas of content he asks students questions about" is also nonjudgmental. To suspend judgment does not require that we look without any bias—we cannot. Our likes and dislikes as well as what we think is important cannot be suspended. But what we can try to suspend is our attributing success to what we like or indicating that when we find a lot of practices we think are important, we have found a good teacher. 1

nonlinguistic. One of the major categories of mediums, the third characteristic of communication noted with FOCUS; like other categories of mediums, this one is subdivided into three subcategories: those that appeal to the eyes (visual), those that appeal to the ears (aural), and those that appeal to other senses (other). 2, 3, 14, 18

nonlinguistic aural. A subcategory of the medium *nonlinguistic* that contains mediums that appeal to the ear, such as noises or music—*na.* 2, 14, 18

nonlinguistic other. A subcategory of the medium *nonlinguistic* that contains mediums that appeal to senses other than the ears or eyes, such as smell and texture—*no.* 2, 14, 18

nonlinguistic visual. A subcategory of the medium *nonlinguistic* that contains mediums that appeal to the eyes, such as objects or pictures—*nv.* 2, 14, 18

nonteaching setting. Any place where a person is not in some way being shown how to look differently or how to change behavior. During breaks in classes, a classroom can become a nonteaching setting, just as a bar can become a teaching setting if one person starts trying to teach something to another. The same setting can be a teaching setting for one and a nonteaching setting for another, as when two people are listening to the radio, one for the chance to relax and the other to identify the parts of a sonata for an upcoming examination.

objective. Like *Yak,* not in this book.

observation. Looking at what is going on, obviously; but our ideas of what is good or bad and our values sometimes obscure some of what is going on; this book is devoted to making us see differently, partly by trying to suspend our judgments so that we attribute less to what we see. By observing ourselves on tape or reading transcripts we have made we can often see just as much or more as others who observe us can; in this book a system has been introduced to aid in observation. 1, 2, 7, 21, 22

paralinguistic. A major category of medium containing those mediums that are intertwined with language but are not sounds or words, such as tone of voice and gestures and touch—*p.* 2, 12, 18

paralinguistic aural. A subcategory of paralinguistic mediums to note those that appeal to our ears, such as word emphasis or tone of voice—*pa.* 2, 18

paralinguistic other. A subcategory of paralinguistic mediums that contains those that appeal to senses other than the eye or ear, such as touching people, doing things with objects, using space to distance oneself from others—*po.* 2, 14, 18

paralinguistic visual. A subcategory of paralinguistic mediums that appeal to the eye, such as gestures, skin color, posture—*pv.* 2, 3, 10, 14, 18

present. One of the major categories of use, the fourth characteristic noted with FOCUS; when mediums are used to state information directly or ask questions, the communications are coded *p* for *present,* as in *Write this; I live in Chicago; Who discovered America? Columbus; This is a pen.* There are four subcategories of *present: elicit, query, question, state.* 4, 13

procedure. One of the three main categories of content, the fifth characteristic of communication noted with FOCUS. The other categories are *life* and *study.* When mediums are used to call the roll, discipline students, give directions, etc., the communications are coded *p* for *procedure.* Printed material such as these materials would be coded as *procedure* in regular use; if they were an object of study, then they would be coded *study,* of language if language was the aim, of other areas if the area each represents were the object of study: tax forms, train or plane schedules, directions, leases and other legal and administrative communications, room numbers and addresses, either on buildings or envelopes, menus and order forms in catalogs or subscription rates in newspapers and magazines, deposit slips, bank statements and bills, traffic regulations. The subcategories and the episodes they are treated in are noted in the FOCUS table on the inside back cover of this book. 6; 16; 20, p. 436

query. A subcategory of *present,* one of the uses noted with FOCUS; when we ask questions we do not know the answer to, they are coded *pq* for *present query* in FOCUS. 4, p. 101

question. A subcategory of *present,* one of the uses in FOCUS; when we ask questions that do not fit neatly into those we know the answer to and those we do not, they are coded *p?* for *present question* in FOCUS. For example, we may ask "may I help you" because we want to help someone or to be polite. We assume the answer will be *yes* or *no,* but we don't know which. 4, p. 101

reacting move. One of the four major move types; reflexive communications that comment on what others have communicated. They can occur after any other type of move and can occur in strings as well. So, when communications do not initiate or are not elicted by others, they are likely to be reactions. 2, 3, 4, 10, 12.

readability, 10, p. 230

read-and-look-up, 14

reading, 3, 10, 14

redundancy, 10, p. 218

relate. One of the major categories of use. When mediums are used to make inferences or generalizations, they are coded *r* for *relate.* Communications that show more than recall and require one to use some thinking process fit this category of use. The two subcategories are *explain* and *infer—re* and *ri.* 4

reliability, 2, p. 29

reproduce. One of the major categories of use. When mediums are used to repeat what another has done, as in copying or mimicking, or when one changes one medium to another, as when we change print to speech in oral reading and speech to print in a dictation, the communications are coded *d* for *reproduce.*

The two subcategories of *reproduce* are *reproduce same medium—ds*—and *reproduce change medium—dc.* Oral reading, dictation, and making gestures in response to commands are *dc.* Substitution drills, paraphrasing, combining, etc., are coded *ds.* The subcategory *dc* is treated in 14; *ds* is treated in 17.

responding move. One of the four major move types; answering questions, performing tasks that others have set for us, or replying to requests or demands others have made to us. 2, 3, 4, 10

roles, 13

roll or *calling the roll,* 16

rules. Unconscious conventions and habits; generalizations which indicate that, 9 times out of 10, the same thing is likely to happen, given certain conditions. 1, p. 5; 23

set. One of the major categories of use. When mediums are used to communicate models or other items that are referred to by words such as *this, that, it,* and *one,* the communications are coded *s* for *set.* In the communication "This sure didn't fit well," the item the *this* refers to is the set.

In a solicit, the content is often determined by the set. Thus, when a person says "Pick out the nouns in the passage," we know that grammar is the content that is attributed to the set—the passage. Since the printed passage is the stuff to pick the nouns out of, the passage is coded *s* for *set.* A television screen provides material for us to take in and then make communications about. So it sets content.

One way that different types of sets can be distinguished is by the medium used to communicate them; these can be coded *se,* for example. The length can be used too so that those of less than one word could be coded *sl* and extended discourse could be coded *st.* Table 4–3, p. 103 shows some ways to categorize sets. 2, 4, 12

short-term memory, 10; 14, p. 325

silence. A category of medium used to note the deliberate use of wait time, the communication of implicit directions, as when we open a door for a person and wait for the person to enter a room before we do. 3, 4, 14, 18

silent reading, 3, 10

soliciting move. One of the four major move types; asking questions, making requests or demands for others to perform tasks, or answer questions, or act. 2, 4, 5

source. The person or thing that communicates a move. A person in charge is coded *t* for teacher and a person not in charge as *s* for student; when two people communicate as peers, each is coded *s* as well. *O* for other is used to indicate moves not communicated by a person, such as when a buzzer on an alarm clock solicits, or when a computer screen responds with a printed message to a request or instruction we type in. Source, together with target, is the first characteristic coded with FOCUS. The source tells us who or what is communicating. 2, 4, 10, 12, 20, 21, 22

transcription. In this book, transcriptions do not represent the sounds made and so are not in any type of phonetic script. An attempt has been made to note both what is said and what is done or communicated with mediums other than speech. Nonlinguistic and paralinguistic mediums are noted in parentheses. As the background note 2–6, on p. 50, notes, transcriptions are attempts to show reality and are never completely accurate. Background note 2–6 also points out that there are two types of transcriptions in this book. Those that are faithful representations of actual communications are noted with a *T* to indicate actual exchanges. Those that have been altered somewhat to illustrate a point more clearly are not noted with this symbol.

unspecified content. When the content being communicated is not easy to specify, it is coded *u* to indicate this fact. 12, p. 280

unspecified language. When the area of the study of language involves more than three subcategories of language or when it is otherwise unclear what areas of language are being studied, the communications are coded *lu* to indicate these facts. 11

use. The fourth characteristic noted with FOCUS indicates how mediums are used to communicate content. The first major distinction between different uses is made by noting whether the mediums are taken in or produced. In silent reading, smelling, tasting, touching, and looking at pictures, mediums are simply taken in. We *attend* to mediums. In using mediums to produce content, we have five options: *characterize, present, relate, reproduce,* and *set. Use* can also be coded as *content,* 4, p. 108

Psで、dじゃないとき Ps?